Lecture Notes in Artificial Intelligence 12092

Subseries of Lecture Notes in Computer Science

More information about this series at http://www.springer.com/series/1244

Yves Demazeau · Tom Holvoet ·
Juan M. Corchado · Stefania Costantini (Eds.)

Advances in Practical Applications of Agents, Multi-Agent Systems, and Trustworthiness

The PAAMS Collection

18th International Conference, PAAMS 2020
L'Aquila, Italy, October 7–9, 2020
Proceedings

 Springer

Editors
Yves Demazeau 🆔
Centre National de la Recherche Scientifique
Grenoble, France

Juan M. Corchado 🆔
University of Salamanca
Salamanca, Spain

Tom Holvoet 🆔
Catholic University of Leuven
Heverlee, Belgium

Stefania Costantini
University of L'Aquila
L'Aquila, Italy

ISSN 0302-9743   ISSN 1611-3349 (electronic)
Lecture Notes in Artificial Intelligence
ISBN 978-3-030-49777-4   ISBN 978-3-030-49778-1 (eBook)
https://doi.org/10.1007/978-3-030-49778-1

LNCS Sublibrary: SL7 – Artificial Intelligence

This Springer imprint is published by the registered company Springer Nature Switzerland AG
The registered company address is: Gewerbestrasse 11, 6330 Cham, Switzerland

Preface

Research on agents and multi-agent systems has matured during the last decade and many effective applications of this technology are now deployed. An international forum to present and discuss the latest scientific developments and their effective applications, to assess the impact of the approach, and to facilitate technology transfer, became a necessity and was created almost two decades ago.

PAAMS, the International Conference on Practical Applications of Agents and Multi-Agent Systems, is the international yearly tribune to present, discuss, and disseminate the latest developments and the most important outcomes related to real-world applications. It provides a unique opportunity to bring multi-disciplinary experts, academics, and practitioners together to exchange their experience in the development and deployment of agents and multi-agent systems.

This volume presents the papers that were accepted for the 2020 edition of PAAMS. These articles report on the application and validation of agent-based models, methods, and technologies in a number of key application areas, including: advanced models and learning, agent-based programming, decision-making, education and social interactions, formal and theoretic models, health and safety, mobility and the city, swarms, and task allocation. Each paper submitted to PAAMS went through a stringent peer-review process by three members of the Program Committee composed of 136 internationally renowned researchers from 27 countries. From the 64 submissions received, 12 were selected for full presentation at the conference; another 17 papers were accepted as short presentations. In addition, a demonstration track featuring innovative and emergent applications of agent and multi-agent systems and technologies in real-world domains was organized. In all, 17 demonstrations were shown, and this volume contains a description of each of them.

We would like to thank all the contributing authors, the members of the Program Committee, the sponsors (IBM, Armundia Group, EurAI, AEPIA, AFIA, APPIA, FBKI, CINI, CNRS, KUL, AIR Institute, and UNIVAQ), and the Organizing Committee for their hard and highly valuable work. We are thankful for the funding/support from the project "Intelligent and sustainable mobility supported by multi-agent systems and edge computing" (Id. RTI2018-095390-B-C32). Their work contributed to the success of the PAAMS 2020 event.

Thanks for your help – PAAMS 2020 would not exist without your contribution.

April 2020

Yves Demazeau
Tom Holvoet
Juan M. Corchado
Stefania Costantini

Organization

General Co-chairs

Yves Demazeau	National Center for Scientific Research, France
Tom Holvoet	Catholic University of Leuven, Belgium
Stefania Costantini	University of L'Aquila, Italy
Juan Manuel Corchado	University of Salamanca and AIR Institute, Spain

Advisory Board

Bo An	Nanyang Technological University, Singapore
Paul Davidsson	Malmö University, Sweden
Keith Decker	University of Delaware, USA
Frank Dignum	Utrecht University, The Netherlands
Toru Ishida	Kyoto University, Japan
Takayuki Ito	Nagoya Institute of Technology, Japan
Eric Matson	Purdue University, USA
Jörg P. Müller	Clausthal Technical University, Germany
Michal Pěchouček	Technical University in Prague, Czech Republic
Franco Zambonelli	University of Modena and Reggio Emilia, Italy

Program Committee

Emmanuel Adam	University of Valenciennes, France
Natasha Alechina	University of Nottingham, UK
Analia Amandi	University of Tandil, Argentina
Frédéric Amblard	University of Toulouse, France
Francesco Amigoni	Milan Polytechnic Institute, Italy
Bo An	Nanyang Technological University, Singapore
Luis Antunes	University of Lisbon, Portugal
Piotr Artiemjew	University of Warmia and Mazury, Poland
Matteo Baldoni	University of Torino, Italy
Joao Balsa	University of Lisbon, Portugal
Cristina Baroglio	University of Torino, Italy
Nick Bassiliades	University of Thessaloniki, Greece
Jeremy Baxter	QinetQ, UK
Michael Berger	DocuWare AG, Germany
Olivier Boissier	Saint Etienne School of Mines, France
Rafael Bordini	Pontifical University of Rio Grande do Sul, Brazil
Vicente Botti	Polytechnic University of Valencia, Spain
Anarosa Brandao	University of São Paulo, Brazil
Lars Braubach	Universität Hamburg, Germany

Sven Brueckner	Axon AI, USA
Bat-Erdene Byambasuren	University of Science and Technology, Mongolia
Javier Carbó	University Carlos III of Madrid, Spain
Luis Castillo	University of Caldas, Colombia
Sofia Ceppi	University of Edinburgh, UK
Anders Lynhe Christensen	Southern Denmark University, Denmark
Helder Coelho	University of Lisbon, Portugal
Rafael Corchuelo	University of Sevilla, Spain
Luis Correia	University of Lisbon, Portugal
Daniela D'Auria	University of Naples Federico II, Italy
Paul Davidsson	Malmö University, Sweden
Keith Decker	University of Delaware, USA
Yves Demazeau (Co-chair)	National Center for Scientific Research, France
Louise Dennis	The University of Liverpool, UK
Andres Diaz Pace	University of Tandil, Argentina
Frank Dignum	Utrecht University, The Netherlands
Aldo Dragoni	Marche Polytechnic University, Italy
Ahmad Esmaeili	Purdue University, USA
Rino Falcone	National Research Council, Italy
Kary Främling	University of Aalto, Finland
Katsuhide Fujita	Tokyo Agriculture and Technology University, Japan
Naoki Fukuta	Shizuoka University, Japan
Stéphane Galland	Technical University Belfort-Montbéliard, France
Amineh Ghorbani	Delft University of Technology, The Netherlands
Daniela Godoy	University of Tandil, Argentina
Mauricio A. Gomez Morales	University of Texas at San Antonio, USA
Jorge J. Gómez-Sanz	Complutense University of Madrid, Spain
Vladimir Gorodetski	University of Saint Petersburg, Russia
Charles Gouin-Vallerand	University of Québec, Canada
James Harland	Royal Melbourne Institute of Technology, Australia
Salima Hassas	University of Lyon, France
Hisashi Hayashi	Advanced Institute of Industrial Technology, Japan
Vincent Hilaire	University of Belfort-Montbéliard, France
Martin Hofmann	Lockheed Martin, USA
Tom Holvoet (Co-chair)	Catholic University of Leuven, Belgium
Piotr Jedrzejowicz	Gdynia Maritime University, Poland
Yichuan Jiang	Southeast University of Nanjing, China
Vicente Julian	Polytechnic University of Valencia, Spain
Ozgur Kafali	Boğaziçi University, Turkey
Ryo Kanamori	Nagoya University, Japan
Takahiro Kawamura	Toshiba, Japan
Yongho Kim	Argonne National Lab, USA
Franziska Klügl	University of Örebro, Sweden
Matthias Klusch	Center for Artificial Intelligence, Germany
Martin Kollingbaum	University of Aberdeen, UK

Silvia Schiaffino	University of Tandil, Argentina
Holger Schlingloff	Humboldt University, Germany
Michael Ignaz Schumacher	Western University of Applied Sciences, Switzerland
Franciszek Seredynski	Cardinal Stefan Wyszynski University, Poland
Emilio Serrano	Technical University of Madrid, Spain
Leonid Sheremetov	Mexican Institute of Petroleum, Mexico
Viviane Torres da Silva	Fluminense Federal University, Brazil
Leandro Soriano Marcolino	University of Southern California, USA
Kostas Stathis	Royal Holloway University of London, UK
Sonia Suárez	University of La Coruna, Spain
Toshiharu Sugawara	Waseda University, Japan
Simon Thomson	British Telecom, UK
Ingo Timm	University of Trier, Germany
Paolo Torroni	University of Bologna, Italy
Elena Troubitsyna	University of Turku, Finland
Ali Emre Turgut	Middle East Technical University, Turkey
Suguru Ueda	Saga University, Japan
Rainer Unland	University of Duisburg, Germany
Domenico Ursino	University of Reggio Calabria, Italy
Laszlo Varga	Computer and Automation Research Institute, Hungary
Laurent Vercouter	University of Rouen, France
Harko Verhagen	University of Stockholm, Sweden
Jacques Verriet	Organisation for Applied Research, The Netherlands
José R. Villar	University of Oviedo, Spain
Gerhard Weiss	Maastricht University, The Netherlands
Wayne Wobcke	University of New South Wales, Australia
Gaku Yamamoto	International Business Machines, Japan
Pinar Yolum	Bogazici University, Turkey
Neil Yorke-Smith	American University of Beirut, Lebanon
Dengji Zhao	Shanghai Technological University, China

Organizing Committee

Juan M. Corchado Rodríguez	University of Salamanca and AIR Institute, Spain
Fernando De la Prieta	University of Salamanca, Spain
Sara Rodríguez González	University of Salamanca, Spain
Javier Prieto Tejedor	University of Salamanca and AIR Institute, Spain
Pablo Chamoso Santos	University of Salamanca, Spain
Belén Pérez Lancho	University of Salamanca, Spain
Ana Belén Gil González	University of Salamanca, Spain
Ana De Luis Reboredo	University of Salamanca, Spain
Angélica González Arrieta	University of Salamanca, Spain
Emilio S. Corchado Rodríguez	University of Salamanca, Spain
Angel Luis Sánchez Lázaro	University of Salamanca, Spain

Alfonso González Briones	University Complutense of Madrid, Spain
Yeray Mezquita Martín	University of Salamanca, Spain
Enrique Goyenechea	University of Salamanca and AIR Institute, Spain
Javier J. Martín Limorti	University of Salamanca, Spain
Alberto Rivas Camacho	University of Salamanca, Spain
Ines Sitton Candanedo	University of Salamanca, Spain
Elena Hernández Nieves	University of Salamanca, Spain
Beatriz Bellido	University of Salamanca, Spain
María Alonso	University of Salamanca, Spain
Diego Valdeolmillos	AIR Institute, Spain
Roberto Casado Vara	University of Salamanca, Spain
Sergio Marquez	University of Salamanca, Spain
Jorge Herrera	University of Salamanca, Spain
Marta Plaza Hernández	University of Salamanca, Spain
Guillermo Hernández González	AIR Institute, Spain
Luis Carlos Martínez de Iturrate	University of Salamanca and AIR Institute, Spain
Ricardo S. Alonso Rincón	University of Salamanca, Spain
Javier Parra	University of Salamanca, Spain
Niloufar Shoeibi	University of Salamanca, Spain
Zakieh Alizadeh-Sani	University of Salamanca, Spain

Local Organizing Committee

Pierpaolo Vittorini	University of L'Aquila, Italy
Tania Di Mascio	University of L'Aquila, Italy
Giovanni De Gasperis	University of L'Aquila, Italy
Federica Caruso	University of L'Aquila, Italy
Alessandra Galassi	University of L'Aquila, Italy

PAAMS 2020 Sponsors

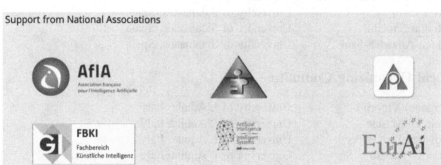

Contents

Regular Papers

An Interruptible Task Allocation Model

Application to a Honey Bee Colony Simulation

Thomas Alves[1]([✉]), Jérémy Rivière[1], Cédric Alaux[2], Yves Le Conte[2], Frank Singhoff[1,4], Thierry Duval[3], and Vincent Rodin[1]

[1] Univ Brest, Lab-STICC, CNRS, UMR 6285, Brest, France
Thomas.Alves@univ-brest.fr
[2] INRAE, UR 406 Abeilles et Environnement, Avignon, France
{cedric.alaux,yves.le-conte}@inrae.fr
[3] IMT Atlantique, Lab-STICC, CNRS, UMR 6285, Brest, France
thierry.duval@imt-atlantique.fr
[4] Groupement de Défense Sanitaire Apicole du Finistère (GDSA29), Brest, France

Abstract. Division of labour is a key aspect of distributed systems, such as swarm robotics or multi-agent systems. Inspired by social insects known for their task allocation capabilities, most of the models rely on two assumptions: 1) each task is associated with a stimulus, and 2) the execution of this task lowers that stimulus. In short, the stimulus is a representation of the amount of work needed on a task. When these assumptions are not true, we need a mechanism to guide the agent in its decision whether to pursue or to interrupt its current task, as there is no diminishing stimulus to rely on. In this article, we propose a model based on the Response Threshold Model and a mechanism based on the agent's intrinsic motivation and internal states, allowing to take into account tasks dissociated from stimuli. Agents use their intrinsic motivation to emulate the priority of tasks not associated with any stimuli, and to decide whether to interrupt or pursue their current task. This model has been applied to simulate the division of labour within a simplified honey bee colony, associated with the constantly adapting physiology of honey bees. Preliminary results show that the task allocation is effective, robust and in some cases improved by the interruption mechanism.

Keywords: Agent-based simulation · Task allocation · Self-organisation

1 Introduction

The ability of social insects to distribute their workforce without any central control has been studied for years. This self-organisation ability to dynamically adapt to its environment allows social insects to be robust to changes and still be able to thrive. In computer science, and more specifically in multi-agent systems, task allocation models adapted from social insects are numerous and effective, applied for example in agent-based simulations [3,22] and in general problem

© Springer Nature Switzerland AG 2020
Y. Demazeau et al. (Eds.): PAAMS 2020, LNAI 12092, pp. 3–15, 2020.
https://doi.org/10.1007/978-3-030-49778-1_1

resolution [16,28]. These models mainly rely on two assumptions: 1) Each task is associated with a stimulus and 2) The execution of this task lowers its stimulus [4]. Thus, internal or external (in the environment) stimulus perceived by an agent triggers the execution of the associated task, lowering the intensity of the stimulus and the probability of doing that same task again. Hence the perceived stimulus can be seen as a representation of the task work needed. However, in some cases, the execution of a task does not affect the amount of the associated perceived stimulus, or there is even a complete lack of association between a task and a stimulus. In that case, we need to find other ways to drive the task allocation algorithm. How can an agent decide whether to keep executing its current task or to interrupt it? In this article, we describe a model able to allocate tasks with no direct connection to stimuli to agents. We notably use agent's intrinsic motivation to decide whether to interrupt a task. We then present an implementation of that model applied to a simplified honey bee colony. In honeybee colonies, there are several tasks dissociated from any stimuli, thus representing an interesting application for the model. For example, the larvae do not emit any stimuli to ask to be fed, but a general stimulus that is more a representation of the brood size. Larva-feeding bees (endorsing a nurse *role*) then have to rely on other mechanisms to evaluate the task priority and to decide whether to keep looking for larvae or seeking other jobs.

2   Related Work

Division of labour occurs when agents have to decide which task to execute in a shared environment. Societies of individuals (or agents) have to find ways to distribute their workforce effectively amongst tasks needed to thrive and survive. In computer science, decentralised control inspired by social insects has been studied for years and has proved to be effective in many applications. In this section, we oversee here what has been done in the field of task allocation models.

In the **Forage for Work** [11] model, the different tasks are scattered in zones. Agents in a given zone try to perform the zone's associated tasks or move randomly. Thus, crowded zones "push" agents to neighbouring zones offering work, resulting in a division of work. When new agents arise in a specific zone and older agents die at a certain age, this rather simple model can recreate age polyethism: agents of the same age are globally doing the same tasks. Newborn agents are taking work offers where they spawned, effectively pushing the older ones away. Following simple rules, an agent can redirect itself in other zones if it cannot find any work to do in its current one. Here, agents have direct access to each task needs. On the other hand, the assumptions that the tasks are scattered in zones and that their stimulus is a representation of the needed work make this model not adapted to the problematic, and need to be refined.

The **Fixed Threshold Model (FTM)** [4] is based on associations between tasks and stimuli. Agent should always execute the task with the higher priority, computed from its score. Each task score is calculated from the intensity of the associated stimulus perceived by the agent, usually computed using a sigmoid.

Let T be the task evaluated by the agent, $F(T)$ the score of the task T, x_T the task's associated perceived stimulus, n an integer for the non-linearity of the function (usually $n = 2$ [20]) and Θ_T a constant named bias used to tweak the function such as when $x_T = \Theta_T$ then $F(T) = 0.5$. The score is calculated with:

$$F(T) = \frac{(x_T)^n}{(x_T)^n + (\Theta_T)^n} \tag{1}$$

The bias Θ is used to alter the perception of the agents. With a given bias, agents are sensitive to the associated stimulus and engage their task earlier than higher bias agents [9]. Each task then has an interruption probability that is randomly tested at each time-step [21]. Then the agent searches a new task using the scores of each task and picks the higher one. Interruption is here completely random and does not reflect the environment nor the agents' capabilities. We believe that better performances can be reached with a more elegant interruption mechanism.

The **Response Threshold Model: Threshold Reinforcement** is based on the FTM. Different works in the 90s [10, 26] proposed to apply some reinforcement to the value Θ, changing the sensitivity of the agents inline. This upgrade of FTM is called a Response Threshold Model (RTM). Widely used to model and drive social insects simulations, it strongly relies on the association between tasks and stimuli in a one to one manner. It also assumes that the execution of the task lowers it's associated stimulus. Otherwise, the agents would execute that task forever. In this article, we are interested in situations where those assumptions are not true. We describe in the next section our model based on RTM and an added mechanism to handle those situations.

3   Proposition: An Interruptible Task Allocation Model

We propose in this section a model based on the Response Threshold Model, in which tasks, activities and actions are defined through a hierarchical subsumption architecture. Our model relies on two mechanisms: 1) the score of each task not associated with any stimuli is based on the agent's current physical state (tools in hand, physiology, physical traits etc.) and 2) An interruption mechanism consisting in: the consideration of the agent's internal motivation in the evaluation of the current task and a systematic evaluation of every available tasks after finishing an action.

3.1   Tasks, Subsumption and RTM

Subsumption architectures have been introduced by Brooks as a way to control robots [5] and are now used in plenty of fields including multi-agent systems. This architecture is organised in stacked layers of behaviour, where each activated behaviour inhibits all the behaviours below it. Topmost layers are prioritised and can be seen as reflexes. Hierarchical subsumption allows a subsumption layer to be another subsumption systems, with layers and conditions. This nesting further improves the adaptability and modality of subsumption system and scales well

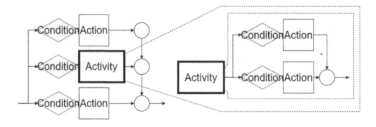

Fig. 1. The hierarchical subsumption architecture represents a task consisting of 2 actions and one activity; the latter consists of 2 other actions, seen on the right.

with increasing complexity [13]. Heckel et al. have shown that this architecture suits well the following definition of the key concepts of task, activity, action and role (based on other's works [1,6]). Figure 1 shows how tasks, activities and actions are defined with a hierarchical subsumption architecture.

An **action** is an uninterruptible piece of work that lasts for a given time. Actions can be cooperative, meaning that they require another agent executing another given action to complete both. Each action has a boolean condition, stating whether it can be executed, as it is a part of a subsumption block.

An **activity** is a set of actions and/or activities building the hierarchical subsumption. Activities also have a boolean condition. Activities can be seen as nodes of a tree where actions are the leaves.

A **task** is a set of piece of work that the agents have to do. Each task of the model is an implementation of the RTM, with an associated threshold and a sigmoid function to compute a score. This score is used by the agent to find the highest priority task.

A **role** is seen as an arbitrary set of tasks, activities or actions. It does not have to match the task's distribution and is more suited to the observer for simplifying the complex mechanisms in place.

3.2 Intrinsic Motivation as Part of the Interruption Mechanism

The first part of the interruption mechanism consists in the use of the intrinsic motivation to help the agent evaluate the usefulness of its current task, and decide whether to pursue it or to choose another one.

For psychologists, motivation is the root of action and a guide for its execution. There are two types of motivation: extrinsic, when a reward is offered by the environment and intrinsic which only has to do with personal needs or expectations [19], like fun or curiosity. Intrinsic Motivation is used in Artificial Intelligence and specifically for learning systems [23], e.g. to help or guide learning agents [2]. Intrinsic motivation can be split up into many different internal stimuli, such as hunger or fear, that trigger behaviours [15], close to what is described in Ethology [10]. When internal stimuli are classified as needs, intrinsic motivation can allow more high-level decision making. Based on the Flow theory [8], an agent struggling in his task feels anxiety and seeks a less difficult task. In the same way, an agent completing an easy task gets bored and moves to more difficult tasks [7]. The competence idea brought by Roohi et al. [18] is, for an agent, the feeling of being in control and able to complete its current task. As such, an agent with a competence level too low seeks an easier task.

In our model, agents do not receive any reward from the environment, so we focus on intrinsic motivation. Tasks in our model can be either *motivated* or not: tasks with no representative stimuli are called motivated, as an agent has to use its intrinsic motivation. Keeping the idea of Flow in mind, our agents can sense whether their current motivated task is useful for the overall system. This can be thought of as a sort of "Desire" in the Belief-Desire-Intention model [17]. Whenever starting a new motivated task, an agent sets its motivation to 1, as fully motivated. Then, the agent executes an action of this task, which may be a **demotivating action**. Upon execution, a demotivating action decrements the agent's motivation. Whenever the agent has finished an action, it computes the score of every tasks it can perform and replaces the score of its current task by its current motivation and picks the higher scored task, as described below. Lowering the agent's motivation makes it more receptive to other tasks.

3.3   Agents and Task Evaluation

Each agent is defined by its internal state, behaviours and capabilities. From these, each agent can achieve a set of tasks, associated with thresholds. Figure 2 shows the decision making of an agent at each cycle, with a systematic evaluation of every available tasks. The agent evaluates first whether its current action is done or not. If it is, the agent selects the task with the highest score. Using the subsumption architecture associated with the selected task, the agent then retrieves the next action and executes it for its full duration. Once done, the whole process is repeated. The re-evaluation of every task at each action completion is key to agents' adaptability. The tasks' thresholds evolve through time and are representative of the agent abilities, whereas the subsumption takes care of the logical approach.

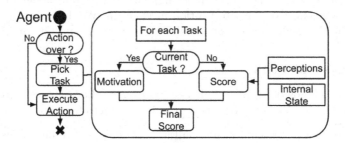

Fig. 2. Decision making of the agent at each cycle.

3.4   Swarm Robotics Example

We present here a theoretical example with swarm robotics to illustrate the mechanisms of our model. The example consists of many robots that can perform two different tasks: foraging (gathering minerals spread around the base), and patrolling around the base. They also have what we call upkeep tasks, such as returning to the base to refuel. The subsumption architecture of the foraging task includes a random movement when no mineral is in sight. This action is a demotivating action: each time a robot executes this action, it lowers its intrinsic motivation and makes it more susceptible to choose another task. When patrolling, the demotivating action is the avoidance of another patrolling bot on the patrol path. This way, patrolling bots auto-regulate themselves.

Robots could use tools that they can pick up and drop-down. Tools modify what robots can do, so picking up a tool changes the bias for all tasks, reflecting the bot internal state. For example, a bot picking up a pickax sees its bias for the foraging task drop-down. Once engaged in the foraging task, not seeing any available mineral fields to harvest (not in sight or already occupied by other bots) lowers the robot's motivation. With a low enough motivation, the robot chooses another task that may require it to change tool.

4   Application: Simulation of a Honey Bee Colony

We implemented a simplified version of a honey bee colony using our model. Bees (are thought to) rely on many stimuli that are not a representation of the priority of a task[1]. For example, in the feeding larva task, larvae emit pheromones no matter how hungry they are[2]. Other tasks (like foraging) are not linked to any external stimuli. The physiological age of a bee determines what key task it can execute, as it needs some biological features (glands - this is equivalent to the "Internal State" of Fig. 2 in our model). Moreover, the physiological age is thought to be a key component of the self-organisation of bees within in the colony, as it can be influenced by hormonal and pheromonal exchanges, as described below. The purpose of this application is then twofold: first, test the role of the physiological age in the division of labour with our model and second, to evaluate the effect of the interruption mechanism. We decided to model two key tasks by the mean of *motivated tasks*: feeding larvae and foraging.

4.1   Agents and Tasks

There are two kinds of agents, adult bees and larvae. Larvae accept food when hungry enough, die when too hungry and emit a contact pheromone called *Ethyle*

---

[1] The source code of the implementation (java), the table of parameters used in the experiments and the scripts (python) used to conduct the statistical analysis (with JASP) can be found on GitHub: https://github.com/Kwarthys/BeeKeeper.

[2] Larvae continuously emit a volatile pheromone called *"E-β-ocimene"*, but recent work has shown that hungry larvae emit more of it and thus attract more workers [12]. Yet, it is still unclear if this stimulus increases the feeding of the larvae.

Oleate (EO) at each time-step. Adult bees, on the other hand, are the agents that have to organise themselves using the *Juvenile Hormone (JH)* in their body to execute the following two motivated tasks: feed the larvae and forage outside. Adult bees also have few upkeep tasks to perform, such as resting or asking/searching for food (see Table 1). Each of these tasks has been described by a hierarchical subsumption architecture (see Fig. 3 for an example).

Table 1. Tasks executed by our adult bee agents. Some tasks are computed using the RTM sigmoid (Eq. 1), but others already mapped in [0; 1] do not need the use of a sigmoid. A non-motivated task behaves exactly as in a classical RTM.

Task name	Input stimulus	Score
Upkeep tasks		
RestTask	Energy	1-Energy
AskFoodTask	Hunger	Hunger
GiveFoodTask	AskFoodStimulus	Sigmoid with bias at 0.5
RandomMoveTask	–	0.2
Motivated tasks		
ForagerTask	–	Sigmoid with bias: 1-JH remapped in [0.3; 1]
FeedLarva	–	Sigmoid with bias: JH remapped in [0.3; 1]

In our model, the scores of the motivated tasks are computed from the current physical state of the agent (see Sect. 3.3). It is particularly true when modelling honeybees: the physiological age of a bee determines what motivated task it can execute. We are insisting on the **physiological** age, as bees can *lower* their age during there lifetime, or *accelerate* their ageing. The physiological age of a bee is given by the amount of *(JH)* in its system, that naturally increases with time. JH guides the physiological development of honeybees: a young bee with low amounts of JH

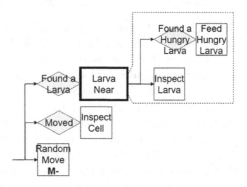

Fig. 3. Hierarchical subsumption describing the "feedLarvae" task. The demotivating action is represented with a "M-"

has the required glands to feed the larvae, and an older bee has the ability to fly to go forage and the glands to process pollen and nectar [24]. Adult bees naturally tend to go foraging outside, pushed by their increasing internal *JH*, but are kept nursing by the brood, the queen and already foraging bees' *EO* (exchanged by contact) [14]. We summed up those interactions Fig. 4. This constant fight of physiological age can nicely balance the workforce between those two major tasks. If foraging bees die outside, less *EO* would be perceived by the young bees inside and some of them would start to age again, restoring the balance.

In nature, a worker can go forage as soon as it is 5 days old but generally starts outside activities around 20. Larvae loss is rare: workers regulate how the queen lay eggs by regulating how they feed her. When they perceive a low resource input, they can almost stop the queen from laying eggs. As we did not model the queen, larva loss will occur and will reflect the efficiency of the colony to allocate its workforce. Moreover, work-

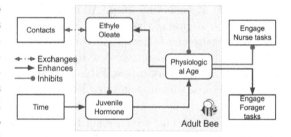

Fig. 4. Physiological dynamics of our simplified adult bee agents. We can see the internal bee variables in the middle and external factors on the left. On the right, we can see how physiological age affects task selection.

ers having to decrease their physiological age is also a rare event. We specifically target those interesting cases, where the colony is deprived of younger adult bees, and, as we did not model a life cycle (no birth, no death, no egg laid), we certainly won't see age polyethism, and thus, bees "classical" life of starting nurse and dying foraging [25].

4.2   Environment and Simulator

The environment is a 2D hexagonal 30 × 30 grid. Each cell has a content (a larva, food, etc.) and may have an adult bee on it. Stimuli are managed at a cell level, where each cell holds an amount of each stimulus. Stimuli are modelled as two major parameters: propagation (their behaviour through space) and dissipation/evaporation (their behaviour through time). When emitting a stimulus, an agent raises the amount of that given stimulus on its cell. Then, at each time-step and for each stimulus, each cell computes its new value using its neighbours' values and its own. The parameters we used for all of our simulations are inspired by biology but calibrated to accelerate the simulations. Hormonal and pheromonal effects can take days to occur, while bees interact and wander through the hive in seconds. We decided to accelerate some effects to obtain results in reasonable simulation time (ranges from x4000 to x6000). For example, larvae are fed about every 2 h [27], but we accelerated that to 2 s. This acceleration brings up a bias, as long term changes are now in the same time scale as quick changes, but won't change the core aspect of what we are demonstrating.

4.3   Experiments and Expected Results

Our first concern is to be sure that the final equilibrium is not influenced by the initial conditions. Moreover, equilibrium should be altered by changing the bee per larva ratio. By putting more larva per worker, we expect to have more worker dedicated to larvae feeding and vice versa. Then we will assess how the interruption mechanism alters the system. We want to assess two hypotheses:

- **H1:** Our model with bee physiology and pheromones can achieve task allocation.
- **H2:** Our interruption mechanism makes the system perform better, enhancing the task allocation. Here, performing better means maximising the time spent foraging AND the larvae survival rate.

We created 5 scenarios (S1 to S5) with different initial conditions that we use to assess those hypotheses. Each scenario is then simulated by bypassing the pheromonal effects (the agents' physiological age is frozen) to assess **H1** or/and bypassing our interruption mechanism (all the tasks are considered as non-motivated) to assess **H2**.

- **S1:** Random age distribution with 150 adult bees and 150 larvae.
- **S2:** 150 adults and 150 larvae but all adult bees start as newborn.
- **S3:** 150 adults and 150 larvae but all adult bees start as old.
- **S4:** Random age distribution with 150 adults and 50 larvae.
- **S5:** Random age distribution with 150 adults and 300 larvae.

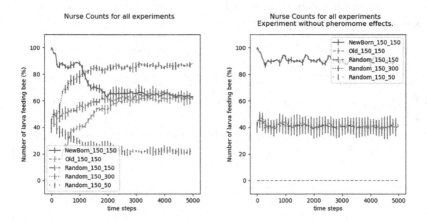

Fig. 5. Here are the different ratios of larva feeding bees of all the experiments (scenarios) we discussed, with and without the Physiology bypass. Each scenario is referred as "InitialDistribution_numberOfBees_NumberOfLarvae".

4.4   Results and Statistical Analysis

With no bypass, S1, S2 and S3 ended with roughly 60% of the colony feeding larvae and about 20% foraging. S4 and S5, when compared to S1, changed the equilibrium. As seen before, the equilibrium for a ratio of adult bee per larva of 1/1 (150 adult bees for 150 larvae, S1) gave us equilibrium at around 60% feeding larvae. A ratio of 1/2 (S5) raises it to almost 90%. A ratio of (S4) 3/1 lowers it to 20%. Figure 5 shows side by side two graphs comparing the different ratios of feeding larva bees amongst the scenarios. We can see on the leftmost graph that S1, S2 and S3 are converging to the same equilibrium, and S4 and S5 have respectively lower and higher equilibrium than the first three. In the rightmost graph, where bee's physiology has been bypassed, we see that the system does not adapt to the scenarios. An ANOVA analysis (Physiology x Interruption, $N = 50$) showed that in some scenarios our interruption mechanism makes the system achieves smaller scores, whereas in others it is the opposite: Table 2 shows an overview of those statistically relevant changes, and the reader will find on Fig. 6 a graphical comparison of the interruption bypass. On the one hand, S1, S2 and S5 are slightly negatively impacted by the interruption mechanism (10% less effective foraging) where the brood care is as effective. On the other hand, in S3 and S4, the interruption mechanism improved the scores by a significant amount.

Table 2. ANOVA analysis, one row for each scenario. The left part holds the impact on the simulation scores of turning on the pheromonal effects, with our interruption mechanism bypassed (computed by scores PhysiologyOn/InterruptionOff - scores PhysiologyOff/InterruptionOff). The right part represents the impact of turning on our interruption mechanism while leaving the pheromonal effects on. Each impact is measured with the nursing score (how much larvae survived) and the foraging score (how many time-steps have been spent foraging).

	Without interruption		With interruption	
	Nursing score	Foraging score	Nursing score	Foraging score
S1	+3% ($p < 0.001$)	−30% ($p < 0.001$)	*Not significant*	−11% ($p < 0.001$)
S2	*Not significant*	0 to 150k ($p < 0.001$)	*Not significant*	−8% ($p < 0.001$)
S3	0% to 68% ($p < 0.001$)	*Not significant*	+37% ($p < 0.001$)	*Not significant*
S4	−32% ($p < 0.001$)	−29% ($p < 0.001$)	+45% ($p < 0.001$)	+35% ($p < 0.001$)
S5	+10% ($p < 0.001$)	−77% ($p < 0.001$)	*Not significant*	−14% ($p = 0.007$)

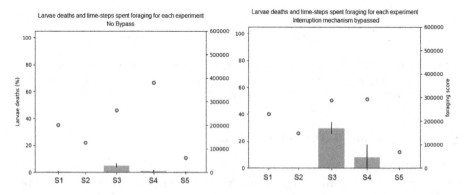

Fig. 6. These graphs show the mean deaths and time-steps spent foraging for each experiment repeated 5 times. The bars show the larvae death rate. The dots shows the number of time steps spent foraging by the colony. The left and right graphs represent the experiments respectively with and without interruption mechanism.

4.5   Discussions

We demonstrated that **H1** is true by changing the starting condition and the bee per larva ratio. However, the statistical analysis we provided only allows us to say that **H2** is true for S3 and S4, where most adaptability is required. The speed at which a demotivating task will cause a task switch is a key parameter. Further work has to be done to calibrate it, but preliminary results show that a faster (up to a point) task switch causes overall better scores, at the cost of individual stability. We would also like to point out that the systematic re-evaluation of all tasks after each action completion could not be bypassed.

5   Conclusion and Perspectives

We proposed here a model based on Response Threshold Model, internal state of the agents and intrinsic motivation to perform task allocation in an environment where not all the tasks have stimuli representing their priority. Modelling the tasks with hierarchical subsumptions and discriminating them using an RTM approach allows us to drive the behaviour of our agents. Tasks contain demotivating actions that represent frustrating behaviours, such as looking for something. Executing a demotivating action lowers the agent's motivation to pursue its current task, making him more sensitive to other tasks. Whenever an agent changes his current task to a motivated task, it resets is motivation. We experimentally showed that our model can reach equilibrium, respond to changing conditions and preliminary work shows that it enhances the effectiveness of the system. Our implementation of this model for a honey bee simplified colony shows a division of labour capabilities. Equilibrium is reached and does not depend on initial conditions, but depends on the adult bee per larva ratio. We intend to enhance the current implementation by adding complexity toward an implementation as close as possible of how honey bee colonies work, further testing the model and its capabilities. We will then compare the behaviour of this implementation with real honey bee colony observations. In parallel we are also implementing the swarm robotics example discussed in Sect. 3.4 to further assess the modality of our proposition.

References

1. Anderson, C., Franks, N.R.: Teamwork in animals, robots, and humans. Adv. Study Behav. **33**, 2–3 (2003)
2. Baldassarre, G., Mirolli, M.: Intrinsically Motivated Learning in Natural and Artificial Systems. Springer, Heidelberg (2013). https://doi.org/10.1007/978-3-642-32375-1
3. Beshers, S.N., Fewell, J.H.: Models of division of labor in social insects. Ann. Rev. Entomol. **46**, 413–440 (2001)
4. Bonabeau, E., Dorigo, M., Theraulaz, G.: From Natural to Artificial Swarm Intelligence. Oxford University Press Inc., Oxford (1999)

5. Brooks, R.: A robust layered control system for a mobile robot. IEEE J. Robot. Autom. **2**, 14–23 (1986)
6. Campbell, A., Wu, A.S.: Multi-agent role allocation: issues, approaches, and multiple perspectives. Auton. Agents Multi-Agent Syst. **22**, 317–355 (2011)
7. Cornudella, M., Van Eecke, P., van Trijp, R.: How intrinsic motivation can speed up language emergence. In: European Conference on Artificial Life. The MIT Press (2015)
8. Csikszentmihalyi, M.: Finding Flow: The Psychology of Engagement with Everyday Life. Basic Books (1997)
9. Dornhaus, A., Klügl, F., Puppe, F., Tautz, J.: Task selection in honeybees - experiments using multi-agent simulation. In: Proceedings of GWAL (1998)
10. Drogoul, A., Ferber, J.: Multi-agent simulation as a tool for modeling societies: application to social differentiation in ant colonies. In: Castelfranchi, C., Werner, E. (eds.) MAAMAW 1992. LNCS, vol. 830, pp. 2–23. Springer, Heidelberg (1994). https://doi.org/10.1007/3-540-58266-5_1
11. Franks, N.R., Tofts, C.: Foraging for work: how tasks allocate workers. Anim. Behav. **48**, 470–472 (1994)
12. He, X.J., et al.: Starving honey bee (*Apis mellifera*) larvae signal pheromonally to worker bees. Sci. Rep. **6**, 1–9 (2016)
13. Heckel, F.W.P., Youngblood, G.M., Ketkar, N.S.: Representational complexity of reactive agents. In: Proceedings of the IEEE Conference on Computational Intelligence and Games. IEEE (2010)
14. Le Conte, Y., Mohammedi, A., Robinson, G.E.: Primer effects of a brood pheromone on honeybee behavioural development. In: Proceedings of the Royal Society of London. Series B: Biological Sciences (2001)
15. Maes, P.: The agent network architecture (ANA). ACM SIGART Bull. **2**, 115–120 (1991)
16. Morley, R.E., Schelberg, C.: An analysis of a plant-specific dynamic scheduler. In: Proceedings of the NSF Workshop on Dynamic Scheduling (1993)
17. Rao, A.S., Georgeff, M.P.: BDI agents: from theory to practice. In: International Conference on Multiagent Systems (1995)
18. Roohi, S., Takatalo, J., Guckelsberger, C., Hämäläinen, P.: Review of intrinsic motivation in simulation-based game testing. In: Proceedings of the CHI Conference on Human Factors in Computing Systems, CHI 2018. ACM Press (2018)
19. Ryan, R.M., Deci, E.L.: Intrinsic and extrinsic motivations: classic definitions and new directions. Contemp. Educ. Psychol. **25**, 54–67 (2000)
20. Schmickl, T., Crailsheim, K.: TaskSelSim: a model of the self-organization of the division of labour in honeybees. Math. Comput. Model. Dyn. Syst. **14**, 101–125 (2008)
21. Schmickl, T., Crailsheim, K.: Analysing honeybees' division of labour in broodcare by a multi-agent model (2008)
22. Schmickl, T., Karsai, I.: Integral feedback control is at the core of task allocation and resilience of insect societies. Proc. Natl. Acad. Sci. **115**, 13180–13185 (2018)
23. Schmidhuber, J.: Formal theory of creativity, fun, and intrinsic motivation (1990–2010). IEEE Trans. Auton. Ment. Dev. **2**, 230–247 (2010)
24. Seeley, T.D.: The Wisdom of the Hive: The Social Physiology of Honey Bee Colonies. Harvard University Press, Cambridge (1995)
25. Seeley, T.D., Kolmes, S.A.: Age polyethism for hive duties in honey bees - illusion or reality? Ethology **87**, 284–297 (1991)

26. Theraulaz, G., Bonabeau, E., Deneubourg, J.L.: Response threshold reinforcements and division of labour in insect societies. Proc. Roy. Soc. B: Biol. Sci. **265**, 327–332 (1998)

27. Winston, M.L.: The Biology of the Honey Bee. Harvard University Press, Cambridge (1991)

28. Zahadat, P., Schmickl, T.: Division of labor in a swarm of autonomous underwater robots by improved partitioning social inhibition. Adapt. Behav. **24**, 87–101 (2016)

RT-BDI: A Real-Time BDI Model

Francesco Alzetta[1] , Paolo Giorgini[1] , Mauro Marinoni[2] ,
and Davide Calvaresi[3](✉)

[1] University of Trento, Trento, Italy
{francesco.alzetta,paolo.giorgini}@unitn.it
[2] Sant'Anna School of Advanced Studies, Pisa, Italy
mauro.marinoni@sssup.it
[3] University of Applied Sciences and Arts of Western Switzerland,
Sierre, Switzerland
davide.calvaresi@hevs.ch

Abstract. Currently, distributed cyber-physical systems (CPS) rely upon embedded real-time systems, which can guarantee compliance with time constraints. CPS are increasingly required to act and interact with one another in dynamic environments. In the last decades, the Belief-Desire-Intention (BDI) architecture has proven to be ideal for developing agents with flexible behavior. However, current BDI models can only reason *about* time and not *in* time. This lack prevents BDI agents from being adopted in designing CPS, and particularly in safety-critical applications. This paper proposes a revision of the BDI model by integrating real-time mechanisms into the reasoning cycle of the agent. By doing so, the BDI agent can make decisions and execute plans ensuring compliance with strict timing constraints also in dynamic environments, where unpredictable events may occur.

Keywords: BDI model · Real-Time Systems · Multi-Agent Systems · Autonomous agents · Real-time multi-agent systems

1 Introduction

Being able to act *in* time, Real-Time Systems (RTS) have been crucial in the technological evolution (in particular, in safety-critical scenarios—e.g., air traffic control). RTS led the development of dependable systems, mainly in predictable environments [10]. Nevertheless, recent studies proposed to adopt RTS' features in *open* environments, detailing opportunities and challenges [3]. On the one hand, RTS lose their efficacy when dealing with highly-dynamic environments. On the other hand, bridging RTS with the Multi-Agent Systems (MAS) approach can create a new generation of systems offering a trade-off in terms of performance and flexibility while ensuring the underlying compliance with strict-timing constraints [11,12,14,21]. In the last decades, MAS researchers developed several agent-oriented languages [5,16,30,32] and frameworks [2,6,8,9,20,26,29]. However, none of them is designed to consider and deal with strict timing constraints explicitly. This lack, among other motivations discussed in [14,25,27,35],

Y. Demazeau et al. (Eds.): PAAMS 2020, LNAI 12092, pp. 16–29, 2020.
https://doi.org/10.1007/978-3-030-49778-1_2

has confined MAS to narrowed application domains rarely employed into the real world. Indeed, most of the real-world applications (especially those safety-critical) cannot operate regardless of time constraints and deadlines.

To overcome such limitations, this paper presents *RT-BDI*, a revision of the *Belief-Desire-Intention* (BDI) cognitive model [31] that integrates real-time notions and mechanisms into the reasoning cycle of the agent. RT-BDI agents are able to make and revise decisions based on the perceived state of the world, their internal state, their computational resources, and the time at their disposal. Moreover, the RT-BDI framework is demanded to either deal with the hardware directly or to run over a real-time operating system (RTOS) able to handle the primitives necessary to ensure compliance with deadlines and reservation.

The remainder of the paper is organized as follows. Section 2 introduces both BDI and RTS basic notions. Section 3 analyzes the relevant state of the art. Section 4 formally describes the proposed model. Section 5 tests the model in a basic case study. Section 6 presents the ongoing work and proposes some future improvements. Finally, Sect. 7 concludes the paper.

2   Background

Belief-Desire-Intention Model - The BDI model [31] is inspired by the theory of human practical reasoning [7], which consists of *deliberation* (deciding the targeted state of affairs), and *means-ends reasoning* (deciding how to achieve it). In BDI, deliberation and means-end are implemented through the notions of *beliefs* (knowledge about itself and the environment), *desires* (objectives), and *intentions* (plans to achieve the committed goals). A *goal* is the instantiation of a desire an agent committed to. A *plan* is a sequence of *actions* that an agent can perform. The decision cycle of a BDI agent consists of *(i) perception* (or inference) of an event's occurrence, which may cause *(ii)* the update of the belief-set of the agent. If a goal is triggered, *(iii)* a set of *relevant* plans are selected from the plans library. Then, *(iv)* the applicability of the plans is checked. Through a selection function, *(v)* a plan is selected, becoming an intention ready to be executed.

Real-Time Systems - RTS are computing systems whose behavior correctness depends not only on the value of the computation but also on the time at which the results are produced [33]. An RTS can provide *soft* and/or *hard* real-time guarantees, which are discriminated in the extent of the damage caused to the system (or its environment) if the result is not delivered on time. In RTS, tasks can be *periodic, aperiodic* or *sporadic*, and each of these task models differ by the regularity of the tasks' activation. Periodic tasks consist of a potentially infinite sequence of regular activations. The activation of aperiodic tasks are irregularly interleaved. Sporadic tasks are a particular case of aperiodic, where consecutive jobs are separated by minimum and maximum inter-arrival time [10]. A possible mapping between RTS tasks and Jade [2] behaviors is proposed in [13].

Real-Time Agent - According to Dragoni et al. [17] a *Real-Time Agent* (RTA) extends and embodies a RT *process*. Thus, its correctness depends both on the soundness and completeness of the code it executes (w.r.t. a certain I/O transfer function) and on its *response time*, which is the interval between the *moment* at which it *starts to be* "executed" and the *instant* at which its *execution* is *completed*. Moreover, focusing on the ontological differences between the concepts of "code" and "process" *acting* in the real world, the authors argued that dealing with *Time* (in both virtual and real environments) is a concrete and basic requirement crucially entangled with *deadlines*, *precedence*, *priority*, and *constrained resources*. RTAs usually operate in highly dynamic environments. Thus, according to Calvaresi et al. [12], the *Earliest Deadline First* (EDF) [10] is the most appropriate real-time compliant scheduling algorithm to power RTAs. However, EDF, as is, can only handle periodic tasks. Therefore, to execute also aperiodic tasks, an RTA should combine it with a bandwidth reservation mechanism [11], such as the Constant Bandwidth Server (CBS) [10] mechanism.

In the context of RTAs and RT-BDI, soft RT means that missing a deadline may cause performance degradation. Conversely, in hard RT, it entails a failure. Our work considers both soft and hard RT guarantees. Providing solely hard RT guarantees in open-world assumption is not reasonable—unless making strong assumptions about the environment [34] and the agents interactions [14]. Hence, a MAS can be considered real-time compliant only if all the agents and their mechanisms (interactions included) operate accordingly [14].

3 Related Work

Since the early 90s, several studies envisioned the need for RT behavior in MAS [18,19,22,28]. Nevertheless, these approaches failed to achieve the overall reliability neglecting the need for the contemporary RT-compliance of the MAS pillars (i.e., scheduler, communication middleware, and negotiation protocol) [14]. In particular, focusing on RT applied to BDI models, [34] and [1], attempted to reach soft RT guarantees for BDI agents by introducing in it RT concepts such as *priority* for goals and *duration* for plans. Nevertheless, since these approaches involve only the deliberative part, they can guarantee a "quick" commitment to an intention, however, still being unable to provide any guarantee on its execution. In [15], the problem of achieving hard real-time compliance is faced by considering an agent composed by in-agents. For every task, an in-agent is responsible for assuring a minimal quality response, while a second in-agent tries to improve this response if there is enough time. However, although this system works under hard real-time constraints, the part responsible for planning - which is the one where BDI is used - is again designed to only operate in the shortest possible time, without providing any compliance with strict RT constraints. In [14], the authors identify in the agent's internal scheduler, communication protocol, and negotiation protocol the fundamental elements characterizing a MAS that, all-together, provide the expected real-time compliance. Since the presented model concerns a single RT-BDI agent, the internal scheduler is the first pillar we focus on. In our BDI model, the scheduler uses RT techniques for both choosing the intentions among the applicable plans, and executing the related tasks, enabling the guarantees for the aimed RT requirements.

4   RT-BDI Model

An agent a is represented by a tuple $a = \{B, D, P, \phi_A, \phi_I\}$, where B, D and P are the set of beliefs, desires and plans of the agent, while ϕ_A and ϕ_I are *selection functions*. ϕ_A chooses a plan (among the applicable ones) to be executed for achieving a selected goal, thus becoming an intention. ϕ_I selects the intention to be executed at each cycle (see Sect. 4.1).

The belief-set B of an agent a is composed of beliefs b. According to Rao [30], if p is a predicate symbol, and $t_1, \ldots, t_k$ are terms, then $p(t_1, \ldots, t_k)$ is a *belief atom*. Therefore, a belief b is a ground belief atom. Yet, differently from Rao, we adopt the closed-world assumption, hence either a knows that p is true, or it assumes p to be false.

The desire-set D of an agent a is a set of desires d defined as a tuple $d = \{b, prec, pr\}$, where $b \in B \cup \overline{B}$ is a *belief literal* (a belief atom or its negation) representing the agent's desire of either achieving or verifying a certain state of the system. *prec* is the set of *preconditions* (i.e., the conjunction of belief literals needed for the activation of the desire) and is formalized as $prec = \bigwedge_{\beta \in \Lambda \subseteq B \cup \overline{B}} \beta$, where β is a belief literal. Finally, pr represents the *priority* of the desire. We intend such a parameter to be a normalized value (e.g., a real number between 0 and 1 to allow priority updates on-the-fly). In particular, pr is used by the selection functions, discriminating most relevant goals for the agent.

When selected by the agent, d becomes a goal. We consider *external goals* (desires activated by a triggering event—e.g., a change in the belief-set or a request made by another agent) and *internal goals* (desires activated by a plan during the execution of an intention, which require the instantiation of a sub-plan). Since such goals must be achieved to complete the execution of the main intention, their activation is not subject to preconditions. Nevertheless, they are still characterized by a priority, which is inherited from the main goal. Moreover, at each instant, a goal is either *active, idle* or *inactive*. A goal is considered active if the agent is actively committed to it. An active goal becomes idle if the corresponding intention requires the achievement of an internal goal. In turn, the internal goal acquires the active state from the parent goal (which remains idle until the internal goal is satisfied). Finally, a goal is inactive if the agent is temporarily unable to achieve it – e.g., because the agent has higher-priority goals to pursue.

An agent a has a library P of plans p. Similarly to Jadex [29], p is composed of a head (containing the goal achieved by the plan, the preconditions for its execution and the context conditions) and a body part (containing a predefined course of action). p is a tuple defined as $p = \{d, pref, prec, cont, body\}$, where d is the triggering desire and *pref* is a cost function sorting the possible plans by preference.

Similar to the desire's definition, *prec* is the set of *preconditions* (the conjunction of belief literals needed for its activation), while *cont* is the *context* i.e., the set of predicates needed to be valid during the entire execution of the plan to prevent its failure. Finally, *body* is a set of sequential actions $\{\alpha_1, \cdots, \alpha_n\}$, where α_j can be either a RT task – e.g., the activation of an actuator – or an internal goal. Inherited from RTS, such tasks can be either periodic or aperiodic [10].

The plans chosen by the means-end reasoning activity become intentions. Since intentions are composed of both internal goals and real-time tasks, we can define them as *partially* instantiated plans. In particular, if the chosen plan requires the achievement of an internal goal g, a suitable plan for achieving g is searched when the execution of the intention reaches such a stage. This mechanism allows the agent to decide which course of action undertake when the satisfaction of the internal goal becomes necessary. However, such an approach also harms the a-priori predictability typical of RTS. A solution to this problem is showed and discussed in Eq. (1).

4.1 Selecting Intentions

Figure 1 shows the agent's reasoning cycle. It starts when the agent perceives new information from the environment or the system. A *Belief Revision Function (BRF)*, which is in charge of preserving the consistency of the belief-set, revises such information. If a new belief corresponds to the precondition of any desire, an external goal is triggered. Moreover, an internal goal can be triggered in case an active intention requires its achievement. Then, all the *relevant plans* are selected and filtered according to the preconditions of such plans, generating the set of currently *applicable plans (AP)*.

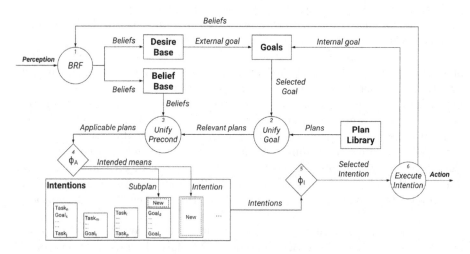

Fig. 1. Reasoning cycle of the agent. Rectangles, circles, and diamonds represent sets, processes, and selections, respectively.

The selection function ϕ_A chooses among AP which plan has to be executed by performing the *schedulability test* of the plans. This analysis is used in RTS to discriminate the feasibility of a task-set based on the processor utilization [10].

According to [24], the *processor utilization factor* U of the agent a is the fraction of processing time spent in the execution of the task set, and at a specific time t is defined by $U(t) = \sum_{\tau_i \in \Gamma(t)} U_{\tau_i}$ with $U_{\tau_i} = C_{\tau_i}/T_{\tau_i}$ where $\Gamma(t)$ is the set of periodic tasks scheduled at time t by the agent, C_{τ_i} is the *computation time* of periodic task τ_i (i.e., the time necessary to the processor for executing the task without interruption), and T_{τ_i} is the activation *period* of the task τ_i, so the fixed time interval after which it repeats.

In particular, according to [10], a task-set of a given agent is feasible if its utilization factor is less or equal than the *least upper bound* (U_{lub}) of the scheduling algorithm used. U_{lub} is the minimum of the utilization factors across all task sets that fully utilize the processor.

Moreover, as mentioned in Sect. 2, to bound the execution of aperiodic tasks and guarantee isolation among periodic and aperiodic tasks, we employ the CBS artifact (also known as server mechanism). Thus, similarly to $U(t)$, the utilization factor of a CBS server S is $U_s = Q_s/T_s$, where Q_s is the maximum budget (i.e., its reserved computational time) and T_s is the period of the server.

Here, we assume that for each "relatable class" of aperiodic tasks (e.g., motion or actuators-related), the designer of the system dedicates a specific server. Due to the sequential execution of the tasks composing an intention, there is at most one server – while all the others are idle – or periodic task running at a time per intention. We define a task-set Γ_i as the set of tasks composing agent's intention to satisfy a goal i. Then, the *Maximum Utilization factor* $\hat{U}_{\Gamma_i}$ of a task-set Γ_i can be defined as $\hat{U}_{\Gamma_i} = \max_{\tau_k \in \Gamma_i} U_{\tau_k}$. Thus, given the sequential nature of the task release within an intention, the higher utilization factor of the tasks composing Γ_i represent the worst case for U_{Γ_i}. By doing so, we *(i)* increase the efficiency of computing the schedulability test (its granularity is per task-set rather than per single task) and *(ii)* grant safety to the system (allowing predictable delays –possibly due to the dynamic nature of EDF– while still ensuring the compliance with the committed deadlines). This approach may appear too conservative (pessimistic). Nevertheless, since the agent does not know a-priori the interleaving of its intentions, it is crucial to provide timing guarantees in RT-settings. However, we plan to optimize this strategy with more effective – yet complex – schedulability policies and mechanisms (see Sect. 6).

Recalling that Γ includes all the task-sets corresponding to the intentions the agent a has committed to, we define $\hat{U}_\Gamma = \sum_{i=1}^{k} max_{\Gamma_i, \Gamma_g \in \Gamma}(\hat{U}_{\Gamma_i}, \hat{U}_{\Gamma_g})$, where i is an external goal and g is an internal goal triggered by the execution of the intention for i. The schedulability test for an applicable plan's task-set AP_i can be formalized as $\Gamma = \Gamma \cup AP_i$, if $\hat{U}_\Gamma + \hat{U}_{AP_i} \leq U_{lub}$.

We define the *remaining utilization factor* as $U_r = U_{lub} - \hat{U}_\Gamma = 1 - \hat{U}_\Gamma$, since $U_{lub} = 1$ when using EDF with CBS. Consequently, $\Gamma = \Gamma \cup AP_i$, if $\hat{U}_{AP_i} \leq U_r$.

At the start of a reasoning cycle, there could be more than one goal pending. Hence, to define the selection function ϕ_A, we revised the well-known multiple-choice knapsack problem [23] in the following variant:

$$\phi_A(AP) = \text{maximize} \sum_{i=1}^{k} pr_i \sum_{j \in AP_i} pref_{ij}x_{ij} \tag{1}$$

$$\text{subject to} \quad \sum_{i=1}^{k} \sum_{j \in AP_i} \hat{U}_j x_{ij} \leq U_r$$

$$\sum_{j \in AP_i} x_{ij} \leq 1 \quad \forall i \mid 1 \leq i \leq k$$

$$x_{ij} \in \{0, 1\} \quad \forall i, j \mid 1 \leq i \leq k \land j \in AP_i$$

where k is the number of goals for which the agent has not committed to an intention yet, pr_i is the priority of the ith uncommitted goal, AP_i is the set of applicable plans for i, $pref_{ij}$ is the value computed by the cost function of the plan $j \in AP_i$, x_{ij} is a binary variable which assumes value one if and only if $j \in AP_i$ is currently taken into consideration.

The selection function ϕ_A complies with the following rules:

(i) Try to schedule (commit to) an applicable plan for each pending goal.
(ii) If (i) is not possible, drop the plans for the goals having less priority.
(iii) Among plans for goals with the same priority, prioritize those that are most preferred by the agent.

Given Eq. (1), $\Gamma = \Gamma \cup \phi_A(AP)$. Finally, we expect that an agent could achieve the same goal with different priorities (depending on the situation). Furthermore, the priority of a committed goal could change on the fly. For instance, a goal could become more urgent upon the occurrence of some condition. Since the agent keeps track of the goals it is currently pursuing, it can easily manage this case. The agent updates the priority of the goal and reschedules its intention—via ϕ_A. In particular, it drops the currently active intention for the goal and chooses a new feasible intention (if it has a higher priority).

4.2 Executing Intentions

Once an agent has committed to a new intention i, it is added to the intention-set I. In the presented RT-BDI model, ϕ_I – which selects the intention to be executed at the next cycle – implements the EDF scheduling algorithm. This approach differs, for instance, from Jason [6], which implements a hierarchical round-robin (RR) as the default intention selection function [13], and JACK [9], which allows choosing between RR and FIFO. EDF has higher fairness among tasks with respect to FIFO (which could lead to blocking task-sets) and is more efficient then RR (which grants fairness but may cause conflicts between interleaved steps in different intentions). For a complete study supporting the employment of EDF in the RT-MAS domain, see [12].

Besides scheduling the current intention in the ready queue, ϕ_I also manages the precedence between tasks belonging to the same task-set. Indeed, the sequentiality of the tasks of an intention (discussed in Sect. 4.1) must be respected to avoid unwanted and unpredictable behaviors. On the one hand, for aperiodic tasks, an action is considered executed when the instance of the corresponding task is completed. Hence, the activation of a successor can be automatically triggered by the termination of its predecessors. Therefore, given the ready queue Ψ^a of an agent a, a task-set Γ_k including an aperiodic task τ_i and its successor τ_j, the current time t and the finishing time f_i of τ_i, $\tau_i, \tau_j \in \Psi^a \Leftrightarrow f_i < t$.

On the other hand, for periodic tasks, the action is considered executed only when the scheduler removes the task from the RT queue (when the last instance of the task is completed).

If the dependency among the instances of periodic tasks is needed (i.e., an instance τ_j^k of task τ_j needs data produced by an instance τ_i^k of task τ_i), non-blocking communication mechanisms must be applied to avoid unbounded delays in tasks execution (e.g., using the Logical Execution Time (LET) paradigm [4]).

5   Example: A Real-Time Autonomous Robot Vacuum

Let us consider the simulation of an in-house automated robot vacuum able to move around, check both levels of battery and garbage container, suck the dirt from the floor, recharge the battery, and empty the garbage container.

5.1   Design of the Agent

The knowledge of both its state and the surrounding environment is crucial for the agent (see Table 1). We assume the robot is equipped with sensors (i.e., proximity, battery level, and cameras) providing the required knowledge (e.g., its current position). Table 2 shows the agent's desire-set and corresponding priorities (based on the goals' relevance). This example shows that both belief atoms and their negations can be a desired state of the system. Furthermore, the same desire can be triggered with a different priority upon the precondition that activated it. In this basic example, we assume 10% to be the minimum battery level necessary to return to the charging station. For this reason, the goal becomes urgent only when such a threshold is reached. However, in a real-world application such a value should be calculated dynamically (position-dependent).

Moreover, recalling that an agent may need to verify the state of the system or its components, goals such as checking(battery) and checking(obstacles) can have remarkably high priority (having a minimum battery level is vital for the robot) and need to be checked continuously.

The internal goals (e.g., currentPos(X,Y) and status(roaming)) are triggered directly by the agent itself, so they have no explicit precondition (e.g., we want the vacuum turning on when a running intention demands for it rather then meeting a precondition). The plans are defined offline by the designer and could involve sub-plans if an internal goal is instantiated within the main plan.

Plan 1 shows a trivial example of a plan aiming at cleaning the bathroom (cleaning kitchen and the bedroom are similar).

Table 1. Agent's belief-set.   **Table 2.** Agent's desire-set containing the possible goals.

Belief atom
clean(kitchen)
clean(bedroom)
clean(bathroom)
kitchenPos(X,Y)
bedroomPos(X,Y)
bathPos(X,Y)
currentPos(X,Y)
sensed(obstacle)
battCharge(B)
contLevel(C)
active(vacuum)
status(roaming)
checking(battery)
checking(obstacles)

Belief literal	Preconditions	Priority
clean(kitchen)	¬(clean(kitchen))	0.6
clean(bedroom)	¬(clean(bedroom))	0.6
clean(bathroom)	¬(clean(bathroom))	0.6
checking(battery)	¬(checking(battery))	0.95
checking(obstacles)	¬(checking(obstacles))	0.95
battCharge(100)	battCharge(10)	0.9
battCharge(100)	battCharge(90)	0.3
contLevel(0)	contLevel(100)	0.6
contLevel(0)	contLevel(10)	0.3
¬(sensed(obstacle))	sensed(obstacle)	0.9
currentPos(X,Y)	–	–
active(vacuum)	–	–
¬(active(vacuum))	–	–
status(roaming)	–	–

Plan 1 Bathroom cleaning

1: **DESIRE:** clean(bathroom)
2: **PREFERENCE:** 2
3: **PREC:** contLevel($C < 80$) ∧ battCharge($B > 40$)
4: **CONT:** contLevel($C < 100$) ∧ battCharge($B > 20$)
5: $g : currentPos(bathPos.X, bathPos.Y)$
6: $g : active(vacuum)$
7: $g : status(roaming)$
8: $g : not(active(vacuum))$

Plan 2 Change position

1: **DESIRE:** currentPos(X,Y)
2: **PREFERENCE:** 2
3: **PREC:** battCharge($B > f$)
4: **CONT:** not(sensed(obstacle))
5: $ac : path \leftarrow calculatePath(X, Y)$
6: $ac : followPath(path)$

Such a plan is applicable only if at the very start the container has enough capacity (i.e., container level does not exceed 80%) and if there is enough battery to perform all the needed operations. Furthermore, at run-time, container and battery levels cannot exceed the respective thresholds. To perform plan 1, the robot has to reach the bathroom, activate the vacuum, roam around the room, and finally, when done, deactivate the vacuum. In plan 2 a possible plan dealing with the currentPos(X,Y) goal is shown. This plan is composed of two actions: (i) calculating the steps needed to reach the destination, and (ii) executing them. Here, the selection of the plan is subject to the charge of the battery: the plan is applicable if f (function approximating the required battery) is enough. Moreover, besides minor obstacle avoidance, if unexpected and considerably obstructive obstacles are encountered, the plan might need an update (demanding a re-planning to the agent) to avoid the obstacle. It is worth noticing that, besides the plan-specific tasks (e.g., calculating the path towards the bathroom), all the other operations are represented as internal goals. This separation between the *main-plan* and its *sub-plans* gives the agent a flexible behavior, since different sub-plans can be chosen depending on the context.

The assignment of the RT parameters (i.e., C and T for the tasks, and Q and P for the servers) is crucial. While task periods are derived from the application requirements (e.g., sampling frequencies, message rate, and physical constraints), the computation time is dependent on platform and implementation. Typical approaches to compute them are the static analysis of the code and the statistical estimation on profiled performances—which go beyond the scope of the paper. Thus, we establish these values approximating the action complexity. For example, to activate and deactivate the vacuum (switching on/off the actuator), we established the minimum computational time possible, $C = 1$. The tasks' computation time and period are specified in Table 3, which shows the complete tasks characterization. τ_1, τ_2 and τ_3 are periodic tasks, τ_4, τ_5 and τ_6 are aperiodic tasks (mapped on the related servers). Albeit the agent reasoning process must be considered as a task itself, we preferred to initially relax this aspect to keep the presented example intuitive. Since τ_4 and τ_5 act similarly on the same component (switching the vacuum on/off), they are assigned to the same server (see Table 4).

Table 3. Agent tasks

Task	Behaviour	C	T
τ_1	Move one step	2	5
τ_2	Check obstacles	1	5
τ_3	Check battery	1	10
τ_4	Vacuum on	1	–
τ_5	Vacuum off	1	–
τ_6	CalculatePath	5	–

Table 4. Agent servers.

Server	Tasks	Q	T
$S_{4,5}$	τ_4, τ_5	1	10
S_6	τ_6	5	20

Table 5. Initial belief-set.

Belief atom
clean(kitchen)
clean(bedroom)
clean(bathroom)
kitchenPos(X_{ki}, Y_{ki})
bedroomPos(X_{be}, Y_{be})
bathPos(X_{ba}, Y_{ba})
currentPos(X,Y)
contLevel(0)
battCharge(100)

Referring to plan 2, $calculatePath(X, Y)$ corresponds to the aperiodic task τ_6, while the action $followPath(path)$ is performed by the periodic task τ_1.

5.2 Execution of the Agent

Table 5 reports the initial predicates composing the belief-set of the agent while Fig. 2 shows the task scheduling of the agent. For simplicity, we assume that the robot can reach its destination in just $n = 1$ steps (hence, periodic task τ_1 is executed only once instead of a variable number of times).

At the very start, the agent commits to two goals: checking(obstacles) and checking(battery). Since the intentions chosen to achieve them are composed by periodic tasks, the corresponding goals are considered achieved when the agent removes them from the ready queue (see Sect. 4.2).

At the time t_0, the agent perceives (or is told that) the bathroom is not clean. This triggers the agent's reasoning cycle, that tries to match this new belief with any desires' precondition, and instantiates the corresponding goal. Searching the possible plans and selecting the best (via ϕ_A), the agent chooses plan 1 with the corresponding Γ_{plan1} composed of $\tau_6, \tau_1, \tau_4, \tau_6, \tau_1, \tau_5$ (sorted by release time). The *roaming* goal is achieved with a plan similar to plan 2, which targets a "covering-an-area" instead of a "direct" path to a pair of coordinates. The schedulability test on the Γ allows an applicable plan to become an intention if $U(t) \leq 1\ \forall t$. For simplicity, we assume that from time t_0 to t_{42}, the goal clean(bathroom) is the only one being instantiated. Being $U_{\tau_2} = 0.2$ and $U_{\tau_3} = 0.1$, the utilization factor of the agent at time t_0 is 0.3. The utilization factors of periodic tasks and servers serving the aperiodic tasks composing the bathroom cleaning's task-set are $U_{\tau_1} = 0.4$, $U_{S_{4,5}} = 0.1$ and $U_{S_6} = 0.25$. Since $U_{\tau_2} + U_{\tau_3} + \hat{U}_{\Gamma_{plan1}} = 0.7 \leq 1$ (the Maximum Utilization factor of plan 1 is at most 0.4, when τ_1 is executing), the agent can always find a feasible schedule. Figure 2 shows a graphical representation of the schedule of Γ produced by EDF.

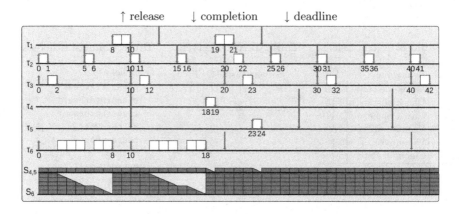

Fig. 2. Representation of agent's task scheduling.

Adopting an RT scheduler in the reasoning cycle of an agent ensures that both hard and soft timing constraints are met. Hence, looking at Fig. 2, at t_4, τ_6 is running. At t_5, when a task with a earlier deadline d is released, it is preempted ($d_{\tau_2} < d_{S_6}$). Then, after τ_2 has executed, the processor completes the execution of τ_6 enabling both to comply with their deadlines, which could be missed in the current BDI implementations [13]. As formalized in Sect. 4.2, managing the precedence among the tasks within the same intention is crucial. Hence, for example, we do not want that the robot starts moving (τ_1) before it has finished to plan the route (τ_6).

6   Future Work

As mentioned in Sect. 4.1, to improve agent's performance ϕ_A should be optimized. Inspired by [11], we aim at adapting their mechanism to compute both real and potential utilization of the agent punctually, leveraging on the commitment (possibly with parallel instances). In particular, ϕ_A will compute the utilization relying on both accepted and pending (under evaluation) plans and tasks. The computation of $U(t)$ needs to be triggered only if interferences occur (e.g., new releases)—being computed according to the related task model. Moreover, we will evaluate possible adaptations of the approach presented in [36] (yet neglecting RT constraints), where the agent selects the intention to be progressed at the action level, possibly increasing the achievable goals. An important step consists of extending the characterization of time from the tasks/plans to the goals level. Besides ensuring compliance with strict-timing constraints (current model), the agent will be able to define whether or not a goal can be satisfied within a time interval, given its resources, capabilities, means, and constraints. Moreover, the RT-BDI model can be extended from single to multi-agent settings. Finally, handling the plan failures will be studied and modeled.

7   Conclusion

We presented RT-BDI, a revision of the BDI model that exploits RT mechanisms to allow its employment in safety-critical applications. The main contribution of this paper consists in the integration of RT mechanisms into the BDI reasoning cycle, involving an RT scheduler in two distinct phases. A schedulability test is first performed to choose a feasible set of intentions to be executed, and then the scheduling algorithm provides the execution order of the actions composing such intentions. This approach opens to promising developments and calls for a simulator to allow verification and validation.

References

1. Alzetta, F., Giorgini, P.: Towards a real-time BDI model for ROS 2. In: CEUR Workshop Proceedings, vol. 2404, pp. 1–7 (2019)
2. Bellifemine, F., Poggi, A., Rimassa, G.: JADE-a FIPA-compliant agent framework. In: Proceedings of PAAM, London, vol. 99, p. 33 (1999)
3. Biondi, A., Nesti, F., Cicero, G., Casini, D., Buttazzo, G.: A safe, secure, and predictable software architecture for deep learning in safety-critical systems. IEEE Embed. Syst. Lett. 1 (2019)
4. Biondi, A., Pazzaglia, P., Balsini, A., Di Natale, M.: Logical execution time implementation and memory optimization issues in autosar applications for multicores. In: International Workshop on Analysis Tools and Methodologies for Embedded and Real-time Systems (WATERS) (2017)
5. Bordini, R.H., Bazzan, A.L., de O Jannone, R., Basso, D.M., Vicari, R.M., Lesser, V.R.: AgentSpeak (XL): efficient intention selection in BDI agents via decision-theoretic task scheduling. In: Proceedings of the First International Joint Conference on Autonomous Agents and Multiagent Systems: Part 3, pp. 1294–1302 (2002)
6. Bordini, R.H., Hübner, J.F., Wooldridge, M.: Programming Multi-agent Systems in AgentSpeak Using Jason, vol. 8. Wiley, Hoboken (2007)
7. Bratman, M.: Intention, Plans, and Practical Reason, vol. 10. Harvard University Press, Cambridge (1987)

8. Bresciani, P., Perini, A., Giorgini, P., Giunchiglia, F., Mylopoulos, J.: Tropos: an agent-oriented software development methodology. Auton. Agent. Multi-Agent Syst. **8**(3), 203–236 (2004)
9. Busetta, P., Rönnquist, R., Hodgson, A., Lucas, A.: Jack intelligent agents-components for intelligent agents in Java. AgentLink News Lett. **2**(1), 2–5 (1999)
10. Buttazzo, G.C.: Hard Real-Time Computing Systems: Predictable Scheduling Algorithms and Applications, vol. 24. Springer, Heidelberg (2011). https://doi.org/10.1007/978-1-4614-0676-1
11. Calvaresi, D.: Real-time multi-agent systems: challenges, model, and performance analysis (2018)
12. Calvaresi, D., et al.: Timing reliability for local schedulers in multi-agent systems. In: RTcMAS@ IJCAI, pp. 1–15 (2018)
13. Calvaresi, D., et al.: Local scheduling in multi-agent systems: getting ready for safety-critical scenarios. In: Belardinelli, F., Argente, E. (eds.) EUMAS/AT -2017. LNCS (LNAI), vol. 10767, pp. 96–111. Springer, Cham (2018). https://doi.org/10.1007/978-3-030-01713-2_8
14. Calvaresi, D., Marinoni, M., Sturm, A., Schumacher, M., Buttazzo, G.: The challenge of real-time multi-agent systems for enabling IoT and CPS. In: Proceedings of the International Conference on Web Intelligence, pp. 356–364. ACM (2017)
15. Carrascosa, C., Bajo, J., Julián, V., Corchado, J.M., Botti, V.: Hybrid multi-agent architecture as a real-time problem-solving model. Expert Syst. Appl. **34**(1), 2–17 (2008)
16. Dastani, M.: 2APL: a practical agent programming language. Auton. Agent. Multi-Agent Syst. **16**(3), 214–248 (2008)
17. Dragoni, A., Sernani, P., Calvaresi, D.: When rationality entered time and became a real agent in a cyber-society, vol. 2280, pp. 167–171 (2018)
18. Hayes-Roth, B.: Architectural foundations for real-time performance in intelligent agents. Real-Time Syst. **2**(1–2), 99–125 (1990)
19. Holt, J., Rodd, M.G.: An architecture for real-time distributed artificial intelligent systems. Real-Time Syst. **6**(1–2), 263–288 (1994). https://doi.org/10.1007/BF01088628
20. Huber, M.J.: JAM: a BDI-theoretic mobile agent architecture. In: Proceedings of the Third Annual Conference on Autonomous Agents, pp. 236–243. ACM (1999)
21. Julian, V., Botti, V.: Developing real-time multi-agent systems. Integr. Comput.-Aided Eng. **11**(2), 135–149 (2004)
22. Julian, V., Carrascosa, C., Rebollo, M., Soler, J., Botti, V.: SIMBA: an approach for real-time multi-agent systems. In: Escrig, M.T., Toledo, F., Golobardes, E. (eds.) CCIA 2002. LNCS (LNAI), vol. 2504, pp. 282–293. Springer, Heidelberg (2002). https://doi.org/10.1007/3-540-36079-4_25
23. Kellerer, H., Pferschy, U., Pisinger, D.: The multiple-choice Knapsack problem. In: Kellerer, H., Pferschy, U., Pisinger, D. (eds.) Knapsack Problems, pp. 317–347. Springer, Heidelberg (2004). https://doi.org/10.1007/978-3-540-24777-7_11
24. Liu, C.L., Layland, J.W.: Scheduling algorithms for multiprogramming in a hard-real-time environment. J. ACM (JACM) **20**(1), 46–61 (1973)
25. Logan, B.: An agent programming manifesto. Int. J. Agent-Orientated Softw. Eng. **6**, 187–210 (2017)
26. Morley, D., Myers, K.: The spark agent framework. In: Proceedings of the Third International Joint Conference on Autonomous Agents and Multiagent Systems, vol. 2, pp. 714–721. IEEE Computer Society (2004)

27. Müller, J.P., Fischer, K.: Application impact of multi-agent systems and technologies: a survey. In: Shehory, O., Sturm, A. (eds.) Agent-Oriented Software Engineering, pp. 27–53. Springer, Heidelberg (2014). https://doi.org/10.1007/978-3-642-54432-3_3

28. Musliner, D.J., Durfee, E.H., Shin, K.G.: CIRCA: a cooperative intelligent real-time control architecture. IEEE Trans. Syst. Man Cybern. **23**, 1561–1574 (1993)

29. Pokahr, A., Braubach, L., Lamersdorf, W.: Jadex: a BDI reasoning engine. In: Bordini, R.H., Dastani, M., Dix, J., El Fallah Seghrouchni, A. (eds.) Multi-Agent Programming. MSASSO, vol. 15, pp. 149–174. Springer, Boston, MA (2005). https://doi.org/10.1007/0-387-26350-0_6

30. Rao, A.S.: AgentSpeak(L): BDI agents speak out in a logical computable language. In: Van de Velde, W., Perram, J.W. (eds.) MAAMAW 1996. LNCS, vol. 1038, pp. 42–55. Springer, Heidelberg (1996). https://doi.org/10.1007/BFb0031845

31. Rao, A.S., Georgeff, M.P.: Modeling rational agents within a BDI-architecture. KR **91**, 473–484 (1991)

32. Rodriguez, S., Gaud, N., Galland, S.: SARL: a general-purpose agent-oriented programming language. In: 2014 IEEE/WIC/ACM International Joint Conferences on Web Intelligence (WI) and Intelligent Agent Technologies (IAT). IEEE (2014)

33. Stankovic, J.A., Ramamritham, K. (eds.): Tutorial: Hard Real-time Systems. IEEE Computer Society Press, Los Alamitos (1989)

34. Vikhorev, K., Alechina, N., Logan, B.: The ARTS real-time agent architecture. In: Dastani, M., El Fallah Segrouchni, A., Leite, J., Torroni, P. (eds.) LADS 2009. LNCS (LNAI), vol. 6039, pp. 1–15. Springer, Heidelberg (2010). https://doi.org/10.1007/978-3-642-13338-1_1

35. Winikoff, M.: Challenges and directions for engineering multi-agent systems. arXiv preprint arXiv:1209.1428 (2012)

36. Yao, Y., Logan, B.: Action-level intention selection for BDI agents. In: Proceedings of the 2016 International Conference on Autonomous Agents & Multiagent Systems, pp. 1227–1236. International Foundation for Autonomous Agents and Multiagent Systems (2016)

Routing Model Evaluator

Vince Antal, Tamás Gábor Farkas, Alex Kiss, Miklós Miskolczi,
and László Z. Varga$^{(\boxtimes)}$ (iD)

Faculty of Informatics, ELTE Eötvös Loránd University, Budapest 1117, Hungary
lzvarga@inf.elte.hu

Abstract. We expect that the traffic will be almost optimal when the
collective behaviour of autonomous vehicles will determine the traffic.
The route selection plays an important role in optimizing the traffic.
There are different models of the routing problem. The novel intention-
aware online routing game model points out that intention-awareness
helps to avoid that the traffic generated by autonomous vehicles be worse
than the traffic indicated by classical traffic flow models. The models are
important, but their applicability in real life needs further investigations.
We are building a test environment, where the decision making methods of the different models can be evaluated in almost real traffic. The
almost real traffic runs in a well known simulation platform. The simulation platform also provides tools to calculate a dynamic equilibrium
traffic assignment. The calculation needs long time and a lot of computing resources. The routing model evaluator contains an implementation
of the routing model which determines the routes for the vehicles. The
route selections are injected into the simulation platform, and the simulation platform drives the vehicles. The first results of the investigations
with the routing model evaluator show that the route selection of the
intention-aware routing model will be able to bring the traffic close to a
dynamic equilibrium in real time.

Keywords: Autonomous vehicles · Route selection · Dynamic
equilibrium

1 Introduction

From a computer science point of view, the road traffic is a large-scale and open
multi-agent system that tries to solve the *routing problem*. The routing problem
is a network with traffic flows going from a source node to a destination node.
The traffic is routed in a congestion sensitive manner. The participants of the
traffic want to optimise their trips.

There are different formal models for the routing problem. A model describes
the possible actions of the participants, and the available information that they
can use to select the best action. The participants are assumed to be rational,
in the sense that each participant selects an action which is the best response to
the expected actions of the other participants. A model involves a solution concept [9] which forecasts the possible outcomes of the problem if the participants

© Springer Nature Switzerland AG 2020
Y. Demazeau et al. (Eds.): PAAMS 2020, LNAI 12092, pp. 30–41, 2020.
https://doi.org/10.1007/978-3-030-49778-1_3

are rational. The most common solution concept is the equilibrium concept. The system is in equilibrium, if none of the agents can select another action to achieve better results from its own point of view. A basic assumption of traffic engineering is that the traffic flows are assigned to possible paths in accordance with an equilibrium, which is either a static equilibrium [1,27] or a dynamic equilibrium [13,17]. The equilibrium is an important concept, because none of the agents has an incentive to deviate from the equilibrium, therefore the equilibrium seems to be a stable state of the system, although it may not be optimal.

We are interested in the route selection of autonomous vehicles, and we would like to know how the formal models for the routing problem can support the trustworthy decision making of real-world autonomous agents. We assume that autonomous vehicles can safely avoid obstacles on their way, so we assume that in this sense they are trustworthy. We are interested in the trustworthiness of their route selection. If the route selection strategy of the model makes the agents select routes which are close to the equilibrium, then we can trust that model.

In Sect. 2, we shortly overview the models of the routing problem. In Sect. 3, we describe the architecture of the Routing Model Evaluator. In Sect. 4, we describe a scenario to be used for the evaluation of the intention aware online routing game model. The evaluation is in Sect. 5. Finally, we conclude the paper in Sect. 6.

2   Related Work: Routing Models and Traffic Simulators

Routing Game. From algorithmic game theory point of view [14], the routing problem is a network with source routing, where end users simultaneously choose a full route to their destination and the traffic is routed in a congestion sensitive manner [19]. The solution concept of the routing game is the *equilibrium* concept. If some restrictions are applied to the model, then the existence of equilibria and an upper limit on the price of anarchy are proved. The drawback of the classic game theory model is that it assumes full knowledge of the game, it describes static situations and decisions are on the flow level.

Evolutionary Routing Game. The evolutionary dynamics of games [29] is usually investigated in repeated games where the agents receive feedback by observing their own and other agents' action and cost, and in the next game they change their own action based on these observations to decrease their cost [2,7,20]. If the initial traffic flow assignment has at least some traffic flow on each path of the static routing game, then the traffic flow assignment converges to the Nash equilibrium of the static routing game. The repeated routing game has similar limitations as the algorithmic game theory model: decisions are on the flow level.

Queuing Network. The *non-atomic queuing network* [5] is a way of investigating how non-atomic traffic flows evolve over time. The solution concept for the queuing model is the *dynamic equilibrium all the time* [5], which corresponds to the *Nash equilibrium over time* defined in [11]. The queuing model does not have load-dependent cost of the edge if the queue is empty and the inflow is below the maximum capacity, because in this inflow range the edge has a constant delay. Therefore the queuing model is not a full extension of the static routing game to the time dimension. Regarding the practical applicability for autonomous vehicles, the queuing model has similar limitations as the static routing game. The queuing model assumes the idealistic situation where the agents have complete knowledge of the current and the future states of all queues and edges. In addition, a general queuing network is a complex system which may not reach a dynamic equilibrium over time.

Online Routing Game. The online routing game model [24] contains elements of the routing game model, the queuing model and the concept of online mechanisms [16]. The online routing game model may comprise other important aspects as well: feedback from the traffic network, intention-awareness and intention aware prediction. In the online routing game model [24], the traffic flow is made up of individual agents who follow each other, and the agents of the traffic flow individually decide which path to select, depending on the real-time situation.

Intention-Aware Online Routing Game is a special type of online routing game, where the agents can perceive their environment as described above, and in addition they also receive aggregated information about the intentions of other agents in the system. The agents communicate their intentions to a service. The service aggregates the data about the agent collective, and it sends a feedback to the agents [3]. The feedback is a forecast of future traffic durations, and the agents who are still planning their route use this information to make decision. The *intention-aware* [28] and the *intention propagation* [4] approaches are based on this scheme. Many results in different dynamical games show that many games exhibit complex unpredictable behaviour, or in the best case, they converge to a cycle [15]. Online routing games are complex games that tend to cycle around a kind of equilibrium, and this fluctuation is measured empirically [26].

Traffic Simulators. There are macroscopic and microscopic traffic simulations. Macroscopic simulations deal with aggregated elements of the traffic system, like traffic flows. Microscopic simulations deal with individual elements of the traffic system, like individual vehicles. The main model in microscopic traffic simulation software is the car following model [18] which simulates real driving behaviours. The car following model assumes that a vehicle maintains a safe space and time gap between itself and the vehicle that precedes it. The routing game model is a good approximation of the macroscopic simulation, and the online routing game is a good approximation of the microscopic simulation. A free and open simulation software is the SUMO (Simulation of Urban MObility) traffic simulation suite [12]. Because traffic simulation software is not a formal model, it does not have its own solution concept. However, the SUMO simulation software gives tools to find a dynamic equilibrium in an iterative way. The SUMO simulation software provides two methods to converge to a dynamic equilibrium during the iteration process: the Iterative Assignment (Dynamic User Equilibrium) method of [8] and the classic logistic regression method [10].

There are advanced 3D simulators like the CARLA Simulator [6], the LGSVL Simulator[1] and the MATISSE (Multi-Agent based Traffic Safety Simulation sys-tEm) [23]. These simulators require powerful computers with GPU video cards, because they provide realistic 3D views which can be used to generate camera and LIDAR sensor data. The main focus of these simulators is on the agent-environment interactions, like the sensor data and the local control of the vehicle. Our focus is on the routing level control, and we want to be able to run our sim-ulator on less powerful computers. The AgentDrive simulator [21,22] is closer to our aims, however it focuses mainly on aspects like trajectory planning, collision avoidance, and cooperative lane changing. Our simulation software is different from these simulators, because our focus is specifically on the evaluation of the above mentioned online routing game model in a realistic environment.

3   Architecture of the Routing Model Evaluator

Logical Architecture. The logical architecture is shown in Fig. 1. The envi-ronment of the agents is represented by the map. The map contains the road network, as well as the traffic rules like allowed speed, yielding, traffic lamps, etc. Vehicle agents are associated with the vehicles. Vehicle agents have hori-zontally layered hybrid agent architecture. The driving layer is responsible for the reactive behaviour, like following the road, keeping the distance from other cars, turning at crossings, etc. This reactive behaviour is executed by the SUMO simulation software. The route selection layer is responsible for the proactive behaviour, which is the planning of the route of the vehicle in accordance with the intention-aware online routing game model. The prediction agent receives the intentions of the vehicle agents and makes predictions of future travel durations.

Software Architecture. The software architecture is shown in Fig. 2. First, we shortly describe the components of the architecture, then we show how they work together.

SUMO[2] is an open source, highly portable, microscopic and continuous road traffic simulation package designed to handle large road networks [12]. The SUMO system is responsible for both the two-dimensional view and for micro-managing the vehicles, such as changing lanes, keeping the required following distance and complying with the traffic rules.

ORG Model. The ORG Model component is the implementation of the Online Routing Game model in C#. Given a network of roads and a list of traffic flows, the model's responsibility is to select the route for the agents according to one of the four available routing methods. A road is described by its origin and

---

[1] https://www.lgsvlsimulator.com/.
[2] https://sumo.dlr.de/index.html.

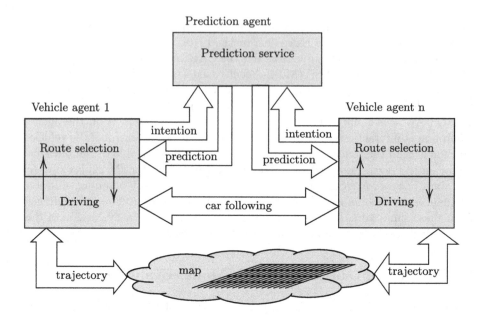

Fig. 1. Logical architecture

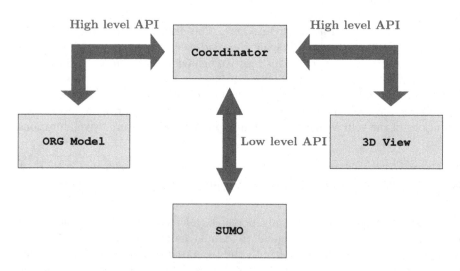

Fig. 2. Software architecture

destination nodes, as well as its cost function given as $VarCost \times flow + FixCost$ where $flow$ is the traffic flow currently entering the road and $VarCost, FixCost$ are constants. Each traffic flow entering the road network is described by its origin and destination node, as well as the intensity of the flow. The ORG Model supports the following four routing methods:

- Shortest: This method searches for the shortest available path between the two nodes by using Dijkstra's method and the *FixCost* of each road.
- Fastest: The fastest-method utilizes the same algorithm as the shortest-method, but it uses the cost reported by the last agent exiting that road.
- Detailed prediction [25]: The detailed prediction method takes into account all the intentions already submitted to the prediction service, and then it computes what will happen in the future if the agents execute the plans assigned by these intentions, and then in computes for each route in the network the predicted travel durations by taking into account the predicted travel durations of the roads.
- Simple prediction [25]: The simple prediction method also takes into account all the intentions already submitted to the prediction service, and then it computes what will happen in the future. However when the simple prediction method computes for each route in the network the predicted travel duration, then it takes into account only the latest predictions for each road.

Coordinator. The Coordinator is written in Python, and it establishes a connection with all of the other components. It reads a map downloaded from Open-StreetMap[3], and it sends the map to the other components of the system. When the Coordinator receives a command from the ORG Model, stating that a new vehicle shall be spawned at a given lane, the Coordinator translates this information into a format that is understood by the SUMO system, then forwards this request. The communication between the 3D View and the SUMO system is similar: the coordinates of the vehicles are requested from the SUMO system then transmitted to the view periodically. The communication between the Coordinator and the SUMO system is accomplished with low level API calls with the use of TraCI (*Traffic Control Interface*)[4], which is a Python library provided by the SUMO system. The communication in both the 3D View's and the ORG Model's direction is achieved by using high level API calls using commands in the JSON format.

3D View. The 3D View component provides a 3D overview of the simulation. It's implemented with the ThreeJS[5] JavaScript library, and it runs on most modern browsers. The user can select a desired vehicle, then follow it until it reaches its destination while traversing its path calculated by the ORG Model. By using the directional keys, the user can also move the camera to a given location. The user can also select a top-down view similar to the 2D view found in the SUMO system.

At the end of the simulation both the ORG Model and the Coordinator produces log files. The log file of the ORG Model contains statistics from the online routing game model. The log file of the Coordinator contain statistics from the SUMO execution.

---

[3] https://www.openstreetmap.org/.

[4] https://sumo.dlr.de/docs/TraCI.html.

[5] https://threejs.org/.

The user interface of the Routing Model Evaluator during the simulation is shown in Fig. 3. The 3D View is on the left-hand side of the figure, the SUMO simulator is on the right-hand side of the figure.

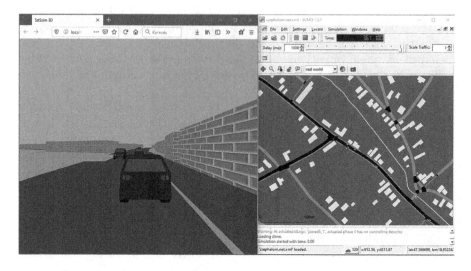

Fig. 3. User interface of the Routing Model Evaluator.

4   Experimental Setup

The Routing Model Evaluator is demonstrated in a real-world scenario. This scenario was investigated in an abstract form in [25], and now it is investigated using the real-world simulation. A critical region of Budapest (shown in Fig. 4) was loaded into the Routing Model Evaluator. Commuter cars enter the town at the upper part of the map, and basically all of them must go through the point in the lower-right part of the map. This is the source-target pair of the experiment.

In order to compute the parameters of the cost functions of the online routing game model, the average travel durations of the different routes at different flow intensities were measured from the SUMO simulation using the routing strategy of SUMO. A linear function is matched to this data. The resulting parameters are: $FixCost = 0.72 \cdot length \div speed$ and $VarCost = 0.0015 \cdot length$, where $length$ is the length of a road in meters and $speed$ is the maximum allowed speed in meter$\div$second on the road from the map. The minimum following distance of the cars is determined uniformly for all roads by the maximum traffic flow intensity that SUMO is able to insert into this network without delay. This intensity is 30 car$\div$minute.

The experiment simulates a 90 min long rush hour period with an additional 17 min long initial period to populate the road network. Several experiments were run at different incoming traffic flow values from 5 car$\div$minute to 30 car$\div$minute

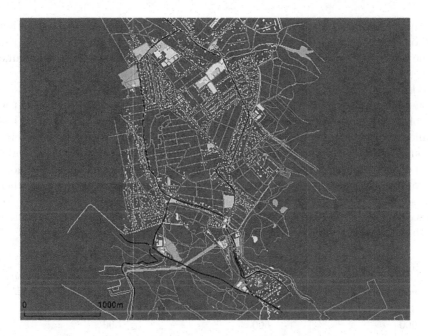

Fig. 4. Map in SUMO showing the real-world scenario of the experiment

in steps of 5. The routes of the cars were selected by the online routing game model, and the cars were driven on their routes by the SUMO system. The travel duration of the cars were recorded during the whole experiment by the SUMO system. The relative deviation, as well as the minimum, the maximum and the average of the travel durations were computed from the recorded values by the Coordinator module of the Routing Model Evaluator.

We used the "duaiterate" tool[6] of SUMO to compute the (approximate) probabilistic dynamic user equilibrium. This concept is described in the documentation of the "duaiterate" tool. We ran this tool until the probabilistic relative deviation was below 0.001, which is a recommended low value. Then we ran the resulting probabilistic traffic assignment in SUMO to record the actual travel durations when the routes are selected in accordance with these probabilities. Then we computed the relative deviation, as well as the minimum, the maximum and the average of the recorded travel durations. These are the reference values for the experiment.

5   Evaluation

Our hypothesis is that the route selection of the formal online routing game model brings the real-world system (represented by the SUMO simulation) to the dynamic user equilibrium which is computed by the duaiterate tool.

---

[6] https://sumo.dlr.de/docs/Demand/Dynamic_User_Assignment.html.

The travel durations of the above experiment for the different route selection methods are shown in the diagrams of Fig. 5. If the routes are selected by the online routing game model, then the average travel durations are almost the same as in the case of the duaiterate route assignment. The maximum values are a little bit higher and the minimum values are a little bit lower in the case of the online routing game model. However, the relative deviations are still better in the case of the online routing game model. There are no big differences between the detailed and the simple prediction methods in this almost real-world experiment, although the simple prediction method performed a little bit better in the model based experiment of [25]. The reason for this might be because in this experiment the routes originate from a real map and they are segmented to much smaller road sections. The relative deviations are shown in the diagrams of Fig. 6. We can see that the route selection of the online routing game model achieves similar results as the dynamic user equilibrium of the duaiterate program.

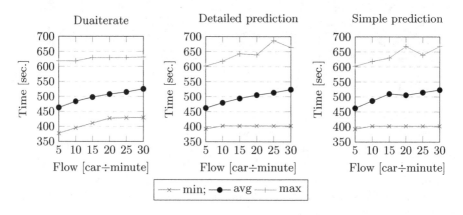

Fig. 5. Travel durations in the experiments.

As discussed in the architecture section, the route selection of the online routing game model runs interleaved with the SUMO simulation. The Routing Model Evaluator can run the SUMO simulation faster than real-time on an average laptop. This means that the route selection method of the online routing game model can be applied in autonomous vehicles.

The execution of the duaiterate traffic assignment program may take more than 30 min on the same laptop in the case of 30 $car \div minute$ traffic flow intensity. The duaiterate program assigns the route for each vehicle in advance for the 107 min long experiment. The duaiterate program cannot be applied in real-time in autonomous vehicles.

This experiment confirms our hypothesis that the model based route selection may bring the real-world system close to the dynamic user equilibrium, and in addition, the model based route selection can be applied in autonomous vehicles.

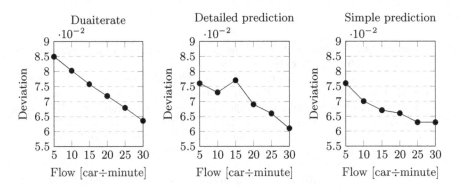

Fig. 6. Relative deviations of the travel durations in the experiments.

6   Conclusion

In this paper we have reported on a tool to investigate the practical applicability of formal models for the routing problem. The intention-aware online routing game model is implemented in the Routing Model Evaluator (RME). The RME builds up a formal model from real-world OpenStreetMap data. The OpenStreetMap data is also loaded into the SUMO simulator which realistically simulates how cars follow their routes. The SUMO simulator uses car following models, while the formal routing model uses mathematical functions. The SUMO simulator includes the duaiterate tool to iteratively compute a dynamic equilibrium of a traffic scenario. The dynamic equilibrium is the outcome of rational agent behaviour. The iterative process of the duaiterate tool runs for long time and cannot be applied in autonomous vehicles. The RME can execute the route selection of the intention-aware online routing game model for each vehicle faster than real-time. Our hypothesis is that the intention-aware online routing game model produces similar traffic as the dynamic equilibrium assignment of the duaiterate tool. This hypothesis was confirmed in a real-world scenario.

Further research will focus on adjusting the formal model to the parameters of the real-world and on including additional real-world components, like e.g. traffic lamps. The adjustments could use machine learning techniques. We think that the online routing game model is able to cope with this, because it has the capabilities of both the queueing model and the classic routing game model.

Acknowledgement. The work of V. Antal, T.G. Farkas, A. Kiss, and M. Miskolczi was supported by the European Union, co-financed by the European Social Fund (EFOP-3.6.3-VEKOP-16-2017-00002). The work of L.Z. Varga was supported by project no. ED_18-1-2019-0030 (Application domain specific highly reliable IT solutions subprogramme), and implemented with the support provided from the National Research, Development and Innovation Fund of Hungary, financed under the Thematic Excellence Programme funding scheme.

References

1. Beckmann, M.J., McGuire, C.B., Winsten, C.B.: Studies in the Economics of Transportation. Yale University Press (1956)
2. Blum, A., Even-Dar, E., Ligett, K.: Routing without regret: on convergence to Nash equilibria of regret-minimizing algorithms in routing games. In: Proceedings of the 25th ACM Symposium on Principles of Distributed Computing, PODC 2006, pp. 45–52. ACM, New York (2006). https://doi.org/10.1145/1146381.1146392
3. Claes, R., Holvoet, T.: Traffic coordination using aggregation-based traffic predictions. IEEE Intell. Syst. **29**(4), 96–100 (2014). https://doi.org/10.1109/MIS.2014.73
4. Claes, R., Holvoet, T., Weyns, D.: A decentralized approach for anticipatory vehicle routing using delegate multi-agent systems. IEEE Trans. Intell. Transp. Syst. **12**(2), 364–373 (2011). https://doi.org/10.1109/TITS.2011.2105867
5. Cominetti, R., Correa, J., Olver, N.: Long term behavior of dynamic equilibria in fluid queuing networks. In: Eisenbrand, F., Koenemann, J. (eds.) IPCO 2017. LNCS, vol. 10328, pp. 161–172. Springer, Cham (2017). https://doi.org/10.1007/978-3-319-59250-3_14
6. Dosovitskiy, A., Ros, G., Codevilla, F., Lopez, A., Koltun, V.: CARLA: an open urban driving simulator. In: Proceedings of the 1st Annual Conference on Robot Learning, pp. 1–16 (2017)
7. Fischer, S., Vöcking, B.: On the evolution of selfish routing. In: Albers, S., Radzik, T. (eds.) ESA 2004. LNCS, vol. 3221, pp. 323–334. Springer, Heidelberg (2004). https://doi.org/10.1007/978-3-540-30140-0_30
8. Gawron, C.: An iterative algorithm to determine the dynamic user equilibrium in a traffic simulation model. Int. J. Mod. Phys. C **09**(03), 393–407 (1998). https://doi.org/10.1142/s0129183198000303
9. Halpern, J.Y., Moses, Y.: A procedural characterization of solution concepts in games. J. Artif. Intell. Res. **49**, 143–170 (2014). https://doi.org/10.1613/jair.4220
10. Hosmer Jr., D.W., Lemeshow, S., Sturdivant, R.X.: Applied Logistic Regression, 3rd edn. Wiley, Hoboken (2013)
11. Koch, R., Skutella, M.: Nash equilibria and the price of anarchy for flows over time. Theory Comput. Syst. **49**(1), 71–97 (2011). https://doi.org/10.1007/s00224-010-9299-y
12. Lopez, P.A., et al.: Microscopic traffic simulation using SUMO. In: 2018 21st International Conference on Intelligent Transportation Systems (ITSC). IEEE, November 2018. https://doi.org/10.1109/itsc.2018.8569938
13. Merchant, D.K., Nemhauser, G.L.: A model and an algorithm for the dynamic traffic assignment problems. Transp. Sci. **12**(3), 183–199 (1978). https://doi.org/10.1287/trsc.12.3.183
14. Nisan, N., Roughgarden, T., Tardos, E., Vazirani, V.V.: Algorithmic Game Theory. Cambridge University Press, New York (2007). https://doi.org/10.1017/CBO9780511800481
15. Palaiopanos, G., Panageas, I., Piliouras, G.: Multiplicative weights update with constant step-size in congestion games: convergence, limit cycles and chaos. In: Proceedings of the 31st International Conference on Neural Information Processing Systems, pp. 5874–5884. Curran Associates, USA (2017). https://doi.org/10.5555/3295222.3295337
16. Parkes, D.C.: Online mechanisms. In: Algorithmic Game Theory, pp. 411–439. Cambridge University Press (2007). https://doi.org/10.1017/CBO9780511800481

17. Peeta, S., Ziliaskopoulos, A.K.: Foundations of dynamic traffic assignment: the past, the present and the future. Netw. Spat. Econ. **1**(3), 233–265 (2001). https://doi.org/10.1023/A:1012827724856

18. Pourabdollah, M., Bjarkvik, E., Furer, F., Lindenberg, B., Burgdorf, K.: Calibration and evaluation of car following models using real-world driving data. In: 2017 IEEE 20th International Conference on Intelligent Transportation Systems (ITSC). IEEE, October 2017. https://doi.org/10.1109/itsc.2017.8317836

19. Roughgarden, T.: Routing games. In: Algorithmic Game Theory, pp. 461–486. Cambridge University Press (2007). https://doi.org/10.1017/CBO9780511800481

20. Sandholm, W.H.: Potential games with continuous player sets. J. Econ. Theory **97**(1), 81–108 (2001). https://doi.org/10.1006/jeth.2000.2696

21. Schaefer, M., Čáp, M., Vokřínek, J.: AgentDrive: agent-based simulator for intelligent cars and its application for development of a lane-changing assistant. In: Alonso-Betanzos, A., et al. (eds.) Agent-Based Modeling of Sustainable Behaviors. UCS, pp. 143–165. Springer, Cham (2017). https://doi.org/10.1007/978-3-319-46331-5_7

22. Schaefer, M., Vokřínek, J., Pinotti, D., Tango, F.: Multi-agent traffic simulation for development and validation of autonomic car-to-car systems. In: McCluskey, T.L., Kotsialos, A., Müller, J.P., Klügl, F., Rana, O., Schumann, R. (eds.) Autonomic Road Transport Support Systems. AS, pp. 165–180. Springer, Cham (2016). https://doi.org/10.1007/978-3-319-25808-9_10

23. Torabi, B., Al-Zinati, M., Wenkstern, R.Z.: MATISSE 3.0: a large-scale multi-agent simulation system for intelligent transportation systems. In: Demazeau, Y., An, B., Bajo, J., Fernández-Caballero, A. (eds.) PAAMS 2018. LNCS (LNAI), vol. 10978, pp. 357–360. Springer, Cham (2018). https://doi.org/10.1007/978-3-319-94580-4_38

24. Varga, L.: On intention-propagation-based prediction in autonomously self-adapting navigation. Scalable Comput.: Pract. Exp. **16**(3), 221–232 (2015). http://www.scpe.org/index.php/scpe/article/view/1098

25. Varga, L.Z.: Two prediction methods for intention-aware online routing games. In: Belardinelli, F., Argente, E. (eds.) EUMAS/AT-2017. LNCS (LNAI), vol. 10767, pp. 431–445. Springer, Cham (2018). https://doi.org/10.1007/978-3-030-01713-2_30

26. Varga, L.Z.: Dynamic global behaviour of online routing games. In: Weyns, D., Mascardi, V., Ricci, A. (eds.) EMAS 2018. LNCS (LNAI), vol. 11375, pp. 202–221. Springer, Cham (2019). https://doi.org/10.1007/978-3-030-25693-7_11

27. Wardrop, J.G.: Some theoretical aspects of road traffic research. Proc. Inst. Civil Eng. Part II **1**(36), 352–378 (1952)

28. de Weerdt, M.M., Stein, S., Gerding, E.H., Robu, V., Jennings, N.R.: Intention-aware routing of electric vehicles. IEEE Trans. Intell. Transp. Syst. **17**(5), 1472–1482 (2016). https://doi.org/10.1109/TITS.2015.2506900

29. Weibull, J.W.: Evolutionary Game Theory. MIT Press Ltd., Cambridge (1997)

The DigForSim Agent Based Simulator of People Movements in Crime Scenes

Alessandro Biagetti[1], Angelo Ferrando[2], and Viviana Mascardi[1(✉)]

[1] University of Genova, Genoa, Italy
biagettialessandro@virgilio.it, viviana.mascardi@unige.it
[2] University of Liverpool, Liverpool, UK
angelo.ferrando@liverpool.ac.uk

Abstract. Evidence analysis is one of the Digital Forensics tasks and involves examining fragmented incomplete knowledge and reasoning on it, in order to reconstruct plausible crime scenarios. After more than one year of activity within the DigForASP COST Action, the lack of real data about movements of people in crime scenes emerged as a major limitation to the need of testing the DigForASP prototypes that exploit Artificial Intelligence and Automated Reasoning for evidence analysis.

In this paper we present DigForSim, an Agent Based Modeling and Simulation tool aimed at producing synthetic, controllable data on the movements of agents in the crime scene, in form of files logging the agents' position at given time points. These log files serve as benchmarks for the DigForASP reasoning prototypes.

Keywords: Agent Based Modeling and Simulation · Evidence analysis

1 Motivation and Background

In 2001, the attendees of the First Digital Forensic Research Workshop published a report entitled "A Road Map for Digital Forensic Research"[1] where Digital Forensics (DF) was defined as "*the use of scientifically derived and proven methods toward the [...] analysis, interpretation, [...] and presentation of digital evidence derived from digital sources for the purpose of facilitation or furthering the reconstruction of events found to be criminal*".

Evidence analysis involves examining fragmented incomplete knowledge and reconstructing and aggregating complex scenarios involving time, uncertainty, causality, and alternative possibilities. In order to overcome the limitations due to the lack of established methodologies for digital evidence analysis, the "Digital Forensics: Evidence Analysis via Intelligent Systems and Practices" (DigForASP) Action was funded[2]. The challenge addressed by DigForASP is to reason

---

[1] www.dfrws.org/sites/default/files/session-files/a_road_map_for_digital_forensic_rese arch.pdf.

[2] CA17124, https://digforasp.uca.es, funded for four years starting from 09/2018 by the European Cooperation in Science and Technology (COST, www.cost.eu).

© Springer Nature Switzerland AG 2020
Y. Demazeau et al. (Eds.): PAAMS 2020, LNAI 12092, pp. 42–54, 2020.
https://doi.org/10.1007/978-3-030-49778-1_4

on evidences on crimes and their perpetrators collected from various electronic devices in order to reconstruct possible events, event sequences and scenarios related to the crime. The evidences elaborated in DigForASP are not raw ones (possibly damaged chips, mobile phones, etc): DigForASP tools will operate on data extracted from these physical evidences, already transformed into some digital, machine and human readable form. In particular, DigForASP aims to analyze data related to people movements in the crime scene, and to produce plausible scenarios and hypotheses by reasoning on them via techniques rooted in Artificial Intelligence and Automated Reasoning. These techniques are reliable, verifiable, and explainable, which makes them understandable by, and useful for, law enforcement, investigators, public prosecutors, lawyers and judges.

After more than one year of activities, and despite the DigForASP networking results which went beyond the initial expectations, it became clear that there is one main obstacle to the large scale experimentation of the prototypical tools designed and implemented within the COST Action: the *lack of real(istic) traces of movements of people, including suspects and crime perpetrators, based on real(istic) crimes*. While digital forensics datasets exist, their aggregation level is too high: DigForASP needs data modeling movements of individuals in crime scenarios both at the urban level, and at the building/apartment one. Magistrates, digital forensics experts, and investigators have access to movements logs extracted from mobile phones, video-surveillance cameras, and other devices, but it is needless to say that such extremely sensible data are protected by government laws that prevent their usage – at least "as they are" – outside the legal process, even under Non Disclosure Agreements. Unfortunately, anonymizing these data is difficult and time consuming: it requires a careful manual inspection to make sure that places, individuals, and court case will not be recognized.

In this paper we present DigForSim, an Agent Based Modeling and Simulation (ABMS) tool designed and implemented to produce *realistic* and *controllable* synthetic data logging people's movements in user-defined environments modeling a city, a borough, or a house. These synthetic data will be used as benchmarks while testing the reasoning prototypes developed in DigForASP. The idea of using ABMS for data generation is not new [18] but, to the best of our knowledge, has never been adopted in the DF domain. Controlling the way in which such benchmarks are produced and being able to enforce situations of interest to emerge ("`alice` and `bob` were in the same place for more than 5 min, in three different occasions"), is a main requirement to properly assess the reasoning process performed by the DigForASP prototypes ("given that `alice` and `bob` were in the same place for more than 5 min, in three different occasions, they might know each other, might have exchanged information or stuff, and might be partners in crime").

Although this paper is centered around DigForSim, we also present two early stage offline reasoning prototypes, DigForReas-J and DigForReas-P, which allow us to exemplify the complete DigForASP data flow. DigForSim and DigForReas-J are fully implemented and are available under LGPL license from GitHub[3].

2   Related Work

DF Tools and Datasets. Many tools for extracting and analyzing evidences from digital devices exist, such as Autopsy[4], SIFT[5], the Oxygen Forensic Suite[6]. These applications operate at the device level, extracting event logs and other pieces of information from tablets and smartphones: the DigForASP reasoning tools have a different scope and come into play after these analyses have been carried out. W.r.t. datasets, those used in DF either provide data that (might) come from devices' sensors like the NIST Image Group dataset[7] and the IARPA Janus Benchmarks[8], or collect and present statistical information on crimes that took place in cities or states, such as the London Crime Data 2008–2016[9], with no details on the dynamics of each crime, and no traces of movements of the involved people.

ABMS Tools. ABMS is, according to some scientists, "a third way of doing science" [2]: it can be exploited when aspects of the real world are not physically accessible and allows scientists to make in vitro experiments when experimenting with the real system is prohibited due to safety or legal reasons [14]. Many tools suitable for modeling and simulating high numbers of agents exist. Some of them like GAMA [20], MASON [13], Netlogo [22], were born with ABMS in mind. Others, like Jade [3], Jason [4], and Jadex [16], were born with agents and MASs in mind; they can be used for ABMS purposes, although their principal aim is different. Finally, there are tools conceived for purposes other than ABMS, that turned out to be very suitable for ABMS as well. As an example, Gazebo[10] is a robot simulator that was used for testing intelligent agents for Ambient Assisted Living applications [19] and Unity[11], born with video games in mind, has indeed been exploited for ABMS in a wide range of domains [12,15,21]. The strengths of Unity for ABMS are its precise implementation of physics laws, its collision detection embedded capabilities, its native support to shortest paths computation and realistic movement simulation and rendering, and its efficiency.

---

[3] https://github.com/VivianaMascardi/DigForSim   and   https://github.com/Vivia naMascardi/DigForReason, respectively; Alessandro Biagetti's Master Thesis (with many experiments, figures and screenshots that could not be inserted in this paper for space constraints) and a link to a video showing DigForSim at work are also available in the DigForSim repository.

[4] https://www.sleuthkit.org/autopsy/.

[5] https://digital-forensics.sans.org/community/downloads#overview.

[6] https://www.oxygen-forensic.com/en/.

[7] https://www.nist.gov/itl/iad/image-group/resources/biometric-special-databases-and-software.

[8] https://www.nist.gov/programs-projects/face-challenges.

[9] https://www.kaggle.com/jboysen/london-crime.

[10] http://gazebosim.org/.

[11] https://unity.com/.

ABMS for DF. ABMS is extremely appropriate to simulate and analyze phenomena within the criminology and digital forensics domain as shown for example by [5] where the spatial dynamics of crime are simulated and [6], where simulation of crime prevention strategies are presented. The state of the art in agent-based modeling of urban crime is represented by [9], published in 2019, whose authors observe that Agent Based Modeling (ABM) *"has the potential to be a powerful tool for exploring criminological theory and testing the plausibility of crime prevention interventions when data are unavailable, when they would be unethical to collect, or when policy-makers need an answer quickly"*. The 45 papers reviewed in that survey, however, do not take the "indoor level modeling and simulation" into account, and – according to the survey's authors – most of them lack detail sufficient to enable replication and many do not include a clear rationale for modeling choices, parameter selection or calibration. DigForSim is a first step toward overcoming these limitations: it can be freely downloaded, used, and extended, hence ensuring replicability of experiments, and the granularity of the simulated environment (indoor, city, state) only depends on the environment model input by the user. The simulation parameters are few, and their rationale is explained in this paper.

Virtual Reality Simulators for DF. The literature on virtual reality simulators for crime analysis, forensic investigation, and law enforcement briefing and training, is vast [7,10,11]. Many virtual reality simulators use Unity to reconstruct a crime scene (usually one room, apartment, or house) in all its details including furniture, lighting, obstacles, objects, accesses like windows or manholes. The reconstructed scene may be real for investigation purposes or invented for training purposes. The goal of these simulators is to allow human beings involved in the investigation to reason on how the suspect(s) might have entered and moved inside the scene, and might have perpetrated their crime. Differently, DigForSim simulates movements of possibly many individuals in 3D environments that are not necessarily realistic in their rendering and whose dimension may go far besides the house; the DigForSim outputs will feed the reasoning process of the DigForASP reasoners, not that of human beings.

3   DigForSim Requirements and Design

Figure 1 (left) presents the context where DigForSim is meant to be used, which emerged from the requirements elicitation and analysis carried out during the DigForASP meetings and which drove its design. DigForSim should

1. allow the user to define and/or import the 2D/3D environment modeling the crime scene via an *environment configuration file*;
2. allow the user to configure the simulation by setting the number and types of involved agents via a *simulation configuration file*;
3. allow "agents under scrutiny", i.e. named agents whose behavior will be subject to queries and reasoning by the DigForASP reasoning prototypes, to be defined in a simple way, but still giving the user the possibility to associate

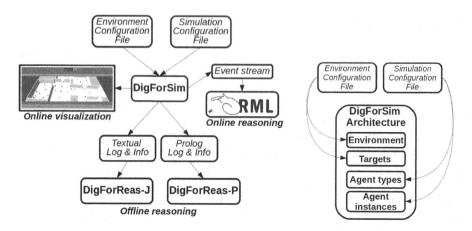

Fig. 1. DigForSim context and data flow (left), and DigForSim architecture (right).

with each agent a target-driven path to be followed in the crime scene. Time spent in specific places within the environment should also be configurable ("start from the kitchen and stay there for 5 min, move to the sitting room and stay there for 10 min, go back to the kitchen..."), along with speed. To model crime scenes, it also emerged as a useful feature the ability for one agent to follow another agent, hence associating a moving target, rather than a pre-defined path, with agents;

4. allow other agents with random movements to be (optionally) inserted into the crime scene, to add noise and make it less predictable and more realistic; this may be especially useful for urban scenarios;

5. adopt an ABMS implementation tool ensuring that the basic laws of physics are respected: agents model human beings and hence they cannot pass through walls, they cannot fly, and if they have to move from one target to another in their path, they have to find an admissible route in the environment that allows for that movement;

6. output a stream of events for feeding online reasoning tools; in particular, the use of runtime verification engines based on computational logic, like RML[12] [8] – although not yet addressed – was considered as a very good option to monitor what is going on in the simulated environment;

7. produce benchmark data, in form of log files, for testing the DigForReas-* offline tools.

The possibility to visualize the crime scene dynamics via a GUI was not actually a requirement, but turned out to be a welcome side-effect of using existing ABMS tools, which already support visualization.

Figure 1 (right) shows the architecture of DigForSim. The environment is characterized by some 2D or 3D map read from a file, plus a set of "targets", namely places or elements in the environment, or even other agents, that the

---

[12] https://rmlatdibris.github.io/.

agents may need to reach. These targets are mandatory elements in the design because the agents' behavior is driven by a sequence of targets to reach, along with the amount of time to spend close to each of them.

The agents themselves can have different types, and for each type, an arbitrary number of instances should be created. In particular, DigForSim must support the definition of *agents under scrutiny*, whose behavior is specified by the user and that may represent criminals, partners in crime, hitmen, policemen, victims, etc., and *wandering agents* that populate the scene with no special purpose apart from making it more believable. If not needed, wandering agents can be ruled out from the simulation.

Wandering agents influence the way the other agents move, for instance by forcing other agents to avoid them. They are characterized by the following properties:

- **wandering radius:** the radius of the area where the agent moves;
- **time:** how much time the agent spends in the area defined by the wandering radius: when the time expires, the agent randomly moves to another area;
- **speed:** fast, medium, slow.

Agents under scrutiny can be configured with the following properties:

- **name:** a unique identifier for the agent;
- **speed:** fast, medium, slow;
- **shape and/or color:** some visible feature which makes the agent distinguishable from the others, in the simulation visualization;
- **starting point:** the coordinates where the agent is spawn at the beginning of the simulation;
- **movements:** the path that the agent will follow, consisting of a sequence of targets – including other agents – among those available in the environment.

Information about where agents under scrutiny are in each time instant must be produced and logged by DigForSim.

Choice of the Implementation Tool. A careful analysis of available ABMS tools has been carried out to select the most suitable one for implementing DigForSim. Given that the behavior of agents, even those under scrutiny, is simple, and that – at least for the first DigForSim release – explicit communication among agents was not required, we excluded tools like Jade which are born for modeling sophisticated communicating agents, possibly spread on different machines. For the same reason we excluded Jason and Jadex, suitable for modeling the agent mental state and reasoning mechanism, but even too powerful for simple target-driven moving agents. These three frameworks were disregarded also because, while the integration of a simple 2D environment would be possible (many Jason examples involve agents wandering on a bidimensional grid), the burden of integrating a complex and "physics-compliant" 3D environment would be entirely on the DigForSim programmer.

We considered the possibility to adopt either NetLogo or Unity, and we implemented preliminary prototypes and we run experiments with both of them. Unity natively supports the definition of agents as characters inside the simulations. Thanks to the NavMeshAgent component[13], agents capable of moving inside virtual environments can be easily defined. The built-in support to physical laws provided by Unity, along with the built-in shortest path computation for allowing agents under scrutiny to move from one target to the next one, were decisive factors in opting for Unity. Although having a GUI was not a requirement, the support offered by Unity to visualization and rendering is definitely more solid and realistic than the one offered by NetLogo. Among the drawbacks of Unity, we may mention its steep learning curve and its hardware requirements, much more demanding than NetLogo's ones.

4   DigForSim Implementation

Modeling the Crime Scene. The 2D or 3D model of the crime scene can be created directly inside Unity, where all the objects of the virtual scene can be modeled and positioned. Alternatively, it can be generated using an external tool, and then imported and modified, if needed, inside Unity. We experimented both approaches. As an external tool we used Blender[14], a free and open source 3D creation suite. Figure 2 shows a 3D Blender model imported into Unity and populated with targets (red cylinders) and agents. Wandering agents are rendered as green capsules and agents under scrutiny are rendered as capsules with other colors. The representation of the environment, the agents and the targets is basic, as a realistic rendering is not a DigForSim goal. Throughout the paper we will present examples related with crime scenes inside houses, rather than in urban scenarios, given that building-level simulations are the less widespread and the most needed in DigForASP. The creation of 3D city models is also supported.

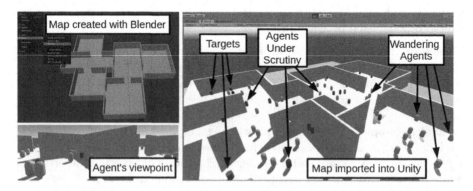

Fig. 2. A Blender model imported in Unity and populated with targets and agents. (Color figure online)

---

[13] https://docs.unity3d.com/ScriptReference/AI.NavMeshAgent.html.
[14] https://www.blender.org.

Configuring the Simulation. Both the wandering agents and the agents under scrutiny have been implemented in Unity using C#. To configure the simulation, the user does not need to write a single line of C# code: he/she just needs to write a configuration file containing the following pieces of information:

- **log time interval:** sets the time lapse in simulated seconds between the emission of the events describing the state of the simulation (namely, where each agent under scrutiny is in that time instant) and the logging of these events in the log files;
- **target creation:** sets the list of objects that can be put in the scene; some targets might appear in the path associated with agents under scrutiny;
- **wandering agents:** sets the total number of wandering agents, which may be zero if they are not needed or suitable for the simulation purposes, and allows the user to split them into three categories according to their speed (slow, medium, fast); as an example, a configuration line `FastWanderingAgents: 30 3 1 20` means that 30% agents are fast, their speed in 3 meters per second, their wandering radius in 1 meter, and they will stay 20 s within that radius, before moving to another area;
- **agents under scrutiny:** sets the list of agents under scrutiny involved in the simulation; for each such agent, the name, the color used for rendering it, the speed expressed in meters per second, the area where it is going to be spawn, and the path expressed ad a list of couples containing target location and time to spend in that location, are provided.

```
Log Time Interval:                Agents Under Scrutiny:
3                                 Alice red 1.5 Kitchen
                                      Phone 4
Target Creation:                  Bob blue 1.5 Corridor
Table DiningRoom                      Phone 1 Charlie 1 Kitchen 3
Phone Bedroom1                    Charlie yellow 2.0 Bedroom1
                                      DiningRoom 2
Wandering Agents:                 ...
AgentsInSimulation: 5             Jack black 1.8 DiningRoom
FastWanderingAgents: 30 3 1 20        Stairs 0 Bathroom 1 Kitchen 3
MediumWanderingAgents: 40 2 1 20
SlowWanderingAgents: 30 1.5 1 5
```

An example of configuration file for DigForSim is shown above. The time interval for emitting and logging the events is set to 3 s; one table is positioned in the dining room and one phone in bedroom 1; the number of wandering agents is set to 5 split in the three categories; and ten agents under scrutiny, Alice, Bob, ..., Jack, with different colors, different starting points, and different paths are created. For instance Bob, rendered via a blue capsule starts its activity in the Corridor, then it goes where the Phone is, it remains there for 1 s, then it goes where Charlie is and spends 1 s there, and finally goes to the Kitchen, where it remains for 3 more seconds. Bob's path highlights the main features of DigForSim: agents can reach rooms (the kitchen), objects positioned in rooms (the phone), but also agents whose position, at the time of reaching them, depends on how simulation evolved. To enforce an agent to follow a very precise and constrained path, many objects (also "fake" ones) should be positioned in the environment, and be enclosed in the agent's path. To model the agent changing pace, longer or shorter stops should be associated with the targets in its path. A criminal agent following its victim can just have the victim as its target; a policeman can have the criminal as its target. Finally, the time lapse of the event emission and logging can be decided by the user: the longer, the fewer information the online and offline reasoning tools will count on in order to answer the user queries.

Despite its simplicity, the configuration file allows the user to control what agents should do, giving them more or less freedom, depending on the benchmarks to be produced. The randomness of the simulation only depends on the presence of wandering agents, which move randomly and which may interfere with movements of agents under scrutiny. Without wandering agents, the same configuration leads to the same simulation, and hence to the same log files.

Running the Simulation and Producing Log Files. When the environment has been loaded into DigForSim and the configuration file has been successfully parsed, the simulation may start. Events stating the position of each agent at each time tick are generated for online reasoning, and the log files are continuously updated. The simulation stops when all the agents under scrutiny have completed their tasks.

Data for DigForReas-J are formatted in the following way:

```
TotalNumberOfAgents: 14 EndingTime: 117.03
Agent: Alice Position: (139.6, 0.1, 35.3) in Kitchen Time: 0
Agent: Bob Position: (23.6, 1.7, 10.6) in Bathroom Time: 0
...
```

The same data formatted as Prolog facts for DigForReas-P look like

```
totalNumberOfAgents(14).
endingTime(117.03).
agent('Alice' , 139.6, 0.1, 35.3, 'Kitchen' , 0).
...
```

5   Experiments and Conclusions

The DigForASP COST Action is actively working to access real log files, carrying out information similar to that produced by DigForSim. Such real log files are not available to the DigForASP members yet: we are indeed using DigForSim logs to test the DigForReas-J and DigForReas-P prototypes which answer questions that mimic those usually asked by magistrates to the DF experts. Checking whether DigForSim can reproduce real scenarios would require to have real data from real scenarios available to compare with, which is not currently the case.

Questions of interest are: "Is it possible that *agentX* and *agentY* met between 3.00PM and 3.10PM?", "Where was *agentW* between 2.00 and 2.20?", "Did *agentZ* pass through *roomA*?", and so on. Hence, the following question patterns are supported by both DigForReas-J and DigForReas-P:

Q1: Where did *agent1* and *agent2* meet between *time1* and *time2*?
Q2: Who did *agent1* meet?
Q3: Where *agent1* was between *time1* and *time2*?
Q4: Where has *agent1* been?
Q5: Who did visit *area1* between *time1* and *time2*?
Q6: Who did visit *area1*?

In DigForReas-J, these questions can be formulated through a user-friendly GUI which guides the user and shows the results of the queries.

DigForReas-P is implemented in SWI-Prolog; it can be accessed via command line and supports more sophisticated reasoning patterns. As an example, via the "all solutions" `findall` Prolog predicate and some basic Prolog programming skill, complex queries like "Which agents exited the kitchen and re-entered it after moving to another room?" can be issued:

```
findall( ag(X, Room, T1, T2, T3),
         (agent(X, _, _, _, 'Kitchen', T1),
          agent(X, _, _, _, Room, T2), T2 > T1, Room \= 'Kitchen',
          agent(X, _, _, _, 'Kitchen', T3), T3 > T2), List).
```

DigForSim and DigForReas-J have been tested with various scenarios, different numbers of agents, and different kinds of questions following the patterns presented before.

The first experiments that were carried out, and which required a large amount of human time, were qualitative ones. They consisted in manually inspecting the logs produced by DigForSim and checking whether they were consistent with the simulation configuration, and in (successfully) verifying that the answers output by DigForReas-J were consistent with the data in the logs. To this aim the DigForReas-J GUI shown in Fig. 3 was exploited; in the screenshot, the question submitted to DigForReas-J via the GUI is whether Gaston and Giuseppe met, and where. The answer is a list of all the time instants the two agents met, along with the information about where they met. The manual inspection confirmed that the answer was correct.

These experiments were followed by quantitative ones, aimed at assessing the performance and scalability of DigForSim and DigForReas-J, and were run on a machine with Intel Core i5 7600 @ 3.50 GHz QuadCore, 16 GB Dual-Channel @ 1067 MHz. In the first of these experiments the environment was a two floor house consisting of living room, dining room, kitchen, bathroom, two bedrooms and a corridor. The configuration file is the one presented in Sect. 4 with 10 agents under scrutiny (**Alice**, **Bob**, ..., **Jack**), 5 wandering agents, and a log time interval of 3 s. The simulation completed after 117.03 s. A fragment of the log file generated for DigForReas-J is shown in Sect. 4.

In order to assess DigForSim's performance, we carried out further different experiments where we played with the dimensions of the environment, the number of rooms, the number of wandering agents and the number of agents under scrutiny involved in the crime scene. For space constraints we cannot report all the details of the experiments: they can be found in the documents available in the DigForSim repository on GitHub. As expected, the size of the environment influences DigForSim's performances the most. We tested the performance with

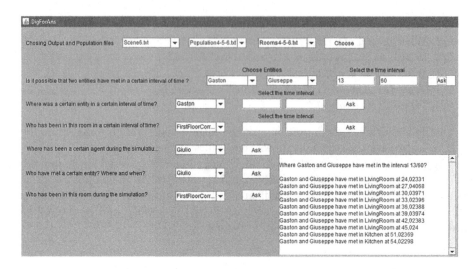

Fig. 3. The DigForReas-J GUI.

the same number of agents and objects, and different environments. In all cases, with a larger environment the time required to compute the paths from one target to another increased.

Concluding Remarks. Despite the large availability of urban crime spreadsheets and of images and video data for DF purposes, no datasets modeling plausible movements of criminals in the crime scenes, in particular when crime scenes are indoor, exist. DigForSim addresses this lack of data, which represents an obstacle to the benchmarking of reasoning tools implemented by the DigForASP partners and by ourselves. DigForReas-J and DigForReas-P are two among those tools. Although they are still at an early prototype stage, they allowed us to address the full DigForASP pipeline, from configuring the simulation, to reasoning on the simulated evidences. The experiments we carried out, besides showing that the tools provide the expected answers, also show that their performances scale up well, when tens of agents are involved. DigForSim is not meant to run simulations with hundreds of agents. Being targeted at reproducing specific crimes, the agents under scrutiny are usually less than 20.

As part of our future work, we plan to extend DigForSim allowing for the definition of the agents under scrutiny as Belief-Desire-Intentions (BDI [17]) agents; this would allow us to model the cognitive stage of the agents, their goals, intentions, and motivations, hence obtaining more realistic simulations where the psychological dimension is also taken into account. We are exploring two ways to achieve this target. The first is to create a bridge between Unity and Jason. We discussed this possibility with one of the developers of Jason, Prof. R. Bordini, and he agrees that this option might be hard to implement, but feasible. Jason is in fact implemented in Java, and tools exist for converting .jar files into

.net dynamic libraries[15], that could be used inside Unity. The second way is to re-implement a BDI-style reasoning engine directly inside Unity, by exploiting UnityProlog, an ISO-compliant Prolog interpreter for Unity3D[16].

We also plan to enrich the simulation in Unity – and the DigForSim configuration file – by adding objects that the agents can pick, move, and leave. Interactions with doors and windows, that could be initially locked and that only some agents could open or close, could be also useful since changing the state of doors and windows would make paths available or unavailable, in a dynamic way.

Finally, we plan to design more complex question patterns that can be expressed in linear time temporal logic (LTL), and extend the DigForReas-* reasoners to deal with them. To this aim, we will adapt the approaches to temporal reasoning on event traces we are familiar with because of our ongoing research on runtime verification [1] to the DigForSim log files.

Acknowledgements. This paper is based upon work from COST Action DigForASP, supported by COST (European Cooperation in Science and Technology). We acknowledge all the DigForASP partners for the exciting and constructive discussions.

References

1. Ancona, D., Ferrando, A., Mascardi, V.: Comparing trace expressions and linear temporal logic for runtime verification. In: Ábrahám, E., Bonsangue, M., Johnsen, E.B. (eds.) Theory and Practice of Formal Methods. LNCS, vol. 9660, pp. 47–64. Springer, Cham (2016). https://doi.org/10.1007/978-3-319-30734-3_6
2. Axelrod, R.: The Complexity of Cooperation: Agent-Based Models of Competitionand Collaboration. Princeton University Press, Princeton (1997)
3. Bellifemine, F.L., Caire, G., Greenwood, D.: Developing Multi-agent Systems with JADE. Wiley, Hoboken (2007)
4. Bordini, R.H., Hübner, J.F., Wooldridge, M.: Programming Multi-agent Systems in AgentSpeak Using Jason. Wiley, Hoboken (2007)
5. Bosse, T., Gerritsen, C.: Agent-based simulation of the spatial dynamics of crime: on the interplay between criminal hot spots and reputation. In: AAMAS (2), pp. 1129–1136 (2008)
6. Bosse, T., Gerritsen, C.: Comparing crime prevention strategies by agent-based simulation. In: IAT, pp. 491–496. IEEE Computer Society (2009)
7. Conway, A., James, J.I., Gladyshev, P.: Development and initial user evaluation of a virtual crime scene simulator including digital evidence. In: James, J.I., Breitinger, F. (eds.) ICDF2C 2015. LNICST, vol. 157, pp. 16–26. Springer, Cham (2015). https://doi.org/10.1007/978-3-319-25512-5_2
8. Franceschini, L.: RML: runtime monitoring language: a system-agnostic DSL for runtime verification. In: Programming, pp. 28:1–28:3. ACM (2019)
9. Groff, E.R., Johnson, S.D., Thornton, A.: State of the art in agent-based modeling of urban crime: an overview. J. Quant. Criminol. **35**(1), 155–193 (2019)

---

[15] https://sourceforge.net/projects/ikvm/.
[16] https://github.com/ianhorswill/UnityProlog.

10. Howard, T.L.J., Murta, A.D., Gibson, S.: Virtual environments for scene of crime reconstruction and analysis. In: Visual Data Exploration and Analysis VII, pp. 41–48 (2000)
11. Karabiyik, U., Mousas, C., Sirota, D., Iwai, T., Akdere, M.: A virtual reality framework for training incident first responders and digital forensic investigators. In: Bebis, G., et al. (eds.) ISVC 2019. LNCS, vol. 11845, pp. 469–480. Springer, Cham (2019). https://doi.org/10.1007/978-3-030-33723-0_38
12. Liberman, A., Kario, D., Mussel, M., et al.: Cell studio: a platform for interactive, 3D graphical simulation of immunological processes. APL Bioeng. **2**(2), 026107 (2018)
13. Luke, S., Cioffi-Revilla, C., Panait, L., Sullivan, K., Balan, G.: MASON: a multi-agent simulation environment. Simulation **81**(7), 517–527 (2005)
14. Madey, G., Kaisler, S.H.: Computational modeling of social and organizational system (2008). www3.nd.edu/~gmadey/Activities/CMSOS-Tutorial.pdf
15. Mascarenhas, S., Guimarães, M., Prada, R., et al.: A virtual agent toolkit for serious games developers. In: 2018 IEEE CIG Conference, pp. 1–7, August 2018
16. Pokahr, A., Braubach, L., Lamersdorf, W.: Jadex: a BDI reasoning engine. In: Bordini, R.H., Dastani, M., Dix, J., El Fallah Seghrouchni, A. (eds.) Multi-Agent Programming. MSASSO, vol. 15, pp. 149–174. Springer, Boston, MA (2005). https://doi.org/10.1007/0-387-26350-0_6
17. Rao, A.S., Georgeff, M.P.: BDI agents: from theory to practice. In: Lesser, V.R., Gasser, L. (eds.) Proceedings of the 1st International Conference on MAS, pp. 312–319. The MIT Press (1995)
18. Renoux, J., Klügl, F.: Simulating daily activities in a smart home for data generation. In: WSC, pp. 798–809. IEEE (2018)
19. Sernani, P., Claudi, A., Calvaresi, P., Accattoli, D., Tofani, R., Dragoni, A.F.: Using 3D simulators for the ambient assisted living. In: AI-AM/NetMed@ECAI, pp. 16–20 (2014)
20. Taillandier, P., et al.: Building, composing and experimenting complex spatial models with the GAMA platform. GeoInformatica **23**(2), 299–322 (2018). https://doi.org/10.1007/s10707-018-00339-6
21. Wang, Z., et al.: Cooperative ramp merging system: agent-based modeling and simulation using game engine. SAE Int. J. Connected Autom. Veh. **2**, 115–128 (2019)
22. Wilensky, U., Rand, W.: An Introduction to Agent-Based Modeling: Modeling Natural, Social, and Engineered Complex Systems with NetLogo. MIT Press, Cambridge (2015)

Personal Data Privacy Semantics in Multi-Agent Systems Interactions

Davide Calvaresi, Michael Schumacher, and Jean-Paul Calbimonte[✉]

University of Applied Sciences and Arts Western Switzerland (HES-SO),
Sierre, Switzerland
jpcik@hevs.ch

Abstract. In recent years, we have witnessed the growth of applications relying on the use and processing of personal data, especially in the health and well-being domains. Users themselves produce these data (e.g., through self-reported data acquisition, or personal devices such as smartphones, smartwatches or other wearables). A key challenge in this context is to guarantee the protection of personal data privacy, respecting the rights of users for deciding about data reuse, consent to data processing and storage, anonymity conditions, or the right to withhold or delete personal data. With the enforcement of recent regulations in this domain, such as the GDPR, applications are required to guarantee compliance, challenging current practices for personal data management. In this paper, we address this problem in the context of decentralized personal data applications, which may need to interact and negotiate conditions of data processing and reuse. Following a distributed paradigm without a top-down organization, we propose an agent-based model in which personal data providers and data consumers are embedded into privacy-aware agents capable of negotiating and coordinating data reuse, consent, and policies, using semantic vocabularies for privacy and provenance.

Keywords: Privacy ontologies · Agent data privacy · Semantic agents

1 Introduction

Protecting data privacy and complying with privacy policies is of utmost importance, especially when handling sensitive personal information. Beyond personal datasets, including demographic information, or medical history records, nowadays, the digitization era has opened the way for a large number of data acquisition alternatives. Ranging from applications installed in smartphones to well-being sensors embedded in smartwatches, or social network data collected on our behalf, the amount of sensitive information directly or indirectly collected by users and third-parties has experienced enormous growth. This trend entails several ethical and legal challenges, which cannot be isolated from the technological implications behind the acquisition of these datasets [3].

The European Union introduced and adopted in 2018 the General Data Protection Regulation (GDPR), a comprehensive legislation body that has had

© Springer Nature Switzerland AG 2020
Y. Demazeau et al. (Eds.): PAAMS 2020, LNAI 12092, pp. 55–67, 2020.
https://doi.org/10.1007/978-3-030-49778-1_5

an enormous impact on how personal data is collected, stored, processed, and shared [26]. The legal enforcement of GDPR is also transforming how digital solutions, applications, and systems handle sensitive data. For instance, the need for explicit consent for the use of data, the right to timely receive all data collected for oneself, or the right to completely delete personal data are specified in this law, forcing technical solutions to be provided following the regulations. Although many privacy-preserving and GDPR compliant frameworks have been designed and implemented in the last few years [2], most of these rely on centralized enforcement and compliance, often assuming full control inside the boundaries of a siloed system. For instance, this is the case with clinical studies, in which acquisition instruments, such as wearable devices, have built-in restrictions to guarantee compliance. This is also the case within the boundaries of a hospital, in which both monitoring devices and electronic health records are designed to respect privacy regulations. However, these approaches disregard the decentralized nature of data interactions in larger scope scenarios. Having full control in a top-down fashion is not feasible in more complex environments such as crowd-sourcing, or public data collection in which no central authority can be the sole entity in charge of data protection. Furthermore, even when centralized data privacy is enforced, the representation of data privacy needs, consent, purpose, etc. lacks the expressiveness and machine-understandable semantics required to provide automated management of personal data handling.

In this paper, we propose the adoption of decentralized agent-based data privacy negotiation, coordination, and enforcement, using semantic representations of personal data privacy conditions and handling. More precisely, we define a set of minimal personal data privacy interaction requirements among agents and the design principles of privacy-aware agent interactions regarding personal data handling. Then, we propose a conceptual architecture in which these interactions are translated into multi-agent protocol specifications, annotated with semantic information about the purpose, recipient, processing, and consent of the personal data. We base this specification in the Data Privacy Vocabulary (DPV) [19], developed by the Data Privacy Vocabularies and Controls Community Group, hosted under the umbrella of the W3C organization.

The remainder of the paper is organized as follows: Sect. 2 provides a motivating use-case and elaborates requirements. Section 3 presents the design principles of a MAS personal data privacy. Section 4 elaborates on data privacy semantics in agent(s) interactions. Section 5 summarizes the related work. Finally, Sect. 6 concludes the paper and proposes a road-map for future steps.

2   Personal Data Privacy Interactions

When sharing, reusing, or processing personal data, privacy concerns surface at different stages, and specific regulations need to be considered at each of them. For example, Fig. 1 considers a use case in physical rehabilitation, where motion monitoring sensors are used to track exercise and physical activity from a patient [4,5]. Following a traditional approach, the patient will sign a general consent for data collection and processing, which will be managed by the clinic or hospital to which the physiotherapist is affiliated. After this consent is signed, the wearable sensors can collect data that will be forwarded to the monitoring system managed by the physiotherapist. In turn, such data can also be linked to the electronic health record of the patient, and later shared with other healthcare professionals within the hospital or clinic.

Fig. 1. Requests from a physiotherapist to patients' data, according to a general consent. This implies no customization of consent conditions, and disregards the decentralized nature of sensing applications.

In this scenario, the patient (or subject) has granted permission to several actions and activities, many of which are probably not exactly clear or transparent. Therefore the following questions can be raised:

- Can the subject timely access all collected data during the interventions?
- Is the subject able to opt-out of specific processing/monitoring activities?
- Can the subject establish restrictions on types of data to be collected/reused?
- How can the subject trace the actions and data access of healthcare providers?
- Can the subject limit read/write access to specific healthcare providers?
- Is the subject given the possibility of deleting or withdrawing her data completely or partially?
- Can the user dynamically change the consent conditions, including restrictions on specific data handling purposes?
- Can the subject be notified of risks or evidence of privacy breach or other undesired activities?

Most of these questions can be linked to regulations in data protection laws. In particular, for the EU, GDPR precisely establishes a legal framework to guarantee that subjects can have satisfactory answers to all these questions. For instance, concerning the possibility of deleting one's data, GDPR introduces the right to be forgotten [26]: *"The data subject shall have the right to obtain from the controller the erasure of personal data without undue delay"*. In the use-case mentioned above, the broad consent given by the patient leaves little space for fine-grained management of personal data, resulting in activities (e.g., processing, data reuse, profile learning) which will be somehow hidden to the patient. Although this is generally based on the assumption of a trusted relationship, nowadays people are more and more aware of the importance of privacy, and on the potential benefits of having access not only to one's data but also to the trace of usage of that data. Moreover, given the potential complexity of data privacy regulations, people may often require assistance to fully grasp the implications of individual consent grant decisions. At the same time, it is also needed to provide users with the means to keep track of data usage and risks, while allowing integration even among different healthcare institutions. Considering that in many cases, patients may desire to share personal data among different clinics and hospitals, their privacy preferences should be able to be transmitted and enforced across institutional and administrative boundaries.

Taking into account these considerations, we formulate the following requirements for establishing personal data privacy in a decentralized environment:

R1: *Data handling actors:* Before establishing any privacy interactions, a shared understanding of actors and processes for data handling must be established. This model, following legal regulations such as the GDPR, must formulate who are the data controllers, subjects, recipients, and what are the possible data handling processes that they may activate. These actors must be able to establish their own goals with respect to the data (e.g., compliance, privacy policies), have their own knowledge or state, as well as a set of potential actions or intentions.

R2: *Decentralized interactions:* The different actors in charge of personal data handling must specify the possible interactions among them, without the need of a centralized entity governing their decisions. Considering that a data controller (e.g., sensor data collection on behalf of a clinical provider) may need to request consent acceptance to a subject (e.g., a patient), none of these actors should be imposed decisions regarding the negotiation of the data access conditions nor should be able to take them independently.

R3: *Semantic data privacy modelling:* To have meaningful interactions among data privacy controllers and subjects, it is essential to rely on the standard and human/machine-understandable models that represent data handling purposes, processes, consent, and other data privacy characteristics. These models must be specified using semantic representations, which can embed interpretable logic that can be later used for enforcing data privacy policies. Semantic vocabularies—aligned with current legislation such as the GDPR—are required to attain this degree of interpretability.

R4: *Interaction protocols:* The interactions must follow a well-defined pattern, specified as a set of behaviors, so that they allow the negotiation or collaboration among different entities. For example, if a clinical study requires crowd-sourcing personal data from a given population, a surrogate entity may emit a call-for-data, including consent and policy conditions, to which potential data providers could emit "accept" or "reject" interactions, followed –if positive– by periodic data collection messages.

R5: *Legal compliance:* All interactions among entities dealing with personal data must comply with the applicable legal framework, e.g., GDPR in the EU.

Furthermore, once the interaction model has been established under these conditions, it is also important to enforce the following aspects, directly regarding the handling of personal data privacy:

R6: *Verification:* It should be possible that all entities participating in data privacy interactions can verify the compliance to regulations. This verification should be automatized, even if across institutional boundaries, thanks to the semantic representation of policies and handling conditions.

R7: *Tracking:* It must be possible to keep track of all interactions, as well as reuse, access, processing, and handling events across the lifetime of personal datasets.

R8: *Explainability:* Controllers should expose explainable and understandable interfaces for all data handling processes. This should allow users and subjects in general to have a clear understanding of data workflows and implications in privacy.

R9: *Transparency:* Controllers should be able to timely communicate any event of importance to subjects, concerning data privacy, such as risks, breaches, compromises, or any other potentially relevant circumstance.

R10: *Granularity:* It must be possible to choose the granularity at which personal data handling is performed. This includes the ability to select the purpose(s) for which data processing is requested, who has access and under which conditions, what are the potential data recipients, what type of reuse or publication is permitted, which technical measures will be applied, such as storage means, deadlines, etc.

3   Design Principles for MAS Personal Data Privacy

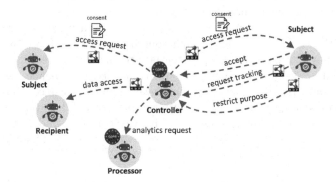

Fig. 2. Personal Data Privacy Agents. The controller may emit access request to subject agents. Negotiation, including consent may happen through agent interactions.

Considering the challenges and requirements enumerated previously, we propose a set of principles for establishing decentralized data privacy interactions among personal data providers, recipients, and managers. This set of principles is based on the adoption of the multi-agent system (MAS) paradigm, which has several properties that match the challenges of complex personal data exchange and reuse. First, the notion of MAS already implies the necessary degree of autonomy for agents, which can embody different types of data handling entities. Second, it naturally allows agents to set their own goals, which in terms of data privacy can include specific policies, consent conditions, red lines regarding privacy, etc. Similarly, for data controllers, it may allow defining goals regarding the quality/quantity of data or de-anonymization guarantees. A third aspect refers to the possibility of establishing negotiating protocols and collaboration patterns among agents, which may translate to consent requests, data tracking petitions, right to be forgotten enforcement, etc. Finally, the agent paradigm permits the exchange of common knowledge, or beliefs, which can be crucial for personal data handling in complex scenarios, thanks to the usage of standard and semantically rich ontologies representing data privacy specifications. We identify three main design principles detailed in the following, and partially illustrated in Fig. 2.

Decentralized Agents: All participating entities in personal data privacy interactions are modelled as autonomous intelligent agents. Following the nomenclature of the GDPR we identify four main types of actors: *data controllers*, *subjects*, *recipients*, and *processors*. Controllers refer to people, organizations, or authorities that govern and decide about the purpose and processing of personal data. Subjects are the persons to which the data is related, while recipients are the people or entities to which the personal information is disclosed. Processors are those persons or entities that perform any processing of the personal data on behalf of the controller. Other classes of agents may exist, such as third parties or authorities, complementary to the main four (Fig. 2). Each of these agents has its own set of goals, w.r.t. personal data handling. For example, a patient may require that all data that is shared with other agents should be only for academic research, or that it should be fully anonymized, or that it should exclude any profiling processing activities, etc. Notice that even under anonymization, re-identification is still possible through combination of different data sources, and agents may consider modelling potential attacks and contemplate countermeasures. These agents also have their own knowledge or beliefs, which may include metadata regarding the personal datasets under their control (e.g., for the data controllers), or the tracking activities of personal data (e.g., for a data subject). The agent knowledge can be arbitrarily complex, and it is the agent who decides which elements of it can be shared with other agents, and for which purposes.

Shared Semantic Vocabulary: The semantic interoperability among these agents is dictated by the use of a common ontology (or set of ontologies) establishing a common model for representing privacy data. This is a fundamental principle for the establishment of meaningful interactions among decentralized agents, given that there is not necessarily a sole authority governing the agent requests and responses. In this work, we advocate the use of the Data Privacy Vocabulary

(DPV)[1], an ontology developed by the Data Privacy Vocabularies and Control Community Group, under the scope of the W3C (see Fig. 3). This vocabulary, although not yet published as a standard, is a GDPR-based model supported by a group of academic, industrial, and administrative institutions, with a high potential for adoption in a wider scope [19]. The model vocabulary includes the definition of the main concepts regarding personal data handling, including consent, purpose, processing, legal basis, controllers, and recipients, among others.

Fig. 3. Main classes of the Data Privacy Vocabulary [19]

Data Privacy Agent Interactions: Having defined the agents and the semantics of the data that sets personal data privacy policies, the third main aspect refers to the specification of interactions in this context. In principle, we base the definition of these interactions in existing FIPA protocols. For instance, a data consent request can be embedded in a request interaction protocol, or a data crowd-sourcing request can be represented as a ContractNet protocol — thus, extending current approaches such as [15] which leverages on weighted aggregation of the encrypted users' data via homomorphic cryptosystems or applications for mobile crowdsensing such as CarTel, ParkNet, BikeNet, and DietSense [8] (Fig. 4).

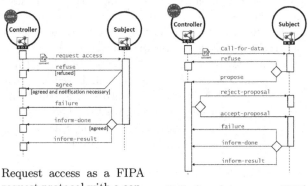

Request access as a FIPA request protocol with a consent.

Call for data as a FIPA ContractNet cfp.

Fig. 4. Agent data privacy interactions as FIPA protocols.

---

[1] https://www.w3.org/ns/dpv.

We identify a non-comprehensive minimum set of interactions listed below:

- Controller requests personal data (with consent) to a specific subject.
- Subject provides personal data (with a consent granted).
- Controller calls for personal data to a set of individuals represented by their subject agents.
- Subject selects only a certain purpose for data handling.
- Subject rejects request for data.
- Subject grants access to personal data only for a certain purpose.
- Subject/Controller customizes permissions and access rights.
- Controller tracks personal data reuse and processing.
- Subject deletes or withholds own personal data.
- Subject/controller verifies personal data use and policy.
- Subject objects to data reuse or processing.
- Subject requests access to own personal data collected (and metadata).
- Controller notifies about data breaches or risk.

4   Data Privacy Semantics in Agent Interactions

As specified in the previous section, the semantic representation of personal data privacy information provides the foundations for interactions among heterogeneous agents. Regarding the specification of the interactions, these can be embedded into standard FIPA protocols[2].

Data controllers, generally in charge of data handling activities, have the possibility of requesting personal data from a subject, providing data to a recipient, initiating data collection, establishing ad requesting consent proposals, requiring access rights, verifying policies, requesting processing activities, etc. Similarly, a data subject agent can request personal data tracking results, withhold personal data, reject access requests, choose which data purposes to apply to, request access to all collected data, etc. All of these interactions can be semantically represented, using models such as RDF, which allows the representation of information as triples (subject, predicate, object).

For example, in Listing 1.1, we illustrate how a FIPA-based interaction can be encoded in JSON-LD format. This interaction, based in the ContractNet protocol represents a request for data from a controller, to which different agents representing data subjects can answer through a bid. The message content, in this case, is a reference to a consent that subjects would need to agree with (in case of acceptance to participate in the data collection).

---

[2] http://www.fipa.org/repository/.

```
{ "prov:generatedAtTime": "2020-02-01T04:00:00.000Z",
  "@id": "ex:callForActivityData",
  "@graph": [
  { "@id": "ex:callForData1",
    "ag:permormative": "ag:CallForProposals",
    "ag:sender": "ex:controller1",
    "ag:protocol": "ag:ContractNet",
    "ag:ontology": "http://w3id.org/ns/dpv#",
    "ag:content": "ex:consentPatient1"   }] }
```

Listing 1.1. Call for data representation in RDF JSON-LD format

All personal data handling activities, such as processing, data access request, consent management, etc., can also be represented using RDF. In Listing 1.2, we provide an example of data collection represented in RDF. Following the DPV ontology, it specifies the data controller (e.g., a hospital), the subject (e.g., a specific patient). It also indicates that the data to collect is about physical health; the purpose is for academic research and includes a consent.

```
ex:dataRequest a dpv:PersonalDataHandling ;
  dpv:hasDataSubject      ex:patient1 ;
  dpv:hasPurpose          [a dpv:AcacemicResearch] ;
  dpv:hasProcessing       [a dpv:Collect];    dpv:hasLegalBasis    [a dpv:Consent];
  dpv:hasDataController    ex:hospital1;       dpv:haRecipient       ex:physician3;
  dpv:hasPersonalDataCategory [a dpv:PhysicalHealth];
  dcterms:title           "Personal Data Collection for clinical study ..." .
```

Listing 1.2. Data handling represented in RDF Turtle format.

Regarding the consent itself, it follows a similar structure as any data handling. In the example of Listing 1.3, the consent establishes three different purposes for data analysis: academic research, economic research, and personalized recommendations. Indeed, for instance, in a clinical study, analytics can be performed for research, but also to create recommendations that would benefit the patient. However, by examining this consent, the subject agent may choose only to authorize the analysis of data for academic research, banning the use for any commercial purpose. This enables fine-grained control over his/her own data.

```
ex:consentPatient1 a dpv:Consent ;
  dpv:hasDataSubject ex:patient1 ;
  dpv:hasPurpose          [a dpv:AcacemicResearch], [a dpv:CommercialResearch],
                          [a dpv:CreatePersonalizedRecommendations] ;
  dpv:hasProcessing [a dpv:Analyse];
  dcterms:title           "Consent for Health data analysis in a clinical study ..." ;
  dpv:hasDataController   ex:hospital1;
  dpv:haRecipient      ex:physiotherapist1;
  dpv:hasPersonalDataCategory [a dpv:PhysicalHealth].
```

Listing 1.3. Consent represented in RDF Turtle format.

About the processing of data, the provenance ontology (PROV-O) provides a complementary set of classes and properties, which allows providing details about different types of data transformation activities. In Listing 1.4, we include an example of a data analytics task for personal data of a patient. The trace of the data analytics enables linking original datasets with processed results, which later can be requested by the data subject.

```
ex:dataAnalysis a dpv:Analysis ;
  dpv:hasDataSubject      ex:patient1 ;
  prov:used               ex:patientDataset1 ;
  dcterms:title           "Data Analysis activity for patient data ..." ;
  prov:isAssociatedWith   ex:dataScientist1;
  prov:wasStartedAtTime   "2020-01-11T04:00:00.000Z".
ex:analyticsResults a prov:Entity ;
  prov:wasGeneratedBy ex:dataAnalysis;  prov:wasDerivedFrom  ex:patientDataset1.
```

Listing 1.4. Data analysis represented in RDF Turtle format.

5   Related Work

A large number of previous works have addressed the research problem of integrating privacy into multi-agent systems [16,23]. Although multiple challenges have been discussed, studied, and addressed in these works, an analysis of the state of the art highlights that the inclusion of clear semantics for representing personal data handling has constantly been missing. Even if several ontologies in this domain have been proposed [19], the inclusion of these within the context of applicable legislation (e.g., GDPR) and the interactions among agents has never been considered before. While some architectural propositions and even full implementations have incorporated agents as a central component of privacy-aware systems [10,13,20,27], these generally lack the capability of having defined clear interactions in a decentralized manner, even across heterogeneous systems. Some other aspects have also been explored (i.e., the verification of privacy policies [14], or the establishment of transparent tracking of provenance [11,25]). Many of these efforts are complementary to our approach, which could benefit from trust and explainability mechanisms [6,7,12], which have shown to be relevant to satisfy high standards in privacy regulations. Table 1 summarizes previous works wrt. the previously discussed aspects.

Table 1. Related works. "+" signs indicate wider availability and maturity.

Aspect	Maturity level		
	Conceptual	Implementation	Validation
Agent architecture: [16,20,27]	+++	+	+
Decentralized interactions: [10,13]	+	+	−
Semantic modelling: [9,19,21,24]	++	−	−
Interaction protocols: [1,17,22]	+	−	−
Legal compliance: [18,28]	+	+	−
Verification: [14]	++	+	−
Tracking: [11,25]	+	+	−
Explainability: [7,12]	+	−	−
Transparency: [6,20]	++	+	+
Granularity: [10,19,27]	++	+	−

6 Conclusions and Roadmap

The enforcement of data privacy, especially for sensitive information in the health domain, is nowadays legally binding, thanks to current regulations such as the GDPR. Applications and systems dealing with personal data are obliged to follow these directives, even more so in consideration of the broader availability of wearable and sensing devices that collect data about individuals and can potentially make it available for different purposes. Adopting a different perspective, as opposed to top-down approaches for data privacy compliance, in this paper, we introduced a vision for decentralized personal data privacy interactions. This approach is founded on the principles of multi-agent systems, which introduce autonomy, decentralization, and negotiation as essential aspects that allow the establishment of interactions among independent agents, even if they have different goals related to privacy and the use of data. Moreover, we have introduced the use of semantic data models, and, in particular, the DPV ontology, to enable heterogeneous agents to specify privacy policies and consent. Regarding potential threats, differential privacy or techniques related to k-anonymity or l-diversity can be used to model adversary agents for which privacy agents can progressively develop protection strategies.

This abstract agent model for data privacy handling introduces an overview of how agents can establish relationships and negotiation activities related to data privacy, even though it leaves the question of implementation and deployment of such a system for future work. The challenge of taking this vision to a deployable solution has not to be underestimated. We foresee the following research opportunities in future works:

(i) The design of domain-specific **vocabularies/ontologies** that describe detailed data processing conditions, purposes and data handling policies;
(ii) The development of **multi-agent environments** that implement the interactions described above, deployable in mobile and sensing devices.
(iii) The study and implementation of agent **negotiation protocols** that automate the personal data privacy workflows, such as consent updates, compliance to user preferences, etc.;
(iv) The specification and validation of **consent and policies** for data privacy, checking automatically for compliance with regulations;
(v) The **validation and evaluation** of the proposed model, in a real environment and including the verification of strict legal compliance (GDPR).

References

1. Biskup, J., Kern-Isberner, G., Thimm, M.: Towards enforcement of confidentiality in agent interactions. In: Proceedings of the 12th International Workshop on Non-Monotonic Reasoning (NMR 2008), pp. 104–112 (2008)
2. Bourgeois, J., Kortuem, G., Kawsar, F.: Trusted and GDPR-compliant research with the internet of things. In: Proceedings of the 8th International Conference on the Internet of Things, pp. 1–8 (2018)

3. Bruschi, D.: Information privacy: not just GDPR. Comput. Ethics-Philoso. Enquiry (CEPE) Proc. **2019**(1), 9 (2019)
4. Buonocunto, P., Giantomassi, A., Marinoni, M., Calvaresi, D., Buttazzo, G.: A limb tracking platform for tele-rehabilitation. ACM Trans. Cyber-Phys. Syst. **2**(4), 1–23 (2018)
5. Calvaresi, D., Calbimonte, J.P.: Real-time compliant stream processing agents for physical rehabilitation. Sensors **20**(3), 746 (2020)
6. Calvaresi, D., Dubovitskaya, A., Retaggi, D., Dragoni, A.F., Schumacher, M.: Trusted registration, negotiation, and service evaluation in multi-agent systems throughout the blockchain technology. In: WI 2018, pp. 56–63. IEEE (2018)
7. Calvaresi, D., Mualla, Y., Najjar, A., Galland, S., Schumacher, M.: Explainable multi-agent systems through blockchain technology. In: Calvaresi, D., Najjar, A., Schumacher, M., Främling, K. (eds.) EXTRAAMAS 2019. LNCS (LNAI), vol. 11763, pp. 41–58. Springer, Cham (2019). https://doi.org/10.1007/978-3-030-30391-4_3
8. Ganti, R.K., Ye, F., Lei, H.: Mobile crowdsensing: current state and future challenges. IEEE Commun. Mag. **49**(11), 32–39 (2011)
9. Jutla, D., Xu, L.: Privacy agents and ontology for the semantic web. In: AMCIS 2004 Proceedings, p. 210 (2004)
10. Kanaan, H., Mahmood, K., Sathyan, V.: An ontological model for privacy in emerging decentralized healthcare systems. In: 2017 IEEE 13th International Symposium on Autonomous Decentralized System (ISADS), pp. 107–113. IEEE (2017)
11. Kifor, T., et al.: Provenance in agent-mediated healthcare systems. IEEE Intell. Syst. **21**(6), 38–46 (2006)
12. Kraus, S., et al.: AI for explaining decisions in multi-agent environments. arXiv preprint arXiv:1910.04404 (2019)
13. Krupa, Y., Vercouter, L.: Handling privacy as contextual integrity in decentralized virtual communities: the privacias framework. Web Intell. Agent Syst.: Int. J. **10**(1), 105–116 (2012)
14. Léauté, T., Faltings, B.: Privacy-preserving multi-agent constraint satisfaction. In: International Conference on Computational Science and Engineering, vol. 3, pp. 17–25 (2009)
15. Miao, C., et al.: Cloud-enabled privacy-preserving truth discovery in crowd sensing systems. In: Proceedings of the ACM Conference on Embedded Networked Sensor Systems, pp. 183–196 (2015)
16. Mivule, K., Josyula, D., Turner, C.: An overview of data privacy in multi-agent learning systems. In: The Fifth International Conference on Advanced Cognitive Technologies and Applications, pp. 14–20 (2013)
17. Moraffah, B., Sankar, L.: Privacy-guaranteed two-agent interactions using information-theoretic mechanisms. IEEE Trans. Inf. Forensics Secur. **12**(9), 2168–2183 (2017)
18. Palmirani, M., Martoni, M., Rossi, A., Bartolini, C., Robaldo, L.: PrOnto: privacy ontology for legal compliance. In: Proceedings of the 18th European Conference on Digital Government (ECDG), pp. 142–151 (2018)
19. Pandit, H.J., et al.: Creating a vocabulary for data privacy. In: Panetto, H., Debruyne, C., Hepp, M., Lewis, D., Ardagna, C.A., Meersman, R. (eds.) OTM 2019. LNCS, vol. 11877, pp. 714–730. Springer, Cham (2019). https://doi.org/10.1007/978-3-030-33246-4_44

20. Piolle, G., Demazeau, Y., Caelen, J.: Privacy management in user-centred multi-agent systems. In: O'Hare, G.M.P., Ricci, A., O'Grady, M.J., Dikenelli, O. (eds.) ESAW 2006. LNCS (LNAI), vol. 4457, pp. 354–367. Springer, Heidelberg (2007). https://doi.org/10.1007/978-3-540-75524-1_20

21. Sanchez, O.R., Torre, I., Knijnenburg, B.P.: Semantic-based privacy settings negotiation and management. Future Gener. Comput. Syst. (2019)

22. Sannon, S., Stoll, B., DiFranzo, D., Jung, M.F., Bazarova, N.N.: "I just shared your responses" extending communication privacy management theory to interactions with conversational agents. Proc. ACM HCI **4**, 1–18 (2020)

23. Such, J.M., Espinosa, A., García-Fornes, A.: A survey of privacy in multi-agent systems. Knowl. Eng. Rev. **29**(3), 314–344 (2014)

24. Thangaraj, M., Ponmalar, P.P., Sujatha, G., Anuradha, S.: Agent based semantic internet of things (IoT) in smart health care. In: Proceedings of the International KMO Conference on the Changing Face of Knowledge Management Impacting Society, pp. 1–9 (2016)

25. Vázquez-Salceda, J., et al.: EU PROVENANCE project: an open provenance architecture for distributed applications. In: Annicchiarico, R., Cortés, U., Urdiales, C. (eds.) Agent Technology and e-Health. WSSAT, pp. 45–63. Springer, Heidelberg (2007). https://doi.org/10.1007/978-3-7643-8547-7_4

26. Voigt, P., Von dem Bussche, A.: The EU General Data Protection Regulation (GDPR). A Practical Guide, 1st edn. Springer, Cham (2017). https://doi.org/10.1007/978-3-319-57959-7

27. Wimmer, H., Yoon, V.Y., Sugumaran, V.: A multi-agent system to support evidence based medicine and clinical decision making via data sharing and data privacy. Decis. Support Syst. **88**, 51–66 (2016)

28. Yee, G., Korba, L.: An agent architecture for e-services privacy policy compliance. In: 19th International Conference on Advanced Information Networking and Applications (AINA 2005) (AINA Papers), vol. 1, pp. 374–379. IEEE (2005)

Towards Real-Time Crowd Simulation Under Uncertainty Using an Agent-Based Model and an Unscented Kalman Filter

Robert Clay[1]([✉]) [iD], Le-Minh Kieu[1,2] [iD], Jonathan A. Ward[3] [iD],
Alison Heppenstall[1,4] [iD], and Nick Malleson[1,4] [iD]

[1] Leeds Institute for Data Analytics, University of Leeds, Leeds LS2 9JT, UK
r.clay@leeds.ac.uk
[2] Department of Civil and Environmental Engineering, University of Auckland,
1010 Auckland, New Zealand
[3] School of Mathematics, University of Leeds, Leeds LS2 9JT, UK
[4] School of Geography, University of Leeds, Leeds LS2 9JT, UK
http://lida.leeds.ac.uk, http://www.cee.auckland.ac.nz/,
https://eps.leeds.ac.uk/maths, https://environment.leeds.ac.uk/geography

Abstract. Agent-based modelling (ABM) is ideally suited to simulating crowds of people as it captures the complex behaviours and interactions between individuals that lead to the emergence of crowding. Currently, it is not possible to use ABM for *real-time* simulation due to the absence of established mechanisms for dynamically incorporating real-time data. This means that, although models are able to perform useful offline crowd simulations, they are unable to simulate the behaviours of crowds in real time. This paper begins to address this drawback by demonstrating how a data assimilation algorithm, the Unscented Kalman Filter (UKF), can be used to incorporate pseudo-real data into an agent-based model at run time. Experiments are conducted to test how well the algorithm works when a proportion of agents are tracked directly under varying levels of uncertainty. Notably, the experiments show that the behaviour of unobserved agents can be inferred from the behaviours of those that are observed. This has implications for modelling real crowds where full knowledge of all individuals will never be known. In presenting a new approach for creating real-time simulations of crowds, this paper has important implications for the management of various environments in global cities, from single buildings to larger structures such as transportation hubs, sports stadiums, through to entire city regions.

Keywords: Agent-based modelling · Unscented Kalman Filter · Uncertainty · Data assimilation · Crowd simulation

This project has received funding from the European Research Council (ERC) under the European Union's Horizon 2020 research and innovation programme (grant agreement No. 757455), through a UK Economic and Social Research Council (ESRC) Future Research Leaders grant [number ES/L009900/1], an ESRC-Alan Turing Fellowship [number ES/R007918/1] and is part of the Leeds Institute for Data Analytics (LIDA) Data Scientist Internship Programme 2018/19, funded by the Alan Turing Institute.

© Springer Nature Switzerland AG 2020
Y. Demazeau et al. (Eds.): PAAMS 2020, LNAI 12092, pp. 68–79, 2020.
https://doi.org/10.1007/978-3-030-49778-1_6

1   Introduction

Agent-based modelling has become a popular tool for simulating the behaviour of crowds. While existing agent-based crowd simulation models are effective at analysing 'what-if' scenarios for the development of policies, they are not yet capable of simulating crowds in *real time*. Instead, models that are calibrated to historical data, are often projected forward in time to make a prediction independently of any new data that might arise [19]. Uncertainty is inherent in the underlying system—e.g. in the precise locations of individuals in a crowd, or in the choices that they make when faced with decisions—so even a well-calibrated model will diverge from the true state of the underlying system. Without the ability to adapt a simulation model to the current system state, it is very difficult to use the model to support any crowd management policies in real time. A mechanism is required that readily allows the incorporation of real-time data into an agent-based model. Such a mechanism would allow for the real-time analysis of pedestrian flows around urban spaces.

This paper, which is part of a wider programme of work[1], introduces a new and novel approach that can be used to update the state of an agent-based model in response to new data in *real time*. This is achieved through the use of *Data assimilation* (DA) [5]; a widely used method in fields such as meteorology, hydrology and oceanography, but rarely attempted for use in agent-based modelling. The paper makes use of a simple crowding model, *StationSim*, and a particular DA method, the *Unscented Kalman Filter* (UKF), to show how DA can be used to reduce the uncertainty in a real time simulation of a crowd. Although the work here only considers the uncertainty in the agents' spatial locations, the algorithm could be used to estimate any other agent parameter or generalised to other types of agent-based models. To quantify the errors precisely and to allow experiments with different types of observations, the identical twin experimental framework [18] is used. The contribution of this paper is twofold. First, to the best of the authors' knowledge, this is the first study that aims to adapt and apply the UKF to incorporate real-time data into an agent-based model. Second, we evaluate the accuracy of the UKF with limited information about the crowd, i.e. only some 'individuals' in the crowd are tracked, with future work extending the algorithm to the use of aggregate observation data.

2   Relevant Research

In recent years, efforts have been made to develop methods that will allow agent-based models to react to real-world observations. Examples of these approaches are often developed under the banner of 'Data-Driven Agent-Based Modelling' (DDABM), which itself emerged from a broader work in data-driven application systems [2]. A number of recent attempts have been made to allow agent-based models to react to new data [6–8,10–13,18–20]. However, whilst promising these applications all exhibit a number of limitations that this work will begin to

---

[1] http://dust.leeds.ac.uk/.

address. These include: the need for manual calibration [11] (which is infeasible in most cases); models with only a few agents and/or limited interactions [6,18]; assumptions that agent behaviours can be proxied by simple regression models [20] (which precludes the addition of more advanced behavioural models); the dynamic optimisation of parameters but not the underlying model state [10] (which might have diverged substantially from reality); the use of agent-based models that are simple enough to be approximated by an aggregate mathematical model [7,19] (which undermines the importance of using ABM in the first place); and the use of a data assimilation method whose computational complexity explodes with increasing model size [6,9].

3   Methods

3.1   Overview

The aim of a Data Assimilation (DA) method is to use current, real-world observations to update the internal state of a model. In this manner, "all the available information" [14] is used to and create a combined representation of the system that is closer to the true state than either the observations or the model in isolation. The DA approach differs from typical agent-based parameter estimation/calibration because DA is used to update the *internal state* of the model, not just the values of its parameters. The DA process works as follows:

1. The *forecast* step involves running the simulation (an ABM in this case) forward up to the point that some new observational data become available. In effect this creates a *prior* estimate of the current system state;
2. The *analysis* step involves using the new observations, and their uncertainties, to update the prior, creating a posterior that has combined the best guess of the state from the model *and* the best guess of the state from the observations. The number of model iterations that occur between analysis steps is termed the DA 'window'.

There are a range of DA methods that have been developed, including the Successive Corrections Method, Optimal Interpolation, 3D-Var, 4D-Var, and various variants of Kalman Filtering [5]. Here a UKF is chosen due to its efficiency relative to similar methods, such as the particle filter. However, it requires the strong assumption of Gaussian distributed innovations. Research is needed into the conditions under which the UKF performs well as this approach could potentially reduce the number of calculations for larger scale agent-based models (i.e. large numbers of individual agents) without a significant loss of accuracy.

3.2   The Agent-Based Model: *StationSim*

StationSim is an agent-based model of pedestrian movement. The model has been designed specifically to be simple—at least in comparison to more comprehensive crowd simulations—because the aim here is to experiment with the data assimilation method, not to accurately simulate a pedestrian system. That said, the data assimilation algorithms are not tied to *StationSim* so could be easily adapted for new systems such as traffic dynamics or disease spread.

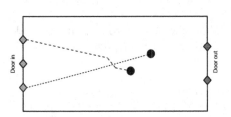

Fig. 1. The *StationSim* environment with 3 entrance and 2 exit doors.

The model contains three entrances and two exits. N agents are created upon initialisation, with each agent assigned an entrance and exit at random. Each agent has a desired maximum speed which is also chosen randomly from a Gaussian distribution. The simulation ends when all N agents have entered and exited the simulation environment. Agents interact when slowly moving agents block the paths of the faster moving agents. When 'collisions' occur, the faster agent makes a random binary choice whether to overtake the slower agent by moving around them to the left or the right. This random choice causes crowding to emerge at different times and locations each time the model is executed. A more comprehensive description of the model can be found in [9], and the model code is available in full from the project repository[2] (Fig. 1).

3.3   Data Assimilation with the Unscented Kalman Filter (UKF)

Kalman Filtering is a well-known data assimilation technique. Ensemble Kalman filtering is an adaptation to the basic filter that can be applied to nonlinear models [19]. In this paper we focus on the Unscented Kalman Filter (UKF) [17]. The UKF uses *statistical linearisation*, whereby a number of 'sigma points' are chosen deterministically to preserve the first two moments of the distribution of states in the model state-space, which is assumed to be Gaussian. These sigma points are passed directly through the nonlinear model and a weighted combination yields the mean and covariance of the updated state. This produces estimates with smaller errors relative to the extended Kalman filter [4].

Let $x_i \in X \subseteq \mathbb{R}^n$ denote the model state at the discrete observation time t_i, where $i \in \mathbb{N}$. We assume that the model state is updated according to the difference equation,

$$x_{i+1} = f(x_i, q_i), \tag{1}$$

where process noise q_i is a random variable with known probability distribution that captures the stochasticity of the model. The transition function f represents the agent-based model's stepping mechanism, which for *StationSim* moves each agent towards its desired exit whilst avoiding collisions with other agents. The

---

[2] The *StationSim* model, specifically, can be found at: https://git.io/JvJSm. The code to run the experiments conducted here can be found at https://git.io/JvJSq.

observation vector $y_k \in Y \subseteq \mathbb{R}^m$ is determined from the state-vector via

$$y_{i+1} = h(x_{i+1}, r_i), \tag{2}$$

where r_i captures the sensor noise. The mean and covariance of x_i is denoted by $\hat{x}_i$ and P_i respectively. Similarly the mean and covariance of y_i by $\hat{y}_i$ and Q_i respectively.

Given the expected values of the state and observation vectors, $\hat{x}_i$ and $\hat{y}_i$, and their corresponding covariance matrices, P_i and Q_i at time t_i, data assimilation proceeds via two steps [16,17].

1. In the *forecast* step, a sample of k *sigma points* $\mathcal{X}_i^{(j)}$, for $1 \leq j \leq k$ are computed deterministically about the mean state $\hat{x}_i$. The sigma points are then evolved independently forward in time via (1) to give $\mathcal{X}_{i+1}^{(j)} = f(\mathcal{X}_i^{(j)}, q_i)$. The forecast of the expected state $\hat{x}_{i+1}$ at time t_{i+1} is given by a weighted sum of the sigma points $\mathcal{X}_{i+1}^{(j)}$ using the Unscented Transform function [15]. Forecasts for the observation vector can be computed in a similar way using (2), as well as the covariances and cross-covariances.
2. The *analysis* step, following the observations at time t_{i+1}, follows the standard Kalman filter using the expected value of the state vector $\hat{x}_{i+1}$ and covariance P_{i+1}.

These steps are then iterated until the final observation. The UKF requires user choices for both the type of sigma points used and the mean weightings in the forecast step. For simplicity, we use the standard choice of Merwe's Scaled Sigma Points and their corresponding weightings. In addition to the expected values of the state and its covariance, the set of $k = 2m + 1$ sigma points is constructed using three tuning parameters α, β, and κ. The concept is similar to that of an m-dimensional confidence interval, using a central mean sigma point as well as $2p$ outer sigma points centred about the mean some distance away depending on the covariance structure. Given our high-dimensional state-space, we adopt the recommended values in [17] for $(\alpha, \beta, \kappa) = (1, 2, 0)$. We also choose values for the process and sensor noise as n/m dimensional identity matrix structures I_n and I_m respectively. Other parameter values are listed in Table 1.

Table 1. Main parameters used in the experiments

Number of agents	n	$[10, 20, 30]$
Number of experiments (repetitions)	N	30
Observation noise	σ^2	0.5^2
Data assimilation 'window'	f	5
Tuning parameters	α, β, κ	$[1, 2, 0]$
Proportion of agents observed	p	$[0.25, 0.5, 0.75, 1.0]$
Process/Sensor noise	q_i/r_i	I_n/I_m

3.4   Error Metrics

Recall that the paper follows an 'identical twin' experimental framework, such that the *StationSim* model is first run once in order to create pseudo-real observations which are assumed to be drawn from the real world. This allows the true state of the system to be known, and hence precise errors to be calculated. In reality the true system state cannot be known precisely.

Assume we repeat an experiment N times where the ith experiment has n_i agents and t_i time steps. For some agent $j \in 1, ..., n_i$ at time $k \in 1, ..., t_i$ we analyse the efficacy of the UKF using the Euclidean distance between each agents' true (x_{jk}, y_{jk}) and UKF predicted $(\hat{x}_{jk}, \hat{y}_{jk})$ Cartesian coordinates (Eq. 3). This provides a matrix of distances $d_{t_i \times n_i}^i$ with each column representing an agents error over time and each row representing the spread of agent errors at each time point. We calculate an agent error vector $\tilde{x}_j^i = (\tilde{x}_0^i, \tilde{x}_1^i, ..., \tilde{x}_{n_i}^i)$ for the ith experiment with the jth element representing the median error for the jth agent (jth column of d). We use medians here to avoid bias caused by taking the means of heavily right skewed agent error distributions.

$$d_{t_i \times n_i}^i = d_{jk}^i = \sqrt{(x_{jk} - \hat{x}_{jk})^2 + (y_{jk} - \hat{y}_{jk})^2} \tag{3}$$

$$\tilde{x}_j^i = \underset{k \in 1,...,t_i}{\mathrm{median}}(d_{jk}^i) \tag{4}$$

For multiple runs we calculate the grand median error vector $\bar{x} = (\bar{x}_1, \bar{x}_2, ..., \bar{x}_N)$ where the ith element represents the median of mean agent errors for the ith model run.

$$\bar{x}_i = \underset{j \in 1,...,n_i}{\mathrm{median}}(\tilde{x}_j^i) \tag{5}$$

We then use this as a sample to gain a measure of the UKF's general efficacy given certain parameters. We use both the raw sample and the sample mean for boxplots and choropleths respectively.

4   Results

4.1   Overview of the Experiments

The aim of the experiments is to provide a better understanding of the conditions under which the UKF reliably estimates the 'true' state of a simple pedestrian system. Two experiments are conducted[3]. The first compares the three different approaches to the problem of real-time optimisation to quantify the improvements offered by data assimilation under different conditions. The observational data used are the locations of a sample of the pseudo-true agent population

---

[3] This work was undertaken on ARC3, part of the High Performance Computing facilities at the University of Leeds, UK.

generated initially by *StationSim*, which is analogous to tracking individuals in a crowd. The second experiment investigates the proportion of agents who are being tracked. This is to understand the amount of information that is required about the underlying system for successful assimilation. Future work will also experiment with aggregate counts of people (e.g. population density) at different spatial locations. This is similar to the types of observations that are available from real systems.

4.2   Experiment 1: Benchmark

This experiment is designed to determine the improvement that filtering offers over an entirely data-driven approach (i.e. pure observation without any model) or an entirely model-based approach (i.e. pure prediction without observations). It also establishes suitable values for the observational noise that is added to the pseudo-truth data and explores the impacts of different data assimilation window sizes, f, i.e. the number of model iterations between data assimilation updates. Using these values, we establish a suitable benchmark under which the UKF performs well. The chosen population size ($n = 30$) is large enough that crowding occurs without excessive computational complexity. For each model run we calculate the grand median distance between each 'true' agent position and its estimate and take a further scalar median of 30 model repetitions ($N = 30$ is sufficient to capture the variability in the results within a reasonable computation time).

Figure 2 presents these scalars over varying noises and assimilation rates. We assume that the noise added to the pseudo-real observations (sensor noise) and the uncertainty associated with the individuals in *StationSim* (the process noise) are treated equally, so the UKF relies on both predictions and observations performing similarly well[4]. Figure 2a shows the error of the *best performing* metric (observation, model, or UKF) and it is evident that when there is no observation noise then the observations in isolation give the best estimate of the pseudo-true system evolution (the yellow area in the left of the grid). Conversely, when observation noise is very high then the *StationSim* prediction provides the best (albeit relatively poor) estimate because it is not confounded by noisy observations (the red area to the right of the grid). However, when the observation noise is not extreme, the UKF gives a more accurate prediction than the model or the observations in isolation (the blue area in the middle of the grid). Figure 2b shows the same information, but illustrates the errors associated with the three approaches simultaneously, rather than just the error of the best performing approach.

For the remaining experiments we set the data assimilation window size and measurement noise to be 5 and 0.5 respectively. These parameters show the UKF performing consistently well.

---

[4] In practice, noise assumptions can be tailored to improve performance, but under high dimensional scenarios such as this it can prove difficult to optimise. This provides a strong motivation for further adaptions to the UKF particularly adaptive filtering [1].

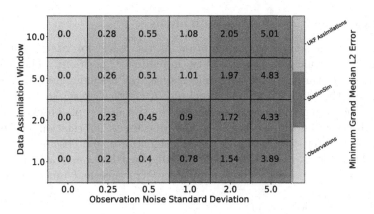

(a) The error of the best performing approach (observation, prediction, or UKF).

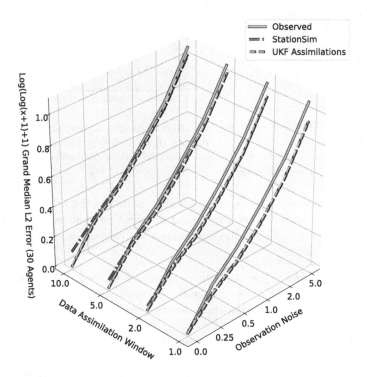

(b) Comparison of all three approaches, not just the best performing one.

Fig. 2. Errors of estimated agent positions against 'true' positions comparing: (1) observations in isolation; (2) *StationSim* predictions in isolation; and (3) UKF predictions (assimilation of *StationSim* predictions and observations) with different data assimilation window sizes and levels of observation noise. (Color figure online)

4.3   Experiment 2: Tracking Individuals

Here we show a simple implementation of the UKF for *StationSim* under a scenario in which we track every individuals' positions. The UKF is then 'stressed' through inducing uncertainty by assuming only some proportion of the crowd can be tracked. A further test is to ascertain whether the filter can both estimate the positions of observed agents and unobserved agents of which it has no direct information. When initialising the filter we randomly assign agents to be observed or unobserved. This allows us to observe how well the UKF can track unobserved agents using only its propagated covariance structure and initial conditions.

With observation frequency and noise parameters decided, we look at the behaviour of a typical *StationSim* example using diagnostics from a single run with 30 agents of which a proportion of 0.5 (50%) are observed. This is illustrated in Fig. 3 which shows the pseudo-true positions of *StationSim* agents and their UKF predicted counterparts. As expected, the estimated positions of observed agents are consistently close to their true positions with small errors introduced through the observation noise. Unobserved agent predictions, however, are much less consistent. Histograms of the L2 error for unobserved agents illustrate a very long tailed distribution split between low error and high error agents. Hence the unobserved agents can be generally grouped into two categories:

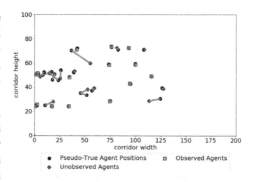

Fig. 3. An example StationSim run showing the performance for observed agents as well as both common and outlier unobserved agents.

- **Common agents**, whose behaviour is similar to some subset of observed agents, exhibit strong cross-covariances between similar agents in the UKF covariance structure allowing them to orientate themselves with reasonable accuracy.
- **Outlier agents**, who have no similar agents to reference, have no strong cross covariances and as such have no points of reference resulting in a drift from the true positions. This lack of reference points comes from either an agent being too fast, too slow, or getting stuck in a crowd.

We now extend our diagnostics to multiple UKF runs. We have three population sizes ($n \in [10, 20, 30]$) and assume noisy GPS style position data for some proportion of agents between 0.25 and 1.0 (25% to 100% of observed agents). We repeat each run 30 times taking a sample of the grand median agent errors (see Eq. 5) for each population n and proportion p. As a quick performance overview, the median of each sample providing scalar values for each (n, p) pair is also taken. Figure 4 illustrates the overall error for all agents (4a) and the errors of just the unobserved agents (4b). For the observed agents (not shown) there is very little error—approximately 0.5 ± 0.03—suggesting the UKF uniformly fits these observed agents well. As the proportion of observed agents increases beyond 0.25, the overall estimate (4a) improves. Although an increase is to be expected, the improvement is nonlinear. Figure 4b shows that the error of unobserved agents, specifically, goes down as a larger proportion of agents are observed. Hence the rapid overall improvement occurs because the filter not only knows the positions of a larger number of agents, but is also able to better estimate the positions of the *unobserved agents* using solely its propagated covariance structure. As a slight note of caution, there is a large variation in the error of the unobserved agents, therefore using a single median value to represent the overall success of the filter masks some of this variation.

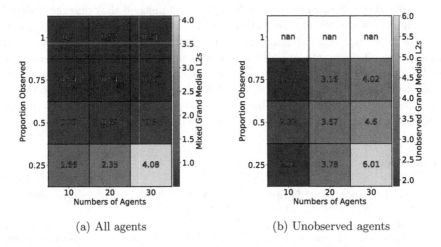

(a) All agents   (b) Unobserved agents

Fig. 4. Grand agent error choropleths for all agents (a) and unobserved agents only (b).

5   Conclusion

This paper has developed an Unscented Kalman Filter (UKF) that can be used to perform data assimilation on an agent-based model. Although previous efforts have used particle filters for this task [6,8,9,13,18] and variants of the Kalman filter for simpler models [19], this is the first time that an unscented Kalman filter has been used to optimise an agent-based model that includes heterogeneous, interacting agents. Importantly, the UKF is able to predict the locations of the agents with relatively little information about the crowd. This is encouraging for its application to real crowd systems where only limited information is typically available. Furthermore, the UKF has the potential to incorporate real-time data into larger scale and more realistic ABMs, in comparison to other data assimilation methods, because the UKF uses only a limited number of sigma points and is hence less likely to require large, computationally expensive ensembles.

There are inevitably drawbacks to the approach that will be addressed in future work. The calculation of sigma points requires finding the square root of the state covariance matrix which is the main computational bottleneck of the algorithm. This becomes a problem for high dimensional cases where alternatives such as the Ensemble Kalman Filter (EnKF) become preferable. The Square Root Unscented Kalman Filter (SRUKF) [16] has been proposed as a solution to this and while even faster than the UKF it suffers from major stability issues for high dimensional cases [3]. Other hyperparameter choices, such as the process and sensor noise covariance structures, are important to prevent filter divergence in high dimensional cases. Adaptive filtering [3], which updates these parameters over time in search of an optimum might be useful. Furthermore, the classical UKF assumes conjugate Gaussian priors and likelihoods, which limits its flexibility in comparison to similar methods such as the Particle Filter.

Despite these drawbacks, the UKF is clearly a method that deserves further research into its efficacy for conducting data assimilation with agent-based models. This paper has laid important groundwork. Immediate future work will: (1) evaluate the efficiency of the UKF in comparison to competing methods such as the Particle Filter and Ensemble Kalman Filter; (2) experiment with observations of different types (such as crowd densities or population counters rather than individual traces); and (3) begin to apply the method on a more realistic crowd system using a more realistic agent-based model.

References

1. Berry, T., Sauer, T.: Adaptive ensemble kalman filtering of non-linear systems. Tellus A: Dyn. Meteorol. Oceanogr. **65**(1), 20331 (2013)
2. Darema, Frederica: Dynamic data driven applications systems: a new paradigm for application simulations and measurements. In: Bubak, Marian, van Albada, Geert Dick, Sloot, Peter M.A., Dongarra, Jack (eds.) ICCS 2004. LNCS, vol. 3038, pp. 662–669. Springer, Heidelberg (2004). https://doi.org/10.1007/978-3-540-24688-6_86
3. Deng, F., Chen, J., Chen, C.: Adaptive unscented kalman filter for parameter and state estimation of nonlinear high-speed objects. J. Syst. Eng. Electron. **24**(4), 655–665 (2013)
4. Gelb, A.: Editor. applied optimal estimation (1974)
5. Kalnay, E.: Atmospheric Modeling, Data Assimilation and Predictability. Cambridge University Press, Cambridge (2003)
6. Kieu, L.M., Malleson, N., Heppenstall, A.: Dealing with uncertainty in agent-based models for short-term predictions. Roy. Soc. Open Sci. **7**(1), 191074 (2020). https://doi.org/10.1098/rsos.191074
7. Lloyd, D.J.B., Santitissadeekorn, N., Short, M.B.: Exploring data assimilation and forecasting issues for an urban crime model. Eur. J. Appl. Math. **27**(Special Issue 03), 451–478 (2016). https://doi.org/10.1017/S0956792515000625

8. Lueck, J., Rife, J.H., Swarup, S., Uddin, N.: Who goes there? using an agent-based simulation for tracking population movement. In: Winter Simulation Conference, 8–11 December 2019. National Harbor, MD, USA (2019)

9. Malleson, N., Minors, K., Kieu, L.M., Ward, J.A., West, A.A., Heppenstall, A.: Simulating Crowds in Real Time with Agent-Based Modelling and a Particle Filter. arXiv:1909.09397 [cs], September 2019

10. Oloo, F., Safi, K., Aryal, J.: Predicting migratory corridors of white storks, ciconia ciconia, to enhance sustainable wind energy planning: a data-driven agent-based model. Sustainability **10**(5), 1470 (2018). https://doi.org/10.3390/su10051470

11. Othman, N.B., Legara, E.F., Selvam, V., Monterola, C.: A data-driven agent-based model of congestion and scaling dynamics of rapid transit systems. J. Comput. Sci. **10**, 338–350 (2015). https://doi.org/10.1016/j.jocs.2015.03.006

12. Schoenharl, T., Madey, G.: Design and implementation of an agent-based simulation for emergency response and crisis management. J. Algorithms Comput. Technol. **5**(4), 601–622 (2011). https://doi.org/10.1260/1748-3018.5.4.601

13. Tabataba, F.S., et al.: Epidemic forecasting framework combining agent-based models and smart beam particle filtering. In: 2017 IEEE International Conference on Data Mining (ICDM), pp. 1099–1104. IEEE, New Orleans, LA, November 2017. https://doi.org/10.1109/ICDM.2017.145

14. Talagrand, O.: The use of adjoint equations in numerical modelling of the atmospheric circulation. In: Griewank, A., Corliss, G.F. (eds.) Automatic Differentiation of Algorithms: Theory, Implementation, and Application, pp. 169–180. SIAM, Philadelphia (1991)

15. Uhlmann, J.K.: Dynamic map building and localization: New theoretical foundations. Ph.D. thesis, University of Oxford Oxford (1995)

16. Van Der Merwe, R., Wan, E.A.: The square-root unscented Kalman filter for state and parameter-estimation. In: 2001 IEEE International Conference on Acoustics, Speech, and Signal Processing. Proceedings (Cat. No. 01ch37221), vol. 6, pp. 3461–3464. IEEE (2001)

17. Wan, E.A., Van Der Merwe, R.: The unscented Kalman filter for nonlinear estimation. In: Proceedings of the IEEE 2000 Adaptive Systems for Signal Processing, Communications, and Control Symposium (Cat. No. 00EX373), pp. 153–158. IEEE (2000)

18. Wang, M., Hu, X.: Data assimilation in agent based simulation of smart environments using particle filters. Simul. Model. Pract. Theory **56**, 36–54 (2015). https://doi.org/10.1016/j.simpat.2015.05.001

19. Ward, J.A., Evans, A.J., Malleson, N.S.: Dynamic calibration of agent-based models using data assimilation. Royal Soc. Open Sci. **3**(4), 150703 (2016). https://doi.org/10.1098/rsos.150703

20. Zhang, H., Vorobeychik, Y., Letchford, J., Lakkaraju, K.: Data-driven agent-based modeling, with application to rooftop solar adoption. In: Proceedings of the 2015 International Conference on Autonomous Agents and Multiagent Systems. AAMAS 2015, International Foundation for Autonomous Agents and Multiagent Systems, Richland, SC, pp. 513–521 (2015)

The JaCa-Android Framework
for Programming BDI-Based Personal
Agents on Mobile Devices

Angelo Croatti$^{(\boxtimes)}$ and Alessandro Ricci

Computer Science and Engineering Department (DISI), Alma Mater
Studiorum – Università di Bologna, Via dell'Università, 50, Cesena, Italy
{a.croatti,a.ricci}@unibo.it

Abstract. Nowadays, smart mobile applications are a medium allowing
more and more for developing (part of) complex software systems, featuring interactive behaviour and exhibiting different degrees of autonomy and flexibility. In agents and MAS literature, Personal Assistant
Agents represent the area that mostly can benefit from the availability
of frameworks allowing for easily developing native agent-based applications able to exploit features offered by smart mobile and wearable
devices. This paper discusses the JaCa-Android framework, a version of
JaCaMo redesigned to natively run over mobile devices equipped with
Google Android operating system. Exposing native features to observe
and perceive the real-time user context and act accordingly, the framework is oriented in particular to the development of smart mobile apps as
BDI-based personal assistant agents offering a proper layer of abstraction
for this specific purpose.

Keywords: Agents · BDI · JaCaMo · Personal agents · Google
Android

1 Introduction

Personal assistants are a well-known application of software agents [25]. Existing proposals and technologies have been developed for different kinds of purposes and capabilities, from scheduling joint activities [1,23,33], monitoring and
reminding users of key timepoints [10,31], sharing key information, assisting in
negotiation decision support [20]. Generally speaking, with personal assistants
the user is engaged in a cooperative process in which human and computer agents
both initiate communication, monitor events, and perform tasks [21].

Among the others, personal assistants running on *mobile* and *wearable*
devices, possibly interacting with services on the Internet, are the main case
today. This has been made possible thanks to the remarkable development that
these technologies witnessed in the last decade, which lead to the explosion of
the market about mobile software applications or mobile *apps*. We argue that

© Springer Nature Switzerland AG 2020
Y. Demazeau et al. (Eds.): PAAMS 2020, LNAI 12092, pp. 80–92, 2020.
https://doi.org/10.1007/978-3-030-49778-1_7

this greatly enhanced the level of applicability of personal assistants technology, which can be applied to a broader set of application domains, for different kinds of purposes and complexity, depending on the *level of assistance* to be provided.

From a software engineering perspective, this motivates the need and opportunity of introducing platforms that simplify the development and execution of personal assistant agents on mobile and wearable platforms, and more generally, of those mobile apps that can be framed as *agents* by the user, as a digital assistant helping them to do some task. In this *mobile apps as agents* perspective, the term *agent* is used as a coarse-grained concept to refer to personal assistant agents whose "assistance" functionalities can greatly vary—from simple, domain-specific cases to complex, general-purpose ones.

In this paper, we discuss JaCa-Android, a platform for developing and executing mobile apps as agents in the Android environment. The platform is based on JaCaMo [7], a well-known framework for Multi-Agent Programming that combines Jason, for programming autonomous BDI-agents, CArtAgO, for programming environment artifacts, and MOISE for programming multi-agent organizations[1].

The remainder of the paper is organized as follows. In Sect. 2 the background on personal assistant agents designed to be executed on mobile and wearable devices is explored, and a review of related frameworks devoted to bringing agents and MAS on the top of mobile platforms is presented. Then, in Sect. 3 the JaCa-Android framework is described from a software architectural perspective, introducing its main abstractions for developing personal assistant apps. Finally, two different applications domains where the framework has been used to develop software personal assistants are proposed in Sect. 4 to conclude the paper.

2   Background and Related Work

Existing works in the literature about personal assistant agents either focus on cognitive models and architectures or specific applications, i.e. personal assistant agents developed for specific domains (e.g. [16,17,22,24,32]). As far as authors' knowledge, there few works about frameworks for *programming* personal agents on existing mobile/wearable platform technologies. Conversely, there are several works about enabling the development of mobile apps/systems using existing agent programming platform/technology. First examples in agent literature include 3APL-M [19], porting programs written in 3APL [18] on mobile devices based on J2ME environment. An attempt to put together agents and mobile devices was proposed in 2008 with the ANDROMEDA platform [2,3], a framework enabling the development of agents based on the *agent-π* meta-model over Android. In 2011, the vision of MOA (*Micro-agents on Android*) was proposed in [15] as a porting of the lightweight μ^2 framework to the Android platform.

---

[1] Currently in JaCa-Android, the organization dimension – provided in JaCaMo by MOISE – has not been considered yet because at the moment it is not relevant for the *mobile apps as agents* vision. Nonetheless, future improvements will include the full JaCaMo stack.

In this case, agent-based apps can access Android functionalities allowing for the development of mobile applications designed in an agent-oriented manner. Also, [5,34] report another interesting attempt to combine agents and Android proposing a JADE add-on for Android as a platform for porting JADE agents on Android-equipped mobile devices. In particular, this solution result from an evolution of the JADE-LEAP project, a proposal of the early 2000s for running JADE agents on the first Java-enabled phones of the time [6]. Finally, in 2017, a work for porting the ASTRA agent-oriented language on the Android platform for developing context-sensitive mobile application has been proposed in [27].

These works typically do not consider specific issues related to the design and development of personal assistant agents, being more focused on providing an agent-based platform to develop mobile applications. Viceversa, the work on JaCa-Android presented in this paper aims at providing some programming support useful for developing personal agents application, in the *mobile apps as agents* perspective. This is done by introducing a layer of artifacts modelling the *context* of the user, based on information retrieved by sensors and services available on the mobile platform and the cloud. From this point of view, this work is related to the existing literature about context-aware systems [4] with an agent-based approach (e.g. [28]).

3   The JaCa-Android Framework

From a programming point of view, the design and the development of Mobile Apps as agents – in the meaning of the agent-oriented paradigm (AOP) and with particular devotion to those apps acting as a personal assistant agents – needs to be supported by proper frameworks allowing to manipulate first class concepts like agents and able to build systems that can be easily deployed on mobile and wearable devices. Two are the alternatives to build this kind of frameworks: (1) introducing agent model directly into standards mobile applications frameworks,i.e. the Android Framework with the addition of new dedicated first-class abstractions; or (2) allowing to an agent-oriented framework to run on the top of the other mobile application developing frameworks.

In the case of the JaCa-Android framework presented here, we have opted for the second one. Using JaCa-Android it is possible to run agent-based applications and systems on the top of the Android platform proposing a proper level of abstraction to design each application as a MAS using related basic concepts (e.g., agent, artifact, etc.) and avoiding to deal with the Android abstractions (e.g., activity, service, intent).

After its first appearance in literature [29], the JaCa-Android framework has been experimented in different research projects and used to build real-world applications, extended and revised as well. So, in this work we present a completely redesigned architecture for the framework considering our experience in designing and programming mobile apps through the BDI approach. The framework has been deeply re-engineered and adapted both for new needs of the novel smart applications and with a particular interest for designing personal assistant agents rather than having a general-purpose framework. Moreover, respect

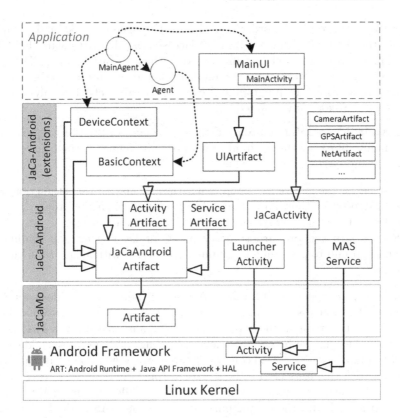

Fig. 1. JaCa-Android Framework coarse-grained architecture and main components.

to the first architecture of JaCa-Android – where a separated middleware was used to keep a shared set of artifacts used by agents of all installed apps to interact with the Android O.S. – the current version of the framework adopts a completely different approach, reducing significantly its complexity and offering a more fluid approach for developing applications.

3.1 Architectural Design

The JaCa-Android framework runs on top of a JaCaMo runtime, extending it with the required abstractions to make possible the design and the execution of MASs over the Android platform. Figure 1 shows an abstract representation of the complete framework, starting from the Android Framework level. As well as JaCaMo, being fully developed in Java, the JaCa-Android runtime runs as a standard Android app and can be deployed in each device with the proper/selected subset of Android O.S. versions.

Generally speaking, the design phase is rooted on the A&A meta-model [26] which allows to conceive an application: (i) choosing the set of agents to include on the base of the application needs and (ii) by properly identifying the set of artifacts to introduce in order to facilitate the agents' works and to interact with the Android Framework and device sensors. In particular, the JaCa-Android programming model is mainly based on the integration of the BDI-based Jason language and interpreter – to implement and execute agents – and the CArtAgO framework – to program and execute the artifact-based environment where agents are logically situated.

From Android to JaCa-Android. Two of the main abstractions representing main building-blocks of the Android Framework are defined within the concepts of *Activity* and *Service*. In particular:

– an *Activity* is the main entry point of an Android app for the interaction with the user, proposing an ad-hoc user interface and having a proper lifecycle presenting the execution states between which it can transit;
– a *Service* is a general-purpose entry point for keeping an app running in the background to perform long-running operations without providing a user interface.

Because one of the goals of the JaCa-Android framework is to hide as much as possible all Android abstraction, its general-purpose layer is in charge of offering proper abstraction to allow the developer to design a mobile app as a MAS. As in JaCaMo, the system can be designed defining the agent's behaviours and coding artifacts. Following the Android constraint according to which an app that wants to interact with the users need to be started through an activity, to execute the MAS in JaCa-Android a proper built-in activity – called `LauncherActivity` – has been designed with the unique purpose to run the MAS in the background, encapsulated in a dedicated built-in service (the `MasService`). So, from the programmer perspective, the app's application logic starts after the execution of the MAS and related agents.

After the starting phase, each agent can use proper artifacts – e.g. an instance or an extension of the `ActivityArtifact` – to create, focus and manage android activities properly encapsulated in CArtAgO artifacts exposing ad-hoc observable properties and operations. In other words, main android abstractions are encapsulated within proper artifacts that can be exploited by agents to build and control the mobile app. The implementation of these artifacts is responsible for managing the android app lifecycle, demanding to proper thread operations and functions call according to their nature, as required by the Android Framework. Other custom artifacts can be used as usual in a JaCaMo application.

JaCa-Android First Example. As a basic example to give a taste of the usage of the JaCa-Android framework, here we present a simple *hello world* application, where a simple personal agent observes the user's GPS position – obtained by the mobile device related sensor – and detects when the user reaches its home. Apart from few details (mainly, the configuration file defining the MAS structure and the user interface layout), the code reported in the figure is the only code to be written by a developer and, trough the support of the JaCa-Android framework, it can be compiled in an APK[2] file to be deployed on an Android device. Entering into details, in Fig. 2 is reported a portion of the code of the agent responsible for creating the user interface (UI) and for detecting when the user is nearby its home—the agent has the belief about where the user's home is in terms of GPS location. The definition of the UI is demanded to the MainUI artifact reported in Fig. 3, encapsulating a request to the Android Framework to build a dedicated activity with a particular layout—to this purpose see the init() function of the artifact that simply require the initialization of the activity given a layout defined in the activity_mainui.xml resource file. When the UI is ready to be used – in the android terminology, when it has been created and brought to the foreground also enabling the user's interaction – the artifact notifies agents with a dedicated observable property named ui_ready. In fact, each artifact extending the ActivityArtifact template, makes observable for agents all events related to the managed activity and its related UI. It's worth clarifying the need to introduce the setup() internal operation for each artifact built extending the ActivityArtifact one. In the Android framework, when a new activity is created, many actions (e.g., attaching a UI layout) must be done before the activity was instantiated. Despite this, the initialization of its UI's components and many other actions must be done after its creation. With this in mind, each ActivityArtifact can be designed assuming that the JaCa-Android framework executes its init() function before the creation of the related activity, that is followed by the execution of the setup() one—that can be used, e.g., to initialize UI elements. Finally, because Android requires that each update to the UI must be done by the Main Thread (aka the *UI Thread* of each activity), the JaCa-Android offers several functions to be used to bypass this constraint (see, e.g., the showMessage() operation in Fig. 3 that calls the setLabelText() function to update a property of an UI element).

3.2   Extensions for Designing Personal Assistant Agents

The JaCa-Android framework architecture described so far qualifies it as a general-purpose framework to design and develop a mobile android app as multi-agents systems. Nevertheless, this framework has been designed with the main goal to facilitate the development of personal assistant agents. So, a particular devotion has been reserved in the analysis and the design of a layer of dedicated first class abstractions to ensure to agents the ability to observe the user context and acting accordingly to it. In fact, to design a personal assistant, the first exigence is about exposing to it all information and belief about the *user context* letting the agent reason and plan considering those informations. A personal assistant agent is a context-aware system. Referring to personal assistants in execution over mobile and wearable devices, the plenty of sensors offered by these devices, their multiple ways to communicate over several different networks and to connect to many other devices, and finally specific computational capabilities

---

[2] An Android Package (APK) is an archive containing all resources and libraries of an Android app along with its binary code.

```
homeLocation(44.147470, 12.235730).

nearbyHome(Lat,Lon,Res) :- ...

!init.

+!init
  <- makeArtifact("mainUI","app.MainUI",[],MainUI);
     focus(MainUI);
     println("MainUI artifact created & focused.").

+ui_ready [artifact_name(Id,MainUI)]
  <- println("MainUI ready.");
     focusBasicContex("GpsLocation", 1.5).

+gpsPostionUpdate(Lat,Lon)
  : nearbyHome(Lat,Lon,Res) & Res == True
  <- !sayWelcomeHome.

+!sayWelcomeHome
  <- showMessage("You are nearby your home!").
```

Fig. 2. A portion of the MainAgent source code in Jason.

```
public class MainUI extends ActivityArtifact {

  public static class MainUIActivity extends JaCaActivity { }

  public void init() {
    super.init(MainUIActivity.class, R.layout.activity_mainui);
  }

  @INTERNAL_OPERATION
  protected void setup() { //Init here your UI! }

  @OPERATION
  public void showMessage(final String text) {
    setLabelText(R.id.messageLabel, text);
  }
}
```

Fig. 3. A snippet of the MainUI artifact.

embedded in mobile devices enable the possibility to incredibly enrich the user context even considering only the single device. In other words, a mobile device held by a user can be considered an efficacious source of information for learning and reason about the user context.

Technically speaking, the JaCa-Android Framework offers a set of CArtAgO artifacts developed with the goal to make agents aware of the user context that can be understood through the mobile/wearable device where the app is in execution. Among others, two of these artifacts are the BasicContext and the DeviceContext ones. In particular, the first one is dedicated to offer to agents the possibility to observe, e.g., the real-time location of the user obtained by the GPS, informations from the device camera to reason on what the user is currently looking to, informations about nearby devices (and possibly other users) considering nearby detected Bluetooth devices, and so on. Conversely, the second one is dedicated to letting agents observe changes in device sensors' values, e.g., changes in the orientation of the accelerometer or the gyroscope, changes related to the light sensor and so on.

These artifacts are available to agents as a singleton as it happens for the basic artifact of a CArtAgO workspace. Each agent can autonomously decide if and when focus a particular context information receiving observable properties updates, exploiting proper operations offered by the artifacts. Nevertheless, we haven't excluded the possibility for a programmer to extend the behaviour of those context artifacts to adapt them to application logic exigences introduced by specific functionalities of the target wearable/mobile devices of the developed app.

3.3   A Development Supporting Tool

To date, the reference IDE for developing Android application is *Android Studio*[3], an open-source IDE based on IntelliJ IDEA developed by Google. To facilitate the usage of the JaCa-Android framework, a plug-in for Android Studio has been developed with the aim to enable the design of each mobile app as a multi-agent system hiding as much as possible the android layer and related abstractions. Practically, this tool allows for:

- adding the JaCa-Android nature to a generic android project, *reconfiguring* it to a JaCaMo-like project, introducing few commands to generate agents and artifacts source code templates;
- supporting the syntax highlighting for the Jason code natively;
- using an ad-hoc view for managing android permissions and other features related to the app avoiding to deal with the manifest of the app.

Currently, the Android Studio plug-in is in an early stage of development, but we have planned to improve it soon to make the design of mobile apps as agents effective and simple as much as possible. In particular, several tools will be developed to make effective the debugging of agents and mas over mobile and wearable devices. Moreover, specific artifacts for building and run dedicated mobile user interfaces to be used to inspect the real-time state of the agent's belief bases will be taken into account for both debugging and testing purposes.

---

[3] https://developer.android.com/studio/.

4   Applications and Case Studies

Apart from several basic examples, the JaCa-Android framework currently has been used to develop some case studies within different heterogeneous application domains where the introduction of personal assistant agents can bring a relevant improvement of the humans' work. In particular, a first case study is related to the healthcare area where a personal medical assistant has been developed for supporting medics in tracking activities performed during emergency management and for alerting them considering the patient real-time status and context. Secondly, another relevant application where the framework has been used is about the design of personal assistant agents able to assist and guide a user within smart mixed reality environments, e.g. like the new concepts of industries and companies as envisioned by the fourth industrial revolution (aka Industry 4.0).

With these case studies, we want to propose and describe two relevant scenarios where the introduction of personal agents could become even more relevant if we consider all benefits obtained in terms of context perception/observation through mobile and wearable technologies. Whit this in mind, we aim to underline how much, nowadays, the availability of agent-based frameworks devoted to the development of personal agents on the top of mobile platforms – like JaCa-Android – become very important to respond to exigencies and requests of the next future smart environments. Following paragraphs will briefly describe such two case studies, focusing on the offered perspective in terms of the application of these kinds of frameworks and avoiding to entering in design and implementation details. Despite this, some basic prototypes in those directions have been already developed and tested.

4.1   A Personal Medical Assistant for Tracking Activities and Alerting

In this case study [11,12] we are interested in exploring the design and development of Personal Assistant Agents that assists healthcare professionals in their individual and cooperative work inside a hospital. In this case, we refer to such personal agents as Intelligent Personal Medical Digital Assistant (PMDA).

The design of a PMDA depends on the specific role of the assisted professional – nurses, doctors, rescuers, etc. – each one providing specific requirements and challenges. In spite of this, it is possible to devise some basic functionalities and capabilities that are useful in general for PMDAs. In particular:

- identification of the context where the user is acting and of the elements that can be relevant for the user's activity. Examples: identifying the room where the user currently is, the patient who is currently the target of the activities, etc.;
- the (anytime/anywhere) capability of retrieving and presenting relevant data for the user's activity, by interacting with the hospital information system (HIS) and devices;

- notification of messages to the user (examples include, e.g., messages sent by other colleagues, warning generated automatically by the system about some situation);
- support for setting up remote audio-video communication.

In the context offered by this case study, the JaCa-Android framework has been used for the design and the development of a PMDA to assist the Trauma Leader – a physician responsible for performing a trauma resuscitation in the hospital emergency department. In particular, the PMDA is responsible for taking notes (tracking) of each action performed by the trauma leader and alerting him/her considering context and patient's vital signs evolution over time. This goes towards the idea of physicians assisted by personal agents working in smart hospitals, in which software personal agents are exploited along with enabling technologies (wearable and pervasive computing, augmented reality, etc.) to create novel smart environments to support individual and cooperative work of healthcare professionals.

4.2   A Smart Guide for Mixed Reality Environments

This case study [13,14] is devoted to exploring the applicability of personal assistant agents to the context of Mixed Reality (MR). In an MR-based environment a user is immersed in a reality where digital things and physical ones are blended in a hybrid multi-user shared space. A main interesting feature of a personal agent is the capability to consider part of its context and belief *what the user sees* in real-time. That is, an agent is capable of observing and initiating user interaction with the environment (which is meant here to include also perceptions). This allows framing new kind of pro-active assistance in which personal assistants reason not only about the context of the user, but about what the user is perceiving – and not perceiving – from that context, what he/she is looking at, etc. Considering also the augmented reality level shaping the mixed reality where users and personal agents are immersed in, the kind of assistance of personal assistant agents can also include the possibility to interact with/-manipulate the augmented entities enriching the physical space, possibly shared with other users (and personal agents) situated in the same space. For instance, a personal assistant agent could automatically annotate them with virtual notes on the physical environment where its user is working – e.g., on physical objects used by the users – as a memo for the user himself or useful for implicitly coordinating with other users, perceiving those virtual signs. Differently from a generic mobile augmented reality (MAR) browser, a personal assistant agent could show only those augmented elements that the agent knows to be relevant according to users' goals and needs for current activity, so functioning a smart guide when moving in complex smart environments.

5   Conclusions

The design and development of personal assistant agent exploiting mobile/wearable devices and platforms as their execution environment call for proper abstraction layers that allow governing related programming complexities. Accordingly, in this paper, we described the JaCa-Android agent-based platform, which enables the design of mobile android apps as agents. Although JaCa-Android is a general-purpose platform, its architecture contemplates specific abstractions to be used to develop personal assistant agents involved within the user real-time context observation. Personal assistant agents will be a main ingredient of the next-future smart environments and, for this reason, its is important to develop novel technologies and to improve existing ones to make their development easier and effective, especially in the AOP perspective. Moreover, in such future smart environments, the introduction of personal assistants offers interesting new research challenges also for the entire agent community, partially tackled in related research contexts about eyewear computing [9], cognition-aware computing [8], activity-based computing [30], and many others. These agents are meant to build dynamically a model about what the user is perceiving, and use this knowledge along with the information about user's goals, the state of ongoing activity, the actual state of the physical environment, to provide a proactive and smart assistance, possibly anticipating and notifying problems and suggesting actions to do.

References

1. Shintani, T., Ito, T., Sycara, K.: Multiple negotiations among agents for a distributed meeting scheduler. In: Proceedings of the Fourth International Conference on MultiAgent Systems (ICMAS-2000), ICMAS 2000, pp. 435-436. IEEE Computer Society, Washington, DC (2000)
2. Agüero, J., Rebollo, M., Carrascosa, C., Julián, V.: Developing intelligent agents on the android platform. In: Sixth European Workshop on Multi-Agent Systems (EUMAS 2008), pp. 1–14 (2008)
3. Agüero, J., Rebollo, M., Carrascosa, C., Julián, V.: Does android dream with intelligent agents? In: Corchado, J.M., Rodríguez, S., Llinas, J., Molina, J.M. (eds.) International Symposium on Distributed Computing and Artificial Intelligence 2008 (DCAI 2008), pp. 194–204. Springer, Heidelberg (2009). https://doi.org/10.1007/978-3-540-85863-8_24
4. Baldauf, M., Dustdar, S., Rosenberg, F.: A survey on context-aware systems. Int. J. Ad Hoc Ubiquit. Comput. 2(4), 263–277 (2007)
5. Bergenti, F., Caire, G., Gotta, D.: Agents on the move: jade for android devices. In: Santoro, C., Bergenti, F. (eds.) WOA. CEUR Workshop Proceedings, vol. 1260. CEUR-WS.org (2014)
6. Bergenti, F., Poggi, A., Burg, B., Caire, G.: Deploying FIPA-compliant systems on handheld devices. IEEE Internet Comput. 5(4), 20–25 (2001)
7. Boissier, O., Bordini, R.H., Hübner, J.F., Ricci, A., Santi, A.: Multi-agent oriented programming with JaCaMo. Sci. Comput.Program. 78(6), 747–761 (2013)
8. Bulling, A., Zander, T.O.: Cognition-aware computing. IEEE Pervasive Comput. 13(3), 80–83 (2014)
9. Bulling, A., Cakmakci, O., Kunze, K., Rehg, J.M.: Eyewear computing – augmenting the human with head-mounted wearable assistants (Dagstuhl Seminar 16042). Dagstuhl Rep. 6(1), 160–206 (2016)

10. Chalupsky, H., et al.: Electric elves: applying agent technology to support human organizations. In: Proceedings of the Thirteenth Conference on Innovative Applications of Artificial Intelligence Conference, pp. 51–58. AAAI Press (2001)

11. Croatti, A., Montagna, S., Ricci, A.: A personal medical digital assistant agent for supporting human operators in emergency scenarios. In: Montagna, S., Abreu, P.H., Giroux, S., Schumacher, M.I. (eds.) A2HC/AHEALTH -2017. LNCS (LNAI), vol. 10685, pp. 59–75. Springer, Cham (2017). https://doi.org/10.1007/978-3-319-70887-4_4

12. Croatti, A., Montagna, S., Ricci, A., Gamberini, E., Albarello, V., Agnoletti, V.: BDI personal medical assistant agents: the case of trauma tracking and alerting. Artif. Intell. Med. **96**, 187–197 (2019)

13. Croatti, A., Ricci, A.: Developing agent-based pervasive mixed reality systems: the mirage framework. In: Demazeau, Y., An, B., Bajo, J., Fernández-Caballero, A. (eds.) Advances in Practical Applications of Agents, Multi-Agent Systems, and Complexity: The PAAMS Collection, pp. 301–304. Springer International Publishing, Cham (2018)

14. Croatti, A., Ricci, A.: A model and platform for building agent-based pervasive mixed reality systems. In: Demazeau, Y., An, B., Bajo, J., Fernández-Caballero, A. (eds.) PAAMS 2018. LNCS (LNAI), vol. 10978, pp. 127–139. Springer, Cham (2018). https://doi.org/10.1007/978-3-319-94580-4_10

15. Frantz, C., Nowostawski, M., Purvis, M.K.: Micro-agents on android: interfacing agents with mobile applications. In: Dechesne, F., Hattori, H., ter Mors, A., Such, J.M., Weyns, D., Dignum, F. (eds.) AAMAS 2011. LNCS (LNAI), vol. 7068, pp. 488–502. Springer, Heidelberg (2012). https://doi.org/10.1007/978-3-642-27216-5_37

16. Freed, M., et al.: RADAR: a personal assistant that learns to reduce email overload. In: Proceedings of the 23rd National Conference on Artificial Intelligence, AAAI 2008, vol. 3, pp. 1287–1293. AAAI Press (2008)

17. Garlan, D., Schmerl, B.: The RADAR architecture for personal cognitive assistance. Int. J. Softw. Eng. Knowl. Eng. **17**(02), 171–190 (2007)

18. Hindriks, K.V., De Boer, F.S., Van der Hoek, W., Meyer, J.J.C.: Agent programming in 3APL. Auton. Agents Multi-Agent Syst. **2**(4), 357–401 (1999)

19. Koch, F.: 3APL-M platform for deliberative agents in mobile devices. In: Proceedings of the Fourth International Joint Conference on Autonomous Agents and Multiagent Systems, AAMAS 2005, pp. 153–154 (2005)

20. Li, C., Giampapa, J.A., Sycara, K.P.: Bilateral negotiation decisions with uncertain dynamic outside options. IEEE Trans. Syst. Man Cybern. Part C **36**(1), 31–44 (2006)

21. Maes, P.: Agents that reduce work and information overload. Commun. ACM **37**(7), 30–40 (1994)

22. Mark, B., Perrault, R.: CALO: Cognitive assistant that learns and organizes (2005)

23. Modi, P.J., Veloso, M., Smith, S.F., Oh, J.: CMRadar: a personal assistant agent for calendar management. In: Bresciani, P., Giorgini, P., Henderson-Sellers, B., Low, G., Winikoff, M. (eds.) AOIS -2004. LNCS (LNAI), vol. 3508, pp. 169–181. Springer, Heidelberg (2005). https://doi.org/10.1007/11426714_12

24. Oh, J., Meneguzzi, F., Sycara, K.: ANTIPA: an agent architecture for intelligent information assistance. In: Proceedings of the 2010 Conference on ECAI 2010: 19th European Conference on Artificial Intelligence, pp. 1055–1056. IOS Press, Amsterdam (2010)

25. Okamoto, S., Scerri, P., Sycara, K.: Toward an understanding of the impact of software personal assistants on human organizations. In: Proceedings of the Fifth International Joint Conference on Autonomous Agents and Multiagent Systems, AAMAS 2006, pp. 630–637. ACM, New York (2006)

26. Omicini, A., Ricci, A., Viroli, M.: Artifacts in the A & A meta-model for multi-agent systems. Auton. Agents Multi-Agent Syst. **17**(3), 432–456 (2008). https://doi.org/10.1007/s10458-008-9053-x

27. Russell, S., Doyle, O., Collier, R.W.: Developing android applications using agent-oriented programming. In: 2017 12th International Conference on Intelligent Systems and Knowledge Engineering (ISKE), pp. 1–7, November 2017

28. Sadeh, N.M.: MyCampus: an agent-based environment for context-aware mobile services. In: AAMAS - First International Joint Conference on Autonomous Agents and Multi-Agent Systems. Press (2002)

29. Santi, A., Guidi, M., Ricci, A.: JaCa-android: an agent-based platform for building smart mobile applications. In: Dastani, M., El Fallah Seghrouchni, A., Hübner, J., Leite, J. (eds.) LADS 2010. LNCS (LNAI), vol. 6822, pp. 95–114. Springer, Heidelberg (2011). https://doi.org/10.1007/978-3-642-22723-3_6

30. Sukthankar, R., Davies, N., Siewiorek, D.P.: Activity-based computing. IEEE Pervasive Comput. **7**(undefined), 20–21 (2008)

31. Tambe, M.: Electric elves: what went wrong and why. AI Mag. **29**(2), 23–27 (2008)

32. Tur, G., et al.: The CALO meeting assistant system. IEEE Trans. Audio Speech Lang. Process. **18**(6), 1601–1611 (2010)

33. Wagner, T., Phelps, J., Guralnik, V., VanRiper, R.: Coordinators: coordination managers for first responders. In: Proceedings of the Third International Joint Conference on Autonomous Agents and Multiagent Systems, AAMAS 2004, vol. 3, pp. 1140–1147. IEEE Computer Society, Washington, DC (2004)

34. Weihong, Y., Chen, Y.: The development of jade agent for android mobile phones. In: Lu, W., Cai, G., Liu, W., Xing, W. (eds.) Proceedings of the 2012 International Conference on Information Technology and Software Engineering, pp. 215–222. Springer, Heidelberg (2013). https://doi.org/10.1007/978-3-642-34531-9_23

Assisted Parameter and Behavior Calibration in Agent-Based Models with Distributed Optimization

Matteo D'Auria[1]([⊠]), Eric O. Scott[2], Rajdeep Singh Lather[2], Javier Hilty[2], and Sean Luke[2]

[1] Università degli Studi di Salerno, Salerno, Italy
matdauria@unisa.it
[2] George Mason University, Washington D.C., USA
{escott8,rlather,jhilty2}@gmu.edu, sean@cs.gmu.edu

Abstract. Agent-based modeling (ABM) has many applications in the social sciences, biology, computer science, and robotics. One of the most important and challenging phases in agent-based model development is the calibration of model parameters and agent behaviors. Unfortunately, for many models this step is done by hand in an ad-hoc manner or is ignored entirely, due to the complexity inherent in ABM dynamics. In this paper we present a general-purpose, automated optimization system to assist the model developer in the calibration of ABM parameters and agent behaviors. This system combines two popular tools: the MASON agent-based modeling toolkit and the ECJ evolutionary optimization library. Our system distributes the model calibration task over very many processors and provides a wide range of stochastic optimization algorithms well suited to the calibration needs of agent-based models.

Keywords: Agent-based models · Model calibration · Evolutionary computation

1 Introduction

In an agent-based model, many *agents* (computational entities) interact to give rise to emergent macrophenomena. Agent-based models (ABMs) are widely used in computational biology, social sciences, and multiagent systems. An important step in developing an agent-based model is *calibration*, whereby the model's parameters are tuned to produce expected results. Agent-based models can be challenging to calibrate for several reasons. First, agents often have numerous and intricate interactions, producing complex and difficult to predict dynamics. Second, the agents themselves may be imbued with *behaviors* that need to be tuned: and thus the parameters in ABMs may not just be simple numbers but computational structures. Finally, ABMs are often large and slow, which reduces the number of trials one can perform in a given amount of time.

© Springer Nature Switzerland AG 2020
Y. Demazeau et al. (Eds.): PAAMS 2020, LNAI 12092, pp. 93–105, 2020.
https://doi.org/10.1007/978-3-030-49778-1_8

Despite its importance, ABM calibration is often done by hand using guess-work and manual tweaking, or the model is left uncalibrated because the model's complexity makes it too difficult for the modeler to perform the calibration! For example, in [6] approximately half of the surveyed models performed no calibration at all.

In this paper we consider the task of *automated agent-based model calibration*. We marry two tools popular in their respective fields: the MASON agent-based simulation toolkit [10], and the ECJ evolutionary optimization library [20]. MASON is an efficient ABM simulation tool which can be serialized and encapsulated in a single thread, making it a good choice for massively distributed model optimization, and ECJ has facilities critical to ABM optimization: it can perform distributed evaluation on potentially millions of machines, and it has a wide range of stochastic optimization facilities useful for agent-based modeling.

We will begin with an introduction to the ABM model calibration problem and discuss previous work in model calibration and optimization. We will next provide some background on ECJ and MASON, then present our approach to massively distributed ABM calibration, including examples that provide insight into the breadth of the approach.

2   Agent-Based Modeling and MASON

Agent-based models are often used to simulate large groups of interacting entities, such as flocks of birds, swarms of robots, warring nations, people flowing through airport checkpoints, and so on. In particular, an ABM describes the *interactions* among the agents, and the complex macrophenomena that arise as a result.

MASON and GeoMASON. MASON is a popular, high-performance, open-source ABM library. MASON maintains a real-valued discrete event schedule that stores agents waiting to respond to time-based events, and one or more *fields*, that is, representations of spatial relationships between arbitrary objects (possibly including agents themselves). Basic provided fields include continuous spaces, various kinds of grids, and networks. MASON comes with extensive optional GUI visualization facilities for agents, objects, and fields in 2D and 3D.

GeoMASON augments MASON with Geospatial Information Systems (GIS) facilities in the form of vector and raster geospatial data, including spatially organized fields, visualization, and data manipulation utilities. GeoMASON can model agents that use earthbound objects and features such as networks of roads or rivers, vegetation, and topology, and is often used to study both social behavior and its response to natural processes such as rainfall and erosion.

3   Model Calibration and Evolutionary Optimization

Testing a model for correctness involves several steps. First, the model is *verified*, that is, it is debugged. Second, the model is *calibrated*, where its parameters are iteratively adjusted to minimize error between its output and some standard provided by the modeler. This standard can be many things, such as: the opinions of a domain expert observing the model, published benchmark values, or a sample of real-world data. Finally, the model is *validated* by comparing its results to a much more significant body of real-world data.

We focus here on model calibration. This is essentially an optimization task: the modeler repeatedly tries new settings of parameters until he finds ones that minimize error. Model parameters are of several kinds, only some of which are used in the calibration process. Consider the following four parameter types:

1. Parameters fixed to constants because their values are known beforehand.
2. Parameters fixed to constants because they are part of the canonical theory that the model developer is trying to demonstrate.
3. Parameters whose values are unknown, or can only be guessed at.
4. Parameters for which we wish the model to be *insensitive*. These are important but less common.

The calibration task is largely concerned with the third and fourth kinds, and particularly the third one: tuning parameters with unknown or unknowable values. Unfortunately, these parameters may exhibit significant nonlinearity, complex linkage with other parameters, and stochasticity. All this may demand many repeated tests of the model, but ABM models can take a long time to run. For this reason, automated calibration of agent-based models is desirable.

Historically model developers have resorted to linear and nonlinear gradient-based optimization approaches, even as simple as gradient descent. These techniques can fail with agent-based models for two reasons. First, such models may have large numbers of local optima. Second, these models may not yield a gradient, either because it is unknown or because the space is not metric: for example, a parameter might be a tree or an edge in a graph. Nominal categorical values (such as race or religion) may cause related problems.

The classical approach to optimization of data of this kind is to use a *stochastic* optimization procedure such as hill-climbing, simulated annealing, or an evolutionary computation method such as a genetic algorithm. The evolutionary computation family is particularly attractive because it is efficiently and massively distributed. This allows us to optimize a model by running many trials in parallel.

ECJ. ECJ is an open-source stochastic optimization toolkit which emphasizes evolutionary computation techniques [20] and is one of the most popular tools in the evolutionary computation community. ECJ can run in a single process and can be distributed across a very large number of machines. ECJ has a many optimization features, such as customizable representations of candidate solutions (*individuals*), facilities for massively distributed model evaluation, and a wide range of optimization algorithms, some of which we will highlight later.

4   Related Work

Because of their complexity, many ABMs are calibrated by simply fixing the parameters in advance using known real-world parameters. But whenever the quality of a model's overall behavior can be assessed, such as using the opinion of a domain expert (as in [7]), or via comparison to real-world output, we might instead optimize one or more model parameters to fit it. When a model has (≤ 3) free parameters, researchers often optimize them with ad-hoc manual tuning, or by reviewing the outcome of an exhaustive parameter sweep (grid search) [1].

Automated model calibration will require an optimization algorithm. Evolutionary algorithms and related stochastic optimization algorithms are well-established approaches to calibrating free parameters for many kinds of models, and have been used to tune models of neuron behavior [19,23], agriculture [12], and textile folding [13], among many others. In the ABM community evolutionary algorithms have been used to calibrate a number of models [4, ch. 10]. Many are based on an ad-hoc variation of the genetic algorithm [2,15,16]. ABMs often also have multiple conflicting objectives that need to be optimized simultaneously. Some authors have applied multi-objective evolutionary algorithms [14,18], but have rarely used state-of-the-art methods (such as NSGA-III or MOEA/D). These techniques make it increasingly possible to tackle complex and high-dimensional problems, but take effort to implement properly.

Only a handful of software tools are available that allow researchers to apply optimization techniques to ABMs without needing to implement their own calibration framework from scratch. The *BehaviorSearch* module in NetLogo supports simple multithreaded optimization of model parameters via a few classic metaheuristics—hill climbing, simulated annealing, and a genetic algorithm [22], and a few basic solution representations. This tool can only be applied to the small, computationally inexpensive models typical of NetLogo, and cannot be distributed across machines, nor applied to noisy objective functions. The Open-MOLE framework (https://openmole.org) can distribute parallel simulations of a model across several kinds of clusters, either following a master-worker parallelization model or with island models. OpenMOLE supports models implemented in arbitrary languages and offers a Scala-based scripting language so that the calibration can be controlled from within a unified GUI. Its optimization algorithms are limited to classic GAs and NSGA-II, but it offers a few advanced features, such as a strategy for handling noise in the objective function.

The field of evolutionary computation has grown to encompass many techniques that perform considerably better than traditional GA-style algorithms or are applicable to a wider variety of tasks. A notable example is CMA-ES, which performs efficient vector-space optimization [5]. The wider EA family also includes many techniques for evolving complex computational structures, such as programs and neural networks [9,21].

Some general-purpose evolutionary algorithm frameworks exist that offer massively distributed algorithms and configuration options useful for optimizing computationally expensive ABMs. The Evolving Objects (or EO) framework has long filled this role for C++ programmers [8]. The ECJ framework we use here has traditionally filled a similar role for Java programmers.

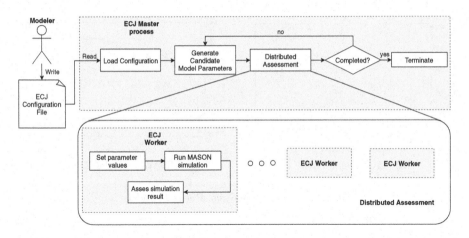

Fig. 1. Automated model calibration workflow using distributed ECJ and MASON.

5 Approach

As agent-based models become more common and more detailed, an automated approach to calibration will be increasingly needed. We envision the automation process to work as follows. The modeler first builds the simulation, then assigns values to those parameters he knows or wishes to be fixed. A distributed system then optimizes the remaining parameters as best it can against criteria specified by the modeler. The modeler then examines the results: if they are poor, this could be due to bugs in the model, or insufficient model complexity to demonstrate the modeler's hypothesis, or a hypothesis that is wrong. Accordingly, the modeler revises the simulation and resubmits it to the system to be recalibrated.

To do this procedure, we merged ECJ and MASON to take full advantage of their technical characteristics. To merge them, it was necessary to make changes to both. Without going into implementation details: first, ECJ was modified so that MASON simulations could be used in the evaluation procedure of a candidate solution. Second, MASON was modified to be able to receive the values of model parameters from outside (that is, from an ECJ process) and to provide the modeler with a way to develop a score function for the simulation (which would then be used by the optimization algorithm).

Figure 1 shows the general workflow of the system. We first define one ECJ process to be the *master*. This process performs the top-level optimization algorithm. When this process has one or more candidate solutions (individuals) ready to be assessed, they are handed to a remote *worker* process. Each candidate solution is simply a set of those agent parameters and behaviors that we wish to test: the worker does this by creating a MASON simulation using those parameters and behaviors, running it some number of times, and assessing its performance. The worker then returns the assessments as the *fitness* (quality) of its tested solutions, and the master uses these results in its optimization procedure.

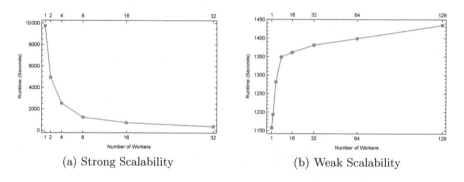

(a) Strong Scalability

(b) Weak Scalability

Fig. 2. Scalability Analysis, Refugee model

The modeler can completely customize this procedure if need be, and we demonstrate one such scenario in Sect. 6.3. But if the modeler's optimization needs only involve global model parameters—as is typical for many ABM calibration scenarios—then we provide a simple alternative. The modeler specifies which parameters of interest to optimize, then selects from a few optimization options, and MASON does the rest: it defines the candidate solution representation as a fixed-length list of the parameters in question, builds the fitness mechanism, creates the evolutionary process, prepares the workers to run the proper simulation and default settings, then sends the candidates to remote workers.

6   Experiments

We begin with a large and nontrivial model drawn from GeoMASON's contributed model library, which we use to demonstrate speedup results for two different approaches to distribution. Then we highlight different capabilities of evolutionary optimization applied to model calibration using proofs of concept with a much simpler (and faster!) model drawn from MASON's demo suite. Finally, we demonstrate the distributed optimization of agent behaviors using genetic programming style parse trees.

6.1   Speedup Demonstration

We first show the efficiency of our distributed model calibration facility on a nontrivial ABM scaled horizontally across a cluster of machines. For this demonstration, we use the *Refugee* model drawn from the contributed models in the GeoMASON distribution. This model can take several minutes to run. *Refugee* explores the pattern of migration of refugees in the Syrian refugee crisis. The model demonstrates how population behavior emerges as the result of individual refugee decisions. The agents (the refugees) select goal destinations in accordance with the Law of Intervening Opportunities and these goals are prone to change with fluctuating personal needs.

We calibrated the model using a simple genetic algorithm from ECJ and assessed candidate solutions by comparing the number of arrivals in each city against real-world data gathered from UNHCR and EU agency databases.

Setup. We calibrated over four real-valued parameters in the model. The model ran for 10,000 steps. We used a genetic algorithm with a tournament selection of size 2, one-point crossover, and Gaussian mutation with 100% probability and a standard deviation of 0.01. We ran the models on a cluster of 24 machines, each with Dual Intel Xeon E5-2670@2.60GHz, 24 GB, Intel 82575EB Gigabit Ethernet, Red Hat Enterprise Linux Server 7.7 (Maipo), OpenJDK 1.8.0. Running on these machines were some $N \leq 276$ MASON worker processes.

Results. We performed *strong* and *weak scalability* analysis. Strong scalability asks how much time is needed for a *fixed size* problem given a *variable number of workers*. Weak scalability asks if an *increasingly difficult problem* can be handled in the same amount of time with a corresponding *increasing number of workers*. All the scalability results are statistically significantly different from one another ($p < 0.01$) as verified by a one-way ANOVA with a Bonferroni post-hoc test.

To do strong scalability analysis we fixed the problem to ten generations, each with 32 individuals, for a total of 320 evaluations. The number of workers was varied from 1 to 32. For 1 to 8 workers we gathered the mean result of ten experiments; for 16 and 32 workers (which ran faster), we gathered the mean result of 20 experiments. Figure 2a displays the speedup results. The *strong scalability efficiency* (as a percentage of the optimum) came to 71.88% using 32 workers to solve the problem.

To do weak scalability analysis, we varied the problem difficulty by adjusting the population size such that, regardless of the number of workers, each worker was responsible for four individuals (and thus four simulation runs) per generation. In all cases, the results reflect a mean of ten experiments. For each optimization process the number of generations was fixed to 10 and the population size varied in $\{4, 8, 16, 32, 64, 128, 256, 512\}$, and thus the number of workers varied as $p \in \{1, 2, 4, 8, 16, 32, 64, 128\}$. Figure 2a shows the weak scalability results. The *weak scalability efficiency* (as a percentage of the optimum) was 83.18.

The previous experiment involved a *generational* evolutionary optimization algorithm: the entire population of individuals had to be evaluated on the remote workers before the next generation of individuals was constructed. We next considered an *asynchronous* evolutionary algorithm to improve efficiency when the model runtime varied greatly. An asynchronous evolutionary algorithm only updates the population a little bit at a time, rather than wholesale, and doesn't need to wait for slowly-running models.

The approach works as follows: there are some N workers and a master with a population of size P. The master first creates random individuals, then assigns each to an available worker. When a worker has completed its assessment, the individual is returned and added to the population, and the worker becomes available for another task. When the population has been fully populated, the master switches to a *steady-state* mode: when a worker is available, the master

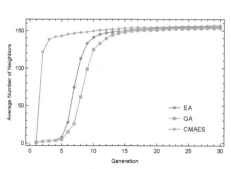
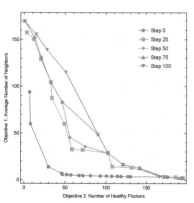

(a) Mean best-so-far performance of a Genetic Algorithm, Evolution Strategy, and CMA-ES on the Flockers domain, averaged over 30 runs.

(b) Pareto Nondominated Fronts (higher values preferred) for a typical run of the two-objective Flockers domain at generations 0, 25, 50, 75, and 100.

Fig. 3. Evolutionary optimization examples

applies the evolutionary algorithm to produce an individual which is then given to the worker to asses. When an individual is returned by a worker, the master selects an existing individual in the population to be replaced by the new individual.

Setup. We compared the generational genetic algorithm from Sect. 6.1 against an asynchronous evolutionary algorithm using a steady-state genetic algorithm. When replacing an individual in the population, the steady-state algorithm selected the least fit individual. In our experiment, there were 128 workers, and the population size was 128: the generational approach was again run for ten generations, while the asynchronous approach was run until it had evaluated 1280 individuals. We performed twenty experiments per treatment. To simulate varying runtimes in the Refugee model, when a model was to be tested we changed the number of simulation steps at random. 1/4 of the time we halved them, 1/4 of the time we left them as normal, and 1/2 of the time we doubled them.

Results. Asynchronous Evolution had a mean runtime of 293.77 seconds; while Generational Evolution had a mean runtime of 437.77 seconds. These results were statistically significantly different ($p < 0.01$) as verified by a one-way ANOVA with a Bonferroni post-hoc test.

6.2 Evolutionary Optimization Examples

So far we have shown speedup results to demonstrate performance: next, we turn to simple examples of some of many evolutionary algorithms approaches afforded by our facility, to illustrate capabilities of the system and justify their value in an ABM. Accordingly, the remaining demonstrations will be mere proofs of concept, and so will not be accompanied by statistical analysis.

Demonstration 1: Different Evolutionary Algorithms. We begin with a demonstration of some different evolutionary algorithms to show breadth. We turn to the *Flockers* model, a standard demo model in the MASON library. This model is a simulation of the well-known *Boids* algorithm [17], where agents develop collective realistic flocking or swarming behaviors.

Flockers has five classic parameters (avoidance, cohesion, consistency, momentum, and randomness) that together define the behaviors of its agents. We optimized over these parameters and assessed the model performance as the mean number of flockers within an agent's neighborhood, averaged over three trials. This is not a hard problem to optimize: the calibration facility need only maximize cohesion. To show the optimizers at work, we fixed every individual in the initial population to represent the opposite situation (minimal cohesion, maximal values for other behaviors).

We ran for 30 generations using a population size of 276, spread over 276 separate workers. We compared three different evolutionary algorithms: the genetic algorithm as described before; a so-called "(46, 276)" *evolution strategy;* and a *CMA-ES* estimation of distribution algorithm with standard parameters. Figure 3a shows the performance of these three algorithms on this simple agent-based model: as expected, CMA-ES performs extraordinarily well.

Demonstration 2: Multi-Objective Optimization. Next, we demonstrate our system's ability to optimize problems with multiple conflicting objectives. The classic approach finds a set of solutions that have advantages or disadvantages relative to one another with respect to these objectives. A solution A is said to *Pareto-dominate* another solution B if A is at least as good as B in all objectives and better than B in at least one objective. The optimal *Pareto Nondominated Front* is the set of solutions not Pareto-dominated by any other solution.

We extended the Flockers model by introducing an "infection" into the population. Healthy flockers have the same behavior as shown in the previous example, but infected flockers will, with some probability, infect their neighbors or be cured. Our new second objective was to maximize the number of healthy flockers. To do this, flockers must stay as far away from each other as possible, putting our new objective in direct conflict with the first one.

We used the NSGA-II [3] multi-objective evolutionary algorithm with four workers and 100 generations, having 24 individuals per generation. Figure 3b shows the improvement in the Pareto front over time for a typical run.

An Aside: Coevolution. Though we do not provide demonstrations of them, it is worth mentioning two other capabilities of our system, which may be of value to an agent-based modeler.

In Sect. 3 we mentioned that one might wish to calibrate a model to be *insensitive to* one or more global parameters (parameter type 4 in that Section).

For example, we might wish agents to perform migration the same way regardless of rain or shine. One attractive evolutionary optimization approach is *competitive coevolution*. Here we optimize the population A against a second *foil* population B of parameter settings simultaneously being optimized to trip up the first population. Thus while A is trying to be insensitive to B, B is searching for corner cases to challenge A.

A related technique, called *cooperative coevolution*, is a popular way to tackle high-dimensional problems. When the number of parameters to optimize is high, the joint parameter space is exponentially too large to efficiently search. Cooperative coevolution breaks the space into N subspaces by dividing the parameters into N groups, each with its own independently optimized population. Individuals are tested by combining them with ones from the other populations to form a complete solution. The fitness of an individual is based on the performance of various assessed combinations in which it has participated. This reduces the search space from $O(a^N)$ to $O(aN)$, but assumes that the parameters in each group are largely statistically unlinked with other groups.

6.3 Optimizing Agent Behaviors

Agent-based models are unusual in that not only do they have (typically global) *parameters* which must be calibrated but agents with *behaviors* that may benefit from calibration as well. Agent behaviors are essentially programs which dictate how the agents operate in the environment and interact with one another. Unfortunately, it is often the case that the modeler does not know what the proper behavior should be for a given agent, or only understands part of the behavior and needs to fill in the blanks with the remainder.

Because we are calibrating agent behaviors and not global model parameters, the modeler must do more than just specify a set of model parameters to calibrate and an optimization algorithm to use. He must also specify the *nature* of the representation of these agent behaviors (in our case below, an array of four parse-trees), and must also write glue code which, when given an individual, *evaluates* its parse trees in the simulation proper.

The evolutionary algorithm community has developed optimization techniques for a variety of agent behavior representations. Out of the box, we can support *policies* (stateless sets of *if→then* rules that determine actions to take in response to the current world situation), *finite-state automata* (as graph structures), *neural networks* (via NEAT), and untyped or strongly-typed "Koza-style" *genetic programming* (or GP) [9]; and provide hooks for a variety of other options.

In this example, we will focus on GP. Here, individuals take the forms of forests of parse trees populated by functions drawn from a modeler-specified *function set*. Functions may have arguments, types, and arbitrary execution order (like Lisp macros). Parse trees typically impact on behavior through side effects among their functions, or by returning some final result via the root of the tree.

Our example is drawn from the *Serengeti* model [11], in which four "lion" agents must capture a "gazelle" in a real-valued toroidal environment. The

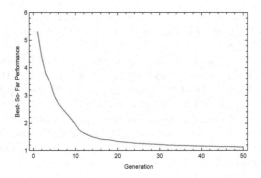

Fig. 4. Mean best-so-far performance, over 30 runs, of genetic programming on the Serengeti model (lower is preferred).

gazelle uses a simple hard-coded obstacle-avoidance behavior to elude the lions, and can move three times as fast as any single lion. The lions can sense the gazelle and each other. Each lion uses a GP parse tree that, when evaluated, returns a vector indicating the direction and speed the lion should travel at that timestep. Thus the behaviors to be calibrated consist of four different parse trees, one per lion.

We used a GP facility closely following the approach in [11], including its function set (we restricted ourselves to the "name-based sensing" and "restricted breeding" variants as described in the paper). We ran the GP algorithm as described, but with a population size of 5760 spread over 276 workers: each worker thus had 20 individuals per generation. Assessment of an individual's parse trees was performed over 10 random trials. Figure 4 shows the mean best-so-far performance of calibrated agent behaviors over 30 runs.

7   Conclusions

We have argued for the importance of automated model calibration for agent-based models. This will become only more pressing as these models increase in complexity and runtime, which will require the use of massively distributed evolutionary optimization tools. We have developed a tool of this kind which combines the popular MASON and ECJ libraries and have shown how their combination can produce a powerful, fully-featured model calibration facility with special capabilities of interest to the agent-based modeler. This preliminary work will be more tested and expanded with other functionalities, like a GUI, also including different types of simulation frameworks besides MASON.

References

1. Batty, M., Desyllas, J., Duxbury, E.: Safety in numbers? Modelling crowds and designing control for the notting hill carnival. Urban Stud. **40**(8), 1573–1590 (2003)

2. Canessa, E., Chaigneau, S.: Calibrating agent-based models using an improved genetic algorithm. In: International Conference of the Chilean Computer Science Society, pp. 25–29 (2014)
3. Deb, K., Agrawal, S., Pratap, A., Meyarivan, T.: A fast elitist non-dominated sorting genetic algorithm for multi-objective optimization: NSGA-II. In: Schoenauer, M., et al. (eds.) PPSN 2000. LNCS, vol. 1917, pp. 849–858. Springer, Heidelberg (2000). https://doi.org/10.1007/3-540-45356-3_83
4. Gilbert, N., Troitzsch, K.: Simulation for the social scientist (2005)
5. Hansen, N., Müller, S.D., Koumoutsakos, P.: Reducing the time complexity of the derandomized evolution strategy with covariance matrix adaptation (CMA-ES). Evol. Comput. 11(1), 1–18 (2003)
6. Heppenstall, A., Malleson, N., Crooks, A.: "space, the final frontier": how good are agent-based models at simulating individuals and space in cities? Systems 4(1), 9 (2016)
7. Johnson, R.T., Lampe, T.A., Seichter, S.: Calibration of an agent-based simulation model depicting a refugee camp scenario. In: Winter Simulation Conference, pp. 1778–1786 (2009)
8. Keijzer, M., Merelo, J.J., Romero, G., Schoenauer, M.: Evolving objects: a general purpose evolutionary computation library. In: Evolution Artificielle (EA), pp. 231–242 (2002)
9. Koza, J.R.: Genetic Programming: On the Programming of Computers by Means of Natural Selection. MIT Press, Cambridge (1992)
10. Luke, S., et al.: The MASON simulation toolkit: past, present, and future. In: International Workshop on Multi-Agent-Based Simulation (MABS) (2018)
11. Luke, S., Spector, L.: Evolving teamwork and coordination with genetic programming. In: Genetic Programming 1996: Proceedings of the First Annual Conference, pp. 141–149 (1996)
12. Mayer, D., Kinghorn, B., Archer, A.: Differential evolution-an easy and efficient evolutionary algorithm for model optimisation. Agric. Syst. 83(3), 315–328 (2005)
13. Mongus, D., Repnik, B., Mernik, M., Žalik, B.: A hybrid evolutionary algorithm for tuning a cloth-simulation model. Appl. Soft Comput. 12(1), 266–273 (2012)
14. Moya, I., Chica, M., Cordón, Ó.: A multicriteria integral framework for agent-based model calibration using evolutionary multi objective optimization and network-based visualization. Decis. Support Syst. 124, 113111 (2019)
15. Nguyen, H.K., Chiong, R., Chica, M., Middleton, R.H., Dhakal, S.: Agent-based modeling of migration dynamics in the Mekong delta, Vietnam: automated calibration using a genetic algorithm. In: IEEE Congress on Evolutionary Computation (CEC), pp. 3372–3379. IEEE (2019)
16. Olsen, M.M., Laspesa, J., Taylor-D'Ambrosio, T.: On genetic algorithm effectiveness for finding behaviors in agent-based predator prey models. In: SummerSim, San Diego, CA, USA, pp. 15:1–15:12 (2018)
17. Reynolds, C.: Flocks, herds and schools: a distributed behavioral model. In: SIGGRAPH, pp. 25–34 (1987)
18. Rogers, A., von Tessin, P.: Multi-objective calibration for agent-based models (2004)
19. Rounds, E.L., Scott, E.O., Alexander, A.S., De Jong, K.A., Nitz, D.A., Krichmar, J.L.: An evolutionary framework for replicating neurophysiological data with spiking neural networks. In: Handl, J., Hart, E., Lewis, P.R., López-Ibáñez, M., Ochoa, G., Paechter, B. (eds.) PPSN 2016. LNCS, vol. 9921, pp. 537–547. Springer, Cham (2016). https://doi.org/10.1007/978-3-319-45823-6_50

20. Scott, E., Luke, S.: ECJ at 20: toward a general metaheuristics toolkit. In: GECCO 2019 Companion (2019)
21. Stanley, K.O., Clune, J., Lehman, J., Miikkulainen, R.: Designing neural networks through neuroevolution. Nat. Mach. Intell. **1**(1), 24–35 (2019)
22. Stonedahl, F.J.: Genetic algorithms for the exploration of parameter spaces in agent-based models. Ph.D. thesis, Northwestern University (2011)
23. Venkadesh, S., et al.: Evolving simple models of diverse intrinsic dynamics in hippocampal neuron types. Front. Neuroinform. **12**, 8 (2018)

Fast and Efficient Partner Selection in Large Agents' Communities: When Categories Overcome Direct Experience

Pasquale De Meo[1] , Rino Falcone[2] , and Alessandro Sapienza[2($\boxtimes$)]

[1] Department of Ancient and Modern Civilizations, University of Messina,
98122 Messina, Italy
pdemeo@unime.it
[2] Institute of Cognitive Sciences and Technologies, ISTC-CNR, 00185 Rome, Italy
{rino.falcone,alessandro.sapienza}@istc.cnr.it

Abstract. When it comes to collaboration within huge agents' networks, trust management becomes a pivotal issue. Defying tool for a fast and efficient partner selection, even in lack of direct information, is of paramount importance, as much as possessing mechanisms allowing a matching between a selected task and a reliable agent able to carry it out. Direct experience plays a big part, nevertheless it requires a long time to offer a stable and accurate performance. In accordance with the literature, we believe that category-based evaluations and inferential processes represent a useful resource for trust assessment. Within this work, by the means of simulations, we investigated how efficient this inferential strategy is, with respect to direct experience, focusing on when and to what extent the first prevails on the latter. Our results show that in some situations it provides even better results.

Keywords: Trust · Inference · Multi-agent systems

1 Background Scenario

We consider a population of agents $\mathcal{A} = \{a_1, \ldots, a_n\}$ which can collaborate by reciprocally delegating the execution of some tasks.

We suppose that any agent $a_i \in \mathcal{A}$ needs to achieve a goal g, which identifies a state of the environment (in short, the *world*) which the agent a_i plans to achieve. The agent a_i can reach the goal g by executing a *task* τ, which affects the world. The most interesting case occurs if the agent a_i want/must delegate the execution of τ.

At an abstract level, each agent possesses some skills and resources, defined here as *features* which determine its ability in carrying out the tasks it has to face. Nevertheless, not all the features associated with an agent are crucial for the execution of τ and the majority of these will not even be necessary. If I were to ask someone to cook for me, it would be interesting to know how fast she/he

© Springer Nature Switzerland AG 2020
Y. Demazeau et al. (Eds.): PAAMS 2020, LNAI 12092, pp. 106–117, 2020.
https://doi.org/10.1007/978-3-030-49778-1_9

is, how good is her/his culinary imagination or if she/he knows how to cook specific dishes; however, knowing that she/he loves reading astrophysics books would not be of any help.

It is therefore a fundamental precondition that an agent a_i identifies which features are necessary to carry out τ. Then, a_i needs a mental representation of any other a_j, which comprises, at least, the subset of the features which are relevant to execute τ. It is also important to underline that just the possession of these features is not enough, it is also very relevant a_j's willingness (following its motivations) to actually realize τ. Of course, two different tasks, say τ_1 and τ_2, require different features to be efficiently addressed.

Thanks to its mental model, a_i is able to estimate the likelihood $\phi(i,j)$ that a_j will positively bring to completion that specific agreed task, for each agent $a_j \in \mathcal{A}$. The function $\phi(i,j)$ measures the *degree of trust* [3] that a_i (hereafter, the *trustor*) puts in a_j (hereafter the *trustee*), i.e., quantifies to what extent a_i is confident that a_j is capable of successfully executing τ.

It is crucial to point out that the assessment of trust is not only *task-dependent* but also *context-dependent*, because external causes may amplify or downsize the trust between the trustor and trustee. For instance, assume that a_i wants to get to the airport one hour before the departure of her/his flight and suppose that a_i is confident that a_j is able to safely drive and she/he is knowledgeable of obstacles to traffic flow (e.g., limited access roads), and thus, a_i puts a high degree of trust in a_j. However, unforeseen circumstances (e.g., a_j stucks in a traffic jam) may prevent a_i from being at the airport at the scheduled time: such an event negatively influence the trust from a_i to a_j, even if, of course, the liability of a_j is limited.

The procedure to select the agent to which the task τ has to be delegated is thus entirely driven from the calculation of the function $\phi(i,j)$: the trustor should select the agent $a_j^\star$ for which $\phi(i,j)$ achieves its largest value, i.e., $j^\star = \arg\max_j \phi(i,j)$. Such a protocol is, unfortunately, infeasible in real-life applications: in fact, a_i is capable of estimating the trust of those agents – in short E_i – with which it interacted in the past and of which it knows features. In real-life applications, we expect that the size of $\mathcal{A}$ is much larger than that of E_i and, thus, the search of a successful partner is likely to end up in a failure.

An elegant solution to the problem of selecting partners in large agent communities is described in [5,6] and it relies on the concept of *agent category* or, in short, *category*.

Broadly speaking, a category is a subset of agents in $\mathcal{A}$ such that each category member possesses homogeneous features. Their unique nature makes categories very interesting and particularly useful. Since the members of a category possess similar features, even their performance concerning the same task will be similar. For sure, we have to consider a certain degree of uncertainty, due to the specific peculiarities of the individuals.

The specific categories to take into consideration change with the context and with the task of interest. For instance, suppose that $\mathcal{A}$ correspond to a community of people working in food service with different roles; chefs, waiters, and sommeliers are possible examples of categories in this context.

Because of the existence of categories, the set of agents that the trustor can evaluate significantly expands in size and it consists of the following type of agents:

1. The aforementioned set E_i, which consists of the agents with which a_i has had a direct experience.
2. The set C_i of agents, such that each agent $a_j \in C_i$ belongs to at least one of the categories $CS = \{C_1, C_2, \ldots, C_p\}$; here we suppose that a_i has had a direct experience with at least one agent in each of the categories in CS.
3. The set of agents R_i with which a_i had no direct experience but which have been recommended to a_i by other agents in $\mathcal{A}$ (for instance, on the basis of their reputation).
4. The set of agents RC_i, such that each agent in RC_i belongs to a category which contain at least one agent in R_i.

Advantages arising from the introduction of categories have been extensively studied in past literature [4–6]: the trustor, in fact, could be able to estimate the performance of any other agent a_j, even if it has never met this agent (and, as observed in [5] without even suspecting its existence), through an *inferential mechanism*.

As the authors of [4] say, it is possible to take advantage of categories just if a few conditions are met. First of all, $\mathcal{A}$ must be partitioned into the categories $\mathcal{C} = \{C_1, C_2, \ldots C_m\}$, classifying the agents according to their features. We assume that this classification is given and accepted by all the agents in $\mathcal{A}$. It must be possible to clearly and unequivocally link a_j to a category c_l. Finally, we must somehow identify the average performance of the category C_l with respect to the task τ: we will discuss in detail in Sect. 3 a procedure to estimate the performance – called true quality – $\theta_l(\tau)$ of the category C_l for task τ.

When all three of these conditions are met, then the category C_l's evaluation can be used for the agent a_j, concerning the task τ since, by definition of category, all agents in C_l will share the same features of a_j and, thus, if the other agents in C_l are able to successfully execute the task τ (or not), we can reasonably assume that even a_j can do it (or not).

Of course, only some of the categories $C_1, \ldots, C_m$ possess the qualities to successfully execute the task τ while others do not. As a consequence, the first step to perform is to *match* the task τ with a set of categories capable of executing τ.

At a basic level, such a matching could be implemented through a function $\psi(C_l, \tau)$ which takes a category C_l and a task τ and returns True if agents in C_l are capable of executing τ, False vice versa. The computation of the function ψ requires an analytical and explicit specification of: *(a)* the chain of actions to perform to execute τ and *(b)* for each action mentioned in *(a)*, the features an agent should possess to perform such an action.

The protocol above easily generalizes to the case in which the trustor has a limited experience (or, in the worst case it has no previous experience): in this case, in fact, the trustor a_i could leverage the sets of agents R_i and RC_i.

2   Related Work

The growing need to deal with bigger and bigger agents' networks makes it difficult to find reliable partners to delegate tasks. It becomes clear that, in such situations, direct experience [9] is not enough to allow us facing this problem. Going beyond this dimension becomes essential, on the light of the knowledge we already have, identifying models and methodologies able to evaluate our interlocutors and possibly to select adequate partners for the collaborative goals we want to pursue.

Several authors proposed trust propagation as a solution to this topic. Trust propagation [8,10] starts from the assumption that if a_i trusts a_j and a_j trusts a_k, then it is reasonable to assume that a_i can trust a_k to some extent. Exploiting this and other assumptions, this technique allows propagating a trust value from an agent to another one, without requiring a direct interaction. The confusion in the reasoning process here is due to the consideration of a generic trust value for an individual, leaving aside the reason why we trust it: the task we want to delegate to it.

Many articles have discussed the use of categories/stereotypes in trust evaluations [7,12]. This is a very useful instrument, allowing to generalize an individual's evaluation, concerning a specific task to other agents owning similar characteristics. It represents a useful proxy for individuating knowledge about specific trustees [11], elicited in particular in all those circumstances precluding the development of person-based trust [1]. Here the intuition is that, given a specific task τ, the performance of the agent we are evaluating are related to the values of the features it needs to carry out the task itself. Along these lines, it is natural to assume that other individual owning similar values, i.e. belonging to the same category, have the same potential to solve τ.

Pursuant to these considerations, our contribution within this work concerns the investigation of how efficient this inferential strategy is, with respect to direct experience, focusing on when and to what extent the first prevails on the latter.

3   Inferring the Quality of Categories

In this section we illustrate our procedure to estimate the performance (in short called the *true quality*) $\theta_l(\tau)$ of agents in the category C_l to successfully execute a particular task τ.

Because of the assumptions of our model (illustrated in Sect. 1), agents belonging to the same category share the same features and, thus, their performances in executing τ are roughly similar; this implies that if an agent $a_j \in C_l$ is able (resp., not able) to execute τ, then we expect that any other agent $a_q \in C_l$ is also able (resp., not able) to execute τ.

In the following, we suppose that agents in C_l are able to execute τ, i.e. in compliance with notation introduced in Sect. 1, we assume that $\psi(C_l, \tau) = \text{True}$. In contrast, if $\psi(C_l, \tau) = \text{False}$, it does not make sense to estimate $\theta_l(\tau)$.

The next step of our protocol consists of selecting one of the agents, i.e., the *trustee*, in C_l to which delegate τ; to this purpose, we could select, uniformly at random, one of the agents in C_l, as illustrated in [5]. However, agents are individual entities and, thus, slight differences in their features exist. Because of these differences, an agent (say a_j) may have better (resp., worse) performance than another agent (say, a_q) in executing τ.

In the light of the reasoning above, the true quality $\theta_l(\tau)$ quantifies the *expected performance of an arbitrary trustee in C_l in the execution of τ.*

We assume that $\theta_l(\tau)$ ranges in $(-\infty, +\infty)$: positive (resp., negative) values of $\theta_l(\tau)$ are an indicator of good (resp., bad) performances.

The first step to compute $\theta_l(\tau)$ consists of modelling the performance $f_j(\tau)$ of an arbitrary agent $a_j \in C_l$ in executing τ. To capture uncertainty in the performance of a_j, we represent $f_j(\tau)$ as a Gaussian random variable with mean μ_j and variance σ_j^2.

The assumption that all of the agents in the same category should reach the same performance implies that $\mu_j = \theta_l(\tau)$ for each agent $a_j \in C_l$.

The variance σ_j^2 controls the amount of variability in the performances of the agent a_j: large (resp., small) values in σ_j^2 generate significant (resp., irrelevant) deviations from $\theta_l(\tau)$. In this paper we considered two options for σ_j^2, namely:

1. *Fixed Variance Model*: we suppose that $\sigma_j^2 = \sigma^2$ for each $a_j \in C_l$.
2. *Random Variance Model*: we suppose that σ_j^2 is a uniform random variable in the interval $[\alpha, \beta]$.

Based on these premises, the procedure to estimate $\theta_l(\tau)$ is *iterative* and, at the k-th iteration it works as follows:

a) We select, uniformly at random, an agent, say a_j from C_l
b) We sample the performance $\hat{f}_j(k) \sim f_j(\tau)$ of a_j

Steps a) and b) are repeated N times, being N the number of agents we need to sample before making a decision. In addition, in Step a), agents are sampled with replacement, i.e., an agent could be selected more than once. The algorithm outputs the average value of sampled performances, i.e.:

$$\hat{\theta}_l(\tau) = \frac{1}{N} \sum_{k=1}^{N} \hat{f}_j(k) \tag{1}$$

Our algorithm actually converges to the true value $\theta_l(\tau)$ as stated in the following theorem:

Theorem 1. *Let N be the number of agents queried by our algorithm and let $\hat{\theta}_l(\tau)$ be the estimation of the true quality $\theta_l(\tau)$ the algorithm returns after N rounds. We have that in both the fixed variance and random variance models $\hat{\theta}_l(\tau)$ converges to $\theta_l(\tau)$ at a rate of convergence of $\frac{1}{\sqrt{N}}$.*

Proof. Let us first analyze the individual agent performances $f_j(\tau)$ and we are interested in computing the mean and variance of $f_j(\tau)$. If we opt for the Fixed Variance Model, then $f_j(\tau)$ is a Gaussian random variable with mean $\theta_l(\tau)$ and the variance is equal to a constant value σ^2. In contrast, if we are in the Random Variance Model, then the estimation of the mean and the variance of $f_j(\tau)$ can be obtained by law of total mean and the law of total variance [2], which state that for two arbitrary random variables X and Y, the following identities hold true:

$$E(X) = E(E(X \mid Y)) \tag{2}$$

$$\text{Var}(Y) = E(\text{Var}(Y \mid X)) + \text{Var}(E(Y \mid X)) \tag{3}$$

We apply Eqs. 2 and 3 to $X = f_j(\tau)$ and $Y = \sigma$; if we condition on $\sigma = \overline{\sigma}$, then $f_j(\tau)$ is a Gaussian random variable with mean equal to $\theta_l(\tau)$ and variance equal to $\overline{\sigma}$ and therefore:

$$E(f_j(\tau)) = E(E(f_j(\tau) \mid \sigma = \overline{\sigma})) = E(\theta_l(\tau)) = \theta_l(\tau)$$

In addition,

$$E(\text{Var}(f_j(\tau) \mid \sigma = \overline{\sigma})) = E(\sigma) = \frac{\alpha + \beta}{2}$$

and

$$\text{Var}(E(f_j(\tau) \mid \sigma = \overline{\sigma})) = \text{Var}(E(\theta_l(\tau))) = \text{Var}(\theta_l(\tau)) = 0$$

which jointly imply

$$\text{Var}(f_j(\tau)) = \frac{\alpha + \beta}{2}$$

As a consequence, independently of the agent a_j, we have that the agent performances $f_j(\tau)$ have the same distribution which we denote as $f(\tau)$. Therefore, in both the Fixed Variance Model and Random Variance Model, the algorithm selects a random sample of agents $Z_1, Z_2, \ldots, Z_N$ of size N in which, for each k such that $1 \leq k \leq N$, Z_k is the average performance of the agent selected at the k-th iteration and it is distributed as $f(\tau)$. The algorithm calculates:

$$S_N = \frac{Z_1 + Z_2 + \ldots + Z_n}{N} \tag{4}$$

Because of the Central Limit Theorem [2], the distribution of S_N gets closer and closer to a Gaussian distribution with mean $\theta_l(\tau)$ as $N \to +\infty$ with a rate of convergence in the order of $\frac{1}{\sqrt{N}}$ and this end the proof.

4 Experimental Analysis

We designed our experiments to answer two main research questions, namely:

RQ₁ What are the benefits arising from the introduction of categories in the selection of a trustee against, for instance, a pure random search or a direct-experience based strategy?

RQ₂ How quickly our algorithm to estimate $\theta_l(\tau)$ converges?

In what follows, we first describe a reference scenario in which our task consists of recruiting a chef from a database of applicants (see Sect. 4.1). Then, in Sects. 4.2 and 4.3, we provide an answer to **RQ₁** and **RQ₂**.

4.1   The Reference Scenario

We assume that features associated with our task are as follows: *(i) Culinary Education*, measured as the (overall) number of hours spent in training courses with qualified chef trainers, *(ii) Expertise*, i.e., the number of years of professional experience, *(iii) Language Skills*, defined as the number of foreign languages in which the applicant is proficient, *(iv) Culture*, measured on a scale from 0 (worse) to 10 (best) and which is understood as the ability of preparing different kind dishes (e.g. fish, meat, vegetarian and so on) in different styles (e.g. Indian, Thai or Italian) and *(v) Creativity*, measured on a scale from 0 (worse) to 10 (best). The list of features is, of course, non-exhaustive. We suppose that each feature is associated with a plausible range: for instance, in Table 1, we consider three potential tasks and the corresponding requirements.

Table 1. Some tasks associated with the recruitment of a professional chef and their requirements

Task	Culinary education	Expertise	Language skills	Culture	Creativity
τ_1	150	5	2	6	7
τ_2	200	4	2	6	6
τ_3	300	4	2	7	6

In the following, due to space limitations, we concentrate only on the task τ_1 and we suppose that five categories exist, namely: *Professional Chefs - C_1*, who are trained to master culinary art. Members in C_1 are able to provide creative innovation in menu, preparation and presentation, *Vegan Chefs - C_2*, specialized in the preparation of plant-based dishes, *Pastry Chefs - C_3*, who are capable of creating chocolates and pastries, *Roast Chefs - C_4*, who have expertise in preparing roasted/braised meats and *Fish Chefs - C_5*, who are mainly specialized in the preparation of dish fishes. Each category consists of 100 agents and, thus, the overall number of agents involved in our experiments is 500. Features associated with categories C_1–C_5 are reported in Table 2.

In our scenario, *only agents in C_1 are able to fulfill τ_1*; agents in other categories are, for different reasons, unable to execute τ_1: for instance, the expertise of agents in categories C_2, C_3 and C_5 is not sufficient while agents forming categories C_3–C_5 correspond to applicants with a high level of specialization in the preparation of some specific kind of dishes (e.g., fish-based dishes) but they are not sufficiently skilled in the preparation of other type of foods and, thus, agents in these categories showcase an insufficient level of culture.

To simplify discussion we suppose that, through a proper normalization, the performance $f(\tau_1)$ (see Sect. 3) of an individual agent as well as the true quality $\theta_l(\tau_1)$ of a category C_l (for l = 1...5) range from 0 to 1. Here, the best performance of an agent can provide (resp., the highest true quality of a category) is 1.

Table 2. Some features associated with categories C_1–C_5

Category ID.	Culinary education	Expertise	Language skills	Culture	Creativity
C_1	250	5	2	8	7
C_2	250	3	2	6	5
C_3	300	3	1	4	5
C_4	100	6	1	4	5
C_5	400	3	1	4	5

4.2 A Comparison of Category-Based Search with Random-Based Search and Direct-Experience Search

In our first experiment, we compare three strategies to search for a trustee, namely: *a) Random-Based Search*: here, the trustor selects, uniformly at random, a trustee to execute τ_1. The trustor measures the performance $f(\tau_1)$ provided by the trustee in the execution of τ_1. *b) Category-Based Search*: here, the trustor considers only agents in the most appropriate category (which in our reference scenario coincides with C_1); as suggested in [5], the trustor selects, uniformly at random, one of the agents in C_1 to act as trustee. Once again, the trustor measures the performance $f(\tau_1)$ provided by the trustee in the execution of τ_1. *(c) Direct-Experience Search*: we suppose that the trustor consults up to B agents in the community, being B a fixed integer called *budget*. The trustor records the performance of each consulted agent but it *does not memorize* its category (it may be that the trustor is unable to perceive/understand the trustee's category). At the end of this procedure, the trustor selects as trustee the agent providing the highest performance $f(\tau_1)$ among all consulted agents. The Direct-Experience Search strategy can be regarded as an evolution of the Random-Based Search strategy in which the trustor learns from its past interactions it uses its knowledge to spot the trustee. Here, the budget B regulates the duration of the learning activity the trustor pursues.

In our experimental setting we considered two values of B, namely $B = 10$ and $B = 30$ and we discuss only results in the Fixed Variance Model with $\sigma = 0.05$ and $\sigma = 0.15$. We applied the Random-Based, the Category-Based and the Direct-Experience Search strategies 20 times; a sketch of the probability density function (pdf) of $f(\tau_1)$ for each strategy is shown in Fig. 1.

As expected, Category-Based Search performs consistently better than the Random-Search one. In addition, the standard deviation of $f(\tau_1)$ in Category-Based Search is much smaller than that observed in the Random-Based strategy and such a behaviour depends on the different degree of matching of categories C_1–C_5 with the task τ_1: in other words, if the trustee is in C_1, the performances it provides are constantly very good; in contrast, in Random-Based Search strategy, the measured performance may significantly fluctuate on the basis of the category to which the trustee belongs to and this explains oscillations in $f(\tau_1)$.

The analysis of the Direct-Experience Search strategy offers many interesting insights which are valid for both $\sigma = 0.05$ and $\sigma = 0.15$. Firstly, notice that if

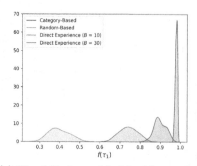
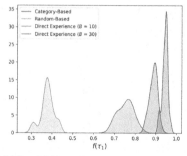

(a) Fixed Variance Model with $\sigma = 0.05$ (b) Fixed Variance Model with $\sigma = 0.15$

Fig. 1. Feedback $f(\tau)$ provided by the trustee

$B = 10$, then the Direct-Experience Search strategy achieves significantly better performances than the Random-Based strategy, which indicates that an even short learning phase yields tangible benefits. If B increases, the trustor is able to see a larger number of agents before making its decision and, in particular, if B is sufficiently large, then the trustor might encounter the best performing agent $a^\star$ in the whole community. In this case, the Direct-Experience strategy would outperform the Category-Based Search strategy: in fact, in the Category-Based strategy, the trustor chooses, uniformly at random, one of the agents in C_1 which provides a performance worse than (or equal to) $a^\star$. In short, for large values of B, the Direct-Experience strategy achieves performances which are comparable and, in some cases, even better than those we would obtain in the Category-Based strategy, as shown in Fig. 1. However, the budget B has the meaning of a *cost*, i.e., it is associated with the time the trustor has to wait before it chooses the trustee and, thus, in many practical scenarios, the trustor has to make its decisions as quick as possible.

It is also instructive to consider a further strategy, called *Mixed-Based Search*, which combines the Random-Based Search strategy with the Category-Based Search strategy.

In Mixed-Based Search, we assume the existence of a *warm-up* phase in which the trustor selects the trustee by means of the Random-Based Search strategy; unlike the Direct-Experience Search strategy, the trustor collects not only $f(\tau_1)$ but it also records the category of the trustee. In this way, the trustor is able to identify (after, hopefully, a small number of steps) the category with the highest true quality, i.e., C_1. From that point onward, the trustor switches to a Category-Based strategy and it selects only agents from C_1. From a practical standpoint, we suppose that a performance $f(\tau_1) \geq 0.6$ is classified as an indicator of good performance (in short, *positive signal*); as soon as the trustor has collected 2 positive signals, it makes a decision on the best performing category and it switches to the Category-Based Search strategy.

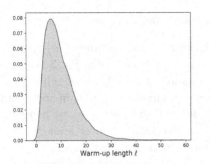 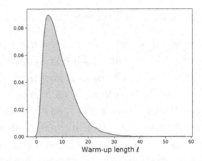

(a) Fixed Variance Model with $\sigma = 0.05$ (b) Fixed Variance Model with $\sigma = 0.15$

Fig. 2. Probability Density Function of the Warm-up length (ℓ) in the Mixed-Search strategy.

We are interested at estimating, through simulations, the length ℓ of the warm-up phase, i.e., the number of agents that the trustor has to contact before switching to the Category-Based search strategy. In Fig. 2 we plot the pdf of ℓ.

Here, the variance σ has a minor impact and we notice that, the pdf achieves its largest value at $\ell \simeq 10$, i.e., 10 iterations are generally sufficient to identify the best performing category.

4.3   The Rate of Convergence of Our Algorithm

We conclude our study by investigating how the Fixed Variance Model and the Random Variance model influence the rate at which our algorithm estimates the true quality $\theta_l(\tau)$ of a category.

To make exposition of experimental outcomes simple, we suppose that $\theta_l = 1$ (which models a scenario in which agents in C_1 showcase an exceptionally high ability in executing τ_1).

We considered the Fixed Variance Model with $\sigma \in \{0.05, 0.1, 0.15\}$ and the Random Variance Model in which σ is uniformly distributed in $[0.01, 0.3]$.

We investigated how $\hat{\theta}_l(\tau)$ varied as function of the number N of queried agents; obtained results are reported in Fig. 3.

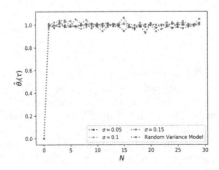

Fig. 3. Variation of $\hat{\theta}_l(\tau)$ as function of N. (Color figure online)

The main conclusions we can draw from our experiment are as follows:

1. Individual agent variability (modelled through the parameter σ) greatly affects the rate at which $\hat{\theta}_l(\tau)$ converges to $\theta_l(\tau)$. Specifically, Fig. 3 suggests that less than 5 iterations are enough to guarantee that $|\hat{\theta}_l(\tau) - \theta_l(\tau)| < 10^{-2}$ if $\sigma = 0.05$. In addition, as σ gets larger and larger, we highlight more and more fluctuations in $\hat{\theta}_l(\tau)$: as an example, if $\sigma = 0.15$ (green line), we highlight the largest fluctuation in $\hat{\theta}_l(\tau)$ and, at a visual inspection, at least $N = 30$ queries are needed to achieve a significant reduction in $|\hat{\theta}_l(\tau) - \theta_l(\tau)|$.

2. An interesting case occurs in the Random Variance Model: in some iterations of the algorithm, agents with a small variability are selected (i.e., we would sample agents with $\sigma \simeq 0.01$) while in other cases agent with a larger variability are selected (here $\sigma \simeq 0.3$). Overall, agents with small variability fully balance agents with high variability and, thus, the algorithm converges to $\theta_l(\tau)$ (red line) generally faster than the case $\sigma = 0.1$ (orange line) and $\sigma = 0.15$ (green line).

5   Conclusions

Highly populated networks represent a useful resource for agents' collaboration, yet the very same agents experience difficulties with trust formation, given the lack of information for evaluating their possible partners. As already proven in the literature, category-based evaluations and inferential processes represent a useful resource for trust assessment, by allowing agents to generalize from trust in individuals to trust in their category and vice versa, basing on their observable features. On that note, we cared about stressing the tight relationship between trust and the specific task, target of the trust itself.

In order to investigate the role of agents' categories, we introduced a simulated scenario, testing in particular the performance of a category-based evaluation, with respect to a random-based search - which it is easily outperformed - and a direct-experience one, showing that, in case of little direct experience, categories grant a better result. Moreover, we proved that, if not available, it is possible to estimate the category' s true quality $\theta_l(\tau)$ in a reasonably short amount of time. Future research will attempt to test these findings on a real data set.

References

1. Adams, B.D., Webb, R.D.: Trust in small military teams. In: 7th International Command and Control Technology Symposium, pp. 1–20 (2002)
2. Bertsekas, D., Tsitsiklis, J.: Introduction to Probability. Athena Scientific (2008)
3. Castelfranchi, C., Falcone, R.: Trust Theory: A Socio-Cognitive and Computational Model, vol. 18. Wiley, Hoboken (2010)
4. Falcone, R., Piunti, M., Venanzi, M., Castelfranchi, C.: From manifesta to krypta: the relevance of categories for trusting others. ACM Trans. Intell. Syst. Technol. (TIST) 4(2), 27 (2013)

5. Falcone, R., Sapienza, A.: Selecting trustworthy partners by the means of untrustworthy recommenders in digitally empowered societies. In: Demazeau, Y., Matson, E., Corchado, J.M., De la Prieta, F. (eds.) PAAMS 2019. LNCS (LNAI), vol. 11523, pp. 55–65. Springer, Cham (2019). https://doi.org/10.1007/978-3-030-24209-1_5

6. Falcone, R., Sapienza, A., Castelfranchi, C.: The relevance of categories for trusting information sources. ACM Trans. Internet Technol. (TOIT) **15**(4), 13 (2015)

7. Fang, H., Zhang, J., Sensoy, M., Thalmann, N.M.: A generalized stereotypical trust model. In: 2012 IEEE 11th International Conference on Trust, Security and Privacy in Computing and Communications, pp. 698–705. IEEE (2012)

8. Guha, R., Kumar, R., Raghavan, P., Tomkins, A.: Propagation of trust and distrust. In: Proceedings of the 13th International Conference on World Wide Web, pp. 403–412 (2004)

9. Hang, C.W., Wang, Y., Singh, M.P.: Operators for propagating trust and their evaluation in social networks. Technical report, North Carolina State University. Department of Computer Science (2008)

10. Jamali, M., Ester, M.: A matrix factorization technique with trust propagation for recommendation in social networks. In: Proceedings of the Fourth ACM Conference on Recommender Systems, pp. 135–142 (2010)

11. Kramer, R.M.: Collective trust within organizations: conceptual foundations and empirical insights. Corp. Reput. Rev. **13**(2), 82–97 (2010)

12. Teacy, W.L., Luck, M., Rogers, A., Jennings, N.R.: An efficient and versatile approach to trust and reputation using hierarchical Bayesian modelling. Artif. Intell. **193**, 149–185 (2012)

Multi-Agent Modelling and Simulation of Hospital Acquired Infection Propagation Dynamics by Contact Transmission in Hospital Wards

Dario Esposito[1(✉)], Davide Schaumann[2], Domenico Camarda[1], and Yehuda E. Kalay[3]

[1] Polytechnic University of Bari, Bari, Italy
{dario.esposito,domenico.camarda}@poliba.it
[2] Jacobs Technion-Cornell Institute at Cornell Tech, New York, USA
davide.schaumann@cornell.edu
[3] Technion, Israel Institute of Technology, Haifa, Israel
kalay@ar.technion.ac.il

Abstract. Hospital-acquired infections (HAI) are recognized worldwide as a major threat to hospital users. In this study, we present the Multi-Agent modelling and simulation of HAI propagation dynamics through exogenous cross-infection by a contact transmission route in a hospital ward. The model relies on the Event Based Modelling and Simulation approach. It is meant to deal with a wide range of pathogen types and scenarios of their spread within a hospital environment, which can be extended to integrate relevant emerging factors in the dynamic evolution of HAIs. The Agent-Based application was validated through a virtual simulation of a case study built in a Unity 3D environment, which generates a real time infection risk map. The simulation represents the building and its users in the situation of HAI risk in a coherent and dynamic system. It allows for the visualization of contamination propagation due to human spatial behaviour and activities. The case study was tested through a what-if scenario, allowing for the real-time visualization of transmission and assessing the effectiveness of different prevention and control measures on pathogen propagation. Of further interest was an understanding of the influences of architectural design and space distribution.

Keywords: Multi-Agent simulation · Hospital Acquired Infection · Decision Support System

1 Introduction

Hospital-acquired infections (HAI), i.e. infections contracted during hospitalization, are recognized as a major threat to hospital users all over the world and are cited as the third most common cause of deaths in the USA [1]. If not always deadly, it can be severely detrimental to patient well-being and contribute to a substantial burden for public health resources. In these circumstances, prevention and control become absolutely vital [2]. To this end, it is essential to improve the current understanding of the dynamics of HAI

© Springer Nature Switzerland AG 2020
Y. Demazeau et al. (Eds.): PAAMS 2020, LNAI 12092, pp. 118–133, 2020.
https://doi.org/10.1007/978-3-030-49778-1_10

spread and to foresee the effects of intervention policies, environmental organization and spatial design, adapting this knowledge domain to features (type of departments, ward architecture, workflow organization and more) of the specific healthcare context of interest.

This work relates to the health risk of a Hospital Acquired Infection (HAI) with an emphasis on the spatial spread of the risk. We present the Event Based modelling and simulation of HAI propagation dynamics through exogenous cross-infection by a contact transmission route in a hospital ward. Our approach relies on the Event Based Modelling and Simulation (EBMS) method which can be calibrated with a high degree of sensitivity for the simulation of spatial behaviour and interaction of agents [3]. The EBMS was expanded to the specific domain of HAI with the aim of representing the mechanism of contamination transmission via a contact route in a spatially explicit, heterogeneously mixed environment and to simulate its propagation dynamics within a hospital ward over time and in space. This considers the profile and behaviour of individuals, the characteristics of pathogens and the role of inanimate objects and spaces. The Agent-Based Model (ABM) works through the variation of one specific agent feature, which is their contamination condition and capacity. This constantly relates to the contamination condition and capacity of other agents (actors and space) through the formalized agents' transmission dynamic.

The potential ABM application was tested through a virtual simulation of a hypothetical case study built in a Unity 3D environment, which is able to generate a real time infection risk map. The simulation represents the building and its users in the situation of HAI risk in a coherent and dynamic environment. It allows for the visualization of contamination propagation due to human spatial behaviour and user activities. A trial case study was tested through a what-if scenario, allowing for the real-time visualization of transmission and evaluating the effect of different control measures and spatial distribution on pathogen propagation. The ABM exploits the effectiveness of intervention policies to prevent and control contamination diffusion, as well providing visualization of their co-presence with others at the same time. Of further interest was an understanding of the influences of architectural design and space distribution.

The proposed ABM proved useful in the study of the dynamics of pathogen circulation (e.g. to visualize clusters of infected patients and patterns of occurrence), as this demonstrated how these may vary depending on initial causes and conditions, the heterogeneity of agents' features and spatially related configurations. A comparison of the experiment's qualitative results is valuable in assessing the effectiveness of the implementation of control strategies, namely practices and procedures (e.g. agent hygiene behaviour and contact precautions), as well as shedding light on possible control protocol breaches during infection outbreak [4]. The working proof of a what-if scenario providing evidence in support of decision-making processes demonstrates the value of the developed framework as a Decision Support System (DSS) in the field of hospital management and design.

2 State of the Art

Agent-Based Models allow researchers to build a comprehensive representation of the real world, with a complete level of detail of agents, intended as people and objects, and their individual characteristics, behaviours, locations and interactions in space. Recently, ABMs have seen a wide growth in many research fields and at the same time, interest in simulating healthcare environments has risen. Several applications of ABMs to hospital environments were designed to address system performances, examining patient flows, admission waiting time, staff workload, economic indicators, and other hospital operational issues [5–8]. However, while there is a rich history of modelling HAIs and despite the fact HAI features fit with the ABM approach, relatively little work exists which applies ABM to the HAI topic [9]. Only in recent years has the HAI domain been investigated with ABM, since the modelling of HAI has been recognized as perhaps the best suited area for ABMs within a healthcare environment. Such a consideration is a consequence of the ABM's ability to address all the crucial components of environment spatial description as well as the agents' social and physical interaction abilities [10–14].

Although previous studies have provided new insights into the relative contributions of various HAI features, these were rooted on fixed assumptions that over-simplify real situations and usually investigated only a few aspects at a time, so losing their grasp on the organized complexity of the phenomenon [15]. Specifically, they suffer from one or more of the following limitations:

- they include only two types of healthcare staff, doctors and nurses, where other healthcare workers (HCWs) and visitors are neglected and often ignore patients' and HCW heterogeneity, spatial behaviours and personal traits;
- they account only for contact transmission through interaction between the patient-physician or patient-HCWs; contact between patients, HCWs and visitors are not considered;
- the contact transmission does not account for the level of risk of the activity in progress between agents and does not consider the specific route of contamination;
- they focus only on transmission between individuals, neglecting the role of the environment and inanimate objects as potential vectors;
- they do not consider pathogen removal via a proper hand hygiene or ward cleaning through decontamination procedures, nor the level of accuracy of such procedures;
- they divide patients into discrete classes, such as colonized or infected and for the healthcare staff into colonized and non-colonized or transiently colonized, without representing these dynamics through continuous states;
- they do not account for the different severity level of an outbreak, nor for different levels of susceptibility of patients or the presence of asymptomatic carriers;
- none of them investigate the impact of different architectural layouts and spatial distribution on the propagation of infections and only a few consider the effective spatial displacements of agents around the ward.

Recently, the Event-Based approach has emerged, based on a Multi-Agent paradigm and this can play an important contributing role. Developed by Schaumann et al. it is based on the Event notion. Events are designed to co-ordinate temporal, goal-oriented routine activities performed by agents. Rather than describing behaviour from the point of view of each actor, events allow for the description of behaviour from the point of view of the procedures that need to be performed to achieve a task [16]. The event system architecture adds to the bottom up structure of the ABM, the capacity to manage the coordinated behaviour of many agents in a top down fashion. Its power to simulate complex and realistic scenarios allows us to apply it in the modelling of HAI spread. Thanks to the Event-Based method, we tried to address many of these under-investigated aspects, above all regarding the spatial spread of contamination. This aims at building a comprehensive system to handle different pathogen types, spreading conditions and architectural and spatial organization within wards.

3   Contamination Transmission Model

Transmissible HAIs are caused by contagious pathogens, and in most cases the pathogens are in the form of bacteria, although viruses and fungi are often involved. We consider the chain of infection which represents the transmission path of an infectious pathogen (see Fig. 1). In fact, despite the variety of pathogens, germs spread from person to person through a common series of events, which we aim to simulate. There are six points at which the chain of the infection can be broken, and a germ can be stopped from infecting another person. The simulation visualizes the mechanism of diffusion of HAIs through a contamination risk map and so suggests where it is feasible to intervene in order to break the chain. In our study, we are interested in modelling and simulating exogenous cross-infection transmitted by contact route. Exogenous cross-infection by contact is direct if the contamination occurs through direct contact between the human source of infection and the human recipient [17]. Exogenous cross-infection by contact is indirect if the contamination occurs through indirect contact via inanimate objects (including equipment), or environmental furniture [1].

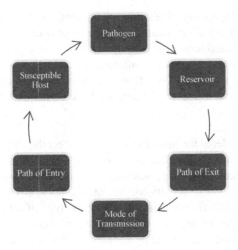

Fig. 1. The chain of infection.

Considering the agent, either actor or space, pathogens and activities, Fig. 2 represents the elements involved in the transmission dynamics and which are needed for contamination propagation.

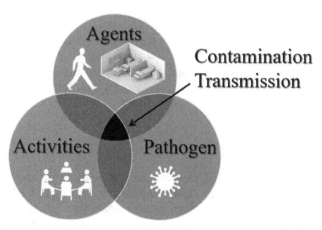

Fig. 2. Components for contamination transmission.

For a reliable simulation we need to model the contamination flow transferred by contact occurring during every single interaction between agents, i.e. through contaminated actors (or actor-space and vice versa) during the development of an activity or during permanence in a shared space. The necessary condition for a pathogen transmission to occur is interaction by touch or by environment between contaminated actors or actors and spaces. Many factors can affect the strength of the transmission flow influencing the contamination status of the receiving actor, changing it from non-carrier to carrier. Two assumptions were made:

- If actors, objects and spaces involved in an event have the same level of contamination, there is no gradient between them and therefore no flow of contamination, thus they will maintain their initial level of contamination.
- If the actors with different levels of contamination enter into contact each other (or with a space or object) there will be a flow of contamination from that with the major level to those with the minor level, increasing the contamination level of the less contaminated.

Moreover, we considered the main factors which affect the strength of the transmission flow of HAI transmission, the characteristics of an activity, the type of pathogen and the compliance and effectiveness of prevention policies, i.e. hand washing or ward cleaning. We introduce "Ty" Type of activity coefficient. Thanks to this we can represent each risk level of acquiring infections which varies with the type of activity, which depends on the need and the type of physical contact between agents. Examples of high-risk activities could be wound care, changing nappies, performing physical examinations, lifting the patient in bed, oral temperature. The second aspect refers to the characteristics of the pathogen. We introduce "Tr" Transmissibility coefficient, which stands for the propagation capacity by contact of a particular pathogen, i.e. its strength in passing from to surfaces and from one host to another. The final feature depends on a compliance with prevention policies, i.e. hand hygiene procedures or ward cleaning. We introduce "Cl"

Cleanness coefficient, indicating the level of cleanliness of the involved actors (objects and spaces). It is a proxy to signify the occurrence or frequency of hand hygiene and ward cleaning as well as the level of accuracy in performing such procedures.

The following equation represents the flow of contamination during a contact between two agents, from the more to the less contaminated. In the Agent-Based Simulation it is automatically calculated every time a potentially infective contact occurs and for its entire duration according to a settable time rate. The form of the flow equation is the same for actor-actor and for actor-space (and space-actor) transmission. In this contamination expression, it is not considered the agent's spatial position variable, since the simulation provides this information in its clear visualisation of an agent's position in space.

$$C2new = C2old + \Delta C(\text{Ty Tr Cl}) \tag{1}$$

- Set C = Contamination level in a range from 0 to 100;
- Actor1 (or Object or Space) starts with C1*old*;
- Actor2 (or Object or Space) starts with C2*old*;
- C1*old* > C2*old*;
- ΔC = C1*old* − C2*old*.

Beyond the variables taken in consideration in the formulation, the duration of actor-actor and actor-space contact is a central factor in the transmission process, as the probability of transmission rises with contact length, as has been verified in literature [17, 18].

This formulation is already able to support a fine-grained level of simulation of the infection dynamics, since it accounts for the contamination variation depending on contact length, which express the increasing risk of being colonized and becoming infected with contact duration increasing (as well as for the permanence inside a contaminated space). This feature in our model signifies that the overall quantity of contamination transmitted by the flow increases over time and is formally expressed by the integer of the transmission flow equation. The duration "Du" of an infective contact is not necessarily the same as the duration of the activity itself, as they are two different concepts, but it must be less or equal to the latter. Being the total length of one contact (between two actors or actor and space) measured in seconds, we have:

$$\frac{dCfinal}{dt} = \int_0^{Du} C2new\, dt$$

Where Du consists of the number of subsequent touch steps (ts). It is equal to:

$$Du = N * ts$$

In our simulation, each touch step is set as equal to 1 s., which approximate real time dynamics. Hence, the flow equation is calculated for every ts of contact and correspondingly the ΔC in the formula is updated following this rate.

The total amount of the transmitted flow during a single contact whose length is equal to Du could be calculated as the sum of the flow for each touch step:

$$Cfinal = \sum_{i=1}^{n} C2new_i$$

Where:

$$C2new_i = C2old_i + \Delta C_i(\text{Ty Tr Cl})$$

To generalize the transmission flow expression in cases of multiple agents, as well as extend it from a discrete to a continuous equation. We suppose n agents (actors, spaces and objects) in our hypothetical ward. Each has its own level of contamination C^i, whose value may change depending on the occurrence of contacts:

$$C \in R^n$$

$$C = \begin{bmatrix} C^1 \\ \vdots \\ C^n \end{bmatrix}$$

Being K parameter:

$$K = (\text{Ty Tr Cl})$$

Therefore, dependent on the type of activity Ty, type of pathogen Tr and level of cleanliness Cl of the more contaminated agent of the two.

The value of contamination of the nth agent will be identical to its previous value plus the difference between its previous value and that of the agent with which it came into contact, multiplied by K. Considering the discrete process for each case of contact, we have a temporal unit, between $n-1$ and n:

$$C_n^i = C_{n-1}^i + \sum_{\substack{j=1 \\ j \neq i}}^{m} \left(C_{n-1}^i - C_{n-1}^j \right) K_{ij} \beta_{ij}$$

with $1 \leq i \in N$

$$\left(C_{n-1}^i - C_{n-1}^j \right) > 0$$

The contact indicator β_{ij} assumes a value of 0 in the case of no contact and a value of 1 where contact occurs; the matrix NxN shows which contacts occur over temporal unit $n-1$ and n. The parameter K_{ij}, describes the strength of contagion in j over i and the zero diagonal matrix NxN, since the agent cannot interact with himself.

Considering the entire duration of contact Δt a differential formula was obtained for (1), which is the extended formulation over continuous time, in which the increase is a derivative.

$$\frac{d}{dt}C(t) = \sum_{\substack{j=1 \\ j \neq i}}^{m} \left(C_{n-1}^i - C_{n-1}^j\right)_+ K_{ij}\beta_{ij}$$

In each contact case, this expression gives the C^i of element i. Thus, at the time t of contact there will be a certain $C^i(t)$. As this is a linear function of C^i, the solution (derived over time) is an exponential function. In cases of a new interaction with contact, the process must be repeated. Thus, the new C^i at the starting time of t will be precisely the value of C^i obtained at the end of the previous interaction.

Extended over the total time of the simulation, we have $\frac{d}{dt}C(t)$ which depends on the simulation history S, standing for the specific sequence of contact events between agents; in fact, due to interaction, the contamination of each agent depends on the contamination of the others. Therefore, we obtain a differential integral function, in the form of a Volterra integral equation, with the following general expression:

$$t \in [0, T]$$

$$\begin{cases} \frac{d}{dt}C(t) = \dot{C}(t) = \int_0^t f(S, C(S))dS \\ C(0) = C_0 \end{cases}$$

According to such formalization the system updates in real time the level of contamination of the agents in any case of contact. From a modelling point of view such equation represents the behaviour result of each agent in his condition of contaminant.

4   Case Study Simulation

HAI contamination happens in contemporary and real-life contexts, i.e. the progression of contamination spread, and the effectiveness of infection control procedures are strictly related to hospital daily life processes, which are implicitly bounded to architectural design. In the simulation of real ward life, some hospital procedures and daily activities are translated in terms of events as system inputs and the contamination risk map, updated every second, is produced as output. The agents' relation law for contamination overlaps with algorithms that guide agents and coordinate multiple agent behaviours, as well as those that regulate unexpected events, which are drawn from the Event Based framework, established by Shaumann et al. for modelling human use of buildings [19].

The EBMS approach combines aspects of Agent-Based and Process-Based models in a coherent simulation. It considers the users and the processes of use of the built space by modelling events, which take place when different user behaviours occur in the same space. [3] The Event is a computational entity that combines information concerning people (who?), the activity they perform (what?) and the spaces they use (where?). To implement our HAI transmission model, we further developed this method, widening its capabilities to fit it within the specific case study of HAI. We chose Unity 3D because of its dynamic visualization capabilities, so that the HAI spreading process could be effectively computed, simulated and visualized at the same time. The platform allows us to profile individuals and their behaviour, characterise the pathogens and the role of furniture and rooms as vectors The HAI transmission function was coded in C# to simulate the effect of the contamination propagation on spaces and actors, during the interactions among such elements. The virtual simulation allows for a real-time dynamic 2D visualization of the building use process and reveals the contamination propagation, through a contamination risk map. To investigate the simulation capability to depict HAI diffusion, a scenario analysis was established. Different preliminary conditions were set up in the dashboard interface and simulation outputs were analysed. The series of events composing the scenario contribute to the infection spread by means of the contamination mechanism that we coded. However, the role of chance in the system exists, both through the occasional opportunities for interactions among actors and the random entrance of visitors.

We chose as a simulation setting the Sammy Ofer Heart Building, Sourasky Tel-Aviv Medical Center, designed by Sharon Architects & Ranni Ziss Architects 2005–2011. This choice is useful because the Cardiology Unit involves multiple categories of users and shows emergent phenomena and behaviour influenced by the organization of spaces and the presence of other people. We collaborated with the internal healthcare staff and management, so that the case study was built with information gathered from real-life observations and on real work procedures and activities carried out within hospital wards. It contemplates several component Actors, Activities, Pathogens and Spaces. Their interaction during the simulation drives the contamination transmission and pathogen propagation.

In our case study, three types of actor populate the virtual setting: HCWs, patients and visitors. They may carry pathogens on their skin, dress and equipment. Their level of contamination is visualized by a range of colours (see Fig. 3).

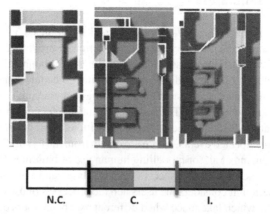

Fig. 3. Actors contamination range of colours. (Color figure online)

- White = Un-colonized status;
- Green and yellow (two sequential levels) = Colonized status;
- Red = Infected.

Initial levels of the contamination status can be set at the start of the simulation for each actor or it can be randomly generated. Two thresholds can be set for each actor. The first accounts for the presence of a minimum level of pathogen, indicating the limit between non-carrier or carrier condition. Where non-colonized actors are non-carrier and colonized or infected are carrier. Carrier actors can contaminate other actors (or spaces) with a lower level of contamination. Each actor is unaware of the actual contamination level of others (or of spaces). The second accounts for the infection limit, indicating the passage between carrier and infected status. Indeed, health care settings are an environment where both infected people and people at increased risk of infection congregate. Patients are constantly exposed to a variety of microorganisms during hospitalization and contact between the patient and a microorganism does not by itself necessarily result in the development of clinical disease. The infection arises from the combination of the Minimal Infective Dose for that kind of pathogen and of the Susceptibility Factor of each actor. Through the designed thresholds we can show the lower or higher risk of HAIs for certain actors, e.g. accounting for the possibility that some of the patients could be more susceptible than others.

Space consists in a layout in which actors can move and perform a set of activities. It reflects a synthesized, slightly modified prototypical Ichilov ward (see Fig. 4).

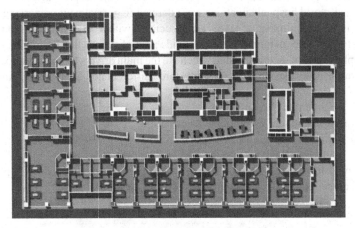

Fig. 4. The synthesized hospital ward plan.

The virtual setting comprises 2 single, 14 doubles and one five-patient room, housing in total 35 patients. The different rooms are connected by a corridor in which the HCWs station is located, adjacent to a central medicine room. To investigate the impact of shared and single rooms, in a scenario dominated by double rooms, two single rooms and a big multi-bed room are introduced. The first two play the role of potential isolation rooms and the latter are designed as an acute treatment room which can be easily found in internal medicine department. Furniture and equipment needed for patient care and treatment procedures are integral part of each space representation. Even if not shown through evident simulated activities, we assume that actors operate in rooms, e.g. patients interacting with objects and furniture, so that the contamination level of the room (space and objects) is affected by their presence and vice versa. Spaces may become vectors through contaminated surfaces, furniture and objects. Hence space shows in real time its contamination level, which is visualized a range of colours (see Fig. 5).

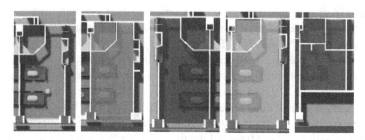

Fig. 5. The range colours for contaminated space. (Color figure online)

In our case study, we assume that neither objects nor spaces are the primary source of contamination but only carriers. Yet, their starting level of the contamination can be set in advance or randomly generated.

To reliably represent the building use processes within the hospital, activities patterns reflecting real-world hospital situations were defined (e.g. treatment processing, nurses and physicians' commitments). Actors are associated with a set of activities to perform in relation to their role. In turn, activities provide a set of actions that drive actors toward the accomplishment of their goals, and which are the main drivers for the infection spread towards actors and spaces. In our case study, three different activity types are simulated:

- Invasive Treatment = Patient Check;
- Non-Invasive Treatment = Medicine Distribution;
- Meeting visitors.

Each one is linked with a certain risk factor Ty. For each type of activity, a plausible length and contact duration were considered (see Fig. 6).

Activity_danger	0,5
Touch_duration	5

Fig. 6. Activity contamination console.

The simulated scenario reveals the propagation dynamic for a chosen type of pathogens. For each simulation run, users may define new features for the pathogens which are essential for the investigation. At the beginning of the simulation two different value of the "Tr" transmissibility coefficient are set. In fact, transmission capabilities of certain pathogens can be different depending on whether transmission occurs between actors or to and from space (surfaces and furniture).

As this is a simulation which condenses hours into a few minutes, the duration of the activities and the contamination map develops at the same rate. Because of this, when an actor reaches the infection level it does not imply that he will suddenly manifest sickness but rather that he is sufficient contaminated to likely develop the disease in the following days. Coherently, the scope of the present study is more to visualize the propagation of pathogens on surfaces and actors without considering their effect on the health, e.g. development of diseases.

5   Scenario Analysis

The case study is represented by a critical scenario with 4 HCWs, 35 patients and 9 visitors, where HCWs act as pathogen spreaders and some highly susceptible patients are inserted (see Fig. 7). At the start, input parameters in the user interface were tested with multiple set-ups to investigate the propagation of pathogens connected with activities with different danger levels, the impact of prevention procedures and the effect of changing the pathogen type. In the following, a significant case of Methicillin-Resistant Staphylococcus Aureus propagation, with baseline patient hygiene, invasive treatments and no ward cleaning, is described. This simulated scenario displays a building use situation where HCWs start from their staff station before moving to the central medicine room to prepare medicines. Afterwards, they move through the patients' rooms to distribute medicines.

In the scenario, three out of four nurses start as carriers and can spread the contamination. Hand hygiene measure was also considered to gain qualitative insights into its relative effect. In the scenario only one HCW strictly adheres to hand hygiene protocol. The simulation shows HCWs starting their respective treatment rounds in three different cohorts. Carrier HCWs 2, 3, 4 contaminate patients with whom they interact one by one. Subsequently, rooms become contaminated due to the presence of contaminated patients. HCW 4 interacts with a highly susceptible patient, further raising his contamination level. The room contaminated by HCW 3 impacts the patients present with the major effect of being a multiple occupancy room. At the same time, the presence of numerous actors in the same room increases the contamination level of the space much faster compared to a double room. Meanwhile, HCW 2 affects patients only marginally and without a considerable effect on susceptible patients. Nor does this affect the space contamination level.

Thanks to the simulation's level of detail and real-time visualisation, it is possible to track the colonized actors directly linked to each HCW. The simulation demonstrates the detrimental effect of the rogue HCWs, 3 and 4, who adhere to Hand Hygiene less than the rest of the medical staff, as well as the remarkable incidence of a compliant HCW 2 who follows prevention protocols. Furthermore, the scenario experimentation proves the valuable role played when cohorting is adopted. If acceptable HCW-to-patient ratios are maintained and if HCWs respect prevention guidelines, they may transmit the pathogen only to the patients assigned to them, unless there are interruptions, e.g. visitors asking for information. It is evident that transmission take place across the cohort,

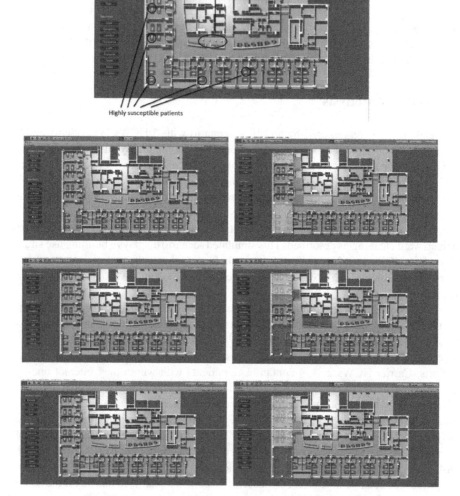

Fig. 7. Contamination risk map without and with spatial layer.

especially when the susceptible patients are mixed with the normal patient population, allowing asymptomatic carriers to remain hidden. This condition is more likely to occur if too many patients share the same HCW, as in cases where the ward is understaffed. Therefore, in dangerous situations, minimizing the size of patient cohorts could be appropriate. The scenario experimentation provides results that are consistent with literature by demonstrating varying degrees of impact within the range of prevention strategies.

6 Conclusions

The study presents an Agent-Based Model and Simulation of HAI transmission by a contact route through exogenous cross-infection and its propagation dynamics in a hospital ward. It is founded on the Event-Based approach by Shaumann et al. which is modelling technique of human building use where spaces, actors and activities are encoded in a computational environment, so that agents' movement and spatial behaviour can be simulated. The nature of the HAI problem domain required to develop the potential of the chosen approach further. The EBMS was extended to consider the HAI phenomenon, i.e. contamination propagation on agents (actors and spaces). Thus, the contamination capacity of each agent, is the element on which pathogen dissemination depends and the formalized transmission relational law between agents drives the propagation dynamic.

To illustrate the potential of the developed ABM, it was tested in a Unity 3D environment by means of trial case study. In the virtual simulation of a hospital ward, the use of space correlates with the contamination propagation through a contact route. In the case study, some hospital procedures and daily activities are coded in terms of events such as system inputs while the contamination risk map is the dynamic output. To demonstrate potential applications of the simulation a case-based scenario was tested, and outputs analysed. The presented scenario was used to illuminate criticalities which, while unlikely, have so dangerous repercussions that the event is much more important than its low probability alone would suggest. In addition to the capacity of the simulation to reveal all kinds of situations occurring in space, i.e. agent-agent and agent-environment interaction, as well as interference and unplanned events, it allows for the real-time visualization of contamination transmission. Although real, this is a threat that is hidden from cognitive agents within the hospital up until its late appearance with symptoms.

The simulation of contact-mediated pathogen contamination permits qualitative estimation of multiple factor impacts: human states, traits, behaviour and activities, patient numbers and distribution, staffing conditions, ward spatial organization, pathogen colonization capacity, frequency of interactions and more. Thus, it visualizes the chain of infection which represents the dynamics of pathogen circulation, while suggesting where it may be more feasible and convenient to operate in order to break the chain. It reveals clusters of infected patients and patterns of spatial occurrence, demonstrating how transmission dynamics change depending on initial causes and conditions and because of spatially related features. Of further interest is the potential to assess the relative merits of different HAI control strategies and procedures, e.g. agent hygiene behaviour and contact precautions. Moreover, it gives us hints on how the spatial design of buildings can affect the risk of HAI. A key potential advantage is to prove that if the human organization does not work, a different design could help. Consequently, the presented approach could help to address the design of future hospital environments and the restructuring of existing ones. The scenario-building mechanism is designed to improve decision-making by providing a consideration of scenario outcomes and their implications. The presented ABM functions as a Decision Support System (DSS), providing evidence in support of underlying decision-making processes, which is the fundamental meaning of hospital management.

The ABM, together with the EBMS technique built in a simulator currently under development, will complement design systems for buildings and should eventually lead to the design of hospitals that are less prone to the outbreak of infections.

Acknowledgments. We wish to thank prof. Jacob Yahav, prof. Francesco Maddalena and prof. Dino Borri for their methodological assistance, as well as the following research group members for their useful comments and insights: K. Date, E. Eizenberg, M. Gath Morad, L. Morhayim, N. Pilosof and E. Zinger.

Author Contributions. Conceptualization, investigation, methodology, formalization and writing D.E.; software D.E. and D.S.; review and editing D.E., D.S. and D.C.; supervision and project administration D.C. and Y.K. All authors have read and agreed to the published version of the manuscript.

References

1. World Health Organization: (WHO) Prevention of hospital-acquired infections (2002)
2. World Health Organisation: (WHO) Practical Guidelines for Infection Control in Health Care Facilities (2004)
3. Schaumann, D., Kalay, Y.E., Hong, S.W., Simeone, D.: Simulating human behavior in not-yet built environments by means of event-based narratives, pp. 1047–1054 (2015)
4. Fatah, C.: Sensitivity analysis for simulation-based decision making: application to a hospital emergency service design. Simul. Model. Pract. Theory **20**, 99–111 (2012)
5. Hutzschenreuter, A.K., Bosman, P.A.N., Blonk-Altena, I., van Aarle, J., La Poutré, H.: Agent-based patient admission scheduling in hospitals (2008)
6. Jones, S.S., Evans, R.S.: An agent based simulation tool for scheduling emergency department physicians. In: AMIA Symposium Proceedings, pp. 338–342 (2008)
7. Cabrera, E., Taboada, M., Iglesias, M.L., Epelde, F., Luque, E.: Optimization of healthcare emergency departments by agent-based simulation. Procedia Comput. Sci. **4**, 1880–1889 (2011)
8. Mielczarek, B., Uziałko-Mydlikowska, J.: Application of computer simulation modeling in the health care sector: a survey. Simulation **88**, 197–216 (2012)
9. Friesen, M.R., McLeod, R.D.: A survey of agent-based modeling of hospital environmentss. IEEE Access **2**, 227–233 (2014)
10. Meng, Y., Davies, R., Hardy, K., Hawkey, P.: An application of agent-based simulation to the management of hospital-acquired infection. J. Simul. **4**, 60–67 (2010)
11. Barnes, S., Golden, B., Wasil, E., Smith, R.H.: MRSA transmission reduction using agent-based modeling and simulation. INFORMS J. Comput. **22**, 635–646 (2010)
12. Temime, L., Kardas-Sloma, L., Opatowski, L., Brun-Buisson, C., Boëllef, P.Y., Guillemot, D.: NosoSim: an agent-based model of nosocomial pathogens circulation in hospitals. Procedia Comput. Sci. **1**, 2245–2252 (2010)
13. Codella, J., Safdar, N., Heffernan, R., Alagoz, O.: An agent-based simulation model for clostridium difficile infection control. Med. Decis. Mak. **35**, 211–229 (2015)
14. Pethes, R., Ferenci, T., Kovacs, L.: Infectious hospital agents: an individual-based simulation framework. In: 2016 IEEE International Conference on Systems, Man, and Cybernetics, SMC 2016, pp. 3434–3439 (2017)
15. Weaver, W.: Science and complexity. Am. Sci. **36**, 536–544 (1948)
16. Schaumann, D., Date, K., Kalay, Y.E., Israel, T.: An Event Modeling Language (EML) to simulate use patterns in built environments (2017)

17. World Health Organisation: WHO Guidelines on Hand Hygiene in Health Care: First Global Patient Safety Challenge Clean Care Is Safer Care. World Health. 30, 270 (2009)
18. Boyce, J.M., Pittet, D.: Morbidity and mortality weekly report: report guideline for hand hygiene in health-care settings recommendations of the healthcare infection control practices centers for disease control and prevention TM. Centers Dis. Control Prev. **51**, 1–45 (2002)
19. Schaumann, D., et al.: A computational framework to simulate human spatial behavior in built environments. In: Proceeding of the Symposium on Simulation for Architecture and Urban Design, pp. 121–128 (2016)

Unsupervised Sleep Stages Classification Based on Physiological Signals

Rahma Ferjani$^{(\boxtimes)}$, Lilia Rejeb , and Lamjed Ben Said

ISGT, SMART Lab, Université de Tunis, 2000 Le Bardo, Tunisia
ferjanirahma@yahoo.com, {lilia.rejeb,lamjed.bensaid}@isg.rnu.tn

Abstract. Automatic sleep scoring has, recently, captured the attention of authors due to its importance in sleep abnormalities detection and treatments. The majority of the proposed works are based on supervised learning and considered mostly a single physiological signal as input. To avoid the exhausting pre-labeling task and to enhance the precision of the sleep staging process, we propose an unsupervised classification model for sleep stages identification based on a flexible architecture to handle different physiological signals. The efficiency of our approach was investigated using real data. Promising results were reached according to a comparative study carried out with the often used classification models.

Keywords: Sleep scoring · Reinforcement Learning · Cooperative agents · Learning Classifier Systems

1 Introduction

Sleep analysis has monopolized the interest of different areas of research in the last decades [3, 25, 38] due to the importance of healthy sleep in establishing a fit life routine. Sleep disposes of several serious abnormalities that threat the individual's life such as sleep apnea, insomnias, hyper-somnias, sleep-related breathing disorders, etc. Thus, sleep analysis is primordial in several diseases' diagnosis and treatments. A mandatory step in sleep analysis is sleep scoring that aims to identify the different stages of a human sleep according to different standards. Most researches assumed that the Rechtschaffen & Kales (R&K) rules are considered as an efficient and most used standard for sleep scoring, thus we identify six sleep stages: Awake stage (W), Non Rapid Eye-Movement (NREM1, NREM2, NREM3, NREM4: from light to deep sleep) and Rapid Eye-Movement (REM) sleep stage [27]. The scoring process is based on polysomnographic recordings (PSG) extracted from a human subject during sleep. The most used physiological signals are Electroencephalogram (EEG), Electromyogram (EMG), Electrooculogram (EOG), Electrocardiogram (ECG), and other indicators such as blood pressure and body temperature. The recordings are traditionally divided into segments of 30-s each, called epochs [22] that are observed and staged manually by a clinician. However, experts need to observe at least the recording 8-h of

© Springer Nature Switzerland AG 2020
Y. Demazeau et al. (Eds.): PAAMS 2020, LNAI 12092, pp. 134–145, 2020.
https://doi.org/10.1007/978-3-030-49778-1_11

continuous sleep and identify over 950 epochs. The process is time-consuming, complex and subjective since it is highly dependent of the expert's preferences. Therefore, many works tried to propose approaches that automatically score sleep based on different standards, criteria and machine learning techniques. However, most of the proposed works are highly dependent on a pre-labeled data thus they are based on supervised learning, deliver implicit models and based on mono physiological signal channel. In this paper, we present a new classification method for automatic sleep stages classification: first, we consider multi physiological signals as inputs; second, our approach is based on a fully unsupervised learning; finally, the proposed approach is able to deliver explicable results that could be evaluated by field experts.

2   Related Work

During the last decade, authors proposed several works to score human sleep automatically based on different machine learning techniques. Among the most used techniques, we distinguish the Artificial Neural Networks (ANNs) where some works [20,30] scored sleep to three main stages: Drowsy, REM sleep and Awake and succeed to reach high rates of successful classification within the 90%. Other works considered five sleep stages: Awake, REM, NREM1, NREM2 and sleep waves sleep (SWS) [6,13,15]. All the previous detailed works were based on a mono EEG recording channel and different ANNs. In order to ameliorate the accuracy rate, other works [2,6,24,32] switched to multiple recording channels where other signals rather than EEG signals were used. The work of Ozsen et al. [24] was based an ANN architecture composed of five multilayer perceptrons ANNs to stage sleep into five stages. They considered three recording channels belonging, respectively, to EMG, EOG, ECG signals. The obtained rate of successful classification was estimated to be 90.93%. Akin et al. [2] had considered EEG and EMG signals and a regression ANN model to reach a 99% of accuracy. In [32], the authors used EEG, EMG and EOG signals to perform their feed-forward ANN and attained 74.7% as an accuracy rate. Artificial Neural Networks were widely used to score sleep and depicted high rated of successful classification but they remain unable to build explicit classification models that deliver explicable results. Consequently, the obtained results could not be evaluated and approved a posteriori by field's experts. Therefore, Chapotot et al. [11] combined an artificial neural network architecture and flexible decision rules to score EEG recordings. In [37], Yildiz et al. presented an Adaptive Neuro Fuzzy Inference System (ANFIS) that succeed to deliver an explicit classification model obtaining an accuracy rate of 98.34%. Koley et al. [19] also proposed a hybrid approach for sleep stages classification by combining Support Vector Machine (SVM) and the One Against All (OAA) and achieved 85% of agreement. To deliver an explicit model, Youssef et al. [17] combined a Multi-agent System (MAS) and two different Learning Classifier Systems (LCS): eXtended Classifier System(XCS) and sUpervised Classifier System (UCS). The model delivered a set of rules reaching 98% of successful classification.

The majority of the existing approaches are supervised methods that depend, highly, on pre-labeled data which considered as an exhausting task. Thus, few works [14,28] proposed unsupervised approaches to assist the work of experts. Ouanes et al. [23] proposed an unsupervised classification model by combining LCSs and ANN to identify sleep stages. The classification was based on unlabeled EEG recordings and the model reached 78.7% of classification agreement. Boostani et al. [9] affirmed that even with the changes of the new sleep manual AASM the identification of some sleep stages requires extra information in addition to EEG. In fact, for the awake sleep stage labeling a high EMG tone and frequent eye movement are present. However, in REM stage lowest muscle movement and rapid eye movement are observed. Zoubek et al. [39] used several classification models trained first by features extracted from only EEG signals to obtain 71% of agreement, then, they added features extracted from EMG and EOG signals to attend about 80% of agreement.

Although the different proposed works for sleep stages classification, there is no consensus on a specific framework for sleep scoring that can handle multiple recording channels, deliver explicable results and generate a relative rules' background. Indeed, the number of the used PSG recordings is very limited, restricted mainly to EEG, EOG and EMG, and most of the works were based only on a single recording channel of EEG [29]. However, the using of multi-signals and multi-derivation of EEG signal led to a better accuracy as shown in [2,11,26]. Generally, the proposed approaches are unable to give results that could be interpreted a posteriori by experts [2,34,37].

Taking advantage of the distributed nature of multi-agent systems and specifically the cooperative MAS that ensures an interactive learning among the different existing agents, we propose a Cooperative Reinforcement Multi-Agent Learning (CRMAL) system for sleep stages classification based on unlabeled data. Multi-agent learning and Reinforcement Learning (RL) have shown their efficiency in solving several real world problems [1,12] where the agent learns interactively how to solve complex problems referring to the environment sensors and feedback. Among the RL techniques, we distinguish the Learning Classifier Systems (LCS) that were successfully applied in different fields thanks to their capability of building explicit models by generating, automatically, their rules set [33]. Therefore, we are interested in LCS to build our adaptive agents.

3   Materials

3.1   DataSet Description

The data set used for sleep analysis is provided by the physio-bank site which contains an important number of databases considered as references for researches working in the medical area [16,23,38]. The sleep data set is formed of 61 polysomnograms (PSGs), each one is accompanied with its annotations file which contains the labels assigned by experts for each epoch. The PSG files contain EEG including Fpz_{Cz} and Pz_{Oz} electrodes location, submental chin EMG and EOG signal records for a whole night for a given subject. They are used to score sleep visually based on Rechtschaffen and Kales rules. Almost 20-h recordings were divided into 30-s epochs. In order to increase the accuracy rate, we created a balanced learning set which contains 1901 epochs for each sleep stage obtained from 20 healthy subjects (10 males and 10 females). The demographic range was between 25 and 34. The physiological signals are stored in a file with a special format which is EDF (European Data Format). This extension represents advantages for researches since it becomes an easy way to store multichannel biological and physical signals.

3.2 Pre-processing and Feature Extraction

Sleep scoring is given by three main steps: Data pre-processing, feature extraction and classification. In this section, we detail the two prior steps of sleep scoring and the used techniques. Since the physiological data may contain artifacts occurred from the body movements and eyelids during sleep, a pre-processing phase is required to obtain only useful data. For that, we used the Blind Source Separation (BSS) technique usually used on signals [10,16] to separate the data spatial components in addition to the SOBI algorithm to seek the pertinent spatial components [18] as indicated in Fig. 1.

The second phase is the feature extraction that allows the extraction of the pertinent classification inputs. To do so, we used the discrete wavelet transform (DWT) extraction technique since it assumes the signal to be non stationary and considers the time variations as the frequency ones. According the to literature, some measures are the most pertinent thus we computed some statical parameters for each used signal.

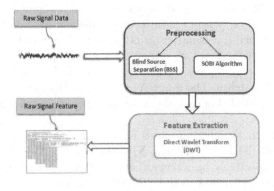

Fig. 1. Preprocessing and Feature Extraction.

4 Learning Classifier Systems

Learning Classifier Systems (LCS) are rule-based systems that combine evolutionary computation with artificial intelligence [33]. Their generalization property and the evolutionary process make them able to efficiently overcome the brittleness of classic expert systems by allowing an automatic building of a rule set. LCS are reinforcement technique that were successfully applied in classification problems, sequential decision problem resolution, knowledge discovery problem and autonomous robotics. Bacardit et al. used LCS to predict protein structure in both [4] and [31]. Llora et al. in [21] were based on LCS to diagnose prostate cancer by classifying Infrared Spectroscopic Image Data.

Knowledge in LCS is represented through a population classifiers. Each classifier is given by three main parameters: condition, action, and a reward. LCS have three types namely: Strength-based systems: **Zeroth Level Classifier System** (ZCS), Anticipation-based systems: **Anticipatory Learning Classifier System** (ALCS) and Accuracy-based systems: **eXtend Classifier Systems** (XCS). We are mainly interested in the XCS since they are the most adequate LCS to real world complex problems.

4.1 eXtended Classifier Systems

The eXtended Classifier System XCS proposed by (Wilson 1995) is a reinforcement learning technique suitable for real world complex problems [35]. XCS uses standard classifier condition-action rules where a condition is presented by a set of binary values. However, Wilson proposed an extension of XCS to surpass this limit [36]. The so-called XCSR deals with numeric inputs which is more appropriate to real world problems. Thus, Each classifier is a condition-action rule given as follows:

- The condition: Is a concatenation of intervals where each interval refers to a specific attribute of the epoch instance i. The interval is represented as follows: $[c_i - s_i, c_i + s_i]$ where c is the center value and s is the spread. For each new epoch instance i, a comparison is made to decide either the classifier's condition matches the input X_i or not. An input X_i is represented by a set of values $x_1...x_n$. If each value x_i verifies the condition: $((c_i - s_i) \leq x_i \leq (c_i + s_i))$ then the input matches. The input X_i consists of the current epoch features extracted using DWT. For each signal agent, an epoch is given by 79 extracted features.
- The action: Each classifier proposes an action that refers to a sleep stage (Wake, NREM1, NREM2, NREM3, NREM4, and REM) and these stages are represented respectively by integers between 0 and 5. For example: 0 refers to the Wake stage, 1 refers to the NREM1 stage, etc.

At the presence of a new input, XCSR builds a matching set $[M]$ of classifiers having the same condition of the input. In the case where the number of xrules in $[M]$ is lesser than the given threshold, the covering operation is performed to generate new classifiers. A prediction value is calculated for each action in $[M]$ among all the classifiers proposing that action in the action set $[A]$. To finally choose an action, two methods are proposed: Exploration (choosing randomly an action among the possible actions) or Exploitation (nominating the action having the highest prediction value). A reward r is returned as a consequence of the made decision to update the parameters of $[A]$. In order to illustrate the functioning of XCS, we propose the scheme in Fig. 2. Each classifier is given by a set of fundamental parameters: prediction reward, prediction error and fitness. The parameters are automatically updated depending on the reward. The latter is given with reference to the proposed action by two possible values: Max payoff (if the proposed action corresponds to the right action) and Min payoff (if the proposed action is wrong).

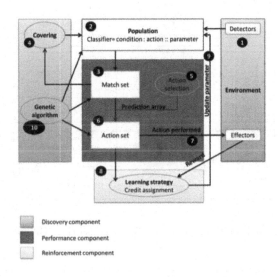

Fig. 2. eXtended Classifier System Architecture [33].

After a number of predefined iterations, the Genetic Algorithm (GA) is performed to update the action sets, to generate new rules for the population and take off useless classifiers if the population is full [7].

5   Proposed Solution

With the objective of establishing an unsupervised sleep classification system based on different physiological signals having heterogeneous natures, our system disposes of two types of agents: Adaptive agents and a supervisor agent. Figure 3 presents the global architecture of the proposed system for a specific epoch's instance i. Each adaptive agent is responsible of a specific physiological signal encapsulating each a XCS classifier. Hence, adaptive agents are given by two main components: Decision making component and Evaluation component. Figure 4 depicts the architecture of an adaptive agent. For each new epoch instance i, each adaptive agent performs its decision process component, given by steps from 1 to 6, to propose the adequate sleep stage. The decision making policy balanced between the total exploration and the exploitation operations. Once each adaptive agent j decide on the common entry instance i, it sends the proposed action W_{ij} to the supervisor agent as cleared in step 7. The latter is responsible of managing the interactive learning of the adaptive agents. The supervisor agent ensures the parallel learning of the existing agents for each instance and handles the reception of all their proposed actions to decide on the wining action WA_i for epoch instance i.

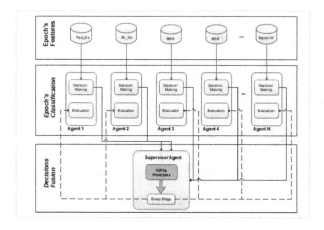

Fig. 3. Unsupervised multi-agent system for sleep scoring: Global Architecture.

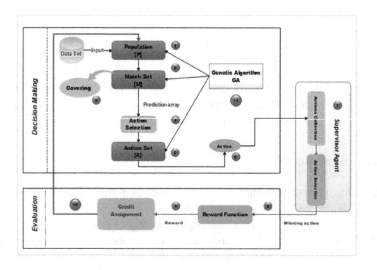

Fig. 4. Architecture of XCS Agent.

Each adaptive agent receives the wining action for the current epoch from the supervisor agent and then performs its evaluation component according to its reward r. Usually, in XCS functioning the reward is given with reference to the proposed action by two possible values: Max_{reward} (if the proposed action corresponds to the right action) and Min_{reward} (if the proposed action is wrong). Instead of assigning either one of two standard rewards, we propose an adaptive reward function:

$$r \leftarrow Max_{reward} - \alpha * |WA_i - A_{ij}|$$

where $(Min_{reward} \leq \alpha \leq Max\_reward)$ is the learning rate. Each adaptive agent will be evaluated accordingly to how much its proposed action is close to the wining one. Once the reward is assigned, step nine is performed to adjust the learning parameters of the signal agent j at epoch i [36]: the prediction P_i, the prediction error ϵ_i, the classifier accuracy K_i and the fitness F_i.

6   Experiments and Results

In order to evaluate the obtained results, we used the Percentage of Correct Classification (PCC) and the confusion matrix. The performance of XCS depends on the setting of some parameters [33]. After some preliminary tests, we found that the following parameters are discriminant in our work:

- Population size $= 6400$,
- The exploration/exploitation rate $= 0.5$,
- Number of iterations 100,000,
- Mutation probability $\mu = 0.06$,
- Genetic Algorithm $\theta_{Genetic} = 50$.

In the aim of evaluating the performance of our distributed approach, we implemented, based on the same real data, a single-agent classification model. The latter is composed of one XCS classifier having, like input, an epoch stream. Each stream is composed of N labeled epochs that refer to N physiological signal sharing the same instance number. The one-agent classification model showed a percentage of correct classification of 63%. Table 1 depicts a comparison between the two approaches by presenting the PCC of each sleep stage.

The PCC provided by the proposed MAS for Awake and NREM2 stages are higher than those delivered by the single agent classification model which can be clarified by Table 2 and Table 3. These tables show, respectively, the confusion matrices obtained from a single agent classification and the results reached using our proposed approach. As can be seen in Table 3 among 1901 epochs of NREM1, 398 epochs are classified as REM while only 159 epochs of NREM1 are classified as REM using the adaptive MAS. Thus, we notice that our approach is efficient to minimize the classification's conflict usually obtained when classifying epochs as NREM1 or REM stages. Indeed, it is always difficult to distinguish between NREM3 and NREM4 [8] as shown in Table 2. However, our method succeed

Table 1. Comparison of the PCC of each sleep stage between MAS and single-agent.

	MAS	Single agent
Awake	91	78.95
NREM1	78.49	68.83
NREM2	78.96	57.68
NREM3	72.65	27.84
NREM4	77.8	32.87
REM	74.75	77.01

to, correctly, classify 1381 epochs among 1901 NREM3 epochs as NREM3 and 1479 epoch among 1901 NREM4 epoch as NREM4 which increases the scoring precision and avoid the side effects of dangerous classification on sleep analysis. One of the main causes of the classification success is the cooperation of different physiological signals especially the EOG signal that helps to avoid the confusion between the Awake and NREM2 stages. Among the works that used the Sleep-EDF database for classification, we note the work of Bajaj et al. [5]. They used the existing PSG signals but based on labeled epochs and reached 92.93% as accuracy rate which reflects the influence and importance of the use of multiple PSG signals. Indeed, our approach, based on the same data, used unlabeled epochs and reached an accuracy rate of 96% which reflects the advantage of using less prelabeled data.

Table 2. Confusion Matrix for single XCS.

Real class	Estimated class					
	Awake	NREM1	NREM2	NREM3	NREM4	REM
Awake	1501	359	9	12	9	11
NREM1	51	1300	115	33	4	398
NREM2	7	370	1100	354	9	61
NREM3	34	16	103	523	1219	6
NREM4	19	2	5	1250	625	0
REM	8	353	64	9	3	1464

In order to evaluate the performance of using unlabeled data, we established a comparison with the work of Ouanes and Rejeb [23]. The comparison was established based on two major criteria. First, the so-called XCSR-based SOM used an eXtended classifier system to train its classifiers. Second, they proposed an unsupervised approach based on EEG signals extracted from the same data set. They used only the fronto-central Fpz_{Cz} channel of EEG. The data set was based on an unlabeled balanced data set composed of 9000 epochs includes 1500 epochs of each sleep stage. They reached an over all accuracy of 78.7%. As can be seen, the using of a set of different PSG signals as well as the interaction among them have enhanced the performance of the sleep stages classification.

Table 3. Confusion Matrix for the proposed Multi-agent System.

Real class	Estimated class					
	Awake	NREM1	NREM2	NREM3	NREM4	REM
Awake	1730	109	12	20	18	12
NREM1	45	1492	144	47	14	159
NREM2	8	154	1501	168	13	57
NREM3	35	23	113	1381	339	10
NREM4	19	5	8	389	1479	1
REM	14	322	125	10	9	1421

7   Conclusion

We have presented a cooperative reinforcement multi-agent learning for sleep stages classification based on unlabeled data. The effectiveness of the proposed approach was tested on real physiological signals. We reached a classification accuracy of 96%. The multi-agent classification system proved its performance in delivering explicit results that could be evaluated a posteriori by field's experts. Indeed, the proposed system provided a flexible architecture that can handle a very large number of learning agents based on different kinds of learning techniques.

References

1. Abbeel, P., Coates, A., Quigley, M., Ng, A.Y.: An application of reinforcement learning to aerobatic helicopter flight. In: Advances in Neural Information Processing Systems, pp. 1–8 (2007)
2. Akin, M., Kurt, M.B., Sezgin, N., Bayram, M.: Estimating vigilance level by using EEG and EMG signals. Neural Comput. Appl. **17**(3), 227–236 (2008)
3. Alickovic, E., Subasi, A.: Ensemble SVM method for automatic sleep stage classification. IEEE Trans. Instrum. Measur. **67**(6), 1258–1265 (2018)
4. Bacardit, J., Stout, M., Hirst, J.D., Sastry, K., Llorà, X., Krasnogor, N.: Automated alphabet reduction method with evolutionary algorithms for protein structure prediction. In: Proceedings of the 9th Annual Conference on Genetic and Evolutionary Computation, pp. 346–353. ACM (2007)
5. Bajaj, V., Pachori, R.B.: Automatic classification of sleep stages based on the time-frequency image of EEG signals. Comput. Methods Programs Biomed. **112**(3), 320–328 (2013)

6. Becq, G., Charbonnier, S., Chapotot, F., Buguet, A., Bourdon, L., Baconnier, P.: Comparison between five classifiers for automatic scoring of human sleep recordings. In: Halgamuge, K.S., Wang, L. (eds.) Classification and Clustering for Knowledge Discovery. Studies in Computational Intelligence, vol. 4, pp. 113–127. Springer, Heidelberg (2005). https://doi.org/10.1007/11011620_8

7. Bernadó-Mansilla, E., Garrell-Guiu, J.M.: Accuracy-based learning classifier systems: models, analysis and applications to classification tasks. Evol. Comput. **11**(3), 209–238 (2003)

8. Berry, R.B., Brooks, R., Gamaldo, C.E., Harding, S.M., Marcus, C., Vaughn, B.: The AASM manual for the scoring of sleep and associated events. Rules, Terminology and Technical Specifications, Darien, Illinois, American Academy of Sleep Medicine (2012)

9. Boostani, R., Karimzadeh, F., Nami, M.: A comparative review on sleep stage classification methods in patients and healthy individuals. Comput. Methods Programs Biomed. **140**, 77–91 (2017)

10. Cardoso, J.F.: Blind signal separation: statistical principles. Proc. IEEE **86**(10), 2009–2025 (1998)

11. Chapotot, F., Becq, G.: Automated sleep-wake staging combining robust feature extraction, artificial neural network classification, and flexible decision rules. Int. J. Adapt. Control Sig. Process. **24**(5), 409–423 (2010)

12. Claus, C., Boutilier, C.: The dynamics of reinforcement learning in cooperative multiagent systems. In: AAAI/IAAI 1998, pp. 746–752 (1998)

13. Ebrahimi, F., Mikaeili, M., Estrada, E., Nazeran, H.: Automatic sleep stage classification based on EEG signals by using neural networks and wavelet packet coefficients. In: 2008 Engineering in Medicine and Biology Society, EMBS 2008. 30th Annual International Conference of the IEEE, pp. 1151–1154. IEEE (2008)

14. Grube, G., Flexer, A., Dorffner, G.: Unsupervised continuous sleep analysis. Methods Find Exp. Clin. Pharmacol **24**(Suppl. D), 51–56 (2002)

15. Hsu, Y.L., Yang, Y.T., Wang, J.S., Hsu, C.Y.: Automatic sleep stage recurrent neural classifier using energy features of EEG signals. Neurocomputing **104**, 105–114 (2013)

16. Kemp, B., Zwinderman, A.H., Tuk, B., Kamphuisen, H.A., Oberye, J.J.: Analysis of a sleep-dependent neuronal feedback loop: the slow-wave microcontinuity of the EEG. IEEE Trans. Biomed. Eng. **47**(9), 1185–1194 (2000)

17. Khaoula, Y., Lilia, R.: Système multiagents pour la classification des stades de sommeil basé sur les signaux physiologiques (2012)

18. Klemm, M., Haueisen, J., Ivanova, G.: Independent component analysis: comparison of algorithms for the investigation of surface electrical brain activity. Med. Biol. Eng. Comput. **47**(4), 413–423 (2009)

19. Koley, B., Dey, D.: An ensemble system for automatic sleep stage classification using single channel EEG signal. Comput. Biol. Med. **42**(12), 1186–1195 (2012)

20. Kurt, M.B., Sezgin, N., Akin, M., Kirbas, G., Bayram, M.: The ANN-based computing of drowsy level. Expert Syst. Appl. **36**(2), 2534–2542 (2009)

21. Llorà, X., Reddy, R., Matesic, B., Bhargava, R.: Towards better than human capability in diagnosing prostate cancer using infrared spectroscopic imaging. In: Proceedings of the 9th Annual Conference on Genetic and Evolutionary Computation, pp. 2098–2105. ACM (2007)

22. Loomis, A.L., Harvey, E.N., Hobart III, G.A.: Distribution of disturbance-patterns in the human electroencephalogram, with special reference to sleep. J. Neurophysiol. **1**(5), 413–430 (1938)

23. Ouanes, A., Rejeb, L.: A hybrid approach for sleep stages classification. In: Proceedings of the 2016 on Genetic and Evolutionary Computation Conference, pp. 493–500. ACM (2016)

24. Özşen, S.: Classification of sleep stages using class-dependent sequential feature selection and artificial neural network. Neural Comput. Appl. **23**(5), 1239–1250 (2013)

25. Phan, H., Andreotti, F., Cooray, N., Chén, O.Y., De Vos, M.: Joint classification and prediction CNN framework for automatic sleep stage classification. IEEE Trans. Biomed. Eng. **6**, 1285–1296 (2018)

26. Piñero, P., Garcia, P., Arco, L., Álvarez, A., Garcıa, M.M., Bonal, R.: Sleep stage classification using fuzzy sets and machine learning techniques. Neurocomputing **58**, 1137–1143 (2004)

27. Quan, S., Gillin, J.C., Littner, M., Shepard, J.: Sleep-related breathing disorders in adults: recommendations for syndrome definition and measurement techniques in clinical research. Editorials. Sleep **22**(5), 662–689 (1999)

28. Rodríguez-Sotelo, J., Osorio-Forero, A., Jiménez-Rodríguez, A., Cuesta-Frau, D., Cirugeda-Roldán, E., Peluffo, D.: Automatic sleep stages classification using eeg entropy features and unsupervised pattern analysis techniques. Entropy **16**(12), 6573–6589 (2014)

29. Schulz, H.: Rethinking sleep analysis: comment on the aasm manual for the scoring of sleep and associated events. J. Clin. Sleep Med.: JCSM: Off. Publ. Am. Acad. Sleep Med. **4**(2), 99 (2008)

30. Sinha, R.K.: Artificial neural network and wavelet based automated detection of sleep spindles, REM sleep and wake states. J. Med. Syst. **32**(4), 291–299 (2008)

31. Stout, M., Bacardit, J., Hirst, J.D., Smith, R.E., Krasnogor, N.: Prediction of topological contacts in proteins using learning classifier systems. Soft Comput. **13**(3), 245 (2009)

32. Tagluk, M.E., Sezgin, N., Akin, M.: Estimation of sleep stages by an artificial neural network employing EEG, EMG and EOG. J. Med. Syst. **34**(4), 717–725 (2010)

33. Urbanowicz, R.J., Moore, J.H.: Learning classifier systems: a complete introduction, review, and roadmap. J. Artif. Evol. Appl. **2009**, 1 (2009)

34. Vural, C., Yildiz, M.: Determination of sleep stage separation ability of features extracted from EEG signals using principle component analysis. J. Med. Syst. **34**(1), 83–89 (2010)

35. Wilson, S.W.: Classifier fitness based on accuracy. Evol. Comput. **3**(2), 149–175 (1995)

36. Wilson, S.W.: Get real! XCS with continuous-valued inputs. In: Lanzi, P.L., Stolzmann, W., Wilson, S.W. (eds.) IWLCS 1999. LNCS (LNAI), vol. 1813, pp. 209–219. Springer, Heidelberg (2000). https://doi.org/10.1007/3-540-45027-0_11

37. Yildiz, A., Akin, M., Poyraz, M., Kirbas, G.: Application of adaptive neuro-fuzzy inference system for vigilance level estimation by using wavelet-entropy feature extraction. Expert Syst. Appl. **36**(4), 7390–7399 (2009)

38. Zhang, B., Lei, T., Liu, H., Cai, H.: EEG-based automatic sleep staging using ontology and weighting feature analysis. Comput. Math. Methods Med. **2018** (2018)

39. Zoubek, L., Charbonnier, S., Lesecq, S., Buguet, A., Chapotot, F.: Feature selection for sleep/wake stages classification using data driven methods. Biomed. Sig. Process. Control **2**(3), 171–179 (2007)

Recommending Learning Videos
for MOOCs and Flipped Classrooms

Jaume Jordán[1]([⊠]) [iD], Soledad Valero[1] [iD], Carlos Turró[2] [iD], and Vicent Botti[1] [iD]

[1] Valencian Research Institute for Artificial Intelligence (VRAIN),
Universitat Politècnica de València, Camino de Vera s/n, 46022 Valencia, Spain
{jjordan,svalero,vbotti}@dsic.upv.es
[2] Área de Sistemas de Información y Comunicaciones,
Universitat Politècnica de València, Camino de Vera s/n, 46022 Valencia, Spain
turro@cc.upv.es
http://vrain.upv.es/

Abstract. New teaching approaches are emerging in higher education, such as flipped classrooms. In addition, academic institutions are offering new types of training like Massive Online Open Courses. Both of these new ways of education require high-quality learning objects for their success, with learning videos being the most common to provide theoretical concepts. This paper describes a hybrid learning recommender system based on content-based techniques, which is able to recommend useful videos to learners and teachers from a learning video repository. This hybrid technique has been successfully applied to a real scenario such as the central video repository of the Universitat Politècnica de València.

Keywords: Learning Recommender System · Learning object · Learning videos · Content-based

1 Introduction

The profile of students has changed in the last decade. They demand new ways of learning, better adapted to their way of life and moving away from classical teaching. Academic institutions must increasingly adapt their teaching methodology to the new required ways, taking into account the opportunities offered by the global world [10,23]. In this way, there has been a great increase in the supply of Massive Online Open Courses (MOOCs) by academic institutions, as well as in the number of students who opt for this type of training [5]. This kind of courses are mainly based on learning objects (LOs). As IEEE propose, a LO is "any entity, digital or non-digital, which can be used, re-used or referenced during technology supported learning" [8]. Thus, MOOCs use different kinds of LOs, being videos the common ones to provide theoretical concepts. In addition, new teaching approaches are emerging in higher education, such as flipped teaching [12,15,19], in which the theoretical contents are studied at home by the students, while the face-to-face sessions are eminently practical,

Y. Demazeau et al. (Eds.): PAAMS 2020, LNAI 12092, pp. 146–157, 2020.
https://doi.org/10.1007/978-3-030-49778-1_12

where the knowledge acquired through problem solving is put into practice. To this end, the teacher indicates to the students which LO they should work on at home before the next face-to-face session. Thus, students are proposed to acquire the theoretical concepts not only through books or specialized articles, but also through audio-visual material.

Universitat Politècnica de València[1] (UPV) is a Spanish Public university which offers undergraduate degrees, dual degrees, masters and doctoral programs. UPV has more than 28000 students. In the last decade, UPV has been promoting new pedagogical methodologies in their degrees, such as flipped teaching [21]. It has also made a great effort in developing MOOCs within the edX platform[2], with more than 2 million enrollments and having three courses in Class Central all time top 100 MOOCs[3].

Students in blended and flipped classroom environments need access to a variety of resources to understand the theoretical concepts required. In order to facilitate this task, UPV has a long time project of digital resources aiming to produce video content as LOs [22]. This video content is managed in the University central video repository, called mediaUPV[4]. This portal is also used for MOOCs and other related projects.

mediaUPV allows UPV teachers to upload and manage video content for students. Students access mediaUPV usually through recommendations of their teachers through the Learning Management System (LMS), but they also access the video portal on their own, and browse through the contents. A relevant feature of mediaUPV against other alternatives (e.g. YouTube) is that videos have been developed by teachers from the institution, so there is a guarantee of the content quality.

While mediaUPV is very important to the institution, its size constitutes a growing problem, because it is increasingly difficult to find the most relevant content for both students to view and teachers to prescribe. Thus, UPV decided to look into a new Learning Recommendation System that could recommend relevant and related videos. This paper describes the proposal of the recommender engine designed and developed, and also its results in production.

This article is structured as follows. In Sect. 2 related works are described. Following, Sect. 3 specifies a description about the LOs to recommend and the potential users of the system. In Sect. 4 the proposed recommender system is explained. Then, Sect. 5 shows the experimental results of the proposed recommender in the mediaUPV portal. Finally, Sect. 6 draws the conclusions and future work of this paper.

2   Related Work

Learning Recommender Systems (LRS) should assist learners in discovering relevant LO than keep them motivated and enable them to complete their learning

---

[1] http://www.upv.es.

[2] https://www.edx.org/.

[3] https://www.classcentral.com/report/top-moocs-2019-edition/.

[4] https://media.upv.es/.

activities [9]. Most of the LRS adopt the same techniques than regular recommender systems [3,7,9,14], such as: *content-based*, in which recommendations are determined considering user profiles and content analysis of the learning objects already visited by the user; *collaborative filtering*, in which recommendations are based on the choices of other similar user profiles; *knowledge-based*, in which it is inferred whether a LO satisfies a particular learning need of the user to recommend it; and *hybrid*, in which recommendations are computed by combining more than one of the above techniques.

In recent years, different approaches have been proposed in order to improve the efficiency and accuracy of the recommendations and retrieval of useful LOs. In this way, in [2], authors provide new metrics for applying collaborative filtering in a learning domain, so users with better academic results have greater weight in the calculation of the recommendations. However, the experiments did not carried out in a learning environment. Other proposals focus on recommending to students those LOs that can be most useful to them, providing solid arguments. This is the case of [14], which combine content-based, collaborative and knowledge-based recommenders using an argumentation-based module to recommend LOs inside a LMS. In this case, information on student profiles and learning styles is also available. An item-based collaborative filtering method is combined with a sequential pattern mining algorithm to recommend LOs to learners in [4]. In this case, LOs are ranked by the students and it is also possible to obtain the browsing sequences made by them. In a similar way, [18] proposes a hybrid knowledge-based recommender system based on ontology and sequential pattern mining for recommendation of LO. Authors can adequately characterize learners and LOs using an ontology, since they have detailed information about them. In [6], the authors propose a method for recommending LOs to a group of individuals, building a unified learner profile which is used to recommend using a collaborative filtering approach.

Besides, other works have been done to improve the accuracy of the searches in mediaUPV. For example, in [17] a semi-supervised method is applied to cluster and classify the LOs of mediaUPV, obtaining specific keywords that represent each cluster. In [20], authors applied a custom approach for indexing and retrieving educational videos using their transcripts, which are available in mediaUPV. Videos are classified in different domains using the method described in [17]. Also, they applied a Latent Dirichlet Allocation algorithm [1] to get a list of topics and their score. User queries are classified in one of the domains, recovering from that cluster those videos whose transcripts are the closest to the query.

As can be seen, most previous work on LRS adopts a hybrid strategy, seeking to harness the strength of each particular technique, overcoming its limitations by using them together. Furthermore, the different strategies that can be applied depend on the data available to describe LOs and users. In our case, a hybrid strategy will also be applied, combining content-based methods. On the other hand, previous experiences on the improvement of searches in the mediaUPV repository show us the usefulness of characterizing LOs using available transcripts and titles.

3   Problem Description

mediaUPV portal started in 2011 and by the end of 2019 it holds 55600 different videos, mainly from STEM topics, with more than 10 million views. From this database, only 13232 are certified as high quality LOs. All these high quality videos have a transcript (with more than 100 characters), a title and an author, however the videos are not classified using any taxonomy and no keywords are associated to them. mediaUPV platform generates the transcripts of what is said in the videos using the poli[Trans] service[5], an online platform for automated and assisted multilingual media subtitling offered by UPV. poli[Trans] service is based on transLectures-UPV Platform [11].

mediaUPV portal is used by students and trainers. The students are mainly formal students of the UPV, but it also receives many visits from anonymous users, who can register in some MOOC offered by the UPV. Moreover, mediaUPV is not connected to the LMS of the UPV, so even though the user is authenticated, it is not possible to know his student profile (e.g. enrolled subjects).

Therefore, the aim of this proposal is to be able to offer recommendations not only to authenticated users but also to anonymous users of the system. In addition, the system should be able to recommend not only students, but also teachers who are looking for suitable material for their students. In all cases, the aim is to be able to offer recommendations on learning videos (LOs) considered by the UPV to be of high quality.

4   Learning Recommender System Proposal

Our LRS is based on two different approaches. On the one hand, a recommender module based on the activity of the user identified in the system, the *profile-based module*. On the other hand, another recommendation module based on the content of the video being watched at the time, the *item-based module*. Thus, the computed recommendations are based on both methods, getting a *hybrid recommendation* system, so the user receives recommendations from videos similar to the one he is currently watching, but also from videos that may interest him due to his viewing history.

In our proposal, LOs/videos are characterized by their title and their transcript. This characterization is used for the calculation of the similarity between the LOs. As transcripts are in different languages, it is possible to recommend videos from different languages.

Because there is a large set of words in the transcript and title of the videos, it is necessary to have an algorithm that filters out the too common words, which do not serve to differentiate the content. Thus, it is possible to focus on

---

[5] https://politrans.upv.es.

the particular words in the entire collection, which serve to identify the content of a video. Therefore, the algorithm chosen is the well-known term frequency - inverse document frequency (tf-idf) [16]. In order to improve the performance of the tf-idf algorithm, also the stop words from the *nltk Python*[6] package are used. Furthermore, some ad hoc words have been added to this package.

The *item-based module* takes only the information from the content of the videos, i.e., there is no information about the users. So, we can consider this module as a recommendation by item-item similarity to be used when a (maybe anonymous) user is watching a video. To do this, we take the characteristics (transcript and title) of each of the videos to calculate the item-item matrix with the tf-idf algorithm. Then, the cosine similarity of two instances of this item-item matrix returns the similarity among the different videos. Cosine similarity calculates the similarity between two n-dimensional vectors by the angle between them in the vector space:

$$cosine\_sim(\overrightarrow{p}, \overrightarrow{q}) = \frac{\overrightarrow{p} \cdot \overrightarrow{q}}{|\overrightarrow{p}| * |\overrightarrow{q}|}$$

The *profile-based module* considers the content information (the terms extracted by the tf-idf algorithm from the transcript and title) of the videos viewed by users. In this way, the recommendations to a user are made based on the similarity among the viewed videos of the user in mediaUPV. In this case, the similarity is calculated using the cosine profile-item matrix.

Finally, our *hybrid recommendation* system consists of the two modules described above, balancing the results of both by means of configurable weights, i.e., w_{IB} for the item-based weight and w_{PB} for the profile-based weight. In this way, the recommendations are made taking into account the intersection of the videos recommended by both modules and completing the rest of the recommendations with the corresponding videos of the modules according to their weight. Also, in cases where there is no user (anonymous) the w_{PB} is set to 0. Likewise, when an authenticated user is not yet watching a video, the w_{IB} is set to 0.

5   Experimental Results

In this section, we explain the experiments carried out with the proposed LRS. On the one hand, we have made tests with data from the videos seen by the users, dividing this data into a training set and a test set (Sect. 5.1). On the other hand, we have taken the parameter configuration of the recommender system that has worked best in this first phase and applied it to recommend in production at the mediaUPV portal; these results are shown in Sect. 5.2.

5.1   LRS Parameter Setting

The data set used in the setting up process is formed by of learning videos viewed by users during an academic year at the UPV, from September 2018 to July 2019.

---

[6] https://www.nltk.org/.

The training data set consists of the data from September 2018 to April 2019, while the testing data set consists of the data from May to July 2019, i.e., 8 months for training and 3 months for testing. The videos considered are those present on the platform until July 2019, after filtering them as described above. Thus, we try to simulate a real scenario, in which the training data represent the past activity of the users, while the test data is formed by the activity of the following 3 months ("future"). Therefore, any recommendation from the recommender that is among the videos that users have actually seen in the test set is considered a success.

We focus on the hybrid recommender engine since it brings together the efforts of the two recommender modules. The weights for each module are set to $w_{IB} = 50\%$ and $w_{PB} = 50\%$. Additionally, in these tests we only consider 5 recommendations since it is the number required by the mediaUPV portal.

We use the well-known precision and recall measures to evaluate the success of the recommender. Precision can be defined as the successful recommendations made (videos that have been viewed by the user in the test set) divided by the number of recommendations made: $precision = \frac{success\_recommendation}{recommendations\_made}$. Recall is defined as the successful recommendations made divided by the number of watched videos in the test set: $recall = \frac{success\_recommendation}{watched\_videos}$.

For our tests we considered a set of *regular users* (*reg_users*) that we define as those who have seen between 10 and 150 videos both in the training and test periods, having 1044 users in this set.

Setting Transcript and Title Features. In this first test, we analyze the success of recommendations for the set of regular users considering different amount of features for the transcript and the title of the video to train the LRS, in order to establish the better amount of both. The graph in Fig. 1a shows the precision and recall for different values of the number of features considered for the transcript, while the number of features for the title is kept at zero.

In general, precision and recall increase slightly as the value of the features for the transcript increases (from 7.2% to 7.7% for precision, and from 1.15% to 1.29% for recall), as would be expected when more information is available from the transcript. The best precision values are with 35000 and 45000 features for the transcript. However, the best recall value is in the case of 35000 transcript features. Therefore, the best configuration for the recommender would be to use 35000 transcript features, since this value achieves higher recall than any other and equals the precision obtained with 45000 transcript features. In addition, the computation of 35000 transcript features is computationally less expensive and, in particular, implies a lower memory cost. It should be noted that, in the experiment made with 35000 transcript features, the number of users who have been recommended successfully is 254 of 1044, i.e., 24.33%.

Figure 1b shows the precision and recall for different values in the number of features considered for the title having the transcript features fixed to 35000. The best values of precision and recall are obtained with the number of features of the title at 0. In addition, both values decrease slightly and in a relatively

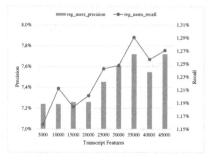
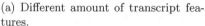

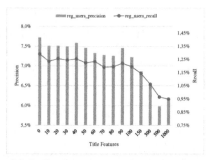

(a) Different amount of transcript features.

(b) Different amount of title features.

Fig. 1. Precision and recall analysis for the regular users set.

uniform way as the number of title features increases. So, apparently it is better to skip the title features. However, it is interesting to analyze this considering the nature of the LOs of mediaUPV. In this way, we have analyzed the set of words that determines the tf-idf algorithm. As we mentioned before, the videos on the platform correspond mainly to university courses, so there is a set of terms that are certainly repetitive in the titles of the videos and do not provide any differentiating information with respect to their content. Among these terms, we find the following: {'analysis', 'calculation', 'control', 'creation', 'data', 'design', 'exercise', 'engineering', 'introduction', 'management', 'mechanism', 'model', 'module', 'practical', 'practice', 'presentation', 'simulation', 'system', 'systems', 'theme', 'unit', 'virtual'}.

Filtering Title Features. In order to increase the precision of the recommendations, we decided to filter the terms of the previous list from the titles of the videos by considering them as stop words. The results of applying this correction can be seen in the Fig. 2b, which shows the precision and recall for 35000 transcript features and different amount of title features. In this case, it can be seen that the best global values of precision and recall are still obtained with 0 title features. However, it should be noted that with 10 title features, for the case where the specified title terms have been filtered out, the precision and recall almost reach this base case, slightly surpassing the case without filtering (with 10 title features). In addition, for values up to 30 title features, the precision and recall are better for the case with filtered terms. However, from 40 title features on, the effect of filtering is diluted and the results are generally slightly worse, and most of the cases slightly worse than the unfiltered case.

Consequently, we can say that filtering has significantly improved the results but it is not enough to make the title relevant. Perhaps it would be necessary a still greater filtering of terms that we have not considered 'common' and that the tf-idf algorithm has not identified as such either. However, since we are considering 35000 transcript terms, the inclusion of 10 to 50 terms from the title can be considered irrelevant after the analysis. Furthermore, it can also be interpreted as a video being better characterized by its own transcript than by its title.

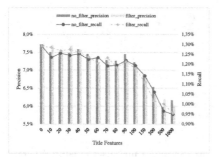

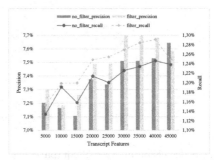

(a) Different amount of title features.

(b) Different amount of transcript features with 10 title features.

Fig. 2. Precision and recall comparison with and without filtering title terms.

Although we have already seen that it is better to skip the title in all cases, we will analyze in detail the difference between filtering the title terms and not filtering them for 10 title terms and different amount of transcript features. Figure 2b shows this comparison (precision and recall) with and without filtering. Precision and recall are significantly better if filtering of title terms is performed in all cases, with the only exception of 45000 transcript features where precision is slightly higher for the unfiltered case (being also the best result for the different transcript values for the unfiltered case of title terms). In this particular case, it could be that by considering only 10 features of the title, but 45000 for the transcript, the effect of the filtering of the title is diluted. However, this is not a very significant difference. On the other hand, as previously observed, the best results, both in terms of precision and recall, are obtained with 35000 transcript features in the case of filtering the title terms.

Hybrid Weights Setting. In Fig. 3 we make a comparison of precision and recall of two different sets of users, using different weights for the recommender modules of our hybrid LRS. We define a first set of users of which we have little knowledge as those who have only seen 1 to 9 videos in the data set (815 users), calling them *new users*. The second set are the *regular users* previously used, formed by users that have already seen between 10 and 150 videos in the data set (1044 users). For all regular users, the best precision and recall is obtained with balanced weights, i.e., $\{w_{PB} = 40\%; w_{IB} = 60\%\}$ and $\{w_{PB} = 60\%; w_{IB} = 40\%\}$. However, for new users, the best precision and recall values are obtained with low w_{PB}, with 15.83% of new users receiving successful recommendations.

Finally, as there is not a previous recommender module in mediaUPV to compare with, we also calculated random recommendations for new and regular

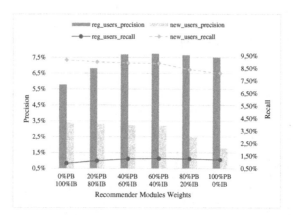

Fig. 3. Precision and recall comparison of regular users and new users, using different LRS modules weights.

users, taking the highest value of 50 different random simulations (since random recommendation obtains 0 successful recommendations in most cases). Thus, a precision of 0.0156% and recall 0.0389% was achieved for regular users, and a precision of 0.0507% and recall 0.0167% for new users.

Discussion. For new users, the item-based module provides better results because low information about their activity is available, so the profile module is not able to offer good recommendations. This is not the case for regular users, since there is enough information about their profiles and therefore, a balanced weight distribution between both modules gives the best results.

Furthermore, we emphasize that even though our hybrid LRS obtains a precision of 7.7% simulating a real environment, 24.33% regular users and 15.83% of new users received some good recommendation. In addition, the precision and recall obtained are significantly better than a random recommendation.

In conclusion, after this analysis we established the parameters of the LRS to be applied in production in the mediaUPV portal as 35000 transcript features, 0 title features, $w_{PB} = 60\%$ and $w_{IB} = 40\%$.

5.2   Production Results

In this section we show the results of the application of the LRS proposed to the mediaUPV portal. It should be noted that mediaUPV did not have a LRS until the application in October 2019 of the one proposed in this work.

In Fig. 4a, we show the number of accesses to the videos of the mediaUPV platform during the year 2019, in which our LRS was applied from October. As can be seen, the existence of the LRS has increased slightly the number of accesses to the videos by the users.

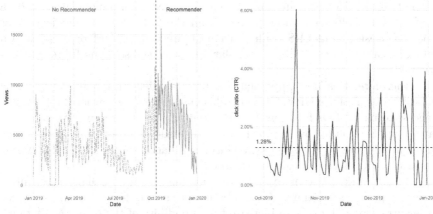

(a) Video access with and without recommender.

(b) Clicks in recommender (CTR).

Fig. 4. Performance measures in production.

A common way in industry to measure relative quality of a recommender
system is the Click-Through Rate (CTR)[7], that measures the percentage of
clicks in the recommender per number of views. As the CTR is used by the ads
industry, there is an ongoing interest in CTR prediction techniques [13]. In the
case of a generic recommender system, anything above 0.35% means you are
doing a good job[8]. As can be seen in Fig. 4b, the CTR is 1.28% on average, with
notable peaks of around 4%. These results can be considered quite satisfactory,
since they imply that the recommendations made to users generate interest in
them.

Finally, we point out the percentage of clicks on each of the recommended
videos according to their order in the list, demonstrating the relevance of this
order to users. Concretely, about 33% of users click on the first video, and more
than half of the users click on the first two recommendations with a distribution
that seems to be heavy tailed. In short, the most relevant video by far for users
is the first one and then the rest of the videos follow a decreasing order of
importance, which also points to a reasonable work of the presented LRS.

6   Conclusions

This work proposes a new hybrid LRS based on content-based techniques capable of recommend learning videos based on viewing history and current video
content. Thus, the LRS proposed is able to recommend not only to authenticated
users but also to anonymous users from the mediaUPV portal, independently if
they are teachers or students.

---

[7] https://en.wikipedia.org/wiki/Click-throughrate.
[8] www.acquisio.com/blog/agency/what-is-a-good-click-through-rate-ctr/.

The hybrid LRS has been applied to a simulated environment, using a data set of learning videos and user profiles from the 2018–2019 academic year at UPV. The best hybrid LRS configuration obtained a 7.7% of precision and a 1.29% of recall, where a 24.33% of regular users received some useful recommendation.

Furthermore, this new approach has been applied in a real scenario, the mediaUPV portal of the UPV. This portal is mainly used by learners and trainers to access to useful LOs for their MOOCs and flipped classrooms. We can state that the application of this hybrid LRS to the mediaUPV portal was positive as it brought an increase in visits to the videos and had a significant CTR of 1.28% on average, with notable peaks of around 4%.

As future work, we want to add a new module based on collaborative filtering, which provides recommendations based on viewing history of users similar to the current one, in order to increase the serendipity of the recommendations. In addition, it would be interesting to evaluate whether to add the classification of the mediaUPV videos obtained by [17] to the current characterization of the videos used by our proposal, which is currently based only on the video transcript.

Acknowledgments. This work was partially supported by MINECO/FEDER RTI2018-095390-B-C31 and TIN2017-89156-R projects of the Spanish government, and PROMETEO/2018/002 project of Generalitat Valenciana. J. Jordán and V. Botti are funded by UPV PAID-06-18 project. J. Jordán is also funded by grant APOSTD/2018/010 of Generalitat Valenciana - Fondo Social Europeo.

References

1. Blei, D.M., Ng, A.Y., Jordan, M.I.: Latent Dirichlet allocation. J. Mach. Learn. Res. **3**, 993–1022 (2003)
2. Bobadilla, J., Serradilla, F., Hernando, A.: Collaborative filtering adapted to recommender systems of e-learning. Knowl.-Based Syst. **22**(4), 261–265 (2009)
3. Burke, R.: Hybrid recommender systems: survey and experiments. User Model. User-Adap. Inter. **12**(4), 331–370 (2002)
4. Chen, W., Niu, Z., Zhao, X., Li, Y.: A hybrid recommendation algorithm adapted in e-learning environments. World Wide Web **17**(2), 271–284 (2012). https://doi.org/10.1007/s11280-012-0187-z
5. van Dijck, J., Poell, T.: Higher education in a networked world: European responses to U.S. MOOCs. Int. J. Commun.: IJoC **9**, 2674–2692 (2015)
6. Dwivedi, P., Bharadwaj, K.K.: e-learning recommender system for a group of learners based on the unified learner profile approach. Expert Syst. **32**(2), 264–276 (2015)
7. Herlocker, J., Konstan, J., Terveen, L., Riedl, J.: Evaluating collaborative filtering recommender systems. ACM Trans. Inf. Syst. **22**(1), 5–53 (2004)
8. Institute and Committee of Electrical and Electronics Engineers: Learning Technology Standards: IEEE Standard for Learning Object Metadata. IEEE Standard 1484.12.1 (2002)

9. Klašnja-Milićević, A., Ivanović, M., Nanopoulos, A.: Recommender systems in e-learning environments: a survey of the state-of-the-art and possible extensions. Artif. Intell. Rev. **44**(4), 571–604 (2015). https://doi.org/10.1007/s10462-015-9440-z

10. Maassen, P., Nerland, M., Yates, L. (eds.): Reconfiguring Knowledge in Higher Education. Higher Education Dynamics, vol. 50. Springer, Heidelberg (2018). https://doi.org/10.1007/978-3-319-72832-2

11. MLLP research group, Universitat Politècnica de València: Tlp: The translectures-upv platform. http://www.mllp.upv.es/tlp

12. O'Flaherty, J., Phillips, C.: The use of flipped classrooms in higher education: a scoping review. Internet High. Educ. **25**, 85–95 (2015)

13. Richardson, M., Dominowska, E., Ragno, R.: Predicting clicks: estimating the click-through rate for new ads. In: Proceedings of the 16th international conference on World Wide Web, pp. 521–530 (2007)

14. Rodríguez, P., Heras, S., Palanca, J., Duque, N., Julián, V.: Argumentation-based hybrid recommender system for recommending learning objects. In: Rovatsos, M., Vouros, G., Julian, V. (eds.) EUMAS/AT -2015. LNCS (LNAI), vol. 9571, pp. 234–248. Springer, Cham (2016). https://doi.org/10.1007/978-3-319-33509-4_19

15. Roehl, A., Reddy, S.L., Shannon, G.J.: The flipped classroom: an opportunity to engage millennial students through active learning strategies. J. Fam. Consum. Sci. **105**, 44–49 (2013)

16. Salton, G., Buckley, C.: Term-weighting approaches in automatic text retrieval. Inf. Process. Manag. **24**(5), 513–523 (1988)

17. Stoica, A.S., Heras, S., Palanca, J., Julian, V., Mihaescu, M.C.: A semi-supervised method to classify educational videos. In: Pérez García, H., Sánchez González, L., Castejón Limas, M., Quintián Pardo, H., Corchado Rodríguez, E. (eds.) HAIS 2019. LNCS (LNAI), vol. 11734, pp. 218–228. Springer, Cham (2019). https://doi.org/10.1007/978-3-030-29859-3_19

18. Tarus, J.K., Niu, Z., Yousif, A.: A hybrid knowledge-based recommender system for e-learning based on ontology and sequential pattern mining. Future Gener. Comput. Syst. **72**, 37–48 (2017)

19. Tucker, B.: The flipped classroom. Online instruction at home frees class time for learning. Educ. Next Winter **2012**, 82–83 (2012)

20. Turcu, G., Heras, S., Palanca, J., Julian, V., Mihaescu, M.C.: Towards a custom designed mechanism for indexing and retrieving video transcripts. In: Pérez García, H., Sánchez González, L., Castejón Limas, M., Quintián Pardo, H., Corchado Rodríguez, E. (eds.) HAIS 2019. LNCS (LNAI), vol. 11734, pp. 299–309. Springer, Cham (2019). https://doi.org/10.1007/978-3-030-29859-3_26

21. Turró, C., Morales, J.C., Busquets-Mataix, J.: A study on assessment results in a large scale flipped teaching experience. In: 4th International Conference on Higher Education Advances (HEAD 2018), pp. 1039–1048 (2018)

22. Turró, C., Despujol, I., Busquets, J.: Networked teaching, the story of a success on creating e-learning content at Universitat Politècnica de València. EUNIS J. High. Educ. (2014)

23. Zajda, J., Rust, V. (eds.): Globalisation and Higher Education Reforms. GCEPR, vol. 15. Springer, Cham (2016). https://doi.org/10.1007/978-3-319-28191-9

Improving Sustainable Mobility with a Variable Incentive Model for Bike-Sharing Systems Based on Agent-Based Social Simulation

Alberto López Santiago(ID), Carlos A. Iglesias$^{(\boxtimes)}$(ID), and Álvaro Carrera(ID)

Intelligent Systems Group, Universidad Politécnica de Madrid,
Avda. Complutense, 30, 28040 Madrid, Spain
alberto.lopezs@alumnos.upm.es, {carlosangel.iglesias,a.carrera}@upm.es
http://www.gsi.upm.es

Abstract. Bike-sharing systems (BSS) have been implemented in numerous cities around the world to reduce the traffic generated by motorized vehicles, due to the benefits they bring to the city, such as reducing congestion or decreasing pollution generation. Caused by their impact on urban mobility, the research community has increased their interest in their study, trying to understand user behavior and improving the user experience. This paper has the goal of analyzing the impact of different policies of incentives on the user experience and their impact on the BSS service. An agent-based simulation model has been developed using data collected from the BSS service of Madrid, so-called BiciMad. Route generation has been calculated based o n OpenStreetMaps. The system has been evaluated, analyzing the results generated on different incentive policies. The main conclusion is that variable incentives outperform the current incentive policy of the service. Finally, a sensitivity analysis is presented to validate the proper variability of results for the model parameters.

Keywords: Bike sharing systems · Incentives · Agent based social simulation

1 Introduction

According to a recent study of the United Nations [20], 55% of the world's population was concentrated in urban areas in 2018. This proportion is expected to increase to 68% by 2050. One of the consequences is increasing congestion in the urban areas that brings other problems such as the increase in air pollution. Since today 64% of all travels are made within urban environments [27], urban mobility demand has exploded, and its improvement has become a global challenge.

The future of urban mobility is foreseen as a transition to integrated mobility [2] that integrates efficiently different types of transport, including new forms

© Springer Nature Switzerland AG 2020
Y. Demazeau et al. (Eds.): PAAMS 2020, LNAI 12092, pp. 158–170, 2020.
https://doi.org/10.1007/978-3-030-49778-1_13

of mobility. Specific attention should be paid to sustainable mobility projects whose objective is to reduce pollution in urban areas [21]. Many fast-moving trends are shaping the future of urban mobility, such as autonomous driving, vehicle electrification, shared mobility, decentralization of energy systems, and smart public transit systems [2].

New shared mobility options (i.e., bike-sharing, car-sharing, and ride-sourcing) complement public transport and are growing in significance [9].

In this article, we pay attention to bike-sharing systems. Numerous companies are supporting their use through the creation of Bike-sharing systems (BSS) [17,29]. Bike-sharing technology has evolved for decades exponentially. As a matter of fact, according to the Bike-sharing World Map [16], in February 2018, there were more than 1500 active BSS all over the globe. However, according to data provided in the European bicycle market research by Confederation of the European Bicycle Industry [5], the adoption of the bicycle is different depending on the country. European countries such as Germany, France, and Great Britain account for more than half of total sales in Europe being the three countries with the highest numbers.

On the other hand, other countries such as Spain, Poland, and Italy barely manage aggregate 20% as a whole. Comparing the first set of countries with the second one, the big difference in the level of sales (+150%) contrasts with the population differences (+50%). One of the main challenges that BSS must face is the demand management, to avoid situations where there is a lack of bicycles for rent or docks to park them and thus causing a deficit of service availability. For this reason, the existence of policies to reduce inequality in the occupation of stations provides benefits to both users and BSS providers [6].

This paper aims at analyzing the bike-sharing service of the city of Madrid, Spain, so-called BiciMad, managed by the Municipal Transport Company of Madrid, *Empresa Municipal de Transportes* (EMT). In particular, we are interested in analyzing alternative incentive models to the models already in use in the city. For this, we have used the data available of this service to develop a realistic simulation model based on multiagent simulation. Then, the variable incentive policy is included in the model. The remainder of this article is structured as follows. Section 2 presents the related works. Section 3 describes the BSS of Madrid, which is used for evaluating our proposal. Section 4 introduces the proposed model, the policies implemented, and the external modules used. Section 5 studies the evaluation of the results obtained. Finally, Sect. 6 closes with a conclusion and outlook.

2   State of the Art

Following systematic review methods [19,23], several questions have been formulated to review the state of the art. Particular emphasis has been put to analyze research papers where the bike-sharing systems have a similar context to our case study.

These questions are the following: (Q1) Does the work deal with bicycle traffic?; (Q2) Does it study a bicycle renting service case?; (Q3) Does it involve

Table 1. State of the art papers. Check mark: yes, empty space: No

Ref			[13]	[14]	[4]	[24]	[15]	[11]	[12]	[28]	[10]	[25]	[22]	[26]	[8]	[7]
Target	Q1		✓	✓	✓	✓	✓	✓	✓	✓	✓	✓	✓	✓	✓	✓
	Q2		✓	✓	✓	✓	✓	✓			✓	✓	✓	✓	✓	✓
	Q3						✓	✓			✓	✓	✓	✓	✓	✓
	Q4		✓	✓	✓	✓	✓	✓	✓		✓	✓	✓	✓	✓	✓
Method	Q5						✓	✓	✓	✓	✓					
	Q6							✓	✓		✓			✓	✓	
	Q7		✓					✓			✓					
	Q8											✓	✓			

a Spanish city?; (Q4) Is real data employed in the study?; (Q5) Does it include a visualization of the traffic simulated?; (Q6) Is there an agent-based social simulation?; (Q7) Does it contrast different policy results?; and (Q8) Does it implement a system of variable incentives? They can be classified into two types: type of target (Q1–Q4) and method used (Q5–Q8). The summary of the selected papers is shown in Table 1.

Several studies use machine learning techniques for predicting bike demand for rebalancing purposes in New York [4,13,14,24], Washington DC stations [24] and Barcelona [11]. The principal used variables are time, speed, traffic as well as meteorological data (e.g., temperature, humidity, and visibility). One of the most used techniques is the applications of clustering methods for stations [4,13] for predicting the over-demand of each cluster.

Agent-based modeling is another popular technique for studying BSSs [3]. These techniques propose bottom-up modeling of the individual behaviour of bikes and stations as well as their interactions. Model realism is frequently validated with real data, as discussed for many cities such as Sydney [12], Salamanca [15], Madrid [10], or Barcelona [26], to name a few. The analysis of traffic flows can help to understand the bike-riders' preferences (e.g., shorter routes [12]) or the impact of factors such as peripheral areas on city traffic [28]. Besides, multiagent models provide the capability to experiment with different policies, such as passive occupation balance [10] and analyze their effects.

Other modeling factors are user satisfaction with the service [22] or their willingness to accept incentives if they contribute to rebalancing the system [25].

Also, machine learning techniques and agent-based mode ling are frequently combined by integrating the predicting capabilities of a machine learning module into a multiagent simulation model. Some examples are the integration of a probabilistic prediction module of station loads [8] using synthetic data or a neural network forecasting model the number of empty parking slots based on a dataset of the city of Valencia [7].

In summary, social behavior around BSSs has been widely studied. However, there are gaps in the possibilities of modifying it. In particular, with variable incentive policies, there are still a large number of variables to be studied in order to optimize results.

3   Case Study

As previously introduced, this work is focused on the study of the BSS of the city of Madrid, Spain, so-called BiciMAD, which is operated by EMT. This service was inaugurated in the summer of 2014 with the novelty of the utilization of electric bicycles. In 2015, the number of stations and bicycles was expanded, reaching the current number of 171 stations and 2028 bicycles. These stations are distributed throughout the city of Madrid in an area of approximately 5×5 km^2.

Table 2. Description of the variables selected from BiciMAD Open Data plaftorm.

Variable	Description
idplug_station	Destination station identifier
idunplug_station	Origin station identifier
travel_time	Trip duration
unplug_hourTime	Time when the bike was rented
user_type	Type of user (subscriber, casual, EMT employee)

(a) Routes Dataset

Variable	Description
id	Station integer identifier
date	Date of recording
name	Station name including address
total_bases	Number of docks at the station
free_bases	Available docks without bikes
dock_bikes	Available docks with bikes
latitude	latitude
longitude	longitude

(b) Stations Dataset

Open data are provided by EMT[1] information about usage by users and hourly records of the state of the stations. This open data service provides two main kinds of data: the trips made during every month, and the situation (i.e., load/occupancy) of the stations with a one-hour time gap. For modeling purposes, data from August to November 2018 have been used. The selected variables for our work are shown in Table 2 and properly subdivided per dataset.

Regarding the trip routes, the variables selected are shown in Table 2a. The most relevant fields for the study we have carried out are the *ids* of origin and destination stations, which show us the route followed by users on every trip. It is also important to track information about the time at which the bicycle was rented. However, due to user privacy terms, only hours are tracked, without providing the minute details. Thus, we will assume an even distribution of trips during that hour. Besides, the duration of the trip is preserved to enable its comparison with the simulation results. Lastly, we keep the variable *user_type*, which indicates the type of user who has made the trip (subscriber, casual, or EMT employee), since these records contain the balancing measures carried out by EMT employees. The trips not belonging to public users are discarded.

---

[1] BiciMAD   Open   Data: http://opendata.emtmadrid.es/Datos-estaticos/Datos-generales-(1).

Regarding the station status, selected variables are shown in Table 2b. Most relevant variables have been identified, and the rest have been filtered. In particular, we use *ids* and *station names* to identify stations and be able to link them with the routes dataset. Also, the *date* variable provides the temporal context. The most relevant variables are *the total bases*, which, along with the information of the bases that are occupied (*dock_bikes*) and the empty ones (*free_bases*), indicate the *base occupation*. Moreover, lastly, the *station position* represented by its *longitude* and *latitude* variables.

A preliminary analysis of the BSS use has been carried out for understanding better the behavior of the system and its users. For this purpose, we have considered the hourly and weekly distribution of trips according to the type of user. The data collected for this study contain information about more than 1.5 million trips made during these four months (August-November 2018), which are distributed according to the user type. The distribution of trips throughout the week can be characterized as follows. For subscribed users, we found a high usage on Monday and Tuesday, which decreases the following two days. The days corresponding to the weekend (Friday, Saturday, and Sunday) show a higher amount of use. As for the EMT employees, we observe a practically homogeneous use throughout the week.

The purpose of the simulation model is to study the effect of implementing a policy of variable incentives for BiciMad, the BSS of Madrid. To do this, we have followed the following methodology based on the methodology described in [23]. The first task has been a *data analysis* of BSS data. Apart from the exploratory analysis previously presented, decision matrices have been created to calculate the points of origin and destination of users. Then, the next phase has been *model construction*. Different agent types have been identified (bike, station, and truck), and their behavior has been specified and implemented, as detailed in Sect. 4.1. The next phase has been *model validation*, where the realism of the model is validated with the real data, as detailed in Sect. 5, which is described in an independent section for the sake of clarity. Once the model is validated, the next phase has been *policy experimentation*. Taking as a baseline the policy used in BiciMad, we have implemented other strategies to see their effects as detailed below.

The data offered by EMT during August and November 2018 have been analyzed to estimate the real behavior of the users. Two logs are provided: trip records and the logs of the station status every hour After filtering the data as described in this section, the resulting dataset includes information about the origin station, destination, time spent in the trip, type of user, and date. Besides, the study has filtered weekends and ha s been focused on the workweek.

4   Model Description

Two probability matrices have been created. These matrices will be used by the agents when deciding their origin and destination stations. In order to achieve a more realistic behavior of the actions of the users, the probabilities will be

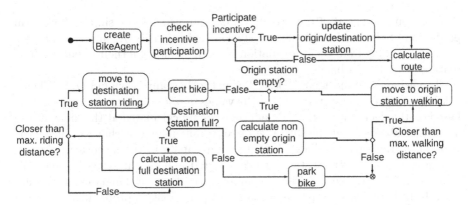

Fig. 1. UML activity diagram for BikeAgent.

calculated based on the time of the system. In this way, it is possible to simulate the use changes according to the time of day.

The first matrix O is the origin station probability matrix. The matrix element O_{hi} represents the probability that a user takes a bicycle from the station i at hour h. This probability has been calculated, as shown in Eq. 1, where N_{hi} is the number of routes whose origin is the station i at hour h, and N_h is the total number of routes at hour h.

$$O_{hi} = N_{hi}/N_{ht} \tag{1}$$

The second matrix is the destination station probability matrix, which has three dimensions. The matrix element D_{hij} represents the probability that a user takes a bicycle from the origin station i to the destination station j at hour h. This probability has been calculated as shown in Eq. 2, where N_{hi} is the number of routes whose origin is the station i and the destination is the station j at hour h and N_h is the total number of routes whose origin is the station i at hour h.

$$D_{hij} = N_{hij}/N_{hi} \tag{2}$$

The number of available bicycles and bases is calculated as the average of the actual records. This value is set at the beginning of the simulation. As the simulation starts at 0 o'clock, this will be the hour used to calculate the average.

4.1   Agents Description

Three types of agents have been identified: BikeAgent, StationAgent, and TruckAgent, which are described below.

The **BikeAgent** is the principal agent of the system. It represents each user of the system that makes use of the BSS service. Its variables contain information about its status, whether the agent is currently on the move, has rented or parked the bike, position, and the route to be carried out. Given that we know the position and speed of the agents, we have implemented a simple short-term prediction of the station's load: the station registers Bike Agents that are less than 10 min away from their destination station, including if their intention. (i.e., renting or parking a bike).

The behavior of the agent is described in the diagram shown in Fig. 1. When a BikeAgent starts, the system assigns the values of origin and destination stations based on the decision matrices. The incentives are calculated at the moment the agent is created, so that the BikeAgent's routes should not be changed during the trip. Then, the agent decides whether to participate in the incentive program, depending on the extra distance to be covered and the incentive offered. We have used the data obtained in the survey carried out by Singla et al. [25] are used. In this survey, an approximation of the participation probability evolution is made, based on the incentive offered and the extra distance. The economic reward offered depends on the scenario. If the agent participates, origin, and destination stations are updated accordingly.

The next step is calculating the route based on a GIS system. Once the route has been calculated, the agent walks to the initial station. When it has arrived, a bike is rented if available. Otherwise, a new origin station is calculated, and the agent walks towards it. This is repeated until the BikeAgent can rent a bike. Once it rents a bike, it rides to the destination station. Finally, it parks the bike at the destination station if it has available bases. If not, it looks for a station with an available base within the area covered by its maximum riding distance and heads for it. If not found, the agent simply waits until the next step. As in the real case, the agent gets the discount associated with the incentive if it rents/parks the bicycle at a station with a lack of bicycles/bases, respectively.

The **StationAgent** acts like a bicycle container. It is also responsible for updating its status. In particular, it should keep updated the load of the station. This load variable will enable the identification of stations needing a balancing action. Based on Ban et al. [1], their value is low if the capacity is less than 30% of the maximum station capacity; high if it exceeds 70% of the maximum capacity; and normal between 30% and 70%. The model has made a simplification, not taking into account the charging time of electric bikes. Therefore the parked bikes are available for rental by another user instantly.

TruckAgent. They are the agents that represent the rental company workers who travel throughout the city, relocating the bicycles between stations. Their primary mission is balancing the station load so that fewer stations are out of service because of a lack of bikes or docks. As far as the truck policy is concerned, there is no precise information on actual usage. It is therefore assumed that the deployed fleet is similar to the hourly distribution of journeys made by company employees. The choice of the station is based on both the distance and the number of bikes or free bases. Due to the nature of the study, the trucks' behavior remains unchanged in every scenario.

4.2 Scenarios Description

Different scenarios have been designed, taking as a reference the actual behavior, to evaluate the effects of the policies.

Base Model (BM): This model simulates the real behavior of BiciMAD, that is, a system that implements an incentive policy with an amount of 0.10€ and the policy of repositioning bicycles with trucks.

Base Model with 0.50€ Incentive Reward (BM50): In this policy, an incentive reward of 0.5€ will be used instead of the existing 0.10€. With this incentive amount, according to Singla et al. [25], a participation of half of the users is achieved. Similarly, according to the study carried out by Ban et al. [1] with an incentive of between 0.5 and 0.6 USD, an average walking distance of about 500 and 600 meters is obtained.

Variable Incentives with Logarithmic Urgency (VI-LOG): A variable incentive policy is now introduced according to the urgency of balancing the station's load. The objective of this type of incentive is to increase user interest during periods of high system load. Two variables are taken into account to calculate the amount of the incentive: the distance to the new station and the short term estimation of that station. This estimation has been calculated as described in the behavior of the BikeAgent in Sect. 4.1. The first step is to determine the price at which agents have a 100% chance of accepting the incentive. We have used the results from the survey carried out by Ban et al. [1]. From this, we obtain data about the influence of the extra distance to be covered and the economic reward. Once this amount is obtained, a level of urgency is stated to apply the policy, based on the current status and short term changes of the concerned station. An approximation is then made, according to a logarithmic distribution, of the level of urgency. The threshold value for action is set at 30% of the station capacity.

$$P_i = B_i - CI_i + CO_i \tag{3}$$

$$U_i = max(min((T + P_i) * log(e), 0.0), 1.0), \quad U_i \in [0, 1] \tag{4}$$

B_i being the number of bicycles or available decks at the station i; CI_i the number of agents intending to rent in a range of fewer than 10 min of the station i; CO_i the number of agents in a range of fewer than 10 min intending to park at the station i; U_i the urgency for the station i; T is the threshold value for action; and P_i the short term estimation for the station i.

According to the urgency calculated for station i and the price for guaranteed participation at a distance m (Pg_m), the price offered to the BikeAgent is adjusted as follows, and the probability of acceptance by the agent is calculated.

$$P_{im} = U_i * Pg_m, \quad P_{im} \in [0, 2] \tag{5}$$

Variable Incentives with Lineal Urgency (VI-LIN): This scenario includes the same policies as the previous case, 0.10€ incentives, variable incentives, and trucks. However, there is a difference in the way the level of urgency is calculated. A linear distribution is now followed according to the number of bikes or docks available in the forecast. The rest of the process for applying the incentive remains unchanged.

$$P_i = B_i - CI_i + CO_i \tag{6}$$

$$U_i = max(min((T - P_i)/(2 * T), 0.0), 1.0), \quad U_i \in [0, 1] \tag{7}$$

This research work has used the agent-based simulation framework MESA[2], an Apache2 licensed Agent-based model (ABM) framework in Python. Its usefulness is to facilitate the creation of agent-based models using built-in core components. It also displays results in a browser-based interface, allowing its subsequent analysis of the resulting data. Regarding route calculation, we have used **OpenRouteService (ORS)**, a library developed by GIScience Research Group[3] in Java, which offers a route calculation service, customizable depending on the vehicle type (bicycle or truck). Finally, a **Tornado Web Server**[4] deployment has been used for providing a visual interface.

5   Evaluation

In order to obtain results, seven simulations of a 4-day use situation have been performed, since the ABM represents 1 min per step. This gives us a total of 5760 steps per simulation. Certain variables are set according to real values to compare the results between behaviors. In particular, the following setting has been used: bike speed (18 km/h), truck speed (40 km/h), number of trips (74.000), the maximum number of trucks (6), truck capacity (20), the maximum walking distance (1 km) and the maximum riding distance (1 km). We have studied the distribution of the trip, the evolution of the station load, the unavailability rate (ratio between failed trips and total trips), and the total profit (the difference between travel income and incentive costs).

Model realism has been evaluated by correlating the distance of both Bici-MAD trips and BM simulated ones Fig. 2b shows the distribution of the trip duration of both BM and BiciMAD datasets. Both define a skew normal distribution, being BM durations average slightly higher. This may indicate a higher real speed than that used in the simulations. Higher dispersion of values in the BM is also observed. Despite the differences, both cases show apparent similarities, so we assume a correct functioning of the BM, and it will be taken as a reference from now on.

The distribution of the **duration** for each model is shown in Table 3a. There are no significant differences between the results of the different scenarios. However, the best results are obtained for BM50, obtaining an average duration of half a minute less than BM. Regarding the **occupancy of the stations** in Table 3b, the data about the number of stations in an unbalanced situation can be found. The best results are obtained for the BM50 scenario with an

---

[2] https://github.com/projectmesa.
[3] https://github.com/GIScience.
[4] https://github.com/tornadoweb/tornado.

Table 3. Unavailability rates and load of stations.

	Trips duration		Unavailability rate	
	μ (sec.)	σ (sec.)	μ (%)	σ (%)
BM	972.53	535.96	0.1024	0.061
BM50	**941.42**	587.67	**0.0507**	**0.034**
VI-LOG	962.29	592.79	0.072	0.044
VI-LIN	951.48	**535.39**	0.0659	0.044

(a) Mean (μ) and standard deviation (σ) of trips duration and unavailability rate.

Scenario	LL μ	LL σ	HL μ	HL σ
BM	34.853	20.37	16.27	9.94
BM50	**25.894**	**17.30**	**10.544**	**8.154**
VI-LOG	33.09	24.92	15.158	9.14
VI-LIN	32.826	19.4	15.26	9.18

(b) Mean (μ) and standard deviation (σ) of the number of low and high load stations. Low Load (LL) and High Load (HL).

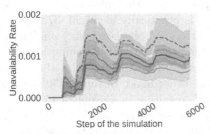

(a) Unavailability rate evolution. Dotted blue BM, orange BM50, green VI-LOG, red VI-LIN.

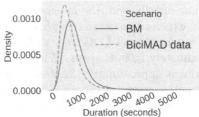

(b) Behavior comparison according to trips duration.

Fig. 2. Failure evolution and trip duration distribution.

Table 4. Morris analysis: values ranges and indices for unavailability rate.

Variable	Value
Bike speed	[10,30] (km/h)
Max. distance walking	[250,1000] (m)
Max. distance riding	[250,1000] (m)
Incentive amount	[0.1,0.5] (€)

(a) Value ranges for Morris analysis.

Parameter	μ	μ^*	σ
bike_speed	-0.00621	0.0086	0.0088
walking_max	**-0.6649**	**0.0664**	**0.0119**
riding_max	-0.01362	0.0136	0.0139
base_incentive	-0.0121	0.0133	0.0112

(b) Morris indices for the unavailability rate.

improvement of 25.7% and 35.2% in the number of low and high load stations, respectively. This stands out against the small improvements achieved by the policy of variable incentives. Peaks can be observed corresponding to the rush hours (17:00 to 20:00). The study of the **unavailability rate**, which can be seen in Fig. 2a and Table 3a, allows us to indicate what percentage of users have not been able to make their journey and therefore have had to leave the system. This ratio has been calculated according to the failed trips with relation to the totals. Where F is the number of failed trips, and S is the number of completed trips.

$$UR = F/(F + S) \tag{8}$$

An agent leaves the system when it is unable to find an available bicycle at its station or elsewhere in its area of action. This area is bounded by the maximum walking distance. When the agent fails to find an available base to park, it decides to wait. The dataset provided by BiciMAD has only the trips completed satisfactorily, so it is not possible to make a comparison. An improvement in the unavailability rate can be observed, especially in the case of BM50, with a 50% reduction. In the case of VI-LOG and VI-LIN models, no assumptions can be made as their levels do not vary significantly from each other.

As for the **total income**, since the trips made in the different models follow the same distribution, the income received is practically identical, 37,000€. As for the expenses associated with the incentives we observe a very similar distribution for the VI-LOG and VI-LIN scenarios with BM, reaching a total of approximately 5,000€ spent. With this, the profit associated with these three scenarios is approximately 32,000€. On the other hand, in the BM50 scenario, the incentive costs are increased to 22,000€, resulting in a profit of 15,000€.

The model has been evaluated using the sensitivity analysis Morris [18] method with the support of the SALib[5] library. Those have been set as output variables: the number of full stations (without available bases) and empty stations (without bicycles), the duration of the journeys, the unavailability rate, and the total income. The study of the variation of these outputs has been focused on the following input variables: the speed of the bike, the maximum walking distance, the maximum riding distance, and the basic incentive offered. There have been generated five trajectories that give us a total of 25 samples of variables that will simulate 4-day of usage of the system. In Table 4a, the value ranges for these parameters are shown.

The maximum walking distance (*walking_max*) is one of the most influential parameters in several outputs, such as the number of empty and full stations or the unavailable rate, Table 4b. This is due to the increase in the number of possible check-in stations. Another variable that stands out is the base amount of the incentive (*base_incentive*), which has a great impact on the number of stations in an unbalanced load and on the system's income. The maximum riding distance mainly influences the duration of the trips, indicating that the waiting time to find a free base is one of its main factors.

6   Conclusions

A multiagent social model has been designed to analyze the influences of passive repositioning policies on a BSS. In this model, four scenarios with different policies have been implemented. We have also tested the influence of increasing the incentive amount in a separate way, even though this reduces the reported income.

---

[5] https://salib.readthedocs.io/en/latest/.

The main contribution is the proposal of a variable incentive policy using the validated simulation model. These incentives are offered during hours of high levels of system use. Simulations show a reduction in the amount of money invested in incentive payments in these scenarios. It also shows better results in balancing the load between the stations and reducing the unavailability rate in making the trips. This policy yields positive results over the reference scenario in every variable studied.

The main future work in this research line is the integration of a machine learning system to forecast user demand on the stations. With this, we will be able to predict inequality in the stations and act before it happens.

Acknowledgments. This research has been funded by the UPM University-Industry Chair Cabify for Sustainable Mobility. The authors want also to thank EMT for providing BiciMad service data.

References

1. Ban, S., Hyun, K.H.: Designing a user participation-based bike rebalancing service. Sustainability **11**(8), 2396 (2019)
2. Bouton, S., Hannon, E., Knupfer, S., Ramkumar, S.: The future(s) of mobility: how cities can benefit. Technical report, McKinsey & Company (2017)
3. Chen, B., Cheng, H.H.: A review of the applications of agent technology in traffic and transportation systems. IEEE Trans. Intell. Transp. Syst. **11**(2), 485–497 (2010)
4. Chen, L., Zhang, D.E.A.: Dynamic cluster-based over-demand prediction in bike sharing systems. In: Proceedings of the 2016 ACM International Joint Conference on Pervasive and Ubiquitous Computing, pp. 841–852. ACM (2016)
5. Conebi: European bicycle market 2017 edition. Technical report, Confederation of the European Bicycle Industry (CONEBI) (2017)
6. Dell'Amico, M., Iori, M., Novellani, S., Subramanian, A.: The bike sharing rebalancing problem with stochastic demands. Transp. Res. Part B **118**, 362–380 (2018)
7. Diez, C., Sanchez-Anguix, V., Palanca, J., Julian, V., Giret, A.: Station status forecasting module for a multi-agent proposal to improve efficiency on bike-sharing usage. In: Belardinelli, F., Argente, E. (eds.) EUMAS/AT -2017. LNCS (LNAI), vol. 10767, pp. 476–489. Springer, Cham (2018). https://doi.org/10.1007/978-3-030-01713-2_33
8. Dötterl, J., Bruns, R., Dunkel, J., Ossowski, S.: Towards dynamic rebalancing of bike sharing systems: an event-driven agents approach. In: Oliveira, E., Gama, J., Vale, Z., Lopes Cardoso, H. (eds.) EPIA 2017. LNCS (LNAI), vol. 10423, pp. 309–320. Springer, Cham (2017). https://doi.org/10.1007/978-3-319-65340-2_26
9. Feigon, S., Murphy, C.: Shared mobility and the transformation of public transit. Technical report. Project J-11, Task 21, American Public Transportation Association (2016)
10. Fernández, A., Billhardt, H., Timón, S., Ruiz, C., Sánchez, Ó., Bernabé, I.: Balancing strategies for bike sharing systems. In: Lujak, M. (ed.) AT 2018. LNCS (LNAI), vol. 11327, pp. 208–222. Springer, Cham (2019). https://doi.org/10.1007/978-3-030-17294-7_16

11. Kaltenbrunner, A., Meza, R., Grivolla, J., Codina, J., Banchs, R.: Urban cycles and mobility patterns: exploring and predicting trends in a bicycle-based public transport system. Pervasive Mob. Comput. **6**(4), 455–466 (2010)
12. Leao, S.Z., Pettit, C.: Mapping bicycling patterns with an agent-based model, census and crowdsourced data. In: Namazi-Rad, M.-R., Padgham, L., Perez, P., Nagel, K., Bazzan, A. (eds.) ABMUS 2016. LNCS (LNAI), vol. 10051, pp. 112–128. Springer, Cham (2017). https://doi.org/10.1007/978-3-319-51957-9_7
13. Li, Y., Zheng, Y., Zhang, H., Chen, L.: Traffic prediction in a bike-sharing system. In: Proceedings of the 23rd International Conference on Advances in Geographic Information Systems, p. 33. ACM (2015)
14. Liu, J., Sun, L., Chen, W., Xiong, H.: Rebalancing bike sharing systems: A multi-source data smart optimization. In: Proceedings of the 22nd ACM SIGKDD International Conference on Knowledge Discovery and Data Mining, pp. 1005–1014. ACM (2016)
15. Lozano, Á., De Paz, J., Villarrubia, G., Iglesia, D., Bajo, J.: Multi-agent system for demand prediction and trip visualization in bike sharing systems. Appl. Sci. **8**(1), 67 (2018)
16. Meddin, R., Demaio, P.: The bike share world map. https://www.bikesharingmap.com (2007). Accessed 10 Nov 2019
17. Mi, Z., Coffman, D.: The sharing economy promotes sustainable societies. Nat. Commun. **10**(1), 1214 (2019)
18. Morris, M.D.: Factorial sampling plans for preliminary computational experiments. Technometrics **33**(2), 161–174 (1991)
19. Nassirtoussi, A.K., Aghabozorgi, S., Wah, T.Y., Ngo, D.C.L.: Text mining for market prediction: a systematic review. Expert Syst. Appl. **41**(16), 7653–7670 (2014)
20. Nations, U.: World urbanization prospects. Technical report, United Nations (2018)
21. Pinna, F., Masala, F., Garau, C.: Urban policies and mobility trends in Italian smart cities. Sustainability **9**(4), 494 (2017)
22. Raviv, T., Kolka, O.: Optimal inventory management of a bike-sharing station. IIE Trans. **45**(10), 1077–1093 (2013)
23. Serrano, E., Iglesias, C.A.: Validating viral marketing strategies in twitter via agent-based social simulation. Expert Syst. Appl. **50**, 140–150 (2016)
24. Singhvi, D., et al.: Predicting bike usage for New York city's bike sharing system. In: Workshops at the Twenty-Ninth AAAI Conference on Artificial Intelligence (2015)
25. Singla, A., Santoni, M., Bartók, G., Mukerji, P., Meenen, M., Krause, A.: Incentivizing users for balancing bike sharing systems. In: 29th AAAI Conference on Artificial Intelligence (2015)
26. Soriguera, F., Casado, V., Jiménez, E.: A simulation model for public bike-sharing systems. Transp. Res. Procedia **33**, 139–146 (2018)
27. Van Audenhove, F.J.E.A.: The future of urban mobility 2.0: imperatives to shape extended mobility ecosystems of tomorrow. Technical report, Arthur D. Little (2014)
28. Wallentin, G., Loidl, M.: Agent-based bicycle traffic model for salzburg city. GI_Forum J. Geogr. Inf. Sci. **2015**, 558–566 (2015)
29. Zhang, Y., Mi, Z.: Environmental benefits of bike sharing: a big data-based analysis. Appl. Energy **220**, 296–301 (2018)

Decentralized Constraint Optimization in Composite Observation Task Allocation to Mobile Sensor Agents

Toshihiro Matsui[✉]

Nagoya Institute of Technology, Gokiso-cho, Showa-ku, Nagoya 466-8555, Japan
matsui.t@nitech.ac.jp

Abstract. Cooperative severance and observation by autonomous multiple mobile sensors have been studied for wide area monitoring, disaster response, and exploration in unsafe zones. In practical situations, sensor agents might be required to perform various composite tasks. To integrate them, the general representation of problems and decentralized solution methods for different requirements are necessary. The distributed constraint optimization problem has been studied as a general and fundamental combinational optimization problem in multiagent systems. Although several studies have applied this approach to sensor networks and teams of mobile sensors, opportunities also exit to apply it to manage composite tasks and utilize decentralized protocols in the sub-tasks in several layers of observation systems. As a case study, we address a cooperative observation system consisting of mobile sensor agents that temporally observe unsafe zones on a floor or a field with obstacles, where the basis of the tasks is the division of observation areas for the agents. We also allocate several tasks with high priority to several agents. We applied a decentralized constraint optimization method to the cooperation for both task allocation and the division of an observation area and experimentally verified our proposed approach in a simulated environment.

Keywords: Mobile sensors · Multiagents · Distributed constraint optimization · Task allocation

1 Introduction

Cooperative severance and observation by autonomous multiple mobile sensors have been studied for wide area monitoring, disaster response, and exploration in unsafe zones. In practical situations, sensor agents might be required to perform such composite tasks as exploration, patrolling, focusing, tracking, and supporting communication channels. To integrate various tasks, the general representation of problems and solution methods for different requirements is necessary,

This work was supported in part by JSPS KAKENHI Grant Number JP19K12117 and Tatematsu Zaidan.

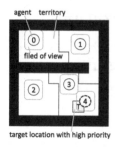
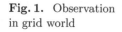
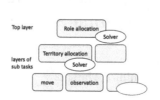
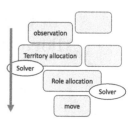

Fig. 1. Observation in grid world

Fig. 2. Hierarchical structure of subtasks

Fig. 3. Flow of processing

even though each subtask is done by dedicated algorithms. Moreover, some part of a subtask can be performed in a decentralized manner by partially employing such a general representation.

The distributed constraint optimization problem (DCOP) [4] has been studied as a general and fundamental combinational optimization problem in multiagent systems. Several studies have applied it to sensor networks and teams of mobile sensors [2,7,14]. In studies, the benefit of the general representation of DCOPs, which can be applied to various resource allocation problems, is employed. On the other hand, opportunities can be identified for applying the approach to manage composite tasks and utilize decentralized protocols in the subtasks in several layers of observation systems.

In a case study toward implementation, we address a cooperative observation system consisting of mobile sensor agents that temporarily observe the unsafe zones on a floor of a building or a field with obstacles. The observation task is based on the division and allocation of the observation area, and the agents explore their own allocated areas. In addition to the basic task, several high-priority tasks are allocated to several agents. We applied a decentralized constraint optimization method for the cooperation, both in the highest layer for task allocation and a lower layer for a subtask to divide the observation area. We experimentally verified our approach in a simulated environment.

The rest of the paper is organized as follows. In the next section, we present the motivating problem domain and introduce the distributed constraint optimization problems as background of our study. We propose a framework of cooperation among mobile sensor agents that perform composite tasks in Sect. 3. The proposed approach is experimentally verified in Sect. 4. We address the issues of solution methods based on pseudo trees for future investigation in Sect. 5 and discuss our proposed approach in Sect. 6. We conclude our study and address future works in Sect. 7.

2 Preliminary

2.1 Example Problem of Multiple Mobile Sensor Agents

In this study, we address a domain of problems with autonomous mobile sensors that cooperatively observe in the hazardous zones on a floor of a building or a field with obstacles. The purpose of the observation includes exploration, patrolling, and focusing on a target. To cooperatively perform composite observation tasks in a decentralized manner, we require a generic framework that represents and solves the decision-making problems in some of the subtasks.

As our first case study toward a practical application, we assume a team of mobile sensor agents that cooperatively explore and focus on several targets in a grid world as shown in Fig. 1. In a lower layer subtask of the system, the agents patrol their observation areas to update their information of the areas. Here, dividing a whole observation area into the territories of agents is a fundamental subtask. In contrast, in the top layer of the system, different prioritized subtasks are allocated to the agents. One of the tasks with higher priority is the observation of specific target locations that have to be temporally allocated to some of agents.

In general cases, including the above tasks, some decision making is necessary for some of lower layer subtasks. The allocation of sub tasks in the top layer is also the decision making. From this perspective, we address decision making in both the division of the observation area into territories and subtask allocation to the agents. We focus on the decision making in part of the problems and formalize them with the fundamental representation of DCOPs. With the formalization, we present an integrated framework of the solution process for decision making in multiple layers of a system.

To concentrate on substantial problems in this study, we assume several background settings. A map of the observation area is given as agents' knowledge, and its information can be dynamically updated with additional methods, if necessary. Some agents temporally stay in a single cell with an appropriate collision avoidance technique. Several details of the communication scheme are beyond the scope of this paper, including how the locations of the special targets are propagated to the agents by a monitoring user or methods above the observation system.

2.2 Distributed Constraint Optimization Problem

The Distributed Constraint Optimization Problem (DCOP) is a constraint optimization problem on a multiagent system, where variables, constraints and objective functions represent the decision of agents and the relationship among them [4].

A standard DCOP is defined by $\langle A, X, D, F \rangle$, where A is a set of agents, X is a set of variables, D is a set of the domains of variables, and F is a set of constraints or objective functions. Variables $X_i \subseteq X$ represent the state or decision of agent $i \in A$. Variable $x_{i,k} \in X_i$ takes a value in a set of discrete values $D_{i,k} \in D$.

Function $f_j \in F$ represents the objective values for the assignments to variables $\{x_0^{f_j}, \cdots, x_m^{f_j}\}$ in the scope of f_j. For minimizing problems, f_j is a cost function $f_j : D_0^{f_j} \times \cdots \times D_m^{f_j} \to \mathbb{N}_0$, assuming f_j takes non-negative integer values. Constraints can be represented with the infinity cost value. The global cost function is defined as the summation of the cost functions for all agents: $F = \sum_{f_j \in F} f_j$. The objective is to find the assignment for the variables that minimizes the value of global cost function. For maximization problems, the objective functions are defined with utility values.

In a simple case, it is assumed that each agent has a single variable, and all functions are binary functions for two variables. This assumption is useful because a problem is represented by a constraint graph where vertices and edges directly represent agents/variables and objective functions. For more practical problems, each agent has multiple variables/vectors that are related by n-ary functions with several extensions.

In addition, the aggregation of objective values can be extended with specific structures. The summation of cost values can be replaced by the maximization. Objective values with a hierarchical structure represent the priority among multiple objectives. In a different class of multi-objective problems, objective values are aggregated for individual agents and represented by objective vectors [9].

The agents cooperatively find a solution that optimizes the aggregated value of the objective function under the constraints using a decentralized solution method with interaction among the agents. Various solution methods for DCOPs have been proposed [4] and can be categorized into exact methods [10,12,13] and inexact methods [2,3,6]. Although the exact methods find optimal solutions, they are not applicable for large scale and complex problems.

Most exact methods need additional graph structures called pseudo-trees that have to be constructed in preprocessing [10,12,13]. A pseudo tree is based on a spanning tree on a constraint graph. Here, edges of the original graph are categorized into tree edges and back edges, where the tree edges are the ones of the spanning tree. This approach is a kind of tree decomposition with cut-edges between upper and lower nodes in a pseudo tree. For each node in a pseudo tree, back edges and a tree edge that connect to upper nodes correspond to variables called separators. The separators are contained in a sub-problem for the node. See the related literature for details.

Inexact methods are relatively scalable and can find quasi-optimal solutions. Several local search methods only depend on groups of neighborhood nodes in constraint graphs and can be employed with simple commitment mechanisms.

2.3   A Decentralized Solution Method

For the first step of a practical domain, applying a local search method, which is based on interaction among neighborhood agents that are directly related constraints, is reasonable, since its control depends on a relatively simple graph structure. We employ a simple local search method based on MGM [4,8] to solve a DCOP. We simplified the protocol with a commitment mechanism for fast convergence. Here, neighborhood agents that are related by a constraint or an objective function communicate and solve a problem. The following is the flow of the solution method.

1. Each agent initializes the parameters for the objectives, the constraints, and the variables of a problem by exchanging their information with its related neighborhood agents.
2. Each agent locally evaluates its assignment to variables under the objectives and constraints.
3. Each agent selects an assignment to its variables that corresponds to the best evaluation value. Then the best value is announced to its neighborhood agents related to the agent.
4. Each agent determines the best evaluation value among its neighborhood agents. Then the best value and the identity of the corresponding agent is sent to its neighborhood agent.
5. The winning agent who has the best evaluation value among its neighbor agents, determines its best assignment, and notifies its neighborhood agents of the termination with its best assignment.
6. Until all the agents terminate or cut-off iteration, the process is repeated from step 2.

For simplicity, we assume a simple barrier synchronization in each communication step including the dedicated processing of subtasks and DCOP solvers by a simulator that can be implemented using several fundamental algorithms. When the problem consists of multiple layers, a solution method is under the solution of the upper layers. Moreover, the entire problem should be designed considering the applicability of DCOP formalization. We address several such problems as a case study.

3 Proposed Framework

3.1 Basic Architecture

The proposed framework consists of multiple layers. In the top layer, agents negotiate to determine their roles. They also negotiate to manage parts of subtasks in several lower layers. Figures 2 and 3 show its architecture. The roles of agents are allocated in the top layer, and in the lower layers, the subtasks of the agents are performed by solving cooperation problems, if necessary. For simplicity, we focus on two contrasting problems that are included in a subtask to divide the observation area into the territories of agents in a lower layer and a process to determine the roles of agents in the top layer. Both problems contain decision making among agents, and those are modeled with DCOPs.

In the whole processing, the solution methods for each layer are performed from preprocessing to post-processing based on the dependence among the subtasks. We focus on how to apply the DCOP approach to a part of several problems in composite subtasks with pre/post-processing.

3.2 Dividing Observation Areas by Agents

Representation of Territories. Agents exclusively divide an entire observation area into territories that they then explore. Here we employ a representation of a grid world with four adjacent cells for the movements of agents. Since

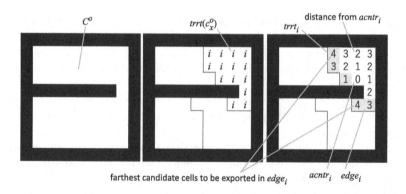

Fig. 4. Notations for territories

the territories are identical as the areas patrolled by moving agents, the size of divided areas should be equalized as possible. The territories can be non-convex, because there might be obstacles on a floor or in a field. We employ a representation of territories that considers the area size similar to the capacity-constrained Voronoi tessellation [1]. However, the size of the territories should be dynamically equalized. For non-convex tessellations that might have no centroid, each generating point is simply approximated to the nearest cell to the averaged coordinate of a tessellation. The approximated generating point is only employed to measure the distance from the tessellation's origin. A map of such distances can be simply computed by a variant of Dijkstra's algorithm.

Each agent appropriately exchanges the information of its territory. Then the agents with neighboring territories trade the edge cells of their territories to balance the size of their areas. In trades, an opposite territory with the maximum difference size between a pair of area is prioritized. In addition, the most remote cells are exported to retain the shape of the exporter's territory as much as possible. Although the size of traded cells is limited to the differences between two territories, the number of the farthest cells is small in most cases. This heuristic method might create small fragments of territories around edges, since it does not ensure that the remotest cells are exported. Instead of that, it prioritizes better balance among area sizes. On the other hand, several other situations, including dynamic environments and changing roles, might also create observation areas that are outside of any territories. Therefore, we allow such territory fragments as incomplete observation areas. An agent who detects non-connected areas purges those areas that are unallocated to any agents. Such unallocated areas are gradually absorbed into neighboring territories during the operation of related agents.

Cooperation to Trade Territories. Most part of the above subtask can be composed as a set of dedicated methods. Even if some conflicts exist among territories, they can be solved with some tie-breakers based on logical time and identifiers of agents related to territory cells. However, for selecting a peer with

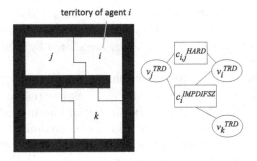

Fig. 5. Problem for territories

whom to trade territory, more negotiation is necessary to avoid inconsistent situations where an importer simultaneously exports edge cells that are adjacent to the imported cells. Such negotiation can be managed with a DOCP.

Here an agent can take two actions: 1) exporting part of its territory to another agent or 2) importing part of the territories from other agents[1]. For exporting, the peer-importer agent corresponds to the maximum difference size of area between two territories. Decision variables represent these actions. The constraints are the consistency between the exporter and importer agents. The objective function is defined as the maximum difference size of areas related to an importer agents to balance the territory sizes.

This problem is only related to agents who perform the subtasks of territories. It is defined with a set of observation area cells C^o to be divided and a set of agents A to be allocated to the cells. For C^o and each cell $c_x^o \in C^o$, several properties are defined as shown in Fig. 4. $trrt(c_x^o)$ denotes a territory of cell c_x^o. $trrt_i$ is a set of the territory cells of agent a_i. $edge_i$ is a set of the edge cells of $trrt_i$. $acnr_i$ is an approximated centroid of $trrt_i$. As mentioned above, most parts of this problem can be addressed with dedicated methods because they are the operation of cells, although it contains a DCOP part. Before solving this problem, agents exchange and update the current state of C^o.

Variables and Constraints. We formalize this problem as a maximization problem. Figure 5 shows the structure of the problem. Each agent $a_i \in A$ has decision variable v_i^{TRD} that represents the decision of importing and exporting territory. v_i^{TRD} takes a value from $D^{TRD} = \{trd^{IMP}, trd^{EXP}\}$. For the case of $v_i^{TRD} = trd^{EXP}$, the destination agent $expDst_i$ who receives a_i's territory is previously determined. It takes an identifier of an agent who has adjacent territory with the maximum difference of territory size such that $\text{argmax}_j \ \max(w_i \times |trrt_i| - w_j \times |trrt_j|, 0)$. Here w_i and w_j are the weight values to define the ability of agents to observe their territory. Although the

---

[1] The actions might cause a small fluctuation in situations that have almost converged. But we allow this situation as dynamics of our system.

weight values can represent the agents' ability, we set the parameters to the same value. In addition, the difference size $expDstSz_i$ for $expDst_i$ is also stored. The information of $expDst_i$ and $expDstSz_i$ are shared by related agents before the cooperation problem is solved.

Hard constraint $c_{i,j}^{HARD}$ avoids inconsistent situations where $v_i^{TRD} = trd^{EXP} \wedge expDst_i = j \wedge v_j^{TRD} = trd^{EXP}$ to assure that a pair of exporter and importer agents avoids contradictory operations around edge cells.

We also define, the following utility value to be maximized. $c_i^{IMPDIFSZ}$: the maximum difference size of territories for all neighborhood agents N_i^{TRRT} of adjacent territories. It is evaluated as $\max_{j \in N_i^{TRRT}} expDstSz_j$ when $v_i^{TRD} = trd^{IMP}$. Otherwise, it is set to zero. $c_i^{IMPDIFSZ}$ aims to prioritizes importer agents whose territories are smaller than neighborhood territories. Here, we employed n-ary functions. It can be easily handled by the local search method with minor modifications, because agents only aggregate the information of their neighborhood agents.

Applying Solution Method. Note that the solution method is a local search where the winning agent fixes its solution at a negotiation step. The information of the neighborhood agents is updated in the beginning of each negotiation step. In this problem, importer agents mainly determine their roles and other exporter agents follow.

After the negotiation, all agents trade a part of edge cells $c \in edge_i$ of their territory. Here, for one neighborhood cell c' of c, $trrt(c') = expDst_i$. In addition, cells c are limited to the cells with the maximum distance from $acnr_i$ to keep the shape of a territory as much as possible. Although this approach is heuristic, it will gradually balance the territories among the agents.

3.3 Allocation of Roles to Agents

Roles of Agents. The mobile sensor agents explore and patrol in their territories when there is no special subtask. Some of them are temporally required to perform other prioritized tasks to focus on or track a specific target area. In the top layer of the system, the allocation of such roles should be performed. As a basic situation, we address a problem where several agents are allocated to high-priority subtasks to observe a special target location.

Here, the inheritance or the exchange of the roles between agents should be considered if possible, since that decision retains several contexts such as territory information and reduces the process of rebuilding them from scratch. Some of the costs of losing the current role and starting a new subtask should be evaluated. These problems can be represented with DCOPs.

An agent chooses one of three actions: 1) exploration, 2) focusing on/tracking a location, and 3) exchanging roles. For these actions, there are several constraints and objectives for avoiding conflict over their roles and reducing the costs for losing roles and the initial cost of new roles. Under the solution of role

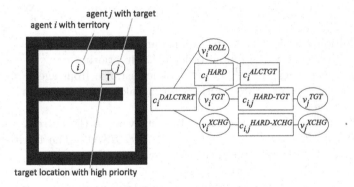

Fig. 6. Problem for roles

allocation problems in the top layer, agents solve other cooperation problems in the lower layers.

Variables and Constraints with Hierarchical Objective Vectors. Since several hierarchical structures are necessary to describe such constraints and objectives, we extend an objective value to a hierarchical vector that represent prioritized objective values. Hierarchical vector **v** consists of objective values. In the case of minimization, the comparison of two vectors of identical length is defined as follows. For hierarchical vectors $\boldsymbol{v} = \{v_0, \cdots, v_k\}$ and $\boldsymbol{v}' = \{v'_0, \cdots, v'_k\}$, $\boldsymbol{v} < \boldsymbol{v}'$ iff $\exists t, \forall i < t, v_i = v'_i \wedge v_t < v'_t$. Operator $>$ is similarly defined.

Here the problem is defined with a set of prioritized subtasks to observe target location $T^p = \{t^p_0, \cdots, t^p_k\}$, set of agents A, and set of roles $R = \{r^{TGT}, r^{TRRT}\}$. r^{TGT} and r^{TRRT} denote the roles for observing a target location and a territory. We formalize this problem as a minimization problem. Figure 6 shows the structure of the problem. Each agent $a_i \in A$ has the following decision variables[2]. v_i^{ROLE}: the role of agent that takes a value from $D^{ROLE} = R$. v_i^{TGT}: target location when $v_i^{ROLE} = r^{TGT}$ that takes a value from $D^{TGT} = T^p \cup \{NOTHING\}$. v_i^{XCHG}: peer agent that exchanges roles. It takes a value from $D^{XCHG} = A \cup \{NOTHING\}$.

The objective is defined as the cost values to be minimized. The following objectives are integrated with a hierarchical vector. The highest ones are the hard constraints. c_i^{HARD}: hard constraint for avoiding inconsistent situations for agent i. For agent a_i itself, condition $v_i^{ROLE} = r^{TGT} \wedge v_i^{TGT} = NOTHING$ or $v_i^{ROLE} = r^{TRRT} \wedge v_i^{TGT} \neq NOTHING$, is a violation. $c_{i,j}^{HARD-TGT}$: hard constraint for agents a_i and its neighborhood agent a_j that previously determined its solution. The assignment to variables of a_i cannot be inconsistent with the decision of agent a_j. $v_i^{TGT} = v_j^{TGT}$ is a violation. $c_{i,j}^{HARD-XCHG}$: hard constraint

---

[2] Although they can be more compactly represented, we prefer to directly represent some structures.

for agents i and j that resembles $c_{i,j}^{HARD-TGT}$. $v_i^{XCHG} \neq j \wedge v_j^{XCHG} = i$ is a violation.

In addition, the following cost values are also evaluated. The cost values below are shown in a descending order of their priority. c^{ALCTGT}: cost for a allocated target when $v_i^{ROLE} = r^{TGT}$. The distance from agent a_i to target location of v_i^{TGT} is evaluated. Otherwise, it takes zero. It selects the nearest agent to a target.

$c^{DALCTRRT}$: cost for a deallocated territory when the current role of a_i is r^{TRRT} and $v_i^{ROLE} \neq r^{TRRT} \wedge v_i^{XCHG} = NOTHING$. The territory size of a_i is evaluated. Otherwise, it takes zero. It keeps the context of territory by exchanging its role with other agents, if possible. Actually, this information is also evaluated by peer agents by exchanging related information in a preprocessing.

Applying Solution Method. Similar to the problem for the division of observation areas, agents exchange information to initialize the allocation problem. Then, negotiation steps are repeated until the termination by updating the information of the problem. Winner agents gradually fix their solutions. After the negotiation, each agent performs with a new role. When an agent of role r^{TRRT} cannot exchange its role, its territory is purged as an unallocated area. Other agents of role r^{TRRT} gradually absorb the unallocated area.

3.4 Moving and Observation

As fundamental additional features, moving and observation subtasks are performed without cooperative decision making. Each agent sets its subgoal at each step based on its role. When an agent is allocated to a target location, the subgoal is set to the location. Otherwise, an agent selects its subgoal so that the agent can observe a cell whose observed time step is older than a threshold value. One of candidate cells nearest to the current location of the agent becomes the next subgoal. Agents employ the shortest path-finding algorithm to determine the paths to their subgoal locations.

Each agent observes its field of view and updates the information of the corresponding cells of a map at each step. Here we assumed that the field of view is the location of an agent and its neighboring eight cells. Each cell has a time stamp that records the steps at which it was recently observed.

3.5 Neighborhood Limitation

In practical cases, neighborhood agents should be limited to consider communication range and to reduce the size of the local problems, although the accuracy of solutions might decrease. The limitation, which affects both the pre-process and the main solution process of DCOPs, also depends each type of subtasks.

Here we assume that each agent cooperates with the limited number of other agents closer to the agent. For the problem of dividing observation areas, each agent exchanges information of them with the particular agents. It is assumed that the other information can be gradually propagated. The neighborhood agent that can be an opponent of a territory trade is also limited to the particular agents that directly exchanges the observation area information. The range should include the agents of adjacent territories.

For the problem of role allocation to specific target locations, each target location is initially related to some of closer agents from the target location. For simplicity, we assumed an overlay communication channel or a mechanism for announcing target locations to part of agents. The neighborhood agents who cooperate to determine the roles are also limited to the particular agents.

4   Evaluation

We experimentally investigated our proposed approach in a simulation environment to illustrate the fundamental activity of the proposed framework as our first study. The simulation environments were the grid worlds of 10×10 and 15×15 with four and ten agents. We assumed a situation where agents are initially located around a special area such as an entrance. Then, the agents move toward their territories or special target locations according to solutions of cooperation problems in each step. We set the cutoff iteration of the DCOP solution process to 20 for both role allocation and territory division. The entire process was repeated until 50 steps. The experiment was performed on a computer with Core i-7-7700@3.60 GHz, 32 GB memory and Windows 10. The computational time of our experimental implementation was 96 s for the case of 15×15 grid and ten agents without neighborhood limitation.

4.1   Results of Basic Dynamics

We first show examples of dynamics of the system related to the problems on which we focus. Figure 7 and 8 (a) show the division of the observation areas. Here, the initial territories of the agents are the initial locations of them. Each territory gradually grows by absorbing the neighboring non-allocated areas by a operation of subtask. Territories are simultaneously traded by solving DCOPs to determine importer and exporter pairs.

Figure 8 (b) shows the time curves of the territory sizes. Here a target location appeared and then moved at steps 20 and 30. For simplicity, the locations of the agents were fixed to their initial locations that are the same as the case of Fig. 7 (b). At step 20, the roles of agents are changed to capture a target location at (5, 5) shown in Fig. 7 (a), and the nearest agent 3 is allocated to the target location. Then at step 30, the role to capture a moved target location (2, 2) is allocated to the nearest agent 0. In this case, an action exchanges the roles of agents 0 and 3, and the territory of agent 0 was inherited by agent 3.

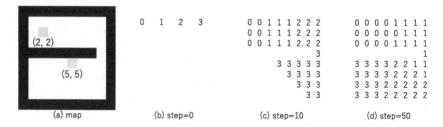

Fig. 7. Territories (4 agents) Black and white/grey cells in (a) represent obstacles and floors. The numbers in (b)-(d) correspond to identifiers of agents and represent territories of the agents. The initial locations of agents are identical to the initial territories in (b). The coordinate of left-top cell is (0, 0).

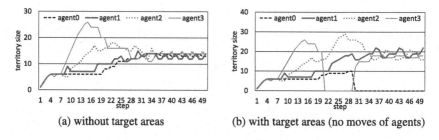

Fig. 8. Size of territories (4 agents)

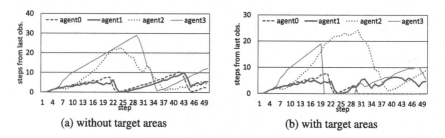

Fig. 9. Freshness of observation area (4 agents)

4.2 Results with Additional Features

Next we show the results with additional features of our system. Agents move and update the observation information of their areas based on roles and territories. Figure 9 shows an example of the update of observed information in the territories. After the territories have almost converged, the update of observed information is also relatively stable.

The results in Fig. 10 and Table 1 show the case of ten agents. Here, three target locations were appeared and and changed at three steps. We limited the number of neighborhood agents. Table 1 (a) shows the size of local problems, and Table 1 (b) shows the number of agents for each ratio of territory size in

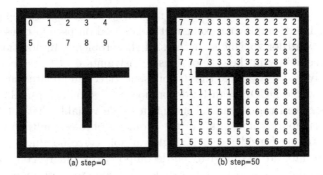

Fig. 10. Territories (10 agents) The numbers correspond to identifiers of agents and represent territories of the agents.

Table 1. Limitation of neighborhood agents (10 agents)

(a) size of local problems

max. nbrs.		10	4	3
nbrs. dcop trrt.	ave.	2.6	2.1	1.7
	max.	5	4	3
nbrs. dcop role	ave.	7.4	2.6	1.4
	max.	9	8	5
iter. dcop trrt.	ave.	4.5	3.7	3
	max.	9	9	9
iter. dcop role	ave.	7.4	5.2	2.7
	max.	9	8	5
num. role xchg.		3	5	4

(b) ratio of territory size

max. nbrs.	ratio of trrt. size					
	0-	0.1-	0.2-	0.3-	0.4-	0.5-1
10	131	193	44	11	1	0
4	141	177	52	7	0	0
3	146	166	40	18	1	0

comparison to the whole observation area. Those results were accumulated for all simulation steps. Although the number of iterations is relatively small due to the local search method, in the case of no limitation of neighborhood agents, more interaction is required. On the other hand, in this setting, the influence to the solution quality by the limitation was not so significant as shown in Tables 1 (a) and (b). However, we found that in more larger problems, the limitation caused a separation of agents who have adjacent territories of large size. To avoid a lock in the trade of territories due to this issue, the communication of such agents should be maintained by a routing or a formation of agents considering their communication range.

5 Consideration for Pseudo-tree-based Solution Methods

We employed a relatively simple local search method. Although the above DCOPs for two tasks have several dedicated structures, it can be easily handled by the local search methods with minor modifications of aggregation operation. On the other hand, employing exact methods based on pseudo trees might not be straightforward for specific structures of the problems. In addition, there is the issue of scalability in the case of dense constraints.

As an analysis, we evaluated the size of pseudo trees and related sub-problems by assuming whole DCOPs can be decomposed by standard pseudo trees. For the problems of territories, each agent has a single variable that related to the variables of neighborhood agents. For the problems of roles, multiple variables of an agent are simply considered as a single variable corresponding to the agent. All the constraints are assumed to be decomposed by binary constraints, and edges in constraint graphs are integrated for the same pairs of nodes. Similar to the evaluation shown in Sect. 4.2, we also evaluated the cases where number of neighborhood agents are limited. In such cases, multiple connected components in a constrained graph and corresponding pseudo trees might be generated. We arranged the connected components so that any components do not overlap each other.

Table 2 (a) shows the size of pseudo trees. This result is evaluated for the same case shown in Sect. 4.2, and contains the situations where all agents are independent. We assumed that agents are independent when there are no neighborhood territories, or when there are no targets. Note that the system was driven with local search methods, and pseudo trees in different situations for simulation steps were evaluated. As shown in Table 2 (a), the number of separator variables for the problem of territories was relatively small. Namely, there are relatively small number of back edges in pseudo trees. On the other hand, for the problems of roles, most variables are contained in a separator due to constraints for targets that are shared by all related agents. Table 2 (b) shows the number of solutions that are evaluated by each agent. Here, the size for the case of local search is also shown. In the case of pseudo trees for the problems of roles, the size of solution space is intractable without approximation due to multiple variables and a number of separators.

One might think that for relatively small problems, solution methods based on pseudo trees can be directly applicable. However, there are several issues that were ignored by the above assumption of standard pseudo trees. Here we note them for future investigation. In the case of problems of territories, the maximum difference size among peers of territories is aggregated for each agent. These problems can be considered asymmetric multi-objective problems. In a global view, the difference values should be separately aggregated and sorted for all the agents. This requires some additional techniques even though there might be opportunities to employ standard pseudo trees. Similarly, some part of the problems for roles also can be considered multiple objectives for agents, because the cost values including the allocation and deallocation of tasks are related to individual agents. To globally prioritize them, additional data structure of aggregation will be necessary. It reveals the difficulty to design the problems with practical structures when standard exact solution methods that require strict description of problems are employed. Since the aggregation operation in

Table 2. Problem size based on pseudo trees (10 agents)

(a) size of pseudo trees

max. nbrs.			10	4	3
dcop trrt.	num. psd. trees	total	69	66	96
		ave.	1.38	1.32	1.92
	height	ave.	3.46	3.44	2.11
		max.	7	7	7
	sz. separators	ave.	1.30	0.99	0.76
		max.	3	2	3
dcop role	num. psd. trees	total	131	198	275
		ave.	2.62	3.96	5.5
	height	ave.	2.82	0.85	0.53
		max.	9	5	3
	sz. separators	ave.	3.69	1.32	0.69
		max.	9	4	2

(b) number of solutions in sub-problems

local search				
max. nbrs.		10	4	3
dcop trrt.	ave.	2	2	2
	max.	2	2	2
dcop role	ave.	66.0	17.6	10.1
	max.	80	72	48

pseudo tree				
max. nbrs.		10	4	3
dcop trrt.	ave.	5.8	4.4	3.8
	max.	16	8	16
dcop role	ave.	1.17E+18	4.06E+05	2137.6
	max.	1.07E+19	5.60E+07	23040

simple local search methods can be easily modified, it is often useful in practical cases.

6 Discussion

Many dedicated solution methods can solve practical problems. On the other hand, the design of how such solution methods can be integrated is not straight forward. We addressed such situations with the distributed constraint optimization approach as relatively generic representations and simple solution methods. Several subtasks contain decision-making problems, particularly in decentralized processing. Some of these problems can be handled with constraint optimization approaches. From this point of view, we also addressed a subtask that divided an observation area into territories of agents. In addition, in a practical case, the problem should be designed with solution methods based on local search so that the solution gradually improved with the steps of the entire framework. It means that the reactive dynamism of a system can be captured as a local search scheme. In each step of the system, exact solution methods and non-monotonic local search methods can be applied.

We applied a simple local search method that has a commitment mechanism and only depends on the information of neighborhood agents. Although several exact solution methods might be applicable, those methods generally need additional graph structures such as pseudo-trees that require more effort to implement preprocessing. Moreover, the constraints of global problems can be dense in practical domains. Because the time/space complexity of exact methods based on pseudo-trees is exponential with the tree width of pseudo-trees, several approximation methods are necessary for the dense problems. In such cases, solution quality decreases, and more implementation of additional methods is necessary. Therefore, in several early studies of DCOP application domains, relatively simple solution methods have been applied [5,14]. There will be opportunities to apply more sophisticated but relatively complex solution methods in our future work.

We employed different problems and solvers for different layers, although our design is based on similar simple approaches. When sub-problems are relatively separated from other problems, this approach reasonably reduces the size of individual problems and might perform at different timings based on their load. On the other hand, objectives with a hierarchical structure can be integrated with vectors, as shown for case of role allocation problems.

In practical structured applications, the problem design depends on specific domains with dedicated sub-algorithms. However, a generic representation helps to describe several parts of cooperation problems that are included in different layers of system. We addressed this case with fundamental problems, as the first step to implement such frameworks on an actual platform with multiple robots.

As a different approach, reinforcement learning methods are employed for several tasks of robots including path finding. While the learning methods experimentally obtain policies of sequential actions, DCOP approach is beneficial as a basis to describe decision making and allocation problems in cooperative systems. Several studies have addressed the integration of DCOPs and Reinforcement learning [11]. Both approaches will also be integrated in practical frameworks. Auction and mechanism design approaches are applied to several resource allocation problems with selfish agents. On the other hand, we basically assume a cooperative system in this work. There might be opportunities to optimize the fairness among agents with specific criteria and solution methods.

7 Conclusion

We applied a distributed constraint optimization approach to a framework of a cooperate observation system with mobile sensors for role allocation and composite subtasks. As a first case study toward implementation, we investigated how some cooperation problems can be described and solved with DCOPs as a general problem representation. We focused on a fundamental scheme of task allocation among agents in the highest layer and cooperation of agents in a lower layer subtask. Opportunities exist for designing other subtasks and allocating of them to agents with a similar approach.

Future work will evaluation and analyze of more practical composite problems with tighter relations. Verification with actual implementation is another goal of our study.

References

1. Balzer, M., Schlömer, T., Deussen, O.: Capacity-constrained point distributions: a variant of Lloydf's method. In: ACM SIGGRAPH 2009 (2009)

2. Béjar, R., et al.: Sensor networks and distributed CSP: communication, computation and complexity. Artif. Intell. **161**(1–2), 117–147 (2005)
3. Farinelli, A., Rogers, A., Petcu, A., Jennings, N.R.: Decentralised coordination of low-power embedded devices using the max-sum algorithm. In: 7th International Joint Conference on Autonomous Agents and Multiagent Systems, pp. 639–646 (2008)
4. Fioretto, F., Pontelli, E., Yeoh, W.: Distributed constraint optimization problems and applications: a survey. JAIR **61**, 623–698 (2018)
5. Fioretto, F., Yeoh, W., Pontelli, E.: A multiagent system approach to scheduling devices in smart homes. In: Proceedings of the 16th Conference on Autonomous Agents and MultiAgent Systems, pp. 981–989 (2017)
6. Hatano, D., Hirayama, K.: DeQED: an efficient divide-and-coordinate algorithm for DCOP. In: IJCAI 2013, Proceedings of the 23rd International Joint Conference on Artificial Intelligence, Beijing, China, 3–9 August 2013, pp. 566–572 (2013)
7. Jain, M., Taylor, M.E., Tambe, M., Yokoo, M.: DCOPs meet the real world: exploring unknown reward matrices with applications to mobile sensor networks. In: IJCAI 2009, Proceedings of the 21st International Joint Conference on Artificial Intelligence, Pasadena, California, USA, 11–17 July 2009, pp. 181–186 (2009)
8. Maheswaran, R.T., Pearce, J.P., Tambe, M.: Distributed algorithms for DCOP: a graphical-game-based approach. In: the International Conference on Parallel and Distributed Computing Systems, pp. 432–439 (2004)
9. Matsui, T., Matsuo, H., Silaghi, M., Hirayama, K., Yokoo, M.: Leximin asymmetric multiple objective distributed constraint optimization problem. Comput. Intell. **34**(1), 49–84 (2018)
10. Modi, P.J., Shen, W., Tambe, M., Yokoo, M.: Adopt: asynchronous distributed constraint optimization with quality guarantees. Artif. Intell. **161**(1–2), 149–180 (2005)
11. Nguyen, D.T., Yeoh, W., Lau, H.C., Zilberstein, S., Zhang, C.: Decentralized multi-agent reinforcement learning in average-reward dynamic DCOPs. In: 28th AAAI Conference on Artificial Intelligence, pp. 1447–1455 (2014)
12. Petcu, A., Faltings, B.: A scalable method for multiagent constraint optimization. In: 19th International Joint Conference on Artificial Intelligence, pp. 266–271 (2005)
13. Yeoh, W., Felner, A., Koenig, S.: BnB-ADOPT: an asynchronous branch-and-bound DCOP algorithm. In: 7th International Joint Conference on Autonomous Agents and Multiagent Systems, pp. 591–598 (2008)
14. Zivan, R., Yedidsion, H., Okamoto, S., Glinton, R., Sycara, K.: Distributed constraint optimization for teams of mobile sensing agents. Auton. Agent. Multi-Agent Syst. **29**(3), 495–536 (2014). https://doi.org/10.1007/s10458-014-9255-3

Comparing the Performance of Message Delivery Methods for Mobile Agents

Andrei Olaru$^{(\boxtimes)}$ (iD), Dragoş Petrescu, and Adina Magda Florea (iD)

University Politehnica of Bucharest, 060042 Bucharest, Romania
{andrei.olaru,adina.florea}@cs.upb.ro, dragos.petrescu@stud.acs.pub.ro

Abstract. Deploying a large number of mobile agents in scenarios where agents migrate frequently and/or exchange messages frequently requires methods for message delivery that are adequate to these specific situations. Deciding on which message delivery model to use, and whether a newly developed model is better than existing ones, may be difficult without an experimental testbed for comparison. This paper presents a framework for the comparison of message delivery models dedicated to mobile agent systems. The framework allows the generation of large, difficult scenarios, in which different methods may be evaluated side-by-side, revealing trade-offs between success rate, delivery time, and resource consumption. The architecture of the framework is designed to quickly integrate new models and to allow the direct deployment of a model implementation in real-life applications. As validation, we have integrated the implementation of several well-known delivery models and made comparisons between these models, from different points of view.

Keywords: Multi-agent systems · Mobile agents · Models and abstractions for MAS

1 Introduction

Mobile agents enable computation to be performed on a remote machine, by an autonomous entity that is able to travel between different hosts, thus avoiding both the difficulties of remote procedure calls and the high bandwidth required to move, from one machine to another, data instead of code. Beyond current applications of mobile agents in high-performance computing [2], wireless sensor networks [6,14], and fog computing [4,16], Future use includes large-scale wireless sensor networks and smart city infrastructures, which require that the protocols for messaging between agents scale up with the number of agents, nodes, and messages, and with the frequency of agent migration.

While they migrate, mobile agents need to be able to receive messages, from either fixed agents or other mobile agents. A *message delivery model* (sometimes called a *message delivery protocol* in the literature) is a set of rules and methods

This research was supported by grant PN-III-P1-1.2-PCCDI-2017-0734.

Y. Demazeau et al. (Eds.): PAAMS 2020, LNAI 12092, pp. 188–199, 2020.
https://doi.org/10.1007/978-3-030-49778-1_15

describing how to deliver a message sent from one agent to another that is identified by its name, in a distributed deployment, considering that the destination agent is mobile and is able to migrate between different hosts (or nodes). When mobile agents decide dynamically where to move next, it is challenging to create a *message delivery model* such that messages reach a rapidly moving agent in a timely manner. In the case of a large number of mobile agents that change host frequently, trade-offs exist between latency, reliability, performance, and network load. While many message delivery models have been surveyed from a qualitative point a view [15,17], choosing the appropriate model also requires a comparison of experimental results.

This paper introduces a framework for the comparison of message delivery models for multi-agent systems featuring mobile agents. We present the architecture of the framework, together with tools for analyzing the outcomes of simulated large-scale experiments. The result is an environment which developers can use to evaluate the advantages and trade-offs of either pre-implemented or newly developed models quickly and efficiently, using numerical comparisons for relevant criteria. The framework is implemented in Java and it is open-source.[1]

Based on characteristics such as number of agents and nodes, processing power of nodes, latency of the network, and frequency with which agents send messages or with which agents migrate, we generate a large number of scenarios for the simulation of the given conditions.

We have implemented several models for message delivery. All the implementations are available to the framework through the same API and can transferred to real-life MAS frameworks, such as the FLASH-MAS framework [12], or the popular Jade framework, as MTP instances. The implemented models have been evaluated on the same scenarios and evaluated according to the same metrics – message delivery success rate, mean delivery time, and network load. These metrics quantify the criteria presented by Virmani and by Rawat [15,17], and are also inspired by the work of Deugo [8]. Based on the results, we were able to make quantitative comparisons between the models and observe which model is more appropriate for each situation, whether we are dealing with a high rate of migration, or a large number of messages, or a resource-constrained network.

The next section presents work related to the subject of this paper. Section 3 introduces the architecture of the framework and its main features. Section 4 covers the comparison between several existing message delivery models, together with experimental results and discussion. The last section draws the conclusions.

2   Related Work

Existing models for message delivery in mobile agent systems have been previously surveyed and compared. Deugo [8] compares several classic delivery models from a theoretical point of view, without actual experiments. Virmani [17] and Rawat et al. [15] make qualitative comparisons of the state-of the art models

---

[1] The implementation is freely available as a Github repository at https://github.com/dragospetrescu/mobile_agents_system_simulator.

at the time. However, no means of quantitative comparison are offered. In the qualitative analyses, the features that are evaluated are generally a subset of the following: solution to the tracking problem (when an agent moves after the message is sent, but before the message reaches it), guaranteed message delivery, support for asynchronous communication, delivery in reasonable time, and transparency of location. However, without any quantization of these criteria, one cannot evaluate the trade-offs between features, such as whether a not-so-perfect success rate is a fair trade-off for other advantages, such as a good delivery time.

Message delivery models for communication in mobile agent systems are generally built around several well known schemata:

- the *centralized* solution, in which one server is tracking the whereabouts of all agents and forwards their messages accordingly; this is improved by the *home server scheme* where different servers are assigned to different partitions of the agent set, offering a more balanced solution than centralization [18];
- *blackboard* solutions, in which agents need to visit or contact the blackboard explicitly in order to get their messages [3,5];
- *forwarding proxy* solutions, in which each host remembers the next location to which an agent migrated, and messages will be forwarded along the path of the agent [7]; the *shadow protocol* combines the proxy model with the home server model by using proxies but agents regularly send updates of their location to their home server [1]; a combination of forwarding proxies and location servers is used by MEFS [9].

Mobile agents are currently used in several application areas, the most relevant being distributed computing (including here HPC and fog computing) and wireless sensor networks. In distributed computing, agent-based applications generally use centralized messaging or centralized directories [4]. However, experiments are only performed using a relatively small number of agents, a case for which the centralized server solution works fine. If the applications were to scale up to larger numbers of agents (e.g. in the thousands), the central server would become a serious bottleneck. In wireless sensor networks, mobile agents are used to gather information from WSN nodes. Some works only use mobility along a pre-calculated itinerary, with no communication [14]. In the cases where communication is needed, centralized communication methods are used, many times using Jade [6,13]. This works for small setups or for when the number of messages is low, but is not adequate to city-scale WSNs.

Research also exists in the field of distributed computing regarding distributed messaging [10], however these are made to support only fixed message receivers, which are not able to migrate through the network. This makes the problem that we address specific to the field of mobile multi-agent systems.

3   Framework Architecture

We see the implementation of a message delivery model as a system distributed across all hosts, which is able to pick a message from one agent in the system

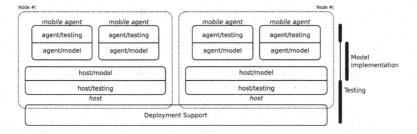

Fig. 1. The structure of elements in a deployment with two hosts, each on one machine, and 4 agents, two for each host.

and deliver that message to a mobile agent which is its destination, wherever that agent may be located at the current time.

In a distributed mobile multi-agent system, there exist 3 types of elements: mobile agents, hosts (or nodes), and what we call *deployment support*, which is able to actually send data through the network from one host to another, and is able to provide information about the network.

The architecture of the framework was built around the following principles:

- there should be a clear separation between the implementation of the message delivery model and the implementation of application-specific or framework-specific components of the multi-agent system;
- one should be able to change the message delivery model without changing the structure of the agents, making the application agnostic with respect to the delivery model that is used;
- one should be able to transfer the implementation of the delivery model from the framework to an actual MAS deployment, making the delivery model agnostic with respect to whether it runs in a simulation or in real-life.

This results in a modular structure which makes the implemented components be reusable across situations and between simulated and actual deployment.

For both the agents and the hosts we have integrated the separation described above, resulting in the following elements result (see also Fig. 1):

- the delivery *model* implementation; this implementation should be deployable in a real MAS application framework;
  - the *agent/model* segment is the part of a mobile agent which is model-specific and is able to communicate with the corresponding *host/model* segment; it stores any information which model-specific but must travel together with the agent;
  - the *host/model* segment contains all functionality that is dependent of the model, but is fixed to the machine, e.g. the registration of agents located on the host, or the routing of messages to or from the agents on the host;
- the *testing* components, including everything outside of the delivery model implementation, and which is used to evaluate the model;

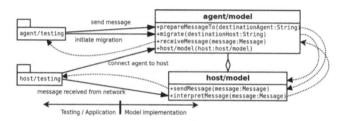

Fig. 2. A UML class diagram, also describing the interactions between the model implementation and the testing components.

- the *agent/testing* segment is the part of a mobile agent which participates in evaluating the message delivery model; the agent/testing segment generates and initiates the sending of messages, or initiates the migration to other hosts, all according to the settings in the evaluation scenario; the agent/testing segment is homologous to an application-specific agent in a real deployed application.
- the *host/testing* segment contains all functionality that is fixed to the host, but is independent of the delivery model, e.g. packing and unpacking of mobile agents when they migrate from or to the host;
- the *deployment support* contains all the elements that simulate a real deployment, such as the capacity to delivery messages between machines;

The resulting structure of the framework is layered. Messages are transmitted as follows:

1. according to the evaluation scenario, the *agent/testing* segment of a mobile agent generates a message and passes it to the *agent/model* segment of the same mobile agent;
2. the *agent/model* implementation performs model-specific processing on the message and passes it to the local *host/model* segment of the host;
3. the *host/model* decides the network identifier of the host at the next hop and passes the message to the *host/testing* segment of the host, which passes it to *deployment support*;
4. at every intermediate hop (if required by the model), the message is passed to the local *host/model*, which decides on the next hop;
5. on the host which is the destination of the message, the *host/model* passes the message to the *agent/model* segment of the appropriate agent;
6. the *agent/model* segment passes the message to the *agent/testing* segment of the same mobile agent, which updates the statistics related to delivery success rate and delivery time.

Similarly, when an agent wishes to migrate, it informs the local *host/testing*, which packs the agent as a message and passes it to the local *host/model*, which routes it the same as with any message; when this special message arrives on the destination host, the local *host/testing* will unpack and deploy the agent and the local *host/model* will register the migration.

There may be other messages that travel through the system, which are not initiated by the *testing* components, but by *model* components, according to the specific message delivery model. Such messages may be disseminating updates on the location of agents or attempting to resend messages that have not been delivered.

In order for a developer or researcher to evaluate a new model one must only implement two Java classes – one for the *agent/model* part and one for the *host/model* part of the model implementation. The interfaces which these classes must implement contain a minimum of required methods: the `agent/model` must contain a method to create and send a message, a method to receive a message from the `host/model`, and a method to initiate the migration to another host; the *host/model* must contain a method to send a message to another host (via *deployment support*) and a method to interpret a message coming from another host. The exact communication between the *agent* and the *host* parts of the model implementation is not imposed. These relationships are presented in Fig. 2.

3.1 Experimental Scenarios

The proposed framework supports the automatic generation of evaluation scenarios with the purpose of estimating the performance of the various message delivery models in real life.

Time in an evaluation scenario is discrete, quantified by means of *time units*. In a time unit, each node is able to process a given amount of messages, and on each direct connection between nodes a message travels for a given length. For easier interpretation of results, the scenarios presented in this paper simulated a complete network with edges of varying length, but other network layouts may be specified in the configuration of experiments. Some delivery models require the network to be divided into regions. This is also done by the scenario generation component. While messages could have different sizes, larger sizes can be simulated by several unit-sized messages.

For each delivery model, about 1000 scenarios were generated, considering combinations of the following parameters:

- the number of nodes in the deployment – with values of 10, 50, 100;
- the number of agents in the scenario – with values of 2, 10, 100, and 200;
- the probability of an agent migrating to another node in a given time unit – with values of EXTREMELY LOW, LOW, NORMAL, HIGH, and EXTREMELY HIGH, each value assigned to a probability between 1 in 1000 and 1 in 10;
- the probability of an agent sending a message to another agent in a given time unit – with values of EXTREMELY LOW, LOW, NORMAL, HIGH, and EXTREMELY HIGH, each value assigned to a probability between 1 in 100 and 1 (the highest probability is when an agent sends one message in each time unit);
- the "CPU" power of hosts, specifying how many messages a host can process in a time unit – with values of EXTREMELY LOW, LOW, NORMAL, HIGH, and EXTREMELY HIGH, each value assigned to a number of 1 to 50 messages processed in every time unit;

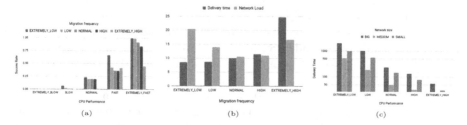

Fig. 3. (a) The success rate of Central Server Schema, depending on CPU power and migration frequency. (b) The delivery time (in time units) and the network load (in number of messages on the network in a time unit) for the Shadow Protocol, for various migration frequencies. (c) The performance of RAMDP, in terms of delivery time (on a log scale), depending on CPU power and network size.

The framework is used via a command-line interface offering arguments specifying the JSON files describing the hosts, the agents and the network, as well as values for migration frequency, message frequency, processing power, and the duration of the simulation. The configuration files for hosts and agents may contain per-host/per-agent values for processing power and for migration and messaging frequency. The framework is able to automatically generate all of the necessary JSON files, randomly, based on several parameters. Using files, however, as opposed to generating the scenario at every execution, allows for improved repeatability of experiments.

The results of one evaluation scenario are returned after the specified number of time units, as a tuple of 4 values which we use as comparison criteria, as detailed in the next section.

4   Comparison of Message Delivery Models

In order to demonstrate how our framework is able to handle comparison between message delivery models, we have implemented several such models and compared the experimental results of their evaluation.

In the comparison, we focused on how well various models handled difficult scenarios, characterized by limited processing power, increased number of messages, or increased probability of migration. For each evaluation scenario, we have used average parameters for all but a chosen characteristic of the scenario, and we have varied that characteristic in order to evaluate its impact on the performance of the model. As comparison criteria we use 4 values which the framework computes for each scenario or for an entire batch of scenarios.

The **message delivery rate** is the ratio of messages successfully delivered during the entire simulation, over the total number of sent messages:

$$Delivery\ rate = \frac{number\ of\ messages\ which\ have\ been\ delivered}{total\ number\ of\ sent\ messages}$$

The **mean message delivery time** is average number of time units it takes to deliver a message:

$$Time = \frac{\sum_i^{message} message\ delivery\ time\ for\ message\ i}{total\ number\ of\ messages}$$

The **mean network load** is the average number of messages which are in transit over the network, over the entire time of the simulation:

$$Load = \frac{\sum_i^{steps} number\ of\ messages\ in\ transit\ at\ time\ unit\ i}{number\ of\ steps}$$

The mean time during which messages that do not get to be delivered stay in the network or on the hosts, before being discarded, is computed as:

$$Time_{failures} = \frac{\sum_{failed\ messages} time\ spent\ in\ transit}{number\ of\ failed\ messages}$$

In order to validate the presented framework, we have implemented several known message delivery models from the literature. For each model, we have run 1000 scenarios with various configurations of the parameters. Each experiment ran for 100,000 time units, of which 30,000 time units were left for messages to be delivered, with no new messages being sent. We have grouped message delivery models into two categories [8]:

- *asynchronous* models, where it is the message that travels through the network, trying to reach its destination agent (leading to the chasing problem); such models are CS, FP, HSS, MDP, and MEFS (in some cases);
- *synchronous* models, where it is the destination agent that needs to synchronize with the source of the message or with the host where the message is currently stored and, once synchronized, the message is delivered immediately, so that messages spend almost no time traveling through the network; such models are RAMDP, Blackboard, and MEFS (in some cases).

For **asynchronous models**, we have analyzed how the success rate, the network load, and the delivery time are influenced by migration frequency and message frequency. Figure 4 presents these results, from which we can derive some useful insights into the situations various models are adequate for. In this comparison, the number of agents was large and CPU power has been relatively limited, in order to observe the efficiency of the models.

The **Central Server Scheme (CS)** model is characterized by the existence of a particular, central, server, which knows the locations of all agents. When agent migrate, they notify the central server. Every message that is sent between agents passes through the central server, which forwards it to the host where the destination is located. The central server is the bottleneck of the system and the performance of the system relies on the performance of the central server machine (as seen in Fig. 3 (a)). While the migration frequency has a moderate impact on performance, increasing the number of messages decreases performance abruptly (see Fig. 4 (b)), because all messages queue on the central server and don't get to be delivered. For situations where the number of messages is reasonable and reliability is not required at 100%, CS is well suited.

The **Home Server Scheme (HSS)** improves CS by distributing the central registry to several servers, with each agent being assigned to a specific home server [18]. Home servers know the distribution of agents among servers. HSS generally has good performance, but delivery time increases when there is a large number of agents, because, as with CS, performance is limited by the performance of individual nodes.

In the **Forwarding Proxy Protocol (FP)**, an agent leaving a host leaves a proxy on the host, pointing to its next location [7]. A message must 'chase' an agent in order to reach it. FP is the only completely decentralized model, among the models compared. FP has very good success rate even when the number of messages is very large. Its advantage comes at the cost of long delivery times and high network usage, even when the migration frequency or the number of messages are moderate. However, if reliability is needed, FP is the best choice. Other models based on FP add home servers, which need CPU performance in order to route messages.

The **Shadow Protocol** combines HSS and FP features, with agents using proxies but periodically updating their location on their home server (the 'shadow') [1]. The shadow forwards the message to the last location that it knows and from there the message chases the agent via proxies. Performance of the Shadow Protocol is better than FP when migration frequency increases, but is worse when the number of messages is large. The results in Fig. 3 (b) show how a lack of migration is related to higher network load, as more frequent migration leads to more frequent refresh of the information in the shadow, and therefore better performance. Being pseudo-centralized, performance of the Shadow Protocol can benefit from increased CPU performance for home servers. If the number of messages is not very high, Shadow offers good all-around performance.

The **Message Efficient Forwarding Schema** also combines centralized server features with forwarding proxies, introducing more reliability by placing forwarding proxies on hosts where it migrates from, and also changing its registration from the old host to the new host in order to increase efficiency [9]. MEFS has similar results to FP.

Message Delivery Protocol (MDP) uses a hierarchical structure to track the location of agents and to route messages in the system [11]. The structure, however, needs to be created specifically for each particular deployment. MDP is quite reliable when there are many messages, has good delivery times and does not load the network. It never achieves perfect reliability, but it is a good trade-off if short delivery times and low network usage are required.

We can observe that, when CPU power is limited, no asynchronous model handles a large number of messages too well, except maybe FP, which comes with other disadvantages for less stressful scenarios. For the case of very frequent messaging, MDP is a good choice.

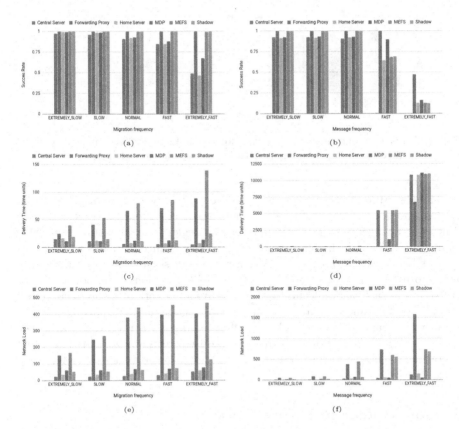

Fig. 4. Comparison of asynchronous models, for 100 nodes and 200 agents. On the left, migration probability varies between 1‰ and 10%, with messaging probability of 10%. On the right, messaging probability varies between 1% and 100%, with migration probability of 1%.

For **synchronous** models, we have analyzed how the success rate, the network load, and the delivery time are influenced by migration frequency. For these models, we have not presented a comparison where the messaging frequency varies, because their performance is not influenced by the number of messages – an agent retrieves all its messages received until that point at once. For the same reason, except for MEFS, which is a hybrid model, the network load is also quite low, as messages don't chase agents, but just wait on a host until an agent retrieves them.

In the **Blackboard** model, every node hosts a blackboard where agents leave messages [3]. An agent which is the destination of a message needs to move to the host where the message is stored in order to receive it. Lacking a specific action from the part of the agents to visit all hosts, the success rate of message delivery is low, and only increases when agents migrate frequently, having the opportunity to visit more hosts.

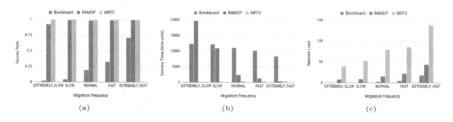

Fig. 5. Comparison of synchronous models, for 100 nodes and 200 agents, when migration probability varies between 1‰ and 10%, and messaging probability is 10%.

The **Reliable Asynchronous Message Delivery Protocol (RAMDP)** groups agents in regions and each region has a blackboard for messages [5]. Whenever an agent migrates, it informs the region and in return it receives its messages. As with the blackboard model, performance increases when agents migrate frequently, also because an agent receives messages only after it migrates and informs the region server. The design of the regions is important, as is visible in the case displayed in Fig. 3 (c), where a network of medium size offers the best performance because the number of regions is more adequate to the number of agents and nodes. RAMFS offers good success rate, especially when the frequency of migration is higher. As message retrieval is related to agent migration, agents that don't migrate don't get to receive their messages very often (Fig. 5).

5   Conclusion and Future Work

We have presented a framework for the experimental evaluation of message delivery models in a variety of scenarios, allowing users to compare the performance of various models and to ascertain which model is adequate for a specific situation. We have integrated the implementation of several delivery models and compared their performance in stressful scenarios. We were able to draw several conclusions related to the suitability of the models for various usage situations.

The framework does not currently support evaluating the robustness of a model when faced with network failure, faulty implementation, or agents that crash unexpectedly, nor the impact of the adoption of open systems, in which agents are able to enter and leave freely. This is a part of future work.

We intend to extend the framework with further metrics, for instance for analyzing CPU consumption, as opposed to only limiting CPU usage. We intend to develop the tools needed to analyze hosts individually, or by regions, as opposed to evaluating metrics across all hosts.

References

1. Baumann, J., Rothermel, K.: The shadow approach: an orphan detection protocol for mobile agents. Pers. Ubiquit. Comput. **2**(2), 100–108 (1998)

2. Benchara, F.Z., Youssfi, M., Bouattane, O., Ouajji, H.: A new scalable, distributed, fuzzy c-means algorithm-based mobile agents scheme for HPC: SPMD application. Computers **5**(3), 14 (2016)
3. Cabri, G., Leonardi, L., Zambonelli, F.: Mobile-agent coordination models for Internet applications. Computer **33**(2), 82–89 (2000)
4. Chang, C., Srirama, S.N., Buyya, R.: Indie Fog: an efficient Fog-computing infrastructure for the Internet of Things. IEEE Comput. **50**(9), 92–98 (2017)
5. Choi, S., Kim, H., Byun, E., Hwang, C., Baik, M.: Reliable asynchronous message delivery for mobile agents. IEEE Internet Comput. **10**(6), 16–25 (2006)
6. Derakhshan, F., Yousefi, S.: A review on the applications of multiagent systems in wireless sensor networks. Int. J. Distrib. Sens. Netw. **15**(5), 1550147719850767 (2019)
7. Desbiens, J., Lavoie, M., Renaud, F.: Communication and tracking infrastructure of a mobile agent system. In: Proceedings of the Thirty-First Hawaii International Conference on System Sciences, vol. 7, pp. 54–63. IEEE (1998)
8. Deugo, D.: Mobile agent messaging models. In: Fifth International Symposium on Autonomous Decentralized Systems, ISADS 2001, Dallas, Texas, USA, 26–28 March 2001, pp. 278–286. IEEE Computer Society (2001)
9. Jingyang, Z., Zhiyong, J., Daoxu, C.: Designing reliable communication protocols for mobile agents. In: 2003 23rd International Conference on Distributed Computing Systems Workshops, Proceedings, pp. 484–487. IEEE (2003)
10. John, V., Liu, X.: A survey of distributed message broker queues. CoRR abs/1704.00411 (2017). http://arxiv.org/abs/1704.00411
11. Lazar, S., Weerakoon, I., Sidhu, D.: A scalable location tracking and message delivery scheme for mobile agents. In: 7th Workshop on Enabling Technologies (WETICE 1998), Infrastructure for Collaborative Enterprises, CAUSA, Proceedings, 17–19 June 1998, Palo Alto, pp. 243–249. IEEE Computer Society (1998)
12. Olaru, A., Sorici, A., Florea, A.M.: A flexible and lightweight agent deployment architecture. In: 22nd International Conference on Control Systems and Computer Science, Bucharest, Romania, 28–30, pp. 251–258. IEEE (2019)
13. Outtagarts, A.: Mobile agent-based applications: a survey. Int. J. Comput. Sci. Netw. Secur. **9**(11), 331–339 (2009)
14. Qadori, H.Q., Zulkarnain, Z.A., Hanapi, Z.M., Subramaniam, S.: Multi-mobile agent itinerary planning algorithms for data gathering in wireless sensor networks: a review paper. Int. J. Distrib. Sens. Netw. **13**(1), 1550147716684841 (2017)
15. Rawat, A., Sushil, R., Sharm, L.: Mobile agent communication protocols: a comparative study. In: Jain, L.C., Behera, H.S., Mandal, J.K., Mohapatra, D.P. (eds.) Computational Intelligence in Data Mining - Volume 1. SIST, vol. 31, pp. 131–141. Springer, New Delhi (2015). https://doi.org/10.1007/978-81-322-2205-7_13
16. Roman, R., López, J., Mambo, M.: Mobile edge computing, Fog et al.: a survey and analysis of security threats and challenges. Future Gener. Comput. Syst. **78**, 680–698 (2018)
17. Virmani, C.: A comparison of communication protocols for mobile agents. Int. J. Adv. Technol. **3**(2), 114–122 (2012)
18. Wojciechowski, P.T.: Algorithms for location-independent communication between mobile agents. In: Proceedings of AISB 2001 Symposium on Software Mobility and Adaptive Behaviour (2001)

Application of Agent-Based Modelling to Simulate Ribosome Translation

Gael Pérez-Rodríguez[1,2,3] ⓘ, Beatriz T. Magalhães[1,3,4] ⓘ, Nuno F. Azevedo[4] ⓘ,
and Anália Lourenço[1,2,3,5(✉)] ⓘ

[1] ESEI, Department of Computer Science, University of Vigo, Edificio Politécnico,
Campus Universitario As Lagoas s/n, 32004 Ourense, Spain
{gaeperez,analia}@uvigo.com, beatriztmagalhaes95@gmail.com
[2] CINBIO, The Biomedical Research Centre, University of Vigo, Campus Univesitario
Lagoas-Marcosende, 36310 Vigo, Spain
[3] SING, Next Generation Computer Systems Group, Galicia Sur Health Research Institute,
SERGAS-UVIGO, Vigo, Spain
[4] LEPABE, Department of Chemical Engineering, Faculty of Engineering, University of Porto,
Rua Dr. Roberto Frias, 4200-465 Porto, Portugal
nazevedo@fe.up.pt
[5] CEB, Centre of Biological Engineering, University of Minho, Campus de Gualtar,
4710-057 Braga, Portugal

Abstract. Translation is a key process in the cell that encompasses the formation of proteins. However, how the translation mechanisms are affected by physiological changes is yet to be determined. *Saccharomyces cerevisiae* is one of the most used microorganisms to express recombinant proteins, showing great industrial/commercial value. Modelling the translation process in this yeast can thus bring forward novel insights into its mechanisms and how they are affected by changes in the environment. The present work introduces an agent-based model describing the elongation step of the translation process in the yeast. The simulated and theoretical elongation times were almost identical, with a standard deviation of 0.0018%, demonstrating the usefulness of the model to simulate this type of scenarios. Results also show a negative correlation between tRNA levels and estimated decoding times of codons, in accordance with biological knowledge. The model holds considerable potential to help unveil new ways of manipulation and thus increase the production of economically relevant yeast-derived products, namely biopharmaceuticals. Further development will address more complex scenarios, such as ribosome queuing or all the phases in the translation process.

Keywords: Agent-based model · Biology · Translation · Protein elongation · Model description · Simulation

1 Introduction

Computational modelling aims to realistically simulate and study the behaviour of complex systems, based on known variables of their components and interplay, to discover

© Springer Nature Switzerland AG 2020
Y. Demazeau et al. (Eds.): PAAMS 2020, LNAI 12092, pp. 200–211, 2020.
https://doi.org/10.1007/978-3-030-49778-1_16

non-trivial knowledge and test new hypotheses [1]. Computational models are of particular interest to Life Sciences because they provide an alternative when *in vivo* and *in vitro* experimentation are not possible or too costly, and the complexity of the problem averts analytical resolution [2]. In this context, agent-based modelling (ABM) is one of today's popular methodologies to model biological scenarios. It relies on the concept of autonomous agents, which are characterized by behavioural rules (logical and mathematical) and interact in a simulation environment (i.e. a source of local information with a set of initial and boundary conditions).

The premise of ABM is to study the behaviour of individual components, which is driven by local interactions, to be able to understand the system as a whole. This modelling mimics closely the mechanisms of stimulus and response observed in Biology. Therefore, ABMs have the potential to replicate the cellular system at its minimum components and help to understand the linkage from molecular level events to the emerging behaviour of the system. Furthermore, the agents can be defined at multiple temporal and spatial scales, and many relevant features, such as molecular diffusion, spatial location and molecular crowding, can be taken into account [3].

Recent works show the usefulness and broad range of application of ABM in Biology. For example, one study presented an ABM to assess the best strategy to capture the real structure of conjugative plasmid propagation in a bacterial population [4]. Another work proposed an ABM to simulate enzymatic reactions at experimentally measured concentrations while incorporating stochasticity and spatial dependence [5]. ABM was also used to help explain why phenotypic switching of individual cells in biofilms may occur at different times [6]. Other work presented SimFI, an ABM to simulate the co-circulation of two distinct pathogens in the human population, to better understand pathogen interactions in epidemiology [7]. Likewise, ABM was applied to assess single-molecule transport across the cell envelope of *Escherichia coli* [8].

The present work contributes to this line of work by proposing and validating a new ABM that supports the stochastic simulation of the translation process in *Saccharomyces cerevisiae* (*S. cerevisiae*). *S. cerevisiae* is the main yeast used to express nearly-all recombinant proteins and yeast-derived products currently available on the market but shows limited recombinant protein productivity [9]. Thus, understanding the translation process in the yeast may unveil new ways of manipulation to increase the production of economically relevant proteins, such as biopharmaceuticals.

1.1 Biological Context

Translation is a crucial process in Biology that results in the formation of a polypeptide chain. The information carried by a messenger ribonucleic acid (mRNA) is decoded by a ribonucleoprotein complex, the ribosome. First, the ribosome identifies the start codon (i.e. the AUG sequence) of the mRNA molecule and then continues reading the open reading frame (ORF), three nucleotides (i.e. one codon) at a time. Once the stop codon is reached, a protein is formed.

While the general mechanism of translation is fundamentally known, the response of the different stages to physiological changes is yet to be determined and could lead to a better understanding of how translation errors can result in disease or abnormal phenotypes. Modelling the translation can thus bring forward novel insights into the mechanisms behind the process, such as translation rates [10].

The new model proposed here tackles some of the key steps of the process (illustrated in Fig. 1). The representation of the translation process starts immediately after the binding of the small ribosomal subunit (40S) to the big ribosomal subunit (60S), which forms the 80S ribosomal subunit. The translation of an mRNA chain depends on the adaptor molecules, i.e. transfer RNAs (tRNAs), which transport the amino acids (AAs), i.e. the precursors of the final polypeptide chain, and bind to complementary codons of the mRNA. The first AA of any peptide chain is methionine (met). However, before hybridization of the tRNA-met or ₁tRNA, the complex must encounter a Eukaryotic translation initiation factor 2 (eIF2), which acts as a transporter of the ₁tRNA towards the mRNA chain being translated by the ribosome [11]. Once the ₁tRNA reaches the ribosome, the elongation phase can take place and further aminoacyl-tRNAs can attach themselves to the ribosome, according to the order defined in the mRNA codons. Once the AA is linked to the nascent peptide chain by peptidyl links, the tRNA is released to find another AA. Once the stop codon is reached, the elongation phase is complete. More than one ribosome can be attached to the same mRNA, albeit in different sections of the chain [12]. For simplicity reasons, the current model describes one mRNA per ribosome.

Fig. 1. Simplified elongation process. When a free Eukaryotic initiation factor (eIF2) collides with a free met-tRNA or ₁tRNA, the complex is transported towards the ribosome. The ₁tRNA-eIF2 complex hybridizes with the start codon (AUG) of the mRNA, starting the elongation phase of the translation process. The eIF2 factor then detaches from the ₁tRNA as a new aminoacyl-tRNA binds to the next codon. A peptidyl link is formed between the first and second amino acids. As new amino acids are transported by the tRNAs to the ribosome, the peptide chain is elongated until a stop codon is reached. Adapted from Magalhães et al. [10].

For a more detailed description of all the currently known stages of the process and of what data is needed for a complete modelling attempt please refer to Magalhães et al. [10].

2 Methods

The description of the ABM follows the updated version of the Overview, Design concepts and Detail (ODD) protocol [13, 14]. The model was developed in Java language using the Multi-Agent Simulator Of Neighborhoods (MASON) framework (version 20) [15]. The simulations were executed on a computer with an AMD Ryzen 5 1600 CPU @

3.20 GHz and 16 GB of RAM DDR4 @ 2133 MHz running Windows 10 Professional 64 bits. The Microsoft Excel software (version 2016) was used for all data analysis and graphic representations.

2.1 Purpose of the Model

The objective of this model is the stochastic simulation of the translation process in S. cerevisiae. The case study is a protein of 41 amino acids, specifically the plasma membrane ATPase proteolipid 1 (PMP1) [16]. PMP1 is a small single-membrane span proteolipid, which acts as a regulator for the ATPase pump [17]. The protein was chosen due to it is a key protein in the cell, to maintain its internal gradient of H+ and, thus its membrane potential, which in turn drives the uptake of several substances [18].

The model only represents the elongation phase of the translation process, during which the tRNA transports AAs towards the ribosome to form a polypeptide chain. The order of binding of the tRNAs to the ribosome, however, must be in accordance with the codon order of the mRNA being translated. For the proposed case study, the model simulates the translation process of one ribosome.

2.2 Entities, State Variables, and Scales

There are three main types of agents in the model, namely: the aminoacyl-tRNA, the translation factor (TF) and the ribosome. In turn, the aminoacyl-tRNA type is divided into 65 different agents, each one with their own state variables and concentration. To reduce computational costs, all the tRNAs presented in the model have their corresponding AA attached, therefore there are no free AAs in the cytoplasm, and the tRNAs are in their aminoacyl-tRNA form. The presented agents are characterized by the set of state variables listed in Table 1. Similarly, the environment and the biological model are characterized by the set of state variables presented in Table 2.

The theoretical values and the formulas used to calculate the radius, the molecular weight and the diffusion rate of the agents were retrieved from the work of Magalhães et al. [10]. The population of each aminoacyl-tRNA was considered equal to the number of tRNAs in the cell, which was calculated according to the codon usage in the aforementioned work. These population values range from 10 to 268 agents in the simulation.

The proposed environment represents a three-dimensional continuous cytoplasm of the S. cerevisiae cell. The spatial scale is the micrometre while the temporal scale is the second. This computational environment is a cube with a side length of 330 μm representing a sub-volume of a S. cerevisiae cell [19]. These dimensions consider some extra space to ensure all the agents can be positioned in the environment. The rate of conversion from simulation time (i.e. timesteps) to biological time (i.e. seconds) was 2.05E+09 timesteps/s, as previously described in the work of Pérez-Rodríguez et al. [5].

2.3 Process Overview and Scheduling

After the simulation is initialized, the processes listed in Fig. 2 are executed every timestep in the presented order, until the stop condition is reached, i.e. the ribosome performs the elongation phase of translation.

Table 1. State variables of the agents.

Variable	Type	Example value	Units	Constant
All agents				
ID	Long	Unique for each agent	–	Yes
Name	String	Ala-A-UGC	–	Yes
Type	String	aminoacyl-tRNA, TF or Ribosome	–	Yes
Color	String	#b8e6df	–	Yes
Radius	Double	1.0–11	μm	Yes
Molecular weight	Double	9,075 – 138,270	μm	Yes
Diffusion rate	Double	0.18 – 1.0	μm^2/s	Yes
Total distance	Double	1,224,356.50	μm	No
Direction	Double3D	<0.0, 0.0, 0.0>	–	No
Current location	Double3D	<0.0, 0.0, 0.0>	–	No
Desired location	Double3D	<0.0, 0.0, 0.0>	–	No
Initial position	Double3D	<0.0, 0.0, 0.0>	–	Yes
Final position	Double3D	<0.0, 0.0, 0.0>	–	No
Action performed	Boolean	False	–	No
Is alive	Boolean	True	–	No
Aminoacyl-tRNA				
Is activated	Boolean	True	–	No
Amino acid	String	UAC	–	Yes
Ribosome				
mRNA*	Stack <String>	<UAC, UGA...>	–	No

The processes of updating model variables and setting new agents in the environment are performed by a high-level controller just before and after the agents execute their behaviours, respectively. This controller is also the one that checks and executes the corresponding events among the agents.

2.4 Design Concepts

Basic principles: In this model, the elongation phase of the translation process in the yeast is represented for a protein of 41 AAs. Modelling such mechanism might offer novel insights into the translation rates at the codon level. For instance, if the total elongation time obtained with modelling is shorter than the theoretical one, this might indicate that there might be pauses during the elongation process or that the elongation rates for each codon are different.

Table 2. State variables of the environment and the model.

Variable	Type	Example value	Units	Constant
Environment				
Width	Double	340.0	μm	Yes
Length	Double	340.0	μm	Yes
Height	Double	340.0	μm	Yes
Model				
Wait time	Long	2,215,015	timestep	No
Population size	Map<String, Integer>	<Ribosome, 1>	–	No
Dead agents	Map<Agent, Long>	<TF, 980,457>	timestep	No
Agents information	Map<String, Agent>	<TF, TF>	–	Yes

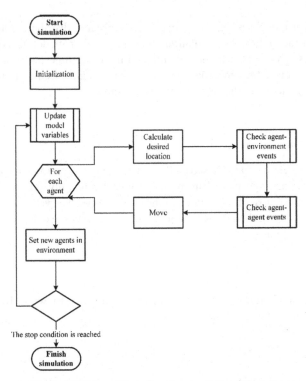

Fig. 2. Workflow illustrating the simulation schedule.

Emergence: The amount of time required to complete the elongation phase is dependent on the number of aminoacyl-tRNAs present in the simulation, i.e. the higher the number of appropriate aminoacyl-tRNAs, the lower the time to finish the elongation phase.

Sensing: The agents are assumed to know their own type, their status (i.e. alive or not) and whether they have performed an action in the current timestep. In the case of the itRNA and the aminoacyl-tRNA agents, they also know if they are active (i.e. they can attach to the ribosome). Lastly, the ribosome knows which position/codon in the mRNA it is occupying.

Interaction: There are four major interactions in the simulation, as follows: (*i*) activation, i.e. when a itRNA and a TF collide; (*ii*) deactivation, i.e. when a itRNA-TF collides with a ribosome and the itRNA frees the associated TF (*iii*) elongation, i.e. when the correct aminoacyl-tRNA and a ribosome collide; and (*iv*) rebound, i.e. when two agents collide and none of the above events occurs. Every agent can only perform one action per timestep. For example, if an agent performs an activation event during the timestep T, it will not be able to move or do any other interaction till $T + 1$.

Stochasticity: The initial location and direction of the agents are completely random in each execution.

Observation: For model testing and calibration, the spatial distribution and the agent displacement at the end of the simulation are observed. For model analysis, the total amount of timesteps to finish the simulation and the exact timestep when an elongation interaction occurred are recorded. Three simulations are executed to minimize the deviation of the data due to the stochasticity of the model.

2.5 Initialization

First, the environment is created based on its own variables as described in Table 2. Then, the agents are created and placed in the environment randomly following a uniform distribution, to cover most of the volume of the environment. The variables of the agents are also initialized using their corresponding biological values, except for the direction variable that is random.

2.6 Input

The model input and initialization are based on the parameters shown in Table 1 and the environmental parameters in Table 2.

2.7 Submodels

The following submodels are executed every timestep in the simulation.

Update model variables: This submodel is executed before any agent in the simulation executes its logic. The high-level controller is responsible for updating the population size in the model (variable in Table 2), i.e. specify the number of agents in the environment. Furthermore, it also eliminates any dead agent from the environment and updates the corresponding variable in the model (Table 2).

Check agent-environment events: The objective of this submodel is to check the collision between an agent and the environment boundaries to calculate the rebound and to change the direction of the agent. The collision and rebound logic are intended to fulfil common biophysics and biochemical laws and assumptions [20, 21], guaranteeing that agent movement complies with the Brownian motion of molecules [22].

Check agent-agent events: The objective of this submodel is to check and execute the following interactions among agents (Table 3).

Table 3. Interactions among agents.

First agent	Second agent	Interaction	Result
TF	Deactivated $_i$tRNA	Activation	The TF captures the $_i$tRNA and set its activated state to true. The TF is removed from the environment
Activated $_i$tRNA	Ribosome	Deactivation	The $_i$tRNA collides with the ribosome, frees the associated TF, and sets the activated state to false. A new TF appears
Activated aminoacyl-tRNA	Ribosome	Elongation	The aminoacyl-tRNA transfers its amino acid to the ribosome. Then, the aminoacyl-tRNA set its activated state to false
Any	Any	Rebound	Both agents change their direction

The activation interaction is only performed if the $_i$tRNA has the activation state set to false. If this interaction occurs, the TF captures the $_i$tRNA agent and sets its activated state to true. Additionally, the TF state is set to false, to be removed from the environment during the submodel update model variables.

The deactivation interaction is only performed if the $_i$tRNA has the activation state set to true. If this interaction occurs, the $_i$tRNA sets its activated state to false and then a new TF is created in the simulation.

The elongation interaction is only performed if the aminoacyl-tRNA is complementary with the current codon in the mRNA being translated. If this interaction is successful, the aminoacyl-tRNA changes its activated state to false and binds to the ribosome. Lastly, a wait time value is calculated using the following equation (Eq. 1).

$$wait\ time = \frac{(elongation\ time - current\ timestep)}{number\ of\ amino\ acids} \tag{1}$$

where *elongation time* is the theoretical time to make the translation in timesteps (i.e. *elongation time* $= 8.2E + 09$), the *current timestep* stands for the timestep in which the interaction occurs and the *number of amino acids* represents the total number of AAs in the case study (i.e. *number of amino acids* = 41).

This wait time is calculated and accumulated in the corresponding model variable whenever an elongation interaction is performed to avoid having timesteps with no activity. This strategy considers the elongation as instantaneous and accumulates the expected duration. At the end of the simulation, this value is added to the total timesteps to be in accordance with the translation theoretical time. The other molecules remain in the same position during this period of time, i.e. assuming process ergodicity.

If any of the previous interactions are not successful or any pair of other molecules collide, then the rebound interaction is performed. Both collision and rebound logics remain the same as in the previous submodel. Otherwise, the agents will move normally.

3   Results and Discussion

Figure 3 summarizes the results of the simulations, including their average. Figure 3A shows the seconds in which an elongation occurred whilst Fig. 3B presents the number of seconds elapsed between two interactions. Note that, the y-axis (in seconds) does not include the accumulated wait time.

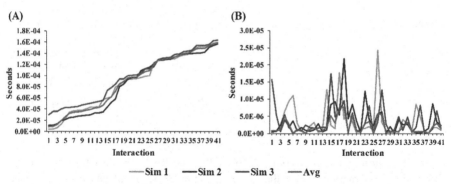

Fig. 3. Simulation results for each replicate and their average. The y-axis does not include the accumulated wait time. (A) Plot showing the seconds in which an elongation interaction occurs. (B) Plot showing the number of seconds between elongation interactions.

Considering that the accumulated wait time is not considered in Fig. 3A, the average time to finish the simulation was ~1.59E−04 s (i.e. 325,815 timesteps using the conversion factor). Otherwise, the average time to finish the simulation was ~4 s (i.e. 8,200,148,588 timesteps using the conversion factor). This time is almost identical to the theoretical value of 4 s (i.e. 8,200,000,000 timesteps) [23] differing by no more than 0.0018% in the whole spectrum of simulations.

Regarding Fig. 3B, model stochasticity led to variations in the time between elongations. The mean value of time was 5.7E−07 s (i.e. 1,175 timesteps) with a maximum value of 7.7E−06 s (i.e. 15,766 timesteps) and a minimum value of 9.2E−08 s (i.e. 189

timesteps). The average time to perform the activation of the ribosome was 6.6E−06 s (i.e. 13,649 timesteps). Additionally, the Pearson correlation coefficient was used to study the association between the abundance of each tRNA with the rate of elongation of the respective codon. Results show a negative correlation of −0.6, i.e. the higher the concentration of tRNAs, the fastest the elongation rate for the corresponding codon. This is consistent with a previous study that showed that there is a significant correlation between tRNAs' concentrations and the codons estimated decoding time [24]. The non-perfect correlation can be explained by factors such as a non-absolute correlation between tRNA levels and codon frequency, which may be a mechanism of translation regulation, different aminoacyl-tRNA accommodation times or peptidyl transfer times.

4 Conclusion

This work introduced a novel ABM to simulate the translation process in *S. cerevisiae* having as a case study the PMP1, a protein of 41 amino acids. In particular, the model represents one of the three phases presented in the translation, i.e. the elongation phase, during which the tRNA transports AAs towards the ribosome to form a polypeptide chain.

The generated results were in accordance with the theoretical data with a low deviation value, highlighting the capabilities of the model to represent this type of biological scenarios. Not only that, results showed a negative or inverse correlation between the levels of tRNA and the codon decoding times. Therefore, the proposed model holds considerable potential for future, more complex analyses, such as changing the concentrations of the represented agents, to study the degree at which the process is affected. Ideally, the entire complexity of the elongation phase should be modelled. Initial future attempts will focus on adding all the ribosomes present in yeast cells and ribosome queuing (i.e. when more than one ribosome is translating the same mRNA), based on data extrapolated from ribosome profiling studies. This should allow the study of pausing during elongation due to ribosome trafficking. Further on, the remaining factors involved in the elongation phase and the translation of other proteins, specifically those with industrial relevance, should also be included in the model to bring it as close to reality as possible. To further increase the complexity, the entire translation mechanisms, i.e. the pre-initiation, initiation and termination phases, and even the post-translational stages should also be modelled. Additionally, the model can be applied to other biological systems, such as other yeasts, microorganisms, or even more complex organisms.

Acknowledgements. This study was supported by the Portuguese Foundation for Science and Technology (FCT) under the scope of the strategic funding of UIDB/04469/2020 unit, BioTec-Norte operation (NORTE-01-0145-FEDER-000004) funded by the European Regional Development Fund under the scope of Norte2020 - Programa Operacional Regional do Norte, and of the PhD Grant SFRH/BD/143491/2019. Additionally, it received funding through Base Funding - UIDB/00511/2020 of the Laboratory for Process Engineering, Environment, Biotechnology and Energy – LEPABE - funded by national funds through the FCT/MCTES (PIDDAC).

References

1. Brodland, G.W.: How computational models can help unlock biological systems (2015). https://doi.org/10.1016/j.semcdb.2015.07.001
2. Castiglione, F.: Agent based modeling and simulation, introduction to. In: Meyers, R. (ed.) Encyclopedia of Complexity and Systems Science. Springer, New York (2009). https://doi.org/10.1007/978-0-387-30440-3_13
3. Foffi, G., Pastore, A., Piazza, F., Temussi, P.A.: Macromolecular crowding: chemistry and physics meet biology. Phys. Biol. **10**, 40301 (2013). https://doi.org/10.1088/1478-3975/10/4/040301. (Ascona, Switzerland, 10–14 June 2012)
4. García, A.P., Rodríguez-Patón, A.: A preliminary assessment of three strategies for the agent-based modeling of bacterial conjugation. In: Overbeek, R., Rocha, M.P., Fdez-Riverola, F., De Paz, J.F. (eds.) 9th International Conference on Practical Applications of Computational Biology and Bioinformatics. AISC, vol. 375, pp. 1–9. Springer, Cham (2015). https://doi.org/10.1007/978-3-319-19776-0_1
5. Pérez-Rodríguez, G., Gameiro, D., Pérez-Pérez, M., Lourenço, A., Azevedo, N.F.: Single molecule simulation of diffusion and enzyme kinetics. J. Phys. Chem. B. **120**, 3809–3820 (2016). https://doi.org/10.1021/acs.jpcb.5b12544
6. Pérez-Rodríguez, G., Dias, S., Pérez-Pérez, M., Fdez-Riverola, F., Azevedo, N.F., Lourenço, A.: Agent-based model of diffusion of N-acyl homoserine lactones in a multicellular environment of Pseudomonas aeruginosa and Candida albicans. Biofouling **34**, 335–345 (2018). https://doi.org/10.1080/08927014.2018.1440392
7. Arduin, H., Opatowski, L.: SimFI: a transmission agent-based model of two interacting pathogens. In: Demazeau, Y., An, B., Bajo, J., Fernández-Caballero, A. (eds.) PAAMS 2018. LNCS (LNAI), vol. 10978, pp. 72–83. Springer, Cham (2018). https://doi.org/10.1007/978-3-319-94580-4_6
8. Maia, P., Pérez-Rodríguez, G., Pérez-Pérez, M., Fdez-Riverola, F., Lourenço, A., Azevedo, N.F.: Application of agent-based modelling to assess single-molecule transport across the cell envelope of E. coli. Comput. Biol. Med. (2019). https://doi.org/10.1016/J.COMPBIOMED.2019.02.020
9. Porro, D., Sauer, M., Branduardi, P., Mattanovich, D.: Recombinant protein production in yeasts (2005). https://doi.org/10.1385/MB:31:3:245
10. Magalhães, T.B., Lourenço, A., Azevedo, N.F.: Computational resources and strategies to assess single-molecule dynamics of the translation process in S. cerevisiae. Brief. Bioinform. (2019). https://doi.org/10.1093/bib/bbz149
11. Kapp, L.D., Lorsch, J.R.: GTP-dependent recognition of the methionine moiety on initiator tRNA by translation factor eIF2. J. Mol. Biol. **335**, 923–936 (2004). https://doi.org/10.1016/j.jmb.2003.11.025
12. Diament, A., Feldman, A., Schochet, E., Kupiec, M., Arava, Y., Tuller, T.: The extent of ribosome queuing in budding yeast. PLoS Comput. Biol. **14**, e1005951 (2018). https://doi.org/10.1371/journal.pcbi.1005951
13. Grimm, V., Berger, U., DeAngelis, D.L., Polhill, J.G., Giske, J., Railsback, S.F.: The ODD protocol: a review and first update. Ecol. Modell. **221**, 2760–2768 (2010). https://doi.org/10.1016/j.ecolmodel.2010.08.019
14. Grimm, V., et al.: A standard protocol for describing individual-based and agent-based models. Ecol. Modell. **198**, 115–126 (2006). https://doi.org/10.1016/j.ecolmodel.2006.04.023
15. Luke, S., Cioffi-Revilla, C., Panait, L., Sullivan, K., Balan, G.: MASON: a multiagent simulation environment. Simul. Trans. Soc. Model. Simul. Int. **82**, 517–527 (2005). https://doi.org/10.1177/0037549705058073

16. PMP1 - Plasma membrane ATPase proteolipid 1 precursor - Saccharomyces cerevisiae (strain ATCC 204508/S288c) (Baker's yeast) - PMP1 gene & protein. https://www.uniprot.org/uniprot/P32903. Accessed 09 Jan 2020

17. PMP1 Protein|SGD. https://www.yeastgenome.org/locus/S000000619/protein. Accessed 15 Jan 2020

18. Palmgren, M., Morsomme, P.: The plasma membrane H+ -ATPase, a simple polypeptide with a long history. Yeast **36**, 201–210 (2019). https://doi.org/10.1002/yea.3365

19. Yamaguchi, M., Namiki, Y., et al.: Structome of Saccharomyces cerevisiae determined by freeze-substitution and serial ultrathin-sectioning electron microscopy. J. Electron. Microsc. (Tokyo) **60**, 321–335 (2011). https://doi.org/10.1093/jmicro/dfr052

20. Millington, I.: Game Physics Engine Development: How to Build a Robust Commercial-Grade Physics Engine for your Game. CRC Press, Boca Raton (2010)

21. Palmer, G.: Physics for Game Programmers. Apress (2005). https://doi.org/10.1007/978-1-59059-472-8

22. Cecconi, F., Cencini, M., Falcioni, M., Vulpiani, A.: Brownian motion and diffusion: from stochastic processes to chaos and beyond. Chaos. **15** (2005). https://doi.org/10.1063/1.1832773

23. Siwiak, M., Zielenkiewicz, P.: A comprehensive, quantitative, and genome-wide model of translation. PLoS Comput. Biol. **6**, e1000865 (2010). https://doi.org/10.1371/journal.pcbi.1000865

24. Dana, A., Tuller, T.: The effect of tRNA levels on decoding times of mRNA codons. Nucleic Acids Res. (2014). https://doi.org/10.1093/nar/gku646

Intent Recognition from Speech and Plan Recognition

Michele Persiani$^{(\boxtimes)}$ and Thomas Hellström

Umeå University, Umeå, Sweden
{michelep,thomash}@cs.umu.se

Abstract. In multi-agent systems, the ability to infer intentions allows artificial agents to act proactively and with partial information. In this paper we propose an algorithm to infer a speakers intentions with natural language analysis combined with plan recognition. We define a Natural Language Understanding component to classify semantic roles from sentences into partially instantiated actions, that are interpreted as the intention of the speaker. These actions are grounded to arbitrary, hand-defined task domains. Intent recognition with partial actions is statistically evaluated with several planning domains. We then define a Human-Robot Interaction setting where both utterance classification and plan recognition are tested using a Pepper robot. We further address the issue of missing parameters in declared intentions and robot commands by leveraging the *Principle of Rational Action*, which is embedded in the plan recognition phase.

Keywords: Intent recognition · Plan recognition · Natural Language Understanding · Semantic Role Labeling · Algorithms

1 Introduction

Intent recognition has been recognized as a crucial task in past and recent research in cybernetic systems [7,14,15], especially when humans are teaming along with artificial agents [5]. The ability to predict other agents' future goals and plans allows for proactive decisions, and relates to several system requirements, such as the need of an enhanced collaboration mechanism in human-machine interactions, the need for adversarial technology in competitive scenarios, ambient intelligence, or predictive security systems [5,15]. In this paper we focus on intent recognition for robotics, in scenarios where a person and a robot are present, yet the results have a broader applicability.

In robotics, the ability to predict users enables proactive behavior, ultimately giving the robots the ability to understand and coordinate actions with their users, even when only partial information is given [5,19]. In this paper we propose a method to infer user intent from speech, which is often a preferred mode of interaction in human-robot interaction [16]. Firstly, a series of utterances by the user are classified into partially instantiated PDDL [10] actions by using

© Springer Nature Switzerland AG 2020
Y. Demazeau et al. (Eds.): PAAMS 2020, LNAI 12092, pp. 212–223, 2020.
https://doi.org/10.1007/978-3-030-49778-1_17

Semantic Role Labeling [8]. The actions are then grounded into PDDL planning instances, and the user's intent is inferred using a plan recognition algorithm constrained to consider only plans containing the classified actions. The proposed method allows for discovery of intents beyond the scope of single sentences (achieved through, for example, a shallow classification of a sentence), by computing intents contextually to the task domain, in the form of a goal and a plan. Being able to reason on goals and plans using also context variables is necessary when attempting to describe or infer an agent behavior [5,14].

The rest of the paper is organized as follows. In Sect. 2 we introduce give background and related work for our proposed algorithm. Section 3 describes the intent recognition algorithm, followed by Sect. 4 in which we evaluate an implementation of the algorithm, both statistically by testing it in different planning domains, and experimentally using a Pepper robot. Finally, in Sect. 5 we give some conclusive remarks.

2   Background

In robotics, intent recognition can be performed using several modalities, such as video [9], gestures [12], eyeball movements, affect information in speech [4], and speech. When inferring intentions, raw input must be first transformed into data structures that are suitable for inference, such as action frames [2,18]. We refer to this as the process of grounding to the task domain. After grounding, various inference tools can be applied. For example, in [3], utterances are processed by mapping semantic roles into ad-hoc action frames using machine learning techniques. Semantic frames, such as the ones described in FrameNet [1], can be transformed to robot actions using sets of lexical units [18]. These units connect grammatical relations found in sentences to the different frame elements. With this approach, all core arguments must be present for the frames to be utilizable.

Pre-trained language models can also be utilized when inferring intentions from speech. Chen et al. [6] map semantic frames to robot action frames by using a language model trained on semantic roles, showing how large language models can be used to obtain the likelihood for the frames arguments. Their proposed *Language-Model-based Commonsense Reasoning* (LMCR) assigns a higher probability to the instruction *"Pour the water in the glass."* than to *"Pour the water in the plate."*. Thus, when the planning component is searching for an object to pour water into, it will prefer a glass rather then other objects. The LMCR is used to rank candidates for complete action frames by testing the different combinations of the available objects.

Inferred actions typically must have all arguments specified before they can be part of an executable plan. However, we can usually not expect all parameters to be fully specified in user utterances. In this regard our approach stands in contrast with other solutions (e.g. [6,17]) where the possible combinations of objects are exhausted or searched to retain only the most likely combination as candidate arguments. We instead allow for missing arguments to be present in the action frames, leveraging then the planner to infer them as the arguments that would allow the whole inferred intention to be the least costly. Intentions are thus infused at parameter level with the *principle of rational action* i.e. intentional agents prefer optimal plans when evaluating different alternatives [19].

3   Method

We formally define an agent's intention as a goal $\hat{g}$ together with an action plan $\hat{\pi}$ the agent is committed to while pursuing $\hat{g}$ [19]. The sequence of actions $\hat{\pi}$ can either be a complete plan achieving $\hat{g}$ or a partial plan directed towards it. Intent recognition thus becomes the task of inferring $\hat{g}$ and $\hat{\pi}$ from a set of observations $o \in O$:

$$\hat{g}, \hat{\pi} = \underset{g \in G, \pi \in \Pi}{\operatorname{argmax}} P(g, \pi | o), \tag{1}$$

where G and Π are the set of possible goals and the set of possible partial plans respectively, O is the set of possible sets of observations. $\hat{g}$ and $\hat{\pi}$ are the arguments that maximizes the likelyhood of the intent recognition model $P(G, \Pi | O)$.

We additionally introduce an explicit grounding model $P(A|O)$ that is used to map raw observations to the task space as grounded actions. Furthermore, we add the assumption that the inferred plan is independent of the observations given the set of grounded actions $a \in A$. The formulation of the intent recognition model becomes:

$$P(G, \Pi | O) = \sum_A P(G|\Pi) P(\Pi|A) P(A|O) P(O). \tag{2}$$

Hence, a partial plan for the agent is first inferred from the grounded observations. Then, the plan is used to infer the agent's goal. Note that if the plan inference always infers complete plans, no inference of the goals is needed. Assuming that the agent behaves rationally, the inferred plan is the optimal plan achieving $\hat{g}$, and that contains the set of grounded actions $a \in A$.

We designed a method to infer the user's intention by grounding the utterances to sets of actions defined in a PDDL domain [10]. Semantic role labeling is used to extract semantic frames from the utterances. Each frame is then classified into a partially instantiated PDDL action to form the set $a \in A$. Inferred actions are then used to infer the speaker's intent $\hat{g}, \hat{\pi}$ using plan recognition.

Missing parameters in classified PDDL actions are automatically inferred by the planner as the ones that would make the speaker's inferred plan $\hat{\pi}$ least costly. For example, if the user utters "Give me something to drink" without specifying which glass to use, plan recognition will select the one that is most convenient to reach. The following example illustrates the process in more detail.

Parsing the utterance "Give me something to drink" may yield the following semantic parsing:

```
(define (domain cups)                  (define (problem cups-3-cups)
    (:requirements                         (:domain cups)
        :strips :typing :equality)         (:objects
    (:types cup - object)                      blue-cup yellow-cup red-cup)
    (:predicates                       ;;tag e:blue-cup   bow:blue,cup
        (finish ?c - cup))             ;;tag e:yellow-cup bow:yellow,cup
;;tag  e:drink bow:drink               ;;tag e:red-cup    bow:red,cup
;;roles e:drink role:ARG2                  (:init )
    (:action drink                     ;;goal (finish blue-cup)
        :parameters (?c - cup)         ;;goal (finish yellow-cup)
        :precondition ()               ;;goal (finish red-cup)
        :effect (finish ?c))           )
    )
)
```

Fig. 1. Example of specification of a PDDL domain and problem instances. In green the annotations performed on the entities $e \in E$. The annotations *tag* and *roles* allows to map bag of words into entities, while every *goal* annotation specifies a possible goal for plan recognition. (Color figure online)

- *verb:* give, *patient:* something to drink, *recipient:* me
- *verb:* drink *patient:* something

Assuming that the PDDL domain description contains the actions

- (**give ?to - agent ?i - item**)
- (**drink ?a - agent ?what - beverage ?from - item**)

the utterance may be classified as the partially instantiated actions

$$a = \{(\textbf{give me } None), (\textbf{drink } None \ None \ None)\}, \tag{3}$$

with the semantic roles of type *verb* mapped to the action names, and semantic roles *me* mapped to the first argument of **give**. Suppose that G contains two possible user goals: to be served food or to be served a drink. Then, the inferred plan $\hat{\pi}$ will have as goal to drink, as it is the least costly goal achieved with a plan constrained to contain a. Furthermore, when using partially instantiated actions the planner will select as the parameters that were set as ***None*** the objects belonging to the planning instance that would make the plan least costly.

3.1   Utterance Classification

For a given PDDL domain and problem definition, we define Act as the set of unique action names, and Obj as the set of all unique objects names. $E \subseteq (Act \cup Obj)$ is the selected subset of entities that are usable to instantiate PDDL actions from semantic roles. In order to map the semantic roles to an action parameter list in the correct order, we specify for every action $a \in (Act \cap E)$ a mapping between semantic roles and parameter indices:

$$M : A \times roles \rightarrow index \cup None. \tag{4}$$

For example, we can define that for the action **drink ?c - cup**, in the simplified drinking domain shown in Fig. 1, the semantic role *instrument* is associated to the 1st parameter. The mapping M allows to map semantic roles to the parameters of the annotated actions. M is manually created by annotating the PDDL action descriptions.

Additionally, for finding the correct entities mentioned in the utterance we classify the semantic roles into entities by using a bag of words classifier. The training set for the classifier is obtained by manually annotating the PDDL domain. Figure 1 shows how a drinking domain is potentially annotated. Table 1 is the corresponding obtained dataset. Additional data is generated by data augmentation techniques (see Sect. 3.1) to improve generalization and robustness of classification. The dataset resulting from the annotation process contains records for the entities $e \in E$ only.

Table 1. Every action or object in the set of entities E is annotated with a bag of words that are used together with the object type as input for the entity classifier. E, the classifier's target label set, contains the PDDL unique names of the annotated entities.

$X_0 = $ **Bag of words**	$X_1 = $ **Type**	$E = $ **Id**
blue, cup	cup	blue-cup
red, cup	cup	red-cup
yellow, cup	cup	yellow-cup
drink	action	drink

For every record in the dataset, every word in $x \in X_0$ is encoded into its corresponding word-vector. $x \in X_1$ and $e \in E$ are categorical features encoded using one-hot-vectors. The target classes for the classifier are the unique PDDL labels of the entities in E. The described dataset is used to train a softmax classifier $P_e(E|X_0, X_1)$ that is used to instantiate PDDL actions from semantic roles by the following algorithm:

$$\hat{a} = \underset{e \in E}{\mathrm{argmax}} P_e(e|b_{\mathbf{verb}}, \mathbf{action})$$

$$\forall i, \hat{e}_i = \underset{e \in E}{\mathrm{argmax}} P_e(e|\{w\}_i, type_i), e_i \neq \hat{a}, M(\hat{a}, type_i) \neq None. \qquad (5)$$

This sequence of classifications results in an action identifier $\hat{a}$ and a list of associated parameters $\{\hat{e}\}$. For a given action, not all of its semantic roles present in $M(\hat{a}, .)$ might be mentioned in the utterance and the missing ones will appear as $None$ in the partially instantiated action. Additionally, semantic roles for which $M(\hat{a}, .) = None$ are discarded.

Notice that SRL could return multiple parsing for a given sentence, one for every verb it contains. In this case we run Algorithm 5 for every different parsing. This also allows to have multiple action declarations in the same sentence, such as in the case of *I'll go to the supermarket and buy maccaroni*, where SRL would produce a parsing for the verbs *go* and *buy*.

Data Augmentation. Data augmentation refers to a synthetic increase of the training data in order to increase the size of the dataset and thus the generalization capabilities for the trained model. For every entry in the original dataset we create $N = 1000$ synthetic entries by replacing, in every new record, the words in X_0 with random synonyms found using WordNet. Additionally, for every bag of word, N random words are added. Thus, the description of every object is expanded to the neighboring regions in word vector space by synonyms, while the injected random words increase the robustness of classification [20].

Negative Action Class. As described above, Algorithm 5 will always attempt to match bag of words with entities belonging to the problem. This is not always desirable, especially for auxiliary verbs such as *am* in phrases like *I am repairing my skateboard*, where SRL might label *am* as a verb and Algorithm 5 would thus return the action with similiar name (e.g. **eat**), resulting in a spurious action for the subsequent computations. For this reason, we allow for semantic roles to be classified as *None*. To detect such cases, the classifier is modified to allow the detection of outliers in its hidden layer, by a combination of regularization and Radial Basis Functions (RBF). In the case an input is detected as an outlier, the corresponding computation of the PDDL action or parameter is not performed.

In order to detect outliers, during training the classifier's hidden layer is regularized such that $\mathbf{h} \sim N(\mathbf{0}, \mathbf{1})$, as this helps in giving the data points a silhouette suitable for RBF when evaluated at the hidden layer of the classifier.

After training the regularized classifier, for every target class $e_i \in E$ a centroid c_i (and associated variance σ_i) is computed by averaging the vectors $\mathbf{h}$ generated by the training set. For every c_i only the rows with $e = e_i$ are taken. A Gaussian RBF network is then created with activation

$$\mathbf{a} = e^{\frac{-\|\mathbf{h}-\mathbf{c}\|^2}{\sigma^2}}, \tag{6}$$

with $\|.\|^2$ being the euclidean distance. Using the above defined RBF network, a bag of word is detected as outlier if $\max \mathbf{a} < T$, with T being a threshold hyper-parameter of the model.

3.2 Intent Recognition Through Plan Recognition

We apply a method similar to [11] that explicitly allows for partially instantiated actions to be present in the set of observations O, rather than allowing only fully instantiated ones. As the set of observations O we use the trajectory of past actions together with the partially instantiated actions gathered from sentence classification $a \in A$. We treat past observations and uttered actions in different ways, therefore splitting the set O into two parts, O_p and O_f. O_p is constrained to appear in a given sequence, as past observations are gathered in a specific order. For the uttered (possibly) future actions O_f no order is enforced instead. From an instance $P = (G, I, A)$ (G: goal, I: initial conditions, A: available actions), a sequence of observed past actions O_p, and a set of partially instantiated future actions O_f, we obtain two modified planning instances $P' = (G', I, A')$ and $P'' = (G'', I, A')$ that are used to compute $C[G + O]$ and $C[G + \neg O]$ respectively, where:

- $A' = A$ with action effects modified as:
  $\forall a \in A'$
  - effects(a') = effects$(a) \cup p_a \to e_0$ if $a \in O_p$ and is the first of the list (i.e. $n = 0$)
  - effects(a') = effects$(a) \cup p_a \wedge e_{n-1} \to e_n$ if $a \in O_p$ and $n \geq 1$
  - effects(a') = effects$(a) \cup p_a \to f_a$ if $a \in O_f$
  - effects(a') = effects(a) otherwise.
  - $p_a = \wedge_i (x_{ai} = arg_{ai})$ if arg_{ai} is specified for action i
  - $p_f = \cup_i f_i$
- $G' = G + O = G \cup e_n \cup p_f$, where e_n is the effect predicate of the last action in O_p, and p_f the conjunction of all of the effect predicates of the actions in O_f.
- $G'' = G + \neg O = G \cup \neg e_n \cup \neg p_f$

Every classified action $\hat{a}$ coming from the Natural Language Understanding component is inserted into the set of future observations O_f. Due to how partially instantiated actions are treated inside P' and P'', these actions receives an additional effect of the type

$$\wedge_i (x_{\hat{a}i} = arg_{\hat{a}i}) \to f_{\hat{a}}, \tag{7}$$

with $f_{\hat{a}}$ entering the set of goal predicates when computing $C[G+O]$. In this way, when computing this cost, the planner will also attempt to satisfy the actions $\hat{a}$ with the generated plan. For $C[G + \neg O]$ instead, the planner will be asked to not take actions $\hat{a}$. Notice that Eq. 7 is applied only to the parameters that are being specified in the action $\hat{a}$, and for which a valid semantic role was classified.

To compute the probability distribution for the goals, and hence of the intents, we pass the cost difference through a softmax layer obtaining $P(G_i|O) = \gamma e^{-\theta \Delta C_i} P(G)$, being $\Delta C_i = C[G_i + \neg O] - C[G_i + O]$, γ the normalizing factor and θ an hyper-parameter of the model, $P(G)$ the prior probabilities of the goals.

4   Evaluation

The evaluation of our proposed system is divided into two parts. Firstly, the developed plan recognition algorithm is evaluated statistically on different planning instances of high complexity. Statistical evaluation is done to quantify how partially instantiated actions alone contribute in the recognition of the correct goal. Then, we implement speech recognition together with image recognition on a Pepper robot, and evaluate intent recognition in human-robot interaction trials.

4.1 Evaluation of Plan Recognition with Partially Instantiated Actions

We evaluate our modified plan recognition algorithm, using only partially instantiated actions as observations, on the following planning domains. Our goal is to show how partially instantiated actions scale (i.e. how many specifications the user should give) when inferring goals in complex domains.

Logistics. In this well-known domain, a fleet of trucks and airplanes has to deliver packages from starting locations to destination ones. There exists different roads or flight routes in which subsets of trucks or airplanes belong to, and trucks and airplanes can move only in between nodes belonging their corresponding route system. The domain has 10 goals, each of them requiring to deliver 2 packages randomly picked from a set of 10 packages. There are 6 possible actions: *load-truck, load-airplane, unload-truck, unload-airplane, drive-truck, fly-airplane*, each of them having 3 arguments.

Blocks World. In this domain there is a table and several blocks on it. Blocks can be stacked on top of each other with the help of a gripper. There are 5 possible goals each of them being a set of towers of blocks. Only one action is possible, *stack-from-to*, that has 3 arguments.

Hospital. In the hospital domain a nurse has to inject drugs to the patients admitted at the hospital. Several rooms are dedicated for the patients and are spread over 3 floors. A set of elevators allow the nurse to change floor. The drugs are all initially stored in a storage room, and every patient requires a specific mixture of drugs. In addition, time constraints determine at which hour of the day the patients should receive their injections. The domain has 12 goals, each of them being the treatment of 2 patients. Patients, rooms, drugs and hours are chosen randomly when the domain is generated. There are 5 possible actions: *take-medicine, wait-for-hour, inject-drug, move, take-elevator*, with a mean number of arguments of 3.2.

For the three domains, each trial is carried as follow: a random goal is selected and an optimal plan A for it is generated. With a parameters $\alpha \in [0,1]$ we selected the percentage of actions in A to keep and use for O_f (always at minimum one action was kept), with another parameter $\beta \in [0,1]$ we specified the percentage of parameters to keep for every action. Retained parameters and actions are randomly selected at every trial. Every goal was tested in equal measure, and for every possible combination of α and β 10 trials were averaged.

Statistical results (Fig. 2) show how both α and β are important in plan recognition. When no parameter is specified ($\beta = 0$) the recognition gives the lowest accuracy values independently of α. In blocks world, being only one action present, this results in random guess performance; in logistics, this performance is slightly above random guess. Given that at least a parameter is specified ($\beta \geq \frac{1}{3}$ in our proposed scenarios), α becomes the dominating factor for the recognition accuracy, as better shown in the right column of Fig. 2.

For practical scenarios, a relevant case is when only one action is specified together with few parameters (e.g. $\alpha = 0$, $\beta \geq \frac{1}{3}$). In this case in the obtained accuracy is in the 20–60% range. Thus, if we expect a limited amount

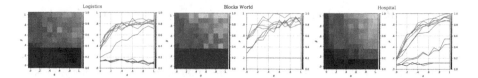

Fig. 2. Results of the statistical evaluation. The matrix on the left shows the tested combinations of values for α and β. Color, from black to white, indicates the obtained accuracy for every combination. On the right is plotted the accuracy in finding the correct goal using different values of α. Every different line correspond to a different value of β. (Color figure online)

of uttered commitments, the introduction of the set of ordered observations O_p is an important factor for achieving high accuracy. Nevertheless, notice that this is a pessimistic measure as in the benchmarks, actions and parameters are chosen randomly, while during real interactions we can expect the observed agent more likely to communicate informatively rather than randomly. Additionally, having the possibility of selecting the classifiable actions, we can ensure that only the actions that are pivotal for the plan recognition problem are expressible an utterances. No such constraint was present in the benchmarks.

4.2   Evaluation in an HRI Setting

In order to test intent recognition in an interaction with a robot, we implemented the described system in an HRI setting using a Pepper robot. In the proposed scenarios, an experimenter stands in front of Pepper and interacts with it using speech. Utterances are detected through the Google Speech API, and classified into PDDL actions using Algorithm 5. Additionally, based on the presence of different objects in the current visual scene, the truth value of selected predicates inside the planning instance is modified. Visual objects are detected using a classifier pre-trained on the YOLO dataset [13]. Figure 3 shows the full developed architecture.

Two different scenarios are evaluated: a *Groceries* scenario where inference on contextual elements is used to discriminate between the user intentions buying food or buying cigarettes. The second *Cups* scenario is created to verify how, given an utterance with partial specifications, missing parameters in the corresponding PDDL action are correctly inferred.

Groceries Setting. In this hypothetical setting the planning instance is programmed to detect whether the speaker in going to buy groceries or cigarettes. Through every trial, the user is asked to state what he is going to do. The possible choices are to buy from the grocery store, to eat food, or to smoke. The possible goals are to eat or to smoke.

Depending on the presence of food on the table in front of Pepper, the corresponding predicates expressing availability for that particular food are set inside the planning instance.

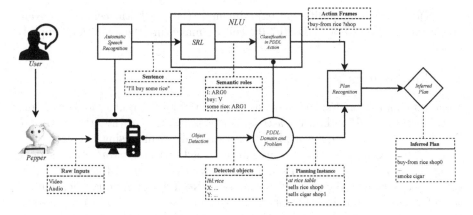

Fig. 3. Main architecture of the implemented system. Audio and video from the Pepper robot are streamed to a workstation where visual objects are identified and audio converted to text. Detected objects are used to modify the planning instance, while speech is classified into partially instantiated actions. The result is used to infer the speaker's intent through plan recognition.

The annotation of the PDDL domain and problem with semantic roles and bag of words is performed in a similar fashion as the one shown in Fig. 1. The expected outcomes of the trials are:

- If the user utters that he wants to go to the supermarket or buy food, the inferred goal depends on the predicate **(at rice fridge)**, which is set to true if a visual object of type *cup* or *bowl* is detected. In such case, the inferred goal is set to smoke, and otherwise to eat.
- If the user utters that he wants to cook or eat, the inferred goal is to eat, expressed by the predicate **(consumed rice)**.
- If the user utters that he wants to smoke, the inferred goal is to smoke, expressed by the predicate **(consumed cigar)**.

Cups Setting. In this setting the user can ask for a drink from three different cups on the table, each one with a different associated cost to reach. The only action that is accessible through speech is *drink*, with one optional parameter specifying which cup to use. There are three possible goals, achieved by the drink action using the different cups. The expected outcomes of the trials are:

- If the user says that he wants to drink, without specifying a cup, the goals have equal probabilities as no discriminating information is present. The inferred goal is returned as to drink from the blue cup.
- If the user specifies any cup for drinking, the inferred goal is to drink with the mentioned cup.

During the experiments the algorithm behaved as expected, and the robot inferred different intentions based on the perceived contextual variable.

A video showing the different experimental trials for both scenarios is available at https://youtu.be/33Dinfh7_0Y (please make sure the address is properly typed).

5   Conclusions

W proposed an algorithm to infer a speaker's intention from utterances and context. The proposed method is based on the classification of the utterances into PDDL actions, followed by a plan recognition algorithm using classical planning. Matching of parts of the utterance to actions and parameters is done using semantic role labeling. Recognized utterances are used to infer the partial plan and goal of the speaker, or to guide execution of actions when part of the information is missing. The proposed system allows to utilize utterances in a contextual way, and depending on the state of the planning instance they lead to different inferred intentions. In our HRI experiments the robot reacts to the user utterances by simply telling the goal it inferred. More complex type of reactions are also possible and are left for future research. The major benefit with our approach is that the intentions do not have to be hardcoded for combinations of a large number of contextual states, but is rather intelligently inferred by the robot in a way that scales both with number of possible intents and contextual variables.

We discuss the issue that when instantiating robot commands all of required parameters must be present in order for the commands to be executed. With the support of a planning domain, partially instantiated actions allow instead to take advantage of the principle of rational action, thus inferring missing parameters as the ones that would yield the most optimal intention. This method is in contrast with other approaches where the combinations of available objects are exhausted or searched in order to find the best match.

Evaluation showed how partially instantiated actions positively contribute to inference of the correct goal. For complex scenarios they yield a fair accuracy only when present in fairly large numbers. Additionally, the system was implemented in an HRI setting using a Pepper robot, and we verified its correct operation in several simplistic but relevant experiments.

Future research include incorporation of a dialogue manager to create/mediate intentions, of multiple agents in the inferred intentions, and collection of a structured knowledge-base for planning domains and annotations, possibly testing grounding algorithms that generalize over them.

Acknowledgments. This work has received funding from the European Union's Horizon 2020 research and innovation program under the Marie Skłodowska-Curie grant agreement No 721619 for the SOCRATES project.

References

1. Baker, C.F., Fillmore, C.J., Lowe, J.B.: The berkeley framenet project. In: Proceedings of the 17th International Conference on Computational Linguistics-Volume 1, pp. 86–90. Association for Computational Linguistics (1998)

2. Bastianelli, E., Castellucci, G., Croce, D., Iocchi, L., Basili, R., Nardi, D.: Huric: a human robot interaction corpus. In: LREC, pp. 4519–4526 (2014)
3. Bensch, S., Jevtić, A., Hellström, T.: On interaction quality in human-robot interaction. In: International Conference on Agents and Artificial Intelligence (ICAART), pp. 182–189 (2017)
4. Breazeal, C., Aryananda, L.: Recognition of affective communicative intent in robot-directed speech. Auton. Robots 12(1), 83–104 (2002). https://doi.org/10.1023/A:1013215010749
5. Chakraborti, T., Kambhampati, S., Scheutz, M., Zhang, Y.: Ai challenges in human-robot cognitive teaming. arXiv preprint arXiv:1707.04775 (2017)
6. Chen, H., Tan, H., Kuntz, A., Bansal, M., Alterovitz, R.: Enabling robots to understand incomplete natural language instructions using commonsense reasoning. CoRR (2019)
7. Demiris, Y.: Prediction of intent in robotics and multi-agent systems. Cogn. Process. 8(3), 151–158 (2007). https://doi.org/10.1007/s10339-007-0168-9
8. He, L., Lee, K., Lewis, M., Zettlemoyer, L.: Deep semantic role labeling: what works and what's next. In: Proceedings of the 55th Annual Meeting of the Association for Computational Linguistics (Volume 1: Long Papers), pp. 473–483 (2017)
9. Kelley, R., Browne, K., Wigand, L., Nicolescu, M., Hamilton, B., Nicolescu, M.: Deep networks for predicting human intent with respect to objects. In: 2012 7th ACM/IEEE International Conference on Human-Robot Interaction (HRI), pp. 171–172, March 2012
10. McDermott, D.: PDDL-the planning domain definition language (1998)
11. Ramírez, M., Geffner, H.: Probabilistic plan recognition using off-the-shelf classical planners. In: Twenty-Fourth AAAI Conference on Artificial Intelligence (2010)
12. Rani, P., Liu, C., Sarkar, N., Vanman, E.: An empirical study of machine learning techniques for affect recognition in human-robot interaction. Pattern Anal. Appl. 9(1), 58–69 (2006)
13. Redmon, J., Divvala, S., Girshick, R., Farhadi, A.: You only look once: unified, real-time object detection. In: Proceedings of the IEEE Conference on Computer Vision and Pattern Recognition, pp. 779–788 (2016)
14. Schaefer, K.E., Chen, J.Y., Wright, J., Aksaray, D., Roy, N.: Challenges with incorporating context into human-robot teaming. In: 2017 AAAI Spring Symposium Series (2017)
15. Sukthankar, G., Geib, C., Bui, H.H., Pynadath, D., Goldman, R.P.: Plan, Activity, and Intent Recognition: Theory and Practice. Newnes, London (2014)
16. Teixeira, A.: A critical analysis of speech-based interaction in healthcare robots: making a case for the increased use of speech in medical and assistive robots. In: Speech and Automata in Health Care, pp. 1–29 (2014)
17. Tellex, S., et al.: Understanding natural language commands for robotic navigation and mobile manipulation. In: Twenty-Fifth AAAI Conference on Artificial Intelligence (2011)
18. Thomas, B.J., Jenkins, O.C.: Roboframenet: verb-centric semantics for actions in robot middleware. In: 2012 IEEE International Conference on Robotics and Automation, pp. 4750–4755. IEEE (2012)
19. Tomasello, M., Carpenter, M., Call, J., Behne, T., Moll, H.: Understanding and sharing intentions: the origins of cultural cognition. Behav. Brain Sci. 28(5), 675–691 (2005)
20. Wei, J.W., Zou, K.: Eda: Easy data augmentation techniques for boosting performance on text classification tasks. arXiv preprint arXiv:1901.11196 (2019)

Planner-Guided Robot Swarms

Michael Schader$^{(\boxtimes)}$ and Sean Luke

George Mason University, Fairfax, VA 22030, USA
{mschader,sean}@gmu.edu

Abstract. Robot swarms have many virtues for large-scale task execution: this includes redundancy, a high degree of parallel task implementation, and the potential to jointly complete jobs that a single agent could not do. But because of their distributed nature, robot swarms face challenges in large-scale coordination, task serialization or ordering, and synchronization. We investigate the use of a central automated planner to guide a robot swarm to perform complicated, multistep operations normally beyond the capabilities of purely decentralized swarms. The planner orchestrates the actions of task groups of agents, while preserving swarm virtues, and can operate over a variety of swarm communication and coordination modalities. We demonstrate the effectiveness of the technique in simulation with three swarm robotics scenarios.

Keywords: Coordination and control models for multi-agent systems · Knowledge representation and reasoning in robotic systems · Swarm behavior

1 Introduction

Robot swarms have long been difficult to control. In 2004, Gerardo Beni coined the term "swarm robotics" [1] and wrote, "Ultimately, after algorithms for task implementation have been devised, the practical realization requires robustness and this is the result of proper control. Swarm control presents new challenges to robotics engineers." In 2012, Brambilla et al. [3] reviewed hundreds of papers in the field and concluded, that "[d]ue to the lack of a centralized controller, it is in general very difficult to effectively control a swarm once it starts operating." Today there is still little ability to specify what a swarm should accomplish and how to have it meet that requirement. A centralized element could solve the control problem by providing a clear point of interface between a human specifying goals and the swarm fulfilling them, and by monitoring and adjusting the swarm's behavior as conditions change. But it is not well understood how introducing a limited amount of central control would affect those virtues that flow from decentralization.

We explore the notion of marrying a distributed behavior-based swarm with a centralized planner. Swarms permit parallelism, redundancy, and simple agent definitions, while central planning provides coordination for nontrivial tasks

© Springer Nature Switzerland AG 2020
Y. Demazeau et al. (Eds.): PAAMS 2020, LNAI 12092, pp. 224–237, 2020.
https://doi.org/10.1007/978-3-030-49778-1_18

involving sequencing and heterogeneous behavior which are very difficult for swarms to do on their own.

This work sits at two different intersections within research and practice. First, in autonomous robotics, there is a long-standing tension between *deliberative* approaches, in which agents choose actions based on a model of the world around them, and *reactive* methods, in which sensor input is closely coupled to behavior without extraneous intermediate layers. A *planner-guided swarm*, described here, is a hybrid architecture combining planning (model-driven deliberation) with reactivity (robots with only local knowledge following simple rules) to get the best of both worlds.

Second, in multi-robot systems, there is a dichotomy between centralized and decentralized architectures. Many multi-robot implementations in industry use a fully centralized approach, with each robot directed in real time by a master controller. Swarm robotics, on the other hand, focuses on independent agents executing simple behaviors that add up to emergent results. A planner-guided swarm preserves the flexibility and robustness of a swarm while adding a bit of centralized direction in order to achieve far more complicated results.

In this paper we first survey the work done by other researchers on the challenge of swarm control and show that no one has previously explored the addition of a central planner to a decentralized swarm. Next, we describe the overall architecture and individual components of our planner-guided swarm concept. We explain how this architecture works with different communication modalities and is independent of the internal design of the agents. Finally, we lay out three very different scenarios that we used to test the capabilities of the system in simulation, and explain how the experiments showed the value of our approach.

2   Previous Work

The most common method seen in the literature to program robot swarms is carefully crafting finite state machines that run on each agent. For example, [10] used regular languages to define Finite-State Automata (FSA) dictating agent behavior. [12] developed a Probabilistic Finite State Machine (PFSM) that used a potential field to drive swarm robot search behavior. [13] progammed swarms by generating behavior trees.

Considering fully decentralized methods, [16] pushed pure pheromone swarm robotics to the limit by implementing the five tasks of classic compass-straightedge geometry, suggesting an upper bound on what such a swarm can accomplish reasonably efficiently without the addition of at least some global knowledge and interaction. [18] applied Embodied Evolutionary Robotics (EER) methods to the development of swarm agent behavior that leads to desired emergent outcomes; tasks were limited to navigation and foraging, and centralized planning was not considered.

Combining reactive and centralized ideas, [21] created a swarm control mechanism in which a subset of the robots was given global information and special influence over the others, occupying a midpoint between centralized and decentralized approaches. [4] developed a decentralized framework for Multi-Agent Systems planning using Hierarchical Task Networks (HTNs) but not emphasizing swarm concepts.

Others have focused on higher-level issues in lightly-centralized swarm design. [6] examined the tradeoffs between microscopic (robot-level) and macroscopic (swarm-level) design and engineering, proposing a hybrid solution. [8] built a top-down systems engineering approach to planning and operating swarms of UAVs.

In the area of multi-agent coordination, [5] created a formal protocol for swarm robots to exchange information about stigmergic values and activities, showing a potential building block for a planning system to interface with pheromone swarms. [20] presented multiple biologically-inspired algorithms for coordinated motion on real robots using pheromone-like signals to influence their behavior. [9] explored the use of response thresholds in determining when agents in a swarm should change behavior.

Task allocation has been examined from several perspectives. [22] proposed the use of a market-based mechanism for swarm robots to acquire task assignments, in which self-interested agents participate in a virtual economy. [2] implemented virtual pheromones in robots built on the Belief-Desire-Intention framework (BDI). [14] used the Artificial Bee Colony (ABC) algorithm to assign tasks in a multi-agent system, achieving results comparable to other methods but with greater efficiency.

[19] developed Termes, a swarm construction system. A compiler takes an architectural specification (with some important constraints) as input and generates a specialized plan for a swarm of robots to build it. They simplify as many aspects of the environment as possible, using custom blocks that are placed in an iterative fashion. Once the plan is loaded onto the robots, all interaction is stigmergic (by where blocks have been placed).

[7] developed AntLab, a centralized multi-robot system which decomposes problems and directs varying numbers of robots to solve them. It is flexible in terms of what tasks it performs and how it handles adding or removing robots from its set of workers. However, it is not a swarm: the individual robots have their motions and activities planned in advance by a central controller, and there is no communication among the robots.

3   Method

It is clear that classic swarm mechanisms can be used to accomplish certain tasks in the real world. However the tasks explored in previous work, such as coverage, foraging, and navigation, are generally simple and known to be well suited to decentralized solutions. It is not clear how to elicit sophisticated behavior from a swarm in situations that require coordinated, simultaneous activity.

The gap we identified in the literature is the lack of research into hybrid architectures that separately address high-level and low-level behavior. Previous

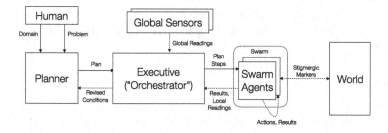

Fig. 1. Planner-guided robot swarm architecture

work explores methods to design and deploy swarm agent behaviors intended to achieve certain goals, but without the ability to monitor and manage the swarm's actions at runtime. Other work features explicit central control of each individual agent in order to optimize its activity, but sacrifices swarm characteristics such as redundancy and local-only communication in the process. Our innovation is to split the swarm design work into high-level planning and low-level behavior implementation, map planning actions to specific behaviors, and build an architecture that manages emergent behavior to achieve desired ends.

The collection of agents used in our approach is truly a swarm, and we focus on this subset of multiagent systems. The individuals are homogeneous, communicate only locally, have a small number of simple behaviors, and exhibit emergent behavior that advances the system toward a goal. They are guided by an external component that adjusts behavioral parameters for groups of agents within the swarm. This guidance is driven by the output of an automated planner. The plan domain and problem definitions are written by a human controller, and the agent behaviors and the mapping from plan actions to agent activity are developed for the situation at hand; all other aspects (agent internals, communication modality, monitoring mechanisms) are generalized and can be used in any scenario.

The architecture of our approach is shown in Fig. 1. The process begins with a *human* creating a domain definition that describes how the world works in classical planning terms, and a problem definition that lays out the initial and goal states. These definitions are given to the *planner*, which devises a sequence of (potentially parallel) actions that will achieve the desired result. The planner submits the plan to the executive component, called the *orchestrator*, which maps the actions in the plan to specific behaviors for the agents to perform. The orchestrator divides the *swarm agents* into task groups, and then transmits the first set of instructions to them. The agents operate according to the parameters they have been given, with overall progress emerging from their activity. The agents may employ stigmergy (communication via changes made to the *world*) and other swarm-type mechanisms to transmit information, such as pheromones, direct interaction, and short-range communication. The orchestrator monitors the swarm's progress through any combination of data returned by the agents and *global sensors* that track conditions in the world. When the orchestrator determines that the current plan step has been completed, it issues the next set of instructions, advancing until the plan has been completed and the goal state achieved.

3.1   Planner

A human creates Planning Domain Definition Language (PDDL) files that specify the domain (the predicates available to evaluate the world and the actions the agent can take to change it) and the problem (the initial and goal states) [17]. These files are fed into the planner, which generates a plan in the form of a sequence of actions that will change the world from the initial state to the goal state. These plans may be sequential or parallel. This capability is exposed as the function MakePlan(*domain, problem*).

In our experiments we used the Blackbox planner [11]. It is well suited to our purposes in that it accepts and emits standard PDDL, generates parallel plans with any number of simultaneous actions, is available for each major operating system, and is highly performant. Nothing in our method is dependent on the particulars of Blackbox; any PDDL-based planner will do.

3.2   Orchestrator

The orchestrator is the interface to the multi-agent swarm. To draw a comparison with the classic three-tiered agent architecture, the orchestrator is the Executive, ensuring that the output of the Deliberator (the planner) is executed and monitored properly. This component transforms plans into sequenced actions that the agents can perform, loosely oversees progress without explicitly conducting the individuals in the swarm, and potentially makes plan and assignment adjustments if tasks are not being accomplished.

Agent Setup. The orchestrator divides the set of agents into however many task groups are called for in the scenario. This size of each group may be the same based on splitting up the total number of agents, or may vary depending on how many are needed for each task. The orchestrator tells each agent which task group it is in, and from then onward, the agents know which group instructions to follow. In some situations it is useful to have a task group that is not given any instructions, but rather serves as a communications medium by having its agents wander around exchanging information with others that are performing specific tasks.

Action to Behavior Translation. The mapping of plan actions to agent behaviors is determined at design time for the scenario. For each action listed in the domain definition, the developer implements code that determines what parameters need to be given to the agents to have them execute the appropriate behavior. For example, an action to open a door might translate to the agent behavior of traveling to the correct button and pressing it, while an action to build a wall could become a set of parameters instructing the agents to wander looking for wall material and bringing it to a designated location.

Progress Monitoring. After the orchestrator issues actions to the task groups, it monitors for completion of the plan step. One way it can do this monitoring is via the agents, counting the number reporting success or tracking other observations that the agents bring back. An alternative method is to use global sensors: mechanisms that allow the orchestrator to directly assess the state of the world in order to know when success has been achieved. Upon learning of step completion, either through diffused knowledge carried by the agents or through direct observation, it moves onto the next step. Ultimately, the orchestrator recognizes when the goal state has been attained.

Regardless of the problem definition or the communication modality, the core algorithm executed by the orchestrator is the same. While there is a step in the plan remaining, we iterate as follows. First, for each action in the step, we convert this action into a concrete agent behavior. Then the task is assigned to an available task group, and the action completion criteria are added to *conditions*. Second, we wait until every condition in *conditions* has been met.

3.3   Agents

The agents are the members of the swarm. They perform actions in the world based on their programming and the guidance they receive from the orchestrator. When accomplishing the objective requires collaboration among the agents, it may be top-down, in which the planner instructs different groups to take actions that complement each other, e.g. one pushes a button to open a door while another goes through it. Alternatively, it may be bottom-up, in which the agents themselves interact to perform a function, such as joining up to move an object. (See Sect. 4.3 for our experiment that included both).

In our conceptual model, there are no restrictions on the internals of the swarm agents. The only requirement is for them to receive behavior parameter information from the orchestrator and adjust their activity accordingly. Our implementation uses state machines to transition among various behaviors, with variables (such as destinations and object types) that are set based on the orchestrator's messages. Note that the orchestrator has no knowledge of these internal states. Agents can also be built using a subsumption architecture, or with complex deliberation, or with any other mechanism that allows them to act on guidance from the orchestrator.

For each scenario (or real-world situation), we craft a planning description of the domain (e.g. locations, objects, constraints) as well as the low-level behaviors of the agents (such as move, pick up, put down). We then create a mapping of domain actions to agent behaviors ("move block A to location 2" becomes "search for an A-type object, pick it up, navigate to location 2, put it down"). Next we implement any needed success criteria checks ("Is location 2 full of A-type objects?"). Finally, we specify the problem in planning domain terms and send the swarm to do the job.

3.4 Communication Modalities

The planner-guided approach depends on having some means of communication between the orchestrator and the agents: the agents need to receive guidance based on the plan, and they need to transmit status updates back to the orchestrator. There are several different communication modalities typically used by swarms, so we have accommodated all of them in our architecture and experiments (see Sect. 4.1):

1. *Broadcast*: The agents instantly learn the particulars of the action they need to execute, and transmit their results directly back to the home base. This method is fast and effective, but it depends on a permissive communications environment and a one-to-many architecture with limited scalability.
2. *Direct Interaction*: Messages diffuse through the swarm by being exchanged when individuals make physical contact with each other or the home base. A variant of this is *Local Interaction*, in which messages are also sent peer-to-peer, but with a relaxed proximity requirement (nearby rather than touching).
3. *Pheromones*: Information is embedded in the environment and sensed when agents pass over it; this removes the need to be in the same place at the same time.

4 Experiments

We have developed three different scenarios in the course of this work, each emphasizing different multiagent control challenges. Our intent is to show that the planner-guided swarm approach is effective and scalable over a variety of situations, and with several different communication mechanisms. (Future work will address other challenges such as responding to unexpected events). The first scenario, *Blocks World*, demonstrates complex sequencing; the second, *MarsOne*, shows a more realistic (albeit on Mars) exploration and construction environment; and the third, *Airlocks*, is a locked-room situation requiring both micro- and macro-level coordination and sequencing.

Each scenario is defined by a domain definition and problem definition formalized in PDDL and shown in the Appendix (Section 6). We ran all the simulations using the MASON multiagent simulation toolkit [15], collecting the number of steps needed to succeed under each treatment.

4.1 Blocks World: Complex Parallel Manipulation in Idealized Space

The first scenario, Blocks World, provides us with a well-understood proving ground for testing the integration of classical planning with a robotic swarm. The actions need to be performed in a correct complicated sequence in order to succeed. Some steps of the plan allow actions to be performed in parallel, offering a valuable speedup in completion time. However, other steps have dependencies which don't permit full parallelization, and the swarm needs to handle this

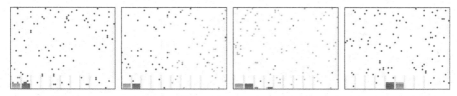

(a) The Swarm starts re-arranging blocks so the top ones end up on the bottom

(b) The agents complete Step 1, word gets back, and the next action spreads

(c) All the agents have moved onto Step 2 and are moving the blocks as directed

(d) Ultimately, the blocks are rearranged as specified and the task is completed

The blue and green dots represent agents on even- or odd-numbered steps. The gray/brown shaded pieces make up the eight different blocks. The thin vertical lines are walls.

Fig. 2. Stages of the Blocks World scenario (Color figure online)

effectively. This challenge showed that we could perform interleaved parallel and serial tasks with a swarm.

Blocks World is derived from the classic planning problem using labeled blocks that can be placed on a table or on each other (Fig. 2). In the swarm simulation, each block consists of several objects that can each be moved by an agent. Walls separate the block sources and destinations in order to force ordered planning to rearrange them efficiently. The domain definition allows up to four actions to take place concurrently, equivalent to having four hands grabbing, holding, and placing blocks in the environment. The initial state features two stacks of four blocks each (ABCD and EFGH, from bottom to top). The goal is to have two stacks in the same order, except with the bottom block of each moved to the top position (BCDA and FGHE).

In this scenario, we use four task groups, correlating conceptually to four manipulator arms that can move blocks simultaneously. The orchestrator translates each of the actions defined in the domain (PICK-UP, PUT-DOWN, UNSTACK, and STACK) to an agent directive. PICK-UP and UNSTACK are mapped to foraging-type behavior in which the agent explored the area looking for the specified type of block. PUT-DOWN and STACK are mapped to the inverse: seeking a destination and depositing the right type of block there. The completion criteria are based on counting the number of blocks picked up or deposited correctly for each action.

The agents are controlled by two parameters: which kind of block to seek, and where to place the type of block they were holding. For example, "PICK-UP H" translates to "find an item of type H and pick it up", while "STACK H G" becomes "if holding an item of type H, navigate to the site above the G blocks and drop it off". The agents have two states, Exploring and Carrying, and two parameters, what to find and where to put it. While Exploring, they use whatever means are at their disposal to find the specified item. Once they find it, they switch to Carrying, and work to bring their carried objects to the

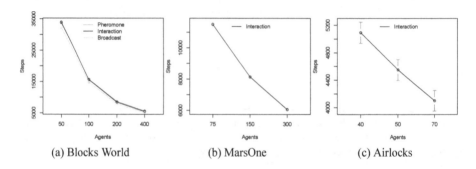

Fig. 3. Mean steps to completion of scenario

destination. Upon reaching it, they drop off their items and resume Exploring. The agents navigate collaboratively using pheromone gradients; each lays down a trail upon leaving a site in order to help others find the same location.

We tested this scenario using three different communication mechanisms explained in Sect. 3.4: Broadcast, Direct Interaction, and Pheromone Encoding. For each modality, we varied the number of agents from 50 up to 400 to observe the effect on the average number of steps needed to reach the goal state (Fig. 3a). We performed 1000 runs of each treatment and verified for statistical significance using the two-tailed t-test at $p = 0.05$ with the Bonferroni correction.

As the Blocks World scenario with various communication mechanisms was run with increasing numbers of agents, swarm performance improved until leveling off. This was due to interference caused by having too many agents in a contained space. The strong similarity of the curves for the three different information exchange modalities indicates that performance is hardly affected by the means of transmission. This implies that the planner-guided approach to swarm control is flexible and not dependent on any particular communication architecture.

4.2 MarsOne: Simulated Autonomous Construction with Dependencies

Compared to the first scenario, the second provides a more physically realistic environment with more meaningful objectives to accomplish. MarsOne is based on plans to build a Martian colony in advance of human explorers by using autonomous robots (Fig. 4). In the MarsOne domain, a ship contains equipment components for an antenna, a machine that can produce ice blocks, and the modules for the base. Useful rocks are strewn about the area, and a distant hill provides an ideal radio transmission point. As per the problem definition, the planner-guided swarm is required to find the hill, bring the antenna components to it and assemble them, emplace the base modules, build the ice-making machine, collect the ice blocks it produces and use them to build a wall around the base, and finally gather rocks and put them around the ice wall.

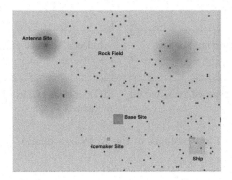

Fig. 4. Initial state of the MarsOne scenario

The actions and success criteria are more sophisticated and open-ended than in Blocks World. For example, ice blocks can only be collected as they are produced, one at a time; ice and rock must be placed into concentric rings in the right sequence. This greater complexity only applies to the planner; the agents and the mapping to their actions are as simple as those in Blocks World, with COLLECT and DEPOSIT-AT instructions working like PICK-UP and PUT-DOWN in the previous scenario. Each action specifies a type of object and a source or destination, e.g. "COLLECT base-parts ship" means "find the ship and pick up a base part", and "DEPOSIT-AT base-parts base" means "if carrying a base part, find the base and put it down there". DEPOSIT-AT-SURROUNDING works exactly like DEPOSIT-AT from the agents' perspective; the distinction between the two is needed to force proper sequencing by the planner (for the ice wall to surround the base and the rock wall to surround the ice wall, the ice wall must be built first).

We tested this scenario using the Direct Interaction communications mechanism and varied the number of agents from 75 up to 300 to observe the effect on the average number of steps needed to reach the goal state (Fig. 3b). We performed 1000 runs of each treatment and verified for statistical significance using the two-tailed t-test at $p = 0.05$ with the Bonferroni correction. This challenge showed whether the planner-guided swarm approach could handle believable, less-idealized situations that were very different from the more abstract world in the first scenario. Under testing, the swarm was able to execute the planned steps and reach the goal state.

4.3 Airlocks: Mandatory Coordination Among Partitioned Task Groups

The third scenario, Airlocks, has a sequence of rooms behind locked doors (Fig. 5). The agents needs to move rocks from the Room 0 starting area (on the far left), through Room 1 and Room 2, into Room 3 (on the far right). These rocks are heavy and can only be moved by pairs of agents working in unison. Each of the doors has a button that opens it as long as an agent is holding

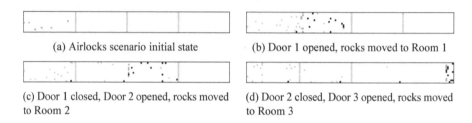

(a) Airlocks scenario initial state   (b) Door 1 opened, rocks moved to Room 1

(c) Door 1 closed, Door 2 opened, rocks moved   (d) Door 2 closed, Door 3 opened, rocks moved
to Room 2   to Room 3

Fig. 5. Stages of the Airlocks scenario

the button. Once the button is released, that door closes. Finally, only one of the three doors can be open at a time. Note that the agents in this scenario can not rely on physical contact to transfer information, because closed doors would partition the swarm into separate regions. For this reason, they have a short-range transmission capability (a 3-square radius) that allows them to communicate through closed doors. The domain definition captures the mutually exclusive relationship among the door states; the problem definition simply states that the world begins with the doors closed and the rocks in Room 0, and should end with the rocks in Room 3.

We tested this scenario using Direct Interaction and varied the number of agents from 40 up to 70 to observe the effect on the average number of steps needed to reach the goal state (Fig. 3c). We performed 1000 runs of each treatment and verified for statistical significance using the two-tailed t-test at $p = 0.05$ with the Bonferroni correction.

The Airlocks scenario requires coordination among the agents at two different levels. From the whole-swarm perspective, the opening and closing of each door has to be synchronized with the movement of the agents through it, and with the state of the other doors. From the individual perspective, agents need to coordinate with each other to collaboratively transport the heavy rocks (using a grab-and-hold approach). This challenge examined the planner-guided swarm's ability to operate with mandatory coordination requirements while executing a centrally-developed plan. Testing showed that the swarm could solve this problem while scaling up successfully.

5 Conclusions and Future Work

The planner-guided swarms were highly effective at solving all three scenarios. These different situations were handled with no change to the core algorithm of the orchestrator, and only minor practical adjustments to the low-level agent behaviors. The swarm performed similarly well when tested with various communications modalities, showing that the concept is independent of any specific information exchange mechanism. These experiments demonstrated the generality of the approach and its applicability to a wide variety of environments.

As future work, we will explore solving the problem of retrograde behavior (some agents being stuck on a previous plan step); ensure swarm robustness via task re-allocation, adjusting communications strategies, and other methods; and demonstrate that coordination under planning can be performed to accomplish tasks reliably and efficiently. This work will show for the first time a flexible, reusable solution to the inverse problem of controlling emergent swarm behavior without sacrificing robustness or low-level decentralization.

6 Appendix: PDDL Files

Blocks World domain and problem definitions

```
(define (domain BLOCKS-WORLD) (:requirements :strips :typing) (:types block)
   ;; Actions ending with "N" are expanded by a preprocesor into "pick-up1", "pick-up2", etc.
   (:predicates (on ?x - block ?y - block) (ontable ?x - block) (clear ?x - block) (handempty) (holding ?x - block))
   (:action pick-upN :parameters (?x - block) :precondition (and (clear ?x) (ontable ?x) (handempty))
   :e ect (and (not (ontable ?x)) (not (clear ?x)) (not (handempty)) (holding ?x)))
   (:action put-downN :parameters (?x - block) :precondition (holding ?x)
   :e ect (and (not (holding ?x)) (handempty) (clear ?x) (ontable ?x)))
   (:action unstackN :parameters (?x - block ?y - block) :precondition (and (on ?x ?y) (clear ?x) (handempty))
   :e ect (and (holding ?x) (not (handempty)) (clear ?y) (not (clear ?x)) (not (on ?x ?y))))
   (:action stackN :parameters (?x - block ?y - block) :precondition (and (holding ?x) (clear ?y))
   :e ect (and (not (holding ?x)) (handempty) (not (clear ?y)) (clear ?x) (on ?x ?y))))

(define (problem REORDER) (:domain BLOCKS-WORLD) (:objects a b c d e f g h - block)
   (:init (handempty) (clear d) (clear h) (ontable a) (ontable e) (on d c) (on h g) (on c b) (on g f) (on b a) (on f e))
   (:goal (and (on a d) (on e h) (on d c) (on h g) (on c b) (on g f))))
```

MarsOne domain and problem definitions

```
(define (domain MARS-ONE) (:requirements :strips :typing) (:types group thing site)
   (:predicates (at ?t - thing ?s - site) (reachable ?s - site) (carrying ?g - group ?t - thing)
         (surrounds ?t - thing ?s - site) (empty ?g - group) (discoverable ?s - site)
         (produces ?s - site ?parts ?output - thing) (encloses ?outsite ?insite - site))
   (:action collect :parameters (?g - group ?t - thing ?s - site) :precondition (and (empty ?g) (reachable ?s) (at ?t ?s))
   :e ect (and (not (empty ?g)) (carrying ?g ?t) (not (at ?t ?s)))
   (:action deposit-at :parameters (?g - group ?t - thing ?s - site) :precondition (and (carrying ?g ?t) (reachable ?s))
   :e ect (and (empty ?g) (not (carrying ?g ?t)) (at ?t ?s)))
   (:action deposit-at-surrounding :parameters (?g - group ?t - thing ?outsite ?insite - site)
   :precondition (and (carrying ?g ?t) (reachable ?insite) (reachable ?outsite) (encloses ?outsite ?insite))
   :e ect (and (empty ?g) (not (carrying ?g ?t)) (surrounds ?t ?insite) (not (reachable ?insite)) (at ?t ?outsite)))
   (:action activate :parameters (?s - site ?parts ?output - thing)
   :precondition (and (produces ?s ?parts ?output) (at ?parts ?s)) :e ect (and (at ?output ?s)))
   (:action discover :parameters (?g - group ?s - site) :precondition (and (empty ?g) (discoverable ?s)) :e ect (and (reachable ?s))))

(define (problem BUILD-BASE) (:domain MARS-ONE) ; References to "groupN" are expanded into "group1", "group2," etc.
   (:objects groupN - group rocks - thing scattered - site ship antenna icemaker base
         ice-wall rock-wall antenna-parts icemaker-parts base-parts ice-blocks)
   (:init (empty groupN) (produces icemaker icemaker-parts ice-blocks) (reachable ship) (reachable icemaker)
         (reachable scattered) (reachable rock-wall) (reachable base) (reachable ice-wall) (at antenna-parts ship)
         (at icemaker-parts ship) (at base-parts ship) (at rocks scattered) (discoverable antenna)
         (encloses ice-wall base) (encloses rock-wall ice-wall))
   (:goal (and (at antenna-parts antenna) (at base-parts base) (surrounds ice-blocks base) (surrounds rocks ice-wall))))
```

Airlocks domain and problem definitions

```
(define (domain AIRLOCKS) (:requirements :strips :typing)
   (:predicates (opened-r1) (opened-r2) (opened-r3) (closed-r1) (closed-r2) (closed-r3) (in-r0) (in-r1) (in-r2) (in-r3))
   (:action open-r1 :precondition (and (closed-r1) (closed-r2) (closed-r3)) :e ect (and (opened-r1) (not (closed-r1))))
   (:action open-r2 :precondition (and (closed-r1) (closed-r2) (closed-r3)) :e ect (and (opened-r2) (not (closed-r2))))
   (:action open-r3 :precondition (and (closed-r1) (closed-r2) (closed-r3)) :e ect (and (opened-r3) (not (closed-r3))))
   (:action close-r1 :precondition (opened-r1) :e ect (and (not (opened-r1)) (closed-r1)))
   (:action close-r2 :precondition (opened-r2) :e ect (and (not (opened-r2)) (closed-r2)))
   (:action close-r3 :precondition (opened-r3) :e ect (and (not (opened-r3)) (closed-r3)))
```

```
(:action move-to-r1 :precondition (and (in-r0) (opened-r1)) :e ect (and (not (in-r0)) (in-r1)))
(:action move-to-r2 :precondition (and (in-r1) (opened-r2)) :e ect (and (not (in-r1)) (in-r2)))
(:action move-to-r3 :precondition (and (in-r2) (opened-r3)) :e ect (and (not (in-r2)) (in-r3))))

(define (problem MOVE-ROCKS) (:domain AIRLOCKS) (:init (in-r0) (closed-r1) (closed-r2) (closed-r3)) (:goal (in-r3)))
```

References

1. Beni, G.: From swarm intelligence to swarm robotics. In: Şahin, E., Spears, W.M. (eds.) SR 2004. LNCS, vol. 3342, pp. 1–9. Springer, Heidelberg (2005). https://doi.org/10.1007/978-3-540-30552-1_1

2. Bottone, M., Palumbo, F., Primiero, G., Raimondi, F., Stocker, R.: Implementing virtual pheromones in BDI robots using MQTT and jason (short paper). In: 2016 5th IEEE International Conference on Cloud Networking (Cloudnet), pp. 196–199. IEEE (2016)

3. Brambilla, M., Ferrante, E., Birattari, M., Dorigo, M.: Swarm robotics: a review from the swarm engineering perspective. Swarm Intell. **7**(1), 1–41 (2013)

4. Cardoso, R.C.: A decentralised online multi-agent planning framework for multi-agent systems (2018)

5. Chibaya, C.: An XSet based protocol for coordinating the behaviour of stigmergic ant-like robotic devices. In: Proceedings of the 2015 Annual Research Conference on South African Institute of Computer Scientists and Information Technologists, p. 9. ACM (2015)

6. Durand, J.G.D.S.: A methodology to achieve microscopic/macroscopic configuration tradeoffs in cooperative multi-robot systems design. Ph.D. thesis, Georgia Institute of Technology (2017)

7. Gavran, I., Majumdar, R., Saha, I.: Antlab: a multi-robot task server. ACM Trans. Embed. Comput. Syst. (TECS) **16**(5s), 190 (2017)

8. Giles, K.: Mission based architecture for swarm composability. Technical report, Naval Postgraduate School Monterey United States (2018)

9. Kanakia, A.P.: Response threshold based task allocation in multi-agent systems performing concurrent benefit tasks with limited information (2015)

10. Kaszubowski Lopes, Y.: Supervisory Control Theory for Controlling Swarm Robotics Systems. Ph.D. thesis, University of Sheffield (2016)

11. Kautz, H., Selman, B.: BLACKBOX: a new approach to the application of theorem proving to problem solving. In: AIPS98 Workshop on Planning as Combinatorial Search, vol. 58260, pp. 58–60 (1998)

12. Khan, M.S., HASAN, M., Ahmed, T.: A new multi-robot search algorithm using probabilistic finite state machine and Lennard-Jones potential function (2018)

13. Kuckling, J., Ligot, A., Bozhinoski, D., Birattari, M.: Behavior trees as a control architecture in the automatic modular design of robot swarms. In: Dorigo, M., Birattari, M., Blum, C., Christensen, A.L., Reina, A., Trianni, V. (eds.) ANTS 2018. LNCS, vol. 11172, pp. 30–43. Springer, Cham (2018). https://doi.org/10.1007/978-3-030-00533-7_3

14. Liu, H., Zhang, P., Hu, B., Moore, P.: A novel approach to task assignment in a cooperative multi-agent design system. Appl. Intell. **43**(1), 162–175 (2015). https://doi.org/10.1007/s10489-014-0640-z

15. Luke, S., Cioffi-Revilla, C., Panait, L., Sullivan, K.: Mason: a new multi-agent simulation toolkit. In: Proceedings of the 2004 Swarmfest Workshop, vol. 8, pp. 316–327. Michigan, USA (2004)

16. Luke, S., Russell, K., Hoyle, B.: Ant geometers. In: Proceedings of the European Conference on Artificial Life 13, pp. 100–107. MIT Press (2016)
17. McDermott, D., et al.: PDDL-the planning domain definition language (1998)
18. Pérez, I.F.: Distributed Embodied Evolutionary Adaptation of Behaviors in Swarms of Robotic Agents. Ph.D. thesis, Université de Lorraine (2017)
19. Petersen, K.H., Nagpal, R., Werfel, J.K.: Termes: an autonomous robotic system for three-dimensional collective construction. In: Robotics: Science and Systems VII (2011)
20. Shirazi, A.R.: Bio-Inspired Self-Organizing Swarm Robotics. Ph.D. thesis, University of Surrey, United Kingdom (2017)
21. Trabattoni, M., Valentini, G., Dorigo, M.: Hybrid control of swarms for resource selection. In: Dorigo, M., Birattari, M., Blum, C., Christensen, A.L., Reina, A., Trianni, V. (eds.) ANTS 2018. LNCS, vol. 11172, pp. 57–70. Springer, Cham (2018). https://doi.org/10.1007/978-3-030-00533-7_5
22. Yusuf, F.: Multi robot task allocation using market based approach. Ph.D. thesis, Universiti Tun Hussein Onn Malaysia (2015)

A MAS-Based Approach for POI Group Recommendation in LBSN

Silvia Schiaffino[1]([✉]), Daniela Godoy[1], J. Andrés Díaz Pace[1],
and Yves Demazeau[2]

[1] ISISTAN (UNCPBA-CONICET), Tandil, Argentina
silvia.schiaffino@isistan.unicen.edu.ar
[2] Laboratoire d'Informatique de Grenoble (CNRS), Grenoble, France

Abstract. Location-based recommender systems (LBRS) suggest friends, events, and places considering information about geographical locations. These recommendations can be made to individuals but also to groups of users, which implies satisfying the group as a whole. In this work, we analyze different alternatives for POI group recommendations based on a multi-agent system consisting of negotiating agents that represent a group of users. The results obtained thus far indicate that our multi-agent approach outperforms traditional aggregation approaches, and that the usage of LBSN information helps to improve both the quality of the recommendations and the efficiency of the recommendation process.

Keywords: Group recommender systems · Location-based social networks · Multi-agent systems · Negotiation

1 Introduction

Location-based social networks (LBSN), like *Foursquare* or *Yelp*, take advantage of the advances in communication technologies to enable users to share their geographical location, look for interesting places (POIs, Points Of Interest) and share content and opinions about these places. In this context, location-based recommender systems (LBRS) generally make recommendations to individual users. However, going to a restaurant or visiting a museum are activities that are usually done in groups. Group recommender systems can provide recommendations to a group of users trying to fulfill the expectations of the group as a whole and to satisfy the individual preferences of all group members [10].

Most approaches for group recommendation make use of different aggregation techniques: (i) generating a group profile that combines individual user profiles (profile aggregation), (ii) aggregating recommendations obtained for each group member, such as in ranking aggregation (recommendation aggregation), or (iii) aggregating individual ratings using approaches such as minimizing misery or maximizing average satisfaction (preference aggregation). Although these approaches have been widely applied, they still present some shortcomings. On

© Springer Nature Switzerland AG 2020
Y. Demazeau et al. (Eds.): PAAMS 2020, LNAI 12092, pp. 238–250, 2020.
https://doi.org/10.1007/978-3-030-49778-1_19

one hand, some aggregation techniques, such as least misery and average, can generate recommendations that might not reflect the group preferences correctly. On the other hand, the decision-making process of the group and the group dynamics [7] (such as users' influence or trust relationships) are not comprehended by the aggregation techniques [10] (ch. 22). We believe that these aspects are important in domains like POI recommendation, in which group members generally discuss and analyze their options for achieving a consensus. Thus, taking the group dynamics into account can help to further personalize recommendations.

Modeling a LBRS as a multi-agent system (MAS) is a more adequate solution, as a negotiation among cooperative agents could replace aggregation techniques, thus helping to overcome their limitations. Along this line, in [15] we proposed a MAS-based approach for group recommendation called MAGReS (Multi-Agent Group Recommender System), which relies on the agents to select those individual recommendations that will be part of the group recommendations. In MAGReS, which was evaluated in the movies domain, each user in a group is represented by a personal agent, which knows the user's preferences and acts on her behalf when trying to agree on items (POIs) with other agents. In order to reach agreements, the agents engage in a cooperative negotiation process.

In the POI domain, group LBRS can leverage on an additional layer of information provided by the LBSN, which includes users' social and geographical relationships, in order to generate better POIs suggestions for the group. In this paper we analyze different alternatives for POI group recommendation and compare our MAGReS approach to two traditional aggregation approaches: aggregation of preferences/ratings, and aggregation of recommendations. Additionally, to determine the usefulness of the LBSN information, we study how the geographical relationships of group members influence the neighbors selection process. The experiments were conducted using the Yelp[1] dataset. The results obtained thus far suggest that: i) our MAS-based approach outperforms traditional aggregation approaches, and ii) the usage of LBSN information helps to improve the quality of the group recommendations while also making the neighbors selection process more efficient.

The rest of the article is organized as follows. In Sect. 2 we describe related works. In Sect. 3 we introduce the MAGReS approach for group recommendation. In Sect. 4 we present an evaluation of our approach against existing approaches. Finally, in Sect. 5 we give the conclusions and outline future work.

2   Related Work

Most group recommendation strategies are based on the aggregation of recommendations, preferences or profiles [10]. Adaptations of the recommendation aggregation functions are proposed in [1,16,18]. In [16] the authors present a group POI recommendation method (GA-GPOI) that combines users' gregariousness, i.e. the degree of association between users in a community, activity,

---

[1] http://www.yelp.com/dataset/challenge.

and sign-in times. Zhu et al. [18] consider the rationality of the location, based on distance and the intra-group influence when making group decisions about POIs. The group decision strategy aims to reach a consensus on the POIs based on a function that aggregates the recommendation results taking into account group relevance and group disagreement. Experiments reported in [1] with a hybrid RS that combines the group geographical preferences, category and location features, and group check-ins for generating group suggestions, yield to the conclusions that models with categorical or geographical information performed better than those not using these features. Also, the combination of individual recommendations with aggregation functions underperforms the group models.

Preference aggregation implies to obtain group models to generate predictions. An example is the SPTW-GRM model [9], which creates a common group profile including the common location categories of their members. Thus, the location category with the higher repetition in the group profile shows the users' interests towards such location type and it has more impact on POI recommendations than those with lower repetition. The CGAR approach uses a hierarchical Bayesian model to recommend activities to groups [8]. CGAR uses topic models to mine activities from location information and group preference from user-group membership information, and then a matrix factorization to match the latent feature space of a group to the latent features of locations.

Finally, a profile aggregation approach is presented in [5]. The structure of groups visiting POIs is used for identifying which groups are likely to visit a place, assuming that the group size and structure affect the POI selection (e.g., some places are visited by large groups and others are preferred by small groups).

3   POI Group Recommendation

Our proposed approach, called MAGReS (*Multi-Agent Group Recommender System*), consists of a MAS in which each agent represents a group member. It was initially developed for group recommendation of movies [15], but it can be extended to other domains like POIs. Instead of using traditional aggregation techniques (such as average or least misery), MAGReS relies on a MAS for selecting those individual recommendations that will be part of the group recommendations.

In MAGReS, each agent has access to a user profile that contains the user's preferences regarding POIs. Each agent is capable of (i) predicting the rating the user would assign to a POI not yet rated, and (ii) generating a ranking of potentially interesting POIs for the user. Initially, the user's preferences are the ratings assigned by the user to the POIs she rated in the past. Also, the agent keeps information about the user's social network and geographical information about the places rated or marked as "check-ins". A general overview of our approach is shown in Fig. 1. At the core of MAGReS is a negotiation process in which *User Agents* try to reach a consensus on the most satisfying items for the group. Although several negotiation protocols are available, only a few of them address two important properties for us, namely: (i) mimic the negotiation

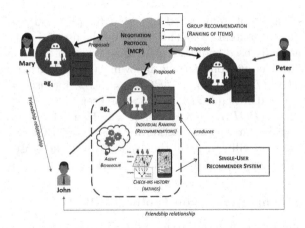

Fig. 1. MAGReS approach for recommending POIs to groups

process followed by humans, and (ii) be suitable for multi-lateral negotiation. On this basis, we chose the *Monotonic Concession Protocol* (MCP) [3] for the approach. In MCP, a set of cooperative agents negotiate over proposals in order to reach consensus over those proposals to guide the negotiation.

Formalizing the problem, let $A = \{ag_1, ag_2, ..., ag_n\}$ be a finite set of N cooperative agents, and let $X = \{x_1, x_2, ...x_m\}$ be a finite set of potential agreements or proposals, each one of them containing a POI (item) that can be recommended to one of the agents. Each agent $ag_i \in A$ has a *utility function* $U_i : X \to [0, 1]$ that maps proposals to their satisfaction value. In our approach, each agent ag_i relies on a single-user recommender system SUR_i, to generate a ranking containing the POIs it can propose. The ranking is sorted in descendant order according to the utility value of the item, and all the candidate proposals with a utility value lower than a certain threshold are discarded. Thus, the set X can be seen as the union of the rankings produced for all the agents, plus a special agreement called *conflict deal*, which yields utility 0 for all the agents and will be chosen as the worst possible outcome (when no agreement is possible).

For example, in the domain of LBSNs let us assume that a group of three friends wants to go to a restaurant together and there is a set of P possible restaurants to be chosen. According to MAGReS, each user is assigned to a personal agent that handles her profile. For simplicity, a user profile includes only ratings over (a subset of) the possible restaurants. A user rating $rt_i(item)$ is a value (in the range $[0, 1]$ where 0 means dissatisfaction and 1 means high satisfaction) assigned by the user i to the given POI or restaurant. Additionally, the utility/satisfaction function yield by each agent $ag_i \in A$ is defined as follows:

$$U_i(x_j) = \begin{cases} rt_i(x_j) & if\ x_j \in R_i \\ SUR_i(x_j) & if\ x_j \notin R_i \end{cases} \quad (1)$$

where R_i is the list of items rated by user i (or ag_i) and $SUR_i(x_j)$ is the rating predicted (in case item x_j was not rated by the user i, i.e. x_j is not in R_i) by the SUR_i internally used by ag_i for generating its list of candidate proposals.

In this context, let us consider the following (initial) situation: ag_1 manages ratings $<rt_1(POI1) = 0.6, rt_1(POI2) = 0.8>$ for user #1, ag_2 manages $<rt_2(POI1) = 0.4, rt_3(POI3) = 0.6>$ for user #2, and ag_3 manages $< rt_3(POI2) = 0.2, rt_3(POI3) = 0.8>$ for user #3. Then, $A = \{ag_1, ag_2, ag_3\}$ is the MAS that carries out the negotiation for the "best" POI or restaurant to visit (i.e., the one that will satisfy all the agents). Since these users are friends, we also assume they are related in a social network.

3.1 The Monotonic Concession Protocol (MCP)

MCP [3] is a multi-lateral negotiation protocol for cooperative agents. It is intended to mimic, in a simplified way, the negotiation process carried out by humans when trying to make agreements on topics. The agents engage in negotiation rounds, each agent making proposals of items that need to be assessed by the other agents, until an agreement is reached or the negotiation finishes with a *conflict*. The agents abide by predefined rules that specify the range of "legal" moves available at each agent at any stage of the process. These rules are related to: (i) the agreement criterion, (ii) which agent makes the next concession (after a round with no agreement), and (iii) how much an agent should concede. The protocol assumes that an agent cannot influence the negotiation position of others, and it assigns quantitative utilities to proposals. For more details about the MCP instantiation for MAGReS, please refer to [15].

At the beginning, each agent makes an initial proposal according to a predefined strategy. For example, if the agent employs an *Egocentric* concession strategy, it might propose its "favorite" or top-ranked item. After that, the initial proposals of all agents are exchanged in order to determine if an agreement over one of those proposals can be reached. The notion of *agreement* or deal is defined in terms of the utility of a given proposal. There is an agreement if one agent makes a proposal that is at least as good for any other agent as their own current proposals. In case of a deal, the proposal that satisfies all the agents is returned as the group recommendation. But, if no agreement can be reached, one (or more) of the agents must concede. A concession means that an agent looks for an inferior proposal in terms of its own utility, with the hope of reaching a deal. A *concession decision rule* decides which agent should make a concession, and which proposal should be proposed is determined by a *concession strategy*. If none of the agents can concede, the process finishes with no-agreement (the *conflict deal* is returned). One way for selecting the agent(s) that must concede is to apply the Zeuthen strategy [17], based on the concept of *willingness to risk conflict* (WRC).

Various strategies are discussed in the literature for deciding on the item the conceding agent(s) should propose in the next negotiation round [3]. Some possible strategies are: *Strong concession* (the proposal is strictly better for each of the other agents), *Weak concession* (the proposal is better for at least one of

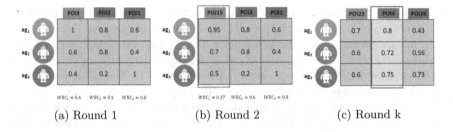

Fig. 2. MCP negotiation example over POIs

the other agents), *Utilitarian concession* (the proposal increases the sum of utilities of the other agents), *Egalitarian Concession* (the minimum utility amongst the other agents increases), *Nash Concession* (the product of utilities of the other agents increases), and *Desires Distance* (DD) that we proposed in [15] to mitigate the problems of the Nash and Utilitarian strategies. DD attempts to measure how far a candidate proposal is with respect to the desires of the others.

Coming back to our example, let us suppose that the initial proposals of ag_1, ag_2 and ag_3 are $POI3$, $POI2$ and $POI1$ respectively (see Fig. 2a) and the agents follow the DD concession strategy. According to the *multilateral agreement criterion*, there is no agreement as none of the proposals satisfies all the agents, and thus one agent must make a concession. According to the concession decision rule, ag_1 must concede as she has the lowest WRC value. At the beginning of *Round 2*, ag_1 proposes $POI15$, which has a dd_{value} lower than that of her previous proposal ($dd_{value}(POI3) = 0.8$ vs. $dd_{value}(POI15) = 0.6$. Once again, there is no agreement and one agent must make a concession. The process repeats until reaching *Round k* , in which ag_2 proposes $POI4$. As $POI14$ satisfies all the agents, it is successfully is selected as the group recommendation.

3.2   Considering Information from the LBSN

Given the variety of data contained in LBSNs, there is a need for developing recommender systems that take advantage of different data sources to enhance recommendations. For example, the traditional collaborative filtering (CF) method, which relates users to items through ratings or opinions provided by users, could be applied straightforwardly to build LBRS. However, CF considers neither the possible friendship relationships nor the geo-localization dimension. In [11], we proposed strategies for including LBSN information when recommending POIs to individual users in a CF context. User-based CF approaches recommend items (e.g. POIs) based on similar users' (called neighbors) preferences. Since user-based CF trusts neighbors as information sources, the quality of recommendations depends directly on the ability to select those neighbors. Our hypothesis was that LBSNs provide rich information for establishing relationships beyond similarity, which enhances the selection of potential neighbors and thus improves the estimation of preferences during the recommendation process.

From experiments using the Foursquare dataset, we concluded that the relationships among users and the use of geo-localization data (among other LSBN elements) allow LBRS to select users that are potentially useful for prediction, particularly in small neighborhoods (up to 100 users). The best performing strategy for selecting neighbors was to choose users from those that share visited places with the target user. This happened because users that tend to visit the same places usually have similar tastes. Notably, this strategy not only reduced the prediction error but also involved the evaluation of fewer users in the prediction step of the CF approach. These findings led us to include LBSN information in MAGReS to improve the recommendations of POIs to groups.

4   Experimental Evaluation

This section reports on the experiments carried out to evaluate our proposal for POI group recommendation. We used a dataset corresponding to the Yelp Dataset Challenge. *Yelp* is a LBSN based on the users' check-ins and the dataset includes information about: businesses, reviews, users, friendship relationships and tips. For the purpose of the experiments we used check-ins for the Arizona state (US). Also, we only considered users having at least 9 check-ins (or ratings). We compared the recommendations resulting from traditional group recommendation techniques against those produced by agent negotiation. As baseline for this comparison, we implemented two RS based on traditional approaches from the literature: i) TRADGRec-PA, a GRS that uses preference aggregation [10] (ch. 22); and ii) TRADGRec-RA, a GRS that relies on aggregation of recommendations produced for each group member. This baseline is based on [4](ch. 2), which generates a recommendation containing k items for each group member and then combines them into a single recommendation. We also implemented a variant of MCP, known as the *One-Step protocol* [12] in which all the negotiations occur in one single round. The agents simply interchange their proposals (one proposal each) and seek for an "agreement", with no concession.

4.1   Evaluation Metrics and Setup

The goal of the proposed approach is not only to increase group satisfaction but also to make group members uniformly satisfied. Thus, the effectiveness of the recommendations was measured in terms of three satisfaction metrics that can be computed both at the item and recommendation (i.e., a list of items recommended) levels. In all the metrics, the term $S_i(x_j)$ represents the satisfaction level of the group member u_i over the item x_j, and it is computed as the rating for the pair $<u_i, x_j>$ predicted by the SUR (if u_i has rated x_j with a rating r_{u_i,x_j} in the past, then $S_i(x_j) = r_{u_i,x_j}$). The prediction is computed according to the Eq. 2, and also according to the similarity metric chosen for the experiment.

$$r_{u_i,x_j} = \bar{r_{u_i}} + \frac{\sum(r_{u_k,x_j} - \bar{r_{u_k}}) \times Similarity(u_i, u_k)}{\sum | Similarity(u_i, u_k) |} \tag{2}$$

Group Satisfaction (GS): measures the satisfaction of the group with respect to an item (or a list of items) being recommended. The satisfaction is equivalent to the estimated preference (or rating) of the user/group for the item.

– item level: the group satisfaction for an item x_j is computed as explained in Eq. 3, where n is the number of group members ($| g |$) in the group (g) and $S_i(x_j)$ is the satisfaction of group member u_i over item x_j.

$$GS(x_j) = S_g(x_j) = \frac{\sum_{i=1}^{n} S_i(x_j)}{n} \tag{3}$$

– recommendation level: the GS of a recommendation r consisting of k items ($r = <x_1, ..., x_k>$) is computed as the average of the GS of each item in r.

Members Satisfaction Dispersion (MSD): assesses how uniformly the group members are satisfied by either a single item x_j or a recommendation r. The lower the MSD is the more uniformly satisfied the group members will be.

– item level: as it can be seen in Eq. 4, the MSD for an item x_j is computed as the standard deviation of the group members satisfaction.

$$MSD(x_j) = \sqrt{\frac{\sum_{i=1}^{n}(S_i(x_j) - S_g(x_j))^2}{n}} \tag{4}$$

– recommendation level: the MSD for a recommendation r that consists of k items is computed as the average of the MSD for each item in r.

Fairness: metric [14] for evaluating a recommendation of an item (x_j) to a group is defined as the percentage of group members satisfied by the recommendation (Eq. 5). To determine which users are satisfied, a threshold th is set to 3.5 stars (out of 5 stars, the equivalent to 0.7 out of 1) and any group member with a satisfaction value above that threshold is considered satisfied. We kept $th = 0.7$ and extended this metric for a recommendation r of k items. The fairness of a recommendation r of k items is the average of the fairness of the items.

$$fairness(g, x_j) = \frac{| \bigcup_{u_i \in g} : S_i(x_j) > th |}{n} \tag{5}$$

The objectives of the experiments were two-fold: i) to compare the recommendations generated by MAGReS, TRADGRec-PA and TRADGRec-RA in the POI domain; and ii) to study how the usage of LBSN information can affect the recommendations generated by MAGReS and the baselines. The execution of

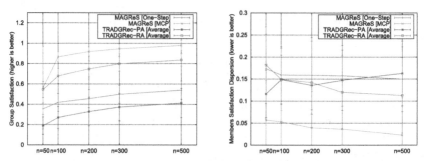

(a) Average GS per approach and neighbor-(b) Average MSD per approach and neigh-
hood size   borhood size

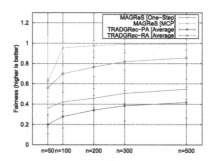

(c) Average fairness per approach and
neighborhood size

Fig. 3. Experimental results for the NN strategy.

the experiments involved 6 steps, for each approach, as follows: 1) we randomly generate n groups for the test, in which the group members have to be direct friends in the social network; 2) we determine the number of (k) items to be recommended; 3) we configure the environment by: (a) selecting the SUR and neighborhood selection strategies, and (b) parameterizing each approach; 4) we run each approach to generate a group recommendation containing k items for each of the n groups involved in the test; 5) we evaluate the recommendations via the GS, MSD and fairness metrics; 6) we compare the approaches by computing the average and standard deviation of the metrics.

In total, we create 45 groups of 3, 4 and 5 people (15 groups of each size). The amount of recommendations (k) is set to 10, which is a common parameter in the literature (top-10) [4,6]. The SUR used by the 3 approaches is the user-based CF recommender implemented on the Mahout framework[2] along with the *Pearson (weighted) similarity metric*. With regard to the *neighborhood selection*

---

[2] http://mahout.apache.org/.

strategies, we analyze two alternatives: *NearestN* (NN) and *NearestNUserZone* (NNUZ). NN is available in Mahout framework and it does not use LBSN information, while NNUZ [11] uses geolocation information to select the neighbors of a user. This strategy works by first computing the "movement area" (i.e., the area in which the places the user has rated and usual visits are) of each user, and then selects the neighbors of the target user among those within a certain *radius* (parameter), independently of the ratings they have given to the same POIs. In both strategies, we test with 5 neighborhood sizes (N): 50, 100, 200, 300 and 500. As for *NNUZ*, we use three different values for the radius parameter: 1, 3 and 5 kms. More details of the configurations used for the different algorithms are provided in the project site[3].

4.2   Results

Next, we summarize the main results obtained when comparing the recommendations generated by MAGReS, against those generated by TRADGRec-PA and TRADGRec-RA when using the two neighborhood selection strategies (NN and NNUZ). Space limitations preclude us from including all the performed experiments and results, but they are described in the project site.

Figure 3 shows the results for the NN strategy. As it can be seen, independently of the size of the neighborhood (n), *MAGReS [MCP]* outperforms *TRADGRec-PA [Average]* and *TRADGRec-RA [Average]* in terms of GS (group satisfaction), as all the recommendations produced by the former had a higher GS than the recommendations generated by the latter two. Additionally, *MAGReS [One-Step]* is only able to outperform *TRADGRec-PA [Average]*, but it fails to do so when compared to *MAGReS [MCP]* and *TRADGRec-RA [Average]*. This can be explained by how the One-Step protocol works.

Regarding MSD and fairness, Tables 1b and 1c show that *MAGReS [MCP]* outperforms all the other approaches. This indicates that *MAGReS [MCP]* recommendations not only have a higher group satisfaction (GS) score, but also satisfy the group members more uniformly (because of the lower MSD score) and ensure that a higher percentage of the group members will be satisfied with the recommendation (due to the higher fairness score).

For the NNUZ strategy, we obtained similar results as in the NN strategy, except when the *zone radius* (*zr*) parameter was set to 1 (i.e. 1 km). As shown in Table 1, *MAGReS [MCP]* outperformes all the other approaches for GS, MSD and Fairness for any neighborhood size, when *zr* was set to 3 or 5. When *zr* was set to 1, despite the neighborhood size (*n*) chosen, we found similar trends as in *NN [n = 50]*: many group recommendations were empty, which lowered the averages and increased the deviations for all metrics (GS, MSD and Fairness).

---

[3] https://github.com/sschia/magres.

Table 1. Experimental results for the NNUZ strategy

Group Satisfaction	MAGReS [One-Step]	MAGReS [MCP]	TRADGRec-PA [Average]	TRADGRec-RA [Average]
NNUZ [n=50,zr=1]	0.3642±0.0829	0.4727±0.4159	0.0914±0.1161	0.5334±0.1294
NNUZ [n=50,zr=3]	0.3627±0.0781	0.6548±0.3573	0.1595±0.1043	0.5453±0.1173
NNUZ [n=50,zr=5]	0.3732±0.0827	0.5946±0.3888	0.1714±0.1078	0.5686±0.0987
NNUZ [n=100,zr=1]	0.3986±0.0895	0.5075±0.4263	0.1245±0.1509	0.5745±0.1245
NNUZ [n=100,zr=3]	0.4031±0.0923	0.7572±0.3043	0.2200±0.1411	0.6051±0.1137
NNUZ [n=100,zr=5]	0.4069±0.0751	0.8380±0.1884	0.2280±0.1300	0.6369±0.1144
NNUZ [n=200,zr=1]	0.4142±0.0847	0.5741±0.4197	0.1822±0.1962	0.6164±0.1266
NNUZ [n=200,zr=3]	0.4383±0.0899	0.8173±0.2667	0.2617±0.1792	0.6738±0.1138
NNUZ [n=200,zr=5]	0.4456±0.0924	0.8680±0.1965	0.2634±0.1584	0.6882±0.0977
NNUZ [n=300,zr=1]	0.4211±0.1026	0.5554±0.4272	0.1920±0.2008	0.6363±0.1310
NNUZ [n=300,zr=3]	0.4467±0.1029	0.8124±0.2958	0.2813±0.1902	0.6957±0.1004
NNUZ [n=300,zr=5]	0.4487±0.0932	0.8787±0.1997	0.2761±0.1837	0.7064±0.1055
NNUZ [n=500,zr=1]	0.4423±0.1215	0.5621±0.4314	0.1993±0.2086	0.6353±0.1321
NNUZ [n=500,zr=3]	0.4578±0.0924	0.8373±0.2712	0.2987±0.1921	0.7110±0.0908
NNUZ [n=500,zr=5]	0.4850±0.1022	0.9088±0.1514	0.2817±0.1720	0.7248±0.1206

(a) Average GS per approach and neighborhood size

Members Satisfaction Dispersion	MAGReS [One-Step]	MAGReS [MCP]	TRADGRec-PA [Average]	TRADGRec-RA [Average]
NNUZ [n=50,zr=1]	0.1600±0.0850	0.0768±0.1384	0.0752±0.0870	0.2364±0.1118
NNUZ [n=50,zr=3]	0.1693±0.0665	0.0499±0.0758	0.1155±0.0878	0.2147±0.0898
NNUZ [n=50,zr=5]	0.1610±0.0827	0.0532±0.1023	0.1314±0.0907	0.1970±0.0939
NNUZ [n=100,zr=1]	0.1863±0.0839	0.0745±0.1528	0.0914±0.0991	0.2426±0.0963
NNUZ [n=100,zr=3]	0.1606±0.0724	0.0435±0.0787	0.1316±0.1906	0.1906±0.1139
NNUZ [n=100,zr=5]	0.1360±0.0834	0.0467±0.0829	0.1326±0.0848	0.1922±0.0950
NNUZ [n=200,zr=1]	0.1882±0.0949	0.0845±0.1571	0.1221±0.1232	0.2275±0.1211
NNUZ [n=200,zr=3]	0.1674±0.0767	0.0517±0.0930	0.1484±0.1124	0.1954±0.1008
NNUZ [n=200,zr=5]	0.1654±0.0777	0.0406±0.0829	0.1590±0.0092	0.1749±0.1070
NNUZ [n=300,zr=1]	0.1843±0.0939	0.0874±0.1605	0.1336±0.1339	0.2217±0.1122
NNUZ [n=300,zr=3]	0.1639±0.0812	0.0411±0.0822	0.1428±0.0962	0.1958±0.0975
NNUZ [n=300,zr=5]	0.1687±0.0778	0.0413±0.0831	0.1602±0.1119	0.1902±0.0904
NNUZ [n=500,zr=1]	0.2050±0.0887	0.0818±0.1559	0.1391±0.1393	0.2134±0.1156
NNUZ [n=500,zr=3]	0.1747±0.0795	0.0489±0.0865	0.1606±0.0946	0.1824±0.0966
NNUZ [n=500,zr=5]	0.1569±0.0763	0.0482±0.0934	0.1453±0.0960	0.1783±0.0898

(b) Average MSD per approach and neighborhood size

Fairness	MAGReS [One-Step]	MAGReS [MCP]	TRADGRec-PA [Average]	TRADGRec-RA [Average]
NNUZ [n=50,zr=1]	0.3683±0.0844	0.5212±0.4617	0.0956±0.1242	0.5424±0.1419
NNUZ [n=50,zr=3]	0.3654±0.0856	0.7337±0.4046	0.1586±0.1073	0.5511±0.1319
NNUZ [n=50,zr=5]	0.4624±0.0867	0.6502±0.4286	0.1747±0.1139	0.5749±0.1023
NNUZ [n=100,zr=1]	0.4023±0.0934	0.5485±0.4628	0.1266±0.1555	0.5808±0.1343
NNUZ [n=100,zr=3]	0.3997±0.1014	0.8315±0.3355	0.2292±0.1483	0.6109±0.1298
NNUZ [n=100,zr=5]	0.4119±0.0831	0.9130±0.2066	0.2366±0.1392	0.6509±0.1318
NNUZ [n=200,zr=1]	0.4161±0.0898	0.6125±0.4500	0.1817±0.2042	0.6265±0.1426
NNUZ [n=200,zr=3]	0.4378±0.0926	0.8753±0.2887	0.2610±0.1870	0.6806±0.1250
NNUZ [n=200,zr=5]	0.4457±0.0992	0.9263±0.2094	0.2667±0.1662	0.6999±0.1132
NNUZ [n=300,zr=1]	0.4214±0.1065	0.5890±0.4542	0.1892±0.2077	0.6464±0.1454
NNUZ [n=300,zr=3]	0.4431±0.1112	0.8641±0.3139	0.2851±0.1994	0.7037±0.1097
NNUZ [n=300,zr=5]	0.4495±0.0992	0.9310±0.2102	0.2845±0.1946	0.7217±0.1245
NNUZ [n=500,zr=1]	0.4425±0.1260	0.5831±0.4568	0.1947±0.2107	0.6429±0.1435
NNUZ [n=500,zr=3]	0.4493±0.0981	0.8731±0.2968	0.2920±0.2009	0.7166±0.0997
NNUZ [n=500,zr=5]	0.4826±0.1084	0.9503±0.1576	0.2842±0.1769	0.7336±0.1396

(c) Average fairness per approach and neighborhood size

5   Conclusions

In this paper, we analyzed and compared three approaches for POI group recommendation. Differently from works based on aggregation strategies, we propose a MAS that uses negotiation techniques to make group recommendations. Similar to our approach is the one presented in [13] that uses a MAS for generating group recommendations in the POI domain, but with some key differences: it requires "live user intervention" as candidate proposals are generated using a pool of items rated by all the users; the mediator relies on aggregation techniques to compute the group rating of the items; the mediator executes the protocol and generates the proposals; the agents can generate counter-offers and model users' behavior in conflicting situations. We could not compare with it because it requires live user intervention.

The experiments showed two main findings: i) the use of negotiation instead of aggregation techniques can improve the quality of POI recommendations, not only increasing the level of satisfaction of the group but also satisfying group members in a more even way; ii) the information provided by the LBSN about geographical relationships among the users helps to improve the quality of recommendations (for small neighborhoods, e.g., up to 200 neighbors) while also making the neighbors selection process more efficient, as less user-user similarity computations are needed. Although we obtained satisfactory results, our experiments also had some limitations. Our current implementation relies on the users' utility/satisfaction function in the prediction made by the SURs. Along this line, increasing the quality of the predictions by using a different approach [2] could improve the recommendations. Regarding the role of the LBSN we believe that the LBSN information can help to further improve the recommendations if we include such information in the utility function used by the agents. For example, an agent might prefer POIs being closer to the movement area of her user.

Acknowledgements. We thank CONICET PIP Project 112-201501-00030, ANPCyT project PICT 2016-2973, C. Ríos and C. Villavicencio for their support and their work.

References

1. Ayala-Gómez, F., Daróczy, B., Mathioudakis, M., Benczúr, A., Gionis, A.: Where could we go? Recommendations for groups in location-based social networks. In: Proceedings of the ACM on Web Science Conference (WebSci 2017), pp. 93–102 (2017)
2. Boratto, L., Carta, S., Fenu, G., Mulas, F., Pilloni, P.: Influence of rating prediction on group recommendation's accuracy. IEEE Intell. Syst. **31**(6), 22–27 (2016)
3. Endriss, U.: Monotonic concession protocols for multilateral negotiation. In: Proceedings of the 5th International Joint Conference (AAMAS 2006), pp. 392–399 (2006)
4. Felfernig, A., Boratto, L., Stettinger, M., Tkalčič, M.: Group Recommender Systems. SECE. Springer, Cham (2018). https://doi.org/10.1007/978-3-319-75067-5
5. Gottapu, R.D., Sriram Monangi, L.V.: Point-of-interest recommender system for social groups. Procedia Comput. Sci. **114**(C), 159–164 (2017)
6. Karypis, G.: Evaluation of item-based top-n recommendation algorithms. In: Proceedings of the 10th International Conference on Information and Knowledge Management (CIKM 2001), pp. 247–254 (2001)
7. Nguyen, T.N., Ricci, F.: Dynamic elicitation of user preferences in a chat-based group recommender system. In: Proceedings of the SAC 2017, pp. 1685–1692 (2017)

8. Purushotham, S., Kuo, C.-C.J., Shahabdeen, J., Nachman, L.: Collaborative group-activity recommendation in location-based social networks. In: Proceedings of the 3rd ACM SIGSPATIAL International Workshop (GeoCrowd 2014), pp. 8–15 (2014)

9. Ravi, L., Vairavasundaram, S.: A collaborative location based travel recommendation system through enhanced rating prediction for the group of users. Comput. Intell. Neurosci. **2016**, 7 (2016)

10. Ricci, F., Rokach, L., Shapira, B., Kantor, P.B. (eds.): Recommender Systems Handbook. Springer, Boston (2011). https://doi.org/10.1007/978-0-387-85820-3

11. Rios, C., Schiaffino, S., Godoy, D.: A study of neighbour selection strategies for POI recommendation in LBSNs. J. Inf. Sci. **44**(6), 802–817 (2018)

12. Rosenschein, J.S., Zlotkin, G.: Rules of Encounter: Designing Conventions for Automated Negotiation Among Computers. MIT Press, Cambridge (1994)

13. Rossi, S., Di Napoli, C., Barile, F., Liguori, L.: A multi-agent system for group decision support based on conflict resolution styles. In: Aydoğan, R., Baarslag, T., Gerding, E., Jonker, C.M., Julian, V., Sanchez-Anguix, V. (eds.) COREDEMA 2016. LNCS (LNAI), vol. 10238, pp. 134–148. Springer, Cham (2017). https://doi.org/10.1007/978-3-319-57285-7_9

14. Felfernig, A., Boratto, L., Stettinger, M., Tkalčič, M.: Evaluating group recommender systems. Group Recommender Systems. SECE, pp. 59–71. Springer, Cham (2018). https://doi.org/10.1007/978-3-319-75067-5_3

15. Villavicencio, C., Schiaffino, S., Diaz-Pace, J.A., Monteserin, A., Demazeau, Y., Adam, C.: A MAS approach for group recommendation based on negotiation techniques. In: Demazeau, Y., Ito, T., Bajo, J., Escalona, M.J. (eds.) PAAMS 2016. LNCS (LNAI), vol. 9662, pp. 219–231. Springer, Cham (2016). https://doi.org/10.1007/978-3-319-39324-7_19

16. Yuan, Z., Chen, C.: Research on group POIs recommendation fusion of users' gregariousness and activity in LBSN. In: Proceedings of the 2nd IEEE International Conference on Cloud Computing and Big Data Analysis, pp. 305–310 (2017)

17. Zeuthen, F.L.B.: Problems of Monopoly and Economic Warfare. Routledge, Abingdon (1930)

18. Zhu, Q., Wang, S., Cheng, B., Sun, Q., Yang, F., Chang, R.N.: Context-aware group recommendation for point-of-interests. IEEE Access **6**, 12129–12144 (2018)

Agent Programmability Enhancement for Rambling over a Scientific Dataset

Matthew Sell[ID] and Munehiro Fukuda[(✉)][ID]

Computing and Software Systems, University of Washington Bothell,
Bothell, WA 98011, USA
{mrsell,mfukuda}@uw.edu

Abstract. Agent-based modeling (ABM), while originally intended for
micro-simulation of individual entities, (i.e., agents), has been adopted
to operations research as biologically-inspired algorithms including ant
colonial optimization and grasshopper optimization algorithm. Observing their successful use in traveling salesman problem and K-means clustering, we promote this trend in ABM to distributed data analysis. Our
approach is to populate reactive agents on a distributed, structured
dataset and to have them discover the dataset's attributes (e.g., the
shortest routes and the best cluster centroids) through agent migration
and interaction. We implemented this agent-based approach with the
multi-agent spatial simulation (MASS) library and identified programming features for agents to best achieve data discovery. Of importance is
ease of describing when and how to have agents traverse a graph, ramble over an array, and share the on-going computational states. We have
responded to this question with two agent-descriptivity enhancements:
(1) event-driven agent behavioral execution and (2) direct inter-agent
broadcast. The former automatically schedules agent actions before and
after agent migration, whereas the latter informs all agents of up-to-date
global information, (e.g., the best slate of centroids so far). This paper
presents our design, implementation, and evaluation of these two agent
descriptivity enhancements.

Keywords: Agent-based modeling · Programmability · Distributed
data analysis

1 Introduction

Agent-based modeling (ABM) gained its popularity to observe an emergent
collective group behavior of many agents by simulating and gathering their
microscopic interactions. Nowadays ABM is being applied to not only micro-
simulation but also operations research. This extension is known as biologically-
inspired algorithms such as ant colonial optimization (ACO) [1] and grasshopper optimization algorithm (GOA) [13], heuristically effective to compute NP-
hard problems: traveling salesman problem (TSP) and K-means clustering problems. Our focus is to promote this trend in agent-based computation to broader

© Springer Nature Switzerland AG 2020
Y. Demazeau et al. (Eds.): PAAMS 2020, LNAI 12092, pp. 251–263, 2020.
https://doi.org/10.1007/978-3-030-49778-1_20

and scalable data-science problems. Obviously this agent-based approach is not applicable to all problems nor always competitive to major tools in big-data computing including MapReduce, Spark, and Storm[1]. To seek for killer applications, we should first point out that biologically-inspired algorithms walk agents over a given dataset for discovering attributes of the data space, (e.g., the shortest routes and the best cluster centroids). This is distinguished from data streaming in most big-data tools that examine every single data item to compute statistics of the entire dataset, (e.g., sum and average). Based on this observation, we have aimed at facilitating agent-based data discovery by constructing a big data structure over distributed memory and populating agents to ramble over the dataset in parallel.

For the feasibility study, we used our multi-agent spatial simulation (MASS) library where *main()* serves as a data-analyzing scenario while *Places* and *Agents*, two major classes of the MASS library, construct a distributed dataset and populate agents on it respectively. Through our former work [4,7,15], the MASS library demonstrated two programming advantages: (1) enforcing weak consistency among agent computation and (2) allowing users to code agents from the vehicle driver's viewpoint. The former guarantees an automatic barrier synchronization among all agents for their state transitions and migrations each time *main()* gets control back from a parallel function invocation on *Agents*. The latter intuitively navigates agents along graph edges or diffuses them to adjacent array elements. However, we also encountered two challenges in describing agent behaviors where users need (1) to give agents step-by-step actions to take – more specifically what to do before and after their migration to a new vertex or an array element and (2) to emulate inter-agent message broadcast with *main()* that passes arguments to *Agents* functions. This emulation makes it tedious for agents to share on-going computational states, e.g. the shortest route so far in ACO-based TSP or the best centroids in GOA-based K-means.

These challenges are big burdens to non-computing specialists who are interested in simply dispatching agents into their datasets but not coding every single agent behavior. Therefore, we are addressing them by automating parallel invocation of *Agents* functions and facilitating inter-agent message broadcast. This paper presents our design, implementation, and evaluation of these two agent descriptivity enhancements. The rest of this paper consists of the following sections: Sect. 2 details the current challenges in agent descriptivity for pursuing agent-based data discovery; Sect. 3 presents our implementation of event-driven agent behavioral execution and direct inter-agent message broadcast; Sect. 4 evaluates our implementation both from programmability and execution performance; and Sect. 5 concludes our discussions.

2   Challenges in Applying ABM to Distributed Data Analysis

This section emphasizes ABM's superiority over conventional approach to structured data analysis, summarizes our previous endeavor with the MASS library,

---

[1] http://hadoop.apache.org, http://spark.apache.org, http://storm.apache.org.

and clarifies the challenges in agent descriptivity for ABM to be smoothly adopted to distributed data discovery.

2.1 Conventional Approach to Analysis of Structured Dataset

Most big-data computing tools benefit statistical analysis of data continuously streamed as flat texts from social, business, and IoT environments. To extend their practicability to analysis of structured datasets, they provide users with additional services to partition, flatten, and stream multi-dimensional NetCDF data[2] into MapReduce with SciHadoop [2]; to describe and process graphs with GraphX[3] on top of Spark; and to schedule repetitive MapReduce processing over a structured dataset with Tez[4]. Furthermore, some textbooks [8,11] introduce how to process a graph problem with MapReduce and Spark in an edge-oriented approach that reads a list of graph edges, narrows down candidate edges by examining their connectivity, and eventually identifies sub-graphs, (e.g., triangles) in the graph [5]. While these big-data computing tools offered simple programming frameworks for parallel computing and interpretive execution environments, their extension to structured datasets does not always achieve the best programmability and execution performance of data discovery [4]. This is due to their nature of data streaming. For instance, data streaming does not allow data to stay in memory and thus cannot analyze different data relationships through the same streaming operation. Repetitive MapReduce invocations or many Spark transformations would transfer back and forth or swap in and out data between disk and memory, which slows down the execution speed.

As observed above, the key is allowing different analyses to be applied to an in-memory structured dataset. GraphLab followed by Turi [9] maintains a graph structure on Amazon EC2, has each graph vertex access its neighboring vertices' state, and prepares a variety of graph functions in Python. NetCDF4-Python[5] is a Python interface to the NetCDF parallel I/O that is implemented on top of HDF5[6] and MPI-I/O, so that a NetCDF dataset is loaded over a cluster system and accessed in parallel by Python programs. Although these tools handle graphs or multi-dimensional arrays in Python, (i.e., a high-level interpretive environment), they still focus on statistical analysis of graphs and arrays such as vertices/edges counting, summation, and max/min values as well as major machine-learning functions that can be done with data streaming, too.

In contrast to them, our agent-based approach loads a structured dataset in parallel, maintains the structure in memory, dispatches reactive agents onto the dataset, and discovers user-designated data attributes in an emergent group behavior among these agents.

---

[2] https://www.unidata.ucar.edu/software/netcdf/.

[3] http://spark.apache.org/graphx.

[4] http://tez.apache.org.

[5] https://github.com/Unidata/netcdf4-python.

[6] https://support.hdfgroup.org/HDF5/.

2.2 Previous Work with MASS

We have evaluated the feasibility of and challenges in agent-based data discovery, using the MASS library. MASS instantiates a multi-dimensional distributed array with *Places* and initializes it with an input data file in parallel [14]. For a graph construction, we create a 1D array of vertices and initialize the vertices with a file that contains an adjacency list. MASS populates agents on a given *Places* object from the *Agents* class. MASS performs parallel function call to all array elements and agents with *Places.callAll(fid)* and *Agents.callAll(fid)*; data diffusion across array elements with *Places.exchangeAll()*; and agent migration, termination, and additional population with *Agents.manageAll()*. Note that these agent behaviors are scheduled as *migrate()*, *kill()*, and *spawn()* in *Agents.callAll()* and thereafter committed with *Agents.manageAll()*. Listing 1.1 shows *main()* in a typical MASS-based data discovery, which loads a structured dataset into memory (line 4), populates a crawler agent (line 5), lets it start from place[0] (line 6), and schedules its dissemination over the dataset (lines 7–9). Weak consistency or barrier synchronizations are enforced between each statement of *callAll()* and *manageAll()*. Listing 1.2 describes each agent's behavior in *walk()* that examines all edges emanating from the current vertex (line12) and disseminates its copies along each edge (lines 13–16).

Listing 1.1. The main program

```
1 import MASS.*;
2 public class Analysis {
3   public void main(String[] args) {
4     Places dataset = new Places( ... );
5     Agents crawlers = new Agents("Crawler'', dataset, 1);
6     crawlers.callAll(ClawerAgent.init_, 0); // start from place[0]
7     while ( crawlers.hasAgents() ) {
8       crawlers.callAll(ClawerAgent.walk_);
9       crawlers.manageAll();
10 } } }
```

Listing 1.2. Agent behavior

```
1 public class Crawler extends Agent {
2   public static final int init_ = 0; // fid 0 linked to init()
3   public static final int walk_ = 1; // fid 1 linked to walk()
4   public void init( Object arg ) {
5     migrate( ( Integer )arg ); // let it start from place[arg]
6   }
7   public void walk( ) {
8     if ( place.visited == true ) {
9       kill( );
10      return; }
11    place.visited = true;
12    for ( int i = 0; i < place.neighbors.length; i++ ) {
13      if ( i == 0 )
14        migrate( place.neighbor[0] );
15      spawn( place.neighbors[i] );
16 } } }
```

Using MASS, we have so far developed two practical applications and one benchmark test set in data discovery: (a) global-warming analysis based on NetCDF climate data [15], (b) biological network motif search [7], and (c) comparison with MapReduce and Spark in six benchmark programs in graphs, optimizations, and data sciences [4]. Through the development work, we encountered two performance issues in agent management. One is an explosive increase of agent population that consumed a cluster system's memory space. For instance in biological network motif search, 5.5 million agents were spawned in total over $16MB \times 8$ compute instances to find all motifs with size five. The other is too many barrier synchronizations incurred between *Agents.callAll()* and *manageAll()*. To address these problems, we have developed two additional MASS features to improve the execution performance:

1. **Agent population control**: does not keep all *agents* active when they migrate over a dataset, thus allows users to specify the max cap of *agent* population in *MASS.Init(cap)*, serializes agents beyond this cap, and de-serialize them when the population goes down; and
2. **Asynchronous and automatic agent migration**: unlike typical ABM simulation based on synchronous agent execution, will reduce synchronization overheads through *doAll(fid[ ],iterations)*, which automates asynchronous *iterations* of *callAll(fid)* and *manageAll()* invocations.

In [4,5,14], we demonstrated the MASS library's substantial performance improvements with these two new features. However, we have not yet addressed any challenges in agent programmability to pursue agent-based data discovery. Below we summarize two challenges we have identified as well as our solutions to them:

1. **Manual descriptions of agent decision-making logic**: this drawback requires users to precisely give agents step-by-step actions to take. For better descriptivity, agents should invoke their behavioral function automatically before their departure, upon their arrival at a new destination, and when receiving an inter-agent message. As a solution, we annotated *@OnDeparture*, *@OnArrival*, and *@OnMessage* to agent functions to invoke automatically.
2. **Emulation of inter-agent broadcast**: while *Places* can serve as an asynchronous mailbox shared among agents, the synchronous system-wide communication must be emulated at a user level via *main()* that becomes a focal point of collecting return values from and sending arguments to agent functions. We implemented direct inter-agent broadcast in the *Agents.exchangeAll()* function. It allows agents to smoothly share on-going computational states, e.g. the shortest route so far in ACO-based TSP.

3   Agent Behaviors to Support Data Discovery

This section describe our enhancement of agent descriptivity that supports event-driven agent behaviors and inter-agent message broadcast. We also differentiate our implementation techniques from other ABM systems.

3.1   Event-Driven Agent Behaviors

While the MASS library maintains weak consistency that guarantees a barrier synchronization of all agents upon executing *callAll()*, *manageAll()*, or *doAll()*, it is a big burden for users to repetitively invoke agent/place function calls from the *main()* program. Instead, such functions should be automatically invoked when their associated events are fired. Since agents duplicate themselves and ramble over a structured data, their major events are three-fold: agents' departure from the current place, their arrival at a new place, and their duplication. We allow users to associate agent functions with these three events, each annotated with *@OnDeparture*, *@OnArrival*, and *@OnCreation*. We also extend the *doAll(fid[ ],iterations)* function to *doWhile(lambda)* and *doUntil(lambda)*. They fire these events and commit the annotated functions while a given lambda expression stays true or until it sets true. With these features, users can focus on describing event-driven agent behavior rather than orchestrating their invocations.

A question comes up on how to trigger, to keep, and to terminate this event-processing sequence. To get started with agent-based data discovery, users are supposed to first populate agents on a structured dataset through *new Agents(AgentClassName, places)* that schedules their very first invocation of *@OnCreation* function, say *funcA*. They will then trigger *Agents.doWhile(lambda)* just only one time where *lambda* in many cases would be *()→agents.hasAgents()*, which repeats annotated agent functions until all agents are gone. If *funcA* schedules *migrate()* in it, *doWhile()* initiates the agent migration, before and after of which it invokes all *@OnDeparture* and *@OnArrival-*annotated functions, each named *funcB* and *funcC* respectively. If *funcC* schedules *spawn()*, *kill()*, and/or *migrate()*, the new events are continuously fired by *doWhile()*.

Listing 1.3 shows the simplification of the *main()* program with *doWhile*. The main program is completely relieved from agent behavioral orchestration. All it has to do is to initiate their repetitive data analysis (line 6). As we are currently implementing an interactive version of the MASS library with JShell [10], data-science specialists (who do not care of agent implementation) will be able to simply inject off-the-shelf agents into their dataset in an interactive fashion. On the other hand, model designers (who are interested in developing agent-based algorithms) can now clarify about which event will fire a given agent behavior, as shown in lines 2 and 6 in Listing 1.4.

The MASS library is a collection of Places/Agents functions, each called one by one from the main program but executed in parallel over a cluster system and with multithreading. Among them, the center of agent management is *Agents.manageAll()*. It examines all agents that have changed their status in

Listing 1.3. The main program with doWhile

```
6    crawlers.callAll(ClawerAgent.init_, 0); // start from place[0]
7    while ( crawlers.hasAgents() ) {
8      crawlers.callAll(ClawerAgent.walk_);
9      crawlers.manageAll();
```

should be replaced with

```
6    crawlers.doWhile( ()→ crawlers.hasAgents() );
```

Listing 1.4. Agent behavior with agent annotations

```
1 public class Crawler extends Agent {
2    @OnCreation
3    public void init( Object arg ) {
4      ...
5    }
6    @OnArrival
7    public void walk( ) {
8      ...
```

the last *callAll* method through *spawn()*, *kill()*, or *migrate()*. How the *manageAll* function processed them is based on batch processing: (1) spawning all new children, thereafter (2) terminating those that called *kill()*, and finally (3) moving all that called *migrate()*. This in turn means that a barrier synchronization is carried out between each of these three actions, which thus enforces weak consistency. While agent annotation provides users with an option of event-driven programming, the underlying MASS execution model still maintains weak consistency by the *manageAll* function that handles each of *OnCreation*, *OnDeparture*, and *OnArrival* annotations in the order summarized in Table 1. The *eventDispatcher* class in this table uses Java reflection to find each agent's method associated with a given annotation. In an attempt to reduce the effect of using Java reflec-

Table 1. Annotation handling in manageAll

Actions	Annotation handling
(1) spawn	for (Agent agent : agents) eventDispatcher.invoke(OnCreation.class, agent);
(2) kill	no annotation handling

(3) migrate	for (Agent agent : agents)
	    eventDispatcher.invoke(OnDeparture.class, agent);
	 move agents to their new place.
	 ... barrier synchronization among all cluster nodes ...
	 for (Agent agent : agents)
	    eventDispatcher.invoke(OnArrival.class, agent);

tion, the eventDispatcher caches methods associated with each annotation. Our initial testing has shown, as compared with the use of integers representing functions with *callAll* (see lines 2–3 in Listing 1.2), this caching method reduces the impact to an extent where it is of statistical insignificance. Since we focus on data scalability in data discovery rather than speed-up in ABM simulation, this implementation would not negate the advantages that MASS provides.

3.2   Inter-Agent Message Broadcast

In general, it is not easy to deliver a message directly from one to another moving agent. As a solution to inter-agent messaging in MASS, we have originally chosen via-place indirect communication among agents that reside on the same place. In other words, agents use each place's data members as a mailbox. Rather than make a rendezvous, senders deposit their messages to a given place, whereas receivers read or pick them up later by visiting the same place. In many cases when agents disseminate over a graph, most frequent information exchanged among agents are run-time attributes of each place, regarding if the current place, (i.e., a vertex) has been visited or not, if the currently recorded travel distance to this vertex is longer than a new agent's distance traveled, and which vertex is the current vertex's predecessor. Therefore, we believe that the MASS indirect communication can cover many agent-based graph analyses.

However, this indirect communication is expensive to maintain message ordering or memory consistency, and thus cannot cover biologically-inspired optimizations such as ACO, GOA, and particle swarm optimization (PSO) [6]. After every migration of agents, they need to identify the agent temporarily closest to the optimal solution, for the purpose of having other agents follow the best. The details are given in Listings 1.5 and 1.6. The MASS main program (in Listing 1.5) collects the latest agent states from the first *Agent.callAll()* as the return values (line 8) and then scatters the best agent information to the second *Agent.callAll()* as the arguments (line 10). Since the main behaves as the focal point of this collective communication and the best agent sorting operation, the entire agent management code in lines 5–10 cannot be condensed into *doAll(max)*. Therefore, none of agent behavior such as *getState* and *approachToBest* functions in Listing 1.6 can be annotated with *@OnDeparture* nor *@OnArrival*, either.

Listing 1.5. MASS main of PSO

```
 1 main() {
 2   public void main(String[] args) {
 3     Places dataset = new Places( ... );
 4     Agents swarm = new Agents( ''Particle'', dataset, Integer.intValue(args[0]));
 5     Data[] data = new Data[swarm.nAgents()];
 6     for (int i = 0; i < max; i++) {
 7       swarm.manageAll();
 8       data = swarm.callAll(Particle.getState_); // gather each agent's value
 9       Data[] best = min( data ); // find the best value so far
10       swarm.callAll(Particle.approachToBest_, best); // scatter the best value
11 } }
```

Listing 1.6. MASS agent behavior of PSO

```
1 public class Particle extends Agent {
2   int[] bestValue, myValue; // globally best or my current value
3   public Object getState(Object arg) {
4     myValue = {index[0], index[1], place.value};
5     return myValue; // return my current value
6   }
7   public Object approachToBest(Object arg) {
8     bestValue = (int[])arg;
9     x = place.index[0] + updateVelocity( bestValue );
10    y = place.index[1] + updateVelocity();
11    migrate(x, y); // approach to the best agent so far
12 } }
```

To address this problem, we have implemented inter-agent message broadcast, so that each agent can collect the states from all the others directly and identify the best agent so far independently from the main program. The *MASSMessaging* class allows agents to broadcast a message to the other agents or places with *sendAgentMessage(message)* or *sendPlaceMessage(message)* respectively.

Using agent annotations, we deliver a message directly to each agent's or place's method that is annotated with *@OnMessage*. This relieves the main program from collective communication. As demonstrated in Listings 1.7, all agent behavioral coordination in the main is simplified into *doAll(max)* that repeats the *max* times of PSO agent migration. Listings 1.8 describes event-associated PSO agents. The logic to find the best value is moved from the main into the PSO agent (line 11). All the agent logic is clarified with arrival and message events.

Listing 1.7. Simplified PSO (main)

```
5    Data[] data = new Data[swarm.nAgents()];
6    for (int i = 0; i < max; i++) {
7      data = swarm.callAll(Particle.getState_);
8      ...
9      ...
10     swarm.callAll(Particle.approachToBest_, best);
```

should be replaced with

```
5    swarm.doAll(max);
```

Listing 1.8. Annotated PSO (agents)

```
1 public class Particle extends Agent {
2   int[] bestValue, myValue; // globally best or my current value
3   @OnArrival
4   public Object getValue(Object arg) {
5     myValue = {index[0], index[1], place.value};
6     MASSMessaging.sendAgentMessage(myValue);
7   }
8   @OnMessage
```

```
 9   public Object approachToBest(Object best) {
10       bestValue = (int[])arg;
11       if ( myValue[2] > bestValue[2] )
12           // the same logic as lines 9-11 in Listing 1.6
```

Our initial implementation of agent messaging uses Hazelcast [7], an in-memory distributed data grid. Hazelcast was selected for performance, maturity, and ease of connecting nodes together. Our use of Hazelcast for messaging allows for agents to send messages (Java Objects) to either a specific agent, a collection of agents, or all agents. An agent may transmit a message by calling *sendAgentMessage* and providing either an enumerated value for a broadcast or one or more agent ID numbers. The payload is serialized and the destination agents receive the message via a callback that is registered upon agent creation or migration to a different node. An agent method annotated with *@OnMessage* with either no arguments or a single argument with data type matching the payload is invoked and the message is delivered. Message delivery callbacks are queued using the aforementioned *eventDispatcher* so that messaging events are handled at the appropriate time.

3.3   Related Work

RepastHPC [12] and FLAME [3] are two representative platforms to run ABM simulations in parallel on top of MPI.

RepastHPC populates and moves agents over a shared space named *Projection*, which is similar to MASS. It allows users to code agent behavior as a collection of methods and to schedule their invocation events in their execution environment named *Context*. The main program then initiates an entire execution. However, RepastHPC's event scheduling is an enumeration of agent methods to be invoked along a repetitive time sequence. We feel that this scheduling strategy is weaker than MASS that associates each agent method with a named event. RepastHPC has its agents communicate with each other indirectly through *Project*. However, they have no message-broadcast feature.

FLAME views an ABM simulation as a collection of communicating, state-transiting agents statically mapped over MPI ranks. FLAME distinguishes two different languages: XML and C. XML declares agent interfaces and schedules their execution events, while C describes agent behaviors. In similar to RepastHPC, FLAME's event scheduling makes a list of agent methods to invoke. On the other hand, FLAME provides agents with a message box at each MPI rank, so that each agent can broadcast its state to all the others. However, message retrievals must be done within a code block specified in MESSAGE_LOOP. Therefore, FLAME can't invoke a given method upon a message broadcast rather than keep polling messages.

Besides event scheduling and inter-agent message broadcast, RepastHPC and FLAME are not a good choice for distributed data discovery rather than ABM

---

[7] https://hazelcast.com/.

simulation. The reasons are: RepastHPC needs to handle I/O in the main and cannot control agent population; and FLAME needs to enclose all spatial data in each agent [4].

4   Evaluation of Agent Behaviors

We compared the conventional and annotated versions of two MASS applications from the viewpoints of their code descriptivity and execution performance. These applications are agent-based BFS (breadth-first search) and PSO programs.

Our descriptivity comparison focuses on quantitative analysis of their MASS-Java code, in particular regarding their total lines of code (LoC) and boilerplate code (BP). The latter counts the lines of code that is irrelevant to the algorithms but needed to use the MASS library for their parallelization. Table 2 shows our analysis. As expected, both BFS and PSO annotated versions show a 37% to 58% reduction of LoC in the main program due to their simplification of agent coordination into a *doWhile()* or *doAll()* statement. In some cases, however, the number of agent BP lines is not reduced or may even increase slightly because of the addition of annotations.

Table 2. BFS and PSO descriptivity

BFS		Total	Main	Agent	PSO		Total	Main	Agent
Conventional	LoC	160	27	43	Conventional	LoC	139	52	57
	BP	23	10	9		BP	25	15	6
Annotated	LoC	148	17	36	Annotated	LoC	102	22	57
	BP	21	9	9		BP	21	7	11
Reduction	LoC in %	7.5	37	16	Reduction	LoC in %	26.6	57.7	0
	BP in %	9	10	0		BP in %	16	53	-83

Our performance measurements compared both conventional and annotated version of BFS and PSO programs executed on top of the MASS library. Figure 1 visualizes their execution time. In BFS, its annotated version yielded 29% and 9% slow-down as compared to the conventional version when executed with a single thread and four threads respectively. In PSO, we observed a significant performance increase, most likely attributable to a large reduction in message transmission. This reduction in messaging overhead helped to reduce execution time by 83%. Contrary to our expectations, increasing the number of threads for PSO execution actually increased execution time, which we attribute to cache thrashing and memory contention.

While our previous performance evaluations on MapReduce and Spark in [4] used different problem sizes in BFS and PSO, each with 3000 vertices and 600 × 600 places respectively, we estimated their execution performance with 2048 vertices and $3K \times 3K$ places as in Fig. 1. MapReduce and Spark would take 17.4 and 6.9 s in BFS and 79.5 and 562.4 s in PSO respectively. These estimates indicate that the annotated version of MASS performs 2 times slower in BFS but 8+ times faster in PSO than MapReduce and Spark. We are further improving MASS performance for solving graph problems faster.

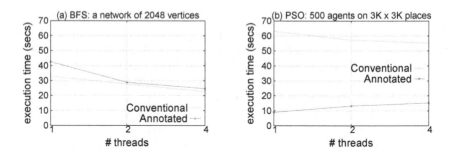

Fig. 1. BFS and PSO execution performance

5   Conclusions

To apply ABM to distributed analysis of structured dataset, we enhanced the MASS library with method annotations and inter-agent message broadcast, which allows data scientists to simply inject off-the-shelf agents from the main program, whereas developers of agent-based algorithms can focus on describing event-driven agent behaviors. Our analysis of agent programmability and execution performance demonstrated a drastic reduction in both LoC and in execution time for messaging-based applications. For non-messaging applications we observed less than a 10% negative performance effect. Additionally, we feel that this new event-driven behavior model more clearly encapsulates agent behavior, thus making the MASS applications easier to understand and easier to maintain.

References

1. Blum, C.: Ant colony optimization: introduction and recent trends. Phys. Life Rev. **2**(4), 353–373 (2005)
2. Buck, J., et al.: SciHadoop: array-based Query Processing in Hadoop. In: Proceedings of SC 2011 (2011). https://doi.org/10.1145/2063384.2063473
3. FLAME. http://www.flame.ac.uk
4. Fukuda, M., Gordon, C., Mert, U., Sell, M.: Agent-based computational framework for distributed analysis. IEEE Comput. **53**(3), 16–25 (2020). https://doi.org/10.1109/MC.2019.2932964
5. Gordon, C., Mert, U., Sell, M., Fukuda, M.: Implementation techniques to parallelize agent-based graph analysis. In: De La Prieta, F., et al. (eds.) PAAMS 2019. CCIS, vol. 1047, pp. 3–14. Springer, Cham (2019). https://doi.org/10.1007/978-3-030-24299-2_1

6. Kennedy, J., et al.: Particle swarm optimization. In: Proceedings of the IEEE International Conference on Neural Networks IV, pp. 1942–1948 (1995)
7. Kipps, M., et al.: Agent and spatial based parallelization of biological network motif search. In: 17th IEEE International Conference on HPCC, New York, pp. 786–791 (2015)
8. Lin, J., et al.: Data-Intensive Text Processing with MapReduce. Morgan & Claypool Publishers, San Rafael (2010)
9. Low, Y., et al.: Distributed GraphLab: a framework for machine learning and data mining in the cloud. In: Proceedings of the 38th International Conference on Very Large Data Bases, Istanbul, Turkey, vol. 5(8), pp. 716–727, August 2012
10. Oracle: Java Platform, Standard Edition, Java Shell User's Guide, Release 9. Technical report E87478–01 (2017)
11. Parsian, M.: Data Algorithms: Recipes for Scaling Up with Hadoop and Spark. O'Reilly, Sebastopol (2015)
12. RepastHPC. https://repast.github.io/repast_hpc.html
13. Saremi, S., Mirjalili, S., Lewis, A.: Grasshopper optimization algorithm: theory and application. Adv. Eng. Softw. **105**, 30–47 (2017)
14. Shih, Y., et al.: Translation of string-and-pin-based shortest path search into data-scalable agent-based computational models. In: Proceedings of Winter Simulation Conference, Gothenburg, Sweden, pp. 881–892, December 2018
15. Woodring, J., et al.: A multi-agent parallel approach to analyzing large climate data sets. In: 37th IEEE ICDCS, Atlanta, GA, pp. 1639–1648, June 2017

Scalable Heterogeneous Multiagent Learning from Demonstration

William Squires[✉] and Sean Luke

Department of Computer Science, George Mason University, 4400 University Dr,
Fairfax, VA 22030, USA
{wsquires,sean}@gmu.edu

Abstract. We present a method of supervised learning from demonstration for real-time, online training of complex heterogenous multiagent behaviors which scale to large numbers of agents in operation. Our learning method is applicable in domains where coordinated behaviors must be created quickly in unexplored environments. Examples of such problem domains includes disaster relief, search and rescue, and gaming environments. We demonstrate this training method in an adversarial mining scenario which coordinates four types of individual agents to perform six distinct roles in a mining task.

Keywords: Learning from demonstration · Multiagent learning · Heterogeneous

1 Introduction

In this paper we introduce an approach to scalable online learning from demonstration of nontrivial, heterogeneous, stateful multiagent and swarm behaviors. The agents in the swarms can coordinate at various levels, and the system can perform scalable load-balancing within the swarm to assign subswarms of heterogeneous agents appropriate for various tasks as called on by the experimenter. This work extends the learning from demonstration method HiTAB, adding an approach to (for the first time) train arbitrarily large, scalable agent swarm hierarchies with agent heterogeneity at every level.

There are many scenarios where training agent behaviors in real-time is highly advantageous. Consider scenarios such as disaster recovery, search, and rescue, which presents considerable challenges: programming and debugging custom behaviors on-the-fly may not be reasonable to do in real-time; and this assumes that the robot handler in the field has sufficient coding skills to achieve this at all. Furthermore, solutions to complex scenarios such as these involve a wide-ranging set of agent capabilities unlikely to be found in a single type of agent and therefore require the coordination of heterogeneous agents to be successful, and this in turn presents a large and complex design space. Finally, these scenarios can span large areas, which may necessitate the need for many heterogeneous teams to work cooperatively.

© Springer Nature Switzerland AG 2020
Y. Demazeau et al. (Eds.): PAAMS 2020, LNAI 12092, pp. 264–277, 2020.
https://doi.org/10.1007/978-3-030-49778-1_21

In scenarios such as these it would be desirable to *instruct* (or if you like, *coach*) the robots how to do various collective behaviors rather than program them. But learning from demonstration in swarms has until recently proven very difficult for two reasons. First, there is the obvious problem of the per-agent *Curse of Dimensionality*: complex and stateful behaviors imply a high-dimensional learning space and thus a large number of training samples, but this cannot be achieved if we wish training to be online. Less obvious but just as problematic is the *Multiagent Inverse Problem*: even if we could formally quantify the emergent macrophenomenon we wished the agents to achieve, in order to learn, the agents require feedback regarding their individual behaviors. While we potentially have a function which tells us the macrophenomena arising from individual agents—that is, a simulator—we lack the *inverse function* which tells us the individual behaviors needed to achieve a given macrophenomenon. Inverse problems like these are classically solved with optimization (reinforcement learning, evolutionary algorithms), and generally must be offline and/or in simulation given the samples involved; but our scenario requires online learning.

HiTAB overcomes these two problems by manually breaking the task into a subtask hierarchy to be trained bottom-up. Agent behaviors are decomposed into behavior hierarchies, and swarms themselves are decomposed to small and manageable groups. This decomposition allows us to project a complex high-dimensional problem space into many spaces of much lower dimensionality; and it also allows us to overcome the inverse problem by reducing the joint task so much that it becomes obvious what micro-behaviors are need to achieve a given (much simpler and more immediate) macrophenomenon.

HiTAB has been applied to homogeneous agent behaviors with arbitrary numbers of agents [6,15,16]; and to heterogeneous agents in small groups or with low heterogeneity [14,17]. However, it has not to date been applied to training complex heterogeneous multiagent behaviors at multiple levels, scaling to large groups, and coordinating agents with distinctly different capabilities and functions. This is because such a problem would demand nontrivial task allocation and heterogeneous swarm organization.

In this work, we consider an extension to HiTAB which makes it possible to train scalable, nontrivial heterogeneous swarms for the first time. Our approach augments HiTAB with, among other things, automated swarm reorganization and task allocation weighted by which heterogeneous capabilities are needed. We begin by discussing related work, and then review the HiTAB training methods introduced in prior work, followed by further extensions introduced in this work. We then introduce a virtual controller hierarchy scaling algorithm which scales the hierarchy at runtime by creating additional controllers based on the number of individual agents, and forming new sub-teams to perform the learned controller behaviors in parallel. Next, we describe a mining scenario created to challenge and highlight the ability of our training method, and then describe how training was performed for the mining scenario. We then describe the experiments performed and discuss the results of those experiments and future work.

2   Related Work

Multiagent Learning from Demonstration. The literature for multiagent learning from demonstration (LfD) outside of HiTAB is quite sparse, and primarily aims to address the complexity of training multiple agents simultaneously. Confidence based LfD was introduced in [4], where robots were trained to cooperatively sort colored balls into the appropriate bin. When a robot was uncertain of the correct action it would request additional demonstration from the trainer. Other work involves learning from the joint demonstration by multiple trainers. In [10], an approach was developed where the individual sequence of actions for each robot is captured and then the sequence of group behaviors is determined through analysis of the individual action sequences over space and time. In [2], robots learn to collaboratively open a door by extracting a template for the behavior and adapting it to doors in other settings. These methods work well for small teams but become dramatically more complex as more robots are added.

Multiagent LfD approaches may be combined with other learning techniques. In [3], LfD is used as a shaping mechanism for the reward function for reinforcement learning while [8] explores a hybrid approach mixing LfD with more traditional machine learning.

Hierarchies and Agents. Hierarchies are a well-known organizational approach for multiagent systems where agents higher in the tree collect increasingly global information and provide instruction to their subordinates [7]. Communication is generally restricted such that subordinate agents communicate information up to parent agents and do not communicate directly with peers, which reduces communication-related scaling problems while also reducing the state information each agent must track.

However, hierarchies can fail due to the loss of a single agent, resulting in multiple single points of failure. These drawbacks are more pronounced when considering hierarchies of real robots [11]. Because of this, most multi-robot coordination algorithms favor decentralized approaches. However, hierarchies can provide a good middle ground between centralized and decentralized coordination [13], and when considering heterogeneous swarms coordination is difficult to achieve without hierarchy [1].

In [5] and [12], heterogeneous swarms used a hierarchical structure to coordinate behaviors between an aerial agent and homogeneous subswarms, extending their capability by providing global information to direct their behavior. The subswarms were able to scale with communication confined to be between subswarm agents and the aerial agent. Multiagent HiTAB operates similarly with regard to the subswarms and communication, but is more flexible in that each subswarm may be a different type of agent.

2.1   HiTAB

Individual Agent Training. Below we provide a brief overview of prior work in HiTAB LfD training methods as an evolution from individual agent, to homogeneous multiagent, and finally heterogeneous multiagent training. To train individual agents [9], the trainer decomposes a behavior into a hierarchical finite-state automata (HFA). The HFA states are agent behaviors, with the lowest level containing only atomic agent behaviors. The HFA transitions represent changes in *features* in the environment. Behaviors and features can be parameterized, for example *GoTo(X)* and *DistanceTo(X)* respectively.

The HFA is trained from the bottom up. At each level the trainer selects features needed for training and binds parameters to *targets* in the environment as needed, for example *GoTo(ClosestAgent)* and *DistanceTo(ClosestObstacle)*. The trainer teleoperates the agent; changing the behavior at the appropriate time, each change generating a training sample including the previous behavior and current feature values. When training is complete the trainer observes the behavior and provides corrective training if needed. Once the behavior works as expected, the behavior is saved for training higher-level FA.

Homogeneous Multiagent Training. To train homogeneous multiagent behaviors [15], first individual agent behaviors are trained, and then a virtual *controller agent* (or boss) is trained to direct agents to perform their trained behaviors as its atomic behaviors. A hierarchy of controller agent behaviors are themselves trained as compositions of these atomic behaviors. When a controller changes to a new atomic behavior, all subordinate agents in its subswarm switch to the corresponding trained behavior.

Heterogeneous Multiagent Training. To train heterogeneous multiagent behaviors [17], virtual controller agents have multiple types of homogeneous agent groups. An atomic behavior in a controller agent corresponds not to a trained behavior learned by its underlings, but to a *set* of top-level behaviors meant to work together. For example, in a group of two agents of type A and one agent of type B, a coordinated behavior C might consist of behavior A_i for each of the A agents and behavior B_j for the B agents. C would correspond to an atomic behavior in the controller agent. When a controller changes to a new atomic behavior, all subordinate agents switch to the appropriate behaviors in the corresponding coordinated behavior set.

The *features* used by an individual agent to determine transitions in its HFA are normally hard-coded sensor capabilities: but what would be the features used by controller agents? [14] introduced *group features* to allow a trainer to quickly define controller features, without programming, by identifying a feature from a subordinate agent group and an aggregator function; for example *Min(At(TheStore))*. Since group features are the features of a controller agent, a higher-level controller can use that feature in a *group feature* of its own, allowing feature information to be passed up the hierarchy.

3   Our Extensions to HiTAB Training

We introduce two extensions to enable training of complex heterogeneous behaviors:

Composite Features. Group features aggregate a feature from one subordinate group or one that is common to all groups, but there are cases where training requires the combination of distinct features from multiple groups. *Composite*

Algorithm 1. Scale Hierarchy by Least Constrained Agent

1: **procedure** SCALEHIERARCHY(*rootgroup*, *agentCnts[]*)
2:     *topCtlr* ← CreateTopController(*rootgroup*)
3:     ComputeRequirements(*topCtlr*)
4:     **if** ¬ MeetsCtrlRqts(*topCtlr*, *agentCnts*, *MIN*) **then**   Abort( )
5:     AllocToController(*topCtlr*, *agentCnts*, *MIN*)
6:     AllocToController(*topCtlr*, *agentCnts*, *PREF*)
7:     AllocToController(*topCtlr*, *agentCnts*, *MAX*)
8: **procedure** ALLOCTOCONTROLLER(*ctl*, *agentCnts[]*, *mode*)
9:     **for all** *grp* **in** *ctl* **do**
10:         **for all** *agentType* **in** *agentCnts* **do**
11:             *computedCnt* ← ComputedGroupRqt(*grp*, *agentType*, *mode*)
12:             *myCnts[agentType]* ← Min(*computedCnt*, *agentCnts[agentType]*)
13:         AllocToGroup(*grp*, *myCnts*, *mode*)
14:         *agentCnts* ← AdjustCounts(*agentCnts*, *myCnts*)
15: **procedure** ALLOCTOGROUP(*grp*, *agentCnts[]*, *mode*)
16:     **if** *grp* is a *individualAgentType* **then**   *agentCnt* ← *agentCnts[individualAgentType]*
17:     **else**
18:         *newControllerCnt* ← 0
19:         **for all** *agentType1* **in** *agentCnts* **do**
20:             *cnt* ← *agentCnts[agentType1]*
21:             *ctlCnt* ← *cnt*/ComputedControllerRqt(*ctl*, *agentType1*, *mode*)
22:             **for all** *agentType2* **in** *agentCnts* **do**
23:                 *cnt* ← *agentCnts[agentType2]*
24:                 *ctlCntMin* ← *cnt*/ComputedControllerRqt(*ctl*, *agentType2*, *MIN*)
25:                 *ctlCnt* ← Min(*ctlCnt*, *ctlCntMin*)
26:             *newControllerCnt* ← Max(*ctlCnt*, *tgtCnt*)
27:         **while** *numControllers*<*newControllerCnt* **do**   CreateController(*ctlType*)
28:         **for all** *ctl* **in** group **do**
29:             *myCnts* ← ControllerCounts(*ctl*, *agentCnts*, *mode*)
30:             AllocToController(*ctl*, *myCnts*, *mode*)
31:             *agentCnts* ← AdjustCounts(*agentCnts*, *myCnts*)
32: **procedure** ADJUSTCNTS(*agentCnts[]*, *allocatedCnts[]*)
33:     **for all** *type* **in** *agentCnts* **do**   *agentCnts[type]* ← *agentCnts[type]* − *allocatedCnts[type]*
34: **procedure** CONTROLLERCOUNTS(*ctl*, *agentCnts[]*, *mode*)
35:     **for all** *type* **in** *agentCnts* **do**
36:         *tgtCnt* ← ComputedControllerRqt(*ctl*, *type*, *mode*)
37:         *myCnts[type]* ← Min(*tgtCnt*, *agentCnts[type]*)

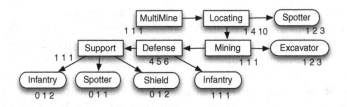

Fig. 1. Mining Behavior Hierarchy. Rectangles are controller groups and rounded rectangles are individual agent groups. Shown with min/preferred/max constraints.

features allow a trainer to, without programming, define a feature that incorporates feature information from multiple individual agent types. We do this by providing a feature name, a list of *group features*, and an aggregation function that combines the group features into a single value. For example, a controller coordinating driverless shuttles (group 0) and passengers (group 1) needs a feature indicating to go to the parking lot if there are at least 10 passengers or there is more than one shuttle at the station; *ReadyToShuttle* is defined as *Min(TenOrMorePassengers, MultipleAtStation)*. Like group features, composite features can be passed up the hierarchy as input to a group feature defined in the parent controller.

Targets with Hierarchy Context. A target in HiTAB is a variable which generalizes a behavior, so we can create general behaviors like "Go to X" rather than concrete behaviors like "Go to the ball" or "Go to George". We define a method for individual agent training where the trainer can quickly define a set of agents within the hierarchy to use as targets. For example, in Fig. 1, training of agents under the *Support* controller may need to reference some agent in the *Infantry* group of the *Defense* controller as a target. Providing a *level* and a *hierarchy subpath*, the trainer can reference any set of agents in the hierarchy. The level defines the starting point of the hierarchy subpath, where level 0 is the immediate parent controller and increases as we move up the hierarchy. The hierarchy subpath is a string of the form *subpath=group[agentNum⟨:subpath⟩],...* defining a list of agent groups under the controller, each having an agent number and an optional nested subpath. Replacing group or agentNum with a wildcard character indicates all groups or all agents respectively. In this way, an agent below the *Support* controller would reference its formation leader with *level=1* and *subpath=1[*]*, corresponding to any *Infantry* agent below the *Defense* controller.

4   Hierarchy Scaling

In this work we train complex behaviors with a relatively small number of agents and then have those behaviors scale, without retraining, to solve large problems given a larger number of individual agents. To do this, we consider the structure of the heterogeneous team, where the size and number of subteams can be increased to improve redundancy and parallelism. The trainer's role in this is to consider an appropriate set of constraints for each subteam by defining its *minimum, maximum,* and *preferred* sizes in operation. In HiTAB, subteams are represented by the agent groups of a virtual controller agent, each including a homogeneous set of individual or virtual controller agents. Given the constraints for each agent group and some allocation of individual agents, we need to adjust agent group sizes to scale the behavior. Scaling a single-level controller is trivial, we simply add available agents to the individual agent groups of the controller (as in [14]). But in a complex agent hierarchy, scaling also involves increasing the size of virtual controller agent groups.

Adding virtual controllers is a difficult problem for the following reasons: First, the number of agents in each agent group must satisfy the *Minimum* and *Maximum* constraints defined by the trainer. We can only add a virtual controller if there are enough individual agents to meet its combined *Minimum* constraints and we can only add individual agents to an existing controller up to the combined *Maximum* constraints. Second, agent types may appear in multiple agent groups of the hierarchy, each having its own constraints for that role in the top-level behavior. And third, we do not know in advance if some type of agent will be much more constrained than others. Below we define a low-cost centralized algorithm to scale an agent hierarchy given the trainer-defined constraints and some allocation of individual agents.

Scale Hierarchy by Least Constrained Agent. Shown in Algorithm 1, the *Scale-Hierarchy* procedure takes a root group of controller agents that run the top-level behavior and an array of individual agent counts. It begins by creating a *dummy* controller containing the root agent group and then recursively computes the individual agent requirements for the three constraint modes (*Minimum, Preferred,* and *Maximum*) for each group and controller in the hierarchy. Then we call *AllocToController* for each constraint mode.

In *AllocToController*, for each agent group we determine how many of each type of agent can be provided given a constraint *mode*. The agent count of each individual agent type is up to the computed group requirement for that type and constraint mode. After allocation to a group is complete, we adjust the individual agent counts to reflect what was allocated and repeat for the next agent group.

The *AllocToGroup* procedure acts in one of two ways. For an individual agent group, the group size is simply increased to the provided agent count. For a controller agent group, we determine how many additional controllers can be added given the available agents and the constraint mode as follows: For each individual agent type, *type1*, we calculate how many controller agents can be created based on the number of *type1* agents and the computed requirement of a controller for that agent type. Within that loop, we check the remaining individual agent types, *type2*, to see how many controllers can be created for that agent type using the *Minimum* constraint. That is, we create additional controllers based on the least constrained agent type so long as the *Minimum* requirements are met for the controller's other individual agent types. If needed, the controller count is reduced so the *Minimum* for the *type2* individual agents is not violated. After calculating the number of additional controllers, we add them to the agent group and then *AllocToController* is called for each controller in the group. Adding the new controllers at the head of the agent group ensures their *Minimum* requirements are met.

5   The Mining Scenario

Demonstrating our learning approach requires a training scenario that is heterogeneous, demands scalability to cover large areas, and requires complex interaction among heterogenous agents. We were unable to find a suitable match in our literature search, so we invented an adversarial mining scenario. In this scenario, *Excavator* agents mine ore from deposits that are located by *Spotter* agents. There are also a number of defensive agent types that cooperate to protect the *Excavator* from adversary agents that seek to stop the mining.

The agent types below are defined by setting attribute values for maximum health and abilities for vision, attacking other agents, shielding attacks from other agents, and what action to take when the agent reaches zero health:

Infantry. This agent can attack other agents but cannot shield attacks.

Spotter. This agent has zero-value attack and shield values, but has increased visual range and a 360-degree field of view. If an *Infantry* agent is associated with a *Spotter*, then it can attack a *spotted* target with 100% accuracy.

Shield. This agent can shield other agents from attack, but cannot attack other agents.

Excavator. This agent has a greater amount of health, no defensive abilities, and is able mine ore from the ore deposits.

Archer. This agent has similar settings to the Infantry agent, but is an adversary to the agents above. When health reaches zero, these agents reappear at spawn points randomly distributed in the environment.

Mining is disrupted when the *Excavator* agent reaches zero health, and resumes when its health is restored (after 1000 time units). When other mining team agents reach zero health, they are disabled for 300 time units, but stay in place to maintain the agent allocations to the scaled hierarchy. *Shield* and *Spotter* agents are not *attackable*, but may be damaged while other agents are being attacked.

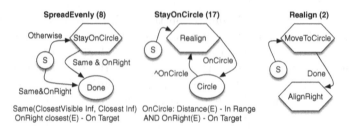

Fig. 2. SpreadEvenly HFA. The samples required to train a behavior is shown in parentheses. Hexagons are trained behaviors; ovals are atomic behaviors.

6   Training the Mining Scenario

To train the mining scenario, we first have to define an agent hierarchy that simplifies training and defines the appropriate subteams. After that we train individual behaviors and then the coordinating behaviors of the virtual controllers.

Defining the Agent Hierarchy. Given the agent types defined above we chose to train the mining scenario behavior using the agent hierarchy shown in Fig. 1. At the lowest level, the *Support* controller includes the supporting agents of a defense team. To provide a reference point for the training of the defensive formation behavior, we add the *Defense* controller where a single *Infantry* agent acts as a *formation leader* for the *Support* agents in the defense team. The *Mining* controller has *Excavator* agents that mine ore and a number of *Defense* teams to protect them from attack. The *Locating* controller has *Spotter* agents that search for available ore deposits for a *Mining* team. At the top level, the *MultiMine* controller is a homogeneous controller of *Locating* teams that perform the mining behavior in parallel. Note that two agent types have multiple roles in the hierarchy, where the agents are trained for both roles and perform the appropriate role based on their placement in the hierarchy during hierarchy scaling.

When defining the hierarchy, we also defined the constraints for *Minimum*, *Preferred*, and *Maximum* agent counts for each agent group. These are shown in Fig. 1 as three integer values next to each agent group. For example, each *Mining* agent has a minimum of four *Defense* agents, with five preferred and 6 at a maximum.

Agent Training. The top-level mining behavior combines *over 150 trained behaviors* for the individual and controller agents, so we will not describe all training here. We provide examples below that are part of the behavior to form agents defensively around *Excavator* agents, with final formation examples shown in Fig. 4. The figure also shows that the formation is scaled based on agent availability.

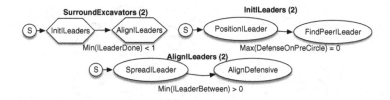

Fig. 3. SurroundExcavators HFA. See also Fig. 2.

Much of the training fell into two categories: training individual agents to position themselves with respect to other agents in the hierarchy and training controller agents to coordinate individual agent behaviors. We describe one instance of each type of training below, highlighting usage of our extensions in this work. Note that all references to *Infantry* agents below are for *formation leader* agents in the second group of the *Defense* controller. Finally, we briefly describe the adversary (*Archer*) behavior.

SpreadEvenly. *Infantry* agents are trained to spread evenly in a circle around *Excavator* agents below the *Mining* controller. When this behavior begins, the agents are already positioned on a circle around *Excavator* agents and a peer *Infantry* agent is visible. The HFA for the *SpreadEvenly* behavior is shown in Fig. 2.

Realign positions the agent at the desired radius to the closest *Excavator* and orients it so that the *Excavator* is directly to the right. *StayOnCircle* circles the closest *Excavator* and realigns if the distance or orientation are not within acceptable limits, which can happen if there are multiple *Excavator* agents to circle. Finally, *SpreadEvenly* moves the agent around the circle until the closest visible peer is also the closest peer. Without further coordination, the agents continue to circle at a relatively even distance because they cannot all be at the stopping condition at the same time.

To train *SpreadEvenly*, we used two different *targets with hierarchy context*. The *Realign* and *StayOnCircle* behaviors are trained with respect to an *Excavator* using *level=1* and *subpath=1[*]*. The *SpreadEvenly* behavior is trained with respect to peer *Infantry* agents using *level=0* and *subpath=0[*:1[*]]*.

SurroundExcavators. The *Mining* controller agent is trained to coordinate *Infantry* agents to position evenly on a circle around its *Excavator* agents. The HFA is shown in Fig. 3, where the ellipses are *joint behaviors* and the features are *group features*.

InitILeaders instructs *Infantry* agents to move to a radius around the closest *Excavator* agent using *PostionILeader* and, when they are all at the proper distance, they are instructed to move around the circle until a peer is visible using *FindPeerILeader*. *AlignILeaders* runs the *SpreadEvenly* behavior described above using *SpreadILeader* and, when all agents are roughly equidistant to their two closest peers, they are instructed to orient outward from the *Excavator* using

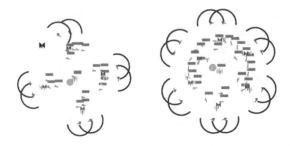

Fig. 4. Mining Formation for 4 and 6 defensive teams

AlignDefensive. The top-level behavior switches from *InitILeaders* to *AlignILeaders* when all of the agents are in a *Done* state.

While no *composite features* were used in training *SurroundExcavators*, two were used in other training to indicate when the defensive formation is complete and mining can start. First, the *DefenseAligned* composite feature in the *Support* controller is the Max of three group features indicating all support agents are on their respective circles around the *Excavator*. This feature is passed up through the *Defense* and *Mining* controllers as the *SupAligned* group feature. The *DefenseAligned* composite feature of the *Mining* controller is the Max of *SupAligned* and the *Max(AlignedRear)* group feature indicating all formation leaders are pointing away from the *Excavators*.

Archer Behavior. The adversary agents are trained with the *AttackMined* behavior, which moves the agent randomly in the environment until it is within 150 units of an ore deposit that is being mined. It then moves toward the closest ore deposit being mined and attacks the *Infantry* and *Excavator* agents near the ore.

7   Experiments

In our experiments we run the top-level mining behavior in environments of two sizes, 580 × 580 and 1080 × 1080 units, with 12 ore deposits. Deposits are randomly distributed in grid locations in the environment and reappear in an open location randomly when depleted. *Archer* agents are randomly distributed in the environment, with 160 in the smaller environment and 555 in the larger environment to keep the density equal. When an *Archer* dies it reappears at one of 18 spawn locations, which are randomly distributed in grid locations at start time. Experiments are run with three allocations of mining agents that result in one, two, and four mining teams respectively after hierarchy scaling.

Baseline Training. We establish a baseline of comparison by training individual agent behaviors for the mining task without a controller hierarchy. For this training we defined an additional agent type, *Seeker*, to perform the *ore seeking* behaviors of the *Spotter* agent. The individual agent behaviors were trained as follows: (1) A *Seeker* agent moves randomly, goes to and attaches to a visible ore deposit with no attached agents, and then repeats the behavior when mining begins on the deposit. (2) An *Excavator* agent moves randomly until it is within 150 units of an attached *Seeker* agent, then goes to, attaches to, and mines the ore deposit, and then repeats the behavior when the deposit is depleted. (3) An *Infantry* agent moves randomly in the environment until within 150 units of active mining, then goes to the mining location and attacks *Archer* agents, and repeats the behavior when the deposit is depleted. (4) A *Spotter* agent moves randomly until it sees an *Infantry* agent, then moves to and follows the *Infantry* agent while keeping it between the nearest *Archer* agent and itself. (5) A *Shield* agent moves randomly until it sees an *Infantry* agent, then moves to and follows the *Infantry* agent while trying to shield it from the nearest *Archer* agent.

The agent allocations for experiments are shown in Table 1, where h is the hierarchical behavior and b is the baseline behavior. At the beginning of each simulation mining teams are randomly distributed, with agents in a 50×50 unit square. Though the baseline agents are not true *teams*, we group them similarly to create a fair comparison at startup. Each experiment was run for 100,000 timesteps. For each environment, we compared the average ore gathered at step 100,000 over 50 runs for the team configurations in the two environments using two-tailed t-tests, p-value = 0.01, with Bonferroni correction.

Table 1. Agent allocations

Allocation	Infantry(h, b)	Shield(h, b)	Excav(h, b)	Spotter(h)	Seeker(b)	Spotter(b)
One Team	8	5	1	7	5	2
Two Teams	16	10	2	14	10	4
Four Teams	32	20	4	28	20	8

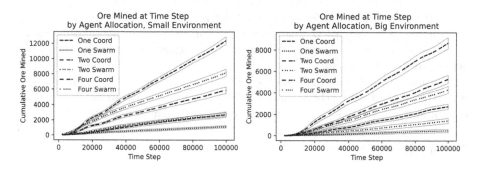

Fig. 5. Mean results for small and large environments. Gray lines are 95% confidence intervals.

Figure 5 shows the mean results with the baseline results having dots indicating the number of teams and the controller hierarchy having dashes indicating the number of teams. In both environments the scaling resulted in a clear but slightly sublinear improvement in results for additional mining teams. The virtual controller hierarchy results in a clear improvement over the baseline behavior. The difference is even more pronounced in the larger environment, with 2 hierarchy teams outperforming 4 baseline teams, suggesting that the added communication and coordination provided by the virtual controller agent hierarchy becomes more important as the environment grows.

In comparing the relative efficiency per team, the increase to four teams shows a small drop in ore mined per team. We attribute this to the increased competition for ore resources. This difference is more pronounced in the big environment, where the cost of teams exploring the same area is higher. Training a top-level behavior to encourage teams to explore other areas of the environment may help to address the decreased efficiency.

8   Conclusions and Future Work

In this work, we successfully trained a complex heterogeneous multiagent behavior and showed that it scales without retraining. We also showed that the virtual controller hierarchy offers a clear benefit over agents attempting to coordinate on their own. We introduced the mining scenario as a means of demonstrating complex and scalable heterogeneous agent training. We also made further refinements to the HiTAB heterogeneous multiagent learning method that were an important part of the mining behavior training.

The *Scale Hierarchy by Least Constrained Agent* algorithm successfully incorporated additional agents, but in empirical testing we noted certain cases where the distribution of available agents was not always balanced. Better hierarchy scaling algorithms could be created to address this, but without applying our method to a greater number of scenarios it is hard to tell if one algorithm would be suitable for all problems.

Finally, the current hierarchy scaling is based on central knowledge of the individual agents and where they are in the environment. While this knowledge is available for a simulation environment, we cannot assume this information is available for robots in a large environment where they are likely to be initially separated from their team.

Future work will center around the creation of a distributed hierarchy scaling algorithm and other methods that will allow the agent hierarchy to be built, scaled, and balanced as agents find each other in the environment.

References

1. Barca, J.C., Sekercioglu, Y.A.: Swarm robotics reviewed. Robotica **31**(3), 345–359 (2013)
2. Blokzijl-Zanker, M., Demiris, Y.: Multi robot learning by demonstration. In: Proceedings of the 11th International Conference on Autonomous Agents and Multiagent Systems-Volume 3, pp. 1207–1208. International Foundation for Autonomous Agents and Multiagent Systems (2012)

3. Brys, T., Harutyunyan, A., Suay, H.B., Chernova, S., Taylor, M.E., Nowé, A.: Reinforcement learning from demonstration through shaping. In: Twenty-Fourth International Joint Conference on Artificial Intelligence (2015)
4. Chernova, S., Veloso, M.: Confidence-based multi-robot learning from demonstration. Int. J. Soc. Robot. **2**(2), 195–215 (2010). https://doi.org/10.1007/s12369-010-0060-0
5. Elston, J., Frew, E.W.: Hierarchical distributed control for search and tracking by heterogeneous aerial robot networks. In: 2008 IEEE International Conference on Robotics and Automation. ICRA 2008, pp. 170–175. IEEE (2008)
6. Freelan, D., Wicke, D., Sullivan, K., Luke, S.: Towards rapid multi-robot learning from demonstration at the robocup competition. In: Bianchi, R.A.C., Akin, H.L., Ramamoorthy, S., Sugiura, K. (eds.) RoboCup 2014. LNCS (LNAI), vol. 8992, pp. 369–382. Springer, Cham (2015). https://doi.org/10.1007/978-3-319-18615-3_30
7. Horling, B., Lesser, V.: A survey of multi-agent organizational paradigms. Knowl. Eng. Rev. **19**(4), 281–316 (2004)
8. Le, H.M., Yue, Y., Carr, P., Lucey, P.: Coordinated multi-agent imitation learning. In: Proceedings of the 34th International Conference on Machine Learning-Volume 70, pp. 1995–2003. JMLR. org (2017)
9. Luke, S., Ziparo, V.A.: Learn to behave! rapid training of behavior automata. In: Proceedings of Adaptive and Learning Agents Workshop at AAMAS 2010 (2010)
10. Martins, M.F., Demiris, Y.: Learning multirobot joint action plans from simultaneous task execution demonstrations. In: Proceedings of the 9th International Conference on Autonomous Agents and Multiagent Systems: Volume 1-Volume 1, pp. 931–938. International Foundation for Autonomous Agents and Multiagent Systems (2010)
11. Parker, L.E.: Multiple mobile robot systems. In: Siciliano, B., Khatib, O. (eds.) Springer Handbook of Robotics, pp. 921–941. Springer, Heidelberg (2008). https://doi.org/10.1007/978-3-540-30301-5_41
12. Pinciroli, C., O'Grady, R., Christensen, A.L., Dorigo, M.: Coordinating heterogeneous swarms through minimal communication among homogeneous sub-swarms. In: Dorigo, M., et al. (eds.) ANTS 2010. LNCS, vol. 6234, pp. 558–559. Springer, Heidelberg (2010). https://doi.org/10.1007/978-3-642-15461-4_59
13. Soule, T., Heckendorn, R.B.: A developmental approach to evolving scalable hierarchies for multi-agent swarms. In: Proceedings of the 12th Annual Conference Companion on Genetic and Evolutionary Computation, pp. 1769–1776. ACM (2010)
14. Squires, W.G., Luke, S.: LfD training of heterogeneous formation behaviors. In: AAAI Spring Symposia (2018)
15. Sullivan, K., Luke, S.: Learning from demonstration with swarm hierarchies. In: Proceedings of the 11th International Conference on Autonomous Agents and Multiagent Systems-Volume 1, pp. 197–204. International Foundation for Autonomous Agents and Multiagent Systems (2012)
16. Sullivan, K., Luke, S.: Real-time training of team soccer behaviors. In: Chen, X., Stone, P., Sucar, L.E., van der Zant, T. (eds.) RoboCup 2012. LNCS (LNAI), vol. 7500, pp. 356–367. Springer, Heidelberg (2013). https://doi.org/10.1007/978-3-642-39250-4_32
17. Sullivan, K., Wei, E., Squires, B., Wicke, D., Luke, S.: Training heterogeneous teams of robots. In: Autonomous Robots and Multirobot Systems (ARMS) (2015)

Multimodal Joke Generation and Paralinguistic Personalization for a Socially-Aware Robot

Hannes Ritschel[(✉)], Thomas Kiderle, Klaus Weber, Florian Lingenfelser, Tobias Baur, and Elisabeth André

Human-Centered Multimedia, Augsburg University, Universitätsstr. 6a, 86159 Augsburg, Germany
{ritschel,kiderle,weber,lingenfelser,baur,andre}@hcm-lab.de

Abstract. Robot humor is typically scripted by the human. This work presents a socially-aware robot which generates multimodal jokes for use in real-time human-robot dialogs, including appropriate prosody and non-verbal behaviors. It personalizes the paralinguistic presentation strategy based on socially-aware reinforcement learning, which interprets human social signals and aims to maximize user amusement.

Keywords: Robot humor · Non-verbal behavior · Personalization

1 Introduction

Humor increases interpersonal attraction and trust in interpersonal communication. It regulates conversations, eases communication problems and helps to cope with critique or stress [19]. Giving robots this ability is an opportunity to create socially intelligent embodied agents, but is also a serious challenge. Humor is complex and generative approaches are faced with many research questions: recognizing the context, estimating the appropriateness in the corresponding situation, generating the humorous content and communicating it successfully.

In the last years, some of these challenges have been investigated. Robots have been sent to theaters [13], presenting Japanese Manzai [11] and stand-up comedy for entertaining the human audience [12]. First steps in personalizing the show to the audience have been made [37], selecting presented contents intelligently according to the audience's visual or auditory reactions. Typically, humorous contents are scripted in advance, outsourcing this complex task to the human. But keeping the diversity of humor, interaction scenarios and dialog topics in mind, an automatic generation of robot humor is desirable. A combination of dynamically generated humor and personalization is desirable [24].

In the text-only domain, several humor generators have been implemented, such as STANDUP [15] for punning riddles. However, humor is multilayered [17]: apart from the text itself, appropriate non-verbal behaviors, such as facial expression and gestures, significantly contribute to successful joke presentation.

© Springer Nature Switzerland AG 2020
Y. Demazeau et al. (Eds.): PAAMS 2020, LNAI 12092, pp. 278–290, 2020.
https://doi.org/10.1007/978-3-030-49778-1_22

Text-To-Speech (TTS) systems do not yet generate humor-specific prosody, nor does the robot add non-verbal behaviors automatically. When presenting humorous contents, it is all about timing, pronunciation and appearance, e.g. to create tension just before telling the punchline of a joke. While recent research investigated the dynamic generation of multimodal ironic robot behaviors, one can find more humor markers in the literature which have not been applied systematically to robotic joke telling yet.

Machine learning is used successfully to adapt the robot's show to the spectators' preferences by selecting scripted contents intelligently. Reinforcement Learning (RL) has become very popular for optimizing social robots' linguistic contents [28,30,31] in recent years, also with focus on humor [37,38].

Building on the STANDUP punning riddle generator, we present an approach for dynamic multimodal joke generation. Our contribution is (1) the identification and (2) systematic implementation of human humor markers for a social robot. Furthermore, we (3) personalize its prosody based on the spectator's audiovisual reactions in real-time. This socially-aware learning process has the ultimate goal of increasing the individual spectator's amusement by tweaking multimodal joke presentation beyond its linguistic content.

2 Related Work

The related work is split up into two sections. First, we take a look at robots entertaining an audience, with focus on scenarios, contents and automated adaptation mechanisms, which help maximizing the spectators' amusement. Afterwards, we outline different humor *markers* in order to equip robots with a natural joke telling strategy. These multimodal social cues have been identified in human interaction to support joke telling and presenting humorous contents.

2.1 Robots Presenting Humor

A very popular comedy show is the traditional Manzai from Japan, which is performed by two entertainers. Hayashi et al. [11] implement a Manzai dialog with two robots. A noise level meter measures human applause and laughter. Both signals are transformed into an estimate of the audience's current amusement (*burst out, laugh, cool down*), which is used to synchronize the communication and movement of each robot with its comedy partner and the audience. Similar is done by Utemani et al. [34], where the content of the show is determined dynamically by keywords from the audience. After searching for newspaper articles on the internet, they are transformed into a Manzai dialog. The generated dialog coordinates both robots' movements, facial expressions and speech output.

Knight et al. [13] use a robot to present a sequence of scripted jokes. During its stand-up comedy, convex programming is used to adapt the presented content to the audience by measuring the current entertainment level. Laughter and applause are recorded with a stage microphone. The audience can evaluate jokes by holding up green or red cards, which are recorded with a camera. Based on

Table 1. Multimodal markers of verbal humor

Modality	Markers
Prosody	Pitch ↑[3,4,6,20,39], Volume ↑[1,4,6,39], Speech rate ↑[1,20,39], Break at punchline [1,3,4,6], Combination of limited pitch range, minor pitch change (syllables, utterance), Syntax and content in the setup of punning riddles [5]
Speech	Laughter [2,7,21]
Facial expr.	Smile [2,7,21] and gaze at the face areas involved in the smile (eyes, mouth) [8,9], Change gaze target to another person [12]

this feedback, the robot dynamically selects the next jokes, which are associated with several attributes. Katevas et al. [12] focus on a robot's non-verbal behaviors during a stand-up comedy show. It presents scripted jokes and utilizes gaze and gestures (e.g. pointing or looking at somebody) to react to acoustic and visual feedback from the audience. Based on the audience's reactions, which are captured with a camera (people's faces) and microphone (laughter/applause), the robot's timing, non-verbal behaviors and answers are adapted.

While aforementioned experiments address larger audiences, research in the context of single spectators optimizes the show for individual preferences. Weber et al. [37] adapt a robot's multimodal joke presentation to the human's sense of humor. The robot presents scripted jokes from different categories and combines them with sounds and grimaces. A reinforcement learning approach selects the best combination while the spectator's smile and laughter are used to shape the reward signal. Ritschel et al. [26] focus on verbal irony in human-robot smalltalk. Based on the user's input the robot dynamically transforms its response into an ironic version with the help of Natural Language Generation (NLG). The authors identify and add typical verbal (prosody) and non-verbal (gaze) robot behavior to successfully support the human in recognizing the presence of irony.

2.2 Multimodal Expression of Humor

The presentation of humor often involves appropriate prosody and non-verbal behaviors, which do not exist out-of-the box with current TTS systems and robots. For example, rolling eyes, winking, extra-long pauses and exaggerated intonational patterns, are crucial in order to support the human in identifying the presence of irony (see [26] for an overview of human irony cues and how to apply them to a social robot). In general, a robots' verbal and non-verbal behaviors have to be synchronized with the text. This also applies to humor: Mirnig et al. [17] point out that humor is multilayered and that the additional robot's modalities contribute to the presentation. According to the authors, adding unimodal verbal or non-verbal, humorous elements to non-humorous robot behavior does not automatically result in increased perceived funniness.

There is no comprehensive overview and transfer of human social cues to the context robot joke telling humor yet. Thus, a collection of *markers* (i.e.,

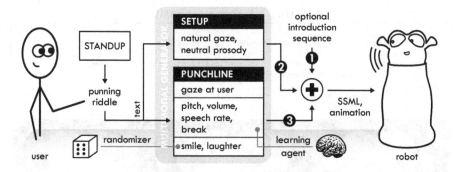

Fig. 1. Overview of the multimodal joke generation approach

characteristics) for verbal humor is compiled in Table 1. It includes conversational humor and canned jokes, but excludes verbal irony. Common markers include increasing pitch, volume and speech rate, often combined with a break at the joke's punchline. Also, an "atypical" prosody with very limited pitch range, as well as special linguistic syntax for the setup of riddles is reported in the literature. Sometimes, short laughter or giggling is performed by the speaker. Facial expressions include smiling or targeted gaze behavior.

3   Multimodal Joke Generation

Figure 1 illustrates the general approach of the socially-aware robotic joke teller. A punning riddle is generated, which consists of two parts: the *setup* (question) and *punchline* (answer). Most of STANDUPs joke types are used (for details and examples see [29]). These two text snippets are transformed into a multi-modal robot performance based on selected markers from Table 1. Speech Synthesis Markup Language (SSML)[1] is used to add prosody and to embed laughter sounds. The robot's face is animated to include gaze behavior and smile. In order to create variety in the created multimodal output, the parameters are randomized to a certain degree. The implementation uses a Reeti robot[2], which offers basic actuators in its face to control the eye ball rotation, eye lids, mouth, ears and head rotation. Since Reeti's internal TTS system does not support SSML the robot's speech is realized with Cerevoice[3], using the male *William* voice.

3.1   Text Generation

As an optional first step, the robot can add an introduction sequence, such as "Did you know this one?" or "The following punning riddle is a real pearl of

---

[1] https://www.w3.org/TR/speech-synthesis/.

[2] http://reeti.fr/index.php/en/.

[3] https://www.cereproc.com/en/products/academic.

Listing 1.1. Generated SSML

```
<speak>
  <s>What do you get when you cross a choice with a meal?</s>
  <break time="1500ms"/>
  <s><prosody pitch="high" rate="fast" volume="loud">A pick-nic.</prosody></s>
  <spurt audio="g0001_019"></spurt>
</speak>
```

Fig. 2. The robot's gaze and facial expressions: a saccade (left), its neutral facial expression when centering on the spectator (middle) and smile (right).

comedy!" When embedded in a human-robot dialog scenario this aims to set the stage for the robot's performance by announcing its intention to tell a joke.

Afterwards, the setup and punchline are generated by STANDUP [15], which is a rule-based generator for punning riddles. It uses different schemas and templates in combination with information about pronunciation and semantic relationships of words. Puns can be generated for given topics or keywords. The following text templates are used in the scenario at hand: *cross* (e.g. "What do you get when you cross X with Y?"), *call* (e.g. "What do you call X that has Y?"), *difference* (e.g. "How is X different from Y?"), *similarity* (e.g. "Why is X like Y?") and *type* (e.g. "What kind of X is Y?"). Here is a generated example: "What do you call a washing machine with a September? An autumn-atic washer."

3.2 Setup

Prosody. The setup's linguistic markers with regards to the syntax and content (see Table 1) are already applied during STANDUP's text generation process. In human joke telling the spoken language is typically accentuated with a combination of limited pitch range, minor pitch change within syllables or the whole utterance (see Table 1). However, since the realization of the presented markers heavily depends on the robot's hard- and software, the implemented prosodic markers are limited by the produced TTS output. Unfortunately, neither the SSML *range* nor the *emphasis* tag show an audible effect with Cerevoice and the *William* voice. Thus, the question's text is directly converted into SSML without additional tags (see the first sentence in Listing 1.1).

Gaze. The robot's gaze behavior during the setup aims to mimic natural human gaze behavior in order to contrast the following punchline. Saccades are frequently implemented in embodied agents since they represent the most noticeable eye movements. They centre the gaze to an object of interest, which causes a rapid shift in eye rotation [32]. In order to mimic this behavior, the robot focuses random points near the spectator's position (see Fig. 2) so that it does not stare at the user the whole time.

3.3   Punchline

Prosody. Speakers typically take a significant break just before telling the punchline (see Table 1). In SSML pauses are specified with the *break* element and a value in milliseconds for best control over their duration. Since there is no clear information about its duration in the literature the robot uses a random value in the range between 1.5 and 2.0 s.

The punchline is often presented with a different pitch, volume and speech rate than the setup (see Table 1). The predefined SSML attribute values *low*, *medium* and *high* are used for pitch manipulation. For volume, the values *soft*, *medium*, *loud* work well. The speech rate is modified with *slow*, *medium* and *fast*. More extreme variants, such as *x-low* or *x-high* result in more synthetic and less natural sounding output. They impair the robot's comprehensibility, in particular compared to the neutral prosody during the setup.

Laughter. The speaker occasionally marks the presented humor with laughing (see Table 1) or giggling after the joke. In Cerevoice *vocal gestures* can be embedded with the non-standard SSML *spurt* tag. These audio samples include different types of laughter, ranging from short giggling to long laughter sounds. When used excessively after every punchline, this appears probably unnatural for the audience, especially if the same sample is used over and over again. Based on the insights by Attardo et al. [2] the probability for laughing is set to 30%. See Listing 1.1 for an SSML sequence with all markers included.

Gaze. Joke tellers often gaze at the face areas involved in the spectator's smile (i.e., eyes and mouth) when presenting the punchline (see Table 1). While the robot mimics natural gaze behavior during the setup, the punchline is accompanied by its head and eyes focusing on the spectator. To this end, the robot's head and gaze center on the spectator in front (see Fig. 2). We did not implement the speaker's change of gaze between different spectators, as observed and used in [12], since the scenario at hand addresses a single person audience.

Smile. Smiling is a frequent human marker when presenting the punchline of a joke (see Table 1). Based on the insights by Attardo et al. [2] the robot uses this marker with a probability of 80% by raising its lip corners. In order to emphasize the smile even more, the robot's large ears are raised (see Fig. 2). After the joke is finished, the robot's face returns to its neutral facial expression.

4   Personalization

Previous experiments adapted the scripted content of robot comedy shows (see Sect. 2) and indicated that personalization can lead to significantly higher amuse-

Fig. 3. Overview of the personalization process

ment. Building on this, we implement a socially-aware reinforcement learning approach [22] for optimizing the robot's paralinguistic joke presentation strategy beyond the linguistic content. While STANDUP provides the opportunity to generate different categories of jokes and since this type of adaptation has already been investigated we focus on the paralinguistic aspects exclusively in order to reduce the complexity for an evaluation and to prevent side effects.

4.1 Overview

Figure 3 illustrates the approach. A multimodal punning riddle is generated and presented. Meanwhile, the user's audiovisual reactions are recorded and interpreted with the Social Signals Interpretation (SSI) framework [36], which detects human laughter and smile. This data serves to compute the reward signal for a RL agent and to optimize the usage of markers for the next joke.

The presented process also aims to algorithmically improve the RL approach by [37] in terms of scalability. A RL agent needs to sequentially explore which action a_t is the best one to execute in a given state s_t according to the environment's reaction $\mathcal{R}_t$ at timestep t. The discrete set of actions $\mathcal{A}$ and discrete set of states $\mathcal{S}$ needs to be as small as possible in order to reduce the required learning time. In contrast to [37] and inspired by [23,27] we encode the robot's prosodic markers directly in the state space instead of modeling them as actions. This allows to model the learning task more compactly.

4.2 Problem Modeling

The robot should learn quickly since the first impression is crucial for the assessment of the audience [37] and preferences may change over time [27]. Therefore, our real-time personalization uses RL with linear function approximation, using a learning rate $\alpha = 0.25$ and discount factor $\gamma = 0.2$. Initially, the exploration rate is set to $\epsilon = 0.5$ and decreased by 0.05 after each time step t.

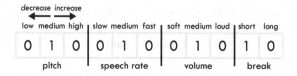

Fig. 4. Initial state (1 = active, 0 = inactive)

State Space. Each state represents the robot's current prosodic presentation strategy. It encodes how the prosodic markers are applied during generation of the robot's multimodal performance, i.e. *pitch, speech rate, volume* and *break*. Smile and laughter are always used according to their probabilities (see Sect. 3.3). A state s_t is defined as a four-tuple $(pitch, speech\ rate, volume, break) \in S$.

The state is converted into the vector $\phi(s_t)$, which is divided into different sections (see Fig. 4). All components in the vector are associated with a specific manifestation of the respective marker: digits are associated with the pitch attributes (*low, medium, high*), with the speech rate (*slow, medium, fast*), with the volume (*soft, medium, loud*) and with the length of the pause (*short, long*). Every marker is one-hot-encoded, i.e. only one manifestation per marker can be active. Figure 4 illustrates the initial state as an example.

Action Space. Two actions exist for every marker: *increase* (↑) and *decrease* (↓), which allow increasing or decreasing pitch, speech rate, volume or break time. Moreover, the action *nop* does not change anything: when the optimal presentation strategy has been found no changes should be made anymore. Switching directly between minima and maxima is excluded by intention. Otherwise, this could result in the robot's behavior appearing strangely. Overall, the available action space $\mathcal{A}$ is defined as the set $\mathcal{A} = \{pitch\ \updownarrow, rate\ \updownarrow, volume\ \updownarrow, pause\ \updownarrow, nop\}$. Actions, which do not have an effect on the state, are excluded (apart from *nop*): if a marker is already set to its minimum or maximum value, it cannot be decreased or increased any further.

Reward. As for the choice of rewarding feedback, laughter has for years been identified as a crucial part of social interaction by traditional conversation analysis [10]. Additionally it is the most evident reaction towards a successful punchline within a joke and is therefore a key element to estimate the user's amusement. Naturally, audible laughter is accompanied by a visual component, i.e., a smiling expression in the facial modality. These human social signals are processed (see Sect. 4.3) to compute the average probability of smiles $\mathbb{E}_{smile}$ and laughter $\mathbb{E}_{laughter}$ from the punchline until 2500 ms after the end of the joke. The additional time is essential to give the user time to understand the joke and to include delayed human reactions into the learning process [37]. Since smiles occur more frequently in humorous situations than laughter [2] the reward function $\mathcal{R}_t : S \times \mathcal{A} \to [0,1]$ at time step t is based on their weighted probabilities:

$$\mathcal{R}_t = \frac{3}{4} \cdot \mathbb{E}_{smile} + \frac{1}{4} \cdot \mathbb{E}_{laughter}.$$

Algorithm. At every RL time step t, the robot selects one of the available actions $a_t \in \mathcal{A}$ according to state $s_t \in \mathcal{S}$, executes it, senses the user's reactions and uses those obtained social signals to compute the reward signal $\mathcal{R}_t$. By employing linear function approximation, the robot has to learn a weight vector $\boldsymbol{\omega}$. The weight vector is used to compute a value $Q(s_t, a_t, \boldsymbol{\omega})$ for every action $a \in \mathcal{A}$ by calculating the dot product of the vector $\boldsymbol{\omega}$ and vectorial representation of the current state $\boldsymbol{\phi}(s_t)$:

$$Q(s_t, a_t, \boldsymbol{\omega}) := \boldsymbol{\phi}(s_t) \circ \boldsymbol{\omega}, \forall s_t \in \mathcal{S}, \forall a_t \in \mathcal{A}$$

In order to allow for learning non-linear dependencies between state values, we make use of the Fourier basis as described in Konidaris et al. [14]. Moreover, to find the optimal weight vector $\boldsymbol{\omega}$, the agent uses the reward $\mathcal{R}_t$ to update the weight vector $\boldsymbol{\omega}_t$ until the strategy converges to the optimal one [33]:

$$\Delta \boldsymbol{\omega}_t = \alpha \big(\mathcal{R}_t + \gamma \max_{a_{t+1}} Q(s_{t+1}, a_{t+1}, \boldsymbol{\omega}_t) - Q(s_t, a_t, \boldsymbol{\omega}_t) \big) \boldsymbol{\phi}(s_t)$$

4.3   Sensing Social Signals

First, we train a custom model offline for recognizing laughter from the audio modality and smiles from video images. To describe the paralinguistic content of voice, Mel Frequency Cepstral Coefficients (MFCC) spectral, pitch, energy, duration, voicing and voice quality features (extracted using the EmoVoice toolbox [35]) are employed. These features were used within an Support Vector Machine (SVM) model trained on excerpts of the Belfast Storytelling Database [16], which contains spontaneous social interactions and dialogs with a laughter focused annotation. Person independent evaluation of the model on the training database showed an unweighted accuracy of 84% for the recognition of laughter frames. For detecting smiles in the video, we apply transfer learning to fine-tune a deep convolutional neural network (VGGFace) by retraining it on the AffectNet facial expression corpus [18].

Based on the trained models audiovisual laughter recognition is carried in real-time during the interaction. The robot continuously captures the spectator's social signals with a headset microphone and webcam and analyzes them with the SSI framework [36]. Bursts of laughter are detected on a frame by frame basis: the audio signal is analyzed within a one-second sliding window that is shifted every 400 milliseconds, resulting in a decision rate of 2.5 Hz. The overall activity is monitored by applying a voice activity transformation to the signals via hamming windowing and intensity calculation. Coherent signal parts (i.e. frames) in which the mean of squared input values – multiplied by a Hamming window – that exceed predefined thresholds for intensity are identified as carriers of vocal activity and therefore serve as input for feature calculation and subsequent classification. Video is captured at a rate of 15 frames per second. Each frame is classified with the neural network model described above and the probabilistic results are averaged with the same sliding window as the audio modality to gain equally clocked classification results from both input signals.

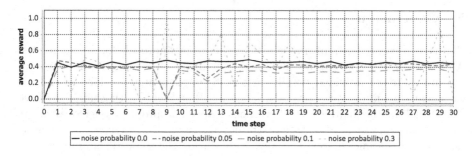

Fig. 5. Simulation results

4.4 Simulation

Several experiments were conducted as a first evaluation of the personalization approach. This is important to check whether the learning approach is implemented correctly and able to adapt to human preferences algorithmically.

Simulated User. Each artificial spectator is initialized with a random preference with regard to the robot's pitch, speech rate, volume and break. These values are unknown by the learning agent, which uses the approach from Sect. 4.2 to find the best presentation strategy. While the simulation does not use the real social signal processing component from Sect. 4.3 the reward is calculated based on simulated amusement. If a feature from the state space matches the simulated user's actual preference, the neutral reward of 0 is increased by 0.25.

Noise. In general, a simulation cannot emulate realistic human behavior. Inspired by [27] we address this issue by adding two kinds of noise: (1) non-deterministic user reactions and (2) sensor hardware and processing noise of the social signal component. The first aims to randomize the spectator's amusement, which will be dependent on more than the robot's joke presentation strategy in real interaction. This is realized by adding a random value the interval $[-1.0, 1.0]$ to the reward. The second addresses noise from the camera and microphone, which result in a wrong interpretation of the sensed human social signals.

Results. The plots in Fig. 5 averages over 30 trials, each consisting of 30 time/learning steps. This is analogous to a study with 30 participants with the robot telling 30 jokes to each of them. The learning task is non-episodic for each artificial user: there are no terminal states, the agent is provided no initial knowledge and the learned policy is reset between each trial. Performance is evaluated for 0% (baseline), 5%, 10% and 30% of noise, which randomizes the reward as described above. Learning without noise results in a pretty stable reward by about 0.5. With increasing noise the overall performance decreases as expected. In average, the reward is still very similar to the baseline most of the time, which indicates that the learning approach is able to cope with noise and outperforms table-based reinforcement learning approaches, such as in [27].

5 Conclusion

We have presented a multimodal joke generation approach for social robots. After identifying appropriate human paralinguistic and non-verbal cues from the literature we provided details on how to implement them for the embodied agent, including gaze, prosody, smile and laughter. Furthermore, we have introduced and simulated a reinforcement learning approach to personalize the robot's paralinguistic presentation strategy for the individual spectator, who is recorded with a microphone and a webcam during the show. This input is analyzed by a deep convolutional neural network and a Support Vector Machine to detect human visual smiles and audible laughter, which serve as a reward for the reinforcement learning process, aiming to maximize human amusement.

Our ultimate goal is to evaluate and to embed this socially-aware generation and personalization process in human-robot dialog, where the variety of conversation topics require to dynamically generate humorous contents on-the-fly. We believe that in real-world interaction scenarios, augmenting the robot with an adaptive artificial sense of humor will increase perceived social intelligence and thus overall result in an improved interaction experience. Future work will also investigate whether the generation and personalization of appropriate non-verbal sounds [25] is able to support a robot's humor presentation, too.

Acknowledgment. This research was funded by the European Union PRESENT project, grant agreement No. 856879.

References

1. Archakis, A., Giakoumelou, M., Papazachariou, D., Tsakona, V.: The prosodic framing of humour in conversational narratives: evidence from Greek data. J. Greek Linguist. **10**(2), 187–212 (2010)
2. Attardo, S., Pickering, L., Baker, A.: Prosodic and multimodal markers of humor in conversation. Pragmat. Cogn. **19**(2), 224–247 (2011)
3. Audrieth, A.L.: The art of using humor in public speaking. Retrieved 20 March 2005 (1998)
4. Bauman, R.: Story, Performance, and Event: Contextual Studies of Oral Narrative, vol. 10. Cambridge University Press, Cambridge (1986)
5. Bird, C.: Formulaic jokes in interaction: the prosody of riddle openings. Pragmat. Cogn. **19**(2), 268–290 (2011)
6. Chafe, W.: Discourse, Consciousness, and Time: The Flow and Displacement of Conscious Experience in Speaking and Writing. University of Chicago Press, Chicago (1994)
7. Gironzetti, E.: Prosodic and multimodal markers of humor. In: The Routledge Handbook of Language and Humor, pp. 400–413. Routledge, London (2017)
8. Gironzetti, E., Attardo, S., Pickering, L.: Smiling, gaze, and humor in conversation: a pilot study. Metapragmat. Humor: Curr. Res. Trends **14**, 235 (2016)
9. Gironzetti, E., Huang, M., Pickering, L., Attardo, S.: The role of eye gaze and smiling in humorous dyadic conversations, March 2015
10. Glenn, P.J.: Initiating shared laughter in multi-party conversations. West. J. Commun. (includes Commun. Rep.) **53**(2), 127–149 (1989)

11. Hayashi, K., Kanda, T., Miyashita, T., Ishiguro, H., Hagita, N.: Robot manzai: robot conversation as a passive-social medium. Int. J. Humanoid Rob. **5**(01), 67–86 (2008)

12. Katevas, K., Healey, P.G., Harris, M.T.: Robot comedy lab: experimenting with the social dynamics of live performance. Front. Psychol. **6**, 1253 (2015)

13. Knight, H.: Eight lessons learned about non-verbal interactions through robot theater. In: Mutlu, B., Bartneck, C., Ham, J., Evers, V., Kanda, T. (eds.) ICSR 2011. LNCS (LNAI), vol. 7072, pp. 42–51. Springer, Heidelberg (2011). https://doi.org/10.1007/978-3-642-25504-5_5

14. Konidaris, G.D., Osentoski, S., Thomas, P.S.: Value function approximation in reinforcement learning using the fourier basis. In: Burgard, W., Roth, D. (eds.) Proceedings of the Twenty-Fifth Conference on Artificial Intelligence. AAAI 2011, San Francisco, California, USA, 7–11 August 2011. AAAI Press (2011). http://www.aaai.org/ocs/index.php/AAAI/AAAI11/paper/view/3569

15. Manurung, R., Ritchie, G., Pain, H., Waller, A., O'Mara, D., Black, R.: The construction of a pun generator for language skills development. Appl. Artif. Intell. **22**(9), 841–869 (2008)

16. McKeown, G., Curran, W., Wagner, J., Lingenfelser, F., André, E.: The belfast storytelling database: a spontaneous social interaction database with laughter focused annotation. In: Affective Computing and Intelligent Interaction, pp. 166–172. IEEE (2015)

17. Mirnig, N., Stollnberger, G., Giuliani, M., Tscheligi, M.: Elements of humor: how humans perceive verbal and non-verbal aspects of humorous robot behavior. In: International Conference on Human-Robot Interaction, pp. 211–212. ACM (2017)

18. Mollahosseini, A., Hasani, B., Mahoor, M.H.: Affectnet: a database for facial expression, valence, and arousal computing in the wild. IEEE Trans. Affect. Comput. **10**(1), 18–31 (2017)

19. Nijholt, A.: Conversational agents and the construction of humorous acts, chap. 2, pp. 19–47. Wiley-Blackwell (2007)

20. Norrick, N.R.: On the conversational performance of narrative jokes: toward an account of timing. Humor **14**(3), 255–274 (2001)

21. Pickering, L., Corduas, M., Eisterhold, J., Seifried, B., Eggleston, A., Attardo, S.: Prosodic markers of saliency in humorous narratives. Discourse Processes **46**(6), 517–540 (2009)

22. Ritschel, H.: Socially-aware reinforcement learning for personalized human-robot interaction. In: Proceedings of the 17th International Conference on Autonomous Agents and MultiAgent Systems. AAMAS 2018, Stockholm, Sweden, 10–15 July 2018, pp. 1775–1777. International Foundation for Autonomous Agents and Multiagent Systems, Richland/ACM (2018)

23. Ritschel, H., André, E.: Real-time robot personality adaptation based on reinforcement learning and social signals. In: Companion of the 2017 ACM/IEEE International Conference on Human-Robot Interaction. HRI 2017, Vienna, Austria, 6–9 March 2017, pp. 265–266. ACM (2017)

24. Ritschel, H., André, E.: Shaping a social robot's humor with natural language generation and socially-aware reinforcement learning. In: Proceedings of the Workshop on NLG for Human-Robot Interaction, pp. 12–16 (2018)

25. Ritschel, H., Aslan, I., Mertes, S., Seiderer, A., André, E.: Personalized synthesis of intentional and emotional non-verbal sounds for social robots. In: 8th International Conference on Affective Computing and Intelligent Interaction. ACII 2019, Cambridge, United Kingdom, 3–6 September 2019, pp. 1–7. IEEE (2019)

26. Ritschel, H., Aslan, I., Sedlbauer, D., André, E.: Irony man: augmenting a social robot with the ability to use irony in multimodal communication with humans. In: Proceedings of the 18th International Conference on Autonomous Agents and MultiAgent Systems. AAMAS 2019, pp. 86–94. IFAAMAS (2019)
27. Ritschel, H., Baur, T., André, E.: Adapting a robot's linguistic style based on socially-aware reinforcement learning. In: 26th IEEE International Symposium on Robot and Human Interactive Communication, pp. 378–384. IEEE (2017)
28. Ritschel, H., Janowski, K., Seiderer, A., André, E.: Towards a robotic dietitian with adaptive linguistic style. In: Joint Proceeding of the Poster and Workshop Sessions of AmI-2019, the 2019 European Conference on Ambient Intelligence, Rome, Italy, 13–15 November 2019. CEUR Workshop Proceedings, vol. 2492, pp. 134–138. CEUR-WS.org (2019)
29. Ritschel, H., Kiderle, T., Weber, K., André, E.: Multimodal joke presentation for social robots based on natural-language generation and nonverbal behaviors. In: Proceedings of the 2nd Workshop on NLG for Human-Robot Interaction (2020)
30. Ritschel, H., Seiderer, A., Janowski, K., Aslan, I., André, E.: Drink-O-Mender: an adaptive robotic drink adviser. In: Proceedings of the 3rd International Workshop on Multisensory Approaches to Human-Food Interaction. MHFI 2018, pp. 3:1–3:8. ACM (2018)
31. Ritschel, H., Seiderer, A., Janowski, K., Wagner, S., André, E.: Adaptive linguistic style for an assistive robotic health companion based on explicit human feedback. In: Proceedings of the 12th ACM International Conference on PErvasive Technologies Related to Assistive Environments. PETRA 2019, Island of Rhodes, Greece, 5–7 June 2019, pp. 247–255 (2019)
32. Ruhland, K., et al.: Look me in the eyes: a survey of eye and gaze animation for virtual agents and artificial systems. In: Eurographics 2014 - State of the Art Reports, pp. 69–91 (2014)
33. Sutton, R.S., et al.: Fast gradient-descent methods for temporal-difference learning with linear function approximation. In: Proceedings of the 26th Annual International Conference on Machine Learning, pp. 993–1000. ACM (2009)
34. Umetani, T., Nadamoto, A., Kitamura, T.: Manzai robots: entertainment robots as passive media based on autocreated manzai scripts from web news articles. In: Handbook of Digital Games and Entertainment Technologies, pp. 1041–1068 (2017)
35. Vogt, T., André, E., Bee, N.: EmoVoice — a framework for online recognition of emotions from voice. In: André, E., Dybkjær, L., Minker, W., Neumann, H., Pieraccini, R., Weber, M. (eds.) PIT 2008. LNCS (LNAI), vol. 5078, pp. 188–199. Springer, Heidelberg (2008). https://doi.org/10.1007/978-3-540-69369-7_21
36. Wagner, J., Lingenfelser, F., Baur, T., Damian, I., Kistler, F., André, E.: The social signal interpretation (SSI) framework: Multimodal signal processing and recognition in real-time. In: 21st International Conference on Multimedia, pp. 831–834. ACM (2013)
37. Weber, K., Ritschel, H., Aslan, I., Lingenfelser, F., André, E.: How to shape the humor of a robot - social behavior adaptation based on reinforcement learning. In: Proceedings of the 20th ACM International Conference on Multimodal Interaction. ICMI 2018, pp. 154–162. ACM (2018)
38. Weber, K., Ritschel, H., Lingenfelser, F., André, E.: Real-time adaptation of a robotic joke teller based on human social signals. In: Proceedings of the 17th International Conference on Autonomous Agents and MultiAgent Systems. AAMAS 2018, Stockholm, Sweden, 10–15 July 2018, pp. 2259–2261. International Foundation for Autonomous Agents and Multiagent Systems, Richland/ACM (2018)
39. Wennerstrom, A.: The Music of Everyday Speech: Prosody and Discourse Analysis. Oxford University Press, Oxford (2001)

A Framework for Verifying Autonomous Robotic Agents Against Environment Assumptions

Hoang Tung Dinh$^{(\boxtimes)}$ and Tom Holvoet

Department of Computer Science, imec-DistriNet, KU Leuven,
3001 Leuven, Belgium
{hoangtung.dinh,tom.holvoet}@cs.kuleuven.be

Abstract. Guaranteeing safety is crucial for autonomous robotic agents. Formal methods such as model checking show great potential to provide guarantees on agent and multi-agent systems. However, as robotic agents often work in open, dynamic and unstructured environments, achieving high-fidelity environment models is non-trivial. Most verification approaches for agents focus on checking the internal reasoning logic without considering operating environments or focus on a specific type of environments such as grid-based or graph-based environments. In this paper we propose a framework to model and verify the decision making of autonomous robotic agents against assumptions on environments. The framework focuses on making a clear separation between agent modeling and environment modeling, as well as providing formalism to specify agent's decision making and assumptions on environments. As the first demonstration of this ongoing research, we provide an example of using the framework to verify an autonomous UAV agent performing pylon inspection.

Keywords: Verification · Model checking · Robotic

1 Introduction

Autonomous robotic agents are often considered as safety-critical. They work in an open environment and need to ensure that their behavior does not harm other entities such as human or properties.

Yet, guaranteeing safety for robotic agent's behavior is difficult. As they often work in an open, dynamic, unstructured and uncontrolled environment, ensuring that the correctness of the agent's behavior holds in all possible situations is non-trivial. The complexity of the environment is a major challenge hindering the formal verification of autonomous agents [11], as achieving a formal and high-fidelity environment model to perform verification is difficult, if not impossible.

Due to the complexity in modeling the environment, researches on formal verification of autonomous agents often focus on a specific and low-fidelity representation of environments such as grid-based [1] and graph-based [13], raising

© Springer Nature Switzerland AG 2020
Y. Demazeau et al. (Eds.): PAAMS 2020, LNAI 12092, pp. 291–302, 2020.
https://doi.org/10.1007/978-3-030-49778-1_23

concerns on the validity of verification results when deploying agent systems in real-world. Recently, environment representations based on Markov decision processes are also used [9,10]. Such representations can capture more complicated behavior of environments but are still not expressive enough to represent, for example, the temporal properties of environments.

In this paper we study the problem of verifying robotic agent's decision making against the specifications of environments. Instead of creating a concrete model of the environment for verification, we verify decision making logics of robotic agents against a set of assumptions, formalized in Linear Temporal Logic (LTL), on the behavior of the environment. The idea of verifying agent's decision making against environment assumptions was introduced in [4]. As having a high-fidelity formal model of the environment is non-trivial while often, not every detail of the environment is relevant to the verification task, it is more realistic and practical to derive a set of necessary assumptions for the agent to guarantee the correctness of its decisions. In addition, from the software engineering perspective, it is desirable to have environment assumptions defined explicitly and formally as they essentially represent the boundary conditions in which the agent system can guarantee its correctness. In contrast, a low-fidelity environment model often consists of many implicit assumptions.

In concrete, our contributions are as follows. We propose a framework to verify the decision making of robotic agents operating in open environments. Our framework provides formalism to represent the discretization logics of the perception information. The environment is represented by a set of LTL assumptions on the perception information before the discretization. We employ the NuXmv model checker that supports various types of systems and model checking techniques, which allows us to represent environments at different levels of fidelity. As the first demonstration of this ongoing research, we provide an example of using the framework to verify an autonomous UAV agent performing pylon inspection.

This paper is organized as follows. Section 2 discusses related work. Section 3 presents a general overview on the architecture of robotic agents. Section 4 describes our proposed framework. Section 5 presents an example of using the framework. Finally, Sect. 6 draws conclusions and outlines future work.

2   Related Work

Formally modeling environments remains one of the most challenging task for verification. Different environment representations were proposed. Aminof et al. [1] propose a framework for verifying multi-agent systems in parameterized grid-environments. Rubin [13] presents a verification framework for mobile agents moving on graphs. In [9,10], the verification of multi-agent systems is performed with environments modeled as Markov decision processes.

In [5,7], the behavior of a homecare robot is verified where the environment is modeled as a set of variables representing high-level sensor information such as the fridge door is being open. Those variables can be set non-deterministically at any time. In [16,17], for the same verification task for a homecare robot, the environment is represented as an agent in Brahms, an agent programming language. The environment model is limited to the non-deterministic choice of actions of the Brahms agent. Morse et al. [12] represent the environment by a probabilistic model where its actors have uncertainty in their actions' outcomes.

A common limitation of these environment representations is that their expressiveness is limited, making it difficult to encode different assumptions on the behavior of environments. So far, there has been little work focusing on formally specifying environments for model checking. Most close to our work is the work of Dennis et al. [4], where they proposed a verification methodology for agent's decision making in which one can specify environment assumptions as logical formulas on the discretized incoming perceptions of the agent. Our work differs from the work in [4] in that beside the decision making of the agent, we also take into account the discretization logics of the perception information in the verification by providing a formalism to represent the discretization logics. By doing so, we allow environment assumptions to be specified on the information before discretization.

3   Robotic Agent Architecture

In this section we provide an overview on the architecture of robotic agents. Similar to other types of agents, robotic agents interact with environments via sensing and acting.

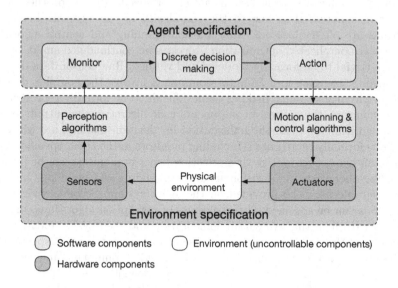

Fig. 1. A typical robotic agent architecture.

Figure 1 illustrates a typical architecture of robotic agents. Robotic agents are cyber physical systems consisting of both software and hardware components. They are equipped with **sensors** that provide raw sensing data about the physical environment. The raw sensing data is then transformed to meaningful information by **perception algorithms** such as localization and obstacle detection. The outputs of the perception algorithms are often continuous data, for example, the location of the agent in a three dimensional Cartesian coordinate system, or events such as commands from human operators. The perception information is then discretized by **monitors** to symbolic information.

The symbolic information is then taken into account by the **discrete decision making** component. The discrete decision making component performs symbolic reasoning, for example, based on well-known Belief-Desired-Intention (BDI) models or planning techniques [8] to select one or several **actions** to execute. An action could be instantaneous, for example, sending a notification or taking a picture, or it could be durative, for instance, moving to a location. When an action is executed, it activates a set of **motion planning and/or control algorithms** that compute and send commands to the agent's **actuators**, which in turns interact with the physical environment.

To verify the agent's decision making, one needs to specify the agent system and the environment in which the agent operates in. As discussed in Sect. 1, we specify the environment as a set of logical assumptions. For the verification problem, we need to define the boundary between the agent specification and the environment specification. The boundary will in turn define how the assumptions on the environment can be specified.

Environments are often modeled based on discrete variables provided by the monitors. The effects of agent actions are either specified based on the discrete variables or ignored. It is due to the complexity of the systems. Perception algorithms are often black-box while motion planning and control algorithms often involve complicated optimization processes on continuous domain, making them non-trivial to be formally modeled and verified. Raw sensor data does not have semantic meaning and actuator commands involve the complex dynamic models of physical systems, making them difficult to be formally represented.

Yet, monitors, the software components that discretize the outputs of perception algorithms to symbolic information for decision making, are white-box and can be formally represented. Including monitors in the agent specification is beneficial in two aspects. First, discretization logics in monitors can be formally verified together with the decision making, extending the boundary in which formal guarantees can be provided on the agent system. Second, environment assumptions can be specified on the outputs of perception algorithms, bringing them closer to the actual system implementation and the physical environment.

Because of these reasons, in our proposed framework, the agent specification includes the monitor components, the decision making component and the action components, as shown in Fig. 1. The other components are considered as the environment in which the agent specification needs to be verified against. The details on the agent specification and environment specification will be discussed in the next section. Note that, monitor components have not received much attention in previous work because previous verification effort only focuses on a specific reasoning technique without considering them being embedded within a system interacting with the physical environment.

4 Verification Framework

In this section we discuss the details of our proposed verification framework. Our framework employs the NuXmv model checker as the computation engine and uses the NuXmv specification language to specify the agent and the environment. We now describe the formalism of the verification framework.

4.1 Discrete Decision Making

We consider discrete decision making components implemented as policies, a popular representation of decision making logic as a result of advanced planning or learning processes [6,14,15]. Note that, our framework is not restricted to this specific decision making representation and can be extended to support different discrete decision making mechanisms such as agent programming languages. For instance, it has been shown in [7] that a complex set of robot decision making rules can be automatically translated to the NuXmv modeling language.

A decision making policy is formally defined as follows.

Definition 1. *A decision making policy is a tuple* $\sum = (\mathbf{S}, \mathbf{A}, \pi)$ *where*

- $\mathbf{S} = \{S_1, S_2, \ldots, S_n\}$ *is a set of n discrete state variables, where each state variable* S_i *takes on values in some finite domain* $Dom(S_i)$*. We call* $\mathbf{S}$ *the state vector.*
- $\mathbf{A} = \{a_1, a_2, \ldots, a_m\}$ *is a set of m actions.*
- $\pi : S_1 \times S_2 \times \cdots \times S_n \to \mathbf{A_{exec}}$ *is a complete function that maps each value of the state vector to a set of actions* $\mathbf{A_{exec}} \in \mathcal{P}(\mathbf{A})$*, where* $\mathcal{P}(\mathbf{A})$ *is the power set of* $\mathbf{A}$*.*

A decision making policy consumes the value of the state vector $\mathbf{S}$ provided by the monitors and decides a set of actions $\mathbf{A_{exec}}$ to be executed at each decision making cycle. The encoding of a decision making policy in a NuXmv specification is straightforward. Each state variable is represented by a NuXmv variable with the enumerated type. One remark is that a decision making policy is often very large with many state-vector-to-action-set mappings. While it is possible to represent each mapping in the NuXmv specification language, it would result in a very large specification which is computationally expensive to verify. Due to that, we first transform decision making policies to a compact format. Since a decision making policy can be seen as a multi-output truth table where the state vector values are inputs and the actions are Boolean outputs, one can apply two-level logic minimization [3] to reduce the truth table to a set of disjunctive normal forms (DNFs), that is, a disjunction of conjunctive clauses. Each DNF represents the condition on the state vector in which an action is executed at each decision making cycle.

We represent each action in the decision making policy as a symbol associated with its corresponding DNF. At each decision making cycle, if the symbol is *true*, that is, the DNF holds, the action is executed. Note that, the compact representation of decision making policies is not the main contribution of this paper. We aim at proposing a general framework in which different discrete decision making mechanisms can be specified and verified.

4.2 Monitor

Monitor components discretize information provided by perception algorithms. At each decision making cycle, each state variable in the state vector is updated by a monitor based on the most recent information received from the perception algorithms. The monitor of a state variable is formally defined as follows.

Definition 2. *A monitor M of a state variable is defined by a tuple $M = (I, S, s_{init}, \delta)$ where*

- *I is a set of inputs. Each input can be either a numerical value, an enumerated type value or an event.*
- *S is a finite, non-empty set of enumerated values. S is the domain of the monitored state variable.*
- *$s_{init} \in S$ is the initial value of the state variable.*
- *$\delta = I \times S \to S$ is the value transition function.*

A monitor is essentially a finite-state machine (FSM) where each state of the FSM corresponds to a value in the domain of the monitored state variable. The three types of monitor inputs cover most of possible information provided by perception algorithms. For example, spatial information such as locations, distances and maps can be represented by numerical values, object classification results can be represented by enumerated type values and notifications from other components or human operators can be represented by events.

Each monitor manipulates the value of the corresponding state variable based on the monitor's inputs. An event input can be represented as a Boolean variable that has the value *true* if the event is triggered. Enumerated type is supported natively in NuXmv and numerical type can be either real number, integer number or bounded integer number, depending on the concrete scenario or the fidelity level of the environment.

In our framework, the inputs of monitors represent the operating environments of agents. For example, a grid-map environment can be encoded using numerical inputs. A detail analysis on the scalability of the proposed framework, for example, how the size of the environment impacts the verification performance, is the subject of future work.

4.3 Environment Assumptions

Instead of building a model for the environment, in the proposed verification framework, one can specify the environment as a set of LTL assumptions on the inputs of monitors and the values of action symbols which represent whether an action is executed at each decision making cycle.

An LTL formula specifies a condition on an infinite execution trace of the system. LTL extends first-order logic with time notion via supporting temporal operators such as *always* (G) and *eventually* (F). In this work we use an extended version of LTL supported by NuXmv that also consists of past operators such as *previous state* (Y). For a complete syntax of the LTL version used, we refer readers to [2].

An LTL formula holds if it is true for every possible infinite execution trace of the system. An LTL property is verified against the conjunction of environment assumptions by checking whether the following LTL formula holds.

$$\phi_{assumptions} \Rightarrow \phi_{property} \tag{1}$$

4.4 Trade-Off Between Completeness and Fidelity

The underlying model checker used in our framework, NuXmv, supports the verification of both finite and infinite systems. The main trade-off between the completeness of the verification and the fidelity level of environment models is made on the specification of numerical variables in the set of monitor inputs I. If a numerical variable has an infinite domain, that is, its type is real or unbounded integer, the system becomes infinite. For infinite systems, NuXmv employs approaches extended from Bounded Model Checking (BMC) to perform verification. BMC verifies a system by searching for a counter-example of a bounded length that violates properties. BMC is incomplete as it might miss a counter-example if the bounded length is not large enough.

For the verification to be complete, the specified system must be finite. As numerical monitor inputs such as distance and battery level are often infinite, one needs to represent them approximately as bounded integers. Doing so makes the system finite at the cost of lowering the fidelity level of environment models. Depending on concrete applications, such approximation might affect the validity of verification results.

5   Example

We demonstrate our framework through an example where an autonomous UAV performs pylon inspection. The mission of the UAV is to autonomously visit predefined inspection points around pylons while taking into account safety requirements. The UAV system in the example was developed within the scope of the SafeDroneWare project[1] and has been deployed in a real UAV platform.

---

[1] https://www.imec-int.com/en/what-we-offer/research-portfolio/safedroneware.

5.1 Monitor Inputs

The following monitor inputs are provided by the perception components.

1. *distance_to_point*[3]: The flying distances between the current position of the UAV to each inspection point. In this model we assume that there are three inspection points.
2. *distance_to_landing_location*: The flying distance between the current position of the UAV to the landing location.
3. *altitude*: The current altitude of the UAV.
4. *battery*: The current battery level of the UAV.
5. *manual_control_on*: A request from the human operator to manually control the UAV.
6. *manual_control_off*: A request from the human operator to stop manually controlling the UAV.
7. *mission_start*: The human operator gives the UAV permission to start the mission.
8. *mission_abort*: A request from the human operator to abort the mission.
9. *configure_mission*: The mission has just been configured.
10. *communication_status*: The status of the communication link, which is continuously monitored by a third-party software component. The communication link can have three states: *stable*, *degraded* and *lost*.
11. *obstacle_detection_status*: The status of the obstacle detection component. A perception component is responsible for monitoring the state of all the hardware and algorithms performing obstacle detection. The state of the obstacle detection component can be either *stable* or *lost*.

The monitor inputs 1–4 are of numerical type, the inputs 5–9 are events and the remaining inputs are of enumerated type.

5.2 Monitors

The decision making policy of the UAV contains 16 state variables. The monitor of each state variable is specified using the NuXmv specification language according to Definition 2. Due to the lack of space, we only discuss three representative monitors. The complete specification is available online[2].

The state variable $S\_manual\_control\_request \in \{on, off\}$ represents whether the human operator wants to control the UAV manually. This state variable is updated based on two events *manual_control_on* and *manual_control_off*. As shown in Fig. 2, every time the UAV receives a *manual_control_on* event, $S\_manual\_control\_request$ turns to *on* until a *manual_control_off* event is received.

The state variable $S\_battery \in \{ok, low, critical\}$ indicates the battery level of the UAV based on predefined thresholds. Figure 3 illustrates the FSM of the monitor for the $S\_battery$ variable.

---

[2] https://github.com/hoangtungdinh/paams20-supplemental-material.

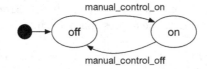

Fig. 2. The FSM for the state variable $S\_manual\_control\_request$.

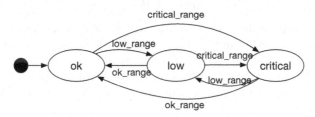

Fig. 3. The FSM for the state variable $S\_battery$. The ranges are defined as follows. $critical\_range : battery < critical\_threshold$ $low\_range : critical\_threshold \leq battery < low\_threshold$ $ok\_range : battery \geq low\_threshold$

The state variable $S\_pylon\_inspection$ keeps track of whether the UAV has inspected all the predefined points. To model the monitor of this state variable, we define an extra variable $point\_index$ to keep track of inspected points. Note that, the UAV must visit the points in a predefined order. Every time the current point is reached, that is, the distance to the point is 0, the value of $point\_index$ is increased. $S\_pylon\_inspection$ turns to $complete$ when all the points are visited. Figure 4 shows the FSMs of $point\_index$ and $S\_pylon\_inspection$ with three predefined inspection points.

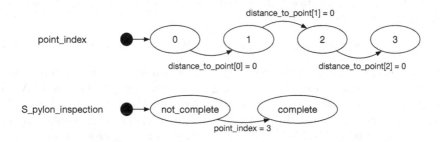

Fig. 4. The FSMs representing $point\_index$ and $S\_pylon\_inspection$.

5.3   Properties and Environment Assumptions

We present three example properties to be verified.

1. The UAV must always land at the predefined landing location.

$$G(altitude = 0 \Rightarrow distance\_to\_landing\_location = 0) \tag{2}$$

2. The UAV must only fly once it has received the `mission_start` event. (The LTL operator O means that the expression holds in at least one previous time step).

$$G(altitude > 0 \Rightarrow O(mission\_start = true)) \tag{3}$$

3. The UAV must eventually visit all the predefined points.

$$F(point\_index = 3) \tag{4}$$

During the verification process, we derive environment assumptions, both by our application knowledge and by counter-examples returned by NuXmv.

The first type of assumptions is the effects of the action execution on the environment. For example, the *altitude* of the UAV will increase when the UAV executes the *take_off* action and will decrease to 0 only when the UAV executes the land action.

$$G(take\_off \Rightarrow next(altitude) > altitude) \tag{5}$$

$$G((next(altitude) = 0 \land altitude > 0) \Rightarrow land) \tag{6}$$

Another assumption is that the UAV only changes its location, that is, the distances between the UAV and other locations are changed, by executing actions involving the movement of the UAV. Also, it can only change its location while it is flying.

$$G((next(distance\_to\_point) \neq distance\_to\_point \lor$$
$$next(distance\_to\_landing\_location) \neq distance\_to\_landing\_location)$$
$$\Rightarrow ((go\_to\_landing\_location \lor manual\_control \lor go\_to\_point) \land \tag{7}$$
$$altitude > 0))$$

We also need to assume that at the beginning, the UAV is landed at the landing location.

$$altitude = 0 \land distance\_to\_landing\_location = 0 \tag{8}$$

Note that, not all properties require the same assumptions. For example, the following assumptions are specifically to guarantee Property 3. For the UAV to complete the inspection, it must eventually receive a *configure_mission* event and a *mission_start* event. In addition, the human operator must never abort the mission, that is, the UAV must never receive a *mission_abort* event.

$$F(configure\_mission = true) \tag{9}$$

$$F(mission\_start = true) \tag{10}$$

$$G\neg(mission\_abort = true) \tag{11}$$

The last example assumption is that eventually, the UAV is never blocked.

$$FG(go\_to\_point \land point\_index < 3 \land$$
$$next(distance\_to\_point[point\_index]) < distance\_to\_point[point\_index]) \tag{12}$$

Due to the lack of space, we do not include all assumptions and properties. However, we believe that the example assumptions and properties are representative enough to understand the proposed framework. We verified the properties with two different models. In the first model, all numerical monitor inputs are specified as of type real. In the second model, all numerical monitor inputs are specified as of type bounded integer so that NuXmv can apply complete model checking techniques. In both models, NuXmv is able to verify all properties and return counter-examples if a property is violated within a few seconds. The generated counter-examples were useful as they helped us realize possible failure situations that we did not think of at the design time. Thanks to the counter-examples, we were able to derive and state explicitly all necessary assumptions for the properties to hold.

6 Conclusions

Verifying autonomous robotic agents is challenging due to the complexity of their operating environments. In this paper, we propose a framework to model and verify the decision making of autonomous robotic agents. The proposed framework makes a clear separation between the agent modeling and the environment modeling. Formalism to specify the discretization logics of the perception information is provided. The environment in the proposed framework is specified as a set of LTL assumptions on perception information. An example of verifying an autonomous UAV performing pylon inspection was provided to demonstrate the usability of the framework.

We experience that many complicated assumptions can be represented in our framework, although it requires expert knowledge in LTL to encode the assumptions. Future studies are required to validate and explore the applicability of the framework on different robotic agent systems, as well as to analyze the computational complexity of the framework. Moreover, patterns for specifying assumptions on different parts of systems such as actions' effects can be derived. We also plan to extend the framework so that it can take into account the verification of motion planning and control components.

Acknowledgment. This research is partially funded by the Research Fund KU Leuven. We thank the anonymous reviewers for their helpful comments.

References

1. Aminof, B., Murano, A., Rubin, S., Zuleger, F.: Automatic verification of multi-agent systems in parameterised grid-environments. In: Proceedings of the 2016 International Conference on Autonomous Agents & Multiagent Systems. AAMAS 2016, pp. 1190–1199. International Foundation for Autonomous Agents and Multiagent Systems, Richland (2016)
2. Bozzano, M., et al.: nuXmv 1.1. 1 User Manual (2016)

3. Coudert, O., Sasao, T.: Two-level logic minimization. In: Hassoun, S., Sasao, T. (eds.) Logic Synthesis and Verification, pp. 1–27. Springer, Boston (2002). https://doi.org/10.1007/978-1-4615-0817-5_1

4. Dennis, L.A., Fisher, M., Lincoln, N.K., Lisitsa, A., Veres, S.M.: Practical verification of decision-making in agent-based autonomous systems. Autom. Softw. Eng. **23**(3), 305–359 (2014). https://doi.org/10.1007/s10515-014-0168-9

5. Dixon, C., Webster, M., Saunders, J., Fisher, M., Dautenhahn, K.: "The fridge door is open"–temporal verification of a robotic assistant's behaviours. In: Mistry, M., Leonardis, A., Witkowski, M., Melhuish, C. (eds.) TAROS 2014. LNCS (LNAI), vol. 8717, pp. 97–108. Springer, Cham (2014). https://doi.org/10.1007/978-3-319-10401-0_9

6. Fu, J., Ng, V., Bastani, F., Yen, I.L.: Simple and fast strong cyclic planning for fully-observable nondeterministic planning problems. In: Twenty-Second International Joint Conference on Artificial Intelligence (2011)

7. Gainer, P., et al.: CRutoN: automatic verification of a robotic assistant's behaviours. In: Petrucci, L., Seceleanu, C., Cavalcanti, A. (eds.) FMICS/AVoCS -2017. LNCS, vol. 10471, pp. 119–133. Springer, Cham (2017). https://doi.org/10.1007/978-3-319-67113-0_8

8. Ingrand, F., Ghallab, M.: Deliberation for autonomous robots: a survey. Artif. Intell. **247**, 10–44 (2017)

9. Kouvaros, P., Lomuscio, A., Pirovano, E., Punchihewa, H.: Formal verification of open multi-agent systems. In: Proceedings of the 18th International Conference on Autonomous Agents and MultiAgent Systems. AAMAS 2019, pp. 179–187. International Foundation for Autonomous Agents and Multiagent Systems, Richland (2019)

10. Lomuscio, A., Pirovano, E.: A counter abstraction technique for the verification of probabilistic swarm systems. In: Proceedings of the 18th International Conference on Autonomous Agents and MultiAgent Systems. AAMAS 2019, pp. 161–169. International Foundation for Autonomous Agents and Multiagent Systems, Richland (2019)

11. Luckcuck, M., Farrell, M., Dennis, L.A., Dixon, C., Fisher, M.: Formal specification and verification of autonomous robotic systems: a survey. ACM Comput. Surv. **52**, 100:1–100:41 (2019)

12. Morse, J., Araiza-Illan, D., Lawry, J., Richards, A., Eder, K.: Formal specification and analysis of autonomous systems under partial compliance. arXiv:1603.01082 [cs], March 2016

13. Rubin, S.: Parameterised verification of autonomous mobile-agents in static but unknown environments. In: Proceedings of the 2015 International Conference on Autonomous Agents and Multiagent Systems. AAMAS 2015, pp. 199–208. International Foundation for Autonomous Agents and Multiagent Systems, Richland (2015)

14. Shalev-Shwartz, S., Shammah, S., Shashua, A.: Safe, multi-agent, reinforcement learning for autonomous driving. arXiv:1610.03295 [cs, stat], October 2016

15. Spaan, M.T.J., Veiga, T.S., Lima, P.U.: Decision-theoretic planning under uncertainty with information rewards for active cooperative perception. Auton. Agents Multi-Agent Syst. **29**(6), 1157–1185 (2014). https://doi.org/10.1007/s10458-014-9279-8

16. Webster, M., et al.: Toward reliable autonomous robotic assistants through formal verification: a case study. IEEE Trans. Hum.-Mach. Syst. **46**, 186–196 (2016)

17. Webster, M., et al.: Formal verification of an autonomous personal robotic assistant. In: Proceedings of the AAAI FVHMS, pp. 74–79 (2014)

Impact of Trust and Reputation Based Brokerage on the CloudAnchor Platform

Bruno Veloso[1,2], Benedita Malheiro[2,3]([⊠]), Juan Carlos Burguillo[4], and João Gama[2,5]

[1] UPT - Portucalense University, Porto, Portugal
[2] INESC TEC, Porto, Portugal
bruno.m.veloso@inesctec.pt
[3] ISEP/IPP – School of Engineering, Polytechnic Institute of Porto, Porto, Portugal
mbm@isep.ipp.pt
[4] ETSET/UVigo – School of Telecommunication Engineering, University of Vigo, Vigo, Spain
j.c.burguillo@uvigo.es
[5] FEP/UP – Faculty of Economics, University of Porto, Porto, Portugal
jgama@fep.up.pt

Abstract. This paper analyses the impact of trust and reputation modelling on CloudAnchor, a business-to-business brokerage platform for the transaction of single and federated resources on behalf of Small and Medium Sized Enterprises (SME). In CloudAnchor, businesses act as providers or consumers of Infrastructure as a Service (IaaS) resources. The platform adopts a multi-layered multi-agent architecture, where providers, consumers and virtual providers, representing provider coalitions, engage in trust & reputation-based provider look-up, invitation, acceptance and resource negotiations. The goal of this work is to assess the relevance of the distributed trust model and centralised fuzzified reputation service in the number of resources successfully transacted, the global turnover, brokerage fees, losses, expenses and time response. The results show that trust and reputation based brokerage has a positive impact on the CloudAnchor performance by reducing losses and the execution time for the provision of both single and federated resources and increasing considerably the number of federated resources provided.

Keywords: Brokerage · Multi-agent platform · Negotiation · Trust & Reputation · Infrastructure-as-a-Service

1 Introduction

Cloud computing aims to simplify the task of planning ahead the provision of storage and computing resources. This computing paradigm provides the flexibility to manage the contracted resources according to the existing workload. According to Gartner (2019), IaaS cloud computing revenues are expected to grow 97 % to a total of 81.5 billion by 2022 [12]. In this context, brokers are

© Springer Nature Switzerland AG 2020
Y. Demazeau et al. (Eds.): PAAMS 2020, LNAI 12092, pp. 303–314, 2020.
https://doi.org/10.1007/978-3-030-49778-1_24

emerging as the preferential middle-ware to match demand and offer between stakeholders. Specifically, IaaS brokers are entities that manage the use, performance and delivery of cloud services, negotiating the relationships between cloud providers and consumers [21]. For SME providers, brokers offer additional business opportunities and simplify the management and integration of disparate cloud services—potentially across different providers—fostering the creation of provider coalitions. In the case of SME consumers, brokers provide seamless partner look-up and invitation as well as Service Level Agreement (SLA) negotiation services, increasing the chances of obtaining the desired resources at the best price and within a given deadline. The goal of CloudAnchor is to support the consumption and provision of IaaS by SME.

While CloudAnchor has been previously reported in [32–34] and [7], this work extends the algorithmic design and experimental evaluation to accommodate Trust & Reputation based services. To improve the performance of CloudAnchor, the algorithm has been enriched with SME profiling, comprising of a decentralised inter-business trust modelling and a centralised fuzzified business reputation service, and the provision of federated resources. The decentralised trust model of peers takes into account all past interactions between pairs of businesses, including invitation/acceptance, SLA negotiation and enforcement outcomes, and not just the usual SLA enforcement results. This novel approach allows consumers to invite providers based on the outcome of past provider/consumer invitation/acceptance ratios as well as provider and consumer SLA establishment/negotiation and enforcement. Regarding the SLA enforcement, the results are provided by the SLA monitoring and enforcement module, which is external to the CloudAnchor platform. Additionally, businesses wanting to use the reputation as a service, which takes into account all intra-business interactions within the platform, have to pay an additional fee. Extensive and in-depth experimental evaluation took place to assess the impact of the new SME profiling and provider federations against the previous implementation.

This paper contains six sections. Section 2 describes related cloud brokerage platforms. Section 3 presents CloudAnchor. Section 4 describes the proposed Trust & Reputation model. Section 5 reports on the tests and discusses the results. Finally, Sect. 6 draws the conclusions and suggests future developments.

2   Cloud Brokerage

A brokerage platform is an information system which provides resource, service or partner brokerage services automatically on behalf of businesses. They are frequently found in business-to-business (B2B) application scenarios where the relationships between businesses are decentralised and include both cooperative and competitive scenarios. Due to this inherently distributed and decentralised nature, brokerage platforms frequently adopt the multi-agent system (MAS) paradigm for modelling businesses. A MAS is, according to Michael Wooldridge (2009), a system composed of a group of interacting agents, which are more proficient together than the sum of their individual competences [36]. Brokers typically offer partner look-up, invitation and acceptance as well as SLA negotiation, establishment, enforcement and termination services. The terms of the service provision are negotiated between provider and consumer in order to establish the binding SLA.

Brokerage platforms are popular in the cloud domain where they manage the use, performance and delivery of cloud services and negotiate relationships between providers and consumers, including the aggregation, customisation and integration of services [11]. For the NIST, a cloud broker may include service intermediation, aggregation/federation and arbitrage [21]. Such tasks require modelling resources (single and federated), businesses and their relationships as well as methodologies for partner discovery, resource negotiation and resource provision [1,6,8,10,15,18,19,23,25,27,28,30,35,37]. Habib, Ries and Mühlhäuser (2010) identify several parameters to select reliable providers [14]: (i) SLA templates; (ii) certification; (iii) portability; (iv) interoperability; (v) location of the data centre; (vi) customer support facilities; (vii) performance tests; $(viii)$ deployment models; (ix) federated identity management; (x) security measures; and (xi) user recommendation, feedback and publicity [1].

3   CloudAnchor

The CloudAnchor brokerage platform presented in [33,34] was designed for the transaction of individual or federated IaaS resources between provider and consumer SME. The platform integrates, among other components, an authentication layer, a brokerage layer, including an automated partner look-up and resource negotiation services; and an abstraction framework, interfacing with different IaaS platforms [22].

This work focuses on the brokerage layer, which orchestrates the interaction between cloud consumers and cloud providers. Figure 1 presents the broker architecture. It is organised in interface, agreement, business and market layers, and comprises five types of specialised agents: (i) interface agents to interact with consumer and provider businesses; (ii) agreement agents to manage SLA instances; (iii) business agents to model consumer and provider businesses; (iv) market delegate agents to negotiate specific resources on behalf of consumer and provider businesses; and (v) layer manager agents responsible for the management of each platform layer. Each business (consumer or provider) is represented in the platform by the corresponding: (i) interface agent located in interface layer; (ii) agreement agent located in agreement layer; (iii) business agent in the business layer; and (iv) an undetermined number of delegate agents involved in specific resource negotiations in the market layer. These agents are identified by a trading code, preventing third parties from intruding in undergoing negotiations.

In terms of the B2B model, the platform implements the standard pay as you go model, $i.e.$, only items that are successfully provided will be paid. In terms of standards, the platform adopts: (i) standard REST Web Service interfaces for the interaction with businesses (via the dedicated interface agents); (ii) Business Process Model Notation to define each business behaviour within the platform;

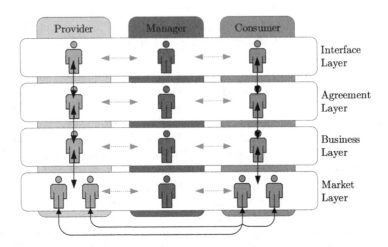

Fig. 1. Brokerage platform architecture

(*iii*) standard specifications for SLA representation; and (*iv*) standard bilateral negotiation protocols. The platform is open (*i.e.*, providers and consumers can register and de-register at will), modular, (*i.e.*, functionalities can be added and removed at will), and scalable (*i.e.*, the platform can be distributed over multiple computing nodes).

The platform processes SME (business registration/de-registration and resource request/offer) and cloud infrastructure (SLA fulfillment/violation) events. These events drive the execution of the business registration and de-registration service, provider look-up and invitation service (resource request), provider resource publication service (resource offer) and SLA termination service (SLA violation/fulfillment). The registration process involves two steps: (*i*) the upload of the business data, including the acceptable brokerage fee range; and (*ii*) the negotiation of the business brokerage SLA (bSLA), including the business brokerage fee. In particular, whenever a consumer requests a new resource via its interface agent (resource request event), it triggers the resource finding process. The consumer business agent automatically looks up and invites providers for negotiation. If the invited provider business agents accept the invitation, dedicated delegate market agents are created by both consumer and provider business agents to negotiate and establish a resource SLA (rSLA). If the providers are unable to provide the resource single-handedly, the platform attempts to create a virtual provider. Virtual providers are temporary coalitions of providers, established on the fly, to provide federated resources, *i.e.*, sets of resources which single providers were unable to provide. The provision of federated resources requires the invitation and negotiation of a coalition SLA (cSLA) between providers willing to meet together large consumer requests. Specifically, it corresponds to the creation of a virtual provider supported by a coalition of providers. When an rSLA terminates, the parties involved (consumer and provider) are notified (fulfillment or violation event).

The provision of a resource results in several payments: (i) the consumer pays the negotiated resource fee (specified in the rSLA) to the provider; (ii) the provider pays the accorded brokerage fee (specified in its bSLA) to the platform; and (iii) the consumer pays the agreed brokerage fee (specified in its bSLA) to the platform. In the case of a federated resource, there is the additional brokerage fee that the federated providers pay to the platform. As a result, when two businesses establish a resource provision contract (rSLA), they must fulfill the agreed brokerage, coalition (in the case of a federated resource) and service provision terms. Whenever a business fails to fulfill an established SLA, it must, according to the default SLA terms, reimburse the partners of all incurred expenses.

This work builds trust and reputation profiles of the businesses registered in CloudAnchor to enhance the performance of the delivered services. Each consumer and provider business agent creates and maintains local trust models of its peers based on the outcomes of the corresponding direct interactions: partner invitation (accepted or rejected), SLA negotiation (success or failure) and SLA enforcement (fulfilled or violated). Furthermore, a fuzzified version of the local trust models is shared with a dedicated RaaS agent, which, in turn, provides a payed business reputation service. These models support all future peer interaction, namely, provider invitation (by a consumer or a virtual provider), provider acceptance and SLA negotiation. From the platform's perspective, the local peer trust models form a decentralised trust system.

4   Trust & Reputation Modelling

Trust is, by default, a subjective property of direct (one-to-one) relationships attributed by a trustor to a trustee and, according to Castelfranchi, implies a decision to rely on someone [5]. Built from the outcomes of past interactions, it is typically intended to be used in future interactions between trustor and trustee. Reputation is obtained from third parties and can be used to characterise new business partners or complement the trust built from first hand information. Together, trust and reputation constitute an extremely important dyadic mechanism of social order and a very cost-effective governance tool for all types of social interactions [31]. These models are widely used on cloud brokers to assess the provider proposals as well as, as referred by Bonatti *et al.*, to filter the best candidates to invite [3].

Pinyol and Sabater (2013) classify reputation and trust models according to: (i) the paradigm, *i.e.* if the model is cognitive or numerical; (ii) the information sources; (iii) the visibility, *i.e.* if the trust can be observed by other agents; (iv) the granularity, *i.e.* the context of the trust information; (v) the source behaviour, *e.g.* credible or deceptive; and (vi) the type of information exchanged [26]. Typically, the trust model is built based on a set of evidence-based features [16]: (i) SLA outcomes [1,2,9,10,13,15,20,23,24,29,35]; (ii) audits [13]; (iii) measurements and ratings [13,15,20,23,24,29]; (iv) self-assessment [9,13,15,23,24,29]; and (v) certificates [13]. However, the majority of B2B brokerage platforms build and rely on trust models [20,24] and/or reputation [15,17,23,24,27,29] models based on the outcomes of SLA enforcement, to support SLA negotiation and, thus, partner selection. The agent-based cloud brokers analysed in Sect. 2 use trust and/or reputation models in the partner discovery stage [10,24,35] and in the SLA negotiation stage [27].

4.1   CloudAnchor Inter-Agent Trust

The CloudAnchor platform was extended with a distributed decentralised trust model, where businesses maintain local (partial and incomplete) trust models of themselves and of the business partners they interacted with (since trust is exclusively based on one-to-one or first hand interactions). Each entity (platform, consumer, provider and virtual provider) builds these local models based on their past common interactions regarding successful invitations, negotiations and SLA. The proposed distributed trust model implements, according to Pinyol and Sabater (2013) [26] classification, a local (granularity), private (visibility) numerical approach (paradigm) based solely on direct interactions (sources). The trust model supports all brokerage stages: provider invitation (I), SLA negotiation (N) and SLA enforcement (E). Each business agent builds corresponding self and partner models. By default, at start up, businesses are fully trusted. For a given brokerage stage S, the local dynamic trustworthiness attributed by the current trustor c to the partner trustee p is given recursively by Eq. 1:

$$T_S(c,p)_n = \frac{n-1}{n} \times T_S(c,p)_{n-1} + \frac{1}{n} \times Out_{S,n} \tag{1}$$

where n is the number of stage S interactions accomplished between c and p, and $Out_{S,n}$ is the binary outcome of the last stage S interaction – success (1) or failure (0). As a result, each business agent builds local partner invitation (I), SLA negotiation (N) and SLA enforcement (E) models: (i) $T_I(c,p)_n$ corresponds to the ratio of acceptances versus invitations to negotiate; (ii) $T_N(c,p)_n$ is the ratio of established versus negotiated SLA; and (iii) $T_E(c,p)_n$ is the ratio of fulfilled versus established SLA. Additionally, businesses maintain their own I, N and E self models. Equation 2 represents, for a given brokerage stage S, the self trustworthiness of business c:

$$T_S(c)_n = \frac{n-1}{n} \times T_S(c)_{n-1} + \frac{1}{n} \times Out_{S,n} \tag{2}$$

where n is the total number of stage S interactions accomplished with all business partners and $Out_{S,n}$ is the binary outcome of the last stage S interaction. In the case of a virtual provider v established on behalf of a consumer c by a coalition of m providers, the self trust $T_S(v)_n$ is obtained through Eq. 3, where $T_S(c,p_i)_n$ corresponds to the current trustworthiness of provider p_i according to consumer c. Equation 3 returns the average trustworthiness of the providers in the coalition as perceived by c.

$$T_S(v)_n = \frac{1}{m} \sum_{i=1}^{m} T_S(c,p_i)_n \tag{3}$$

4.2   CloudAnchor System-Wide Fuzzy Reputation

The platform includes an RaaS agent which maintains the reputation of the registered businesses. This centralised service represents the many-to-one nature of reputation. The reputation values are fuzzified since they rely on incomplete and partial information [4]. Businesses decide at registration whether to accept this service access conditions, which imply the payment of an additional fee.

The RaaS agent uses the fuzzified trustworthiness and justification data periodically received from the registered businesses to build their global reputation model. Equation 4 presents the dynamic reputation score of business c based on the peer feedback received so far:

$$R_S(c) = \begin{cases} \dfrac{N_{HT}}{N_T} & : P_c \neq \emptyset \\ 1 & : P_c = \emptyset \end{cases} \tag{4}$$

where N_{HT} represents the number of justifications in support of high trustworthiness received from all peers, N_T is the total number of justifications (regardless of their fuzzy values) received from all peers and P_c represents the set of peers of business c who volunteered feedback. At start up, businesses enjoy a default reputation of one (1).

Businesses and the RaaS agent share the default fuzzification rules displayed in Algorithm 1. In the case of the fuzzification of the peer trust, $V_S = T_S(c, p)$ and, in the case of the fuzzification of the business reputation, $V_S = R_S(c)$. Businesses can, alternatively, define their own specific fuzzification rules. The HIGH, MEDIUM and LOW values correspond to 1.00, 0.75 and 0.50, respectively.

Algorithm 1: Default Platform Fuzzification Rules

```
rule "FDft-001"
when m: Value( V_S >= 0.90 ) then
     modify( m )  status=Value.HIGH;
end
rule "FDft-002"
when m: Value( V_S( >= 0.80 && V_S < 0.90 ) then
     modify( m )  status=Value.MEDIUM;
end
rule "FDft-003"
when m: Value( V_S < 0.80 ) then
     modify( m )  status=Value.LOW;
end
```

---

5   Tests and Results

Experiments were performed to assess the impact of the trust (T) as well as trust & reputation (T&R) based services in the performance of the platform. T and T&R will be compared against the base algorithm, i.e., without business trust & reputation modelling. This analysis contemplates the global turnover, losses, costs, and negotiation time. The global turnover is the total value paid for the supplied resources, including resource provisioning, brokerage and coalition fees. The global loss corresponds to the brokerage and coalition fees paid regarding faulty services. In terms of hardware, the tests were executed on a platform with one quad-core i7-2600 3.40 GHz CPU with two threads per core, 16 GiB RAM and a 1.8 TiB of storage capacity.

These experiments involved thirty consumers and thirty providers with renegotiation of the brokerage fees. Consumers and providers are grouped into three sets of 10 businesses with 60%, 80% and 100% of average SLA enforcement trustworthiness ($\overline{T_E}$). Each provider holds 1000 resources. Depending on the experiment, each consumer requires 1000 single resources or forty federated resources composed of 25 VM each. Table 1 summarises the carried tests.

Table 1. Tested scenarios

Scenario	Businesses	VM/business	$\overline{T_E}$ (%)
1	30 consumers 30 providers	1000 × 1 Short Term	10 × [60, 80, 100]
2	30 consumers 30 providers	1000 × 1 Long Term	10 × [60, 80, 100]
3	30 consumers 30 providers	1000 × 25 Short Term	10 × [60, 80, 100]
4	30 consumers 30 providers	1000 × 25 Long Term	10 × [60, 80, 100]

The platform holds in fact 120 000 faultless resources since there is an overall 20% resource provision fault rate. When a business violates the terms of an established rSLA, it must reimburse its partner of the negotiated resource price and involved brokerage fees. In the first scenario, each consumer requires 1000 individual resources for a period of 1 month, while, in the second scenario, each consumer requires 1000 individual resources for a period of 5 months.

By default, businesses are fully trusted (100%) at start up. Then, with time, they exhibit a dynamic $\overline{T_E}$ according to the pre-defined fault rate. Each test corresponds to a period of 10 months for the short-term scenario and a period of 30 months for the long-term scenario, where the first 5 months represent the cold-state of the platform and the last 5 or 25 represent the warm operation of the platform. For this reason, this analysis focuses always on the last 5 months of operation. Both experimental scenarios were executed with the base (B), trust (T) and trust & reputation (T&R) based Invitation/acceptance and Negotiation services with bSLA renegotiation.

Table 2 displays the results of the short-term and long-term scenarios with single and federated resources, including the total number of established rSLA, the number of successfully provided resources (VM) as well as the average transacted value $\overline{TV}$ and the average rSLA negotiation time per resource. In the case

Table 2. Lease of single and federated resources

		Single resources			Federated resources		
		B	T	T& R	B	T	T& R
Short Term	rSLA	144 998	88 898	99 465	21 115	24 436	27 924
	VM	95 978	73 626	80 493	13 714	21 649	23 112
	$\overline{TV}$ (€)	62.3	44.2	45.6	61.6	41.7	44.5
	$\overline{\Delta t}$ (ms)	219.6	42.5	38.2	223.4	92.7	56.6
Long Term	rSLA	149 996	92 296	105 673	21 164	25 286	27 426
	VM	95 996	75 653	82 711	13 764	21 953	22 459
	$\overline{TV}$ (€)	62.9	44.9	48.0	61.9	42.5	45.1
	$\overline{\Delta t}$ (ms)	220.7	49.2	48.4	181.5	64.2	59.1

of single resources, the percentage of violated rSLA (difference between the negotiated rSLA and the resources actually provided) is 35 % with the base approach, 17 % with T and 19 % with T&R for short term resources and 19 % with T and 22 % T&R for long term resources. The results show that the highest number of VM is obtained with the base algorithm, the lowest average transacted value with T and, finally, the fastest algorithm with T&R. With federated resources, the highest number of resources is obtained with T&R, the lowest average resource price with T and the fastest rSLA negotiation time with T&R. When considering simultaneously the number of resources provided, the average resource price and average run time, the T&R based services consistently display the best results.

Table 3 assesses the impact of providing T and T&R based services against the base approach, considering turnover, losses, costs, negotiation time and number of single and federated resources successfully leased in both short and long term scenarios. While in the case of single resources all values decrease, losses

Table 3. Impact of trust and reputation based services

		Single resources		Federated resources	
		T	T& R	T	T& R
Short Term	ΔTurn (%)	−46	−39	−4	20
	ΔLoss (%)	−73	−67	−66	−39
	ΔCost (%)	−33	−26	32	48
	ΔVM (%)	−23	−16	58	69
	Δt (%)	−81	−83	−59	−75
Long Term	ΔTurn (%)	−44	−35	1	17
	ΔLoss (%)	−71	−58	−59	−36
	ΔCost (%)	−43	−52	7	−14
	ΔVM (%)	−21	−14	59	63
	Δt (%)	−78	−79	−65	−67

and negotiation time drop significantly. In the case of federated resources, the T and T&R approaches present a considerable reduction of negotiation time, losses and costs as well as an increase in terms of resources provided.

These results illustrate the advantages of providing T and T&R based brokerage and negotiation services. When considering simultaneously the number of resources successfully traded, the negotiation time and the global turnover, costs and losses, T&R based services are the best approach. Specifically, in the case of federated resources, T&R based services outperform all alternatives.

6   Conclusions and Future Developments

The enrichment of CloudAnchor with trust and fuzzified reputation business modelling allowed the refinement of the look-up, invitation, acceptance and negotiation platform services. This novel business model takes all past interactions into account, including provider invitation, resource negotiation and resource provision, and not just the SLA enforcement outcomes. This allows: (i) consumers to invite providers based on the outcome of past invitations, SLA negotiations and SLA enforcements; and (ii) providers to decide whether or not to accept an invitation for negotiation based on the outcome of past SLA negotiation and SLA enforcement. The trust & reputation based results demonstrate the usefulness of the model for SME, displaying stable turnovers and loss decrease. Concerning the T&R model, the results prove that while the turnover and costs are in line with the number of resources provided, the losses and negotiation time decrease considerably. Additionally, in the case of federated resources, the trust & reputation model improves significantly the number of resources provided.

In terms of future developments, the plan is to: (i) enrich SLA templates with new parameters to meet increasing business demands; (ii) create virtual providers at the request of consumers as well as of providers; and (iii) convert SLA into smart contracts by adopting blockchain technology.

Acknowledgements. This work was partially financed by CloudAnchor: Modular Platform for the Integration and Management of Federated Cloud Computing Platforms – projects QREN N. 23151 and «POCI-01-0145-FEDER-006961», and by National Funds through the Portuguese funding agency, FCT – Fundação para a Ciência e a Tecnologia, within project UIDB/50014/2020.

References

1. Amato, A., Di Martino, B., Venticinque, S.: Evaluation and brokering of service level agreements for negotiation of cloud infrastructures. In: 2012 International Conference for Internet Technology and Secured Transactions, pp. 144–149. IEEE (2012)
2. Awasthi, S.K., Vij, S.R., Mukhopadhyay, D., Agrawal, A.J.: Multi-strategy based automated negotiation: BGP based architecture. In: 2016 International Conference on Computing, Communication and Automation (ICCCA), pp. 588–593. IEEE (2016)

3. Bonatti, P., Oliveira, E., Sabater-Mir, J., Sierra, C., Toni, F.: On the integration of trust with negotiation, argumentation and semantics. Knowl. Eng. Rev. **29**(1), 31–50 (2014)
4. Carbó, J., Molina, J.M., Dávila, J.: Trust management through fuzzy reputation. Int. J. Coop. Inform. Syst. **12**(01), 135–155 (2003)
5. Castelfranchi, C., Falcone, R.: Principles of trust for MAS: cognitive anatomy, social importance, and quantification. In: Proceedings of the 3rd International Conference on Multi Agent Systems, pp. 72–79, July 1998
6. Celesti, A., Tusa, F., Villari, M., Puliafito, A.: How to enhance cloud architectures to enable cross-federation. In: Proceedings of the 2010 IEEE 3rd International Conference on Cloud Computing. CLOUD 2010, pp. 337–345. IEEE Computer Society, Washington, DC (2010)
7. Cunha, R., Veloso, B., Malheiro, B.: Renegotiation of electronic brokerage contracts. In: Rocha, Á., Correia, A.M., Adeli, H., Reis, L.P., Costanzo, S. (eds.) WorldCIST 2017. AISC, vol. 570, pp. 41–50. Springer, Cham (2017). https://doi.org/10.1007/978-3-319-56538-5_5
8. Cuomo, A., et al.: An SLA-based broker for cloud infrastructures. J. Grid Comput. **11**(1), 1–25 (2013)
9. Fan, W., Perros, H.: A novel trust management framework for multi-cloud environments based on trust service providers. Knowl.-Based Syst. **70**, 392–406 (2014)
10. Ferrer, A.J., et al.: OPTIMIS: a holistic approach to cloud service provisioning. Future Gener. Comput. Syst. **28**(1), 66–77 (2012)
11. Fowley, F., Pahl, C., Jamshidi, P., Fang, D., Liu, X.: A classification and comparison framework for cloud service brokerage architectures. IEEE Trans. Cloud Comput. **6**(2), 358–371 (2018)
12. Gartner Inc.: Magic quadrant for cloud infrastructure as a service (2019). https://www.gartner.com/doc/reprints?id=1-1CMAPXNO&ct=190709. accessed December 2019
13. Habib, S.M., Hauke, S., Ries, S., Mühlhäuser, M.: Trust as a facilitator in cloud computing: a survey. J. Cloud Comput. **1**(1), 1–18 (2012)
14. Habib, S.M., Ries, S., Mühlhäuser, M.: Cloud computing landscape and research challenges regarding trust and reputation. In: 2010 7th International Conference on Ubiquitous Intelligence & Computing and 7th International Conference on Autonomic & Trusted Computing (UIC/ATC), pp. 410–415. IEEE (2010)
15. He, Q., Yan, J., Kowalczyk, R., Jin, H., Yang, Y.: An agent-based framework for service level agreement management. In: 2007 11th International Conference on Computer Supported Cooperative Work in Design. CSCWD 2007, pp. 412–417. IEEE (2007)
16. Huang, J., Nicol, D.M.: Trust mechanisms for cloud computing. J. Cloud Comput. **2**(1), 1–14 (2013)
17. Irissappane, A.A., Jiang, S., Zhang, J.: A framework to choose trust models for different E-marketplace environments. In: IJCAI, pp. 213–219 (2013)
18. Javed, B., Bloodsworth, P., Rasool, R.U., Munir, K., Rana, O.: Cloud market maker: an automated dynamic pricing marketplace for cloud users. Future Gener. Comput. Syst. **54**, 52–67 (2016)
19. Kertész, A., Kecskemeti, G., Brandic, I.: An interoperable and self-adaptive approach for SLA-based service virtualization in heterogeneous Cloud environments. Future Gener. Comput. Syst. **32**, 54–68 (2014)
20. Kumawat, S., Tomar, D.: SLA-aware trust model for cloud service deployment. Int. J. Comput. Appl. **90**(10), 10–15 (2014)

21. Liu, F., et al.: NIST Cloud Computing Reference Architecture: Recommendations of the National Institute of Standards and Technology. CreateSpace Independent Publishing Platform (2012). (Special Publication 500–292)

22. Meireles, F., Malheiro, B.: Integrated management of IaaS resources. In: Lopes, L., et al. (eds.) Euro-Par 2014. LNCS, vol. 8806, pp. 73–84. Springer, Cham (2014). https://doi.org/10.1007/978-3-319-14313-2_7

23. Messina, F., Pappalardo, G., Rosaci, D., Santoro, C., Sarné, G.: A trust-aware, self-organizing system for large-scale federations of utility computing infrastructures. Future Gener. Comput. Syst. **56**, 77–94 (2016)

24. Pawar, P.S., Rajarajan, M., Dimitrakos, T., Zisman, A.: Trust assessment using cloud broker. In: Zhou, J., Gal-Oz, N., Zhang, J., Gudes, E. (eds.) IFIPTM 2014. IAICT, vol. 430, pp. 237–244. Springer, Heidelberg (2014). https://doi.org/10.1007/978-3-662-43813-8_18

25. Pawluk, P., Simmons, B., Smit, M., Litoiu, M., Mankovski, S.: Introducing STRATOS: a cloud broker service. In: 2012 IEEE Fifth International Conference on Cloud Computing, pp. 891–898. IEEE (2012)

26. Pinyol, I., Sabater-Mir, J.: Computational trust and reputation models for open multi-agent systems: a review. Artif. Intell. Rev. **40**(1), 1–25 (2013)

27. Shakshuki, E.M., Falasi, A.A., Serhani, M.A., Elnaffar, S.: The sky: a social approach to clouds federation. Procedia Comput. Sci. **19**, 131–138 (2013)

28. Sim, K.M.: Agent-based cloud computing. IEEE Trans. Serv. Comput. **5**(4), 564–577 (2012)

29. Stantchev, V., Schröpfer, C.: Negotiating and enforcing QoS and SLAs in grid and cloud computing. In: Abdennadher, N., Petcu, D. (eds.) GPC 2009. LNCS, vol. 5529, pp. 25–35. Springer, Heidelberg (2009). https://doi.org/10.1007/978-3-642-01671-4_3

30. Tordsson, J., Montero, R.S., Moreno-Vozmediano, R., Llorente, I.M.: Cloud brokering mechanisms for optimized placement of virtual machines across multiple providers. Future Gener. Comput. Syst. **28**(2), 358–367 (2012)

31. Urbano, J., Rocha, A.P., Oliveira, E.: A socio-cognitive perspective of trust. In: Ossowski, S. (ed.) Agreement Technologies. Law, Governance and Technology Series, vol. 8, pp. 419–429. Springer, Dordrecht (2013). https://doi.org/10.1007/978-94-007-5583-3_23

32. Veloso, B.: Media content personalisation brokerage platform. Ph.D. thesis, University of Vigo, Vigo, Spain, September 2017

33. Veloso, B., Malheiro, B., Burguillo, J.C.: CloudAnchor: agent-based brokerage of federated cloud resources. In: Demazeau, Y., Ito, T., Bajo, J., Escalona, M.J. (eds.) PAAMS 2016. LNCS (LNAI), vol. 9662, pp. 207–218. Springer, Cham (2016). https://doi.org/10.1007/978-3-319-39324-7_18

34. Veloso, B., Meireles, F., Malheiro, B., Burguillo, J.C.: Federated IaaS resource brokerage. In: Developing Interoperable and Federated Cloud Architecture, pp. 252–280. IGI Global (2016)

35. Venticinque, S., Aversa, R., Di Martino, B., Rak, M., Petcu, D.: A cloud agency for SLA negotiation and management. In: Guarracino, M.R., et al. (eds.) Euro-Par 2010. LNCS, vol. 6586, pp. 587–594. Springer, Heidelberg (2011). https://doi.org/10.1007/978-3-642-21878-1_72

36. Wooldridge, M.: An Introduction to Multiagent Systems. Wiley, Hoboken (2009)

37. Yangui, S., Marshall, I.J., Laisne, J.P., Tata, S.: CompatibleOne: the open source cloud broker. J. Grid Comput. **12**(1), 93–109 (2014)

Formal Verification of Autonomous UAV Behavior for Inspection Tasks Using the Knowledge Base System IDP

Jan Vermaelen$^{(\boxtimes)}$ (ID), Hoang Tung Dinh$^{(\boxtimes)}$ (ID), and Tom Holvoet$^{(\boxtimes)}$ (ID)

Department of Computer Science, imec-DistriNet, KU Leuven,
3001 Leuven, Belgium
{jan.vermaelen,hoangtung.dinh,tom.holvoet}@cs.kuleuven.be

Abstract. Unmanned Aerial Vehicles (UAVs) have become useful tools in industries. In this paper, we verify the behavior of an autonomous UAV executing an inspection task. More specifically, we look into the use of the knowledge base system IDP as a verification tool. We propose an approach for the modeling and verification of the safety-critical UAV and its environment in IDP. The methodology and modeling choices that are beneficial for the performance of the verification task and the readability of the model are denoted. We identify the need for discrete domains and investigate the consequences. Verification is successfully achieved using both Bounded Model Checking (BMC) and Invariant Checking (IC).

Keywords: IDP · Unmanned Aerial Vehicle · Autonomous system · Model · Verification

1 Introduction

In recent years, Unmanned Aerial Vehicles (UAVs) have become increasingly popular in industries. They are, compared to human performance, very fast and agile. The interest arose to use them for various tasks, such as inspection tasks. The UAV can be equipped with an autopilot to automate the process. Companies providing inspection and monitoring services using UAV systems already exist.

The application verified in this research originates from a setting in which a UAV operates on an industrial site, inspecting the state, integrity, and operation of machines, reservoirs, and buildings. The flight goal of the UAV consists of autonomously achieving a visual inspection of artifacts at several predefined locations. Achieving this goal requires the execution of autonomous actions regarding take-off, navigation, height adjustment, capturing images, and landing, as well as the correct scheduling of these actions.

The UAV might be deployed along with human actors and potentially hazardous equipment. Since the UAV is a safety-critical system, safety and productivity properties of its behavior are important. It is interesting, if not essential, to be able to verify these properties to guarantee them to a certain extent. From

© Springer Nature Switzerland AG 2020
Y. Demazeau et al. (Eds.): PAAMS 2020, LNAI 12092, pp. 315–326, 2020.
https://doi.org/10.1007/978-3-030-49778-1_25

a safety point of view, one wants to be able to make sure that things that should never happen, indeed **do not** happen. A straightforward, yet highly relevant example states that the UAV should never fly into other agents or equipment. On the other hand, things one does want to happen, **should** eventually happen, to make sure the pilot gets work done. The UAV should make progress towards its overall flight goal. This distinction will result in the verification of *safety properties* and *liveness properties*, respectively.

For the verification task, we look into the use of IDP[1], a knowledge base system. The modeling language, FO(.), is an extension of traditional First Order logic [5]. It allows for modeling using (inductive) definitions and provides a type system with some built-in types and support for user-defined types. IDP only supports types with discrete domains. This limitation confines the sorts of systems that can be modeled, yet for the application at hand, the consequences should not be too severe. It follows that the result of the verification task is only valid under the assumption that the application can be (and is) modeled correctly in this discrete setting. Furthermore, when using a knowledge base system, the implementation of a concrete verification approach is up to the user. We verify properties using Bounded Model Checking (BMC) and Invariant Checking (IC).

The overall contribution of this work consists of an IDP model of the UAV and its environment. We focus on the advantages and disadvantages of using IDP for verification purposes. Preliminary examples show that IDP can be used, yet only for relatively small systems. *How can IDP be used as a model checking tool for the application at hand? What is the desired approach? To what level of detail can the system be modeled? What precautions can be undertaken to maintain tractability?* We look into the modeling aspect of the application and denote the preferred modeling approaches. To model the system precisely, we keep the state description as concrete as possible. The need emerges to use numerical modeling instead of a higher-level description. When relevant, subtypes are introduced to improve the performance and readability of the model. Non-determinism is addressed to model more realistic, uncertain effects. Finally, the concept of a back loop time path (instead of a linear, finite trace) provides support for stronger guarantees.

The paper is organized as follows. Section 2 discusses other research verifying the behavior of UAVs. Section 3 elaborates on the outline of our model and choices that were made during modeling. Section 4 discusses the results and findings. Section 5 draws the conclusions and outlines future work.

2   Related Work

As mentioned above, it is important to be aware of the safety and productivity properties of a safety-critical system and to be able to verify and guarantee such properties. A lot of research has been going on regarding model checking and verification. In our work, we do not introduce a novel or superior model checking

---

[1] IDP stands for *Imperative Declarative Programming*. More information on IDP and its modeling language can be found here: https://dtai.cs.kuleuven.be/software/idp.

tool or technique. We are merely interested in taking a knowledge base approach for verification purposes, more specifically, using the IDP system. Despite IDP being able to perform verification tasks, little research has been investigating this ability [7]. In this section, we touch upon some verification approaches and applications related to UAV systems. From the point of view of model checking within IDP, the verification of other systems is considered relevant as well.

The techniques we will apply within IDP are majorly based on BMC principles. Biere et al. [3] provide a solid basis regarding a BMC approach. The idea emerges to search for counterexamples of a property to reject this property. If an execution trace of a bounded length is found, in which the property gets violated, the property does not hold. If no counterexample is found, the bound has to be increased until one is found, or until some pre-known upper bound is reached. The property holds if no counterexample can be found.

Torens et al. [12] emphasize the need for verification of UAV software and behavior. Many regulatory rules and certification standards have to be taken into account during the development of the autopilot. This leads to numerous challenges. A NASA case study [10] looks into autonomy software and the issues related to verification. Interesting to note is that behavioral errors are considered more difficult to detect, compared to, for example, implementation errors. The used models form a critical basis. Sirigineedi et al. [11] look into the modeling and verification of a multiple UAV system. The properties are verified using counterexamples. Unlike their approach, our work concerns the properties of the behavior of a single UAV. This approach allows us to focus on the modeling details and choices of the UAV itself. Alhawi et al. [1] investigate the verification of UAV systems, to detect security vulnerabilities. Their work takes into account the communication aspect of the system. We consider the autopilot to reside onboard the UAV. No external communication is required, avoiding another opportunity for failure or attack.

Finally, as elaborated upon by Hoffmann et al. [8], the use of probabilistic model checking can yield more informative results. For this purpose, the probabilistic model checker PRISM [9] is used. Actions can have probabilistic effects, yielding more realistic models, compared to models in IDP. Furthermore, probabilistic guarantees (expressing chances) can be obtained, rather than less informative boolean results (expressing possibilities). However, a sufficiently precise probabilistic model of the effects of actions on the UAV and world is required. Such a precise model can be hard to obtain.

3   Modeling the System

A typical inspection flight roughly looks as follows. The UAV starts at its home base location, landed on the ground, where it is deployed or serviced. When a mission is due, the UAV will take off and rise to an appropriate flight height. At this height, where obstacles are least common and no legal restrictions hold, the most direct path to the inspection location is available. The autopilot will navigate the UAV to the inspection location, actively avoiding (possibly temporal and dynamic) restricted regions representing other UAVs, tall buildings, and restricted airspace. At the inspection location, the UAV will lower to an appropriate inspection height. At this position, inspection is due. Currently, this inspection corresponds with taking a picture of which the processing will be handled offline. After the inspection, the UAV can regain height and travel onward to the next location. This location can be the next inspection location or the home base if no more inspections are due. Furthermore, the UAV is not allowed to enter a height zone above a certain height level, defined by law.

3.1   Modeling in IDP

Before we can verify the properties of a system, the system has to be modeled in IDP. The modeling language FO(.) allows for straightforward modeling of the system and its properties. In IDP, coherent knowledge, expressing (a part of) the model is grouped in a *theory*. The base theories contain the autopilot policy[2] and the UAV and its environment. Furthermore, time is modeled explicitly to support a BMC approach. The obtained model allows us to use IDP to search for execution traces of the UAV that meet certain constraints. We will use this approach to find counterexamples of properties, to reject these properties.

A concrete, numerical representation of the state of the system is deemed to be more informative than a boolean indicative approach. For example, an integer percentage as a representation for the battery level of the UAV can represent the complete battery range. A boolean indication, *battery_below_n_%*, only expresses whether or not a threshold is reached. It does not make sense to discard the fine-grained information present in real systems. This information might be required to model the correct physical behavior. For example, since the battery drains slowly during each action, the UAV will fall to the ground once all power is drained. The disadvantage of keeping track of the detailed information is the need for larger domains, for example, $\{0,1,\ldots,100\}$ *(%)* instead of $\{0,1\}$ *(boolean)*. Large domains are costly in terms of performance. The relevant domains are (manually) modeled as small as possible, while still providing the necessary features.

It has to be said that an integer representation is the most concrete type available in IDP. A more exact, continuous representation might be preferred, but this is not supported. We use discretized values, giving rise to a less precise model. The verification capabilities for the model at hand should not be affected. In general, the precise effects of the actions of a system can not always be modeled using a discrete domain. For some actions, the possible effects might not even be considered to be accurately known. Under the assumption that the actions of the system have accurately known effects, a discretized approach yields a valid model. Conceptually, to achieve a more fine-grained representation, one can increase the size of the relevant domains. For example, represent the distance using centimeters instead of meters. In our model, we generalize over the specific units being used.

---

[2] A policy contains a mapping from every possible state of the system to the action that has to be executed in that state.

3.2   Modeling the UAV and World

The complete model[3] makes use of many (helper) predicates and (helper) functions. The most significant types for defining the (physical) state of the UAV are the following.

Location is a type used to declare the meaning of the different height independent locations at which the UAV can be. This approach is chosen, rather than a 3D discretized world grid, as the latter yields to be intractable in IDP. Without the usage of 3D coordinates in the model, we are not able to represent every possible location. We solely define the world using the distances between the locations. This approach provides all the information needed to model any flight between the locations. *Location* is constructed from the values:

- **Home** being the home base of the UAV.
- **TravelSpace** being the less interesting part of the world through which the UAV can fly to reach the other locations.
- A number of inspection locations **Insp$_n$** at which inspection is due.

An example toy world is shown in Fig. 1. The distances between different locations are fixed in time so that the locations in the world are static. As the UAV flies around in the world, the distances between the UAV and the locations will change deterministically. When the UAV is navigating from location A to location B, the distance between the UAV and location A increases. The distance between the UAV and location B decreases. The distances between the UAV and other locations remain constant. This approach is solely a (physically incorrect) modeling choice and is implemented so that it does not compromise the correctness of the verification task. A physically correct model could be preferred but would require continuous domains and calculations.

The restricted area, which is to be avoided by the UAV, is modeled less explicitly. The distance between the UAV and *RestrictedArea* can change non-deterministically[4] during flight. As a result, the restricted area has no fixed shape. IDP can verify properties using the most diverse and dynamic shapes possible, which can represent (the behavior of) humans and other agents.

Height is a natural number, used to represent the current height of the UAV. As an example illustrates in Fig. 2, *Height* has the following distinct subtypes:

- **GroundHeight** representing the landed position.
- **InspectionHeight** being the lower level of the air space, in which objects are to be inspected.

---

[3] The IDP model of the application at hand is available at https://github.com/VermaelenJan/Model-Checking-Drones-with-IDP/blob/master/model.idp.

[4] Non-determinism in IDP can be achieved by defining a predicate without initializing it. IDP will look for models regarding all possible values (of the relevant domain) for the predicate.

- **FlyHeight** being the higher level of the air space, in which the UAV is more or less free to fly in.
- **RestrictedHeight** being the highest level of the air space, in which the UAV is not allowed to fly, for legal reasons.

This height representation outlines the complete physical air space. Every concrete altitude in the real aerial space is (non-linearly) mapped to one numerical height value and thus to one of these levels. This representation is interesting, both for the readability of the model and for the performance of the verification task. Certain instructions or statements are only relevant for (the domain of) one such region. For example, inspection is due only at *InspectionHeight*. As the computations within IDP can be executed using smaller domains, a performance gain (linear with the reduction) is observed.

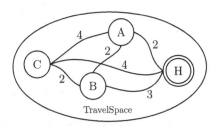

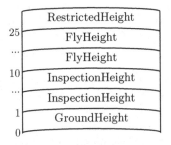

Fig. 1. The locations (Home base H, Inspection Locations A, B and C, and the TravelSpace in between) of a simple toy world are visualized, along with the distances connecting them.

Fig. 2. The height definition is visualized, showing the semantic height zones and the boundaries between them as they are present in a simple toy world.

Power is a natural number, used to represent the quantity of power. This numerical value is, for example, used by helper predicates to determine whether the battery of the UAV is at time step t:

- **AtNormalPower(t)** when normal operation of the UAV is expected.
- **AtLowPower(t)** when the UAV is expected to return home.
- **AtCriticalPower(t)** when the UAV is expected to land immediately.

The numerical value keeps track of the actual power level of the battery. Once the value reaches zero, the UAV can no longer execute any actions since each action requires power to execute. The UAV will start falling to the ground. The effect of this falling is modeled as an unconditional lost of altitude at each consecutive time step.

An intuitive domain to model the *PowerUsage* of the UAV, that is, the power used at each time step, would be the same *Power* domain that is being used for the battery itself. However, the values for *PowerUsage* are typically much smaller than an entire battery worth of power. This makes *PowerUsage* suitable to be modeled as a subtype of *Power*. Analogous to the modeling of the *Height*, the use of a subdomain improves tractability and the readability of the model.

Action is a type used to represent the possible actions that can be executed by the UAV on behalf of the autopilot. The policy (see Sect. 3.3) will be responsible for deciding which actions to execute, based on the state of the system. The possible actions are:

- **MoveTowardsTarget** to (try to) move towards the current *Target* location.
- **MoveAwayFromRA** to (try to) move away from the closest region modeled as *RestrictedArea*.
- **TakePicture** to take a picture at the current position.
- **NoOp** to execute no operation. This action will, for example, occur after the UAV has completed its tasks.
- **Lift** to (try to) gain altitude.
- **Lower** to descend.

The *Move* and *Lift* actions are modeled so that they can fail a (non-deterministic) number of times. Assumptions on the maximum amount of successive or total failures can be set as a function of the weight. A heavy UAV could take longer to lift or move. Furthermore, each action is modeled to have a certain power consumption, gradually draining the battery.

3.3   Modeling the UAV Behavior

As mentioned before, the overall goal of the UAV is to take off at its home base, consecutively fly to the interesting locations and take pictures, to finally return and land back at its home base. The current position (location and height) of the UAV, along with the status of taken pictures and distances to objects, form the relevant input for the policy. In IDP, the instructions that form the policy are represented using a rule-like syntax. As the policy contains dozens of such rules[5], only one, arbitrarily selected rule is denoted here for illustrative purposes. *IF the UAV has sufficient power AND not all pictures are taken yet AND the current location does not have to be inspected (anymore) AND the UAV is at fly height AND the UAV is close to Restricted Area THEN the UAV will (try to) move away from the Restricted Area.* In IDP syntax, this rule is denoted as:

$$\forall t[Time] : Plan(t) = MoveAwayFromRA$$
$$\leftarrow AtNormalPower(t) \land \neg AllPicturesTaken(t)$$
$$\land \neg AtInspectionToDo(t) \land AtFlyHeight(t) \land CloseToRA(t).$$

---

[5] The policy of the application at hand is available at https://github.com/ VermaelenJan/Model-Checking-Drones-with-IDP/blob/master/Policy/Policy.pdf.

Exactly one action must be returned for each possible state of the UAV. We say the policy should be *complete*. This can be verified exhaustively[6] and is enforced by IDP as well. The policy at hand is found to be complete.

3.4   Modeling the Time

We denote two different ways of modeling *Time* by means of what the successor function *Next(Time)* looks like.

Finite Time. A classical time definition can be modeled using a partial successor function. Each time step is mapped to the next one $(0 \to 1, 1 \to 2, \ldots, k - 1 \to k)$. The final time step (k) has no successor. In IDP syntax, *Next(Time)* is modeled as:

$$\forall t[Time] : Next(t) = t + 1 \leftarrow Time(t + 1).$$

Back Loop Time. A total time definition can be achieved by letting the final time step k loop back to any previous one l [3,4]. IDP's knowledge base nature allows it to look for solutions in which states of the system are repeated. Infinite sequences of time steps can be considered, as long as they can be expressed using a (k, l) back loop. The model is extended with:

$$Next(MAX[: Time]) = BackLoopTime.$$

where the value for *BackLoopTime*, representing l, can be chosen by IDP non-deterministically.

3.5   Modeling the Properties

Within IDP, model checking is achieved by BMC. To check property *f*, one adds the statement *not f* to the base system and queries IDP to determine whether the new, extended theory is satisfiable. If the theory is satisfiable, a counterexample is found in which the negation of the property holds. The property is violated and hence does not hold in general. Some properties of the autopilot that are to be verified are the following:

1. The UAV does not fly into restricted areas.
2. The UAV achieves its inspection flight goal.
3. The UAV reaches back home, before running out of battery power.

---

[6] For the policy of the application at hand, proof of completeness is provided at https://github.com/VermaelenJan/Model-Checking-Drones-with-IDP/blob/master/Policy/Completeness%20Policy/policy%20complete.pdf.

Since we need to look for scenarios in which the negation of the property occurs, we extend the theory as follows.

$$\exists t[Time] : Curr\_DistanceToRA(t) = 0. \tag{1}$$

forces IDP to look for a scenario in which at some time step t, the UAV *does* reach the restricted area.

$$\neg \exists t[Time] : AllPicturesTaken(t) \wedge AtGroundHeight(t) \wedge AtHome(t). \tag{2}$$

forces IDP to look for a scenario in which the UAV *never* reaches its goal.

$$\neg(AtHome(MAX[: Time]) \wedge AtGroundHeight(Max[: Time])). \tag{3}$$

forces IDP to look for a scenario in which the UAV *never* returns home.

The properties can be divided into two groups: safety properties (1) and liveness properties (2 and 3). For safety properties, it is sufficient to find a single time step at which the property is violated. For liveness properties, on the other hand, we need to find an example of a complete flight trace in which the liveness goal does not get achieved.

Rather than applying a complete BMC iteration with an increasingly large bound, we opt for a single check with a fixed, well-chosen bound. In IDP, this corresponds to the use of a fixed time domain. In every flight scenario, after the UAV inevitably runs out of battery power, it will end up on the ground and remain there forever. In this final state, a back loop, as discussed in Sect. 3.4, occurs. If a safety property is not violated until this looping state is encountered, the property will not be violated anywhere in the entire execution trace. This statement is concordant with the observation by Biere et al. [4]. Furthermore, the infinite loop can be used to find counterexamples for liveness properties as well. Such a counterexample provides an infinite execution trace in which the liveness goal never gets achieved. Making use of a back loop, we avoid the main drawback of BMC, that is, the need for an endlessly increasing bound. We essentially only apply one BMC step with a sufficiently large bound.

Property 1 can be guaranteed, as no counterexample was found by IDP. Property 2, related to reaching the goal, does not always hold. Depending on the initial battery level and the distances to be covered during flight, counterexamples can be found. Property 3, related to reaching back home, holds under some assumptions. For example, the number of non-deterministically failed actions has to be limited. If the policy takes this limit into account, the estimation it makes, regarding the power needed to return home, will always be sufficient to make sure the UAV can reach back home.

To improve the performance of the verification task, we look into reducing the time domain. We apply an approach related to Invariant Checking, as described by Biere et al. [2]. Only two consecutive time steps are taken into account simultaneously. This approach contrasts with a BMC approach, for which a complete flight scenario has to be considered. Biere et al. [3] state that the three steps in a proof with an inductive invariant are: the base case, the induction step, and the strengthening step. For the base case and induction step, we rely on IDP. As we use the property itself as the inductive invariant, the strengthening step holds trivially. For the base case, we have to check whether the property initially holds. This check is straightforward using a knowledge base tool such as IDP. By adding this requirement to the theory, IDP only looks for models in which the property holds in the initial time step. For the induction step, we apply a simplified BMC approach. We query IDP, looking for a counterexample. If the property holds at the initial time step (base case) and a time succession can be found after which the property is violated, the invariant, and thus the property, does not hold.

4   Discussion

The properties stated in Sect. 3.5 are successfully verified for different concrete initializations of the world. If desired, the properties can easily be checked for different autopilot policies as well. We are able to check for each property whether or not it can get violated, and if so, a counterexample is provided by IDP.

Discretization
Physical domains, such as distance, can easily be discretized. For the application investigated in this research, a discretized approach is adequate. The use of discrete domains is sufficiently concrete, as the level of accuracy depends on the chosen unit (for example, express distance in centimeters instead of meters). Since an arbitrarily high finite precision can be achieved, we do not experience the need for continuous domains.

Back Loop Time
When modeling a realistic UAV, a back loop time structure might seem useless as the battery level decreases at each time step. However, a useful trick arises. Once the battery gets completely drained, a back loop allows us to express infinitely long paths. We can verify the properties using a fixed bound since the need for an endlessly increasing bound is avoided. For example, the bound can be set to a value greater than or equal to the initial battery level divided by the smallest possible power usage per time step.

Performance
As the intention is to execute representative verifications, realistic domain sizes would be desired. However, experience shows that the use of large domains in IDP is disastrous for its performance. As we verify properties imitating a single BMC step, we do not experience any advantages regarding the state explosion problem [6]. The use of smaller domains does not have to compromise the desired principle of concrete verification. An acceptable measure is to reduce the domain sizes but keep them as concrete. The properties will be checked on down-scaled worlds. For the system and properties at hand, it is plausible to assume that if

no violations are found for such worlds, violations will not occur in realistically sized worlds either. This assumption is not valid if the properties depend on large values regarding certain domains.

Furthermore, the (correct) use of types is advantageous for the performance of IDP. Two important types for which *additional* measures regarding the domain size have been taken are the *Height* level of the UAV and the UAV's *PowerUsage* at each time step. In both cases, the use of subdomains succeeds to reduce the bulk of computations within IDP, yielding a performance gain.

Finally, the reduction of time steps by using Invariant Checking is also beneficial for the performance of the verification task. However, there are two major drawbacks. Firstly, only counterexamples with the chosen initialization state can be found. The check should be executed for every state in which violations might occur. Secondly, and perhaps more importantly, it yields that this way of checking properties is only applicable to safety properties, as a result of reducing the time domain. It is impossible to draw conclusions regarding any property of which the violation requires more than one time step succession. To remedy the first drawback, the initialization of the first time step is handed off to IDP to find as many violations as possible. The initial state of the system is set non-deterministically. *All possible* initializations are checked. For this purpose, the use of a knowledge base system is rather convenient. Furthermore, not only the initial state of the UAV but, for example, also the initialization of the distances that define the world can be taken care of by IDP. As a result, an even more complete search can be achieved. Since porting the model from BMC to IC (within IDP) requires no changes, IC only enhances the verification capabilities.

5   Conclusion

We outlined our model for the verification of a safety-critical UAV. Taking into account the assumptions and drawbacks we encountered, IDP can be used as a verification tool. The straightforward and compact way of modeling makes IDP suitable for a high-level approach of verification and facilitates acquiring quick proofs of concept. The counterexamples provided by IDP form excellent guidance for debugging purposes regarding the system at hand.

Using discrete domains, any arbitrary precision can be achieved. However, precise models require large domains, which are disastrous for the performance of IDP. Therefore, verification on down-scaled worlds is preferred. The introduction of a back loop, when possible, allows taking into account infinitely long execution paths. The need for an endlessly increasing bound during BMC is avoided. The use of subtypes yields to be advantageous for both the performance of IDP and the readability of the model. Furthermore, the application of Invariant Checking is also beneficial for the performance of the verification task. However, since Invariant Checking only takes into account two consecutive time steps, it is only applicable for safety properties.

Future work should focus on more realistic modeling of the system. The effects of executed actions and external influences are never precisely known. As mentioned at the end of Sect. 2, probabilistic models are suitable to take into account more realistic effects. To obtain correct claims from such a model, however, the model itself first has to be guaranteed to be correct.

Acknowledgments. This research is partially funded by the Research Fund KU Leuven.

References

1. Alhawi, O.M., Mustafa, M.A., Cordeiro, L.C.: Finding security vulnerabilities in unmanned aerial vehicles using software verification. CoRR abs/1906.11488 (2019). http://arxiv.org/abs/1906.11488
2. Biere, A., Cimatti, A., Clarke, E.M., Fujita, M., Zhu, Y.: Symbolic model checking using SAT procedures instead of BDDs. In: Proceedings 1999 Design Automation Conference (Cat. No. 99CH36361), pp. 317–320, June 1999. https://doi.org/10.1109/DAC.1999.781333
3. Biere, A., Cimatti, A., Clarke, E.M., Strichman, O., Zhu, Y.: Bounded model checking. In: Advances in Computers, vol. 58, pp. 117–148. Elsevier (2003). https://doi.org/10.1016/S0065-2458(03)58003-2
4. Biere, A., Cimatti, A., Clarke, E., Zhu, Y.: Symbolic model checking without BDDs. In: Cleaveland, W.R. (ed.) TACAS 1999. LNCS, vol. 1579, pp. 193–207. Springer, Heidelberg (1999). https://doi.org/10.1007/3-540-49059-0_14
5. Bruynooghe, M., et al.: Predicate logic as a modeling language: modeling and solving some machine learning and data mining problems with IDP3. Theory Pract. Logic Program. **15**(6), 783–817 (2015). https://doi.org/10.1017/S147106841400009X
6. Clarke, E.M., Klieber, W., Nováček, M., Zuliani, P.: Model checking and the state explosion problem. In: Meyer, B., Nordio, M. (eds.) LASER 2011. LNCS, vol. 7682, pp. 1–30. Springer, Heidelberg (2012). https://doi.org/10.1007/978-3-642-35746-6_1
7. Dinh, H.T., Cruz Torres, M.H., Holvoet, T.: Combining planning and model checking to get guarantees on the behavior of safety-critical UAV systems. In: ICAPS Workshop on Planning and Robotics (2018). https://lirias.kuleuven.be/retrieve/509824
8. Hoffmann, R., Ireland, M., Miller, A., Norman, G., Veres, S.: Autonomous agent behaviour modelled in PRISM – a case study. In: Bošnački, D., Wijs, A. (eds.) SPIN 2016. LNCS, vol. 9641, pp. 104–110. Springer, Cham (2016). https://doi.org/10.1007/978-3-319-32582-8_7
9. Kwiatkowska, M., Norman, G., Parker, D.: PRISM: probabilistic symbolic model checker. In: Field, T., Harrison, P.G., Bradley, J., Harder, U. (eds.) TOOLS 2002. LNCS, vol. 2324, pp. 200–204. Springer, Heidelberg (2002). https://doi.org/10.1007/3-540-46029-2_13
10. Schumann, J., Visser, W.: Autonomy software: V& V challenges and characteristics. In: 2006 IEEE Aerospace Conference, pp. 1–6. IEEE (2006)
11. Sirigineedi, G., Tsourdos, A., White, B.A., Żbikowski, R.: Kripke modelling and verification of temporal specifications of a multiple UAV system. Ann. Math. Artif. Intell. **63**(1), 31–52 (2011). https://doi.org/10.1007/s10472-011-9270-x
12. Torens, C., Adolf, F.M., Goormann, L.: Certification and software verification considerations for autonomous unmanned aircraft. J. Aerosp. Inf. Syst. **11**(10), 649–664 (2014)

Pattern-Based Goal-Oriented Development of Fault-Tolerant MAS in Event-B

Inna Vistbakka[1(✉)] and Elena Troubitsyna[1,2]

[1] Åbo Akademi University, Turku, Finland
inna.vistbakka@abo.fi
[2] KTH – Royal Institute of Technology, Stockholm, Sweden
elenatro@kth.se

Abstract. Goal-oriented development facilitates structuring behaviour of complex multi-agent systems. It allows us to represent the required system behaviour as a set of goals to be accomplished by the agents with corresponding functionality. However, in general, the agents might fail and hence, to ensure goal reachability we should augment the goal-oriented framework with fault tolerance mechanisms. In this paper, we propose a formal pattern-based approach to formal modelling of fault tolerant MAS in Event-B. The framework allows us in a systematic and rigorous way to define complex relationships between the unreliable agents and goals. It is illustrated by a case study – a smart warehouse system.

Keywords: Event-B · Formal modelling · Refinement · Goal-oriented development · Multi-agent system

1 Introduction

Development of multi-agent systems is a complex engineering task. The complexity becomes even higher if the agents are unreliable, i.e., might fail to execute tasks. Goal-oriented development [10] framework provides us with a suitable formalism for structuring complex behaviour of MAS. The system behaviour is defined as a number of goals, which might be achieved by system execution. Each goal can be consequently decomposed into a number of subgoals. At a certain level of decomposition, the subgoals can be directly associated with the agent functionalities.

In general, the agents are unreliable, i.e., they might fail to execute the goal assigned to them. In this paper, we propose a number of modelling patterns that allow us by re-association and re-allocation of goals between the agents, achieve fault tolerance. The approach relies on goal decomposition and dynamic goal allocation to agents. To define and monitor complex associations between the goals at different levels of abstraction and unreliable agents, we rely on formal modelling and verification in Event-B [1].

© Springer Nature Switzerland AG 2020
Y. Demazeau et al. (Eds.): PAAMS 2020, LNAI 12092, pp. 327–339, 2020.
https://doi.org/10.1007/978-3-030-49778-1_26

Event-B is a state-based formal framework, which promotes correct-by-construction development by refinement. Refinement-based approach provides a suitable formalization for goal-oriented development, while automated proof-based verification [2] scales for the development of complex MAS.

In this paper, we define a number of modelling and refinement patterns that represent instantiatable solutions for modelling goals, behaviour of agents and fault tolerance mechanisms by goal re-allocation and agent re-association. The proposed approach allows us formally, by proof, demonstrate goal reachability despite agent failures. The approach is illustrated by a case study – a development of smart warehouse system.

2   Formal Modelling and Refinement in Event B

Event-B is a state-based formal approach that promotes the correct-by-construction development paradigm and formal verification by theorem proving. In Event-B, a system model is specified using the notion of an *abstract state machine* [1]. An abstract state machine encapsulates the model state, represented as a collection of variables, and defines operations on the state, i.e., it describes the dynamic behaviour of a modelled system. The important system properties that should be preserved are defined as model invariants. Usually a machine has the accompanying component, called context. A context is the static part of a model and may include user-defined carrier sets, constants and their properties.

The system dynamic behaviour is described by a collection of atomic *events* defined in a machine part. Generally, an event has the following form:

$$\text{event}_e \ \widehat{=} \ \textbf{any} \ \ x_e \ \ \textbf{where} \ \ G_e \ \ \textbf{then} \ \ R_e \ \ \textbf{end}$$

Here event_e is the unique event's name, x_e is the list of local variables, and G_e is the event guard – a predicate over the model state. The body of an event is defined by a *multiple* (possibly nondeterministic) assignment to the system variables. In Event-B, this assignment is semantically defined as the next-state relation R_e. The event guard defines the conditions under which the event is *enabled*, i.e., its body can be executed. If several events are enabled at the same time, any of them can be chosen for execution nondeterministically.

System development in Event-B is based on a top-down refinement-based approach. A development starts from an abstract specification that nondeterministically models the most essential functional system behaviour. In a sequence of refinement steps, we gradually reduce nondeterminism and introduce detailed design decisions. In particular, we can add new events, refine old events as well as replace abstract variables by their concrete counterparts. The *gluing invariants* are used to link the abstract and concrete state variables. A correct refinement ensures that the abstract system's properties are preserved in the concrete one.

The consistency of Event-B models – verification of model well-formedness, invariant preservation as well as correctness of refinement steps – is demonstrated by discharging the relevant proof obligations. Rodin platform [2] provides tool support for modelling and verification in Event-B. In particular, it automatically generates all required proof obligations and attempts to discharge them. When the proof obligations cannot be discharged automatically, the user can attempt to prove them interactively using a collection of available proof tactics.

3   Event-B Patterns for Goal-Oriented Modelling of MAS

In this work we present a combination of the goal-oriented development and the Event-B refinement for modelling distributed MAS. To support the goal-oriented development of MAS in Event-B, we define a set of Event-B specification and refinement patterns that reflect the main ideas of the goal-oriented engineering [10]. Patterns define generic reusable solutions that support development of complex systems. We start by abstractly defining system goals, then we show how to perform goal decomposition by refinement. We define and prove the relevant gluing invariants establishing a formal relationship between goals and the corresponding subgoals. Next we introduce system agents and the required mechanisms to ensure that the system progresses towards achieving its goals.

We propose the following *specification and refinement patterns*:

- *Goal Modelling Pattern*: explicitly defines high-level system goal(s) in Event-B and postulates goal reachability;
- *Goal Decomposition Pattern*: demonstrates how to define the system goals at different levels of abstraction in Event-B (i.e., how to decompose high-level system goal(s) into subgoals and introduce a goal hierarchy);
- *Agent Modelling Pattern*: allows the designers to introduce agents and agent types into a specification as well as associate agents with (sub)goals;
- *Agent Refinement Pattern*: defines nominal and off-nominal agent behaviour.

3.1   Goal Modelling Pattern

We start our development in Event-B by creating a high-level abstract specification. In the abstract model – called *Goal Modelling Pattern* – we focus on specifying the overall system behaviour. Here we aim at specifying the following property: *a system is trying to accomplish the main goal during its execution*.

The dynamic behaviour of the system is modelled by the GOD_MAS_m0 machine. We define a variable $goal \in STATES$ that models the current state of the system goal, where $STATES = \{incompl, compl\}$. The variable $goal$ obtains the value $compl$ when the main goal is achieved. Otherwise $goal$ has the value $incompl$. To abstractly model the process of achieving the goal – specified in the event Reaching_Goal – the variable $goal$ may change its value from $incompl$ to $compl$. The system continues its execution until the goal is reached (see Fig. 1)

3.2   Goal Decomposition Pattern

In our work, we follow the main principles of goal-oriented development approach [10]. After introducing the high-level system goals, we are going to decompose them into a set of corresponding *subgoals*. This process is called *goal decomposition*. The objective of the Event-B *Goal Decomposition Pattern* is to explicitly

Context GOD_MAS_c0
Sets $STATES$
Constants $incompl, compl$
Axioms
    axm1: $STATES = \{incompl, compl\}$

Machine GOD_MAS_m0 See GOD_MAS_c0
Variables $goal, finish$
Invariants
    $finish \in BOOL \wedge goal \in STATES$
    $finish = TRUE \Rightarrow goal = compl$
Events
ReachingGoal $\widehat{=}$
    where $goal \neq compl$
    then $goal :\in STATES$
    end

Finish $\widehat{=}$
    where $goal = compl \wedge finish = FALSE$
    then $finish := TRUE$
    end

Fig. 1. Event-B context GOD_MAS_c0 and machine GOD_MAS_m0

introduce such subgoals into the system specification. Essentially, a subgoal represents a single functional step that the system has to execute to progress towards the goal achievement.

In our *Goal Decomposition Pattern*, we focus on representing the overall system execution as an iterative execution of a set of subgoals. To represent all subgoals that constitute system execution, we introduce a new abstract type (set) $SUBGOALS$ into the model's context.

In the machine part of the first refinement, we define the new variable *subgoal_state* that stores the current execution status of each subgoal:

$$subgoal\_state \in SUBGOALS \rightarrow STATES.$$

Initially, none of the subgoal is completed, i.e., the status of a subgoal is *incompl*. After successful execution, the subgoal's status changes to *compl*. Now the event ReachingGoal of the abstract machine is refined by ReachingSubgoal event, modelling the process of achieving of the corresponding subgoal. Note that this event is parametrised – the parameter sg designates the id of subgoal being processed:

ReachingSubgoal $\widehat{=}$ **refines** Reaching_Goal
    any $sg, result$
    where $sg \in SUBGOALS$
        $subgoal\_state(sg) = incompl$
        $result \in STATES$
    then $subgoals\_state(sg) := result$
    end

While defining the lower-level goals, we should ensure that the high-level goals remain achievable. Hence our refinement pattern should reflect the relation between the high-level goals and their subgoals. Moreover, it should ensure that high-level goal reachability is preserved and can be defined via reachability of the corresponding lower-level subgoals. To establish the relationship between the main goal and subgoals, we formulate and prove the following gluing invariant:

$$goal=compl \Leftrightarrow (\forall sg. \, sg \in SUBGOALS \Rightarrow subgoal\_state(sg) = compl).$$

The invariant postulates that *the main system goal is achieved if and only if all the involved subgoals are successfully completed.*

In general, the proposed *Goal Decomposition Pattern* can be repeatedly used to refine subgoals into the subgoals of a finer granularity until the desired level of detail is reached.

3.3   Agent Modelling Pattern

The proposed *Goal Modelling* and *Goal Decomposition Patterns* allow us to specify the system goal(s) at different levels of abstraction and focus on functional decomposition of the system behaviour into execution of atomic goals. We have deliberately abstracted away from associating these (sub)goals with the specific system agent that perform the goals.

In MAS, (sub)goals are usually achieved by system components – agents – independent entities that are capable of performing certain subgoals. In general, the system might have several types of agents that are distinguished by the type of subgoals that they are capable of performing. Our next refinement pattern – *Agent Modelling Pattern* – allows us to introduce into the system specification agents and their types as well as associate them with goals. For convenience, now we will use both terms low-level goals and subgoals interchangeably.

In the model context associated with this pattern (presented in Fig. 2), we introduce the set *AGENTS* that abstractly defines the set of all system agents. Since the set *AGENTS* contains all possible system agents, they may have different functionalities. In order to associate certain classes of agents with the system goals, which are able to accomplish, first we introduce types of system agents. The function *AType* associates each agent with its respective type:

$$AType \in AGENTS \rightarrow ATYPES,$$

where *ATYPES* is the set that contains all possible types of agents. Similarly, we introduce classifications of system goals:

$$SGType \in SUBGOALS \rightarrow SGTYPES,$$

where *SGTYPES* is the set that contains all possible types of goals.

Context GOD_MAS_c2 extends GOD_MAS_c1
Sets *AGENTS, ATYPES, SGTYPES*
Constants *AType, SGType, A_G_Rel*
Axioms
axm1: $AGENTS \neq \varnothing$
axm2: $ATYPES \neq \varnothing$
...
axm7: $AType \in AGENTS \rightarrow ATYPES$
axm8: $SGType \in SUBGOALS \rightarrow SGTYPES$
axm9: $A\_SG\_Rel \in ATYPES \leftrightarrow SGTYPES$

Fig. 2. Context GOD_MAS_c2

Next we should define a relation between agent types and the corresponding goal types:

$$A\_SG\_Rel \in ATYPES \leftrightarrow SGTYPES$$

In general, a particular agent type might cover several types of goals, i.e., an agent of this type might accomplish several goals.

Knowing the interrelationships between the agent and goals types allows us to check, whether a concrete agent is able to accomplish a specific goal. Therefore, before assigning a certain goal sg to be achieved to some agent ag, we have to check whether it is eligible for this goal. Specifically, we have to check if $AType(ag) \mapsto SGType(sg) \in A\_SG\_Rel$.

Next we also define the dynamic system characteristic between subgoals and agents – *goal assignment*. A subgoal can be "assigned" to an agent that will try to perform this subgoal:

$$Assigned \in SUBGOALS \rightarrowtail AGENTS.$$

Here $\rightarrowtail$ denotes a partial *injection*. The function is injective because we assume that an agent can not perform more than one subgoal simultaneously.

Obviously, only unreached subgoal can be assigned to an agent for execution. This property is formulated as a model invariant:

$$\forall sg. \; sg \in dom(Assigned) \Rightarrow subgoal\_state(sg) = incompl.$$

Moreover, only the agents of a specific type can be assigned for a subgoal execution. We formulate this property by the following model invariant:

$$\forall sg, ag. \; (sg \mapsto ag) \in Assigned \Rightarrow AType(ag) \mapsto SGType(sg) \in A\_SG\_Rel.$$

System should have a possibility to assign a new (sub)goal to an agent. To reflect this in the Event-B specification, we introduce a new event AssignSubgoal (given below). The event represents assignment of a subgoal sg to an agent ag. To make such an assignment, a number of conditions should be satisfied. Firstly, we have to be sure that sg is not yet accomplished, and is not being currently executed by any other agent. Secondly, the type of the agent should be suitable for performing the subgoal sg. Moreover, the agent ag should be idle, i.e., it should not be involved into an execution of another subgoal.

```
AssignSubgoal ≘
  any sg, ag
  where   sg ∈ SUBGOALS
    subgoal_state(sg) = incompl          // the subgoal sg is not yet accomplished
    sg ∉ dom(Assigned)                   // the subgoal sg is not assigned to any other agent
    AType(ag) ↦ SGType(sg) ∈ A_SG_Rel   // the agent ag is able to achieved the subgoal sg
    ag ∉ ran(Assigned)                   // the agent ag has not any other assigned subgoal
  then   Assigned(sg) := ag
  end
```

SubgoalSuccess refines ReachingSubgoal $\widehat{=}$	SubgoalFailure refines ReachingSubgoal $\widehat{=}$
any sg, ag	**any** sg, new_state, ag
where $sg \in SUBGOALS$	**where** $sg \in SUBGOALS$
$subgoal\_state(sg) = incompl$	$subgoal\_state(sg) = incompl$
$ag \in AGENTS$	$ag \in AGENTS$
$(sg \mapsto ag) \in Assigned$	$(sg \mapsto ag) \in Assigned$
then $subgoal\_state(sg) := compl$	**then** $subgoal\_state(sg) := incoml$
$Assigned := \{sg\} \lhd Assigned$	$Assigned := \{sg\} \lhd Assigned$
end	**end**

Fig. 3. Some events of *Agent Modelling Pattern*

Upon receiving the assignment, the agent starts to perform the assigned subgoal. However, while achieving a given subgoal, an agent might fail, which subsequently leads to the failure to perform the assigned subgoal. In case of an agent failure, the failed subgoal might be assign for execution to the next available agent. To reflect this behaviour in our model, we should refine the abstract event ReachingSubgoal by two events SubgoalSuccess and SubgoalFailure (as shown in Fig. 3). They model respectively successful and unsuccessful execution of the subgoal. Here $\lhd$ denotes the domain subtraction relation, i.e. $S \lhd r = \{x \mapsto y \mid x \mapsto y \in r \wedge x \notin S\}$.

3.4   Agent Refinement Pattern

Let us remind that in the *Goal Decomposition Pattern* we have abstractly modelled both nominal and off-nominal system behaviour allowing the system subgoals to be successfully executed or fail. In the *Agent Modelling Pattern*, we have defined agents and their types as well as associate them with goals. Now, we should explicitly represent off-nominal situations such as agent failures or agent disconnections and model their impact on the system behaviour. As a result of these off-nominal conditions, agents usually lose an ability to perform their predefined goals. Thus, in the *Agent Refinement Pattern* we are going to introduce possible agents failures and specify their effects on the subgoal execution.

The set $AGENTS$ defines all possible system agents. We also define a variable $Active$ to associate a subset of active agents in the current system state. Agents are called active if they can carry out the tasks in order to achieve the (sub)goals. Inactive agents are either not currently present in the system or failed and thus incapable to carry out tasks.

To address agent failures and their effect on goal assignment and execution, we introduce the event modelling agent failure and refine old events AssignSubgoal, SubgoalSuccess, SubgoalFailure. The goal assignment can be given only to the active agents. Moreover, the introduced agent failures affect the goal execution. If a certain agent failed it can not continue to perform a given task, in this case its goal should be reassign to another available eligible agent.

Next we will demonstrate how to apply the described patterns in a concrete development of a multi-agent system – a smart warehouse system.

4   Case Study: Smart Warehouse System

4.1   A Case Study Description

A smart warehouse is a fully automated storage and shipment facility. It is equipped with the autonomous robots that can transport labelled goods (called *boxes* for simplicity) between the multi-level shelves and collection points. One of the main goal of a smart warehouse system is to assemble parcels consisting of a number of boxes for shipping.

Each box has an unique RFID tag attached to it. When a box arrives at the warehouse, the warehouse management system (WMS) assigns it the place at which it should be stored.

Each robot has an unique ID known to WMS and collection points. The robot can communicate with WMS and collection points. It receives the orders to bring the box from the corresponding place or fetch it and bring to a collection point. WMS sends the robot both the ID of a place and RFID of the box. WMS also sends the routes to the robots.

A robot communicates with WMS when it fails to complete its operation due to some reasons. It also should send a notification to WMS when it decides to abort its current assignment and move to the charging station.

Due to space limits, in this paper, we only discuss goal-oriented modelling of the following workflow associated with WMS:

- A request to assemble a parcel has arrived to a smart warehouse from the external system responsible for logistic.
- When WMS gets such a request, its chooses a collection point and chooses a subset of idle robots to transport the required boxes to this collection point.
- Upon receiving an assignment, a robot autonomously moves to the box location, picks up the box and returns with the box to the collection point.
- While performing a given task, a robot might fail at any moment. In that case, WMS may assign another idle robot to perform the failed task.
- The current request is considered as completed, when all the boxes for the parcel are delivered to the collection point and the point assembles the parcel.

The described system has a heterogeneous architecture. It consists of different types of agents (robots and collection points) that might fail. The goal of our development is to formally derive a specification of a smart warehouse system and verify that the proposed design ensures goal reachability despite unreliability of the system agents. By relying on the patterns proposed in Sect. 3, next we demonstrate how to define a system goal and decompose it into the corresponding subgoals of finer granularity until the desired level of details is reached.

4.2   Pattern-Driven Refinement of a Smart Warehouse System

In this section we will describe our formal development of a smart warehouse system (SWS) in Event-B. Our development is conducted according to the generic development patterns presented in Sect. 3. Due to space limits, we only highlight the most important modelling solutions of the development.

Initial Model. We start with a very abstract model, essentially representing the behaviour of SWS as a process of achieving the main goal – handling requests for services, arriving from the system responsible for the logistics.

First Refinement. We perform a refinement of the initial model according to the *Goal Decomposition Pattern.* The high-level goal of the considered system is decomposed into a number of subgoals – *to serve arriving requests.*

We represent all possible incoming requests by the abstract set $REQUESTS$ defined in model context. In the machine component SWS_m1, we describe the abstract dynamics of our system. Here we define a variable *requests*, $requests \subseteq REQUESTS$, that represents the received by WMS requests. A variable *request_status* defines their current status:

$$request\_status \in requests \rightarrow STATUS.$$

The event RequestService abstractly represents the process of a request handling. This event is constructed according to the pattern event ReachingGoal (see below). We also define an event RequestArrival modelling arriving of a request.

```
Machine SWS_m1 refines SWS_m0
Sees SWS_c1
Variables requests, request_status
Invariants requests ⊆ REQUESTS ∧ request_status ∈ requests → STATUS ∧ ...
Events

  Initialisation ≙ ...                    RequestService ≙
  RequestArrival ≙                          status anticipated
   any rq                                   any rq, result
   where rq ∈ REQUESTS ∧                    where rq ∈ requests ∧ result ∈ STATUS ∧
         rq ∉ requests                            request_status(rq) = incompl
   then requests := requests ∪ {rq}        then request_status(rq) := result
         request_status(rq) := incompl     end
   end                                       ...
```

Second Refinement. The goal of the second refinement is to model the steps involved into the process of request handling. While performing this refinement we again apply the *Goal Decomposition* pattern. In general, we should use goal decomposition technique until we reach the level of "primitive" goals, i.e., the goals for which we define the classes of agents – robots and collection points – eligible for execution of these goals.

When a new request arrives, WMS chooses a collection point and a number of idle robots to bring the boxes to this collection point. Thus, the high-level goal – *serve a request* – is split into two subgoals – *bring a box* and *assemble a parcel*. Here a subgoal *"bring a box"* should be executed a certain number of times determined by the specificity of a request.

In the second refinement step resulting in the machine SWS_m2, we augment our model with representation of discussed subgoals. New variables *box_status* and *package_status* represent the corresponding current subgoals statuses:

$$box\_status \in BOXES \rightarrow STATUS, \ package\_status \in requests \rightarrow STATUS.$$

The following gluing invariant establishes relation between the initial and the refined models:

$$\forall rq. \ request\_status(rq) = compl \Leftrightarrow (\ \forall bx. \ bx \in package\_boxes(rq) \Rightarrow$$
$$box\_status(bx) = compl) \land package\_status(rq) = compl.$$

The invariant can be understood as follows: the request is considered to be served if and only if all the required boxes are brought and the package is assembled.

The pattern event ReachingSubgoal corresponds to events BringBox and AssemblePackage:

BringBox $\hat{=}$	AssemblePackage **refines** RequestService $\hat{=}$
any bx, rq	**any** $rq, boxes$
where	**where**
$\quad rq \in requests \land bx \in package\_boxes(rq)$	$\quad rq \in requests \land package\_boxes(rq) = boxes$
$\quad box\_status(bx) = incompl$	$\quad \forall bx. \ bx \in boxes \Rightarrow box\_status(bx) = compl \land$
then	$\quad package\_status(rq) = incompl$
$\quad box\_status(bx) = compl$	**then** $package\_status(rq) = compl$
end	**end**

Third Refinement. In our development of SWS, we apply the *Goal Decomposition Pattern* several times. It allows us to divide each high-level goal for a robot into several intermediate goals, which could be translated into robot-level commands. Namely, every robot task – *to bring a box* – is split into several steps: move to the shelf position, pick up a box, move to a conveyor belt, deliver a box, finalize a task. The robot task is completed when the last step is performed. We define all these steps by the corresponding Event-B model events. Similar, we split the collection point behaviour into a number of steps. At this modelling step we have reached the desire level of granularity of our subgoals. In the next refinement we are going to augment our model with a representation of agents.

Fourth Refinement. This refined model is constructed according to the *Agent Modelling Pattern*. As a result, we introduce agents, their types (robots and collections points) and associate agents with the goals.

Fifth Refinement. Finally, we apply *Agent Refinement Pattern* to introduce possible agent failures (both for robots and collection points) and specify their effects on the main goals and subgoals execution (including goal reassigning).

5 Conclusions and Related Work

In this paper, we have presented a formal approach to the development of fault tolerant MAS. It is based on formalizing goal-oriented development in Event-B and defining a set of reusable specification and refinement patterns for representing the essential concepts of goal-oriented development: goals, goal decomposition and goal reachability. The reusable patterns can be instantiated to model goal reachability and goal decomposition at different levels of abstraction for a variety of MAS. Moreover, they allow us to formally define the relationships between the goals and the agents in a dynamic and traceable way. To cope with agents failures and achieve fault tolerance, we have demonstrated how to introduce fault tolerance mechanisms based on the dynamic goal re-allocation from failed agents. Formal modelling and refinement allowed us to prove goal reachability despite agent's unreliability. The approach has been demonstrated by a case study – a goal-oriented development of a smart warehouse system.

By combining goal-oriented and formal development in Event-B, we have created a systematic approach to structuring and formalizing behaviour of complex MAS. Goals define a suitable basis for a hierarchical decomposition of system behaviour, which enables direct and traceable association of low-level goals with agent functionality. In its turn, it facilitates an introduction of fault tolerance mechanisms based on agent health monitoring and dynamic goal re-allocation.

Unlike majority approaches, which rely on model checking for verifying goal reachability, our work is based on proof-based verification and correct-by-construction formal development. We believe that such an approach achieves better scalability and hence enables reasoning about behaviour of MAS with a large number of agents, which is typical, e.g., for multi-robotic applications. As a future work, we are planning to further extend the set of modelling patterns as well as combine this work with our previous works [8,15].

Related Work. MAS represent a popular paradigm for modelling complex and distributed systems. Various methodologies and tools have been proposed for design, development and verification of MAS [4,6,7,11,17]. However these approaches are limited to provide rigorous reasoning about agent behaviour as well as agent interactions. In our work we attempt to formally model each individual agent as well as the dynamic behaviour of the overall system. Moreover, employed Event-B modelling method was capable of rigorously describing all the essential aspects of goal-oriented development paradigm in MAS.

Significant work has been done on goal-oriented requirement engineering approaches. The foundational work on *goal-oriented development* belongs to van Lamsweerde [10]. The proposed KAOS framework [5] introduces a goal-oriented approach for requirements modelling, specification, and analysis as well as addresses both functional and non-functional system requirements. Based on the KAOS framework, Lamsweerde [9] has proposed a method for deriving the software architecture from its requirements.

The Tropos methodology [4] supports analysis and design in the development of agent-based software systems. UML diagrams are used to represent the system goals, agents, their capabilities and interdependencies, as well as system properties and agent interactions. An extension of this work [14] also supports modelling of agent errors and recovery activities.

A significant body of research has been also devoted for translating formal specifications built according to the KAOS goal-oriented method into event-based transition systems. For example, the work [12] presents an approach to use the formal analysis capabilities of LTSA (Labelled Transition System Analyser) to analyse and animate KAOS operational models. The mapping allows the designers to translate goal-oriented operational requirements into a black-box event-based model of the software behaviour, expressed in a formalism appropriate to reason about system behaviours at the architectural level.

Combination of the KAOS goal-oriented framework with the B formalism was presented in [16]. Another study to formalise KAOS requirements in Event-B is presented in [3]. The paper proposes a constructive approach that allows linking of high-level system requirements expressed as linear temporal logic formulae to the corresponding Event-B elements. Similar, Matoussi et al. [13] present works on coupling requirements engineering methods with formal methods. In contrast, in our work we have relied on goals to facilitate structuring of the system behaviour, while connecting them with the required agent behaviour.

References

1. Abrial, J.R.: Modeling in Event-B. Cambridge University Press, Cambridge (2010)
2. Abrial, J., Butler, M.J., Hallerstede, S., Hoang, T.S., Mehta, F., Voisin, L.: Rodin: an open toolset for modelling and reasoning in Event-B. Int. J. Softw. Tools Technol. Transfer **12**(6), 447–466 (2010). https://doi.org/10.1007/s10009-010-0145-y
3. Aziz, B., Arenas, A., Bicarregui, J., Ponsard, C., Massonet, P.: From goal-oriented requirements to Event-B specifications. In: First NASA Formal Methods Symposium - NFM 2009, pp. 96–105 (2009)
4. Bresciani, P., Perini, A., Giorgini, P., Giunchiglia, F., Mylopoulos, J.: Tropos: an agent-oriented software development methodology. Auton. Agents Multi-Agent Syst. **8**(3), 203–236 (2004). https://doi.org/10.1023/B:AGNT.0000018806.20944.ef
5. Darimont, R., Delor, E., Massonet, P., van Lamsweerde, A.: GRAIL/KAOS: an environment for goal-driven requirements engineering. In: Proceedings of the 19th International Conference on Software Engineering, pp. 612–613. ACM (1997)
6. DeLoach, S.A.: Multiagent systems engineering of organization-based multiagent systems. ACM SIGSOFT Softw. Eng. Notes **30**(4), 1–7 (2005). https://doi.org/10.1145/1082983.1082967
7. Ezekiel, J., Lomuscio, A.: Combining fault injection and model checking to verify fault tolerance in multi-agent systems. In: AAMAS 2009, pp. 113–120 (2009). https://dl.acm.org/citation.cfm?id=1558028
8. Laibinis, L., Pereverzeva, I., Troubitsyna, E.: Formal reasoning about resilient goal-oriented multi-agent systems. Sci. Comput. Program. **148**, 66–87 (2017). https://doi.org/10.1016/j.scico.2017.05.008
9. Lamsweerde, A.: From system goals to software architecture. In: Bernardo, M., Inverardi, P. (eds.) SFM 2003. LNCS, vol. 2804, pp. 25–43. Springer, Heidelberg (2003). https://doi.org/10.1007/978-3-540-39800-4_2
10. van Lamsweerde, A.: Goal-oriented requirements engineering: a guided tour. In: RE 2001, pp. 249–263. IEEE Computer Society (2001)
11. Letier, E.: Reasoning about agents in goal-oriented requirements engineering. Ph.D. thesis. Université catholique de Louvai (2001)

12. Letier, E., Kramer, J., Magee, J., Uchitel, S.: Deriving event-based transition systems from goal-oriented requirements models. Autom. Softw. Eng. **15**(2), 175–206 (2008). https://doi.org/10.1007/s10515-008-0027-7
13. Matoussi, A., Gervais, F., Laleau, R.: A goal-based approach to guide the design of an abstract Event-B specification. In: 16th IEEE International Conference on Engineering of Complex Computer Systems. ICECCS 2011, pp. 139–148 (2011)
14. Morandini, M., Penserini, L., Perini, A.: Towards goal-oriented development of self-adaptive systems. In: SEAMS 2008, pp. 9–16. ACM (2008). https://doi.org/10.1145/1370018.1370021. DBLP:conf/icse/2008seams
15. Pereverzeva, I., Troubitsyna, E., Laibinis, L.: Formal goal-oriented development of resilient MAS in Event-B. In: Brorsson, M., Pinho, L.M. (eds.) Ada-Europe 2012. LNCS, vol. 7308, pp. 147–161. Springer, Heidelberg (2012). https://doi.org/10.1007/978-3-642-30598-6_11
16. Ponsard, C., Dieul, E.: From requirements models to formal specifications in B. In: Workshop on Regulations Modelling and their Validation and Verification. ReMo2V 2006. CEUR Workshop Proceedings, vol. 241. CEUR-WS.org (2006)
17. Zambonelli, F., Jennings, N.R., Wooldridge, M.J.: Developing multiagent systems: the Gaia methodology. ACM Trans. Softw. Eng. Methodol. **12**(3), 317–370 (2003). https://doi.org/10.1145/958961.958963

A Study on Automated Receptionists in a Real-World Scenario

Ralf Wolter[2,3(✉)], Koen V. Hindriks[1], Dalya Samur[3], and Catholijn M. Jonker[2]

[1] Vrije Universiteit, Amsterdam, The Netherlands
k.v.hindriks@vu.nl
[2] Delft University of Technology, Delft, The Netherlands
{r.c.Wolter,c.m.jonker}@tudelft.nl
[3] ING, Amsterdam, The Netherlands
ralf.wolter@ing.com, dalyasamur@gmail.com

Abstract. The commercial availability of robots and voice-operated smart devices such as Alexa or Google Home have some companies wondering whether they can replace some current human interactions by using these devices. One such area of interaction is at the reception desk. While both platforms can offer the necessary interaction features to take on the task of an automated receptionist, the question remains as to which platform actual visitors would prefer - body or no body? To this end we created a receptionist agent that can receive visitors with an appointment, presented as either an embodied robot or a disembodied smart display. The agent uses common commercial products and services, and was tested in a real-world environment with real visitors.

The results show no significant difference in visitor preference for either platform.

Keywords: Human-robot interaction · Embodiment · Social agents · Dialogue management · Automated receptionist

1 Introduction

The user experience of people visiting bank branches has not changed much since the inception of the savings bank. A customer enters, waits in line, and states their needs to an employee. If it is a routine request the employee can help directly and the visit ends there. For more important meetings the customer can make a private appointment with a more specialised employee.

While over the years there has been little change in the bank visiting experience, ever-improving communication technology steadily reduced the need for customers to visit the bank branch in person [18]. From telegraph, to telephone, and now internet, increasingly secure and reliable channels allow many routine actions to be performed without visiting the bank. Recent years have even given rise to banks without any branches at all.

As more and more of the routine tasks are taken over by internet and mobile banking applications, the few visits left become more and more important to

© Springer Nature Switzerland AG 2020
Y. Demazeau et al. (Eds.): PAAMS 2020, LNAI 12092, pp. 340–352, 2020.
https://doi.org/10.1007/978-3-030-49778-1_27

both bank and client [21]. The decisions made during the visit could have a large impact on the clients personal future. From the perspective of the bank, it is one of the few times that it has direct face-to-face contact with the customer. As such it is one of the few opportunities to deepen the relationship.

To make the most of these scarce moments of contact, some companies are experimenting with new types of offices [8,9]. Some have replaced counters and stuffy meeting rooms with sitting areas decorated to feel like small living rooms. This is done in order to make a visitor feel welcome and at home. Similarly the receptionist plays a huge role in the customer experience. Making the customer be at ease and engaged and delivering a personalized experience is essential for a good customer relationship [4].

Even when entering a building with such a homely atmosphere, customers could still feel uncertain and uncomfortable if they are unfamiliar with the environment. It is then paramount to engage with these visitors as soon as possible to minimize those feelings [13]. Typically this is the role the receptionist fulfills.

With the recent advancements in robotics and AI, companies have been experimenting with automated assistants and receptionists to further improve customers experience [10,23]. The popularity of humanoid robots such as Softbank's Pepper [20] and smart displays such as Amazon Echo Show [1] make these obvious candidates for automating a receptionist. Speech recognition and generation capabilities allow for direct spoken dialogue between receptionist and visitor, while the electronic nature of the receptionist allows for sending and retrieval of relevant information in the background. With the wide variety of capabilities of these technologies, it is important to investigate which of their features contribute to an effective user experience when they are used as receptionists. One of the most striking difference between the two above-mentioned technologies is that a robot, such as Pepper has a humanoid robot body, while others, such as Alexa, use only voice for the interaction. Given these differences, especially with regard to the impact on deployment cost, it is important to investigate how important it is to give an automated receptionist a body. The availability of these tools raises the question of how important the embodiment is when replacing a counter with an automated receptionist. That is, if, in a real-life setting, we were to replace a reception desk with an automated agent, how important is it to give the agent a body? More precisely we studied:

Research Question: To what extent does providing a body for an automated receptionist contribute to a better user experience?

To this end we created a prototype agent that could handle receiving guests who have appointments. It engages a visitor in a verbal dialogue based on observed dialogues between receptionists and visitors. This agent was given two different housings, a Pepper robot, and a smart display.

The prototype was tested in a real life setting at a recruitment office of ING, a large international banking organization with its head office in the Netherlands. Visitors were almost exclusively job applicants coming in for an interview. Upon entry they were confronted with either a robot or a smart display. Their experiences were analysed in order to determine the effect of a robot body on user experience.

2   Related Work

The value of physicality in interaction fascinated humans even before the invention of robots. Interactions with robots or avatars have been studied and compared to other forms of communication. In these comparative studies some physical aspect of the robot is compared to virtual (visual) alternatives (for examples, see [3,7,14,15,22,24]). In most cases the virtual agent is a digitized avatar of the robot, so in essence an animation of the same robot on a screen.

The social settings studied vary from entertainment and games to informational and directive interactions. These are more extended tasks to the to the task in this research. Some compare an information display to a robot where a more traditional interface is put against a fully physical social robot. Hence, the mode of interaction also differs between the two options. In contrast, the present research takes an between path in which the interaction is performed through spoken dialogue by all parties, but there is no graphic representation of the assistant just a disembodied voice.

These comparisons are also generally studied in artificial lab scenarios. An exception is Lee et al. [16], who studied interactions with a receptionist robot by simple placing it in a busy area. The studies all reported a positive benefit to the physical robot above the virtual in their dependent variable. Bainbridge et al. and Lee et al. [3,15] listed more positive user ratings as a benefit.

Robots have been studied in real-world contexts, e.g., [6,17]. However, these studies were not comparative in nature, but studied the feasibility of having robots act effectively in the chosen situations. These studies have involved not only highly specialised robots such as SAYA [12] and Telenoid [19], but also commercial robots such as Nao, Pepper, Sophia [11] and Emiew3 [2].

To our knowledge, the present experiment is the first in which two automatized receptionists, with body and no body options, welcomed participants in the same experimental context which enables comparison of user experience with a commercial robot and a commercial audio platform.

3   Research Design

To answer the research questions stated in Sect. 1, the experimental design focuses on evaluation of the agent-user dialogue and user experience. Dialogue evaluation relies on transcription logs and classification of the utterances by human experts. User experience is measured by social robotics questionnaires completed by the participants after the interaction.

3.1   Groups and Participants

The participants were all job applicants for positions ranging from technical to human resources oriented. They were asked whether they wanted to participate in the experiment at the invitation to the interview. Due to the sensitive nature of a job interview, participants were informed that participation was voluntary and optional, and had no bearing on the interview.

Forty-six applicants agreed to participate in the experiment. 12 of the participants were female and 34 were male. They were between 22 and 36 years of age with an average age of 27.2. Five of the participants listed high school as their highest completed education, two had received their PhD and thirty-nine were university graduates.

For the experiment participants were divided into two groups. One group interacted with the agent housed in a Pepper robot, the other with the agent housed in the smart display setup. During interview days, the receptionist was setup in the morning and all visitors for the day were received with the same setup. All participants on the same day therefore encountered the same setup and were placed in one of the two groups based on this. Data were not collected from non-participants.

3.2 The Location

The experiment took place in an old farm remodeled as an office. Aside from the bank's human resource department, the building also houses the corporate academy used for training recruits.

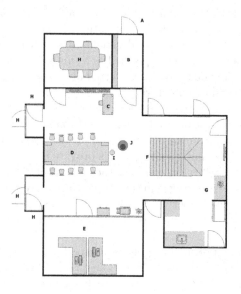

Fig. 1. Floor plan of the reception area.

All visitors enter the building through the main entrance at A and B, shown in Fig. 1. A receptionist located at C receives guests here. Guests are directed to a nearby area D to await an employee.

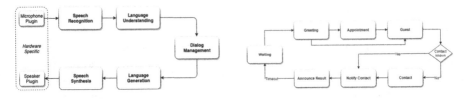

Fig. 2. Agent architecture   **Fig. 3.** Reception dialogue states

For the experiment, the desk at C where the receptionist would normally be sitting was removed. The human receptionist took seat nearby in area E to answer the phone, but not interact with guests. One exception was that when the agent had a fatal breakdown in the dialogue, it asked the visitor to wait and notified the receptionist instead of a proper appointment contact with the appropriate employee.

The agent housing was placed in front of the entrance at location J. A sign was hung on a support beam next to it asking visitors to report to the robot or smart display. The sign gave no instructions as to how this should be accomplished.

3.3 The Agent

The goals for the agent were twofold: First to be able to run different task-based dialogues as needed and secondly to execute the same dialogue independent of the hardware used. The agent is designed as a generic lightweight simple dialogue system. Dialogues can be specified as a simple state machine in a simple description format. This method was preferred above more advanced techniques for its clear predictability and control.

The architecture follows the classical dialog system approach as shown in Fig. 2. The pipeline is implemented as an asynchronous observable stream, each component reacting to incoming messages and producing the next message in the stream. The microphone and speaker plugins provide hardware specific hot spots where the behaviour can be customized to the housing of the agent. Speech recognition, language understanding and speech synthesis are wrapper components linking to commercial cloud services for the related tasks. Dialogue management implements a finite state machine-based execution environment for specifications of states and events.

It is common for spoken dialogue hardware to have some form of speech recognition and speech synthesis built-in. The quality of these pre-packaged solutions varies. So as not to let the quirks of each system influence the results, the designed agent skips the internal speech recognition, language understanding and speech synthesis. Instead, the agent components make use of the Google services for speech, dialogue flow and text-to-speech.

The dialogue manager handles incoming events, outgoing actions and session storage. A specification creates mappings between events and one or more actions based on the current state. Events include activation, semantic input as the result of the language understanding component, errors and timer notifications. Actions can be semantic output, state transition, store input, clear store, and execute plugin. One composite action is defined for selectively executing another action based on an expression. Plugins contain domain specific code, mainly used to communicate with external systems. This set of primitives creates a small specification language sufficient to handle simple task-based dialogues.

3.4   Agent Housing

For this experiment two housings were used for the agent. One is a Softbank Pepper robot and the other custom hardware representing the various smart displays on the market such as Amazon Echo and Google Home. Both have some lightweight plugins written for the specific requirements of the hardware.

In order to ensure that both setups would behave much the same and to control for aspects such as pitch and gender in the experiment, the speech generation and speech synthesis used in both setups are the same. Only the bodily behaviour differs between the setups.

Pepper. Pepper is a humanoid robot created by Softbank. It normally speaks with a high pitched child-like voice and makes contextual gestures. To keep the contextual gestures but speak in the agents (more mature) voice the plugin uses the normal speaking method with volume set to zero, while at the same time playing the audio stream generated by the agent. Audio from Pepper's speakers is directly streamed to the agent. In all other aspects, the default autonomous life feature of Pepper was used.

Smart Display. A custom setup was created for the smart display. Commercially available alternatives have closed-in aspects that allow direct streaming of audio and voice information. This would prevent the use of the agent's voice components. The custom setup used instead a Raspberry Pi Model B with audio capabilities. The plugins used are the generic Linux audio plugins for the agent.

3.5   Dialogue Specification

The model for the reception dialogue was based on a set of observations of human receptionists in action. The receptionists were asked to perform their task as normal while researchers observed. The conversations between receptionist and guest were also recorded.

The result was a set of recordings that give a general idea of how a human approaches this task. These recordings were transcribed and analysed to create a model for the dialogue as the agent should perform it.

In the diagram, shown in Fig. 3, boxes represent states derived from the transcripts. The sequence of events in the observed data always followed a fixed order. First the receptionist greets the guest, then guest are asked whether they have an appointment, followed by asking for the guest's name. Finally the receptionist asks for the contact name, after which the contact is called and the contact's answer is announced.

The data set showed three possible variations of this order. Some guests would tell the receptionist they had an appointment in response to the greeting, by passing the appointment query state. Other guests mentioned the contact's name during the greeting, allowing the contact query state to be skipped. The last variation combined the other two.

The "Greeting" state expects either a greeting intent or an appointment intent for the user. The "Appointment", "Guest" and "Contact" states query the user for the specific information and store this in the session. The "Notify Contact" state makes an external call and "Announce Result" state vocalizes the contact response. These states do not expect any user interaction. The decision state "Contact Known" is specified as a state handling only its activation events with guards to differentiate for the data in the session. The waiting state resets the session.

The model differs from the transcripts gathered from the human-human dialogues in one aspect. When notifying the contact the receptionist would pick up the phone and call the contact. The guest could see and hear this activity. For the dialogue system sending a message to the contact is silent and in the background, providing no clue to the guest as to what is going on. For this reason the system announces to the guest that it will notify the contact.

Repair Strategies. In one transcript shows the guest walked by the receptionist while giving a greeting in passing. Because the initial model was based on only a small set of dialogues, it is possible that a visitor could utter phrases the system has not yet heard. This indicates the need for recovery strategies.

A number of recovery strategies have been identified over the years. These range from repeating the question to giving full help information. Bohus et al. [5] showed that humans mostly employ asking the user to repeat and briefly going through the options of what the user could say.

The recovery strategy employed is a straightforward sequence of strategies. It first asks the users to repeat themselves (AREP), then makes a short suggestion of what to say (TYCS) and finally gives a more complete explanation of the user's options (YCS).

If all recovery actions (AREP, TYCS, YCS) fail to reach the intended result, the conversation is considered to have broken down and the system executes the fallback strategy. The fallback strategy is asking the guest to take a seat in the waiting area and notifying an employee to handle the task in person.

The normal strategy described above is used for states that require important information for the dialogue, such as appointment, guest and contact. A state such as greeting is considered less critical and has a more lenient recovery strategy in which the greeting is first repeated, if the system still does not understand after that it simply moves on to the next state.

3.6   Running the Experiment

The experiment ran for a total of 24 days. All participants were notified a week before about the data collection for the experiment and gave permission for their reception conversations to be recorded.

When a participant entered there was no other contact before engaging with the setup. Participants were expected to figure out where and how to interact with the setup on their own initiative. The only hint was a sign asking them to present themselves to the setup. Researchers observed the interaction of the participants with the setup. The agent automatically recorded and logged the conversation.

After the participant had taken a seat in the waiting area, a researcher approached the participant with the questionnaire. The employee contacts had been asked to wait ten minutes before approaching the participant.

3.7   The Measures

The conversation logs contained the textual transcript of the conversation as made by the agent, its' internal decisions, as well as the entire audio file of the conversation. The audio file was transcribed manually by a research assistant and afterwards compared with the logs for error analysis.

The questionnaires, offered to the participants, consist of three parts. A generic user experience part, namely "UX-questionnaire" [26], a part devoted to the specifics of embodiment, namely the "AttrakDiff questionnaire" [25], and a small number of open-ended questions.

The "UX-questionnaire" by Weiss and colleagues measures user experience focusing on five dimensions: Emotion (EM), Embodiment (EB), Feeling of Security (FoS), Human-oriented Perception (HOP), and Co-experience (COE). Each factor is assessed with five statements which were rated on a 7-point Likert scale.

AttrakDiff is a validated standardized questionnaire to get general insight on UX. This questionnaire is designed to measure four aspects: pragmatic quality of the system (PQ), hedonic quality identification (HQ-I), hedonic quality stimulation (HQ-S), and attractiveness (ATT). PQ describes the usability of the system. HQ-I is the extent to witch the user can identify with the system, and HQ-S is the extent to witch the system can stimulate functions and interactions. ATT describes the perceived quality of the system. This questionnaire consists of word-pairs, e.g. disagreeable - likable. Participants rate on a 7-point Likert scale, where negative word anchor is -3, and the positive anchor pole is 3.

Each of the two setups had its own version of the questionnaire, with the same questions but with the descriptions changed to correctly describe the setup. For the Pepper setup, the questions referred to "the robot", while for the display setup they referred to "the smart display". In all other aspects the two versions were exactly the same.

4   Results

After the initial testing 46 participants were received by the two setups. Of these 43 successfully completed the interaction. The participants included 12 females and 34 males and were between 22 and 36 years of age. In total 18 subjects (5 female, 13 male) interacted with the smart display setup, and 25 (5 female, 20 male) with the Pepper setup.

The error rate for all trials was 0.27. When normalized to the setups, the robot's rate was 0.32, while the smart display's rate was 0.19. The overall recovery rate was 0.94, 0.65 rate after one action, 0.87 after two actions, and 0.94 after the third action. During the course of the experiment, the fallback strategy was executed three times, a 0.06 breakdown rate.

The results for the AttrakDiff questionnaire are presented in Table 1. The values range from −3 to 3 in this scale; hence a mean value above 0 indicates a positive view of the experience, while below 0 indicates a negative view. Overall, the participants evaluated the experience as neutral and there were no significant differences between the two setups.

For the UX-Questionnaire, the values range from 1 to 7. The higher the value, the more positive the participants rated their experience. In this range 4.0 can be considered neutral with values lower than that negative and higher values positive. Table 2 shows a slight positive trend for "Feeling of Security" (FoS) while "Co-experience" (CoE) can be considered slightly negative. Differences between the robot setup and the smart display were not statistically significant.

5   Discussion

During the experiment 46 participants were received. These were serious applicants for job positions who were invited for interview as part of the normal operations of the human resources department. The procedure for the interviews was exactly the same as normal, except for their reception when entering the building, where the experiment was performed. This setup was dependent on the available pool of participants that were invited by the department.

Table 1. Results AttrakDiff

	ATT	HQI	HQS	PQ
Display Mean	0.532	0.357	0.873	0.794
Display S.D.	1.077	0.9754	1.030	0.8405
Robot Mean	0.362	0.259	1.167	0.490
Robot S.D.	0.8802	0.6564	0.7118	0.8619
t value	−0.069	−0.334	0.855	−0.983
p value	0.945	0.7404	0.398	0.332

Table 2. Results UX questionnaire

	COE	EB	EM	FoS	HoP
Robot Mean	2.589	4.390	4.470	5.005	4.227
Robot SD	0.7614	0.8872	0.6400	0.8126	0.8486
Display Mean	3.069	4.111	4.306	4.733	4.589
Display SD	1.143	1.058	0.8250	0.7388	0.6668
t value	−1.423	1.248	1.436	1.299	−1.076
p value	0.163	0.219	0.159	0.201	0.289

It is likely the participants were some form of stress during the experiment as they had their interview afterwards. This may have some influence on the results. We did not control for this variable. An topic requiring an appointment at a financial institution is almost by definition also a high state meeting as it likely involves a significant amount of financial resources. Therefore we made an assumption the participants would yield results similar to the targeted audience.

This brings us to the next question of how participants experienced the two platforms we tested. The questionnaire results show the users to be neither extremely positive, nor extremely negative about their experience.

In the present user experience results, we did not find any significant difference between the two setups. Other researchers have reported better user ratings for embodied agents [3, 15]. We speculate the differences could be the result of the interaction length (about 45 seconds), task related, and/or the limited number of subjects. Looking at the magnitude of the effect further research with much more participants would be needed. A conservative estimate indicated about twenty times the current number is needed.

Such a followup would require a significant investment of time and money. And while we would consider a conclusive answer to the question whether embodiment actually influences the user experience in a financial reception setting to be valuable, other variables to be investigated could be considered at least as valuable.

Another aspect to consider is that the two setups are far from equal in regard to price. A single Pepper unit costs as much a hundred smart display units. This combined with the uncertainty of the actual benefit of embodiment in this context would make such an investment risky at best.

In addition, while the hardware may differ, the actual agent was the same for both setups. This means further development of AI behind the agent is actually independent of the physical representation. This gives us the opportunity to use the inexpensive smart displays to test and experiment. In time, robots could become much cheaper and reliable. Making the transition at that time should still be possible as long as the hardware/software duality remains observed.

One intriguing possibility of the separation between hardware and software is the effect of mobility on the user experience. As the software agent can switch between robot and display for the experiment, it is also conceivable to switch between hardware on the fly during conversation. This would allow the agent to be divorced from its fixed location in the lobby. The agent could move with the user, jumping from hardware to hardware as needed.

A conversation with such a mobile agent could be structured completely different from a fixed agent. It could behave more like an assistant or friend guiding the user instead of a receptionist directing the user. In the end, perhaps we are trying too hard to imitate the receptionist we know instead of finding our own way with all the possibilities our technology offers.

6 Conclusions and Future Work

The experiment used a speech interface for interacting with users. While a lower error rate would be preferable, the overall success rate indicates that the agent can recover from these errors. This shows that technology and voice recognition have evolved far enough to be completely viable even in a noisy environment like a corporate lobby. Break-down in communication was rare and in most cases could be recovered from by repeating the last communication. From the users perspective the experience was neutral, neither positive, nor negative.

The main goal of the experiment was to test to what extent a body contributes to a better user experience with an automated receptionist. A comparison between the two setups indicated no significant difference in the reported user experience between a smart display and a Pepper robot.

The results are inconclusive. This leaves us in uncertainty as to the actual possible benefit of having a body. Given these results we can not recommend investing in expensive Pepper units for commercial automated receptions at scale at this time. The smart displays offer a viable alternative at much less cost and risk. The display can be upgraded to actual robots at a later point in time without serious loss of time and money.

Further research would be needed to reach a clearer picture on the actual benefits of having a body. With the current research design this would take an estimated period of 9 to 12 months assuming the same density of participants.

An other avenue to research would be the effect of agent mobility on the user experience. Combining strategically located smart displays with users smart phones could lead to a different reception experience altogether.

Aside from the mobility of the agent, a locale independent setup would need to change conversation style from the current version. In this experiment it mimics the actual conversation between a human receptionist and a guest. How a conversation could be structured if it no longer followed human conventions and limitations is a question that remains open.

One thing is clear, we have the technology to automate receptions and, at least in regard to our participants, guest are willing to use an automated reception. Implementing an reception agent will alter an organisation. In the extreme case of a fully mobile agent conventional lobbies and receptions desk may disappear as receiving guest becomes an ambient task of the organisation as a whole. The social impact of the could be far reaching and needs to be examined.

Acknowledgments. The authors would like to thank Joost Bosman, Edwin van Dillen and Martijn Schuts for their willing contributions to this project.

References

1. Amazon.com Inc.: Introducing echo show 5: compact smart display with alexa (2019). https://www.amazon.com/gp/product/B07HZLHPKP. Accessed 12 June 2019
2. Baba, A., Kagehiro, T., Koshizuka, H., Togami, M., Yoshiuchi, H.: Robotics solutions opening up new service markets. Hitachi Rev. **65**(9), 433 (2016)
3. Bainbridge, W.A., Hart, J.W., Kim, E.S., Scassellati, B.: The benefits of interactions with physically present robots over video-displayed agents. Int. J. Soc. Robot. **3**(1), 41–52 (2011)
4. Berry, L.L., Wall, E.A., Carbone, L.P.: Service clues and customer assessment of the service experience: lessons from marketing. Acad. Manag. Perspect. **20**(2), 43–57 (2006)
5. Bohus, D., Rudnicky, A.I.: Sorry, I didn't catch that!-an investigation of non-understanding errors and recovery strategies. In: 6th SIGdial Workshop on Discourse and Dialogue (2005)
6. Breazeal, C.: Social interactions in HRI: the robot view. IEEE Trans. Syst. Man Cybern. Part C (Appl. Rev.) **34**(2), 181–186 (2004)
7. Donahue, T.J., Scheutz, M.: Investigating the effects of robot affect and embodiment on attention and natural language of human teammates. In: 2015 6th IEEE International Conference on Cognitive Infocommunications (CogInfoCom), pp. 397–402. IEEE (2015)
8. Dunford, R., Palmer, I., Benveniste, J.: Business model replication for early and rapid internationalisation: the ING direct experience. Long Range Plan. **43**(5–6), 655–674 (2010)
9. Dutta, V.: Banking revisited: key trends reshaping banking in India. Paradigm **7**(1), 103–108 (2003)
10. Etlinger, S., Altimeter, A.: The conversational business (2017). Accessed 14 July 2017
11. Hanson, D.: Commencement 2018 keynote address—David Hanson via robotic proxy Sophia (2018)
12. Hashimoto, T., Kobayashi, H.: Study on natural head motion in waiting state with receptionist robot SAYA that has human-like appearance. In: 2009 IEEE Workshop on Robotic Intelligence in Informationally Structured Space, pp. 93–98. IEEE (2009)
13. Julian, C.C., Ramaseshan, B.: The role of customer-contact personnel in the marketing of a retail bank's services. Int. J. Retail Distrib. Manag. **22**(5), 29–34 (1994)
14. Kennedy, J., Baxter, P., Belpaeme, T.: The robot who tried too hard: social behaviour of a robot tutor can negatively affect child learning. In: 2015 10th ACM/IEEE International Conference on Human-Robot Interaction (HRI), pp. 67–74. IEEE (2015)
15. Lee, K.M., Jung, Y., Kim, J., Kim, S.R.: Are physically embodied social agents better than disembodied social agents?: the effects of physical embodiment, tactile interaction, and people's loneliness in human-robot interaction. Int. J. Hum. Comput. Stud. **64**(10), 962–973 (2006)

16. Lee, M.K., Kiesler, S., Forlizzi, J.: Receptionist or information kiosk: how do people talk with a robot? In: Proceedings of the 2010 ACM Conference on Computer Supported Cooperative Work, pp. 31–40. ACM (2010)
17. Linssen, J., Theune, M.: R3D3: the rolling receptionist robot with double Dutch dialogue. In: Proceedings of the Companion of the 2017 ACM/IEEE International Conference on Human-Robot Interaction, pp. 189–190. ACM (2017)
18. Malhotra, R., Malhotra, D.: The impact of internet and e-commerce on the evolving business models in the financial services industry. Int. J. Electron. Bus. 4(1), 56–82 (2006)
19. Ogawa, K., Nishio, S., Koda, K., Balistreri, G., Watanabe, T., Ishiguro, H.: Exploring the natural reaction of young and aged person with telenoid in a real world. JACIII 15(5), 592–597 (2011)
20. SoftBank Robotics: Pepper (2016). https://www.softbankrobotics.com/emea/en/pepper. Accessed 12 June 2019
21. Swaid, S.I., Wigand, R.T.: The effect of perceived site-to-store service quality on perceived value and loyalty intentions in multichannel retailing. Int. J. Manag. 29(3), 301 (2012)
22. Thellman, S., Silvervarg, A., Gulz, A., Ziemke, T.: Physical vs. virtual agent embodiment and effects on social interaction. In: Traum, D., Swartout, W., Khooshabeh, P., Kopp, S., Scherer, S., Leuski, A. (eds.) IVA 2016. LNCS (LNAI), vol. 10011, pp. 412–415. Springer, Cham (2016). https://doi.org/10.1007/978-3-319-47665-0_44
23. Tuzovic, S., Paluch, S.: Conversational commerce – a new era for service business development? In: Bruhn, M., Hadwich, K. (eds.) Service Business Development, pp. 81–100. Springer, Wiesbaden (2018). https://doi.org/10.1007/978-3-658-22426-4_4
24. Wainer, J., Feil-Seifer, D.J., Shell, D.A., Mataric, M.J.: The role of physical embodiment in human-robot interaction. In: The 15th IEEE International Symposium on Robot and Human Interactive Communication, ROMAN 2006, pp. 117–122. IEEE (2006)
25. Weiss, A., Bernhaupt, R., Lankes, M., Tscheligi, M.: The USUS evaluation framework for human-robot interaction. In: Proceedings of the Symposium on New Frontiers in Human-Robot Interaction, AISB 2009, vol. 4, pp. 11–26 (2009)
26. Weiss, A., Bernhaupt, R., Tscheligi, M., Yoshida, E.: Addressing user experience and societal impact in a user study with a humanoid robot. In: Proceedings of the Symposium on New Frontiers in Human-Robot Interaction, AISB 2009 (Edinburgh, 8–9 April 2009), SSAISB, pp. 150–157. Citeseer (2009)

Navigation of Autonomous Swarm of Drones Using Translational Coordinates

Jawad N. Yasin[1]([envelope]) [ORCID], Sherif A.S. Mohamed[1] [ORCID],
Mohammad-Hashem Haghbayan[1] [ORCID], Jukka Heikkonen[1] [ORCID],
Hannu Tenhunen[1,2] [ORCID], and Juha Plosila[1] [ORCID]

[1] Autonomous Systems Laboratory, Department of Future Technologies,
University of Turku, Vesilinnantie 5, 20500 Turku, Finland
{janaya,samoha,mohhag,jukhei,juplos}@utu.fi
[2] Department of Industrial and Medical Electronics,
KTH Royal Institute of Technology, Brinellvägen 8, 114 28 Stockholm, Sweden
hannu@kth.se

Abstract. This work focuses on an autonomous swarm of drones, a multi-agent system, where the leader agent has the capability of intelligent decision making while the other agents in the swarm follow the leader blindly. The proposed algorithm helps with cost cutting especially in the multi-drone systems, i.e., swarms, by reducing the power consumption and processing requirements of each individual agent. It is shown that by applying a pre-specified formation design with feedback cross-referencing between the agents, the swarm as a whole can not only maintain the desired formation and navigate but also avoid collisions with obstacles and other drones. Furthermore, the power consumed by the nodes in the considered test scenario, is reduced by 50% by utilising the proposed methodology.

Keywords: Autonomous swarm · Multi-agent systems · Agent-based modeling · Swarm intelligence · Leader follower

1 Introduction

Optimising different aspects in swarms of drones such as autonomous navigation, collision avoidance, payload reduction, resource allocation is gaining traction in the research community [1]. The deployment of swarms of UAVs adds remarkable advantages over single UAVs, as the UAVs in a swarm have the ability to work in a collaborative manner, and consequently have demand in various fields ranging from commercial use to search and rescue to military applications, and etc [2–4]. From the general perspective, the nodes or agents in the swarm can be classified

This work has been supported in part by the Academy of Finland-funded research project 314048 and Finnish Cultural Foundation.

Y. Demazeau et al. (Eds.): PAAMS 2020, LNAI 12092, pp. 353–362, 2020.
https://doi.org/10.1007/978-3-030-49778-1_28

as: 1) reactive agents, where agents react to changes in the environment or a signal from another agent; 2) evolutionary agents, these are inspired by evolutionary algorithms and work on the basic principles of reproduction, mutation, recombination, and selection; 3) flocking agents, mimic the behaviour, inspired by e.g., swarms of bees or flocks of birds, moving together; 4) cognitive agents, inspired by the cognitive architecture, enables them to take decisions, process data, and make predictions [5–7].

Formation maintenance and collision avoidance are the most important problems in navigation of a swarm of drones [8,9]. In a formation the relative location of each agent is defined w.r.t. the other agents in the swarm, while the collision avoidance focuses on the path planning for individual agents and is responsible for avoiding any possible collisions between agents within the swarm and the agents and objects in the environment. The methodologies, for maintaining the formation, can be categorised into the following three generic approaches [10,11] : 1) virtual structure, in this approach the drones are collectively considered as a single drone and navigated through the trajectory as such [12–14]; 2) leader-follower, in this approach every drone functions individually and autonomously while maintaining and adjusting its position according to the leader and its neighbours in the formation [15–18]; 3) behavior based approach, where from a pre-defined strategy, one of the numerous behaviours is selected by the drone [19,20]. Furthermore, collision avoidance algorithms can be classified into the following three generic categories: 1) optimization based algorithms are focused on determining the near-optimal solutions for navigational and path planning purposes of each drone relative to other drones or objects in the vicinity, by relying on the already known locations and sizes of the statics objects for an efficient route calculation [21–23]; 2) sense and avoid based, by simplifying the process of collision avoidance to individual detection and avoidance, these have short response times and require much less computational power, individual drones are controlled without the knowledge of other drones paths etc [24–27]; and 3) force-field based, in this technique each drone is considered as a charged particle with attractive or repulsive forces. These attractive/repulsive forces between different drones themselves or drone and obstacles are used to generate the path for the drone to be taken [28,29].

In this paper, the leader-follower based approach is used for the swarm due to its ease of analysis, implementation, scalability, and reliability [18,24]. The focus is cost saving by reducing the processing power and reducing the payload carried by individual drones while still keeping the swarm autonomous and able to navigate to its destination. A global collision avoidance algorithm is defined for the leader agent in the formation. Which is then used by the follower agents in the adaptive autonomous mode to be able to calculate the relative locations/coordinates of the objects in the environment as observed by the leader, hence tackling the generic problem of tracking by a follower relative to the master.

The rest of the paper is structured as follows. Section 2 gives the motivation. Development of the proposed algorithm is described in Sect. 3. Section 4 focuses on simulation results. Finally, Sect. 5 concludes the paper with some discussion and future work.

2   Motivation

There are many scenarios when the intelligent decision making is not required to be done by every single agent in a swarm. Especially when it comes to static environments, not all drones in the swarm need to be equipped with all sensors and similarly all the drones are not supposed to be taking decisions intelligently. As it increases the processing power required by individual drones resulting in decreased battery timing and hence decreased mission life on one charge. For instance in huge warehouses or in cities with high rising buildings, where normally the dynamic variables w.r.t. obstacles approaches to zero, if only one drone i.e., the leader of the swarm, can see and do all the processing required to take the decisions, it takes a lot of processing load off the followers. In this paper we consider this technique to decrease the overall cost of the swarm, e.g., power consumption of sensors, by deliberately activating and deactivating some of the follower sensors in run-time. Taking inspiration from reactive agents [5] and using our proposed technique, for instance, if the leader detects any change in environment or dynamicity, it signals to the followers to turn on the adaptive autonomous high-conscious mode wherein the followers turn on more sensors to pass the critical situation, and later they switch back again to the low-conscious mode. In the case of the high-conscious mode, we utilised the collision avoidance technique in [24], which will be activated and used by individual drones of the swarm. The main motivation behind this is the cost reduction by reducing the power consumption and processing required by every individual drone in an autonomous swarm.

3   Proposed Approach

The general pseudo code of the global leader is given in Algorithm 1. We assume that the UAVs are assigned IDs and the leader-follower connection has established before the mission is started. Using the on-board processing units, each node is executing this top-level algorithm locally. Algorithm 1 starts by checking if the global leader for the swarm has been declared, and declares the leader if it has not been set up yet. After this, the followers are connected to their immediate leaders (Lines 3–8). After this, every node (starting from the leader) sends its coordinates, along with the distance and angle at which an obstacle (if any) has been detected, to its follower (Line 11–14). Based on the received signal and coordinates from *FollowerMode*, the node checks and sets the *Lead_is_Alive* flag depending on if its leader is still functioning properly or not (Line 14). If there's is no response from the leader, the node in question announces itself as its own leader. The node/leader cross-checks the coordinates it received from its follower(s) after the follower has calculated the distances and angles (Line 15). A criticality check is done by analysing if the absolute value of the received coordinates or angles is greater than a certain threshold, in this case the environment is defined as dynamic (Lines 16–18). If the node is itself the global leader or if the environment has been declared as dynamic, then the collision avoidance module is called (Line 20–21). Otherwise, if the node is not the global leader and the environment is not declared as dynamic, the *FollowerMode* module is called (Line 23–24).

In case the node itself is the leader, the timeout signal is not checked; otherwise, every node checks if it is receiving signals constantly from its respective leader. If the leader has not transmitted its coordinates by timeout, the follower declares itself as its leader and turns on its sensors for active collision avoidance maneuvering.

Algorithm 1 Global Leader

1: **procedure** NAVIGATION & OBJECT DETECTION
2:     $Dynamic \leftarrow False$;
3:     **if** $Self.ID == 1$ **then**
4:         $MyLeader \leftarrow Self$;
5:         $Lead\_is\_Alive \leftarrow False$;
6:     **else**
7:         $MyLeader \leftarrow Leader(Self)$;
8:         $Lead\_is\_Alive \leftarrow True$;
9:     **end if**
10:     **while** True **do**
11:         **if** $MyLeader == Self$ OR $Lead\_is\_Alive == False$ **then**
12:             $D_{obstacle}, A_{obstacle} \leftarrow$ Calculate obstacle distance and angles at which the edges lie;
13:         **end if**
14:         $Lead\_is\_Alive, ref.coords \leftarrow$ FollowerMode() $\leftarrow$ send(
            $self.coord, angle, D_{obstacle}, Aobstacle$);
15:         $cal.ref.coords \leftarrow$ Reverse cross-check follower's received coordinates
16:         $CRITICALITYCHECK \leftarrow ref.coords - cal.ref.coords$
17:         **if** $|CRITICALITYCHECK| > Threshold$ **then**
18:             $Dynamic \leftarrow True$;
19:         **end if**
20:         **if** $Lead\_is\_Alive == False$ OR $Dynamic == True$ **then**
21:             $Dynamic \leftarrow$ AdaptiveAutonomousMode();
22:         **else**
23:             **if** $Lead\_is\_Alive == True$ AND $Dynamic == False$ **then**
24:                 FollowerMode();
25:             **end if**
26:         **end if**
27:     **end while**
28: **end procedure**

3.1   Coordinate Calculation

In this function (specified in Algorithm 2), the follower receives the coordinates of the leader and the coordinates of the obstacle detected (if any). If there is no feedback from the leader by the timeout, the node returns false for its leader status (Lines 2–3). This information is then used by the node to declare itself as the leader for the fail safe mode in Algorithm 1 (Lines 21–22). Otherwise, based on its own coordinates, the node calculates the translational coordinates of the obstacle and returns the calculated values to be cross-checked (Lines 6–8), as shown in the Fig. 1 (Table 1).

Algorithm 2 FollowerMode

```
1: procedure FOLLOWERMODE(rcvcoord, rcvangle, dist.obstacle, angle.obstacle)
2:     if !rcvcoord AND Timeout == 3 then
3:         Lead_is_Alive ← False;
4:         return(Lead_is_Alive, self.coords)
5:     else
6:         Lead_is_Alive = True;
7:         self.coords ← Calculate new coordinates;
8:         return(Lead_is_Alive, self.coords)
9:     end if
10: end procedure
```

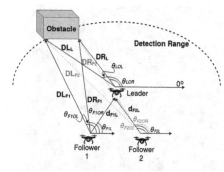

Fig. 1. Distance and direction calculation (Color figure online)

Table 1. Description of variables from Fig. 1

Variables	Description
DR_L DL_L	Distance of right and left edges of the obstacle from leader
DR_{F1} DL_{F1} DR_{F2} DL_{F2}	Calculated distance of obstacle's right and left edges from follower 1 and follower 2, respectively, as observed by leader
d_{F1L} d_{F2L}	Distance of leader from follower 1 and follower 2 respectively
θ_{LOR} θ_{LOL}	Angle at which right and left edges are detected from leader respectively
θ_{F1L} θ_{F2L}	Angle of leader from follower 1 and follower 2, respectively
θ_{F1OR} θ_{F1OL} θ_{F2OR} θ_{F2OL}	Angles at which right and left edges are detected from follower 1 and follower 2, respectively

3.2 Adaptive Autonomous Mode

If there are any obstacle(s) in the detection range, then this mode, Algorithm 3, is called by the leader. If the environment has been declared to be dynamic, then those node(s) which are working individually call this module locally. The system calls for collision avoidance module and keeps on checking the status of the environment (Line 2). In order to successfully avoid collisions, we utilise the collision avoidance technique presented in [24]. As soon as the collisions have been avoided, the status of the environment is set to static and the control is returned to the main module (Lines 3–5).

Algorithm 3 AdaptiveAutonomousMode

```
1: procedure ADAPTIVEAUTONOMOUSMODE()
2:     Collision avoidance (Dynamic);
3:     if !D_obstacle then
4:         Dynamic ← False;
5:         return(Dynamic)
6:     end if
7: end procedure
```

4   Simulation Results

The initial conditions/assumptions for our work are defined as follows:

1. all UAVs have constant ground speeds
2. UAVs obtain their own position vectors using the on-board localization techniques
3. there is no information loss in communication between the UAVs

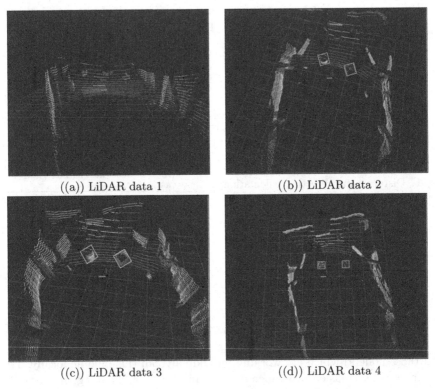

((a)) LiDAR data 1   ((b)) LiDAR data 2

((c)) LiDAR data 3   ((d)) LiDAR data 4

Fig. 2. LiDAR point set at starting point of simulation and when the obstacles are visible (Color figure online)

The LiDAR sensor used in our experiment is Velodyne Puck LITE. The data generated by Velodyne Puck LITE was then used and injected into the simulation platform for visualisation purposes, generation of the obstacle(s), and verification of the proposed algorithm.

Figure 2, shows the LiDAR data from different angles and at different intervals for instance at starting point (Fig. 2(a)), when the obstacles enter detection range (Figure (b)), when the obstacles are in close vicinity (Figure (c) and 2(d)).

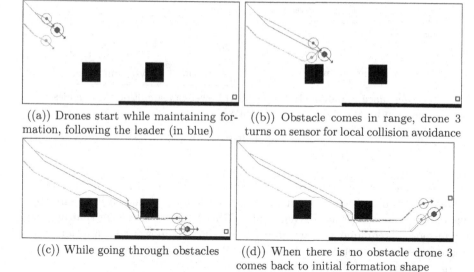

((a)) Drones start while maintaining formation, following the leader (in blue)

((b)) Obstacle comes in range, drone 3 turns on sensor for local collision avoidance

((c)) While going through obstacles

((d)) When there is no obstacle drone 3 comes back to initial formation shape

Fig. 3. Simulation Results at different instances (Color figure online)

In these figures, the position of the drone equipped with LiDAR is shown as the blue, red, and green bars indicating the z, y, and x-axes, respectively.

The simulation results shown in Fig. 3 show the V-shaped formation, in which UAV 1 (blue circle) is the leader (which is getting the data from LiDAR as shown in Fig. 2 and UAV 2 (red) and 3 (green) are followers calculating their coordinates as shown in Fig. 1. Figure 3(b) shows the scenario where the obstacle is within the detection range of the leader but not in its path. However, UAV3 upon performing necessary calculations realises that continuing along the current path will lead to a collision, and hence it deviates away from its original path as can be seen from the traces of the UAVs.

Figures 3(c) and 3(d) show the case when they go through the obstacles. Notice UAV2 does not deviate from its path and maintains the desired position w.r.t. UAV1 even when the second obstacle is close to it. That is because the calculations performed locally by UAV2 indicate that the collision is not possible given that the obstacle is stationary and out of the collision radius. However, after avoiding the second obstacle, UAV3 maintains the pre-defined minimum safe distance from UAV1 since going back to formation is not possible due to the third obstacle in the bottom. When the final destination is moved at runtime, Fig. 3(d), UAV3 comes back to its position in the formation, turns off the sensor, and starts following UAV1 by translating the coordinates transmitted by UAV1. Figure 4(a) shows the distances maintained by the UAVs throughout the simulation.

5000 mAh battery was used in the setup, and the power consumption of one Velodyne Puck LITE is 8 W (in typical conditions). Based on these values we calculated the power consumed by the sensors of all nodes, by tracking the

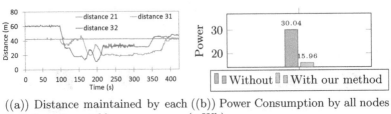

((a)) Distance maintained by each ((b)) Power Consumption by all nodes
drone from its neighbours   (mWh)

Fig. 4. Results

amount of time every sensor on each agent was active or turned on, during the
simulation with and without our proposed methodology (shown in Figure (b)),
where power consumption is given in milli-Watt hours. It is evident that utilising
the proposed technique we can significantly reduce the power consumption of on-
board sensors by approximately 50%, and hence increase the mission duration
on one charge.

5   Conclusion

In this paper, we developed an algorithm for pre-defined formation of multi-
agents in a static environment, where under normal circumstances one agent
can see the surroundings and the other agents blindly follow. However, depending on the scenario the follower(s) can turn on their sensors for safety purposes.
The proof of concept using simulation tools was performed to verify the method
of translational coordinates calculation in a system consisting of multiple agents,
i.e., a swarm of drones. The simulation results shown provide sufficient proof that
the method works reliably in simulated static environments. It is evident from
the results that the proposed algorithm helps reducing the power consumed by
the sensors over time. In the considered test scenario it turned out to be approximately half the power consumed if the sensors are used in a continuous mode. In
general, this power saving naturally depends on the dynamicity/structure of the
environment. In future, we plan to further develop this algorithm by extending it
for moving obstacles and test its usability in dynamic environments. This will be
very interesting to analyse especially when two swarms have to cross paths i.e.,
multi-swarm cross-overs, as only the leader agents of both swarms can communicate, and the follower agents in the respective swarms use the leaders' translated
coordinates.

References

1. Campion, M., Ranganathan, P., Faruque, S.: A review and future directions of UAV
   swarm communication architectures. In: 2018 IEEE International Conference on
   Electro/Information Technology (EIT), pp. 0903–0908, May 2018

2. Murray, R.: Recent research in cooperative control of multi-vehicle systems. J. Dyn. Syst. Meas. Control **129**, 571–598 (2007)
3. He, L., Bai, P., Liang, X., Zhang, J., Wang, W.: Feedback formation control of UAV swarm with multiple implicit leaders. Aerosp. Sci. Technol. **72**, 327–334 (2018). https://doi.org/10.1016/j.ast.2017.11.020, http://www.sciencedirect.com/science/article/pii/S1270963816309816
4. Ladd, G., Bland, G.: Non-military applications for small UAS platforms. In: AIAA Infotech@ Aerospace Conference and AIAA Unmanned... Unlimited Conference, p. 2046 (2009)
5. Mualla, Y., et al.: Agent-based simulation of unmanned aerial vehicles in civilian applications: a systematic literature review and research directions. Future Gener. Comput. Syst. **100**, 344–364 (2019). https://doi.org/10.1016/j.future.2019.04.051, http://www.sciencedirect.com/science/article/pii/S0167739X18328462
6. Gkiokas, A., Cristea, A.I.: Cognitive agents and machine learning by example: representation with conceptual graphs. Comput. Intell. **34**(2), 603–634 (2018). https://doi.org/10.1111/coin.12167, https://onlinelibrary.wiley.com/doi/abs/10.1111/coin.12167
7. Dorri, A., Kanhere, S.S., Jurdak, R.: Multi-agent systems: a survey. IEEE Access **6**, 28573–28593 (2018)
8. Zhuge, C., Cai, Y., Tang, Z.: A novel dynamic obstacle avoidance algorithm based on collision time histogram. Chin. J. Electron. **26**(3), 522–529 (2017)
9. Wang, X., Yadav, V., Balakrishnan, S.N.: Cooperative uav formation flying with obstacle/collision avoidance. IEEE Trans. Control Syst. Technol. **15**(4), 672–679 (2007)
10. Wei, R.: Consensus based formation control strategies for multi-vehicle systems. In: 2006 American Control Conference, pp. 6pp., June 2006
11. Low, C.B., Ng, Q.S.: A flexible virtual structure formation keeping control for fixed-wing UAVs. In: 2011 9th IEEE International Conference on Control and Automation (ICCA), pp. 621–626, December 2011
12. Beard, R.W., Lawton, J., Hadaegh, F.Y.: A coordination architecture for spacecraft formation control. IEEE Trans. Control Syst. Technol. **9**(6), 777–790 (2001)
13. Li, N.H., Liu, H.H.: Formation UAV flight control using virtual structure and motion synchronization. In: 2008 American Control Conference, pp. 1782–1787. IEEE (2008)
14. Dong, L., Chen, Y., Qu, X.: Formation control strategy for nonholonomic intelligent vehicles based on virtual structure and consensus approach. Procedia Eng. **137**, 415–424 (2016). Green Intelligent Transportation System and Safety
15. Oh, K.K., Park, M.C., Ahn, H.S.: A survey of multi-agent formation control. Automatica **53**, 424–440 (2015)
16. Buzogany, L., Pachter, M., D'azzo, J.: Automated control of aircraft in formation flight. In: Guidance, Navigation and Control Conference, p. 3852 (1993)
17. Shen, D., Sun, Z., Sun, W.: Leader-follower formation control without leader's velocity information. Sci. China Inf. Sci. **57**(9), 1–12 (2014)
18. Han, Q., Li, T., Sun, S., Villarrubia, G., de la Prieta, F.: "1-N" leader-follower formation control of multiple agents based on bearing-only observation. In: Demazeau, Y., Decker, K.S., Bajo Pérez, J., de la Prieta, F. (eds.) Advances in Practical Applications of Agents, Multi-Agent Systems, and Sustainability: The PAAMS Collection, pp. 120–130. Springer International Publishing, Cham (2015). https://doi.org/10.1007/978-3-319-18944-4_10
19. Lawton, J.R., Beard, R.W., Young, B.J.: A decentralized approach to formation maneuvers. IEEE Trans. Robot. Autom. **19**(6), 933–941 (2003)

20. Balch, T., Arkin, R.C.: Behavior-based formation control for multirobot teams. IEEE Trans. Robot. Autom. **14**(6), 926–939 (1998)
21. Zhang, X., Liniger, A., Borrelli, F.: Optimization-based collision avoidance. arXiv preprint arXiv:1711.03449 (2017)
22. Pham, H., Smolka, S.A., Stoller, S.D., Phan, D., Yang, J.: A survey on unmanned aerial vehicle collision avoidance systems. CoRR abs/1508.07723 (2015). http://arxiv.org/abs/1508.07723
23. Smith, N.E., Cobb, R., Pierce, S.J., Raska, V.: Optimal collision avoidance trajectories via direct orthogonal collocation for unmanned/remotely piloted aircraft sense and avoid operations. In: AIAA Guidance, Navigation, and Control Conference, p. 0966 (2014)
24. Yasin, J.N., Haghbayan, M.H., Heikkonen, J., Tenhunnen, H., Plosila, J.: Formation maintenance and collision avoidance in a swarm of drones. In: Proceedings of the 3rd International Symposium on Computer Science and Intelligent Control. ISCSIC 2019, Amsterdam, Netherlands. ACM, September 2019
25. Prats, X., Delgado, L., Ramirez, J., Royo, P., Pastor, E.: Requirements, issues, and challenges for sense and avoid in unmanned aircraft systems. J. Aircr. **49**(3), 677–687 (2012)
26. Albaker, B.M., Rahim, N.A.: A survey of collision avoidance approaches for unmanned aerial vehicles. In: 2009 International Conference for Technical Postgraduates (TECHPOS), pp. 1–7, December 2009. https://doi.org/10.1109/TECHPOS.2009.5412074
27. Soriano, A., Bernabeu, E.J., Valera, A., Vallés, M.: Multi-agent systems platform for mobile robots collision avoidance. In: Demazeau, Y., Ishida, T., Corchado, J.M., Bajo, J. (eds.) Advances on Practical Applications of Agents and Multi-Agent Systems, pp. 320–323. Springer, Heidelberg (2013). https://doi.org/10.1007/978-3-642-38073-0_37
28. Albaker, B.M., Rahim, N.A.: Unmanned aircraft collision detection and resolution: concept and survey. In: 2010 5th IEEE Conference on Industrial Electronics and Applications, pp. 248–253, June 2010. https://doi.org/10.1109/ICIEA.2010.5516808
29. Seo, J., Kim, Y., Kim, S., Tsourdos, A.: Collision avoidance strategies for unmanned aerial vehicles in formation flight. IEEE Trans. Aerosp. Electron. Syst. **53**(6), 2718–2734 (2017)

Multi-agent Service Area Adaptation for Ride-Sharing Using Deep Reinforcement Learning

Naoki Yoshida[1,2](✉), Itsuki Noda[2](✉), and Toshiharu Sugawara[1](✉)

[1] Department of Computer Science and Engineering, Waseda University,
Tokyo 1698555, Japan
`n.yoshida@isl.cs.waseda.ac.jp`, `sugawara@waseda.jp`
[2] National Institute of Advanced Industrial Science and Technology,
Ibaraki 3058560, Japan
`i.noda@aist.go.jp`

Abstract. This paper proposes a method for adaptively assigning service areas to self-driving taxi agents in ride-share services by using a centralized deep Q-network (DQN) and demand prediction data. A number of (taxi) companies have participated in ride-share services with the increase of passengers due to the mutual benefits for taxi companies and customers. However, an excessive number of participants has often resulted in many empty taxis in a city, leading to traffic jams and energy waste problems. Therefore, an effective strategy to appropriately decide the service areas where agents, which are self-driving programs, have to wait for passengers is crucial for easing such problems and achieving the quality service. Thus, we propose a service area adaptation method for ride share (SAAMS) to allocate service areas to agents for this purpose. We experimentally show that the SAAMS manager can effectively control the agents by allocating their service areas to cover passengers using demand prediction data with some errors. We also evaluated the SAAMS by comparing its performance with those of the conventional methods.

Keywords: Multi-agent learning · Ride-share service · Deep Q-networks

1 Introduction

The ride-share service is now part of our daily life thanks to the spread of communication technologies and portable smart devices. In this service, everybody can participate as a driver or passenger, and because passengers share taxis with strangers, it is expected to reduce the number of cars on the roads (which also reduces the pollution), fares, operation cost, and traffic congestion. These are advantages for both ride-share companies and passengers [1]; thereby, the number of ride-share services such as Uber[1] and Lyft[2] is rapidly increasing worldwide.

---

[1] https://www.uber.com/.
[2] https://www.lyft.com/.

© Springer Nature Switzerland AG 2020
Y. Demazeau et al. (Eds.): PAAMS 2020, LNAI 12092, pp. 363–375, 2020.
https://doi.org/10.1007/978-3-030-49778-1_29

We believe that future ride-share services will be provided by self-driving taxis that are cost effective and high quality.

However, the appropriate arrangement of agents, which are the programs for self-driving taxis for passenger(s), is a challenging issue due to the imbalance in the time and locations of passengers' demands. In addition, numerous cars in specific locations may result in severe traffic jams [2]. For example, agents have to go to and wait in the most demanded locations, such as stations and airports at busy times, because there they are more likely to be able to pick up passengers. This may be a rational decision from the ride-share company's myopic viewpoint but may lead to the oversupply of taxis in some areas and areas where there are no taxis, leading to a decrease of sales and low service quality. Therefore, a ride-share company has to have a certain coordinated strategy to predict where passengers will appear next and appropriately allocate agents to their own *service areas* where they should wait for passengers.

Meanwhile, a number of demand prediction methods for taxis that gather numerous passengers' trip data by using the global positioning system (GPS) data via intelligent programs in smartphones are proposed [3]. Because such demand prediction data include the estimated number of passengers, their pickup times, locations, and destinations within a few tens of minutes, a number of studies stated that ride-share companies should use these data for giving the next movement instructions to all taxis [4]. However, most current studies assume that demand prediction data are accurate, but accidental and unforeseeable events are always possible in the real world.

Therefore, this paper proposes a control method for a multi-agent ride-share service to decide the service area of individual agents, called the *service area adaptation method for ride share* (SAAMS), using *deep reinforcement learning* (or *deep Q-networks* (DQNs)) and demand prediction data that may contain uncertainty to some degree. The SAAMS manager, which is a centralized learning controller in a ride-share company like that of other studies [4], assigns to the driver agents the service areas where they will wait and provide services for passengers in accordance with the received prediction data, although, in the other studies mentioned above, the controller gives to all taxis the sequences of micro (or minimum-unit) movements, such as moving to one of the neighboring areas or staying at the current place in their simulated environments. Therefore, the SAAMS agent does not care about the detailed paths to the assigned areas when their service areas are reassigned; we assume that such detailed micro movements are determined by individual agents. This approach makes the learning process simpler; thus, it considerably improves the learning speed and the robustness to noisy data in prediction.

We then experimentally evaluated the SAAMS in a simulation environment by comparing it with the conventional method [4]. Our experimental results indicate that the SAAMS learning agent could realize coordinated behaviors and improve the service quality by reducing the passenger's waiting time. We also found that control by SAAMS generated implicit coordinated behavior by deciding the main areas of responsibility and could avoid oversupply and deal with unexpected demands.

2   Related Work

The effective arrangement of vehicles is a key issue in a variety of ride-share systems. Before the 2010s, dial-a-ride problems for on-demand bus systems were the most common studies, so many methods to find (near) optimal solutions to arrange buses for passengers, to, for example, minimize travel time and/or waiting time [5, 6] With the rise of the use of mobile devices, research has shifted to the arrangement problem between passengers and taxis in ride-share services [7,8]. Nakashima et al. [7] proposed a ride-share service system that looked for a reasonable arrangement by (1) sending a passenger's demand to all cars, (2) calculating the expected required time including waiting and travel time, and then (3) allocating the demand to the car whose expected required time is the shortest. They demonstrated that their ride-share system with their proposed arrangement method worked well in the actual system in Hakodate City, Japan. Alonso-Mora et al. [8] formulated the taxi arrangement of the ride-share service as an integer programming framework and proposed a method to find the semi-optimal solutions. This study showed that their solution could reduce by 70 percents the number of taxis in downtown New York required to cover all the taxi demands.

On the other hand, demand prediction method has been studied in the context of bus and taxi services [3], and a few studies proposed ride-share control using demand prediction data [4,9,10]. For example, Miao et al. [4] proposed *receding horizon control* (RHC) in which empty cars are guided to a service area where there is a shortage of cars. RHC was formulated using a linear programming framework and can control empty cars to improve the service efficiency by more than that of the previous studies, which did not take into account any demand prediction data. However, this approach is weak due to the error or dispersion in demand prediction data. Our study attempts to introduce flexibility to the dispersion in the prediction data using the DQN technique.

Of course, there are a number of studies on taxi arrangement problems in ride-share systems using the DQN technique (without using prediction data) to deal with complex environments and diverse demand patterns [9,10], and actually, some studies demonstrated that the performances of their arrangement methods were equal to or higher than those of the previous studies.

Lin *et al.* [10], for example, proposed a method in which the centralized DQN agent instructs the movements of all taxis and evaluates this in the simulation using the actual arrangement data. However, it is hard to learn their behaviors in a complicated environment within a reasonable learning time because the DQN in their method instructs the sequence of micro movements as mentioned in Sect. 1; therefore, such sequences are usually long, leading to a long learning time and instability of learning because the shortest paths may vary over time due to the dynamic nature of traffic conditions. In contrast, the SAAMS manager learns how the service areas of individual agents are covered using the received most up-to-date demand prediction data and the rewards that reflect the achievements of services.

3   Problem Formulation and Model

3.1   Ride-Share Problem

Let $\mathcal{D} = \{1, \ldots, n\}$ be the set of agents, and we introduce a discrete time $t \geq 0$. The environment is described by an $L \times L$ grid ($L > 0$ is an integer) consisting of cells, and each cell represents a $K_x \times K_y$ region (K_x and K_y are approximately 500 meters in our experiments below). Therefore, any numbers of agents and passengers can exist in a cell. Figure 1 shows an example environment, in which orange circles are agents and empty triangles are passengers waiting to move to their destinations. Each agent has the passenger capacity, $Z > 0$, and cannot carry more passengers than Z. Finally, S is the set of states of the environment, and the state at time t is denoted by $s_t \in S$, which includes all agents, the known passengers, the current service areas of all agents, and the updated demand prediction data.

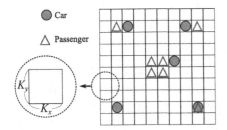

Fig. 1. Environment of ride-share problem.

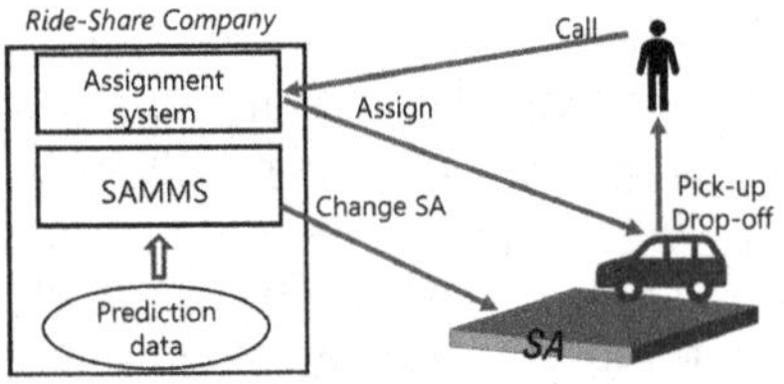

Fig. 2. Architecture of ride-share service with the SAAMS.

The system architecture of our ride-share system is shown in Fig. 2. At time t, the SAAMS manager assigns agent $\forall i \in \mathcal{D}$ to its service area $C_{i,t}$ that is an $T_x^i \times T_y^i$ region of cells, and i's service area is kept until the next adjustment of the service area by the SAAMS manager. Then, i will try to move somewhere it can easily wait in the assigned service area (in our experiments, i tries to move to the center of the area).

Agents can move up, down, left, or right. When $i \in \mathcal{D}$ is assigned to service area $C_{i,t}$, we assume that it immediately tries to drive to the center cell of $C_{i,t}$, and waits for passengers if i is empty; otherwise, i continues the current service to drive to the passengers' destination, and then i drives back to the center of $C_{i,t}$ after they have got off. This behavior of agents indicates that the SAAMS manager indirectly and partly navigates agents by changing the locations of service areas.

When a ride demand from passengers arrives at the ride-share company, the taxi arrangement system immediately finds a *vacant agent*, which is defined as the agent that is empty or has enough vacant seats and is closest to the passenger(s) (Fig. 2). Moreover, we also introduce the expected maximum travel time (EMTT). The ride-share system may assign a car agent to additional passengers if the expected arrival time does not exceed the EMTT by taking the new passengers. If multiple agents are equally close, (1) the agent that has the lowest ID number is selected in the training phase or (2) one agent is selected randomly in the test phase. Then, it moves to the cell where the passengers are waiting, picks them up, drives to their destination, and drops them off there. After that, it returns to its service area specified by the SAAMS. Note that the SAAMS agent does not care about the paths to the passenger's destination and to the service area; these are decided individually by driver agents.

The purpose of our ride-share service is that agents carry as many (groups of) passengers as possible to their destination reasonably quickly in a timely fashion. Because a quick pickup of passengers is essential for a quality service, the SAAMS manager learns the appropriate *assignment* of a service area to each agent. Therefore, the SAAMS's assignment strategy to reduce the average waiting time of passengers using the most-updated demand prediction data is our main concern. Note that because busy locations (cells) where many demands regularly are made require many taxis, the agents' service areas overlap there.

Table 1. List of adjustments for service area.

Name	Manipulation of adjustments
Enlarge	C_i whose size is $T_x^i \times T_y^i$ enlarges to $(T_x^i + 2) \times (T_y^i + 2)$
Shrink	C_i whose size is $T_x^i \times T_y^i$ shrinks to $(T_x^i - 2) \times (T_y^i - 2)$
Up, down, left, right	Move C_i up, down, left, or right (no change in size)
Stay	Keep the current service area

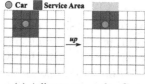

(a) Adjustment *up* for C_i.

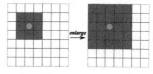

(b) Adjustment *enlarge* for C_i.

Fig. 3. Examples of manipulation for adjusting service area.

3.2 Adjustment of Service Areas

The SAAMS manager adjusts the service areas of agents for a quality service. Let A be the set of the (joint) adjustments of service areas of all agents; adjustment

$a_t \in A$ at time t can be expressed by $a_t = (a_t^1, \ldots, a_t^n) \in A = A^1 \times \cdots \times A^n$, where A^i is the set of adjustments of i's service area. We introduce seven adjustments of service area $A^i = \{enlarge, shrink, up, down, left, right, stay\}$; the details of these adjustments are listed in Table 1. Examples of adjustments up and $enlarge$ are shown in Fig. 3.

Service area C_i is the rectangular space consisting of a number of cells, whose maximum size is $T_x^i \times T_y^i$ (where $T_x^i, T_y^i > 0$ are integers) and minimum is 1×1. If an adjustment for C_i results in a violation of size constraints, it is treated as $stay$. At state s_t, the SAAMS manager decides joint adjustment $a_t \in A$ based on its policy π derived from the DQN and notifies all agents of the resulting service areas.

4   Proposed Method

4.1   SAAMS

The SAAMS uses the centralized DQN whose inputs are the part of the environmental state $s_t \in S$ and outputs are the Q-values for adjustments of service areas for all agents to work efficiently from the viewpoint of the ride-share company.

The design of the reward scheme is crucial to maximize the received cumulative future rewards. We first introduce the following weighted rewards for agent i:

$$r_t^i = w_b b_t^i - w_p d_t^i \quad \text{and} \quad r_t'^i = -w_f f_t^i, \tag{1}$$

where w_b, w_p, and w_f are the rewards' weight parameters whose values are non-negative and real. Reward $b_t(> 0)$ is the number of demands assigned to i at time t, and $d_t^i(> 0)$ is the distance (the number of cells) between i and the location where the assigned passengers are waiting; thus, d_t^i is a cost. Therefore, i receives r_t^i only when it is assigned to the demand at t, and r_t^i can be positive or negative. Meanwhile, $f_t^i(= 0 \text{ or } 1)$ denotes if i's service area C_i has changed, so i receives a negative reward $r_t'^i < 0$ when a_t^i is not $stay$; thus, a large w_f prevents unnecessary adjustment for service areas.

Note that agent i (and so the SAAMS) only receives a positive reward when it is assigned to the demand that arises in C_i during the training phase, so the SAAMS learns to change C_i to cover more predicted cells. However, an enlargement does not necessarily result in a higher r_t^i because i may be assigned to pick up distant passengers. This suggests a trade-off between the size of C_i and the distances to passengers. In addition, the change of C_i always incurs cost $r_t'^i$. Of course, it better that C_i covers the busy locations, but an excessive concentration of agents leads to high competition and ignorance of passengers in areas where there is a shortage of agents, losing opportunities to provide services. Therefore, the SAAMS requires that i needs to learn appropriately both the location and size of C_i on the basis of the demand prediction data.

Table 2. Network architecture.

Layer	Input	Filter size	Stride	Activation	Output
Convolutional	$L \times L \times 61$	2×2	1	ReLu	$L \times L \times 512$
Max pooling	$L \times L \times 512$	2×2	2		$L/2 \times L/2 \times 512$
Convolutional	$L/2 \times L/2 \times 512$	2×2	1	ReLu	$L/2 \times L/2 \times 512$
Max pooling	$L/2 \times L/2 \times 512$	2×2	2		$L/4 \times L/4 \times 512$
FCN	$L/4 \times L/4 \times 512$			ReLu	1024
FCN	1024			Linear	210

4.2   Structure of Network

We use double DQN (DDQN) [11] to suppress the overevaluation. Our DQN consists of two convolutional neural network (CNN) layers and two fully connected neural network (FCN) layers (Table 2). The network's outputs are the action-value pairs of agents to decide the next action a_t^i for $\forall i \in \mathcal{D}$.

The example environment and the associated input fed to the centralized double DQN are shown in Fig. 4. The input consists of:

1. One $L \times L$ grid including the prediction data provided by a certain prediction system in the test phase, as shown in Fig. 4b, which includes the predicted numbers of passengers' demands in the example environment (Fig. 4a). On the other hand, because we can assume that the SAAMS in the training phase knows the actual demand locations where agents already took passengers, the prediction data fed to the DQN are replaced by actual demand data that are successfully assigned to the agents whose service areas included the waiting place. An example of actual demand data is shown in Fig. 4c.
2. $2n$ $L \times L$ grids of the service areas of all agents, $C_{i,t-1}$ and $C_{i,t}$ ($1 \leq i \leq n$, $t \geq 1$).

Note that the locations of agents are not included in the input. Because they may be far from their service areas when they are carrying passengers, the current locations of agents are rarely useful to decide the service areas.

We apply the experience replay to update the weight parameters of DQN. Because samples of DQN are time-series data, DQN is likely to overfit to the frequently appeared samples, and the learning becomes unstable. For this reason, the SAAMS stores the sample as $(s_t, a_t, R(s_t, a_t), s_{t+1})$ in the buffer, where $R(s_t, a_t)$ is $\sum_{i \in \mathcal{D}} r_t^i + r'^i_t$. We also set the replay buffer size d (>0) indicating the number of samples that can be stored in the buffer, and the oldest samples are removed when the buffer overflows. Then, the SAAMS randomly selects U samples from the buffer and feeds them to the DQN to update, where positive integer U is called the *minibatch size*.

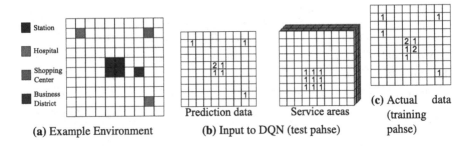

Fig. 4. Environment and examples of prediction data. (Color figure online)

5   Experiments

5.1   Experimental Settings

We evaluated our proposed method experimentally using our simulated environment by varying the error rate in the demand prediction data. Our experimental environment is shown in Fig. 4a, where colored cells express the busy areas. By referring to a report of taxi demands in Tokyo [12], we generated the ride-share demands that appear at one of the busy areas that are *station area, two hospitals, business district,* and *shopping center* whose occurrence ratio is 4:1:1:1 or that appear at random locations. We assume that random demands occur with a probability of $0 \le e_1 \le 1$. We denote the set of cells of busy areas by B. Their destinations are also determined in the same way, i.e., random destinations with a ratio of e_1 and others' destinations (whose ratio is $1 - e_1$) are busy areas whose ratio is also identical to the demand occurrence ratio, but we assume that the start location and destination of each demand are different.

Demands are generated in accordance with the Poisson distribution $\mathcal{P}_o(\lambda)$ every time step, and their start locations are determined using the ratio described above. We will vary the value of λ between 0 and 3.0, where 1.0 and 2.0 correspond to the moderately and very busy periods of time. We assume that the prediction data includes only the numbers of demands at busy locations generated in this way; an example of the prediction data is shown in Fig. 4b, where empty cells mean no demands.

We generated the actual data by adding two types of prediction errors to the prediction data because the predictions are not usually complete. The first type of error is random demands whose occurrence rate is e_1, meaning that unexpected demands possibly occur everywhere because this type of demand in the unbusy area can hardly be predicted. The second type of error expresses the fluctuations of the estimated number of demands at the busy area. This error is measured by distance, $\delta \ge 0$, which is called the *error distance* and defined as

$$\delta = \sum_{x \in B} |p_x - o_x|,$$

Table 3. Setup parameters.

Parameter	Value
Number of agents, n	30
Environment size (km)	5.0
Cell size (km), K_x, K_y	0.5
Riding capacity, Z	2
Max size of service area, T_x, T_y	5
Cost of changing service area, f_t	1

Table 4. Network parameters.

Parameter	Value
Replay buffer size, d	100,000
Learning rate, α	0.0001
Update interval of target network	20,000
Discount factor, γ_q	0.99
Mini batch size, U	64
Initial and final values of ε	1.0, 0.1

where p_x is the expected demand number at cell x in the prediction data and o_x is the number of demands in the actual data. For example, the error distance δ between the prediction and actual data in Fig. 4 is 1 (and there are two random demands). The actual demand data (in the training phase) and prediction data (in the test phase) were fed to the DQN every 10 steps (which corresponds to 30 min).

We set the weight parameters in Formula 1 as $w_b = 1$, $w_p = 0.1$, and $w_f = 0.01$. The EMTT was defined as twice the time required to carry the passengers along the shortest paths from the locations where they declared their demands. The other setup parameters are listed in Table 3. Note that we assumed that the size of a cell (K_x and K_y) is the square of 0.5 Km and one time step corresponds to 3 min, so agents can move to a neighboring cell in one time step on average (Table 4).

To evaluate our proposed methods, we measured the mean (Manhattan) distance between agents and passengers when they are assigned because this distance indicates the passengers' waiting time, which is an indicator to evaluate the quality of the service. We also measured the mean driving mileage during each experimental run. We used the DQN for the SAAMS trained for 8000 epochs (one epoch is 200 steps). Then, these data are compared with those when using the RHC [4] and non-position control (NPC). The RHC tries to move unassigned cars by giving instructions to move to shortage areas on the basis of prediction data. It uses the linear programming framework and was often used to compare its performance with the performances of the methods using DQNs in several papers [9]. Note that agents under the RHC are instructed each movement every certain interval (so 10 steps) if they are empty. The NPC does not use prediction data, and empty agents always drive randomly if they are empty. The experimental data shown below were mean values of 100 runs (epochs).

5.2 Effect of Demand Occurrence Rate

First, we examined the effect of demand occurrence rate λ on the entire performance, especially the quality of service. The mean distances between passengers and agents when they were arranged using the prediction data with the error number $\delta = 0$ and 5 were plotted in Figs. 5 and 6. We set $e_1 = 0.3$ because the

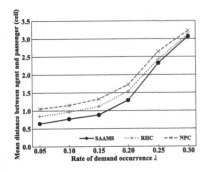

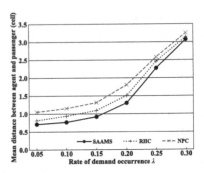

Fig. 5. Mean distance between agents and passengers ($e_1 = 0.3, \delta = 0$).

Fig. 6. Mean distance between agents and passengers ($e_1 = 0.3, \delta = 5$).

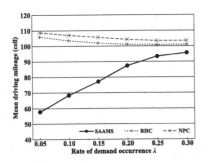

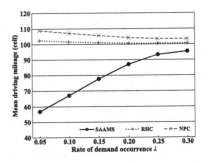

Fig. 7. Total driving mileage per epoch ($e_1 = 0.3, \delta = 0$).

Fig. 8. Total driving mileage per epoch ($e_1 = 0.3, \delta = 5$).

random demands must arise very often and are unignorable. These figures indicate that the mean distance when using the SAAMS was the smallest, resulting in the shortest passengers' waiting times.

Figures 7 and 8 plotted the mean driving mileage per agent in an epoch. We can see that their mean driving mileage was much shorter under the SAAMS control than that under the RHC, which indicates that the SAAMS control could avoid redundant driving and have agents stand ready to take passengers near the cells where passengers are expected to appear. However, agents under the RHC wait for passengers at the expected cells in a slightly concentrated form, and this behavior makes it harder for agents under the RHC to cover the random demands.

5.3   Effect of Errors in Demand Prediction

Figures 9 and 10 indicate how the mean distance between agents and passengers varied with the value of the error distance δ. They show that agents under the SAAMS control could reach the waiting places of passengers much earlier than the case when agents are controlled by the RHC. By comparing these figures, we can say that if e_1 is larger, their differences became smaller; actually, the mean

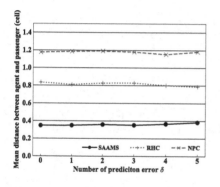

Fig. 9. Mean distance between agents and passengers ($e_1 = 0, \lambda = 1.0$).

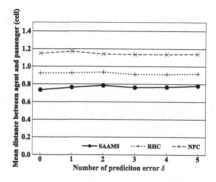

Fig. 10. Mean distance between agents and passengers ($e_1 = 0.3, \lambda = 1.0$).

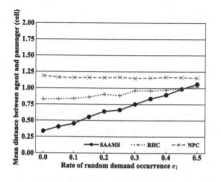

Fig. 11. Mean distance between agents and passengers ($\delta = 0, \lambda = 1.0$).

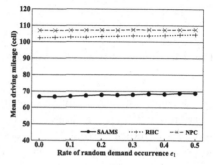

Fig. 12. Mean driving mileage per epoch ($\delta = 0, \lambda = 1.0$).

distances were almost identical when agents were controlled by NPC because they moved randomly when they were empty, so this was the upper bound of the mean distance. They also show that the mean value seemed not to be affected by the value of δ because the large δ affected only the numbers of demand occurrences at busy areas.

On the other hand, the difference of e_1 affects the mean distance, as shown in Fig. 11, which plots the mean distance between agents and passengers when $\delta = 0$ and $\lambda = 1.0$. Because random demands could not be predicted, the mean distances were likely to become larger with the increase of e_1, but the agents controlled by the SAAMS could keep shorter distances than those with other methods. However, the mean driving mileage of each agent per epoch looks almost invariant with e_1, as shown in Fig. 12.

5.4 Difference in Behaviors

To understand the difference in the agents' behaviors when they are controlled by the RHC and the SAAMS, we generated heatmaps (Fig. 13) showing the numbers

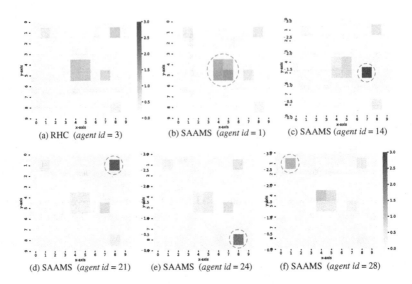

Fig. 13. Number of passengers taking at each cell (heatmap). (Color figure online)

of passengers taken by individual agents at each cell. We only show the data in a certain epoch, but the overall tendency described here was almost identical. Figure 13(a) indicates that the agents took passengers almost proportional to the demand occurrence ratio when controlled by the RHC. Note that we only show the data of the agent whose ID is 3, but the heatmaps of others were also similar so they had the similar behaviors.

On the other hand, agents' behaviors under the SAAMS control were different and could be classified into five groups, as shown in Fig. 13(b)-(f); they were likely to take passengers at the specific locations shown by red circles. The strategy with which agents were split up and took passengers appearing at different places, like these heatmaps, may not be bad but not be the best. However, under the RHC control, agents tended to be concentrated in expected busy areas; thus, their distances to the passengers appearing at unbusy locations became slightly longer. However, the SAAMS allocated the service areas in different locations and indirectly navigated the self-driving agents there. Therefore, they could cover wide areas and could arrive at passengers' locations within shorter times.

6   Conclusion

We proposed the SAAMS for the adaptive control of self-driving agents by using the centralized DQN with demand prediction data in a ride-share service environment. The SAAMS directly controls the agents' service areas where individual agents should wait for passengers to make passengers' waiting times shorter, leading to better service quality for the ride-share service. In addition, the control of the service areas also means the indirect control of movements of all agents. We evaluated the SAAMS in our simulated environment and compared its performance with the performance of other conventional methods. Our experimental results indicate the SAAMS could achieve shorter waiting time and was more robust to errors or noise of prediction data.

We introduced three weight parameters w_b, w_p, and w_f in Formula 1, but their values should be decided or learned in a more flexible way for more effective and higher quality ride-share services. Furthermore, since we assumed that there was only one ride-share company, we will consider the situation in which multiple companies have their own DQNs and analyze the generated competition or coordination structure.

Acknowledgements. This work was supported by JSPS KAKENHI (17KT0044) and JST-Mirai Program Grant Number JPMJMI19B5, Japan.

References

1. Yaraghi, N., Ravi, S.: The current and future state of the sharing economy. SSRN Electron. J. (2017)
2. Erhardt, G.D., et al.: Do transportation network companies decrease or increase congestion? Sci. Adv. **5**(5), Kindly provide volume and page number for Ref. [9], if applicable. (2019)
3. Ke, J., Zheng, H., Yang, H., Chen, X.(Michael): Short-term forecasting of passenger demand under on-demand ride services: a spatio-temporal deep learning approach. Transp. Res. Part C: Emerg. Technol. **85**, 591–608 (2017)
4. Miao, F., et al.: Taxi dispatch with real-time sensing data in metropolitan areas: a receding horizon control approach. CoRR, abs/1603.04418 (2016)
5. Cordeau, J.-F., Laporte, G.: A tabu search heuristic for the static multi-vehicle dial-a-ride problem. Transp. Res. Part B: Methodol. **37**(6), 579–594 (2003)
6. Berbeglia, G., Cordeau, J.-F., Laporte, G.: A hybrid tabu search and constraint programming algorithm for the dynamic dial-a-ride problem. INFORMS J. Comput. **24**, 343–355 (2012)
7. Nakashima, H., et al.: Design of the smart access vehicle system with large scale ma simulation. In: Proceedings of the 1st International Workshop on Multiagent-Based Societal Systems (2013)
8. Alonso-Mora, J., Samaranayake, S., Wallar, A., Frazzoli, E., Rus, D.: On-demand high-capacity ride-sharing via dynamic trip-vehicle assignment. Proc. Natl. Acad. Sci. **114**(3), 462–467 (2017)
9. Oda, T., Joe-Wong, C.: MOVI: a model-free approach to dynamic fleet management. In: IEEE INFOCOM 2018 - IEEE Conference on Computer Communications, pp. 2708–2716, April 2018
10. Lin, K., Zhao, R., Xu, Z., Zhou, J.: Efficient large-scale fleet management via multi-agent deep reinforcement learning. In: Proceedings of the 24th ACM SIGKDD International Conference on Knowledge Discovery & Data Mining, USA, pp. 1774–1783. ACM (2018)
11. van Hasselt, H., Guez, A., Silver, D.: Deep reinforcement learning with double Q-learning. In: Proceedings of the 30th Conference on Artificial Intelligence. AAAI 2016, pp. 2094–2100. AAAI Press (2016)
12. Tokyo Hire-Taxi Association. Result of taxi research in 2018 (2018). http://taxi-tokyo.or.jp/enquete/pdf/research2018.pdf

Demo Papers

Assisting Users on the Privacy Decision-Making Process in an OSN for Educational Purposes

José Alemany[1]([✉]), Elena del Val[2], and Ana García-Fornes[1]

[1] VRAIN, Universitat Politècnica de València, Camino de Vera s/n, Valencia, Spain
{jalemany1,agarcia}@dsic.upv.es
[2] DIIS, Escuela Universitaria Politécnica de Teruel, Teruel, Spain
edelval@unizar.es

Abstract. In online social networks (OSNs), users create and share content to socialize with others. There are some privacy risks that emerge due to the access and/or misuse of this content. We propose a modular approach with an agent-based implementation for assessing the privacy risk of a posting action using soft-paternalism mechanisms. This proposal has been included in a gamified social network called PESEDIA, developed with educational purposes.

Keywords: Online social networks · Privacy decision-making · Scope of the action · Nudging mechanisms · Gamification · Education

1 Introduction

Online social network (OSN) users interact and socialize between them sharing their opinions and comments, supporting their friends and favorite groups, and posting their information, activities, etc. As a result, huge traffic of information is produced daily. The way to control the access and use of this information is via the privacy policies. However, privacy is a concept of disarray for OSN users [7]. Users do not have complete information to assess the consequences of a sharing action in a OSN. Therefore, privacy problems such as the *invisible audience* [6], that refers to the audience a user did not know were looking, or the access to information by unintended users through *resharing actions* of content might also cause a risky privacy situation. These situations might lead users to make wrong decisions with a negative effect on their real life.

2 Main Purpose

This work develops a modular approach for providing users with privacy mechanisms that estimate the potential risk of reaching an unintended audience with a sharing action based on its privacy policy selected. The estimation of the potential risk is introduced to users through well-informed and personalized nudges.

© Springer Nature Switzerland AG 2020
Y. Demazeau et al. (Eds.): PAAMS 2020, LNAI 12092, pp. 379–383, 2020.
https://doi.org/10.1007/978-3-030-49778-1_31

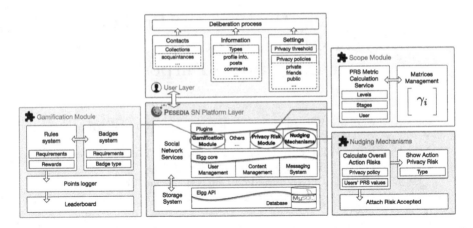

Fig. 1. PESEDIA SN architecture.

In this way, users are a proactive way in the privacy decision-making process. The modules are used by a Privacy-Aware agent that represents the interests of each user in the social network. The agent takes as input the action request, the content of the action, and the audience selected based on social circles and individuals selected. Next, the agent assesses the action of sharing and provides information about the estimated privacy risk associated to the action. This proposal provides a mechanism to enhance users' information privacy without relinquishing the social benefit of using social networks.

3   Demonstration

We developed an OSN called PESEDIA where all the modules and agents were included[1]. PESEDIA acts as a tool for learning and increasing the privacy awareness of its users. Currently, PESEDIA is operative and has been already used in several year editions of the summer school at Technical University of Valencia. It was applied in the context of a 1-month course about privacy management to a teenager population. The main goals of PESEDIA include: (i) the design and development of new metrics to analyze and quantify privacy risks [3]; (ii) the application of methods to influence on users' behaviour towards a safer actions regarding their privacy [2]; (iii) and the evaluation and testing of new proposals with real users. The underlying implementation of PESEDIA uses Elgg[2], which is an open source engine used to build social environments. PESEDIA was designed to be similar to well-known social networks where privacy decisions are taken by users daily like on Facebook. We developed each functionality on PESEDIA through modules following the design principles of Elgg engine (see Fig. 1). These

---

[1] https://pesedia.webs.upv.es/.

[2] https://elgg.org/.

Fig. 2. Examples of PESEDIA's functionality. (Top and middle) Nudges to inform about the estimated risk of a publication. (Bottom) Badges used to offer a visual representation of the learning progress.

modules can be activated and deactivated at any moment from a dashboard. Next, we describe the modules developed that compose this work.

Users' Scope Module. The topological location of a user in the network, how active a user is, user's probability of re-sharing content in the network, and other properties have been studied for analyzing information spreading in networks. From the point of view of determining the privacy risk, or even the social benefit, associated to a user's sharing action, it is interesting to determine if there are influential users in the audience or in the path that information follows. In this module, the PRS (Privacy Risk Score) metric is calculated, which is a metric for estimating the scope of user's actions taking into account (i) his/her position in the social network graph, and (ii) the flows of information previously produced in the social network [3,4]. This module aims to avoid risky privacy situations of access to information by unintended users.

Nudging Module. How the information message is depicted to users is a relevant factor for an effective communication. Effective communication uses clear, short, and relevant messages to support users' decision making. It is necessary to mitigate the potential negative effects of asymmetric information and overcoming the overconfidence biases that may lead to suboptimal decisions. Previous works have already tested the validity of these nudges to cause an effect on users' behavior during the publication in OSNs [1,2,5]. This module is responsible for introducing the privacy risk computed with well-informed reasons to users. Figure 2 (top and middle) shows an example of the nudges developed to inform about the estimated risk of a publication to a user.

Gamification. PESEDIA includes gamification that allows students to learn about privacy risks in OSN through a set of activities. The gamification design included in PESEDIA offers to users the possibility to choose what activities to complete. We have considered game design elements at two levels of abstraction: (i) educational gamification design principles and (ii) game mechanics. The gamification design principles selected are based on the idea of progress. The intention was to present practical lessons in stages that scale by difficulty, but that each user can accommodate to his/her own pace and needs. The game mechanics proposed are based on the following three key elements: Points, Badges, and Leaderboard. Figure 2 (bottom) shows the available badges in PESEDIA that offer a visual representation of the learning progress and are given for special achievements.

4   Conclusions

This paper presents a modular approach with an agent-based implementation for assessing the privacy risk of a posting action. This proposal has been included in a gamified social network called PESEDIA aimed at educating young people on privacy. The modules developed allow an estimation of the risk of a publication having a wider scope than expected and through soft-paternalism mechanisms (nudges) inform the user to make more informed decisions about their publications. In addition, a gamification module has been developed that allows for autonomous learning adapted to the user's pace.

Acknowledgments. This work is partially supported by the Spanish Government project TIN2017-89156-R, and the FPI grant BES-2015-074498.

References

1. Acquisti, A., et al.: Nudges for privacy and security: understanding and assisting users' choices online. ACM Comput. Surv. (CSUR) **50**(3), 44 (2017)
2. Alemany, J., del Val, E., Alberola, J., García-Fornes, A.: Enhancing the privacy risk awareness of teenagers in online social networks through soft-paternalism mechanisms. Int. J. Hum. Comput. Stud. **129**, 27–40 (2019)
3. Alemany, J., del Val, E., Alberola, J., García-Fornes, A.: Estimation of privacy risk through centrality metrics. Future Gener. Comput. Syst. **82**, 63–76 (2018)
4. Alemany, J., del Val, E., Alberola, J.M., Garćia-Fornes, A.: Metrics for privacy assessment when sharing information in online social networks. IEEE Access **7**, 143631–143645 (2019)

5. Alemany, J., del Val, E., García-Fornes, A.: Empowering users regarding the sensitivity of their data in social networks through nudge mechanisms. In: Proceedings of the 53rd Hawaii International Conference on System Sciences (2020)
6. Croom, C., Gross, B., Rosen, L.D., Rosen, B.: What's her face (book)? How many of their facebook "friends" can college students actually identify? Comput. Hum. Behav. **56**, 135–141 (2016)
7. Solove, D.J.: Understanding privacy (2008)

A Demonstration of the Routing Model Evaluator

Vince Antal, Tamás Gábor Farkas, Alex Kiss, Miklós Miskolczi,
and László Z. Varga(✉)

Faculty of Informatics, ELTE Eötvös Loránd University, Budapest 1117, Hungary
lzvarga@inf.elte.hu

Abstract. There are different models of the routing problem. We are building a test environment, where the decision making methods of the different models can be evaluated in almost real traffic. The almost real traffic runs in a well known simulation platform. The route selections are injected into the simulation platform, and the simulation platform drives the vehicles. We demonstrate how the routing model evaluator can be run to evaluate a routing model against a dynamic equilibrium.

Keywords: Autonomous vehicles · Route selection · Dynamic equilibrium

1 Introduction

The routing problem is a network with traffic flows of agents going from a source node to a destination node in a congestion sensitive manner. The agents want to optimise their trips. There are different formal models for the routing problem. A basic assumption of traffic engineering is that the traffic flows are assigned to routes in accordance with an equilibrium, which is either a static equilibrium [9] or a dynamic equilibrium [4]. We are interested in the route selection of autonomous vehicles, and we would like to know how the formal models of the routing problem can support the trustworthy decision making of real-world autonomous agents.

Online Routing Game. The online routing game model [7] contains elements of the routing game model [6], the queuing model [1] and the concept of online mechanisms [3]. In the online routing game model [7], the traffic flow is made up of individual agents who follow each other, and the agents of the traffic flow individually decide which route to select, depending on the real-time situation.

Intention-Aware Online Routing Game is a special type of online routing game, where the agents communicate their intentions to a service. The service forecasts future traffic durations, and the agents, who are still planning their route, use this information to make decision.

Traffic Simulators. The main model in microscopic traffic simulation software is the car following model [5] which simulates real driving behaviours. A free and

© Springer Nature Switzerland AG 2020
Y. Demazeau et al. (Eds.): PAAMS 2020, LNAI 12092, pp. 384–387, 2020.
https://doi.org/10.1007/978-3-030-49778-1_32

open simulation software is the SUMO (Simulation of Urban MObility) traffic simulation suite [2]. The SUMO simulation software gives tools to find a dynamic equilibrium in an iterative way using two methods: the Iterative Assignment (Dynamic User Equilibrium) method and the classic logistic regression method.

The focus of our simulation software is specifically on the evaluation of the above mentioned intention-aware online routing game model in a realistic environment represented by the SUMO simulator.

2   Architecture of the Routing Model Evaluator

The software architecture (see Fig. 1) consist of the SUMO simulator, the Open Routing Game (ORG) Model, the Coordinator and the 3D View. The SUMO system is responsible for both the two-dimensional view and for micromanaging the vehicles, such as changing lanes, keeping the required following distance and complying with the traffic rules. The ORG Model component is the implementation of the Online Routing Game model in C#. Given a network of roads and a list of traffic flows, the model's responsibility is to select the route for the agents according to one of the four available routing methods: shortest, fastest, detailed prediction [8] and simple prediction [8]. The Coordinator is written in Python, and it establishes a connection with all of the other components. It reads a map downloaded from OpenStreetMap[1], and it sends the map to the other components of the system. When the Coordinator receives a command from the ORG Model, stating that a new vehicle shall be spawned at a given lane, the Coordinator translates this information into a format that is understood by the SUMO system, then forwards this request. The communication between the 3D View and the SUMO system is similar: the coordinates of the vehicles are requested from the SUMO system, and then they are transmitted to the view periodically. The 3D View component provides a 3D overview of the simulation. It's implemented with the ThreeJS[2] JavaScript library, and it runs on most modern browsers. At the end of the simulation both the ORG Model and the Coordinator produces log files. The log file of the ORG Model contains statistics from the online routing game model. The log file of the Coordinator contain statistics from the SUMO execution.

3   Running the Routing Model Evaluator

A scenario can be started with the Routing Model Evaluator using the command `main.py -n map.net.xml -c conf.cfg.json --3DView -o out.xlsx`, where the argument `-n` is the name of the map file of the scenario extracted from OpenStreetMap using the SUMO tools, the argument `-c` is the name of the configuration file of the scenario, and the argument `-o` is the name of the output file where the statistics are written. The switch `--3DView` indicates that we want

---

[1] https://www.openstreetmap.org/.

[2] https://threejs.org/.

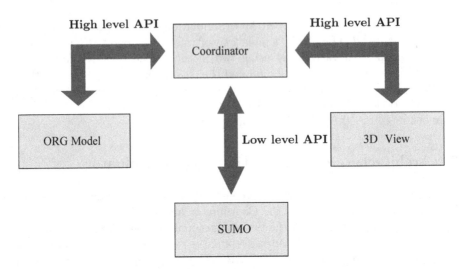

Fig. 1. Software architecture

to have a 3D View. The configuration file contains the parameters of the traffic flows, the duration of the simulation, and the routing strategy to be used by the ORG Model. The routes are assigned to the vehicles in the SUMO simulator by the ORG model. The simulator can be run faster than real-time on an average laptop. The output statistics file will contain the ID, the start time, the end time and the duration of the trip of each vehicle, as well as the minimum, maximum and the average of the duration, together with their standard deviation.

We use the `Sumo\tools\assign\duaIterate.py` program to compute a dynamic user equilibrium of a scenario. We provide the same map as argument `-n map.net.xml`, the same trips as argument `-t conf.trips.xml`, and the convergence is provided as `--max-convergence-deviation 0.001` which is 0.1%. The duaiterate program may run for about 30 minutes on an average laptop. The duaiterate program creates a trip information file for each iteration. The trip information file contains the route assignment for each vehicle for the duration of the simulation. We execute the trip information file of the last iteration in SUMO. The log file of the SUMO simulator is processed with Excel to create the same type of statistics as those created by the Routing Model Evaluator. The statistics are than compared.

4 Conclusion

In this paper we have reported on a tool to investigate the practical applicability of formal models for the routing problem. The intention-aware online routing game model is implemented in the Routing Model Evaluator (RME). The RME builds up a formal model from real-world OpenStreetMap data. The OpenStreetMap data is also loaded into the SUMO simulator which realistically simulates how cars follow their routes. The SUMO simulator uses car following models, while the formal routing model uses mathematical cost functions. The SUMO simulator includes the duaiterate tool to iteratively compute a dynamic equilibrium of a traffic scenario. The iterative process of the duaiterate tool runs for long time and cannot be applied in autonomous vehicles. The RME can execute the route selection of the intention-aware online routing game model for each vehicle faster than real-time. The RME can be used to evaluate different multi-agent route selection strategies against a dynamic equilibrium computed by the SUMO simulator.

Acknowledgement. The work of V. Antal, T.G. Farkas, A. Kiss, and M. Miskolczi was supported by the European Union, co-financed by the European Social Fund (EFOP-3.6.3-VEKOP-16-2017-00002). The work of L.Z. Varga was supported by project no. ED_18-1-2019-0030 (Application domain specific highly reliable IT solutions subprogramme), and implemented with the support provided from the National Research, Development and Innovation Fund of Hungary, financed under the Thematic Excellence Programme funding scheme.

References

1. Cominetti, R., Correa, J., Olver, N.: Long term behavior of dynamic equilibria in fluid queuing networks. In: Eisenbrand, F., Koenemann, J. (eds.) IPCO 2017. LNCS, vol. 10328, pp. 161–172. Springer, Cham (2017). https://doi.org/10.1007/978-3-319-59250-3_14
2. Lopez, P.A., et al.: Microscopic traffic simulation using SUMO. In: 2018 21st International Conference on Intelligent Transportation Systems (ITSC). IEEE, November 2018. https://doi.org/10.1109/itsc.2018.8569938
3. Parkes, D.C.: Online mechanisms. In: Algorithmic Game Theory, pp. 411–439. Cambridge University Press (2007). https://doi.org/10.1017/CBO9780511800481
4. Peeta, S., Ziliaskopoulos, A.K.: Foundations of dynamic traffic assignment: the past, the present and the future. Netw. Spatial Econ. 1(3), 233–265 (2001). https://doi.org/10.1023/A:1012827724856
5. Pourabdollah, M., Bjarkvik, E., Furer, F., Lindenberg, B., Burgdorf, K.: Calibration and evaluation of car following models using real-world driving data. In: 2017 IEEE 20th International Conference on Intelligent Transportation Systems (ITSC). IEEE, October 2017. https://doi.org/10.1109/itsc.2017.8317836
6. Roughgarden, T.: Routing games. In: Algorithmic Game Theory, pp. 461–486. Cambridge University Press (2007). https://doi.org/10.1017/CBO9780511800481
7. Varga, L.: On intention-propagation-based prediction in autonomously self-adapting navigation. Scalable Comput.: Pract. Exp. 16(3), 221–232 (2015). http://www.scpe.org/index.php/scpe/article/view/1098
8. Varga, L.Z.: Two prediction methods for intention-aware online routing games. In: Belardinelli, F., Argente, E. (eds.) EUMAS/AT 2017. LNCS (LNAI), vol. 10767, pp. 431–445. Springer, Cham (2018). https://doi.org/10.1007/978-3-030-01713-2_30
9. Wardrop, J.G.: Some theoretical aspects of road traffic research. Proc. Inst. Civil Eng. Part II 1(36), 352–378 (1952)

JADE/JaCaMo+2COMM: Programming Agent Interactions

Matteo Baldoni⬤, Cristina Baroglio⬤, Roberto Micalizio⬤,
and Stefano Tedeschi$^{(\boxtimes)}$⬤

Dipartimento di Informatica, Università degli Studi di Torino, Torino, Italy
{baldoni,baroglio,micalizio,stefano.tedeschi}@unito.it

Abstract. We present 2COMM, a middleware in which social relation-ships, created during agent interactions, are represented as social com-mitments. These relationships are reified as resources in the agents' envi-ronment, and can be directly manipulated by the agents themselves via standard operations. We show that this perspective induces an agent programming schema that is independent of the actual agent platform. The uniformity of the approach is exemplified in two well-known agent platforms: JADE and JaCaMo.

Keywords: Social commitments · Agent programming · Interaction

1 Introduction

When the autonomy of components is a key requirement, software engineers can choose from a wide number of agent platforms (see, e.g., [5,6]). However, while providing coordination and communication mechanisms, all of them fail in clearly separating the interaction logic from the agent dimension. The way in which agents interact is "hard-coded" into their implementations, with a negative impact on code decoupling and reuse. We claim that an explicit representation of the *social relationships* among agents is beneficial since it improves modu-larity and flexibility. In this work, we practically demonstrate these advantages when social relationships are modeled as *social commitments*. A commitment is a promise that an agent (debtor) makes to another (creditor) to bring about a condition (consequent) when a given context (antecedent) holds. Commitments have a standardized lifecycle, and can be manipulated through some standard operations. By properly selecting the terms of the agreement, an agent can create a commitment so as to entice the cooperation of another agent, while maintain-ing autonomy and low coupling. In particular, we present 2COMM, a framework to define *dedicated commitment artifacts*, seamlessly integrated as resources in the environment where agents are situated. These artifacts *reify* the set of social relationships created during an interaction. Such an approach paves the way for a general, platform-independent, agent programming schema: agents, by directly creating and manipulating commitments, can engage others to cooperate for achieving their goals. As a practical use case, we rely on a distributed logistics scenario.

© Springer Nature Switzerland AG 2020
Y. Demazeau et al. (Eds.): PAAMS 2020, LNAI 12092, pp. 388–391, 2020.
https://doi.org/10.1007/978-3-030-49778-1_33

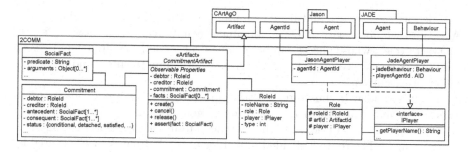

Fig. 1. Excerpt of the 2COMM architecture together with the connectors for JADE and JaCaMo.

2   Main Purpose

This demo presents the main features of 2COMM, which implements the *conceptual architecture* originally presented in [4]. In 2COMM social relationships are first-class programming entities, and the demo shows the practical implications of using these entities from an agent programming perspective. Following the A&A meta-model [8], 2COMM is a middleware that makes social commitments available to agents by means of CArtAgO artifacts [9]. Notably, the approach is not bound to any agent programming platform: to use 2COMM within a specific platform, it is sufficient to realize a dedicated connector. So far, two connectors are available for JADE [5] and JaCaMo [6]. The demo exemplifies how the modeling of interaction in terms of commitments, and grounded on 2COMM, allows to program both JADE and JaCaMo agents in a uniform way.

2COMM is the result of more than four years of work of researchers and students at Department of Computer Science at the University of Torino. Main methodological and practical outcomes are presented in [1–3,7]. The platform is freely available at http://di.unito.it/2comm together with some practical use cases encompassing both JADE and JaCaMo agents.

3   Demonstration

Figure 1 reports an excerpt of 2COMM main components. Each commitment artifact encapsulates a commitment and provides two *roles* that agents can enact: the debtor and creditor of the commitment itself. For instance, by adopting the debtor role, an agent will be able to perform the artifact *operations* for creating or canceling the corresponding commitment. Of course, roles are linked to agents of the specific platform through platform-dependent connector classes. Note that commitments are *observable properties* of artifacts; this means that agents focusing on commitment artifacts are notified whenever a commitment state change occurs. In particular, the infrastructure automatically handles commitment progression according to their standard lifecycle and to the events occurring in the environment. Events that are relevant for the progression of commitments are encoded as *social facts*, and hence maintained within the artifacts themselves. Agent programming with 2COMM amounts, then, to realizing a classical "sense-plan-act cycle", whose phases can be renamed "observe the environment", "activate behaviors according to the state of relevant commitments", and "schedule behavior execution."

Let us consider, to illustrate, a setting in which a *seller* agent sells its products online and ships them to a *customer* agent. Let us assume *seller* needs to rely on multiple couriers for the shipment from the original location A to destination D. The route is divided into three parts: 1) from A to B, covered by truck trk_1; 2) from B to C, covered by plane pln; and 3) from C to D, covered by truck trk_2. The relationships among these agents are captured by the following set of commitments. From a conceptual point of view, these commitments have a precise meaning in terms of mutual expectations between the agents. For instance, c_1 represents the offer that *seller* proposes to *customer*: if *customer* pays 500 for some *goods*, *seller* will deliver them at *customer*'s place D. Since *seller* cannot directly deliver the goods, however, it will likely, and safely, create c_1 only after having established the commitments c_2 and c_3, representing the offers made by the couriers to move the goods along the route. With the former, the *seller* gets a means for moving the goods from A to B by using trk_1. With the latter, instead, the *seller* has an agreement with pln to ship goods from B to D. The last commitment, c_4, encodes an agreement between pln and trk_2 for the shipping of goods from C to D.

$$c_1 : \mathsf{C}(seller,\ customer,\ pay(500, seller),\ at(goods, D))$$

$$c_2 : \mathsf{C}(trk_1,\ seller,\ pay(50, trk_1) \wedge at(goods, A),\ at(goods, B))$$

$$c_3 : \mathsf{C}(pln,\ seller,\ pay(200, pln) \wedge at(goods, B),\ at(goods, D))$$

$$c_4 : \mathsf{C}(trk_2,\ pln,\ pay(50,\ trk_2) \wedge at(goods, C),\ at(goods, D))$$

From a programming point of view, 2COMM allows a programmer to use directly these commitments to guide the implementation of both environment and agents. As concerns the environment, for each commitment, a corresponding commitment artifact is implemented in 2COMM. On the agent side, instead, a programmer is asked to implement the operations on the commitments that are of interest for the agent under development. For instance, while implementing *seller*, the programmer has to consider the creation of commitment c_1 and the reaction to the detachment of c_1 after the payment by the customer. In JADE, this process amounts to equipping each agent with proper behaviors to take the initiative of creating commitments, or to handle those events that, intercepted from 2COMM, are relevant for them (e.g., a commitment status change). The JaCaMo framework, in turn, adopts Jason as agent programming language. In this case, each agent has its own belief base, and a set of plans. Since JaCaMo already integrates CArtAgO, the 2COMM connector enables a direct mapping between the observable properties of commitment artifacts into beliefs of Jason agents. It follows that a change of state in a commitment can be used as a triggering event for agent plans. Similarly, operations on commitment artifacts are directly made available to agents, that can use them in their plans. Note how a programming pattern driven by social relationships emerges: the development of socially responsive JaCaMo agents amounts to equipping them with plans to properly manipulate the commitments in which they are involved.

4 Conclusions

2COMM supports programming heterogeneous interacting agents by following a uniform approach, which decouples the interaction and agent dimensions. Agent programming can leverage the conceptual architecture and general schema outlined in [4]. This feature fulfills the purpose of supporting the development of heterogeneous and open agent systems. Any agent can take part in an interaction with others by simply using properly defined commitment artifacts. The use of 2COMM with Jason and JADE proves that programming agents starting from their desired interaction can be a valuable starting point to build a general methodology useful for open and heterogeneous scenarios. The implementation of a scenario like the logistic one serves the purpose of showing the validity and suitability of the approach both from a conceptual and from a practical standpoint. Indeed, it provides a proof of concept to highlight the benefits coming from the development of socially-responsive agents in a realistic use case.

References

1. Baldoni, M., Baroglio, C., Capuzzimati, F.: A commitment-based infrastructure for programming socio-technical systems. ACM Trans. Internet Technol. **14**(4), 23:1–23:23 (2014)
2. Baldoni, M., Baroglio, C., Capuzzimati, F., Micalizio, R.: Commitment-based agent interaction in JaCaMo+. Fundamenta Informaticae **159**(1–2), 1–33 (2018)
3. Baldoni, M., Baroglio, C., Capuzzimati, F., Micalizio, R.: Type checking for protocol role enactments via commitments. J. Auton. Agents Multi-Agent Syst. **32**(3), 349–386 (2018)
4. Baldoni, M., Baroglio, C., Micalizio, R., Tedeschi, S.: Programming agents by their social relationships: a commitment-based approach. Algorithms **12**(4), 76 (2019)
5. Bellifemine, F., Bergenti, F., Caire, G., Poggi, A.: JADE — a Java agent development framework. In: Bordini, R.H., Dastani, M., Dix, J., El Fallah Seghrouchni, A. (eds.) Multi-Agent Programming. MSASSO, vol. 15, pp. 125–147. Springer, Boston, MA (2005). https://doi.org/10.1007/0-387-26350-0_5
6. Boissier, O., Bordini, R.H., Hübner, J.F., Ricci, A., Santi, A.: Multi-agent oriented programming with JaCaMo. Sci. Comput. Program. **78**(6), 747–761 (2013)
7. Capuzzimati, F.: A commitment-based infrastructure for programming socio-technical systems. Ph.D. thesis, Università degli Studi di Torino, Italy (2015)
8. Omicini, A., Ricci, A., Viroli, M.: Artifacts in the A&A meta-model for multi-agent systems. Auton. Agent. Multi-Agent Syst. **17**(3), 432–456 (2008)
9. Ricci, A., Piunti, M., Viroli, M.: Environment programming in multi-agent systems: an artifact-based perspective. Auton. Agent. Multi-Agent Syst. **23**(2), 158–192 (2011)

SEAMLESS: Simulation and Analysis for Multi-Agent System in Time-Constrained Environments

Davide Calvaresi[✉], Giuseppe Albanese, Jean-Paul Calbimonte, and Michael Schumacher

University of Applied Sciences and Arts Western Switzerland HES-SO, Sierre, Switzerland
{davide.calvaresi,giuseppe.albanese,jean-paul.calbimonte, michael.schumacher}@hevs.ch

Abstract. The correctness of a system operating in time-constrained scenarios leverages on both precision and delivery time of its outcome. This paper presents SEAMLESS, a system enabling the design, simulation, and in-depth analysis of Multi-Agent Systems (MAS). In particular, SEAMLESS allows defining in detail the agents' knowledge (set of tasks it might execute), needs (set of tasks to be negotiated), local scheduler (execution of the task-set), negotiation protocols, possible communication delays, and heuristics related to the parameters mentioned above. This tool is pivotal in the strive to study and realize real-time MAS.

Keywords: MAS simulator · Timing-reliability · MAS analysis

1 Introduction

In time-critical scenarios, compliance with deadlines and response times is imperative. Focusing on the ontological differences between the *execution* of "code" and "process" *acting* in the real world, dealing with *time* (in both virtual and real environments) is a fundamental requirement crucially entangled with *deadlines, precedence, priority,* and *constrained resources*. In the last decades, MAS researchers developed several agent-oriented models, languages and frameworks, although none of them is able to reason and operate *in* time—thus being incapable of considering and dealing explicitly with strict timing constraints [3]. Hence, MAS have been confined in narrowed application domains, rarely employed in the real-time compliant systems. To foster MAS in widening their application domains, there is the need for deeply understanding the behavior of their characterizing algorithms, protocols, and inputs with respect to time. SEAMLESS has been designed as a design, simulation, and evaluation system to fill this gap.

© Springer Nature Switzerland AG 2020
Y. Demazeau et al. (Eds.): PAAMS 2020, LNAI 12092, pp. 392–397, 2020.
https://doi.org/10.1007/978-3-030-49778-1_30

2 Objectives and Requirements

In MAS, the incapability of complying with strict-timing constraints stems from current theories, standards, and technological implementations of the MAS foundations. In particular, traditional agent internal schedulers, communication middleware, and negotiation protocols are co-factors inhibiting real-time compliance [3]. Unlike RTS-algorithms, general purpose (GP) algorithms do not allow mathematical means to provide off-/on-line timing guarantees. Thus, to understand the effects of employing a given algorithm within a specific scenario, we set the following goals: (i) to enable the creation of customizable input (e.g., task-sets and needs); (ii) to allow the customization of the system parameters (see Table 2); (iii) to provide a detailed representation (both graphical and logs) of the simulation's outcome for analytical purposes. Furthermore, we set specific requirements to facilitate the use of SEAMLESS: (i) Accessibility: The system is available online, through a multi-dev responsive Web-interface, not requiring local installation or deployment. (ii) Portability: the software is docker-contained; (iii) OpenSource: The code will be opened in accordance with the funding agency policies.

3 Demonstration

SEAMLESS provides several indicators to characterize the simulation of the designed MAS (Table 1). The parameters can refer to the overall MAS (G), to each agent (S), or both, aggregating values (A) or the trends spanning over the entire simulated time (P).

Table 1. Simulation indicators

Id	Indicator	Description	A/P	G/S
I1	Deadline Miss Ratio (DMR)	Number of deadlines missed by a task	A	S
I2	Lateness (LT)	Extra time required by a task missing its deadline to complete	P	S
I3	Response Time (RTM)	Amount of time required to complete a given task	P	S
I4	Utilization Factor (UF)	Utilization of the Agent's processor	P	G, S
I5	Potential UF (PUF)	Agent's UF variance subject to pending negotiations	P	S
I6	Acceptance Ration (AR)	Ratio among negotiated and accepted task	A	G, S
I7	Task-set Execution (TE)	Graphical representation of the task schedule	P	S

3.1 SEAMLESS Architecture

The components of the SEAMLESS architecture (Fig. 1) are organized in four Docker containers: client (React), server, backend-simulator (Omnetcpp and Node.js Express), database (Postgres), and Redis) orchestrated by Docker compose. The interface enables to register, login, manage the user's details, manage the simulation (create, delete, and edit existing ones), and provides analysis support (i.e., graphical analysis tools and formatted simulation logs). The backend-simulator is an improved and extended version of MAXIM-GPRT [1], which executes simulations of MAS characterized by many new parameters, protocols, algorithms, and heuristics (see Table 2). Task-sets, needs, and parameters can be configured via the web-interface by the user. When the setup is completed, they are organized in JSON files and fed to MAXIM-GPRT. When the execution is completed, the outcome is stored into the DB and linked to the user profile.

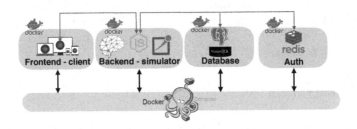

Fig. 1. SEAMLESS architecture.

3.2 SEAMLESS Setup

Table 2 describes the main parameters that can be set via web-interface characterizing the inputs and the system setup. Figure 2 shows their graphical representation. These parameters, as detailed in Table 2, allow indicating the number of agents (P1), task execution capabilities (P2, including id, computation time, arrival time, deadline, period, activation time, etc.), task set (P3), on-demand services (P4), agent needs (P5, e.g. tasks needed to be executed, including their release time), etc. Most of the parameters are fully customizable (including P7–P9), while others have preset options, e.g., the local scheduler (P11) and the negotiation protocol (P10, e.g., Contract Net, Reservation-Based Negotiation, Reservation-Based Negotiation Plus, English Auction, Dutch Auction).

3.3 SEAMLESS Simulation Analysis

SEAMLESS proposes the possibilities of downloading verbose formatted logs and graphical representations of (I1 to I7) and general statistics. Due to space limitations, we can only show a few of them. Figure 3 shows the evolution of I4 of each agent representing a snapshot of the distribution of the computations in the system. Figure 4 shows the actual behavior of P11. The most granular

Table 2. Configurable parameters

Id	Parameter	Description
P1	Number of agents	Number of agents participating in the simulation
P2	Agent knowledge	Set of tasks an agent is able to execute
P3	Agent task-set	Set of running tasks
P4	Agent Services	Set of tasks an agent might execute on demand
P5	Agent Needs	Set of tasks an agent needs, but it is unable to execute
P6	Tasks models	Typology of running tasks
P7	Agent utilization	Load of the agent's CPU [2]
P8	Tasks characterization	The features can be computational time, period, deadline, the number of executions, demander, executor, release time, server, isPublic, isActive
P9	Network delay	Customizable min and max value to define a communication delay among the agents
P10	Negotiation prot	Mechanisms used to negotiate (bid and award) task(s) execution
P11	Local scheduler	Algorithm scheduling the agent tasks/behaviors and related mechanisms (e.g., server) [2]
P12	Heuristics	Policies used by agents to select possible contractors and to award them

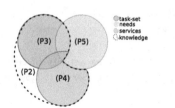 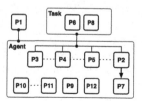

Fig. 2. (a) Venn diagram of P2-5. (b) Graphical representation of a Scenario.

representation of the execution of two periodic tasks (T0 and T5) and two aperiodic (read and write messages) served by the respective servers (S200 and S100). Figure 5a shows I3 of three tasks (P11 - FIFO) and (P11 - CNET). In particular, it is possible to see how the interference provoked by the release of task t_4 impacts on t_0. Moreover, releasing t_8, the task-set becomes unstable, causing the divergence of its response time. Under real-time assumption (EDF+CBS and RBN), the potential P7 is computed by the schedulability test to verify the impact on P7 of possibly accepting a task execution. Figure 5b shows P7 (purple line) and the potential P7 utilization (black line). The agent receives a two proposals in a few seconds. Making its computation the agent decides to bid positively to both. In turn, the bid are accepted, and P7 gets aligned with the potential P7.

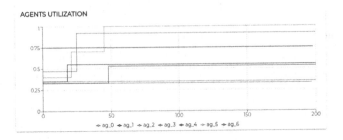

Fig. 3. Utilization (y-axes) of 7 agents over 200 simulated seconds (x-axes).

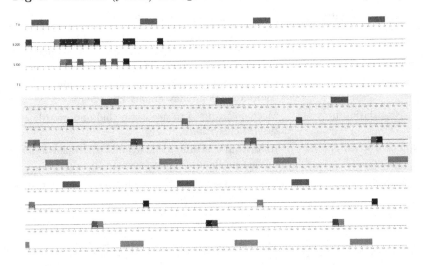

Fig. 4. Graphical representation of the simulated scheduling activity of the Earliest Deadline First (EDF) combined with the Constant Bandwidth Server (CBS) over 200 s.

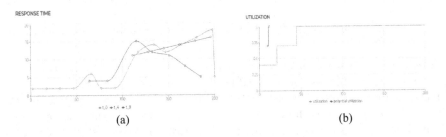

Fig. 5. (a) Response time of tasks t_0, t_4, t_8. (b) Potential and effective Agent's utilization. (Color figure online)

4 Conclusions

SEAMLESS copes with the need for understanding and evaluating the system behavior w.r.t. deadlines of both GP and RT-algorithms. Hence, the proposed system allows to analyze several time-critical performance indicators (see Table 1) employing GP and RT algorithms (see Table 2). SEAMLESS is strategic in supporting the design and analysis of time-critical MAS, enabling future adoption of RT-compliant systems.

References

1. Albanese, G., Calvaresi, D., Sernani, P., Dubosson, F., Dragoni, A.F., Schumacher, M.: MAXIM-GPRT: a simulator of local schedulers, negotiations, and communication for multi-agent systems in general-purpose and real-time scenarios. In: Demazeau, Y., An, B., Bajo, J., Fernández-Caballero, A. (eds.) PAAMS 2018. LNCS (LNAI), vol. 10978, pp. 291–295. Springer, Cham (2018). https://doi.org/10.1007/978-3-319-94580-4_23
2. Buttazzo, G.: Hard Real-Time Computing Systems: Predictable Scheduling Algorithms and Applications, vol. 24. Springer, Heidelberg (2011). https://doi.org/10.1007/978-1-4614-0676-1
3. Calvaresi, D., Marinoni, M., Sturm, A., Schumacher, M., Buttazzo, G.: The challenge of real-time multi-agent systems for enabling IoT and CPS. In: Proceedings of the International Conference on Web Intelligence, pp. 356–364. ACM (2017)

Agent-Based Mixed Reality Environments in Healthcare: The **Smart Shock Room** Project

Angelo Croatti[✉], Manuel Bottazzi, and Alessandro Ricci

Computer Science and Engineering Department (DISI),
Alma Mater Studiorum – Università di Bologna,
Via dell'Università, 50, Cesena, Italy
{a.croatti,a.ricci}@unibo.it

Abstract. Nowadays, the impressive development of smart technologies allows for designing novel kind of Personal Digital Assistant Agents (PDAA) supporting healthcare professionals in their individual and cooperative activities. Such technologies can have a disruptive impact in supporting those pathologies where the enhancement of both physician and the environment could be useful to reduce patient care times and to offer to physician new ways to access information and to be assisted by smart agents. This demo aims to present the prototype of the **Smart Shock Room** project. The project's purpose is to design and develop an innovative environment where smart technologies (e.g. mobile and pervasive computing, Mixed Reality, Vocal Assistants) can revolutionise the management of critical time-dependent pathologies (i.e. traumas) within the hospital emergency department.

Keywords: Healthcare · Personal agents · Mixed reality · Mirror worlds

1 Introduction

In recent years, we assisted to an impressive development and progress of those technologies designed to empower physical environments (i.e., pervasive computing [10]), humans capabilities (i.e., wearable computing [9]) and, more in general, the whole physical reality (i.e., Mixed Reality [2]). Such technologies are nowadays more and more efficient, in other words, ready to be used out of the lab. From an application point of view, they can have a significant impact in enhancing human cognitive capabilities and allowing for rethinking how people work, interact and collaborate. In the literature, such a scenario is inspired by the *mirror worlds* vision proposed by D. Gelernter [4], and recently reconsidered by introducing the agent-oriented paradigm as a modern approach to designing and developing mirror worlds [7].

Beyond Industry 4.0 [8], a main relevant context for the application of convergence of such technologies is healthcare, where the enhancement of the way of

Y. Demazeau et al. (Eds.): PAAMS 2020, LNAI 12092, pp. 398–402, 2020.
https://doi.org/10.1007/978-3-030-49778-1_34

performing care procedures could be impressive. In such a context, we started to design and develop the **Smart Shock Room** project. Its primary purpose is offering an advanced cyber-physical environment, an instance of a mirror world, to support emergency pathologies—in particular, severe traumas. Mirror world's features can be accessed exploiting mixed reality interactions, physical assets enhancement and with the support of cognitive personal agents.

2   Background

In the healthcare emergency context, time-dependent pathologies – i.e., traumas, strokes and heart attacks – are the most critical physicians have to manage. Such pathologies require professional skills, reactivity, quick and coordinated response, fast-paced and accurate decision making. In this context, personal digital assistant agents (PDAA) [5] plays a fundamental role, offering a way to enhance both physicians and the environment where the pathology management takes place. Generally speaking, it is possible to devise some basic functionalities and capabilities that are useful in general for personal assistants in healthcare:

- identification of the context where the user is acting and of the elements that can be relevant for the user's activity (e.g., the room where the user currently is, the patient who is currently target of the activities, ...);
- the (anytime/anywhere) capability of retrieving and presenting relevant data for the user's activity, by interacting with the hospital information system (HIS) and devices (e.g., retrieving the information stored in the Electronic Medial Record, or current value of vital signs);
- notification of messages to the user. Examples include e.g., messages sent by other colleagues (SMS, email, ...), warning automatically generated by the system about some situation;
- support for taking note and track relevant events (even multimedia ones such photos and videos) and support for setting up remote audio-video communication (e.g. requesting the assistance of a colleague).

In the literature, personal assistants are a well-known application of software agents, developed for different kind of purposes and capabilities. Generally speaking, with personal assistants, the user is engaged in a cooperative process in which human and software agents both initiate communication, monitor events, and perform tasks [6]. Considering their application to healthcare, the most critical issue to be addressed is about the interaction between physician and personal agent can take place. The introduction of this technology in a context such as healthcare emergency management requires to be not invasive and as much as possible seamless for physicians. Moreover, they need to have their hands free in order to perform procedures to the patient, so hands-free interactions with software systems (e.g. voice control) are more advisable than others.

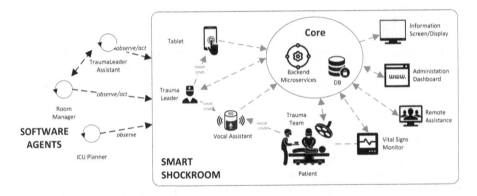

Fig. 1. The Smart Shock Room conceptual representation.

3 The **Smart Shock Room** Project

The Smart Shock Room project[1] born with the main purpose to support the trauma management process enhancing both physician and the environment involved into the management of a traumatised patient. With this demo we want to propose a first taste of the opportunities that such a scenario could bring to healthcare critical pathologies management.

3.1 Features

In a hospital emergency department, the Shock Room is the principal place where trauma management takes place. With the Smart Shock Room project, we want to bring into the shock room advanced technologies nowadays available, to develop an instance of a mirror world efficiently supporting physicians actions in managing traumas. In particular, the idea is to offer to the trauma team of physician involved in the trauma management a set of smart tools accessible both via voice control and manipulating holograms in order to have in full control the ongoing status of trauma. Also, personal agents who live in this smart environment have the capability to assist the team. To better clarify, some features of the Smart Shock Room project are:

- according to physicians vocal requests, a touch-screen display in the Shock Room shows all collected informations (e.g., performed procedures, administered drugs quantities, diagnostics medical reports and images, ...);
- wearing a mixed reality visor, the trauma leader is able to see and manipulate digital representations of anatomic organs obtained from diagnostics result – such as, e.g., computed tomography – referring to it in a complete hands-free modality, without move his/her gaze away from the patient;

---

[1] This project is carried out in collaboration with domain experts and physicians of the Trauma Center of the "M. Bufalini" Hospital in Cesena (Italy).

- personal agents can observe all diagnostics machinery – e.g. the vital signs monitor – alerting in real-time or anticipating possible critical situations;
- the trauma leader can share in any moment the information collected and the ongoing real-time stream of video acquisition obtained by the visor's camera with a remote colleague to be assisted in performing trauma management.

Figure 1 reports a conceptual representation of involved elements and assets in the Smart Shock Room vision.

3.2 Materials

The Smart Shock Room project involves several technologies, both hardware and software, in order to access the smart environment. Personal agents are developed as BDI cognitive agents in JaCaMo [1]. Interaction with the physical environment exploiting mixed reality techniques is performed through the MiRAgE framework [3], allowing for building agent-based pervasive mixed reality environments. Visors like Microsoft Hololens or Meta2 are used to allow interaction with holograms, while Vuzix Blade Smart Glasses allow for virtual elements visualization. The project also involves the usage of vocal assistant tools such as Amazon Alexa. Finally, other standard technologies to build the backend infrastructure as a Service-Oriented Architecture (SOA) are involved.

4 Conclusions

The Smart Shock Room project currently is in a very early stage of design and development. Despite this, the current state of the prototype provides a first taste of improvements smart technologies may inject into the healthcare care process. Moreover, it represents a significant application context for agent-technologies to explore their usage in real complex scenarios. Our idea is to use this project as a first test-bed for the design of general-purpose healthcare smart environment of the next future, in the Healthcare 4.0 perspective.

References

1. Boissier, O., Bordini, R.H., Hübner, J.F., Ricci, A., Santi, A.: Multi-agent oriented programming with JaCaMo. Sci. Comput. Program. **78**, 747–761 (2013)
2. Costanza, E., Kunz, A., Fjeld, M.: Mixed reality: a survey. In: Lalanne, D., Kohlas, J. (eds.) Human Machine Interaction. LNCS, vol. 5440, pp. 47–68. Springer, Heidelberg (2009). https://doi.org/10.1007/978-3-642-00437-7_3
3. Croatti, A., Ricci, A.: Developing agent-based pervasive mixed reality systems: the MiRAgE framework. In: Demazeau, Y., An, B., Bajo, J., Fernández-Caballero, A. (eds.) PAAMS 2018. LNCS (LNAI), vol. 10978, pp. 301–304. Springer, Cham (2018). https://doi.org/10.1007/978-3-319-94580-4_25
4. Gelernter, D.: Mirror Worlds or the Day Software Puts the Universe in a Shoebox: How Will It Happen and What It Will Mean. Oxford University Press Inc., Oxford (1991)

5. Maes, P.: Agents that reduce work and information overload. Commun. ACM **37**(7), 30–40 (1994)
6. Okamoto, S., Scerri, P., Sycara, K.: Toward an understanding of the impact of software personal assistants on human organizations. In: Proceedings of the 5th International Conference on Autonomous Agents and Multiagent Systems. ACM (2006)
7. Ricci, A., Piunti, M., Tummolini, L., Castelfranchi, C.: The Mirror World: preparing for mixed-reality living. IEEE Pervasive Comput. **14**(2), 60–63 (2015)
8. Schwab, K.: The Fourth Industrial Revolution Hardcover. Crown Business (2017)
9. Starner, T.: Project glass: an extension of the self. IEEE Pervasive Comput. **12**(2), 14–16 (2013)
10. Weiser, M.: The computer for the 21st century. SIGMOBILE Mob. Comput. Commun. Rev. **3**, 3–11 (1999)

Demo Paper: Monitoring and Evaluation of Ethical Behavior in Dialog Systems

Abeer Dyoub[1(✉)], Stefania Costantini[1], Francesca A. Lisi[2], and Giovanni De Gasperis[1]

[1] Università degli Studi dell'Aquila, L'Aquila, Italy
Abeer.Dyoub@graduate.univaq.it,
{Stefania.Costantini,giovanni.degasperis}@univaq.it
[2] Università degli Studi di Bari "Aldo Moro", Bari, Italy
FrancescaAlessandra.Lisi@uniba.it

Abstract. In this demo paper, we describe a Multi Agent System (MAS) application for monitoring and evaluation of the ethical behavior of customer service agents in an online chat point w.r.t their institution/company's codes of ethics and conduct. This MAS is realized using the state-of-the-art JaCaMo framework, and can be practically demonstrated to an audience.

Keywords: Multi Agent Systems · Ethical machines · Codes of ethics and conduct

1 Introduction

With autonomous intelligent machines entering rapidly into all spheres of our life, the call is increasing for new methods to engineering machine ethics, or building practical ethical machines which is not just about traditional engineering. With machine ethics, we need to find ways to practically build machines that are ethically restricted, and can also reason about ethics. This on the one hand involves philosophical aspects, but on the other hand the problem has a non-trivial computational nature. Chatbots are software tools designed to simulate how a human would behave as a conversational partner. They are meant to simplify the interaction between human and computer, and may constitute the external interface of intelligent agents. With autonomous chat agents speaking with people, questions of ethical baselines for such technologies has become imperative.

In previous works [1–3], a hybrid logic-based approach was proposed for ethical evaluation of chatbots' behavior, concerning online customer service chat points, w.r.t institution/company's codes of ethics and conduct. The approach is based on Answer Set Programming (ASP) as a knowledge representation and reasoning language, and on Inductive Logic Programming (ILP) as a (white box) machine learning device for learning rules needed for ethical evaluation and

Y. Demazeau et al. (Eds.): PAAMS 2020, LNAI 12092, pp. 403–407, 2020.
https://doi.org/10.1007/978-3-030-49778-1_35

reasoning (references in the aforementioned papers). The system in particular starts from general ethical rules proper of a certain application domain. By means of ILP, and given a set of positive and negative examples of what is ethical/non-ethical in the domain, it will generate more specific rules aimed to evaluate whether the answer provided by the chatbot to a certain user question is ethical or not. After the learning phase, the system will perform an online evaluation of the chatbot's answer to user's questions by means of these rules, with the aid of the ASP reasoner. The reasoner is in fact able to evaluate the rules' elements in practice: e.g., it is unethical to provide manipulative answers involving irrelevant concepts, and the role of the reasoner is to assess relevance in the present context (given a suitable background knowledge base). In case no applicable ethical rules is found concerning present user's question and system's answer, the system is able to start an online incremental learning phase. In this paper, we demonstrate a prototypical system realizing the above mentioned approach, implemented as a Multi-agent System.

Agent-oriented abstractions and multi-agent systems are well known in literature as a programming paradigm for the realization of complex and dynamic systems. Accordingly, our implementation exploits relevant AOSE (Agent-Oriented Software Engineering) existing work for Logical Agents (agent-oriented approaches based on Computational Logic). Namely, we adopt the JaCaMo[1] methodology to design and implement our MAS simulation environment. The first objective behind the development of this MAS is to serve as experimental simulation model, representing the various units (modules) of our system (Fig. 1). This, in fact, provides an insight into system dynamics, rather than just predicting the output of the system based on specific inputs. Simulation is generally recognized as one of the best design support technologies. This model is an initial prototypical approximation of the ethical evaluation framework, and of the real-world online customer service scenarios. The second objective behind this MAS is to address the ethical dataset challenge faced in our work for building practical ethical machines. In fact, scarcity of examples is one of the main challenges in the ethical domain in general. So, we intend to use the same MAS (with some modifications) for the creation of datasets for training.

2   Demonstration

The architecture of the system is described below, and is depicted in Fig. 1:

Our MAS consists of six Jason[2] agents organized as one group. In this group there are six different roles. Each agent plays one of these six roles. Each role is obliged to commit to a particular mission for achieving the global goal of the MAS, which is the ethical evaluation of the customer service agent's answers to customer's requests. The ethical evaluation task is a coordinated task between the six agents in the MAS. Our agents should perform their assigned missions (tasks) in a correct sequential order. Coordination of the execution of joint tasks

---

[1] http://jacamo.sourceforge.net.

[2] http://jason.sourceforge.net/wp/.

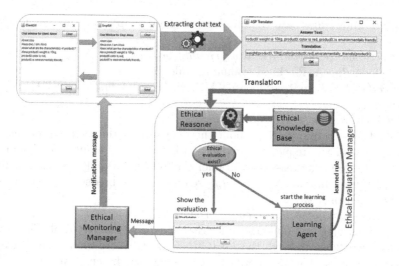

Fig. 1. Ethical Monitoring and Evaluation Framework

is achieved by an organization. Moise[3] is used for programming the organization in our MAS. The agents will interact with each other through message exchange or through environmental shared artifacts programmed using CArtAgO[4]. The environment of our application has five graphical display artifacts of the type *GUIArtifact*, where agents can perceive and update the values of different observable properties. In addition, we have one shared console artifact which is the default console where agents can print messages. These artifacts can be placed in one workspace, or in different workspaces (which is the case especially when the agents and the artifacts are distributed over different nodes in a network). In the rest of this section, we illustrate the behavior of our MAS via a simple example that can be demonstrated to an audience.

The process starts with the simple conversation shown in Table 1. The answer provided by the chatbot (A), containing the use of irrelevant sensitive slogans to manipulate customers, is judged to be unethical, by means of the following process. The *textExtractor agent* will extract the answer text from the chat point and will send it to the *ASPTranslator agent*, which will show it in the *ASPtrans-GUI* artifact, and will translate the composing sentences into ASP Syntax. The result of the translation in our case will be ASP predicates (facts). These facts are sent by the *ASPTranslator agent* to the *ethicalEvaluator agent* (consisting of the reasoning agent and the learning agent), and will be added to its knowledge base (KB). The reasoning agent is currently implemented as a special kind of Jason agent, with a customized knowledge base, which stores the ethical evaluation rules learned during the training phase. It uses these rules together with the current case facts to give the final ethical evaluation; ethical/unethical). It

---

[3] http://moise.sourceforge.net/.

[4] http://cartago.sourceforge.net/.

has in her knowledge base the ontology of the domain including the following fact:

$sensitiveSlogan(environmentally\_friendly(productX))$.

and the following ASP ethical evaluation rule (learned):

$unethical(V1) : -sensitiveSlogan(V1), notrelevant(V1), answer(V1)$.

and the rule:

$ethical(V1) : -answer(V1), notunethical(V1)$.

The agent has no information about the relevance of the adoption of this sensitive slogan for the requested product, so it will safely assume by default the irrelevance. Then, the reasoner will infer the following evaluation as a result:

$unethical(environmentally\_friendly(productX))$ If subsequently we add to the KB of our reasoner the fact:

$relevant(environmentally\_friendly(productX))$.

Then, the reasoner will no longer infer that the answer is unethical. The evaluation result is shown through the *EvalGUI* artifact, where the monitoring agent can perceive it, and send a notification message to the employee agent (chatting agent). When the reasoning agent is not able to give an evaluation (ethical/unethical), this agent will send a message to the *ethicalEvaluator agent* which in turn will send a message to the learning agent. The learning agent once received this message will invoke an artifact that acts as an interface for the learning algorithm. Practically, this interface will be used by human users (an ethical expert of the domain supported by a technical expert). Through this artifact, the following values needs to be given to initiate the learning process: i) The ethical evaluation of the chatting agent's answer (ethical/unethical). ii) The mode declarations which are the patterns for restricting the search space for hypothesis (cf. [1–3] and the references therein). iii) The relevant fact (s) for the ethical evaluation. An example representing the current case scenario will be stored in a 'JSON' file (this file is to be passed to the learning algorithm). In addition the system, starting from the current example, will generate negative examples and add them to the 'JSON' file.

Table 1. Case scenario

Sample conversation
Q: What are the characteristics of productX
A: productX has color red, productX costs 10Euros, productX is environmentally friendly
Case facts
productX has color red
productX costs 10Euros
productX is environmentally friendly

3   Conclusions

In this demo we present our first version of a MAS system for ethical evaluation and judgment. This MAS represents one of the first effective computational applications of Machine Ethics. Therefore, we believe that it has the potential to constitute a basis for the development of intelligent ethical agents. So far, our experiments are still limited due to the absence of a big enough dataset. The present implementation has two limitations: the first one is related to the text-to-ASP translator; the second one is to fully automate the learning process. Lifting these limitations is the subject of future work.

References

1. Dyoub, A., Costantini, S., Lisi, F.A.: Learning answer set programming rules for ethical machines. In: Proceedings of the Thirty Fourth Italian Conference on Computational Logic CILC, Trieste, Italy, 19–21 June 2019. CEUR-WS.org (2019). http://ceur-ws.org/Vol-2396/

2. Dyoub, A., Costantini, S., Lisi, F.A.: Towards an ILP application in machine ethics. In: Kazakov, D., Erten, C. (eds.) Proceedings of the 29th International Conference on Inductive Logic Programming - ILP 2019, Plovdiv, Bulgaria, 3–5 September 2019. LNAI, vol. 11770, pp. 1–10. Springer (2020). https://doi.org/10.1007/978-3-030-49210-63

3. Dyoub, A., Costantini, S., Lisi, F.A.: Towards ethical machines via logic programming. In: Proceedings 35th International Conference on Logic Programming (Technical Communications), ICLP 2019 Technical Communications, Las Cruces, NM, USA, 20–25 September 2019. EPTCS, vol. 306, pp. 333–339 (2019). https://doi.org/10.4204/EPTCS.306.39

A Multi-Agent Simulator for Infection Spread in a Healthcare Environment

Dario Esposito[1]([✉]), Davide Schaumann[2], Domenico Camarda[1], and Yehuda E. Kalay[3]

[1] Polytechnic University of Bari, Bari, Italy
{dario.esposito,domenico.camarda}@poliba.it
[2] Jacobs Technion-Cornell Institute at Cornell Tech, New York, USA
davide.schaumann@cornell.edu
[3] Technion, Israel Institute of Technology, Haifa, Israel
kalay@ar.technion.ac.il

Abstract. A Multi-Agent simulator made in Unity 3D is proposed to track the spread of Hospital Acquired Infections transmitted by contact in hospital wards. The tool generates a real-time contamination risk map for both people and spaces, depending on the profile, behavior and activities of virtual agents, the characteristics of pathogens and the role of inanimate objects and places.

Keywords: Multi-Agent simulation · Hospital Acquired Infection · Decision Support System

1 Introduction

Hospital infections are a critical challenge for the safety requirements of healthcare environments, since they are the principal hazard for hospital users worldwide. If admitted to a hospital, there is an 8% chance of contracting a Hospital Acquired Infection (HAI) and on average, the length of hospital stay increases by 17 days. Furthermore, this occurrence contributes to the development of antimicrobial resistance, which is one of the biggest threats to global health. In US hospitals alone, the Center for Disease Control estimates that HAIs account for an approximate 1.7 million infections and 99,000 associated deaths each year. This contributes to health care costs of $30 billion a year, since almost 10% of inpatient costs are HAI-related [1–3].

A demonstration of a Multi-Agent simulator to track the spread of infection transmitted by contact in hospital wards is presented. The tool generates a real-time contamination risk map for both people and spaces. The simulation visualizes the dynamic propagation of pathogens depending on the profile, behavior and activities of virtual agents, the characteristics of pathogens and the role of inanimate objects and places.

2 Main Purpose

HAI prevention and control programs rely on a normative approach, practitioners' expertise and past experiences. Nevertheless, HAIs lie hidden from cognitive agents up until

© Springer Nature Switzerland AG 2020
Y. Demazeau et al. (Eds.): PAAMS 2020, LNAI 12092, pp. 408–411, 2020.
https://doi.org/10.1007/978-3-030-49778-1_36

their appearance with symptoms. Current strategies are insufficient, as they are mostly counter measures to deal with the problem once it is evident. To establish an effective infection prevention and control system, it is essential to foresee the effects of intervention policies, workflow organization and spatial design. This is critical in order to propose strategies to reduce pathogen propagation beyond an increased adherence to Hands Hygiene and toward a more comprehensive understanding of the role of the environment in contamination (direct: surfaces, equipment and furniture; indirect: effect on human spatial behavior), which to date is impossible to evaluate promptly and is therefore largely underestimated [4].

The simulator adopts an Event-Based approach, which is a modelling method of human building use based on Event Narrative System architecture, whereby spaces, actors and activities are grouped into computational entities. These direct agents' behavior in space [5]. Events allow for the description of behavior from the point of view of the procedures that need to be performed to achieve a task (Fig. 1). This allows for a realistic representation of complex coordinated human activities.

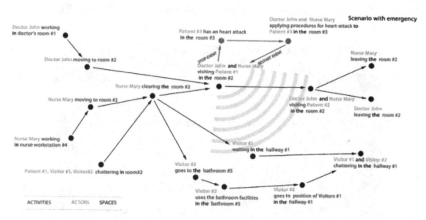

Fig. 1. Example of Event Narrative System architecture in the case of an unplanned event [6].

During the simulation, actors interact with each other and with the environment. This is the mechanism through which HAI transmission occurs. The contamination relational law between agents (either actors or spaces) drives the transmission flow. It varies with the type of activity, the type of pathogen and the cleansing of involved agents, which represents the level of efficacy in hand hygiene or ward cleaning. An expert system is translated into a system function to account for the agents' predisposition in complying with prevention and control procedures (e.g. hand hygiene), depending on human factors (local conditions, perceived barriers, risk awareness). The case study was built with information gathered from real-life observations and on real work activities carried out within hospital wards and was developed considering scientific literature on HAIs [7]. Sessions with hospital managers widened our knowledge on measures and policies to manage HAI spread. The system elements and the transmission law were implemented in C# in a virtual simulation built with a Unity 3D engine.

3 Demonstration

Germs spread from person to person through a common series of spatial events. These follow one another in the chain of infection, which is the transmission path of an infectious pathogen. Therefore, the proposed Multi-Agent Simulator simulates building use by actors in coherent and dynamic situations of HAI risk. This represents exogenous cross-infection transmitted by contact route in a spatially explicit, heterogeneously mixed environment. The initial contamination level for each actor can be set, as well as his susceptible and asymptomatic conditions. Likewise, each space can act as a pathogen source or vector. To demonstrate the potential applications of the simulator, the working proof of a trial HCW carrier scenario is presented. This shows a building use situation where HCWs start from a staff location before moving to the central medicine room to prepare medicines and then move through the patients' rooms to distribute medicines. The simulation displays actors' movements and activities within the hospital ward and visualizes the correlated contamination propagation through a real-time contamination risk map with a range of colors for the increasing level of contamination. This output allows us to understand the dissemination of pathogens over time and space (Fig. 2).

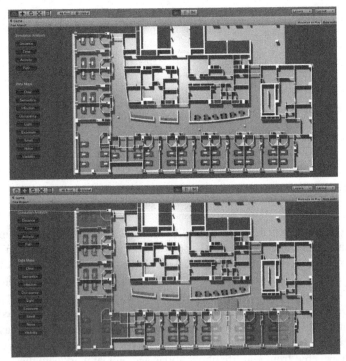

Fig. 2. Contamination risk map: initial and final screenshots from the simulation. (Color figure online)

4   Conclusions

The proposed simulator integrates the system agents in a virtual simulation of building use, correlated with the contamination propagation through a contact transmission route, with real-time results and a data-log. The produced output is a dynamic contamination risk map which visualizes how pathogen diffusion varies depending on a number of factors: initial set up causes and conditions, the heterogeneity of agents' features and spatial layouts, users' spatial behavior and activities, the effect of different prevention and control measures and architectural design and spatial distribution. By depicting the environmental spread of contamination, simulations are more geared toward the reality of the phenomenon. The what-if scenario analysis provides an understanding of different qualitative factors. It reveals clusters of infected patients and patterns of occurrence. It assesses the effectiveness of practices and procedures, e.g. agent hygiene behavior, contact precautions and isolation. It gives insights on how the spatial design of buildings, facilities location and equipment distribution can affect or reduce the risk of HAIs. Thus, the simulator sets up a Decision Support System for the management of safety and health risk in healthcare facilities. It can be employed as a forecasting tool for the evaluation of policy proposals and to address the architectural design of future hospitals and the restructuring of existing ones. Finally, the simulator could be useful in facilitating managers to issue instructions and recommendations to healthcare staff members, as well as using realistic scenarios to act as a knowledge support tool for HCW training.

Author Contributions. Conceptualization, investigation, methodology, formalization and writing D.E.; software, review and editing D.E., D.S.; supervision and project administration D.C. and Y.K. All authors have read and agreed to the published version of the manuscript.

References

1. Klevens, R.M., et al.: Estimating health care-associated infections and deaths in U.S. Hospitals, 2002. Public Health Rep. **122**, 160–166 (2007). https://doi.org/10.1177/003335490712200205
2. Scott, R.D.: The direct medical costs of healthcare-associated infections in U.S. hospitals and the benefits of prevention. In: Centers for Disease Control and Prevention (2009)
3. Davies, J.: Origins and evolution of antibiotic resistance. Microbiol. Mol. Biol. Rev. **74**, 417–433 (2010). https://doi.org/10.1128/MMBR.00016-10
4. Beggs, C.B., Shepherd, S.J., Kerr, K.G.: Increasing the frequency of hand washing by healthcare workers does not lead to commensurate reductions in staphylococcal infection in a hospital ward. BMC Infect. Dis. **8**, 114 (2008). https://doi.org/10.1186/1471-2334-8-114
5. Schaumann, D., et al.: A computational framework to simulate human spatial behavior in built environments. In: Proceedings of the Symposium on Simulation for Architecture and Urban Design, pp. 121–128 (2016)
6. Simeone, D., Yehuda, E., Schaumann, D., Carrara, G.: Adding users' dimension to BIM. In: Morello, E., Piga, B.E.A. (eds.) 11th Conference of the European Envisioning Architecture: Design, Evaluation, Communication, pp. 483–490. Architectural Envisioning Association, Milano (2013)
7. World Health Organization: Prevention of hospital-acquired infections: a practical guide (2002). No. WHO/CDS/CSR/EPH/2002.12

SafeCity: A Platform for Safer and Smarter Cities

Bruno Fernandes$^{(\boxtimes)}$, José Neves , and Cesar Analide

Department of Informatics, ALGORITMI Centre, University of Minho, Braga, Portugal
bruno.fmf.8@gmail.com, {jneves,analide}@di.uminho.pt

Abstract. Smart cities, to emerge as such, must evolve technologically and create means for their citizens to become active actors of the city's ecosystem. With road safety as background, cities must promote and implement new measures to guarantee the safety of its citizens. The goal of *SafeCity* is to foster Smart Cities and, at the same time, allow its users to participate and have access to a set of information about the current and future status of their city. It currently targets those more vulnerable at the road. *SafeCity*'s backend focuses on data collection and on fulfilling the entire Machine Learning pipeline, with a mobile application working as frontend. *SafeCity* offers, among others, traffic flow forecasts, a geofencing service with smart notifications, a city's map based on the quantification of citizens' feelings, and a boredom classifier. A gamification engine is used to support and promote user engagement.

Keywords: Smart Cities · Machine Learning · Deep learning · Geofencing

1 Introduction

Cities, to become smart, must evolve technologically, must implement systems to promote data collection and knowledge creation, and, last but not the least, must create means for their citizens to become active actors of the city's ecosystem. The way to address these issues is not monolithic. Instead, it should be made of several small contributions that, when summed, allow people to have available a set of information that may improve their quality-of-life. To achieve this goal, we must evolve from an Internet of Things (IoT) to an Internet of People (IoP), i.e., an ecosystem where everyone and everything can sense the other and the world, and act upon such data [1].

Road safety, on the other hand, has become a major issue of concern not only for car manufacturers, but also for governments. At its core, it is a very comprehensive and broad topic, ranging from measuring traffic congestion [2] to increasing the safety of motorcyclists or pedestrians [3]. Indeed, at the road one may find actors that differ in a number of characteristics, attributes and idiosyncrasies. Those more vulnerable are known as Vulnerable Road Users (VRUs), with their vulnerability arising from the lack of external protection, age and phycological impairments, among others [4].

© Springer Nature Switzerland AG 2020
Y. Demazeau et al. (Eds.): PAAMS 2020, LNAI 12092, pp. 412–416, 2020.
https://doi.org/10.1007/978-3-030-49778-1_37

2   Main Purpose and Features

The main goal of SafeCity is to allow its users to participate and have access to a set of information about the current and future status of their city in regard to traffic flow, dangerous zones and the feelings of peer citizens towards the city. To achieve such goals, SafeCity makes use of several proprietary technologies, algorithms and Machine Learning (ML) models. The main features that compose SafeCity are:

1. Backend server, hosting two main software agents, completely autonomous, working twenty-four hours seven days a week:

   a. **The Collector**, responsible for the full non-mobile data collection process, it went live on 24 July 2018 and has been collecting data uninterruptedly. It is a modular and configurable piece of software that can, at any time, start collecting data (traffic, weather and pollution, among others) for any city worldwide;

   b. **ML Architect**, responsible for pre-processing all data in other to guarantee that it is ready to be fed to the ML models. It is also responsible for updating and re-training new models. Holds all non-mobile ML models. An hourly job executes the deployed models and disseminates predictions and forecasts.

2. A mobile application that hosts and implements the following services:

   a. **Geofencing**, a location aware service that establishes virtual perimeters for real-world geographic areas. Current available categories include dangerous, high traffic, crowded and polluted geofences. These zones are related to VRUs and aim to notify such users as soon as they enter a zone where their vulnerability increases. It is also possible to create geofences that trigger specific notifications on user's smartphones about road works, concerts or events, just to name a few;

   b. **Feelings Map**, i.e., a city's map based on the feelings of its citizens in regard to certain categories and zones of a city. The feelings' map is made of direct contributions of the community. To quantify positive and negative feelings this service makes use of mathematically modified weighted heatmaps. Users are able to visualize the feelings of the entire community, are able to add their own feelings and are able to see and remove previously added feelings. A recommender system is being developed to recommend zones of a city to *SafeCity* users;

   c. **Traffic Flow Forecaster**, a service that makes use of deep recurrent neural networks, in particular, Long-Short Term Memory Networks (LSTMs), to forecast the traffic flow. To overcome the spatial problem of open source datasets, this service uses its own dataset collected by *The Collector*. The goal is to allow the possibility of knowing, beforehand, how will traffic stand in future hours to enable a cyclist to opt for another hour to cycle, for example;

   d. **Boredom Classifier**, a service that makes use of mobile sensors' data and a ML model to predict and classify user boredom when using the smartphone. This service collects a set of data from the smartphone sensors, cleans it and applies a ML model to predict user boredom when using a smartphone. The current model is deployed within the mobile application When bored, this service is intended to provide users with notifications on to-do lists and relevant articles;

e. **Personality Analyser**, a service that aims to provide to its user a vision of his personality using the OCEAN model. This service, still under development, is able to quantify the user's personality based on a set of data, including the applications the user has installed in his smartphone;

f. **Gamification Engine**, a service to support and promote user engagement. This service consists in a set of levels and points, which are to be given for the successful accomplishment of specified activities such as contributing to the feelings map or using the application. The goal is to have tradable points, i.e., points that may be exchanged for specific discounts in cities' services and products.

3   SafeCity's Demo

SafeCity's mobile app is available at Google's Play store. It targets Android users with, at least, Android 6.0. It is available in the Portuguese and English languages. Figure 1, 2 and 3 depict the main activities, i.e., screens, of the application and the corresponding features.

Fig. 1. From left to right: (a) login activity, (b) main activity after successful login, (c) profile activity allowing the user to see his points and turn on/off several ML engines, and (d) a notification created by the Boredom AI service stating the user is not bored at that time.

Fig. 2. From left to right: (a) geofencing activity, (b) notification after entering a geofence, (c) feelings' map activity and (d) adding a feeling to the feelings' map.

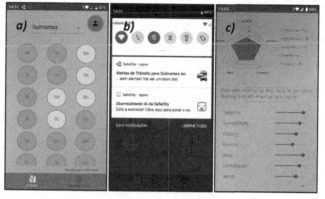

Fig. 3. From left to right: (a) hourly traffic flow predictions for the city of Guimarães, (b) traffic alerts received every morning, and (c) activity where the user can perform and inspect the results of the OCEAN's Big Five personality test.

4 Conclusions

The goal of *SafeCity* is to foster Smart Cities and, with that, allow its users to participate and have access to a set of information about the current and future status of their city. It currently targets those more vulnerable at the road, providing information that may help reducing their vulnerability. A city that has models creating knowledge based on the city's data, that allows citizens to have access to such information, and that allows them to become active actors, will be indeed closer to become a smart one. SafeCity has been recently released, with the goal now being to promote the application as well as focus on improving the used models with new data.

Acknowledgments. This work has been supported by FCT - Fundação para a Ciência e a Tecnologia within the R&D Units project scope: UIDB/00319/2020, being also supported by a doctoral grant, SFRH/BD/130125/2017, issued by FCT in Portugal.

References

1. Fernandes, B., Neves, J., César, A.: Envisaging the Internet of people an approach to the vulnerable road users problem. In: De Paz, J.F., Julián, V., Villarrubia, G., Marreiros, G., Novais, P. (eds.) ISAmI 2017. AISC, vol. 615, pp. 104–111. Springer, Cham (2017). https://doi.org/10.1007/978-3-319-61118-1_14
2. Milanes, V., Villagra, J., Godoy, J., Simo, J., Perez, J., Onieva, E.: An intelligent V2I-based traffic management system. IEEE Trans. Intell. Transp. Syst. **13**(1), 49–58 (2012)
3. Cho, W.: Safety enhancement service for vulnerable users using P2V communications. In: International Conference on Connected Vehicles and Expo (ICCVE), pp. 1002–1003 (2014)
4. European Parliament: Directive 2010/40/EU of the European parliament and of the council of 7 July. Off. J. E.U. **8**, 296–308 (2010)

AGADE Traffic 2.0 - A Knowledge-Based Approach for Multi-agent Traffic Simulations

Jannik Geyer, Johannes Nguyen[(✉)], Thomas Farrenkopf, and Michael Guckert

KITE, Technische Hochschule Mittelhessen, 61169 Friedberg, Germany
{Jannik.Geyer,johannes.nguyen,thomas.farrenkopf,
michael.guckert}@mnd.thm.de

Abstract. AGADE Traffic 2.0 (funded by Karl-Vossloh-Stiftung) is a multi-agent based tool for traffic simulations with focus on modelling dynamic decision-making processes for individual traffic participants. For this purpose, a revised modelling component has been integrated that uses semantic technologies (OWL and SWRL) to express agent behaviour. At the same time, this approach enables new options to make agent behaviour explainable. In this paper, we demonstrate that a rule-based modelling approach combined with a logging mechanism can be applied to provide data that can be used to identify specific emerging behavioural patterns and their consequences for the results of the simulations.

Keywords: Agent behaviour modelling · Multi-agent based traffic simulation · Transparent agent behaviour · Semantic agent modelling

1 Introduction

As multi-agent based systems are an accepted means to conduct traffic simulations, a variety of approaches have been published in the past addressing different purposes and following varying goals [1,2,4,5]. However, an aspect that has so far only been dealt with marginally is the modelling of dynamic decision-making processes for individual traffic participants. In previous work, AGADE Traffic has been introduced as a tool for multi-agent based traffic flow simulation [3]. In this initial state, an architecture was presented in which agents move in geographic networks, for which publicly available map material (*Open Street Map*)[1] is stored in graph databases (*Neo4J*)[2]. The agents of the simulations move in maps visualized by NetLogo. Routing algorithms of the Neo4J graph database are used and traffic flows are reflected into the database so that traffic densities can be taken into account in *routing*. Based on this architecture, AGADE Traffic 2.0 was further developed for the integration of a revised modelling component. This component combines multi-agent systems with technologies from the

---

[1] See https://www.openstreetmap.de/ - (accessed on 04/12/2019).
[2] See https://neo4j.com/ - (accessed on 04/12/2019).

© Springer Nature Switzerland AG 2020
Y. Demazeau et al. (Eds.): PAAMS 2020, LNAI 12092, pp. 417–420, 2020.
https://doi.org/10.1007/978-3-030-49778-1_38

semantic web enabling new options for modelling the behaviour and decision-making processes of individual travellers. The application of ontologies allows for a formal description of concepts (or rather knowledge) in a machine-readable form, about the agents themselves and their environment. These can be complemented by a set of inference rules to formulate more advanced relationships to go beyond the scope of the more object-centric description logic propositions. Computational reasoner technology is then able to draw conclusions based on the knowledge that is formally expressed in OWL, which can be used to portray a decision-making process of travel participants. Traveller behaviour can be modelled with this approach. In the context of mobility, such behaviour can be for instance reactions to dynamically changed travel times scheduling, travel costs or environmental impacts of individual transportation mode. Applied reasoning mechanisms simulate their choice of transportation mode and route. For example, an agent could explicitly avoid a certain transportation mode if these contradict personal preferences (e.g. being CO_2-neutral) and the personal benefit is maximised by cycling. For AGADE Traffic 2.0, the existing NetLogo module has been replaced by self-developed software modules for the visualisation and control of the agents as scaling options (larger maps, higher number of agents, etc.) were limited in the NetLogo environment.

2   Main Purpose

Initially, AGADE Traffic has been introduced as a tool for multi-agent based traffic flow simulation. With the new version 2.0, a revised modelling component has been integrated which allows the system to make use of semantic technologies (ontology and rules). In comparison to other traffic simulation platforms such as MATSim [2], ITSUMO [1], etc., our tool focuses on the effects of dynamic decision-making processes of individual traffic participants. While the main purpose of traffic flow simulation remains, we assume that personal preferences and decisions made by individual traffic participants have major impact on the overall traffic flow. With AGADE Traffic 2.0, the overall objective is to analyse behavioural structures of exactly these individual traffic participants. Moreover, we intend to use this platform to examine the effects of measures, taken by higher-level institutions, on individual travel behaviour in order to optimise the overall network flow. Up to now, we have implemented basic structures for agents to move on map data based on established routing algorithms such as A* that make use of individual cost functions [3]. Furthermore, by integrating the revised modelling component it is now possible to model dynamic decision-making as well as *en route* replanning. In order to create a data basis for elaborate analysis of agent behaviour we have created a modelling structure as well as a mechanism that allows the extraction of active rules leading to decisions made by agents. Apart from this, traffic demand for the simulation can be modelled using an origin-destination matrix. Agents are generated based on either mathematical distributions (e.g. *poisson*) or real-world data for which arrival times and quantities can be specified in detail. For future work, an additional option for activity-based agent generation is in consideration. Locations for the origin-destination matrix can be defined by setting markers per drag and drop on the interactive map in the web-frontend. For each location and its surrounding parking capacities can be specified. The parking slots are calculated in a user-defined radius on the basis of the street segments. The simulation already includes basic multimodal mechanisms e.g. agents travelling by car having to search for appropriate parking options and if necessary walk the remaining distance to the intended target location. At the current state of implementation, travellers can travel by car, bike or walk. Public transport such as bus and train will be added in the future. Besides, relevant key indicators are calculated in the background and visualised using appropriate diagrams. Interactive analysis options were also implemented on the map, such as displaying tracks to see where the agents were driving.

3   Demonstration

As demonstration, we have chosen a real-world scenario of students commuting to the Friedberg campus of Technische Hochschule Mittelhessen on a specific date (25/11/2019). For this purpose, we collected real data for this specific campus site about number of students (total of 2676) enrolled in the study programmes (total of 20) as well as number of staff members (total of 260), and matched this to available lecture schedules for the selected date in order to model demand. As many students are travelling by public transport, a transport mode that has not yet been implemented, we modelled impulses of pedestrians walking from the train station to the university building based on public transport timetables. These impulses represent travellers arriving by incoming trains. In this case, the station is located directly across street from the university. Bus traffic is neglected in this example, because in Friedberg as a small town most of the locations are accessible on foot and by bicycle. We made use of the ontology in order to infer further agent properties and logic rules to model agent behaviour. For example, generated agents characterised by demographic properties are assigned to different agent types (*students, staff* or *residents*) and defined mindsets (e.g default, eco, avoid mainstream, etc.) that determine personal preferences. Based on the situational context in the immediate environment of the agents, decisions are made for transportation mode and routes. Decisions made can change dynamically at any moment during the agent's journey. For this demonstration, we have modelled three categories of rules for concluding further *agent characteristics, transportation mode* as well as *personal preferences*. A logging mechanism outputs active rules into a relational database in order to make agent decisions explainable. At the same time, we calculate statistical key figures such as required travel times per route, created agents per tick, etc. Figure 1 shows a heatmap of agent movements calculated in the simulation. Roads indicated in red show sections that are particularly exposed to high traffic volumes.

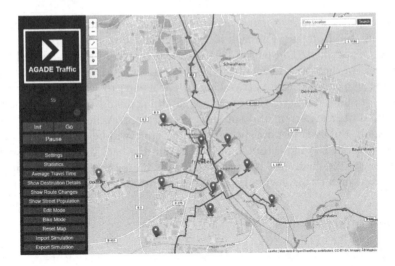

Fig. 1. A heat map of the travel routes for the commuter scenario to the university in Friedberg

4   Conclusion

In this work, we presented AGADE Traffic 2.0 as tool with a refined modelling component for traffic flow simulation. This component extends multi-agent technology by semantic expressiveness in order to model individual travel behaviour. At the same time, this modelling component enables new options to output data about the agent's decision-making processes using appropriate logging mechanisms. With real data, a commuting scenario to the university in Friedberg has been modelled and simulated.

References

1. Bazzan, A.L.C., do Amarante, M.D.B., Sommer, T., Benavides, A.J.: ITSUMO: an agent-based simulator for its applications. In: Proceedings of the 4th Workshop on Artificial Transportation Systems and Simulation, p. 8. IEEE (2010)
2. Horni, A., Nagel, K., Axhausen, K.W.: The Multi-Agent Transport Simulation MATSim. Ubiquity Press, London (2016)
3. Rotärmel, S., Guckert, M., Farrenkopf, T., Urquhart, N.: Agade-traffic. In: Demazeau, Y., Davidsson, P., Bajo, J., Vale, Z. (eds.) PAAMS 2017. LNCS (LNAI), vol. 10349, pp. 355–358. Springer, Cham (2017). https://doi.org/10.1007/978-3-319-59930-4_37
4. Thulasidasan, S., Kasiviswanathan, S., Eidenbenz, S., Galli, E., Mniszewski, S., Romero, P.: Designing systems for large-scale, discrete-event simulations: experiences with the FastTrans parallel microsimulator. In: 2009 International Conference on High Performance Computing (HiPC), pp. 428–437. IEEE (2009)
5. Torabi, B., Al-Zinati, M., Wenkstern, R.Z.: MATISSE 3.0: a large-scale multi-agent simulation system for intelligent transportation systems. In: Demazeau, Y., An, B., Bajo, J., Fernández-Caballero, A. (eds.) PAAMS 2018. LNCS (LNAI), vol. 10978, pp. 357–360. Springer, Cham (2018). https://doi.org/10.1007/978-3-319-94580-4_38

PoVaBiA: A Multi-agent Decision-Making Support Tool for Organic Waste Management

Christelle Hatik[1]([✉])[iD], Mehdi Medmoun[1,2], Rémy Courdier[1][iD],
and Jean-Christophe Soulié[3,4][iD]

[1] University of La Réunion, 15 Avenue René Cassin, Messag Cedex,
97715 Saint Denis, France
christelle.hatik@univ-reunion.fr
[2] Mines Paris Tech, 60 Boulevard Saint-Michel, 75272 Paris, France
mehdi.medmoun@mines-paristech.fr
[3] CIRAD, RU Recycling and Risk, Réunion, 97743 Saint-Denis, France
jean-christophe.soulie@cirad.fr
[4] Recycling and Risk, Montpellier University, CIRAD, Montpellier, France

Abstract. This paper presents an agent-based model, which is developed to support decision-makers in the selection of best biowastes management scenarios. The model simulates biowastes transfers between the production points to farmland and analyses supply/demand balance of organic matter (transformed biowastes) as a complementary organic resources for crops. The system describes the biowastes chain management and contains five main agents: (1) producer agents that generate biowastes, (2) treatment plant agents that transform biowastes into compost or sludge, (3) vehicle agents that collect biowastes from producers to treatment unit and deliver organic matter after transformation by treatment unit to farmland, (4) agricultural sites that need organic matter, and (5) administrative agents that plan schedules of vehicle agents and orders of organic matter. Our aim is to test organizational alternatives at a territory scale to manage this new matter (biowastes transformed) on the economic market. The proposed model is used on a french overseas department in the Indian Ocean: La Réunion island.

Keywords: Multi-agent based simulation (MABS) · Decision support system · Biowaste management

1 Introduction

According to the latest estimations, global annual solid waste generation is expected to rise from 2.01 billion tons in 2016 to 3.40 billion tons by 2050[1]. This fact high-lights the crucial importance of improving waste management. To do that, we have to support decision makers in order to deal with both global

---

[1] http://datatopics.worldbank.org/what-a-waste/.

© Springer Nature Switzerland AG 2020
Y. Demazeau et al. (Eds.): PAAMS 2020, LNAI 12092, pp. 421–425, 2020.
https://doi.org/10.1007/978-3-030-49778-1_39

pollution issues and re-source shortages. In this context, France has defined a new regulation for the management of biowastes. Indeed, in 2025, sorting of biomass at source will be mandatory for all producers (from 'big producers' to citizens) in order to valorize them by composting and/or anaerobic digestion (french Law of Energetic Transition and Green Growth (LTECV)). Valuing organic waste makes the territory less dependent to imports (fertilizers, energy), improve soil quality and reduce the energy mix carbon footprint. Biowaste and green waste management is a strategic issue, especially for islands such as La Réunion which is a French overseas department located in the Indian Ocean. In this context, the 'Agricultural management of biomasses at the Reunion Island scale' (GABIR) project has been created (2017/2020)[2]. Its goal is to make the agricultural sector of La Réunion less dependent on mineral fertilizers (fully imported).

Waste management can be viewed as Complex Adaptive System (CAS) with multiple interconnected stakeholders, with some unpredictable behaviour (negotiation issues, technical failures, etc.) and also various factors (economical, environmental and social). Besides, former research from the French agricultural research and international cooperation organization (CIRAD) proved the relevance of Agent Based Models (ABMs) for modelling and simulating similar systems [1,3].

2   Main Subject

Decision-making support tools for public investments are increasingly arousing the interest among decision-makers and communities, however there are a few

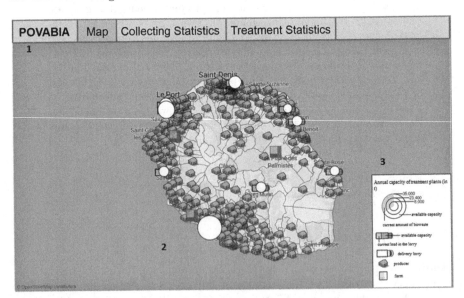

Fig. 1. General view of the simulator with the main pane (1), the map and the spatialized agents (2) and the legend (3).

---

[2] https://reunion-mayotte.cirad.fr/actualites/2018/projet-gabir.

reports on comprehensive waste management system using ABMs and still less apply on biowastes management. Most of them remain focused on the upstream part or restrict their study to the classical landfills or incineration plants [2]. As a way to meet the growing needs for decision-making tools, and inspired by previous models on related topics, we developed the PoVaBia (French acronym for agricultural potential valorization of biowastes) simulation tool through a research partnership gathering the CIRAD and the University of La Réunion (Fig. 1). Based on Anylogic simulation software[3], this spatialized model provides multi-criteria analysis of 1-year long scenarios for organic waste management on La Réunion island.

3 Demonstration

For this demonstration, we will describe the agents we designed, as well as a selection of indicators that can be monitored while the model runs (Fig. 2).

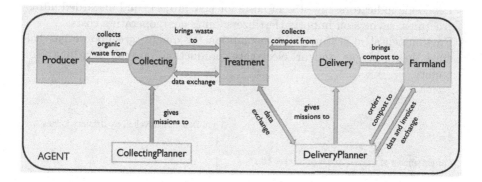

Fig. 2. Model diagram with all the agents involved in the organic waste chain.

Producers are characterized by a location, a waste daily mean production and their type (household, collective restaurant, retailer and food industry). Thus, producers can either be individuals or account for several actors. We decided to choose the second approach because most precise waste statistics are available at the district scale.

Lorries (Collecting and Delivery) are characterized by their capacity. They try to minimize their collecting circuits duration using a constant speed (set to the mean velocity of garbage trucks). The collecting circuits are designed by the Collection Planner. The delivery collecting missions are assigned by the Delivery Planner.

---

[3] www.anylogic.com.

Collection Planner creates a weekly schedule according to producers' attributes (collecting days and city). It then distributes individual circuits to a set of collecting lorries (available and as near as possible from the circuit).

Treatment plants process organic waste according to their type and their yearly capacity. Waste streams are preferentially directed to not full plants in the appropriate area (A plant only handles the waste of a given area).

Delivery Planner stands for a virtual entity which receives organic fertilizers orders from farmers and manages it according to the available amount. It also defines a price for the digestat and compost.

Farmlands ensure the nutrients quality of their fields. This quality is a function of N, P and K concentrations whose consumption rate depends on cultivated species, soil and maturation state. When its value reaches the critical threshold, the agent orders organic matter.

Several relevant criteria are simulated and can be monitored during the simulation and are retrieved at the end (Fig. 3):

- Economic indicators: investment costs for new projects and discarded infrastructures, savings on imports (fertilizers, oil & gas), operating costs.
- Environmental indicators: oil consumption for freight, greenhouse gas balance, heat, biogas and/or electricity production, ground handling, soil quality.

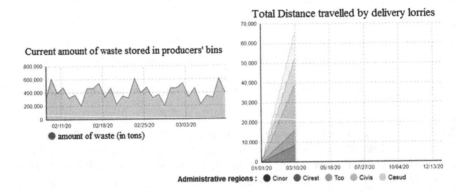

Fig. 3. Running indicators: current waste amount at producers and distance travelled per area

4   Conclusion

PoVaBiA is a ABM which allows to compare several organic waste management scenarios and to predict local consumption tendencies. Since waste management (collection and treatment) has been developed in a generic way, the model is then adaptative according to the data precision and also applicable to others territories. Multi-agent systems such as PoVabiA allow explore complex social and economic simulations and would help designing and predicting the effects of circular economy in terms of goods consumption, pollution and wealth creation.

References

1. Guerrin, F., Paillat, J.M.: Modelling biomass fluxes and fertility transfers: animal wastes management in reunion island. MSSANZ (2003)
2. Meng, X., Wen, Z., Qian, Y.: Multi-agent based simulation for household solidwaste recycling behavior. Resour. Conserv. Recycl. **128**, 535 – 545 (2018). https://doi.org/10.1016/j.resconrec.2016.09.033. http://www.sciencedirect.com/science/article/pii/S0921344916302816
3. Soulie, J.C., Wassenaar, T.: Modelling the integrated management of organic waste at a territory scale. In: Proceedings of MODSIM. Modelling and Simulation Society of Australia and New Zealand (2017)

Dedale: Demonstrating a Realistic Testbed for Decentralized Multi-agents Problems

Cédric Herpson$^{(\boxtimes)}$

Sorbonne Université, CNRS, LIP6, 75005 Paris, France
`cedric.herpson@lip6.fr`

Abstract. The *Dedale* platform is a peer-to-peer multi-agent testbed dedicated to the study of MAS coordination, learning and decision-making problems under realistic hypotheses: Asynchrony, partial observability, uncertainty, heterogeneity, open environments, limited communication and computation. *Dedale* facilitates the implementation of reproducible and realistic experiments in discrete and (3D) continuous environments. Agents can face cooperative or competitive exploration, patrolling, pickup and delivery, treasure(s) or agent(s) hunt problems with teams of dozens of heterogeneous agents. This paper presents the demonstration elaborated in order to exibit the platform's capabilities.

Keywords: Agent testbed · Coordination · Learning · Decision-making

1 Introduction

Existing multi-agents testbeds make unrealistic hypotheses. They either focus on large-scale complex adaptive systems restricted to synchronous environments with no or few communication capabilities [1], or they assume closed-world environments, homogeneous agents and a perfect vision of the system [4,5]. In both cases, these platforms hypotheses make rendering solutions based on them either ineffective or inoperable in real situations. As a result, researchers working on multi-agent coordination, learning and decision-making problems often use their own (unpublished) toy examples environments which make the results difficult to reproduce. Moreover, they usually do not scale to real-life use-cases and can unfortunately turn out to be over-fitting the proposed algorithms.

Dedale[1] aims to facilitate and improve the experimental evaluation conditions of the developed algorithms and to contribute to the progress of the field towards decentralised solutions able to deal with real-world situations.

This demonstration article first presents the strengths of *Dedale* towards this goal (Sect. 2). We then illustrate the platform key capabilities through the configuration, instantiation and analysis of two use-cases standing on hand-made and real-geographically based environments (Sect. 3) before concluding.

---

[1] http://dedale.gitlab.io/.

© Springer Nature Switzerland AG 2020
Y. Demazeau et al. (Eds.): PAAMS 2020, LNAI 12092, pp. 426–429, 2020.
https://doi.org/10.1007/978-3-030-49778-1_40

2   Main Purpose

The purpose of *Dedale* is to provide a platform allowing both the research and teaching communities to tackle decentralized problems under parametrizable but realistic hypotheses and environments. In a companion paper, we defined what we called the 8 fallacies of MAS that such a testbed should avoid:

1. Agents take turns executing each other
2. Agents are homogeneous and run at the same speed
3. Agents have access to unlimited resources
4. Agents are reliable
5. Agents are sure
6. Agents have a global and perfect vision of the system
7. Agents number does not change over time
8. Agents communication respects the 8 fallacies[2] of distributed systems.

Dedale is the first platform to avoid all these unrealistic hypotheses. To create it, we combined the well-known Jade framework [2] with the GraphStream[3] and jMonkeyEngine[4] (Jme3) libraries. While Jade is in charge of the MAS management, GraphStream and Jme are respectively handling the two types of environments provided by Dedale: discrete dynamic graphs and continuous 3D-environments. Through the use of *Dedale*'s API, users' agents will have to evolve and cooperate within the chosen environments to accomplish their goals. We currently allow users to choose the type of open-research problems they wants to study among 3 multi-agent classical use-cases of increasing difficulties:

- Distributed exploration [7],
- Cooperative patrolling and pursuit-evasion games [3],
- Treasure(s) hunt & pickup and delivery problems (PDP)[6].

For each of them, the user can define the topology he wants to work on as well as the number and characteristics of the agents. To properly compare the performances of different proposals to a given problem instance, several evaluation metrics are available: 1) The number of messages exchanged between the agents 2) The number of actions executed and 3) The overall time needed to complete a task. In the treasure-hunt case, the quantity of collected resources is also stored.

To further enhance users' interest in studying realistic multi-agent problems with Dedale, the platform is able to function as a node in a network of peer-to-peer Dedale environments. This gives user' agents the ability to test their robustness against environments - and potentially agents - unknown to their designer. The size, complexity and richness of the distributed environment accessible to agents thus becomes virtually unlimited.

---

[2] The network is secure, reliable, instantaneous, with infinite bandwidth, the topology is fixed and homogeneous, communications costs are non-existent.
[3] http://graphstream-project.org/.
[4] https://jmonkeyengine.org/.

3   Demonstration

As shown in Fig. 1, the platform configuration is done in 2 stages: Definition of the environment in which the agents will evolve then configuration of the agents themselves. Setting up the environment allows to define the type of problem the agents will face. The demonstration aims to present these different aspects.

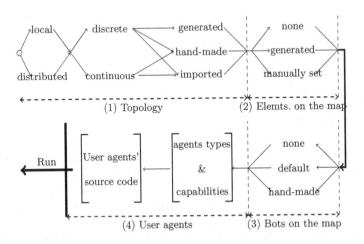

Fig. 1. Dedale platform configuration process. In the upper part the configuration of the environment, in the lower part the configuration of the agents. The 4 steps can be modified independently of each others.

Setting Up an Environment. The user chose to connect or not its environment to the network then select the type of topology he wants (discrete or continuous). In the case of a distributed setup, the choice of the neighbours can be manually set or be left up to the platform. The user can then design, generate, or import from OpenStreetMap a topology. From there he can select the location and type of resources that the environment will posses. We currently offers traps (the agent dies when it touch them) and two types of treasure chest (diamond and gold) with parametrizables detection radius and openning conditions. These may require the cooperation of more than one agent. The setting up of an environment generates two editables files that can easily be modified, shared to, and used by, any Dedale user.

Setting Up Agents. Depending on the use case chosen, the user will choose whether or not to activate the presence of opponents on the map. As detailed in the companion paper, they can be used as intruders for the patrolling case, or as disruptive elements for collecting resources. We will present two of the default behaviors – collecting and moving resources – that make the environment dynamic and decisions uncertain. The user then defines the respective characteristics and capabilities of his agents within the environment (communication radius, transport or resource collection, ...) before linking them to the classes

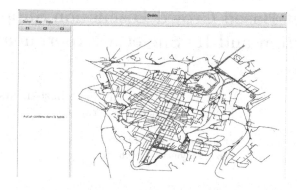

Fig. 2. Real-time view of agents looking for intruders in Aquila

developed to control their behaviours. Once the simulation started, Dedale's interface (Fig. 2) allows users to follow their agents progress in real-time whether regarding their locations or the generated statistics.

4   Conclusion

This demonstration highlighted the realistic hypotheses and the configuration flexibility of *Dedale*. It presented two of the different classes of open research problems that can currently be studied within 2D-discrete and 3D-continuous environments. Coupled with the execution statistics, this demonstration illustrates how easy it is to set up reproducible experiments and obtain comparative measurements of different solutions to a multi-agent problem with *Dedale*.

References

1. Adil, K., Jiang, F., Liu, S., Jifara, W., Tian, Z., Fu, Y.: State-of-the-art and open challenges in rts game-ai and starcraft. Int. J. Adv. Comput. Sci. Appl. **8**(12), 16–24 (2017)
2. Bellifemine, F.L., Caire, G., Greenwood, D.: Developing Multi-agent Systems with JADE, vol. 7. Wiley, Hoboken (2007)
3. Chevaleyre, Y.: Theoretical analysis of the multi-agent patrolling problem. In: Proceedings of the IEEE/WIC/ACM - IAT, pp. 302–308. IEEE (2004)
4. Hausknecht, M., Mupparaju, P., Subramanian, S., Kalyanakrishnan, S., Stone, P.: Half field offense: an environment for multiagent learning and ad hoc teamwork. In: AAMAS Adaptive Learning Agents (ALA) Workshop (2016)
5. Resnick, C., et al.: Pommerman: a multi-agent playground. arXiv:1809.07124 (2018)
6. Savelsbergh, M.W., Sol, M.: The general pickup and delivery problem. Transp. Sci. **29**(1), 17–29 (1995)
7. Shantanu, D.: Graph explorations with mobile agents. In: Flocchini, P., Prencipe, G., Santoro, N. (eds.) Distributed Computing By Mobile Entities. Lecture Notes in Computer Science, vol. 11340, pp. 403–422. Springer, Cham (2019). https://doi.org/10.1007/978-3-030-11072-7_16

Agent-Based Crowd Discussion Support System and Its Societal Experiments

Takayuki Ito(✉), Rafik Hadfi, Jawad Haqbeen, Shota Suzuki, Atsuya Sakai, Naoki Kawamura, and Naoko Yamaguchi

Nagoya Institute of Technology, Gokiso, Showaku, Nagoya 466-8555, Japan
ito.takayuki@nitech.ac.jp

Abstract. Crowd-scale discussion platforms are receiving great attention as potential next-generation methods for democratic citizen platforms [1,2,5,8]. One of the studies clarified the critical problem faced by human facilitators caused by the difficulty of facilitating large-scale online discussions. In order to address this issue, we implement an automated facilitation agent to manage crowd-scale online discussions. An automated facilitator agent extracts the discussion structure from the texts posted in discussions by people. We conduct large-scale social experiments with several cities including Nagoya city in Japan, and the Kabul city in Afganistan. In this demonstration, we present our current implementation of D-agree, a crowd-scale discussion support system based on an automated facilitation agent, and some results on social experiments.

Keywords: Crowd discussion · Facilitation agent · Collective intelligence

1 Main Purpose

1.1 D-Agree: Crowd Discussion Support System Based on Automated Facilitation Agent

Figure 1 outlines D-agree. D-agree is one of the web forum systems where participants can submit their opinions as texts. An automated facilitation agent extracts the discussion structure from the texts posted in discussions by people. We adopted IBIS (Issue-Based Information System) structure [3] as an ideal discussion framework because our aim is to lead discussions through which people can clarify issues, ideas, and debate merits/demerits. IBIS effectively constructs such discussions. Extending any form of argumentative structure is possible [4].

Based on the extracted structure, the facilitation agent posts facilitation messages about the discussion so that the on-going discussion covers enough ideas, merits and demerits. By following the IBIS structure, the agent can encourage people to submit ideas (positions) for an issue, merits (pros) for an idea, and demerits (cons) for an idea as much as possible in order to make comprehensive discussion for the given theme. The structured discussions are stored in the discussion DB, and will be utilized in the future discussion as references.

Y. Demazeau et al. (Eds.): PAAMS 2020, LNAI 12092, pp. 430–433, 2020.
https://doi.org/10.1007/978-3-030-49778-1_41

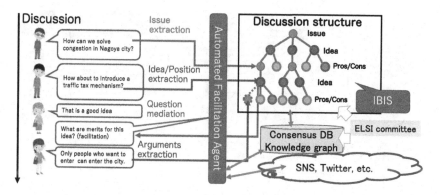

Fig. 1. Outline of D-agree

1.2 Automated Facilitation Agent

We developed automated facilitation agent software that observes the posted texts, extracts their semantic discussion structures, generates facilitation messages, and posts them to the discussion system. The software also filters inappropriate posts.

The facilitation agent consists of two parts: a discussion structure extraction/visualization mechanism and an observing and posting mechanism. To extract the discussion structure, we utilize argumentation mining technologies [7] with BiLSTM, which first captures meaningful sentences and then important words that are IBIS components: issues, ideas, pros, and cons. After that, it identifies the relations among these IBIS components and unifies these relations and components into one discussion structure.

By using the extracted structure, the observing and posting mechanism posts facilitation messages. It has around 200 facilitation rules, which have been carefully collated after consultation with professional facilitators. By matching the rules and the obtained structure, facilitation messages are generated.

1.3 System Architecture and User Interface

The right picture (A) of Fig. 2 presents the architecture. Our current system operates on Amazon Web Services, which are scalable enough even if we have many numbers of discussions. The left picture (B) of Fig. 2 presents the user interface of our system in which a posting form, a discussion board and information boards for the theme, discussion points, and important keywords. Users can input their opinions from the posting form, and the opinions are immediately shown in the discussion board. Theme is the top-level issue. Usually a theme is given by the administrator when the discussion starts. The discussion points are virtual points that an user can obtain when he/she posts and replies, his/her posting is replied, and evaluated.

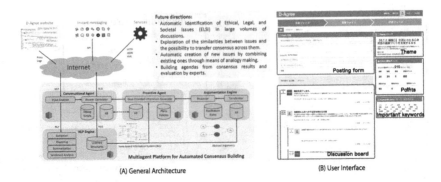

Fig. 2. General architecture and UI (Color figure online)

A web server component manages discussion boards and all data are stored in the database. Users can access to our system through one of the web browsers. We implemented the iPhone and Android applications as well. A red box in Fig. 2 shows the architecture of our automated facilitation agent. The automated facilitation agent consists of 2 main modules. One is the observation and posting module, the other is the discussion structure extraction module. The observation and posting module were implemented by using scalable AWS Cloud Watch and AWS Lambda functions. The discussion structure extraction module extract IBIS structures from the current discussion.

1.4 Social Experiments: Nagoya and Kabul

We conducted a real world experiment with the Nagoya municipal government from November 1 to December 7, 2018. Nagoya City citizens discussed five themes about their city's future. We got 15,199 page views, visits from 798 participants, 157 registered participants, and 432 submitted opinions. We established two phases: a 30-day-discussion and a 7-day phase for agreeing to the summarized ideas. Our automated facilitation agent successfully facilitated discussions among civilians.

In Afganistan, we conducted two social experiment using D-Agree, a kick off social experiment with Kabul city local government officials and a social experiment with Kabul municipal district citizens to find out city issues, prioritizing the problems and come up with possible solution through analyzing the discussed items of experiment discussants. Total number of 426 of citizens participated in 5 selected of Kabul city. The discussion theme jointly created by KM and NITech researcher team. The discussion had just one theme, which was under the title of "What are the challenges and problems within each designated district". We established two working days for each district experiment starting from February 5 to February 14, 2019. We got total number of 1,245-page views, total of 426 registered participants and total number of 1023 posted items jointly by discussants, human facilitators and AI agent facilitator.

2   Demonstration

In our demonstration, participants can log-in the D-agree system by using our laptop computer, and try to submit their opinion in discussions as they like. Our automated facilitation agent responds their inputs, and participants can figure out how it works. We present our demonstration movie (https://bit.ly/2wSyJK3) on another computer. Further, we will present our on-going social experiment in the Kabul city, Afganistan in which the Kabul mayor and real civilian are discussing the future urban planning on Kabul city.

3   Conclusion

We presented our current implementation of a crowd-scale discussion support system based on an automated facilitation agent. The agent extracts discussion structures from online discussions, analyzes the content, and posts facilitation messages. We have also conducted a large-scale experiment in Nagoya and Kabul where our agent worked quite well.

Acknowledgement. This work was supported by the JST CREST fund (Grant Number: JPMJCR15E1).

References

1. Ito, T., Imi, Y., Ito, T., Hideshima, E.: COLLAGREE: a facilitator-mediated large-scale consensus support system. In: ACM Collective Intelligence 2014 (2014)
2. Kawase, S., et al.: Cyber-physical hybrid environment using a largescale discussion system enhances audiences' participation and satisfaction in the panel discussion. IEICE Trans. Inf. Syst. **E101.D**(4), 847–855 (2018)
3. Kunz, W., Rittel, H.W.: Issues as elements of information systems. Technical report (1970). CiteSeerX 10.1.1.134.1741
4. Lawrence, J., Reed, C.: Mining argumentative structure from natural language text using automatically generated premise-conclusion topic models. In: Proceedings of the 4th Workshop on Argument Mining, pp. 39–48 (2017)
5. Malone, T.W., Klein, M.: Harnessing collective intelligence to address global climate change. Innov.: Technol. Gov. Glob. **2**(3), 15–26 (2007)
6. Sengoku, A., et al.: Discussion tree for managing large-scale internet-based discussions. In: ACM Collective Intelligence 2016 (2016)
7. Stab, C., Gurevych, I.: Parsing argumentation structures in persuasive essays. Comput. Linguist. **43**(3), 619–659 (2017)
8. Ito, T., Shibata, D., et al.: Agent that facilitates crowd discussion. In: ACM Collective Intelligence 2019 (2019)

Disaster Response Simulation

Tabajara Krausburg[1,2](✉) , Vinicius Chrisosthemos[1] , Rafael H. Bordini[1] ,
and Jürgen Dix[2]

[1] School of Technology, Pontifical Catholic University of Rio Grande do Sul,
Porto Alegre, Brazil
{tabajara.rodrigues,vinicius.teixeira99}@edu.pucrs.br,
rafael.bordini@pucrs.br
[2] Department of Informatics, Clausthal University of Technology,
Clausthal-Zellerfeld, Germany
dix@tu-clausthal.de

Abstract. We introduce a novel two-dimensional simulator for disaster
response on maps of real cities dealing with logistics and coordination
problems. Our simulator allows to plug-in almost any approach developed for simulated environments and offers functionalities for further
developing and benchmarking. It provides metrics that help the analysis of the performance of a team of agents during the disaster. Our
experiments were conducted for a mud disaster episode and show how
to evaluate different techniques.

Keywords: Disaster response · MAS · Testbed

1 Introduction

Our aim is to provide a realistic simulation environment for benchmarking intelligent software agents in the context of disaster response. We present a novel MAS
simulator especially tailored for disaster response scenarios, where agents control simulated entities that represent autonomous vehicles, human professional
rescuers, and volunteers.

We apply the concepts introduced in [1] to simulations in disaster response
episodes in which developers are free to choose the degree of agent's reasoning
and AI techniques that fit them best, doing so, techniques are not evaluated in
isolation, but as part of a complex system.

The event that triggered the development of our simulator was the collapse
of a dam for mining tailings, inundating with mud all over a sparse area; in
fact, 12 million cubic meters of mining tailings were spread out over more than
46 km [2]—with 225 fatal victims and 68 missing people. We demonstrate how
to use our simulator to compare different AI approaches in a mud disaster
episode. The results show that that our simulator is robust enough for receiving

© Springer Nature Switzerland AG 2020
Y. Demazeau et al. (Eds.): PAAMS 2020, LNAI 12092, pp. 434–438, 2020.
https://doi.org/10.1007/978-3-030-49778-1_42

connections from large team of agents and provides good qualitative evaluation of the teams. The reader can find the code and additional information about this simulator in our repository[1].

2   Main Purpose

To simulate scenarios, one can design an agent-based modelling approach which simulates some predefined behaviour that tackles the problem [5]. Another approach is to provide a problem and ask for solutions from the Multi-Agent System (MAS) community: RoboCup-Rescue [6] is one of the most successful simulators to simulate disaster response episodes. Teams implement their algorithms in ADF modules focusing on certain aspects of the scenario (e.g., task allocation).

An even more general approach is to leave it entirely open to the MAS community to choose strategies and techniques of how to solve the problem. In the multi-agent programming contest [1], the aim is to identify key problems, collect benchmarks, and gather test cases for MAS community, in particular to MAS programming languages. Agents are decoupled from the environment server and interact with it by sending actions and receiving perceptions. Doing so, agents chose strategies and AI techniques that fit them best.

Inspired by [1], our approach is to leave it entirely to the developers of the teams to choose and apply what are the possibly best approaches to address the overall problem: MAS platforms, AI techniques, but also classical techniques can be used and finally be evaluated.

In our setting, there are tasks for rescuing victims (that can die), collecting mud samples, and taking photographs[2]: These are announced by the Centre for Disaster Management (CDM). Some victims may have their location already revealed and others are hidden. Information about the area should be collected and then analysed in order to decide whether there might be victims at that location. The CDM also tags specific locations in which the mud must be sampled.

One important concept in our simulator is the idea of *social assets*. We distinguish between agents that connect before the simulation starts (i.e., regular agents) and agents that connect after the simulation has begun (i.e., social assets). Those agents represent volunteers during the disaster operation and are included/disposed in the simulation on the fly in order to help some other agent.

Three types of movement are supported in our simulated environment: by air, on ground, or in water. The underlying map is a graph consisting of nodes and edges (effected by mud on the ground surface), that could form a route from one place to another. The simulator generates an environment model based on a configuration file that contains information regarding the map, regular agents, social assets, actions, and events. At the beginning, a mud event is always generated (i.e., at the first step), after that, other events may occur dynamically

---

[1] https://github.com/smart-pucrs/MASiRe.
[2] Photo is data that requires further investigation (victims location and state).

over the simulation. The communication between the simulator and a MAS is established by a well-defined protocol so that any MAS platform is able to connect and interact with our simulator as long as it implements the protocol.

Agents play in discrete steps: At each step an action is expected from each connected agent. During the simulation, we collect some metrics that help developers of the MAS and experts to analyse the advantages and drawbacks of the strategies taken while achieving the tasks announced by the CDM.

3   Demonstration

Our aim is to evaluate two approaches in the same disaster scenario: (i) a MAS, depicted in blue, with only very simple reasoning; and (ii) a MAS, depicted in orange, using a coalition formation approach to partition the set of agents.[3] In this scenario, we consider a mud disaster environment in which 30 experts receive tasks from the CDM and have to establish a coordination to perform all announced tasks. The configuration file (easily changeable) is set as follows:

- 500 steps in a match;
- two types of regular agents: *drone* for aerial locomotion (7 agents), and Unmanned Ground Vehicles (UGV) for ground locomotion (23 agents);
- ground vehicles suffer speed reduction of 50% in a zone affected by mud;
- new mud events occur at each step with chance of 2% containing: four to eight mud sample tasks; four to ten photo tasks; and one to three victims.
- each photo has a chance of 80% to reveal one to three victims in that area;
- victims stay alive in the simulation for 50 to 100 steps.

Both approaches have some characteristics in common: Drones are capable of taking photos, analysing them, and collecting mud samples; they prefer collecting photos and analysing them rather than collecting mud samples; UGV are capable of rescuing victims and collecting mud samples; they prefer rescuing victims rather than collecting mud samples.

After completing a task, an agent always returns to the CDM to report on what was done, to recharge, and to choose a new task. Agents use a simple coordination mechanism in order to pick a task. An agent queries if there is no other agent performing that task, then it broadcasts to the other agents that it is now attempting to achieve that particular task.

In the simple MAS, team agents always consider all the active mud events in order to pick a task. They only attempt to execute the first task returned when querying its belief base for known events (preserving the preferences of each role over the tasks). The more sophisticated MAS team makes use of the C-Link algorithm introduced by Farinelli et al. [4], based on hierarchical clustering. We aim to partition the agents for the set of active mud events. After the *coalition structure* is formed, coalition members only act upon the mud event related to the coalition they belong. We generate a new coalition structure every time a new mud event occurs in the scenario, and agents may be reallocated to work on different areas.

---

[3] Both approaches were developed using the JaCaMo platform [3].

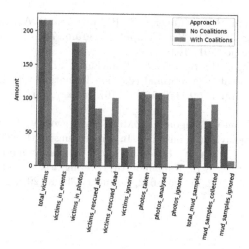

Fig. 1. Metrics for the mud disaster response considering two MAS approaches.

We execute both teams in the same scenario (i.e., same events at the same steps) and collect their performance results which are depicted in Fig. 1. The simple reasoning MAS team rescued more victims alive, but it did not accomplish many mud sample tasks. Drones and UGV always try to achieve their most preferred tasks (i.e., taking photos and rescuing victims respectively), and ignore the rest. In contrast, the coalition formation MAS team accomplished more of the tasks announced by CDM, however, the priority system was applied only locally in the mud regions which led to a higher number of rescued bodies. This shows how to use the simulator's metrics as a guide for decision-making.

4   Conclusions

We have introduced a new disaster response simulator to help experts evaluating different MAS approaches for coordinating autonomous agents and to improve rescue operations. It differs from previous approaches in the literature about simulating disaster response environments by *not constraining* the MAS approach to a few reasoning mechanisms or AI techniques: Any methods can be plugged-in and evaluated. For future work, we aim to expand the range of disasters that our simulator is capable of simulating.

References

1. Ahlbrecht, T., Dix, J., Fiekas, N.: Multi-agent programming contest 2017. Ann. Math. Artif. Intell. **84**(1), 1–16 (2018). https://doi.org/10.1007/s10472-018-9594-x
2. Armada, C.A.S.: The environmental disasters of Mariana and Brumadinho and the Brazilian social environmental law state, August 2019. https://ssrn.com/abstract=3442624

3. Boissier, O., Bordini, R.H., Hübner, J.F., Ricci, A., Santi, A.: Multi-agent oriented programming with JaCaMo. Sci. Comput. Program. **78**, 747–761 (2013). https://doi.org/10.1016/j.scico.2011.10.004

4. Farinelli, A., Bicego, M., Bistaffa, F., Ramchurn, S.D.: A hierarchical clustering approach to large-scale near-optimal coalition formation with quality guarantees. Eng. Appl. Artif. Intell. **59**, 170–185 (2016). https://doi.org/10.1016/j.engappai.2016.12.018

5. Mancheva, L., Adam, C., Dugdale, J.: Multi-agent geospatial simulation of human interactions and behaviour in bushfires. In: Proceedings of the 16th ISCRAM (2019)

6. Visser, A., Ito, N., Kleiner, A.: RoboCup rescue simulation innovation strategy. In: Bianchi, R.A.C., Akin, H.L., Ramamoorthy, S., Sugiura, K. (eds.) RoboCup 2014. LNCS (LNAI), vol. 8992, pp. 661–672. Springer, Cham (2015). https://doi.org/10.1007/978-3-319-18615-3_54

Understandable Teams of Pepper Robots

Avinash Kumar Singh, Neha Baranwal, Kai-Florian Richter,
Thomas Hellström, and Suna Bensch$^{(\boxtimes)}$

Department of Computing Science, Umeå University, Umeå, Sweden
{avinash,neha,kaifr,thomash,suna}@cs.umu.se
http://www.cs.umu.se

Abstract. The term *understandable robots* refers to robots making their actions and intentions understandable (or explainable) to humans. To support understandability of a team of collaborating robots we use natural language to let the robots verbalize what they do and plan to do. Our solution is based on Cooperating Distributed Grammar Systems for plan derivation and a Multi-agent algorithm for coordination of robot actions. We implemented and evaluated our solution on a team of three Pepper robots that work collaboratively to move an object on a table, thereby coordinating their capabilities and actions and verbalizing their actions and intentions. In a series of experiments, our solution not only successful demonstrated collaboration and task fulfilment, but also considerable variation, both regarding actions and generated natural language utterances.

Keywords: Understandable robots · Explainable AI · Multi-agent systems · Natural language generation · Robot teams

1 Introduction

Detection and recognition of human actions and behaviors has for a long time received attention within the Human-Robot Interaction (HRI) community. Robots often are supposed to be able to correctly infer what the humans are currently doing and what they plan to do, in order to support them in service robot scenarios. Robots are becoming increasingly autonomous and capable and it is not evident for an interacting human what the robot does or what it is planning to do and why. The area of understandable or explainable robotics specifically addresses this problem [3]. Failure to take understandability into consideration may affect safety, efficiency, user-experience, and interaction quality in general [1].

We investigate understandability for teams of robots collaborating to solve a common task. While such a robot team will rarely need to communicate verbally with each other for successful coordination, human bystanders might benefit from overhearing verbal dialogues between the robots, describing what they currently

Supported by the Kempe Foundations.

do and plan to do. A robot may ask another robot for help, suggest to other robots to perform actions, or inform the other robots about what it intends to do. Moreover, in a scenario where a team of robots works together with a team of humans, using natural language is a very efficient way to coordinate actions and plans.

We introduce models for collaborative planning, task execution, and the generation of actions and utterances [4]. Our solution is demonstrated on a team of three Pepper robots solving a pick-and-place task by coordinating the work with each other, thereby verbally informing human bystanders.

To the best of our knowledge, architectures supporting verbal understandability for teams of collaborating robots have not been previously investigated. As far as we are aware, there has not been a demonstration of a team of Pepper robots moving objects in a pick-and-place task while speaking.

2   Main Purpose

To support understandability of a team of collaborating and speaking robots we present an approach that is divided into parts: plan derivation and plan execution. The robots first cooperatively derive a plan thereby considering their individual capabilities to perform actions. The derived plan is then executed, also in cooperation between the robots. During plan execution, the robots verbalize what they intend to do or what they request other robots to do. Plan derivation is modelled using the grammar formalism known as Cooperating Distributed Grammar System (CDGS) [2], which is a formal model of blackboard architectures for collaborating multi-agent systems. During plan execution, the robots communicate to decide who should do what and when. The robots generate verbal utterances to explain what is going on to human bystanders. Plan execution and generation of verbal utterances is modelled with an agent-based architecture synchronizing actions and utterances. For more details on our approach we refer the reader to [4].

Our approach is illustrated in Fig. 1, where the autonomous robots silently interact using a virtual blackboard during cooperative plan derivation and execution. The execution comprises interaction with the physical world, and is accompanied by verbal utterances to make the robots' behavior understandable for human bystanders.

3   Demonstration

A derived plan is used as input for plan execution. Our solution comprises a main coordinating component and identical control systems running in parallel on each robot. The coordinating component is given a plan, places it on the blackboard, and starts all robot's control systems.

The robots communicate through the blackboard to execute the plan. In addition to the current plan, a string denoting the action currently scheduled for execution resides on the blackboard.

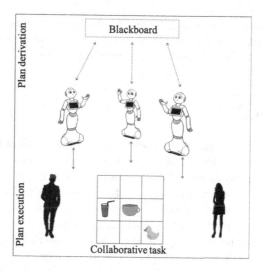

Fig. 1. Illustration of the interaction model in which three robots collaborate to solve a pick-and-place task. See text for details.

To demonstrate the developed models and algorithms, plan execution was implemented on a team of three Pepper robots. Although the Pepper robots are not designed to manipulate objects, we managed to grip and move lightweight objects made with a base of polystyrene foam, and a tip of softer rubber foam that allows for safe gripping. Figure 2 shows the experimental setup.

Fig. 2. Experimental setup showing one of the collaborating robots gripping an object. (Color figure online)

The concurrent execution of our plan execution in all three robots results in several randomized operations. The behavior and verbalization for a given plan varied from one execution to another, and several experiments were therefore conducted for evaluation. Some results are presented in a video demonstration at https://people.cs.umu.se/thomash/understandablerobotteams.mp4 in which the robots have the task to move the red object on cell 7. The video demonstration shows the variability in behaviour and verbalization as well as how obstacle removal is handled.

4   Conclusions

We proposed and evaluated a novel solution for understandable, collaborating robot teams, based on CDGS and a multi-agent algorithm for coordination of actions, and generation of verbal explanations. In our conducted experiments, the robot team successfully collaborated to solve given tasks. The individual robots verbally commented on their own planned actions, and also on actions requested to be performed by other robots. The randomized agent-based approach, together with the under-specified plans, demonstrated considerable variation, both regarding actions and generated utterances. The underlying motivation for the work presented in this paper is understandability for improved safety, efficiency, and user-experience in HRI.

References

1. Bensch, S., Jevtić, A., Hellström, T.: On interaction quality in human-robot interaction. In: International Conference on Agents and Artificial Intelligence (ICAART), pp. 182–189 (2017)
2. Csuhaj-Varju, E., Kelemen, J., Paun, G., Dassow, J. (eds.): Grammar Systems: A Grammatical Approach to Distribution and Cooperation. Gordon and Breach Science Publishers Inc., 1st edn. (1994)
3. Hellström, T., Bensch, S.: Understandable robots - what, why, and how. Paladyn J. Behav. Robot. 9(1), 110–123 (2018)
4. Singh Kumar, A., Baranwal, N., Richter, K.F., Hellström, T., Bensch, S.: Understandable collaborating robot teams. In: 18th International Conference on Practical Applications of Agents and Multi-agent Systems (2020). Submitted

A Practical Demonstration of a Variable Incentive Model for Bike-Sharing Systems Based on Agent-Based Social Simulation

Alberto López Santiago[ID], Carlos A. Iglesias[✉][ID], and Álvaro Carrera[ID]

Intelligent Systems Group, Universidad Politécnica de Madrid,
Avda. Complutense, 30, 28040 Madrid, Spain
alberto.lopezs@alumnos.upm.es, {carlosangel.iglesias,a.carrera}@upm.es
http://www.gsi.upm.es

Abstract. Bike-Sharing Systems (BSSs) have been implemented in numerous cities around the world to reduce the traffic generated by motorized vehicles, due to the benefits they bring to the city, such as reducing congestion or decreasing pollution generation. Caused by their impact on urban mobility, the research community has increased their interest in their study, trying to understand user behavior and improving the user experience. This demonstration shows the simulator developed to analyze the impact of a variable incentive model for BSSs based on Agent-based Social Simulation. The model has been developed using data collected directly from BiciMad, the BSS of the city of Madrid, Spain. The developed simulator uses OpenStreetMaps as a route generator software. The simulated scenario for this demonstration consists of a 7-day series of simulations with different traffic flows to observe the impact of different policies according to different traffic intensity.

Keywords: Bike Sharing Systems · Variable incentive model · Agent-based systems

1 Introduction

There is a growing interest in the Sharing Economy because of its impact on individuals, businesses, and governments. In a particular case, Bike-Sharing Systems (BSSs) bring benefits to users, societies, and the environment, making sustainable mobility an essential pillar of society.

The optimization of these services helps to introduce these services into the routine of the users. One significant problem that should be improved is the lack of availability of the service. This problem is most noticeable during peak hours in areas with a high density of population. This paper studies the implementation of a variable incentive system during those peak hours. During the simulation process, we analyze the availability of the system and the associated cost for the company providing the service.

© Springer Nature Switzerland AG 2020
Y. Demazeau et al. (Eds.): PAAMS 2020, LNAI 12092, pp. 443–446, 2020.
https://doi.org/10.1007/978-3-030-49778-1_44

2   Main Purpose

The objective of this study is to observe the consequences of implementing a system of variable incentives on a BSS during high demand hours. For this purpose, an Agent-Based Model (ABM) model has been developed with Mesa, an open-source tool for Python.

The system implements two different incentive policies: (1) One variable incentive policy is implemented in a station-based system, where the user must access the station to rent/park the bicycle. (2) The system also implements a policy of fixed incentives per day.

These incentives are applied as a discount to the fare of the trip, so that the amount of the discount can never be higher than the cost of the service. In order to benefit from these incentives, users must help to balance the load of the stations. Based on Ban et al. [1], that load balancing can be achieved by renting at a station with a high capacity load (greater than 70%) or by parking at a station with a low capacity (less than 30%).

To measure the influence of the policy, we collect data from the simulation and its agents (users, stations, and employees). The primary variable that we observe is the Quality of Experience (QoE) rate per user/agent, which shows a relationship between trips made successfully and those that could not be completed. Once a bicycle has been rented, it must be returned to a station. The model considers that when a user does not find an available bicycle within his action range, the trip is unsuccessful. The QoE rate is defined according to the following formula.

$$QoE = F/(F + S) \tag{1}$$

where F is the number of failed trips and S is the number of completed trips.

Moreover, due to the nature of the policy in modifying user behavior, the duration of the trips is an important variable. We assume a higher predisposition to shorter trips, so a considerable increase in the duration traveled means a decrease in the QoE perceived by users. Besides, the variation in the number of full stations (with no available slot to park the bike) or empty stations (with no available bikes to rent) will be meaningful in the QoE. Finally, the deviation of incomes can also be observed, showing us the economic benefits perceived by the system operator.

3   Demonstration

Simulation results are stored for its analysis. Table 1 presents the results of the scenario mentioned above. A 7-day series of simulations have been carried out to test the influence of the policies on the system. The simulations have been programmed in different scenarios, according to the traffic flow (30,000, 74,000, and 150,000 trips), both with the variable and the fixed incentive policies. In this way, we can observe the impact of each policy according to traffic intensity.

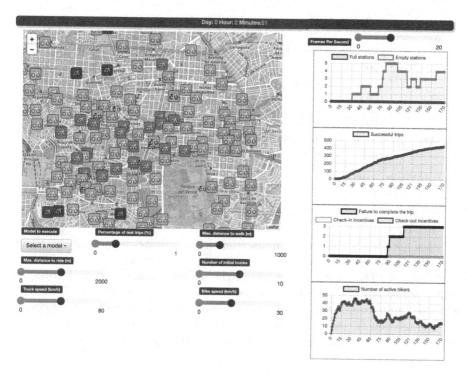

Fig. 1. Visualization of the simulation.

User behavior has been model based on a probabilistic estimation using the real data of trips, provided by the operator company Municipal Transport Company of Madrid, *Empresa Municipal de Transportes* (EMT) on its web portal[1]. Based on that estimation and using the library OpenRouteService (ORS)[2], routes are calculated, enabling a better calculation of the travel times and its visualization through the web interface developed using the Folium library[3].

The simulation system has been deployed as a web application with a graphic user interface that enables the configuration of the model in a fast and intuitive way. This graphical interface also enables the visualization of the simulation results in real-time, as shown in Fig. 1, where the distribution of the station loads along the city of Madrid can be observed. More details can be found in the full paper [2].

According to the results obtained when applying the incentive policy, a growing trend in travel duration can be observed, with 1% and 1.55% for low and medium traffic scenarios respectively. However, for high traffic, a reduction of 3% has been obtained. So we can assume that the implementation of the pol-

---

[1] BiciMAD Open Data Repository: http://opendata.emtmadrid.es/Datos-estaticos/ Datos-generales-(1).

[2] OpenRouteService GitHub Site: https://github.com/GIScience.

[3] Folium GitHub Repository: https://github.com/python-visualization/folium.

Table 1. Output variable results from simulation.

	Variable policy	Trips duration		QoE		Income	
		μ (sec.)	σ (sec.)	μ (%)	σ (%)	μ (€)	σ (€)
30,000 trips	True	755.24	346.32	5.82e−04	3.4e−08	12959.86	71.52
	False	747.71	332.12	6.22e−04	5.54e−08	12971.23	86.76
74,000 trips	True	1083.09	597.5	0.075	2.03e−05	32374.17	98.46
	False	1066.56	570.58	0.103	3.54e−05	32313.79	69.70
150,000 trips	True	1244.39	606.93	0.684	6.85e−04	63852.91	130.77
	False	1281.85	650.97	0.804	8.505e−04	63679.16	136.57

icy does not have a misleading impact on the overall user experience in terms of travel time. In the case of the QoE ratio, a reduction has been obtained in every case. The most outstanding is the average traffic, with a decrease of 27.2%. Regarding the revenues received by the system operator, no differences are observed between the two strategies (with and without policy). One potential explanation is that the higher costs associated with the variable incentive are compensated by the increase in the number of trips.

4   Conclusions

In this paper, we have presented a demonstration of an agent-based system to assess the impact of implementing a variable incentive policy in a BSS. Our main conclusions are that significant improvements are obtained in terms of service availability, not resulting in either a decrease in income or an increase in travel duration.

Acknowledgments. This research has been funded by the UPM University-Industry Chair Cabify for Sustainable Mobility. The authors want also to thank EMT for providing BiciMad service data.

References

1. Ban, S., Hyun, K.H.: Designing a user participation-based bike rebalancing service. Sustainability **11**(8), 2396 (2019)
2. Santiago, A.L., Iglesias, C.A., Carrera, A.: Improving sustainable mobility with a variable incentive model for bike sharing systems based on agent-based social simulation. In: Advances in Practical Applications of Agents, Multi-agent Systems, and Trustworthiness: The PAAMS Collection (2020)

Implementation of a Holonic Multi-agent System in Mixed or Augmented Reality for Large Scale Interactions

Dani Manjah[1]([✉]) [iD], Kaori Hagihara[1], Gillian Basso[2], and Benoit Macq[1] [iD]

[1] Institute of Information and Communication Technologies, Electronics and Applied Mathematics, Avenue Georges Lemaître 4-6, Louvain-La-Neuve 1348, Belgium
{dani.manjah,kaori.hagirara,benoit.macq}@uclouvain.be
[2] Alterface, Avenue Pasteur 11, 1300 Wavre, Belgium
gillian.basso@alterface.com

Abstract. We present a new holonic organizational meta-model that uses the multi-agent approach to design a mixed/augmented reality framework enhancing user-experience for the entertainment industry. Our applied model can control games played by groups in a mixed universe (real and virtual) and a distributed environment (city, theme park, etc.). We will particularly present a game in which visitors can interact and experience varying stories through the introduction of autonomous virtual agents. In our case, characters evolve according to their personality and to the user's inputs. Furthermore, we programmed behaviors for the characters letting their dynamics play the animation rather than programming the animation directly. Our demonstration during PAAMS will show, through a mobile application, new kind of interactions with the system leading to a personalized experience with virtual characters.

Keywords: Human agent interaction · Virtual agents · Serious games · Agent engineering and development tools

1 Introduction

The future of the entertainment industry should bring about changes in the way the user interacts with an amusement system. The shift of the paradigm from scripted systems to autonomous interactive agents comes with complex engineering challenges. Foremost, we need to design a model of an adaptive system allowing to experience scenarios triggered by the behaviour of autonomous agents. In addition, the model should work in various situations and be easily extendable. To meet those requirements, we offer a solution based on a holonic multi-agent approach. The inherent properties of agents such as autonomy and

Supported by Parkar/DGO6 project (#1610130) funded by the Région Wallonne WA LINNOV, Alterface S.A and with the partnership of OpenHub-Empowerhub/ UCLouvain.

Y. Demazeau et al. (Eds.): PAAMS 2020, LNAI 12092, pp. 447–450, 2020.
https://doi.org/10.1007/978-3-030-49778-1_45

reactivity are well suited to reach high degrees of variability and openness in the system [1]. Eventually, the holonic architecture ensures that we could deal with multiple abstraction levels enhancing the scalability of the model. We therefore chose to work with the organizational methodology ASPECS [2]. Once we designed the model, we built a game using *Unity* game engine during which a user could simply (un-)spawn characters. Those characters are autonomous and own their particular BDI. The result is a scalable model and a demonstration proving the feasibility and the validity of the approach.

2   Main Purpose

The challenge we addressed is the design of a scalable and re-usable software that manages interactions between users and a mixed or augmented reality. Our work applies concepts of autonomous behaviours in virtual agents and the concept of storytelling developed in Cavazza et al. [3]. In their paper, Rual et al. and O. Zohreh Akbari encourage the shift in the (game) industry towards an agent-oriented methodology. Indeed, the traditional object-oriented approach is irrelevant when dealing with multiple scenarios, scalability and modularity [4,5]. In order to illustrate the case, imagine an amusement park around the theme of *Star Wars*. One of the attractions is an adventure within a *Galaxy* where virtual citizens and magical creatures are evolving autonomously. Your actions will either make them willing to support your adventure or hinder it. From a software point of view, the system should provide access to the users and keep track of them in the *Universe* (Star Wars amusement park). It should also allow them to interact with any attraction within the system, namely a *World* (Galaxy). In addition, an interactive system requires managed input (light saber) and output devices (screens, mechanical device, etc.). Eventually, within a given *World*, the evolution of *Entities* (autonomous agents) should be supervised. We already see that the system is divided into three parts: *User management*, *World management* and *Interactivity management*. They contribute to each other but they can work individually. Each part constitutes an organization which will be later decomposed in multiple roles (Fig. 1 presents the organization). With this decomposition into organizations and roles, we do not need to know beforehand the implementation of each agent but rather the roles they play. This approach is known as an *organizational approach*. Such organizational approach provides greater modularity and supports heterogeneous languages compared with an agent-centered method [6].

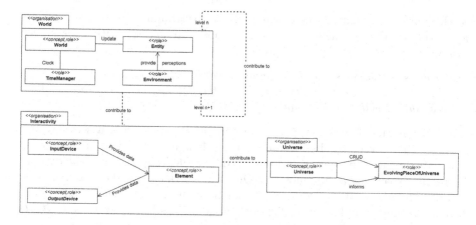

Fig. 1. Fragment of the Organization identification. **World:** manages the interaction between autonomous agents. **Interactivity:** provides a mean for a User to interact directly (i.e. actively) with the World. **Universe:** keeps track of entities status.

3 Demonstration

Our demonstration is a game where users (un-)spawn small characters by exercising a "drag and drop" from a mobile app into a world where the animation is played on a screen (shown in Fig. 2). Once spawned, the characters start to evolve

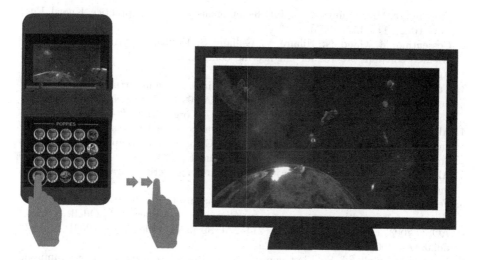

Fig. 2. The user interacts with the system by exercising drag and drop. The animation of the autonomous characters are displayed on a screen. We observe here Hulk following a character as it decided to hit it and another agent moving towards a new position to flee.

in the world according to their own BDI. We programmed several behaviours according to the characters' stress level and interactions with others. For example:

"If my stress level is low, I will move towards friends"
"In case of extreme stress level, I will hit the first character I see unless I am weak then I will move to another position".

The dynamic they follow plays the animation rather than a scripted animation. The player can observe the amusing dynamics (flocking, hunting, etc.) wondering what their agent will do next. Meanwhile, they can alter the dynamics by (un-)spawning at any moment. Our framework can handle n users and m worlds. The MAS was coded in *SARL* for its ease in implementing an organizational model [7] and the visualization (game and mobile app) using *Unity3D* engine.

4   Conclusion

The demonstration is an implementation of a model designed to handle large interactions within a mixed or augmented reality framework. In the "main purpose" section, we showed how modular our model is and its scalability. As a conclusion, we illustrated the exploitation of this model in the scope of amusement parks.

References

1. Wooldridge, M., Jennings, N.R.: Intelligent agents: theory and practice. Knowl. Eng. Rev. **10**(2), 115–152 (1995)
2. Cossentino, M., Gaud, N., Hilaire, V., Galland, S., Koukam, A.: ASPECS: an agent-oriented software process for engineering complex systems. Auton. Agent. Multi-Agent Syst. **20**(2), 260–304 (2010)
3. Cavazza, M., Charles, F., Mead, S.J.: Agents' interaction in virtual storytelling. In: de Antonio, A., Aylett, R., Ballin, D. (eds.) IVA 2001. LNCS (LNAI), vol. 2190, pp. 156–170. Springer, Heidelberg (2001). https://doi.org/10.1007/3-540-44812-8_13
4. Al-azawi, R., Ayesh, A., Obaidy, M.A.: Towards agent-based agile approach for game development methodology. In: World Congress on Computer Applications and Information Systems (WCCAIS), Hammamet (2014)
5. Akbari, O.: A survey of agent-oriented software engineering paradigm: towards its industrial acceptance (2010)
6. Ferber, J., Gutknecht, O., Michel, F.: From agents to organizations: an organizational view of multi-agent systems. In: Giorgini, P., Müller, J.P., Odell, J. (eds.) AOSE 2003. LNCS, vol. 2935, pp. 214–230. Springer, Heidelberg (2004). https://doi.org/10.1007/978-3-540-24620-6_15
7. Feraud, M., Galland, S.: First comparison of SARL to other agent-programming languages and frameworks. Procedia Comput. Sci. **109**, 1080–1085 (2017). In: 8th International Conference on Ambient Systems, Networks and Technologies, ANT-2017 and the 7th International Conference on Sustainable Energy Information Technology, SEIT 2017, 16–19 May 2017, Madeira, Portugal

A Multi-agent Evaluation of Traffic Light Models

Philippe Mathieu[(✉)] , Antoine Nongaillard , and Alexandre Thery

Univ. Lille, CNRS, Centrale Lille, UMR 9189 – CRIStAL, 59000 Lille, France
{philippe.mathieu,antoine.nongaillard}@univ-lille.fr,
alexandre.thery@centrale.centralelille.fr
http://cristal.univ-lille.fr/en/gt/i2c/

Abstract. Urban planning policies are increasingly questioning the problem of the last kilometer. The objective of this demonstration is to show how, with the help of a multi-agent simulation, it is possible to measure the effectiveness of different management strategies for traffic lights. Based on 2 types of environments and 5 different strategies, we show how to evaluate a road infrastructure. The software architecture presented is easily extensible to any kind of traffic light or car behaviors and any map. Our demonstration is carried out with the SUMO simulator with the help of both abstract road maps and real maps from different cities (parts of Nice, Manhattan, Madrid).

Keywords: Simulation · Traffic lights · Smart infrastructures · ICT

1 Introduction

Urban congestion, last kilometer management or pollution caused by road traffic are becoming major problems for our society year after year. In order to make this traffic more fluid, it is now possible to set up intelligent infrastructures that automatically adapt to different situations. "Smart Traffic lights" or Intelligent traffic lights are a vehicle traffic control system that combines traditional traffic lights with an array of sensors and artificial intelligence to efficiently route vehicle and pedestrian traffic [8]. Expected results include a reduction in vehicle waiting times, reduced fuel consumption, reduced toxic emissions or even to reduce speeding in populated areas. Our goal is to show how, with the help of a multi-agent simulation, it is possible to measure the effectiveness of different traffic light strategies and thanks to several metrics, and choose the most suitable one.

The use of multi-agent systems for road traffic simulation is not new. Since the seminal paper of [3] where the authors propose a reservation based system for alleviating traffic congestion at intersections, many other papers have followed the same approach. [1,2,7] with Matisse or [4] with MATsim propose also an interesting distributed control system to reduce traffic jams.

© Springer Nature Switzerland AG 2020
Y. Demazeau et al. (Eds.): PAAMS 2020, LNAI 12092, pp. 451–455, 2020.
https://doi.org/10.1007/978-3-030-49778-1_46

2   Main Purpose

We present here an agent-based infrastructure implemented with the SUMO simulator. SUMO (Simulation of Urban MObility) is an open source, highly portable, microscopic and continuous road traffic simulation package designed to handle large road networks [6]. It allows for inter-modal simulation including crossroads and comes with a large set of tools for scenario creation (see Fig. 1).

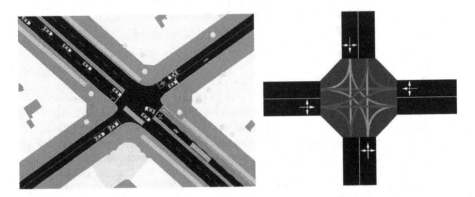

Fig. 1. The simulations presented are carried out with the SUMO software it allows to create our own infrastructure or to import a real map. On the left a crossroads of the city of Madrid. On the right, zoom on a crossroads handling with its possible re-directions.

Within SUMO, our work uses a classical abstract model [5,9] as well as GIS real maps. Our parametric model consists on n verticals $\times$ n horizontal one-way lanes, with a generator at one end (left and top of the grid), and 1 pit at the other end (bottom and right) which implies $2n$ generators and as many wells, and with a traffic light at each intersection (making n^2 lights to be managed), which in SUMO would correspond to one real life light for each of the two incoming lanes. Generators send their vehicles at one of the $2n$ pits randomly. We created 2 kinds of generators: one with a high-frequency spawn rate, and the other a low-frequency one. Each vehicle generated also has one chance out of two to have the ability to drive over the speed limit of the lane (it appears red in the simulation instead of yellow): this is useful for some behaviors we have tested, see below. Each light has two sensors, one on each incoming lane, that can detect the passage of a vehicle and inform the light (they are represented in SUMO by yellow rectangles on the lanes (see Fig. 2)). We run the simulation for every generator combination, which allows $2^{(2n)}$ configuration. With $n = 3$ this leads to 6 generators, 9 lights and 64 possible configurations (exhaustive set). This abstract approach can easily be extended to real situations (see Fig. 3).

3   Demonstration

We have tested five traffic light behaviors: (i) `Timer` switches after a given elapsed time (here 40 s); (ii) `Timer phased` is close to `Timer`, but all neighbor intersection's traffic lights are in opposition; (iii) `Punish` switches to red when a motorist exceeds the speed limit; (iv) `Reward` switches to green when the user complies the speed limit; (v) `Count` is an adaptive traffic light relating to the number of vehicles on standby.

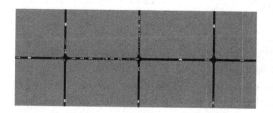

Fig. 2. Our evaluations are tested on an abstract infrastructure. On the left you can see 3 out of our 9 crossroads regulated by traffic lights, and their sensors (yellow rectangles). On the right, a zoom on one of the crossroads in which some vehicles are already engaged. (Color figure online)

The demonstration carried out is illustrated through both the abstract model previously described and on maps from different cities (parts of Nice, Manhattan, Madrid) using the SUMO software (Fig. 2 and Fig. 3). Through this demonstration we show how, with the help of an exhaustive configuration test, it is possible to compare different strategies for intelligent traffic light management. The results obtained for the 64 testing configurations can be summarized as follows:

Fig. 3. On the left a simulation on Manhattan at the intersection of 5th Avenue and Broadway near the Flat iron Building and Madison Square. On the right a zoom on this intersection. You can see the different vehicles blocked at the traffic lights.

Table 1. Results obtained for a light traffic: low-frequency generators spawns one vehicle every 20 ticks, and high-frequency ones spawns one every 10 ticks. Total of cars simulated through the exhaustive sets: 518,400

Traffic light behavior	Timer	Timer phased	Punish	Reward	Count
Mean co2 (g)	358.19	434.90	429.22	513.34	346.75
Mean fuel consumption (ml)	153.97	186.95	184.50	220.67	149.06
Mean waiting time (s)	23.56	48.99	46.35	56.61	10.36
Mean exceeding time (s)	19.90	18.68	18.64	18.48	19.29
Mean exceeding time (%)	17.59	13.14	12.73	13.72	18.19

In Table 1, corresponding to a light traffic, the count behavior has the best overall wait time, the lowest fuel consumption and CO2 emissions. The punish behavior has the lowest relative speeding time. We can now choose a behavior accordingly to a given objective. If the goal is to reduce pollution, count will be chosen. If it is to reduce speeding, near a school for example, punish is the best option. Our method allows to compare traffic lights behaviors for many contexts, and helps greatly in obtaining an objective idea of what behavior will be good at, and what are its limitations.

4   Conclusion

In this paper, we have proposed a multi-agent system for testing intelligent traffic light behavioral strategies. In this model, agents represent vehicles as well as vehicle generators, sensors and lights, each of them having its own behavior. This model allows us to determine the best traffic light strategy according to the desired objective, from reducing pollution to reducing waiting times. It is easily extensible to incorporate other objectives or new behaviors. We have tested different traffic light behaviors on abstract models as well as on real maps of major cities around the world. Depending on the objective to be optimized, it is then possible to know which of the different strategies studied is the most suitable one.

References

1. Bazzan, A.L.C.: A distributed approach for coordination of traffic signal agents. AAMAS **10**(2), 131–164 (2005). https://doi.org/10.1023/B:AGNT.0000049887. 90232.cd
2. De Oliveira, D., Bazzan, A.L.C., Lesser, V.: Using cooperative mediation to coordinate traffic lights: a case study. In: AAMAS 2005, pp. 463–470 (2005)
3. Dresner, K., Stone, P.: Multiagent traffic management: a reservation-based intersection control mechanism. In: AAMAS 2004, pp. 530–537 (2004)

4. Inedjaren, Y., Zeddini, B., Maachaoui, M., Barbot, J.-P.: Modeling a multi-agent self-organizing architecture in MATSim. In: Jezic, G., Chen-Burger, Y.-H.J., Kusek, M., Šperka, R., Howlett, R.J., Jain, L.C. (eds.) Agents and Multi-agent Systems: Technologies and Applications 2019. SIST, vol. 148, pp. 311–321. Springer, Singapore (2020). https://doi.org/10.1007/978-981-13-8679-4_25
5. Jayakumar, G., Gopinath, G.: Performance comparison of manet protocols based on manhattan grid mobility model. J. Mob. Commun. **2**(1), 18–26 (2008)
6. Lopez, P.A.: Microscopic traffic simulation using sumo. In: ITSC 2018, pp. 2575–2582 (2018)
7. Torabi, B., Wenkstern, R.Z., Saylor, R.: A self-adaptive collaborative multi-agent based traffic signal timing system. In: ISC2 2018, pp. 1–8 (2018)
8. Wikipedia. https://en.wikipedia.org/wiki/Smart_traffic_light
9. Wikipedia. https://en.wikipedia.org/wiki/Manhattan_mobility_model

Author Index

Printed in the United States
By Bookmasters